a true crime graphic novel

brian michael bendis

marc andreyko

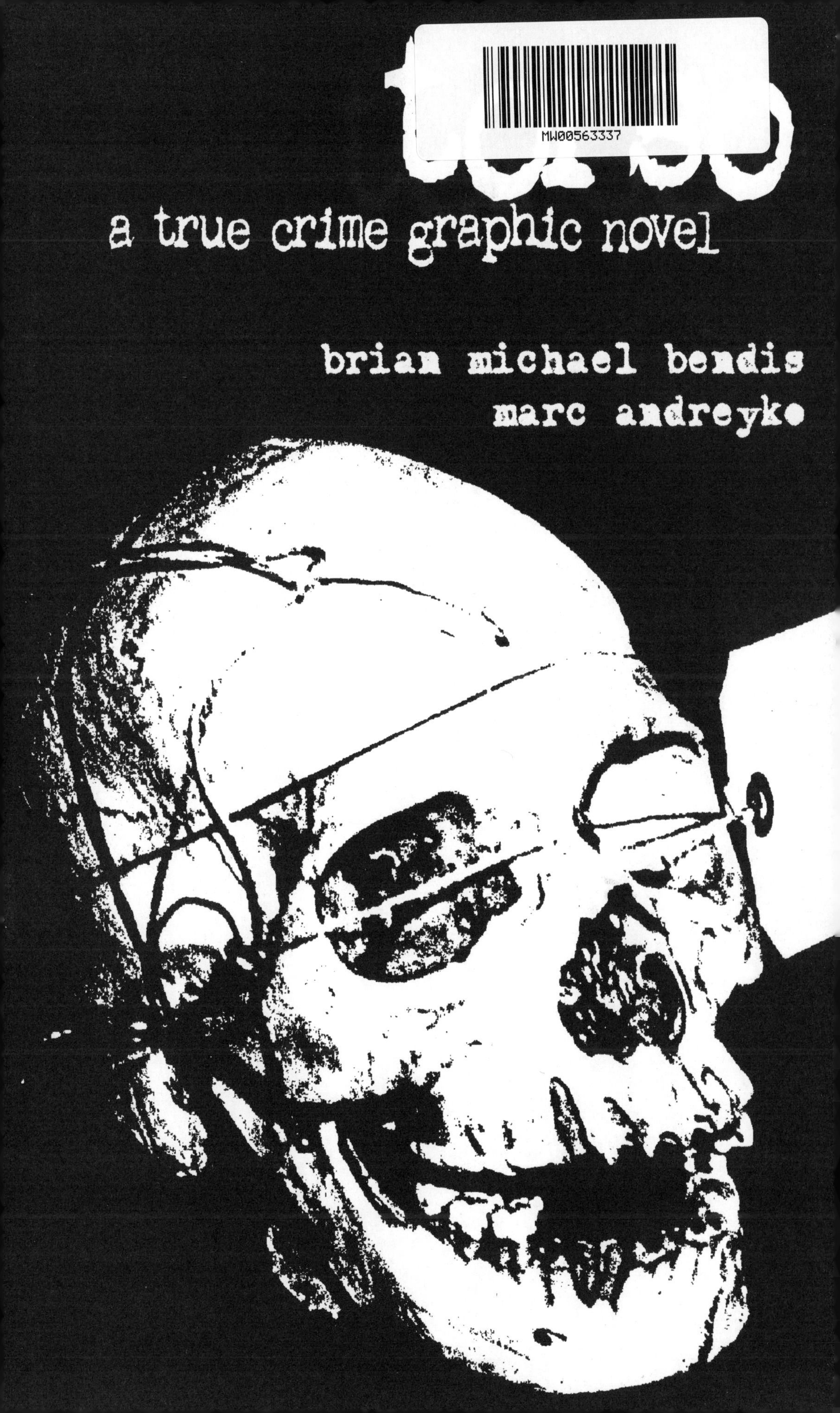

I've actually met Brian Bendis twice for the first time,
though I'm certain he only recalls one of those meetings.
That would be the second one, when he, myself, Brian
Azzarello, and Ed Brubakerall attending the San Diego
Comiconwere somehow convinced to submit ourselves
for a Wizard photoshoot to accompany an article that,
at least at the time, was to be titled "Murder, They Wrote."
To match the inspired title of the article, the concept behind
the photoshoot was to put all of the writers against a white
washed wall in a studio, and shoot pictures of us in black
and white, to serve as mugshots. The order was to look as
stern and hardcore badass as possible. The only one of us
who could really manage it was Azzarello, but that's because
I think he's been in a lineup before, because he certainly knew
what to do; the rest of us faked it pretty good.

Except Bendis.

He couldn't stop grinning.

We're doing this hardboiled crime writers photo sheet, and
there's Bendis, grinning. The photographer is telling him
things like, "You're dog just died," and "I'm sleeping with
your sister," and, "I.R.S. audit" and Bendis is grinning and
chuckling, and every time he tries to put on his stern face,
he gets a fit of the giggles, and the grin comes back.

If you've ever met Bendis, you know the grinit's one
part mania, one part pure amusement, and a huge helping of
Iknowsomethingyouden'tandit'sgonnabiteyourass.
It's a memorable grin. It's an inescapable grin. It's the grin
of an imp who's whacked out on meth and is about to steal
your car for a threestate crime spree.

Which is appropriate, because that's kind of what he does
with his writing. He grabs you and doesn't let go until he's
finished, and he doesn't tell you where he's taking you, either.

Marc Andreyko (who I've never met, and so have no
anecdotes about, sorry) and Bendis do this nowhere better
than in Torso. This whole collection is a fakeout; part
mystery, part procedural, part history and civics lesson,
part Athenian tragedy. The writing here is pure craft, deftly

layered, and never heavyhanded. Not to give anything away,
but take a close look at the interrogation sequence late in
the story to see what I'm talking about. Bendis and
Andreyko do what only the best writers can do give you
a story without spending words; they let the silences speak
for themselves. Creating character in small moments,
and make the moments echo.

The writing is a perfect compliment to the art. Like the writing,
the art itself is layered, images played across one another;
looking at these pages is like looking into a clear pond, where
depth becomes deceptive, and foreground facts are deployed
against an objective and impassive background. Bendis' use
of negative space is remarkable, and becomes as much a driving
force on these pages as the narrative itself.

Comics is, for the most part, not a form of subtlety; the four
color world eschews thought for action, believes that character
comes from only the most banal of conflicts. The current trend
in the industry is to tell "retro" stories, or, to put it in a less
complimentary light, revise history, to retell old stories in a
new light.

The irony is that, in Torso, Bendis and Andreyko have taken
a truly old story and with it done something new, certainly
something that I've never seen before. It is, simply, unique.

And that, if nothing else, should give Bendis yet another
reason to smile. And hopefully, Mr. Andreyko, too.

GREG RUCKA
Los Angeles, August, 2000

Greg Rucka is the acclaimed author of a series of novels about bodyguard Atticus
Kodiak. The first four titles KEEPER, FINDER, SMOKER, and SHOOTING AT
MIDNIGHT are all currently in print from Bantam Books. His comics career began
with the first WHITEOUT miniseries in 1998, and it garnered him an Eisner and a gig as
Batman writer in both comics and novels. He lives in Oregon with his lovely wife,
Jennifer Van Meter, and their son.

dedications

from marc
mom and dad for their
unending and unwavering
love and support

from brian
to alisa because i never
get sick of saying it.

CHAPTER 1

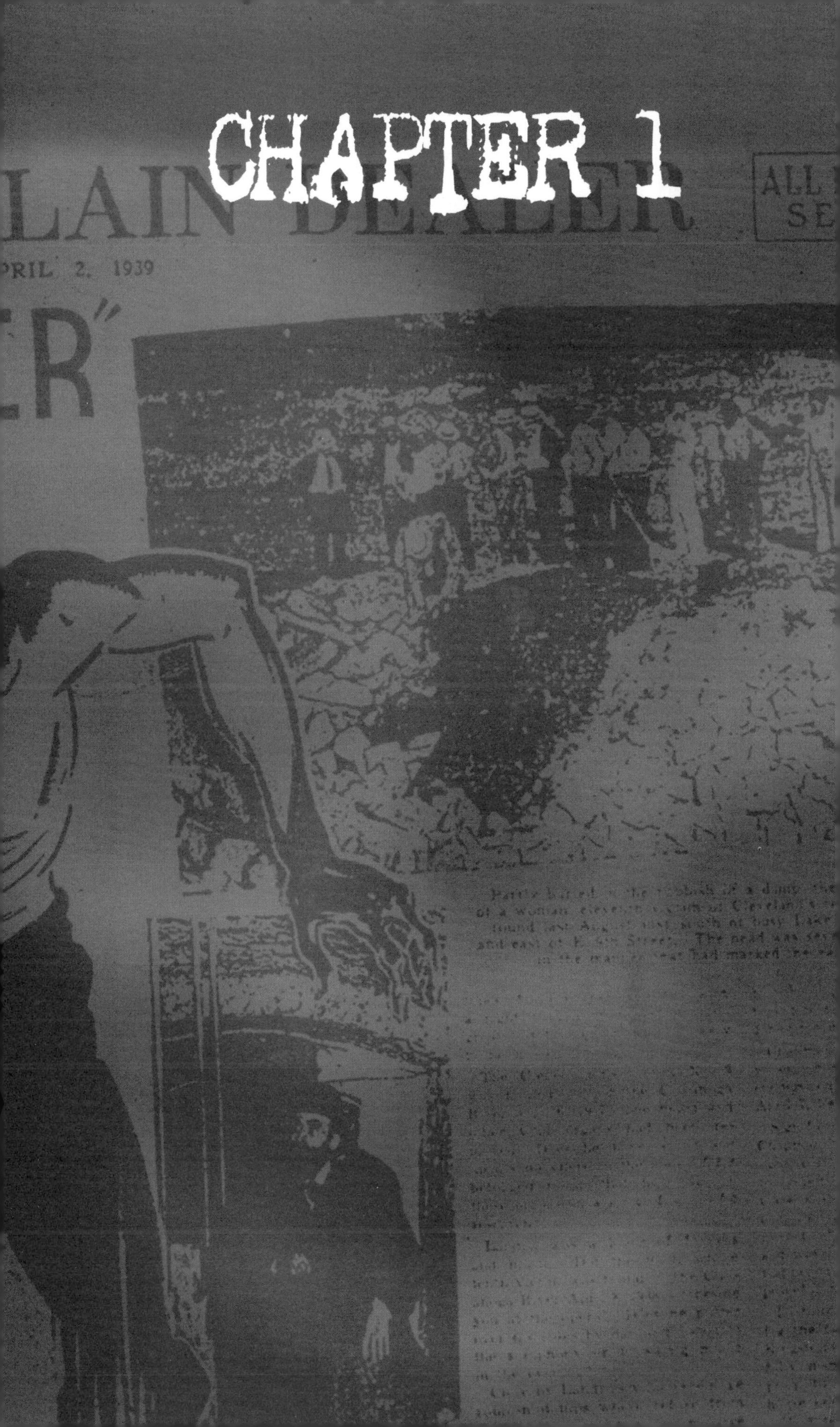
DEALER
2. 1939

image comics presents

TORSO

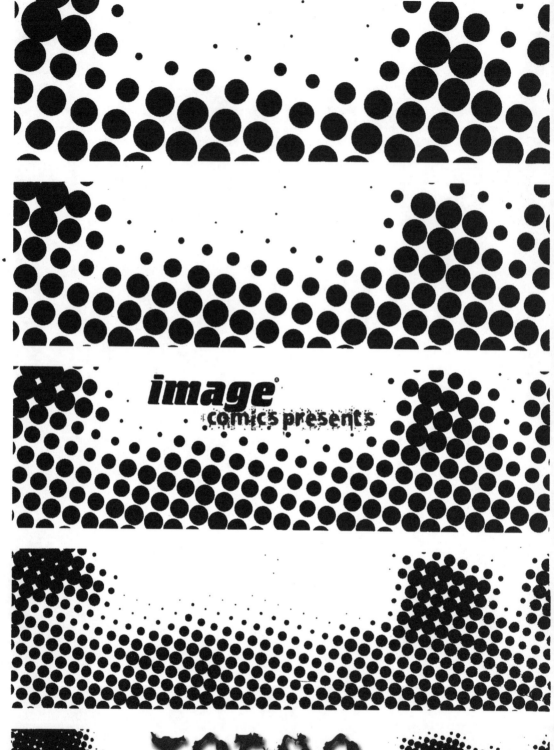

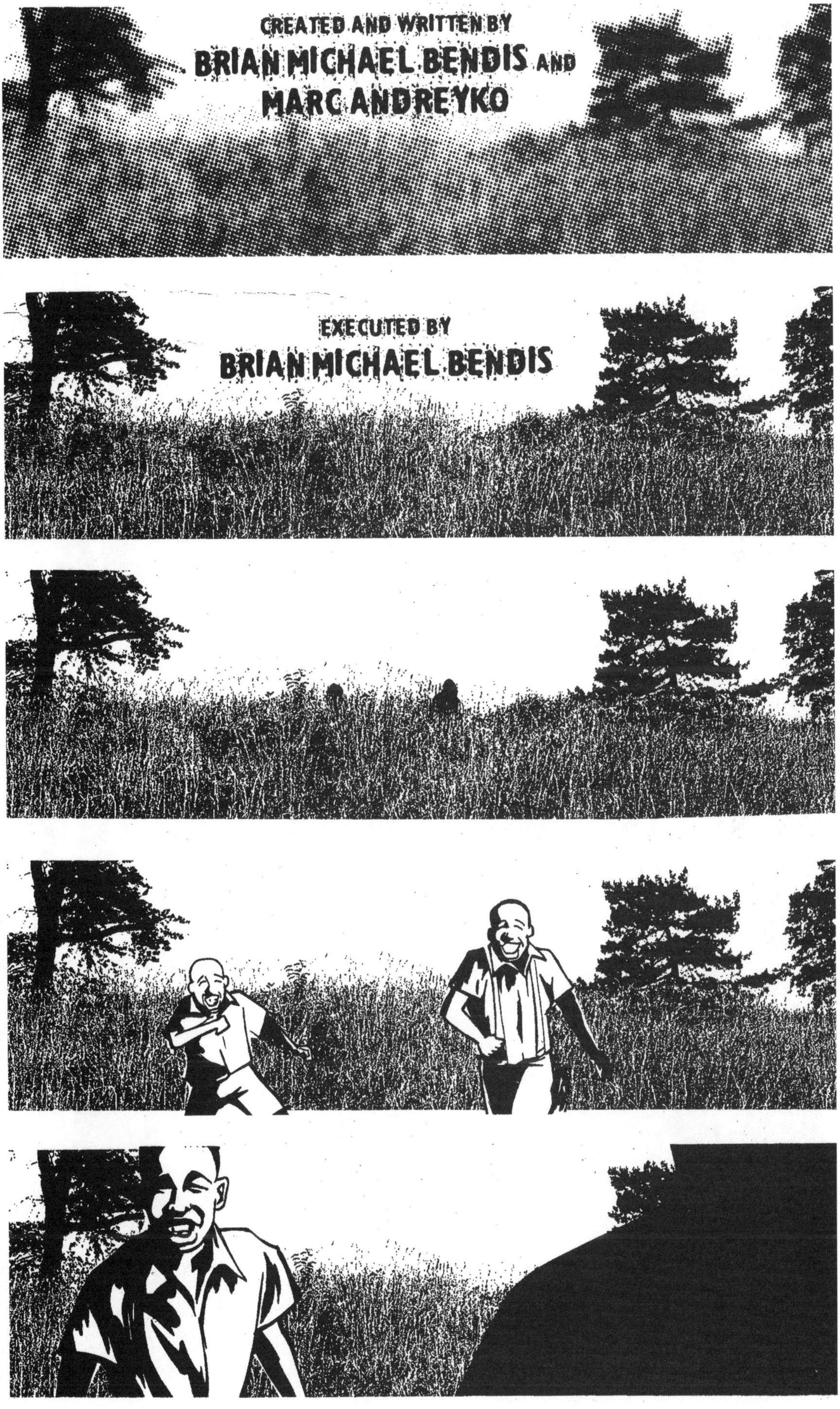
CREATED AND WRITTEN BY
BRIAN MICHAEL BENDIS AND
MARC ANDREYKO
EXECUTED BY
BRIAN MICHAEL BENDIS

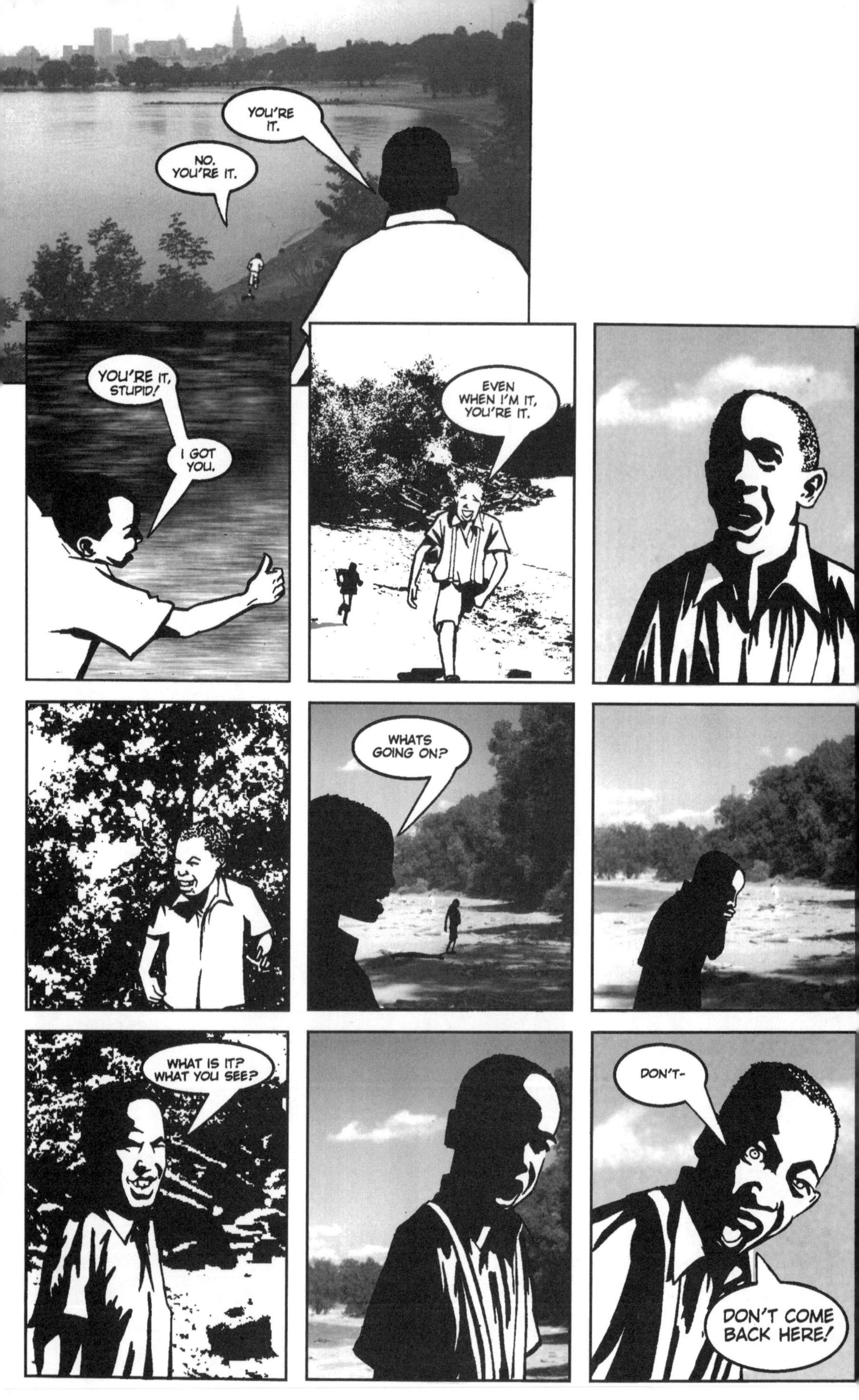
NO, YOU'RE IT.
YOU'RE IT.
YOU'RE IT, STUPID!
I GOT YOU.
EVEN WHEN I'M IT, YOU'RE IT.
WHATS GOING ON?
WHAT IS IT? WHAT YOU SEE?
DON'T-
DON'T COME BACK HERE!

POP
POP
POP
POP

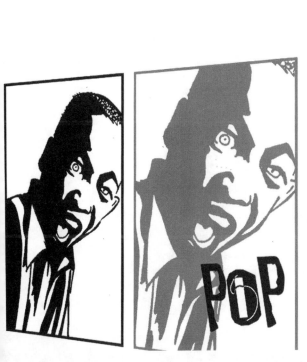

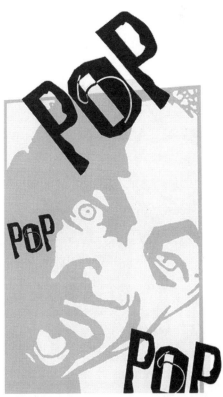

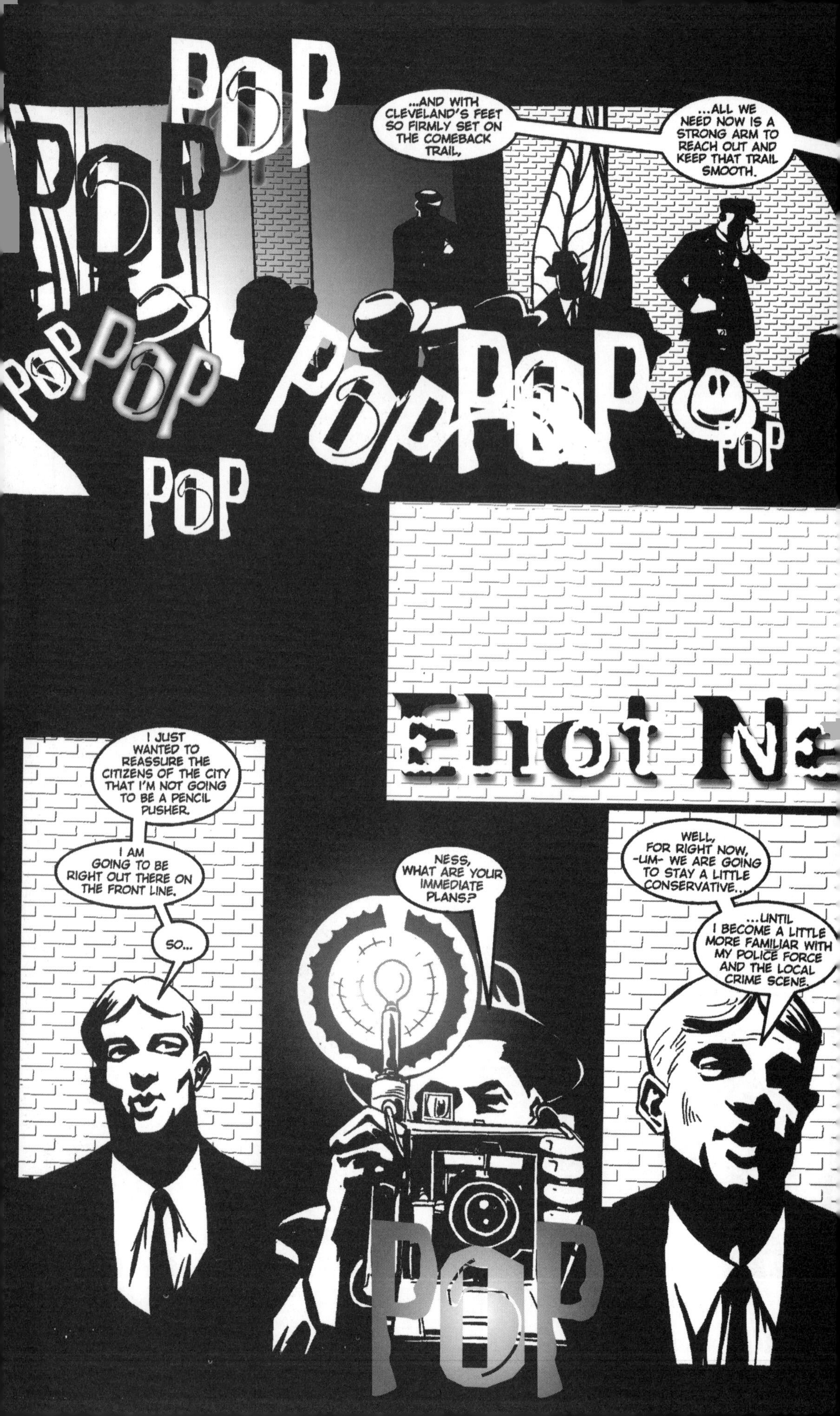
POP POP
...AND WITH CLEVELAND'S FEET SO FIRMLY SET ON THE COMEBACK TRAIL,
...ALL WE NEED NOW IS A STRONG ARM TO REACH OUT AND KEEP THAT TRAIL SMOOTH.
POP POP POP POP POP POP POP
POP
Eliot Ne
I JUST WANTED TO REASSURE THE CITIZENS OF THE CITY THAT I'M NOT GOING TO BE A PENCIL PUSHER.
I AM GOING TO BE RIGHT OUT THERE ON THE FRONT LINE.
SO...
NESS, WHAT ARE YOUR IMMEDIATE PLANS?
WELL, FOR RIGHT NOW, -UM- WE ARE GOING TO STAY A LITTLE CONSERVATIVE...
...UNTIL I BECOME A LITTLE MORE FAMILIAR WITH MY POLICE FORCE AND THE LOCAL CRIME SCENE.
POP

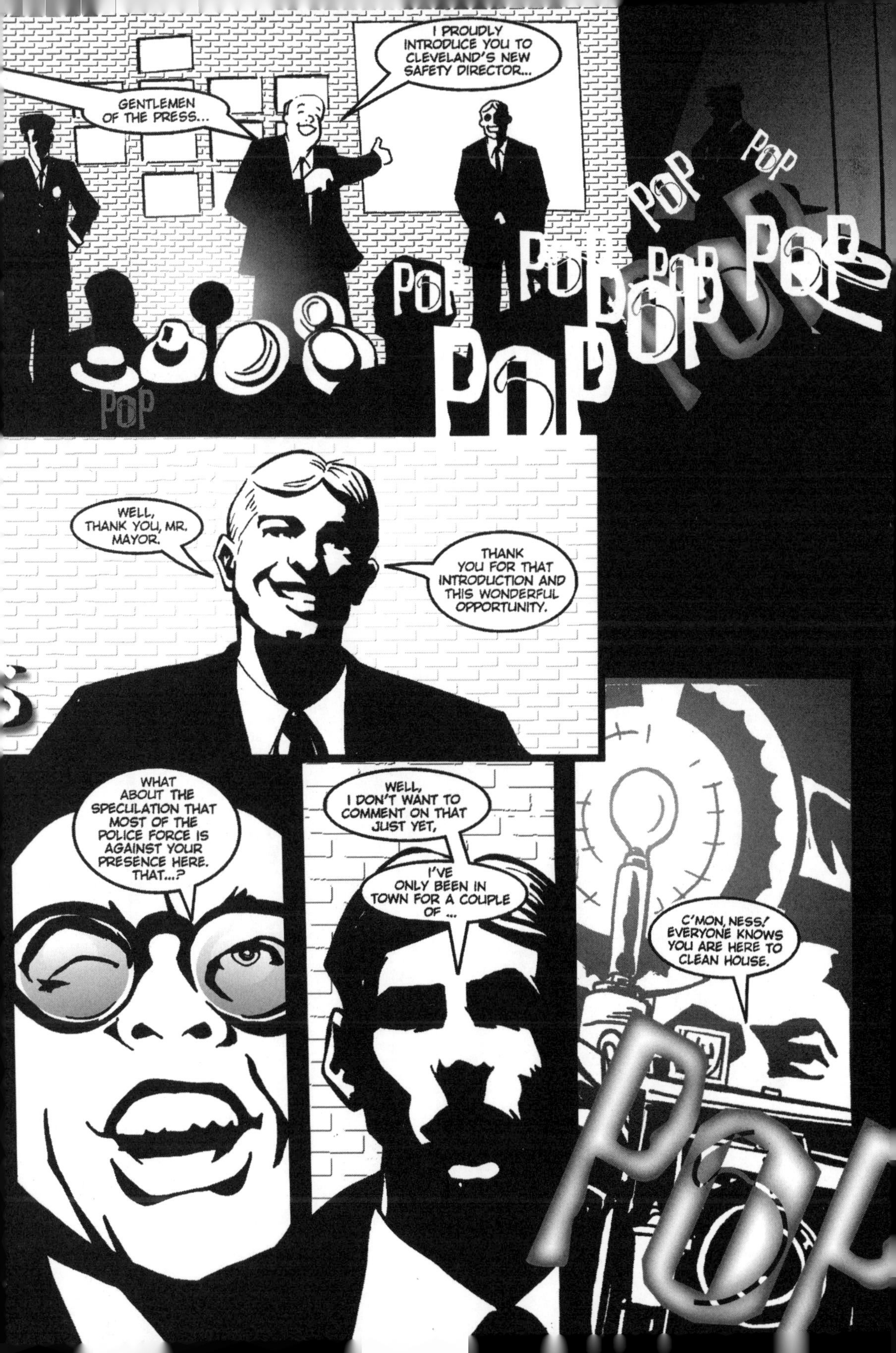
GENTLEMEN OF THE PRESS...
I PROUDLY INTRODUCE YOU TO CLEVELAND'S NEW SAFETY DIRECTOR...
POP
POP
POP
POP
POP
POP
WELL, THANK YOU, MR. MAYOR.
THANK YOU FOR THAT INTRODUCTION AND THIS WONDERFUL OPPORTUNITY.
WHAT ABOUT THE SPECULATION THAT MOST OF THE POLICE FORCE IS AGAINST YOUR PRESENCE HERE. THAT...?
WELL, I DON'T WANT TO COMMENT ON THAT JUST YET,
I'VE ONLY BEEN IN TOWN FOR A COUPLE OF ...
C'MON, NESS! EVERYONE KNOWS YOU ARE HERE TO CLEAN HOUSE.
POP

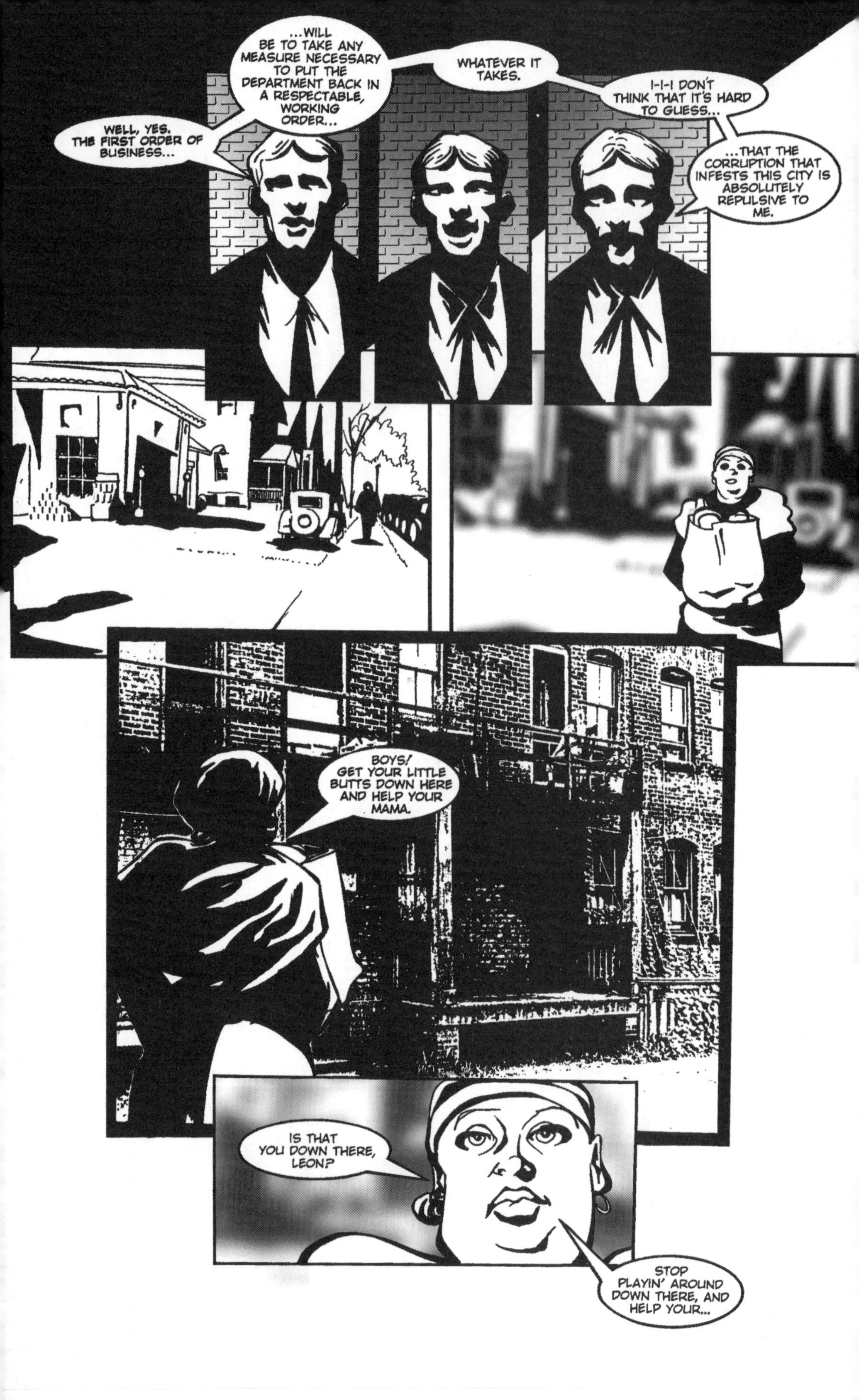
WELL, YES. THE FIRST ORDER OF BUSINESS...
...WILL BE TO TAKE ANY MEASURE NECESSARY TO PUT THE DEPARTMENT BACK IN A RESPECTABLE, WORKING ORDER...
WHATEVER IT TAKES.
I-I-I DON'T THINK THAT IT'S HARD TO GUESS...
...THAT THE CORRUPTION THAT INFESTS THIS CITY IS ABSOLUTELY REPULSIVE TO ME.
BOYS! GET YOUR LITTLE BUTTS DOWN HERE AND HELP YOUR MAMA.
IS THAT YOU DOWN THERE, LEON?
STOP PLAYIN' AROUND DOWN THERE, AND HELP YOUR...

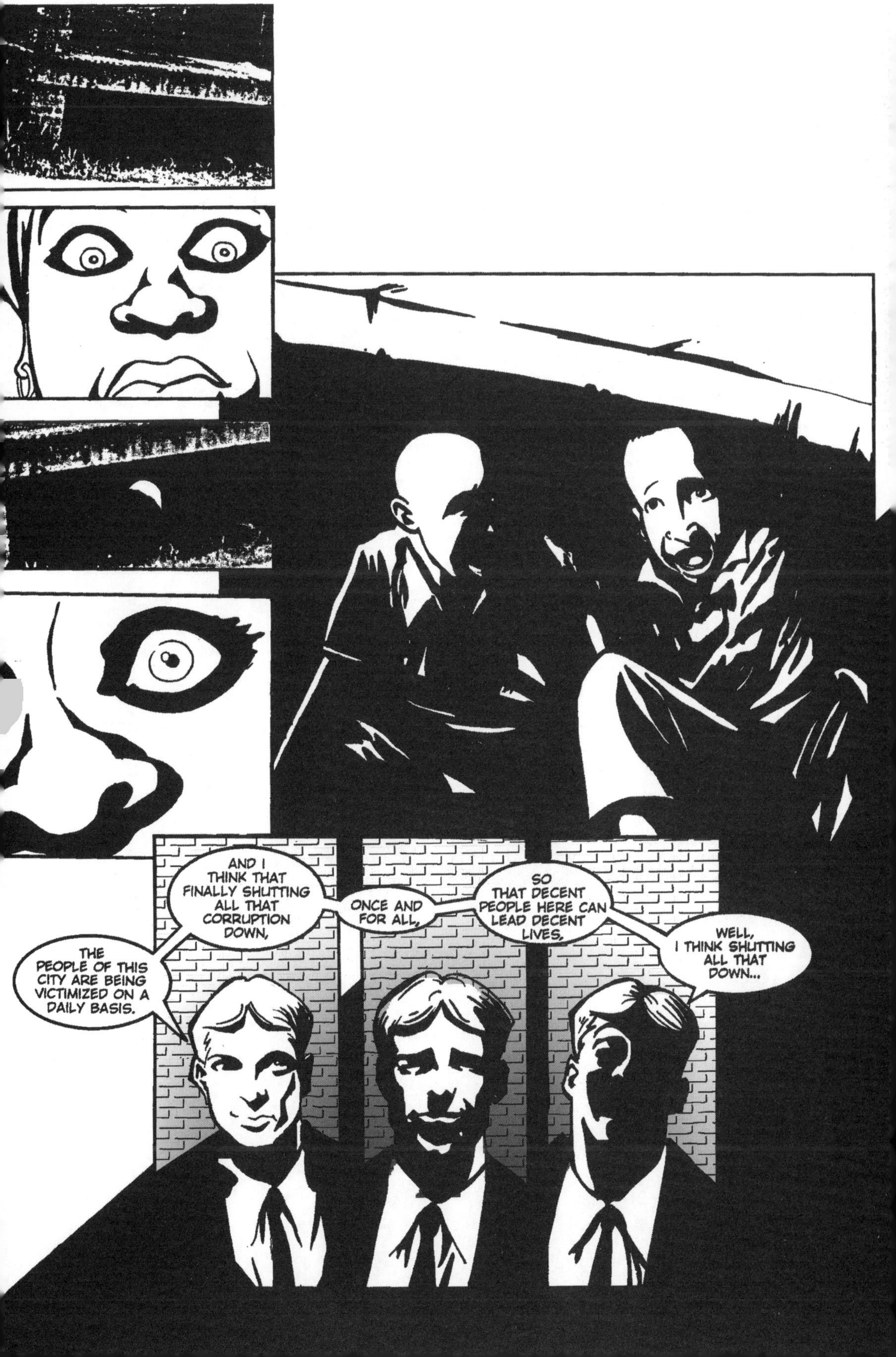
THE PEOPLE OF THIS CITY ARE BEING VICTIMIZED ON A DAILY BASIS.
AND I THINK THAT FINALLY SHUTTING ALL THAT CORRUPTION DOWN,
ONCE AND FOR ALL,
SO THAT DECENT PEOPLE HERE CAN LEAD DECENT LIVES,
WELL, I THINK SHUTTING ALL THAT DOWN...

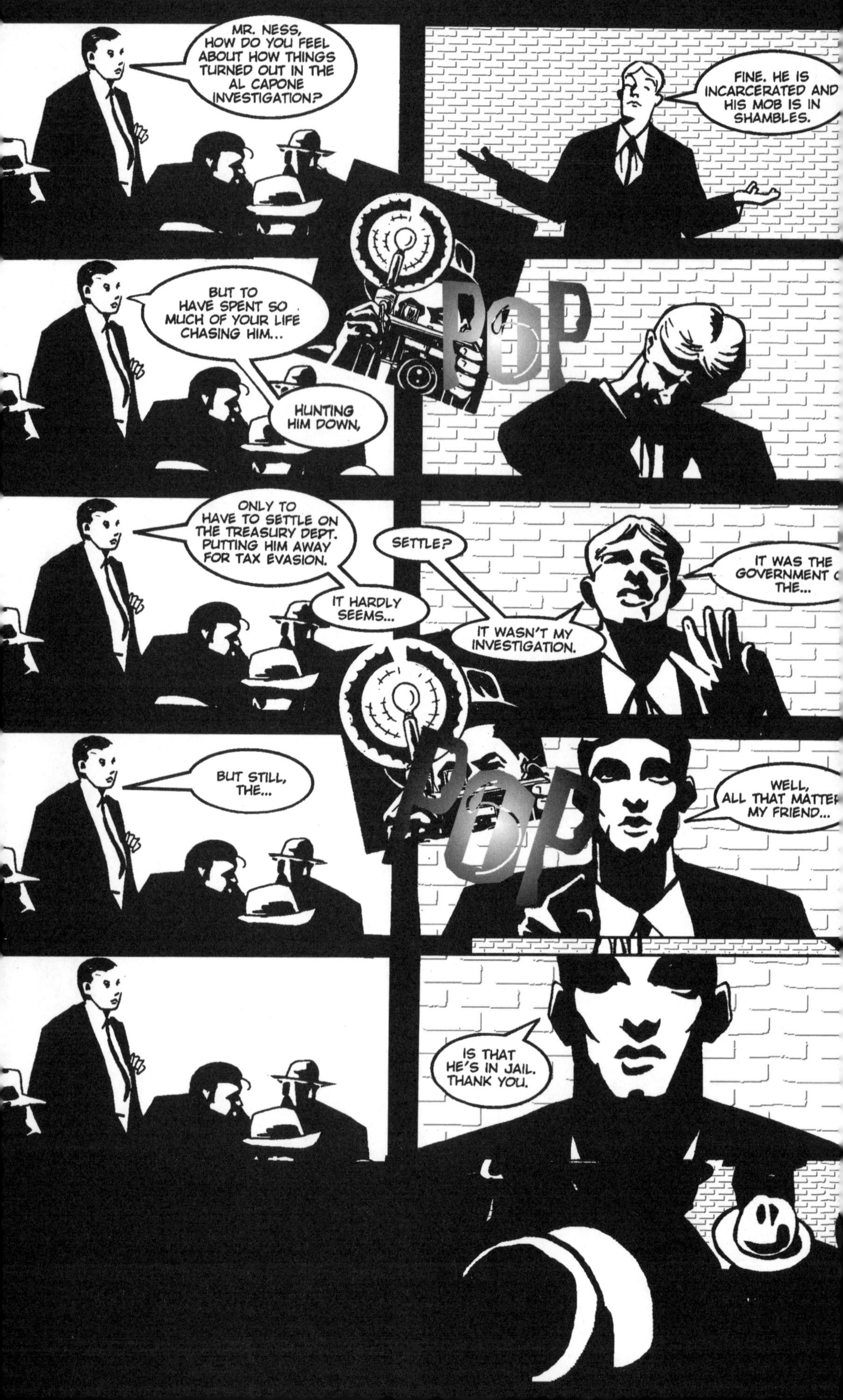
MR. NESS, HOW DO YOU FEEL ABOUT HOW THINGS TURNED OUT IN THE AL CAPONE INVESTIGATION?
FINE. HE IS INCARCERATED AND HIS MOB IS IN SHAMBLES.
BUT TO HAVE SPENT SO MUCH OF YOUR LIFE CHASING HIM...
HUNTING HIM DOWN,
POP
ONLY TO HAVE TO SETTLE ON THE TREASURY DEPT. PUTTING HIM AWAY FOR TAX EVASION.
IT HARDLY SEEMS...
SETTLE?
IT WASN'T MY INVESTIGATION.
IT WAS THE GOVERNMENT
THE...
BUT STILL, THE...
POP
WELL, ALL THAT MATTE
MY FRIEND...
IS THAT HE'S IN JAIL. THANK YOU.

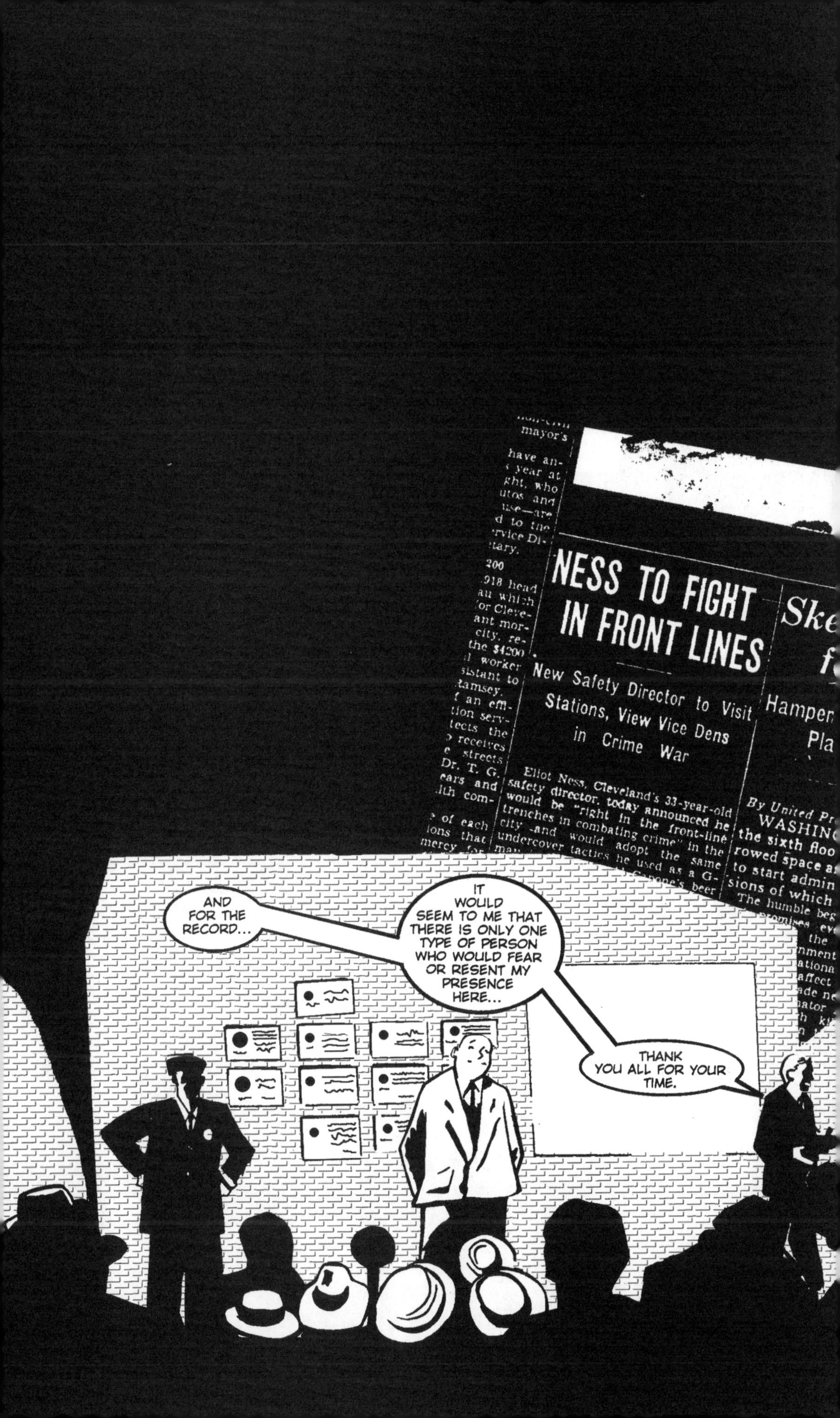
NESS TO FIGHT IN FRONT LINES
New Safety Director to Visit Stations, View Vice Dens in Crime War
Elliot Ness, Cleveland's 33-year-old safety director, today announced he would be "right in the front-line trenches in combating crime" in the city and would adopt the same undercover tactics he used as a G-
By United Pr
WASHIN
the sixth floo
rowed space a
to start admin
sions of which
The humble beg
Hampen
AND FOR THE RECORD...
IT WOULD SEEM TO ME THAT THERE IS ONLY ONE TYPE OF PERSON WHO WOULD FEAR OR RESENT MY PRESENCE HERE...
THANK YOU ALL FOR YOUR TIME.

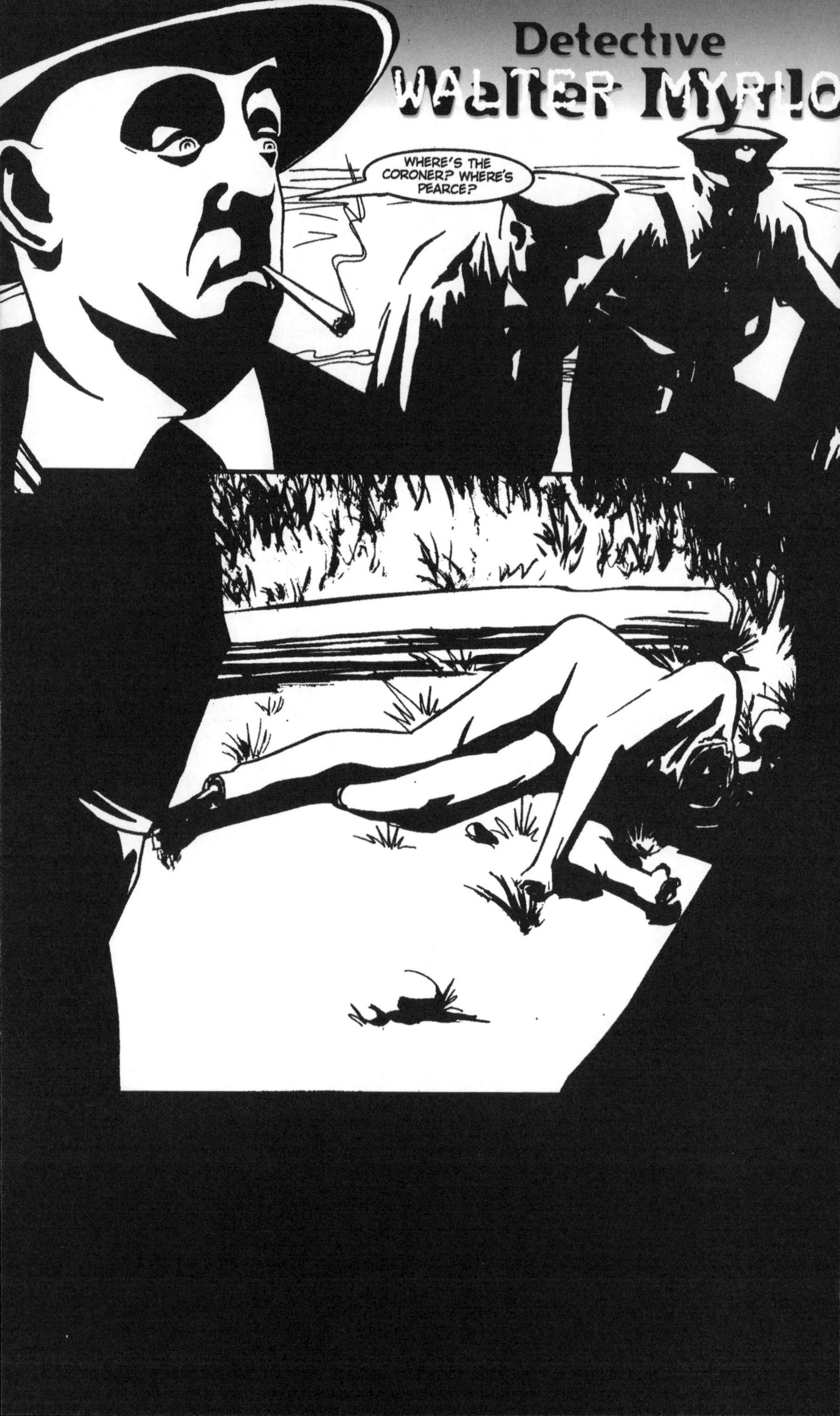
Detective
Walter Myrlo
WHERE'S THE CORONER? WHERE'S PEARCE?

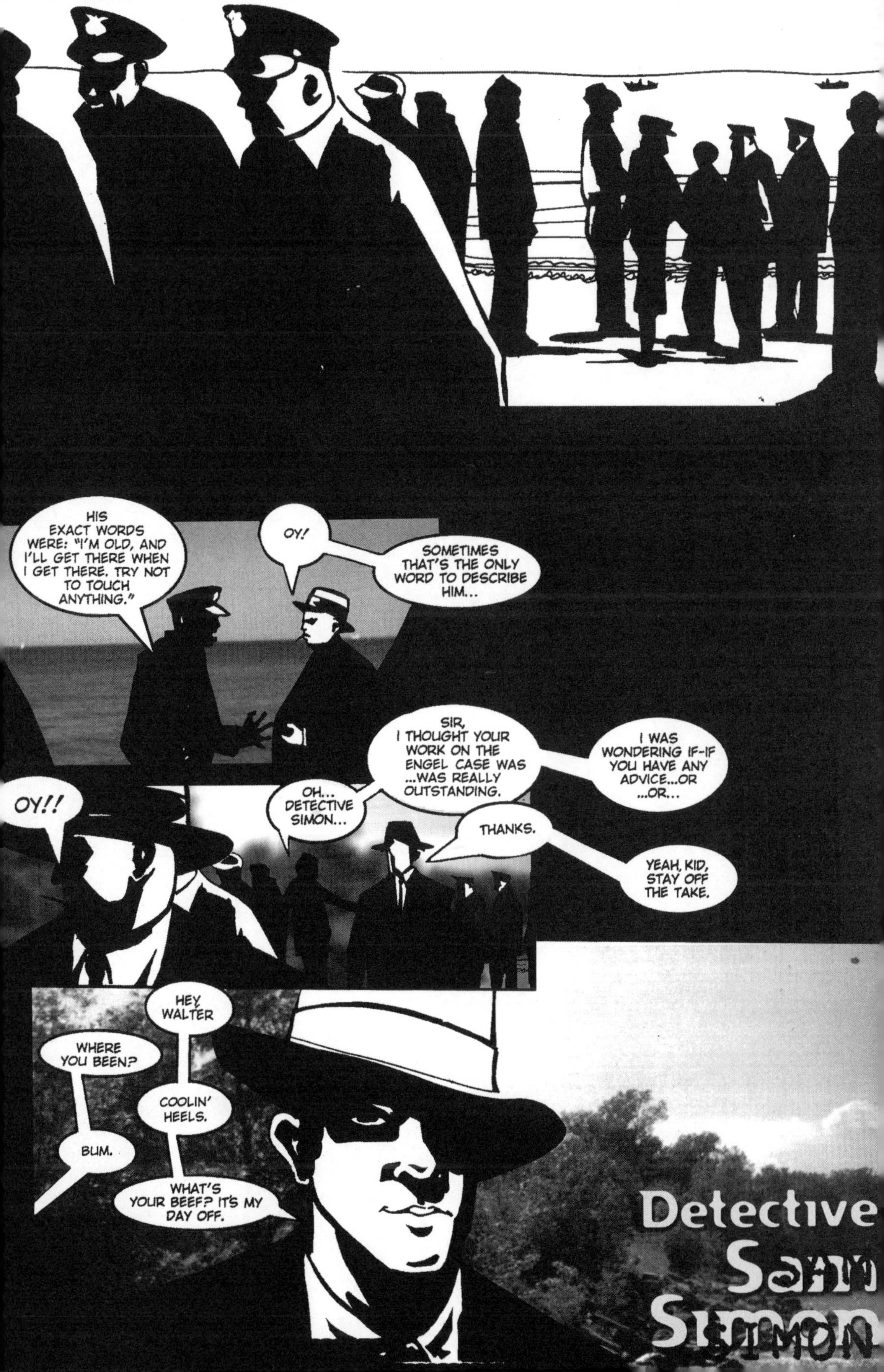
HIS EXACT WORDS WERE: "I'M OLD, AND I'LL GET THERE WHEN I GET THERE. TRY NOT TO TOUCH ANYTHING."
OY!
SOMETIMES THAT'S THE ONLY WORD TO DESCRIBE HIM...
OY!!
OH... DETECTIVE SIMON...
SIR, I THOUGHT YOUR WORK ON THE ENGEL CASE WAS ...WAS REALLY OUTSTANDING.
THANKS.
I WAS WONDERING IF-IF YOU HAVE ANY ADVICE...OR ...OR...
YEAH, KID, STAY OFF THE TAKE.
HEY WALTER
WHERE YOU BEEN?
COOLIN' HEELS.
BUM.
WHAT'S YOUR BEEF? IT'S MY DAY OFF.
Detective
Sam
Simon

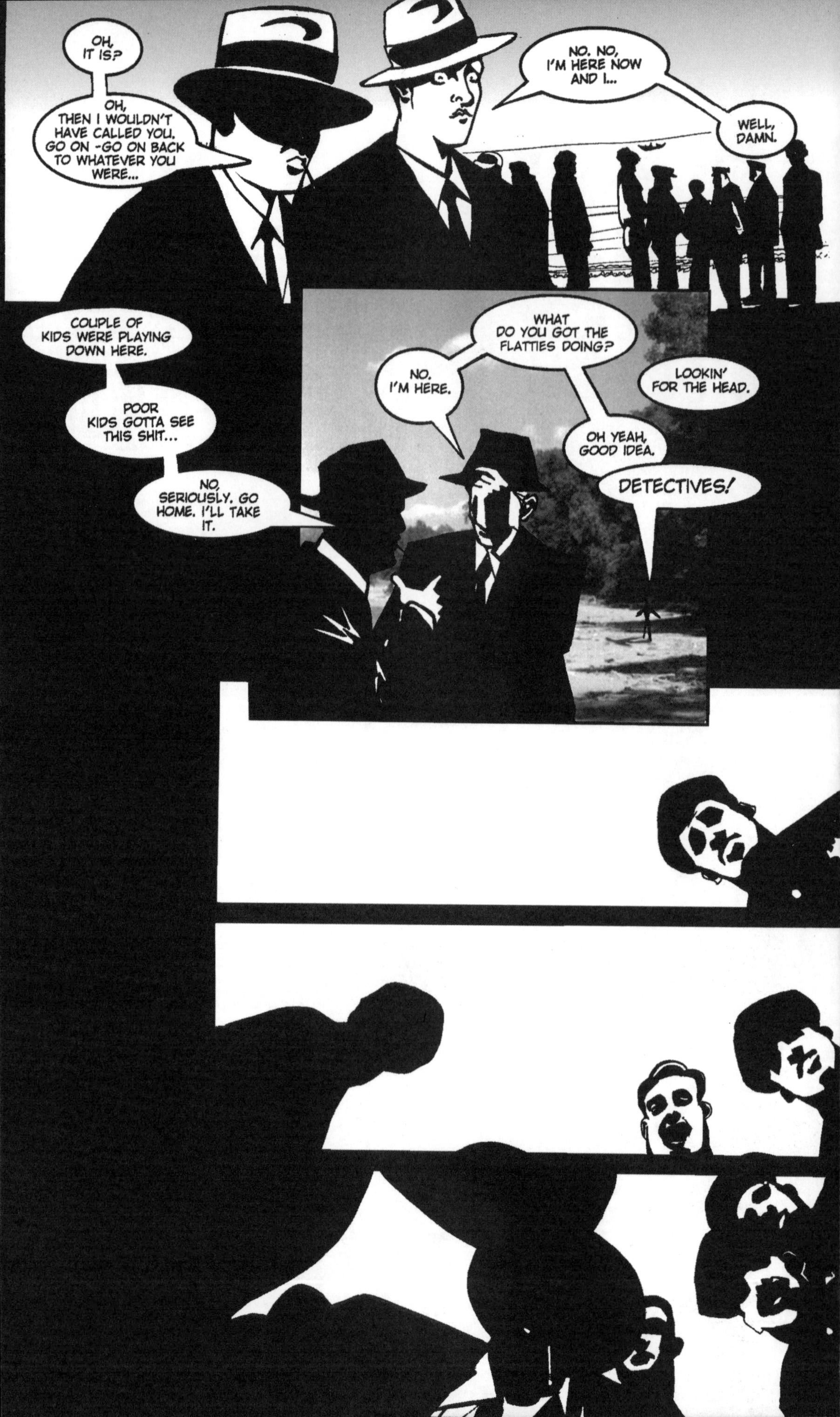

OH, IT IS?
OH, THEN I WOULDN'T HAVE CALLED YOU. GO ON -GO ON BACK TO WHATEVER YOU WERE...
NO. NO, I'M HERE NOW AND I...
WELL, DAMN.
COUPLE OF KIDS WERE PLAYING DOWN HERE.
POOR KIDS GOTTA SEE THIS SHIT...
NO, SERIOUSLY. GO HOME. I'LL TAKE IT.
NO. I'M HERE.
WHAT DO YOU GOT THE FLATTIES DOING?
LOOKIN' FOR THE HEAD.
OH YEAH, GOOD IDEA.
DETECTIVES!

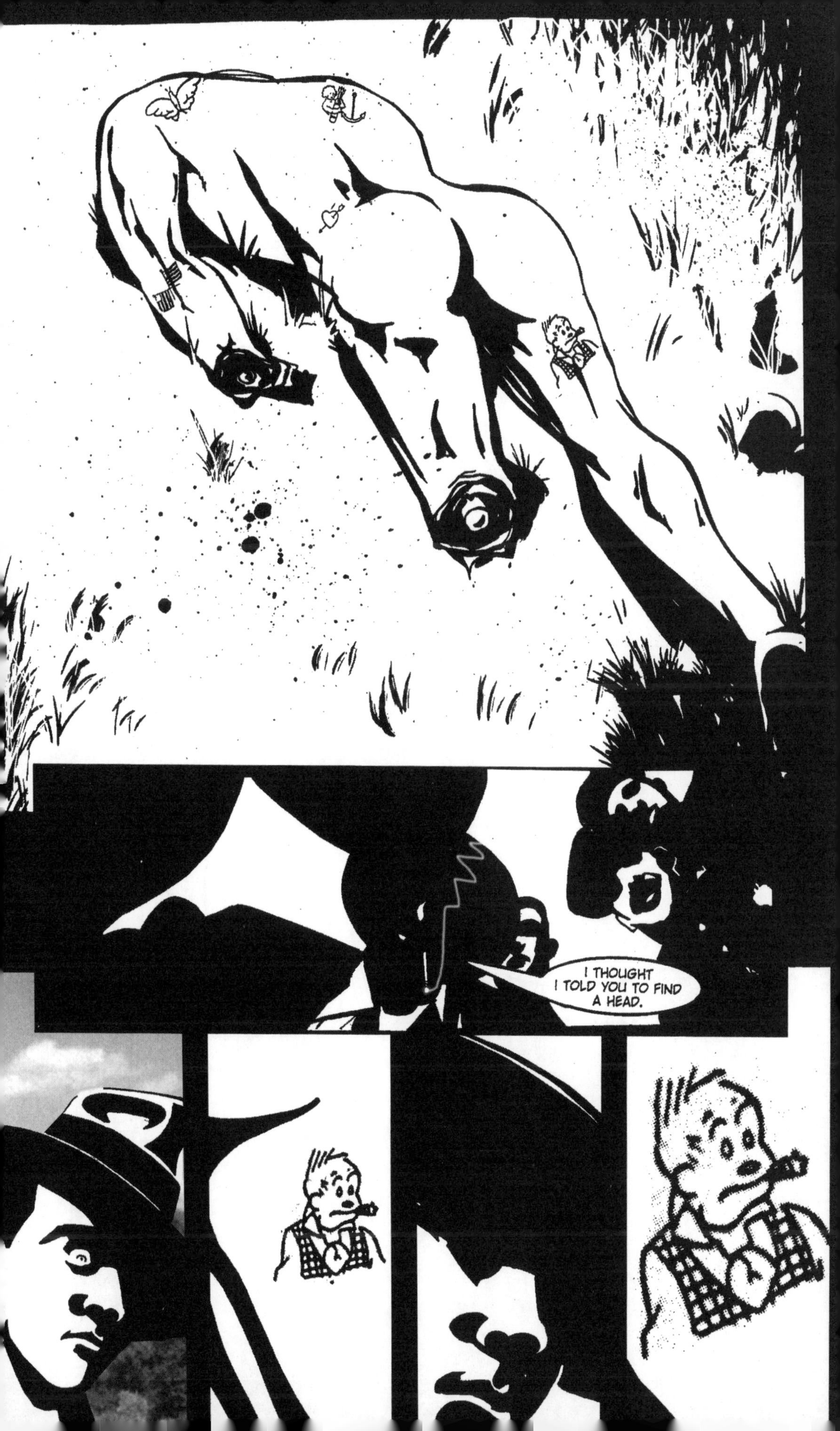
I THOUGHT I TOLD YOU TO FIND A HEAD.

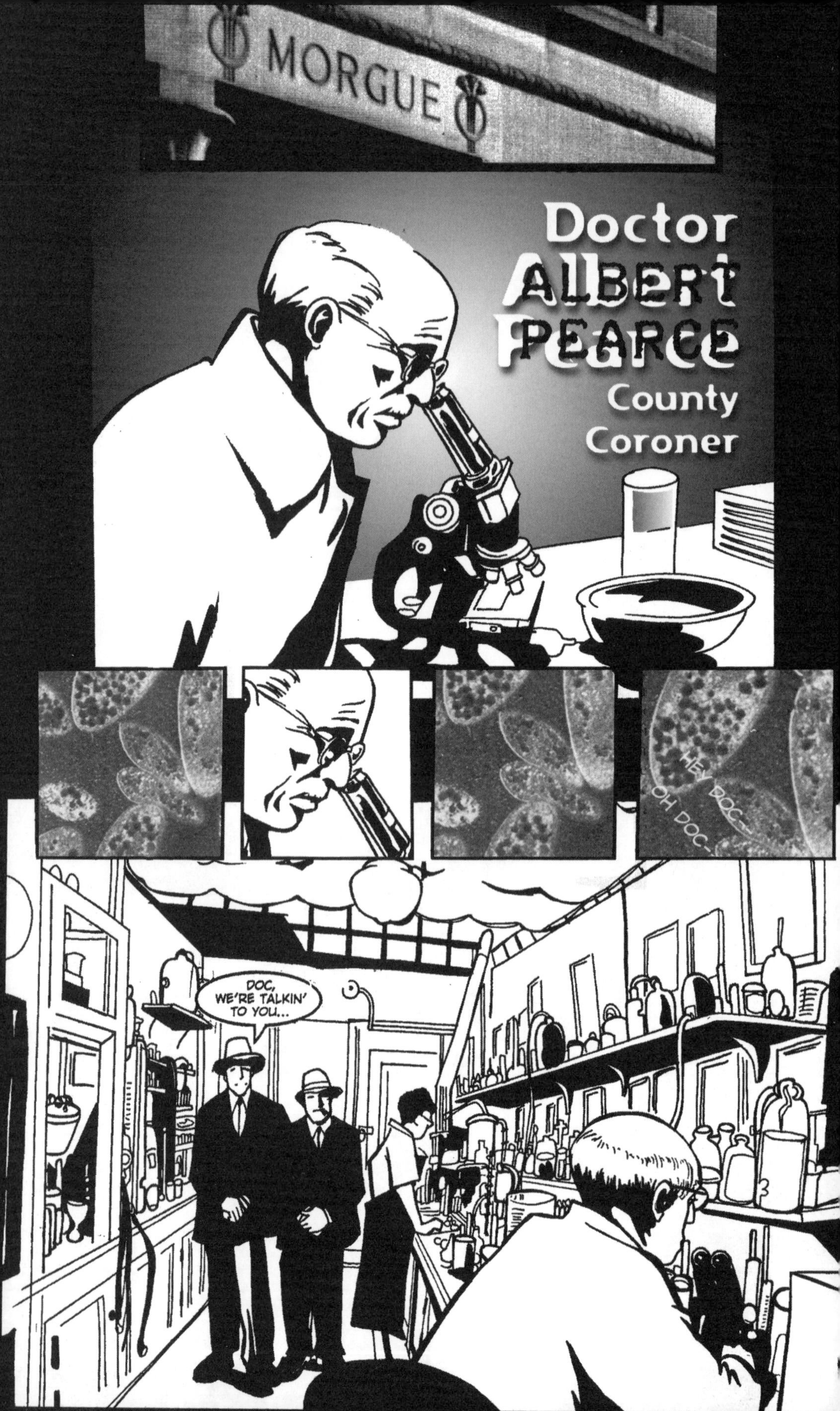
MORGUE
Doctor
Albert
Pearce
County
Coroner
HEY DOC-
OH DOC-
DOC, WE'RE TALKIN' TO YOU...

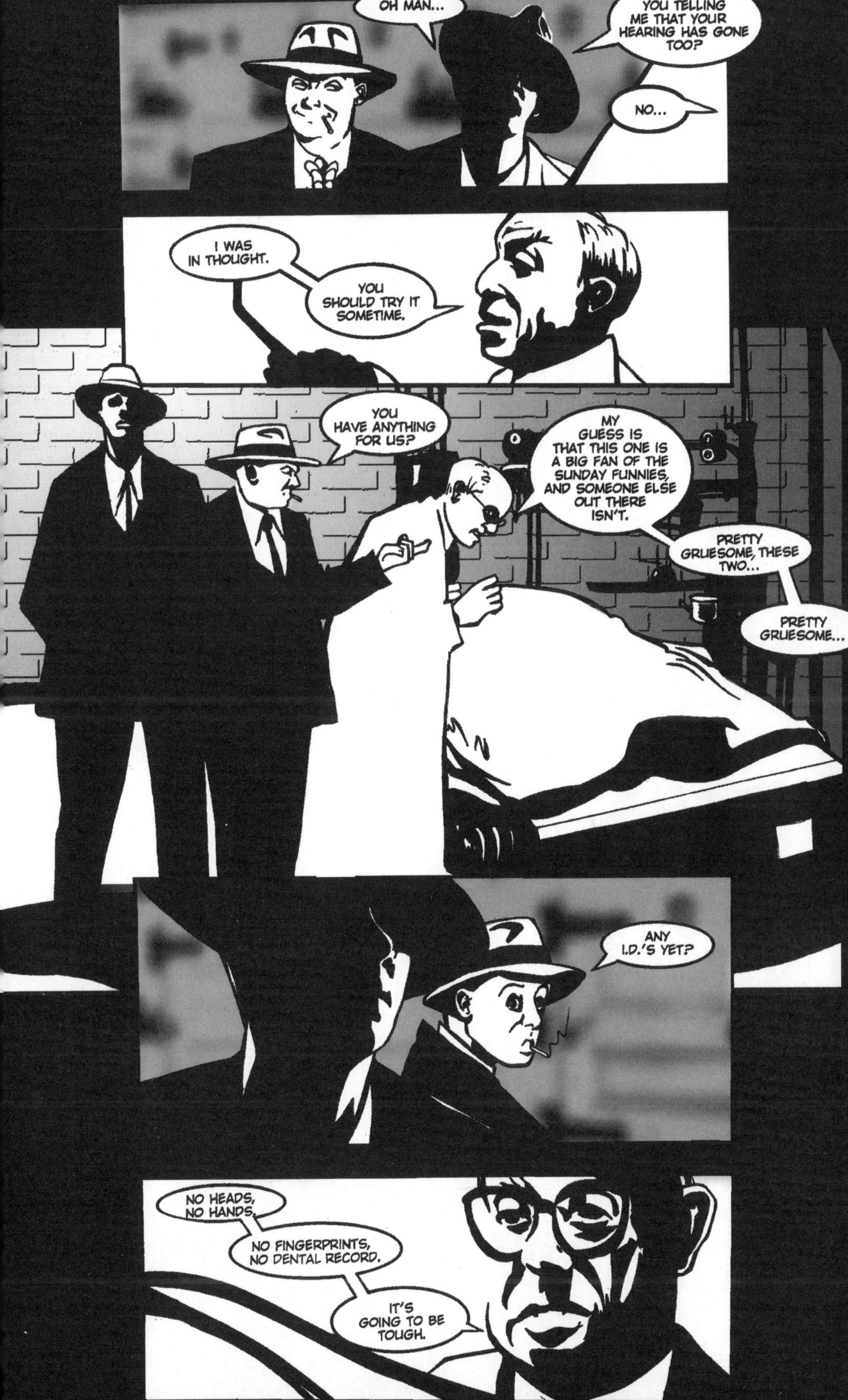
OH MAN...
ARE YOU TELLING ME THAT YOUR HEARING HAS GONE TOO?
NO...
I WAS IN THOUGHT.
YOU SHOULD TRY IT SOMETIME.
YOU HAVE ANYTHING FOR US?
MY GUESS IS THAT THIS ONE IS A BIG FAN OF THE SUNDAY FUNNIES, AND SOMEONE ELSE OUT THERE ISN'T.
PRETTY GRUESOME, THESE TWO...
PRETTY GRUESOME...
ANY I.D.'S YET?
NO HEADS, NO HANDS,
NO FINGERPRINTS, NO DENTAL RECORD.
IT'S GOING TO BE TOUGH.

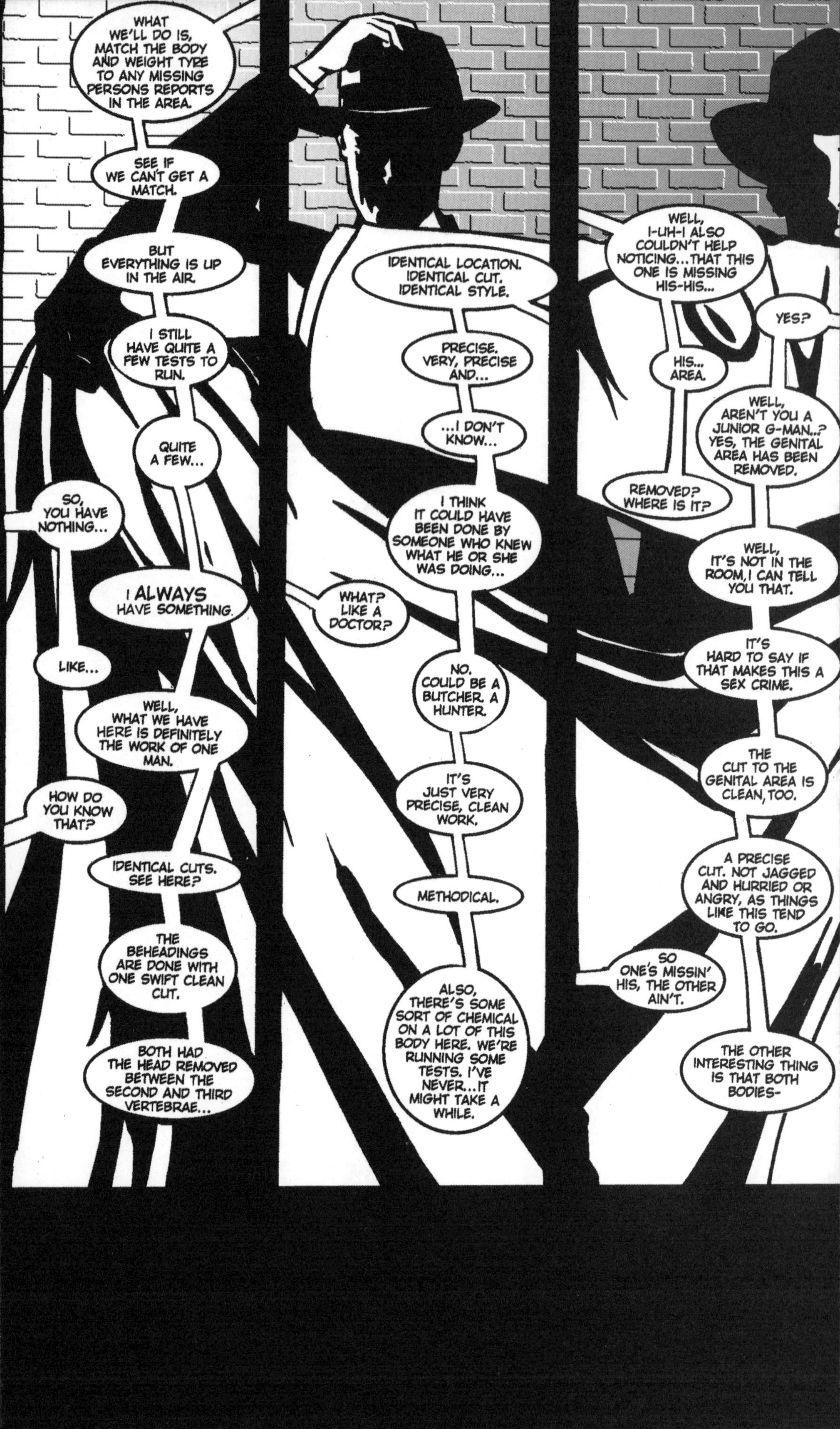
WHAT WE'LL DO IS, MATCH THE BODY AND WEIGHT TYPE TO ANY MISSING PERSONS REPORTS IN THE AREA.
SEE IF WE CAN'T GET A MATCH.
BUT EVERYTHING IS UP IN THE AIR.
I STILL HAVE QUITE A FEW TESTS TO RUN.
QUITE A FEW...
SO, YOU HAVE NOTHING...
I ALWAYS HAVE SOMETHING.
LIKE...
WELL, WHAT WE HAVE HERE IS DEFINITELY THE WORK OF ONE MAN.
HOW DO YOU KNOW THAT?
IDENTICAL CUTS. SEE HERE?
THE BEHEADINGS ARE DONE WITH ONE SWIFT CLEAN CUT.
BOTH HAD THE HEAD REMOVED BETWEEN THE SECOND AND THIRD VERTEBRAE...
IDENTICAL LOCATION. IDENTICAL CUT. IDENTICAL STYLE.
PRECISE. VERY, PRECISE AND...
...I DON'T KNOW...
I THINK IT COULD HAVE BEEN DONE BY SOMEONE WHO KNEW WHAT HE OR SHE WAS DOING...
WHAT? LIKE A DOCTOR?
NO. COULD BE A BUTCHER. A HUNTER.
IT'S JUST VERY PRECISE, CLEAN WORK.
METHODICAL.
ALSO, THERE'S SOME SORT OF CHEMICAL ON A LOT OF THIS BODY HERE. WE'RE RUNNING SOME TESTS. I'VE NEVER...IT MIGHT TAKE A WHILE.
WELL, I-UH-I ALSO COULDN'T HELP NOTICING...THAT THIS ONE IS MISSING HIS-HIS...
YES?
HIS... AREA.
WELL, AREN'T YOU A JUNIOR G-MAN..? YES, THE GENITAL AREA HAS BEEN REMOVED.
REMOVED? WHERE IS IT?
WELL, IT'S NOT IN THE ROOM, I CAN TELL YOU THAT.
IT'S HARD TO SAY IF THAT MAKES THIS A SEX CRIME.
THE CUT TO THE GENITAL AREA IS CLEAN, TOO.
A PRECISE CUT. NOT JAGGED AND HURRIED OR ANGRY, AS THINGS LIKE THIS TEND TO GO.
SO ONE'S MISSIN' HIS, THE OTHER AIN'T.
THE OTHER INTERESTING THING IS THAT BOTH BODIES-

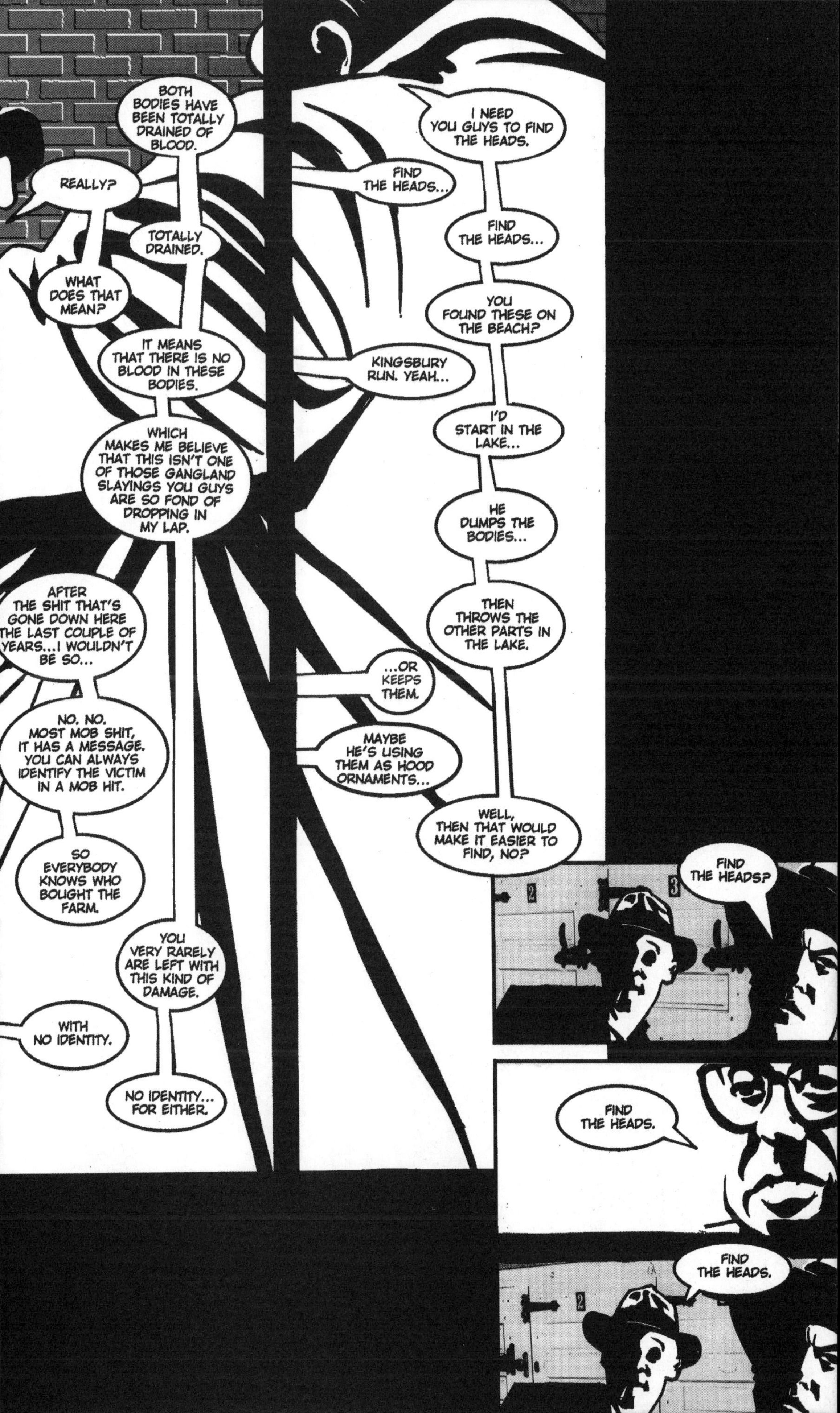

BOTH BODIES HAVE BEEN TOTALLY DRAINED OF BLOOD.
REALLY?
TOTALLY DRAINED.
WHAT DOES THAT MEAN?
IT MEANS THAT THERE IS NO BLOOD IN THESE BODIES.
WHICH MAKES ME BELIEVE THAT THIS ISN'T ONE OF THOSE GANGLAND SLAYINGS YOU GUYS ARE SO FOND OF DROPPING IN MY LAP.
AFTER THE SHIT THAT'S GONE DOWN HERE THE LAST COUPLE OF YEARS...I WOULDN'T BE SO...
NO. NO. MOST MOB SHIT, IT HAS A MESSAGE. YOU CAN ALWAYS IDENTIFY THE VICTIM IN A MOB HIT.
SO EVERYBODY KNOWS WHO BOUGHT THE FARM.
YOU VERY RARELY ARE LEFT WITH THIS KIND OF DAMAGE.
WITH NO IDENTITY.
NO IDENTITY... FOR EITHER.
I NEED YOU GUYS TO FIND THE HEADS.
FIND THE HEADS...
FIND THE HEADS...
YOU FOUND THESE ON THE BEACH?
KINGSBURY RUN. YEAH...
I'D START IN THE LAKE...
HE DUMPS THE BODIES...
THEN THROWS THE OTHER PARTS IN THE LAKE.
...OR KEEPS THEM.
MAYBE HE'S USING THEM AS HOOD ORNAMENTS...
WELL, THEN THAT WOULD MAKE IT EASIER TO FIND, NO?
FIND THE HEADS?
FIND THE HEADS.
FIND THE HEADS.

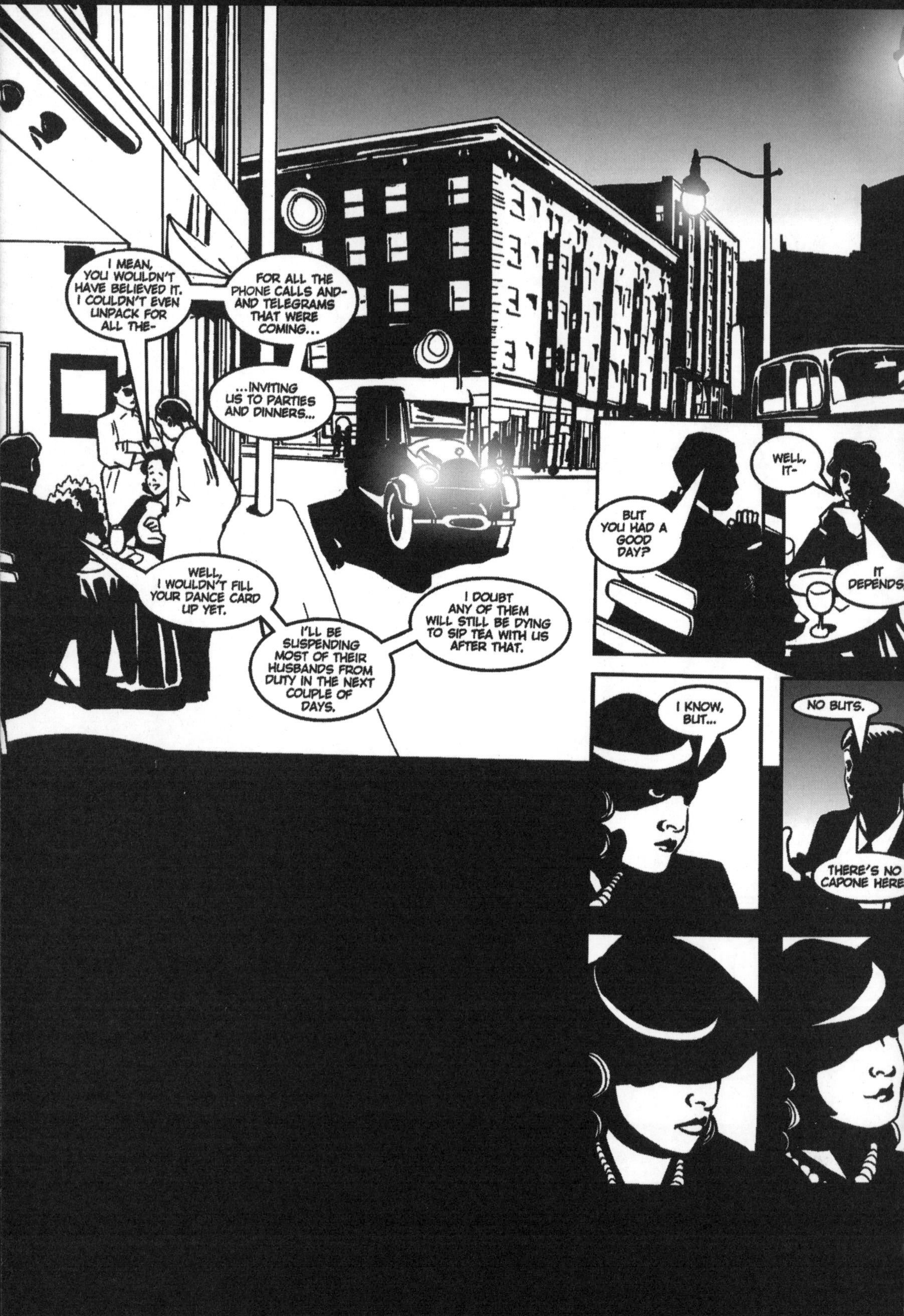
I MEAN, YOU WOULDN'T HAVE BELIEVED IT. I COULDN'T EVEN UNPACK FOR ALL THE-
FOR ALL THE PHONE CALLS AND- AND TELEGRAMS THAT WERE COMING...
...INVITING US TO PARTIES AND DINNERS...
WELL, I WOULDN'T FILL YOUR DANCE CARD UP YET.
I'LL BE SUSPENDING MOST OF THEIR HUSBANDS FROM DUTY IN THE NEXT COUPLE OF DAYS.
I DOUBT ANY OF THEM WILL STILL BE DYING TO SIP TEA WITH US AFTER THAT.
BUT YOU HAD A GOOD DAY?
WELL, IT-
IT DEPENDS
I KNOW, BUT...
NO BUTS.
THERE'S NO CAPONE HERE

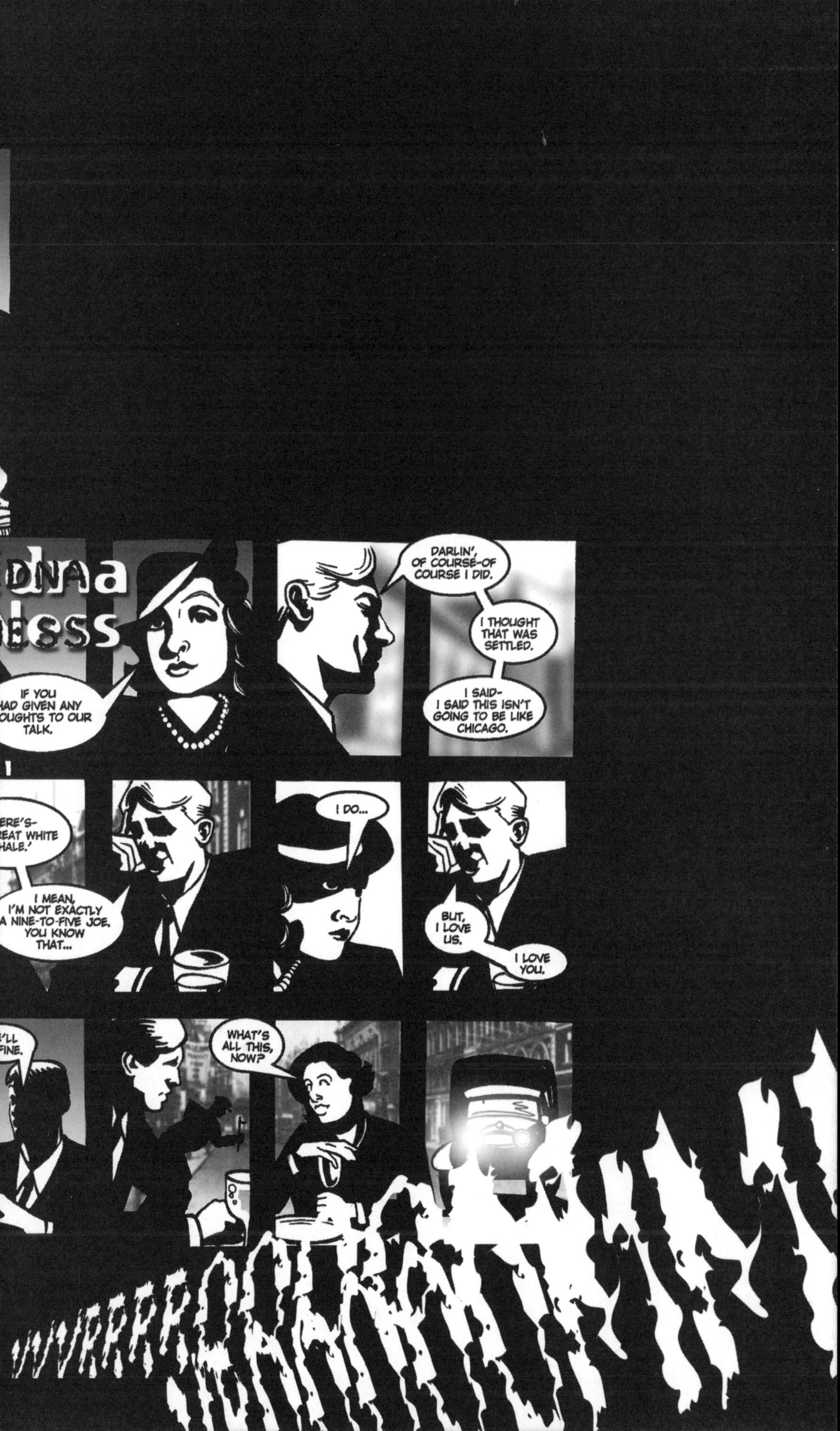

DARLIN', OF COURSE-OF COURSE I DID.
I THOUGHT THAT WAS SETTLED.
I SAID- I SAID THIS ISN'T GOING TO BE LIKE CHICAGO.
I MEAN, I'M NOT EXACTLY A NINE-TO-FIVE JOE. YOU KNOW THAT...
I DO...
BUT, I LOVE US.
I LOVE YOU.
WHAT'S ALL THIS, NOW?

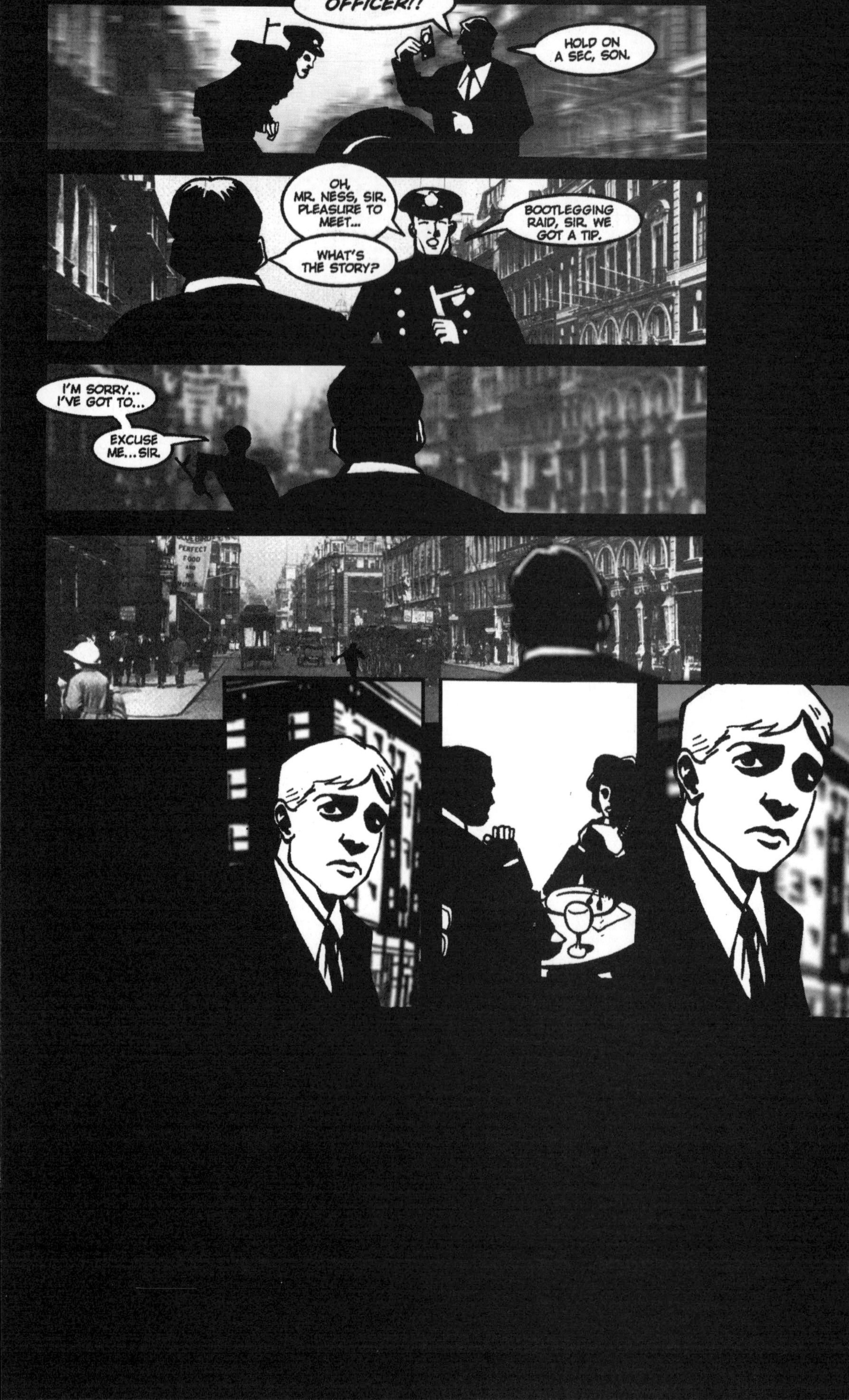
OFFICER!!
HOLD ON A SEC, SON.
OH, MR. NESS, SIR. PLEASURE TO MEET...
WHAT'S THE STORY?
BOOTLEGGING RAID, SIR. WE GOT A TIP.
I'M SORRY... I'VE GOT TO...
EXCUSE ME...SIR.
PERFECT FOOD

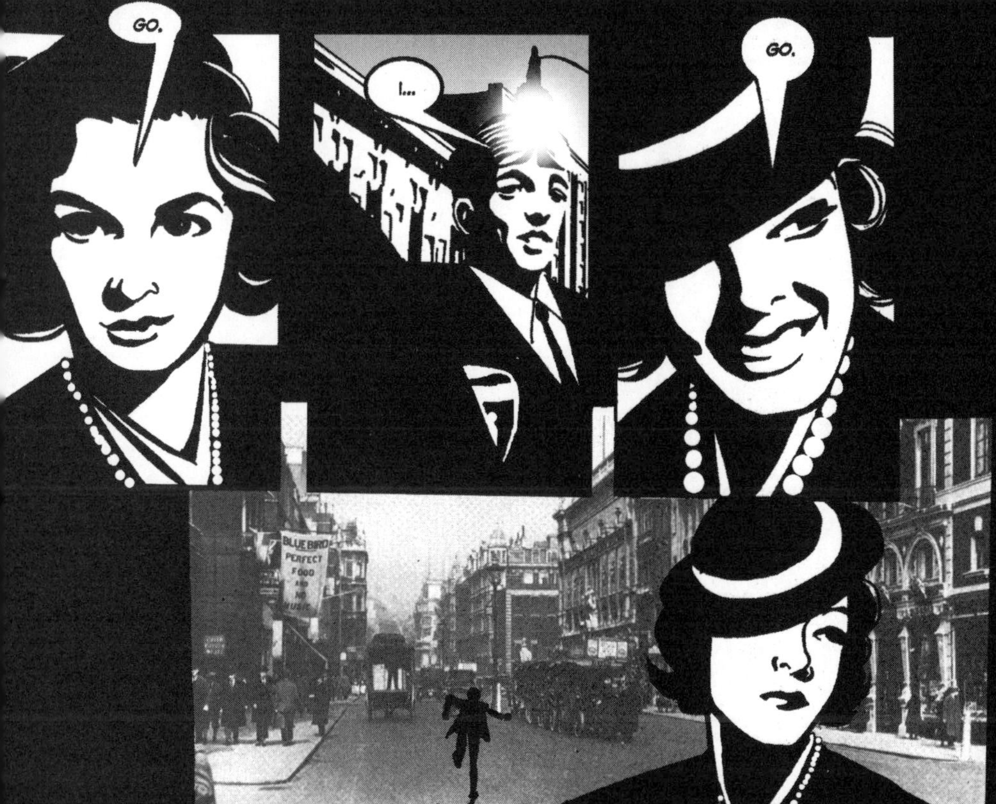
GO.
I...
GO.
BLUEBIRD
PERFECT
FOOD

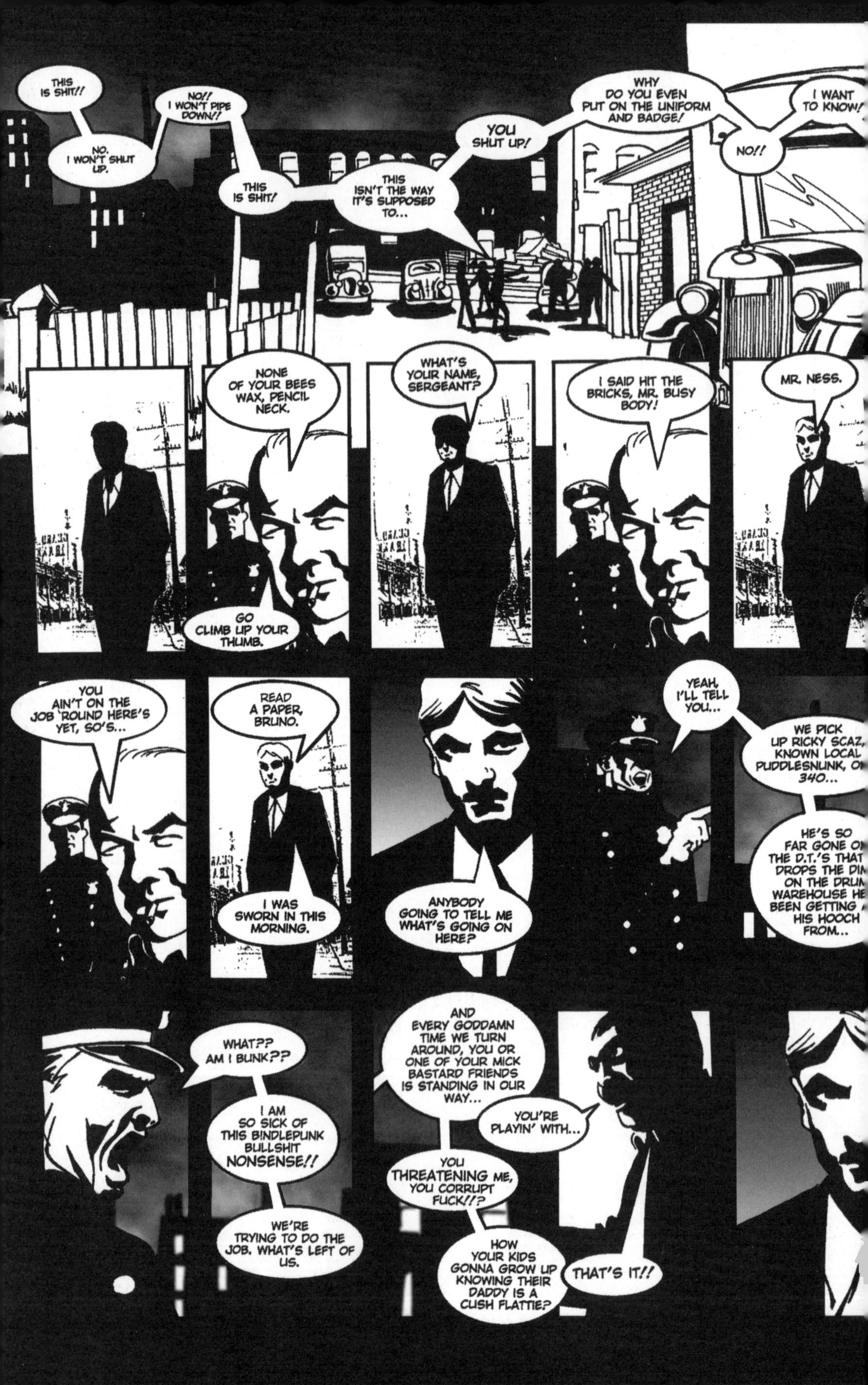
THIS IS SHIT!!
NO. I WON'T SHUT UP.
NO!! I WON'T PIPE DOWN!!
THIS IS SHIT!
THIS ISN'T THE WAY IT'S SUPPOSED TO...
YOU SHUT UP!
WHY DO YOU EVEN PUT ON THE UNIFORM AND BADGE!
NO!!
I WANT TO KNOW!
NONE OF YOUR BEES WAX, PENCIL NECK.
GO CLIMB UP YOUR THUMB.
WHAT'S YOUR NAME, SERGEANT?
I SAID HIT THE BRICKS, MR. BUSY BODY!
MR. NESS.
YOU AIN'T ON THE JOB 'ROUND HERE'S YET, SO'S...
READ A PAPER, BRUNO.
I WAS SWORN IN THIS MORNING.
ANYBODY GOING TO TELL ME WHAT'S GOING ON HERE?
YEAH, I'LL TELL YOU...
WHAT?? AM I BUNK??
I AM SO SICK OF THIS BINDLEPUNK BULLSHIT NONSENSE!!
WE'RE TRYING TO DO THE JOB. WHAT'S LEFT OF US.
AND EVERY GODDAMN TIME WE TURN AROUND, YOU OR ONE OF YOUR MICK BASTARD FRIENDS IS STANDING IN OUR WAY...
YOU'RE PLAYIN' WITH...
YOU THREATENING ME, YOU CORRUPT FUCK!!?
HOW YOUR KIDS GONNA GROW UP KNOWING THEIR DADDY IS A CUSH FLATTIE?
THAT'S IT!!

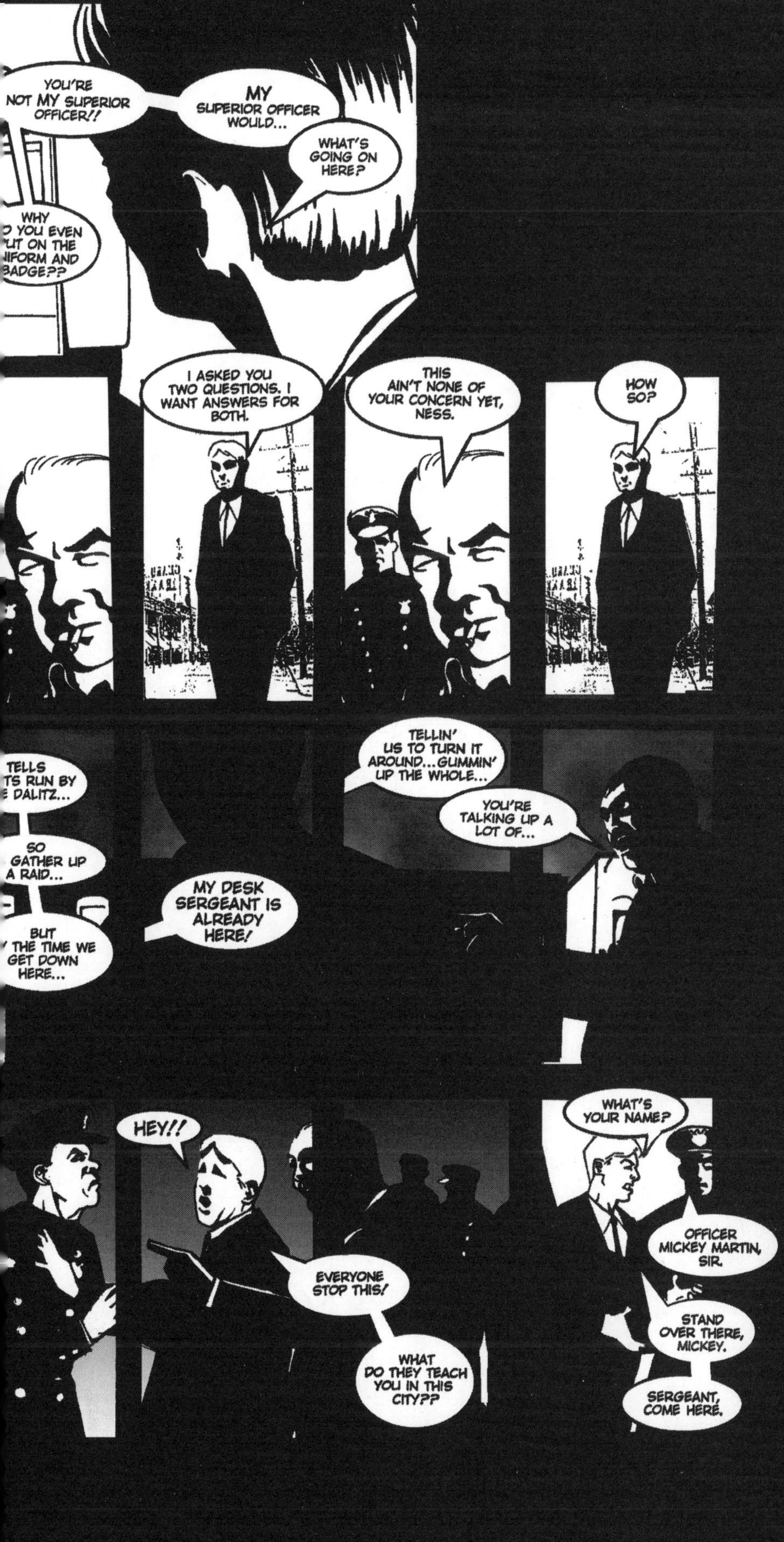
YOU'RE NOT MY SUPERIOR OFFICER!!
MY SUPERIOR OFFICER WOULD...
WHAT'S GOING ON HERE?
WHY
O YOU EVEN
UT ON THE
NIFORM AND
BADGE??
I ASKED YOU TWO QUESTIONS. I WANT ANSWERS FOR BOTH.
THIS AIN'T NONE OF YOUR CONCERN YET, NESS.
HOW SO?
TELLS
TS RUN BY
E DALITZ...
SO
GATHER UP
A RAID...
BUT
THE TIME WE
GET DOWN
HERE...
MY DESK SERGEANT IS ALREADY HERE!
TELLIN' US TO TURN IT AROUND...GUMMIN' UP THE WHOLE...
YOU'RE TALKING UP A LOT OF...
HEY!!
EVERYONE STOP THIS!
WHAT DO THEY TEACH YOU IN THIS CITY??
WHAT'S YOUR NAME?
OFFICER MICKEY MARTIN, SIR.
STAND OVER THERE, MICKEY.
SERGEANT, COME HERE.

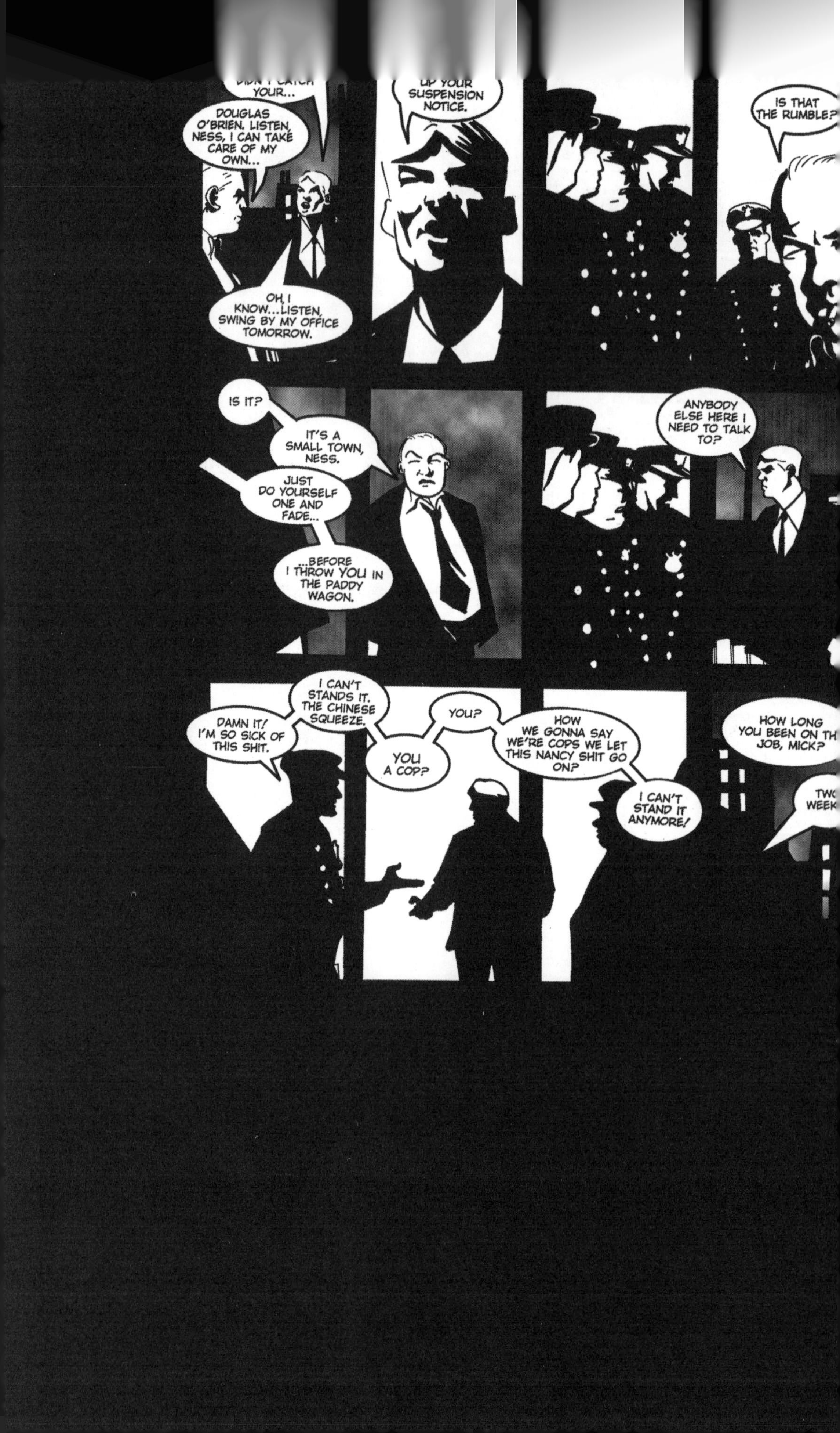
YOUR...
DOUGLAS O'BRIEN. LISTEN, NESS, I CAN TAKE CARE OF MY OWN...
OH, I KNOW...LISTEN, SWING BY MY OFFICE TOMORROW.
SUSPENSION NOTICE.
IS THAT THE RUMBLE?
IS IT?
IT'S A SMALL TOWN, NESS.
JUST DO YOURSELF ONE AND FADE...
...BEFORE I THROW YOU IN THE PADDY WAGON.
ANYBODY ELSE HERE I NEED TO TALK TO?
DAMN IT! I'M SO SICK OF THIS SHIT.
I CAN'T STANDS IT. THE CHINESE SQUEEZE.
YOU A COP?
YOU?
HOW WE GONNA SAY WE'RE COPS WE LET THIS NANCY SHIT GO ON?
I CAN'T STAND IT ANYMORE!
HOW LONG YOU BEEN ON TH
JOB, MICK?

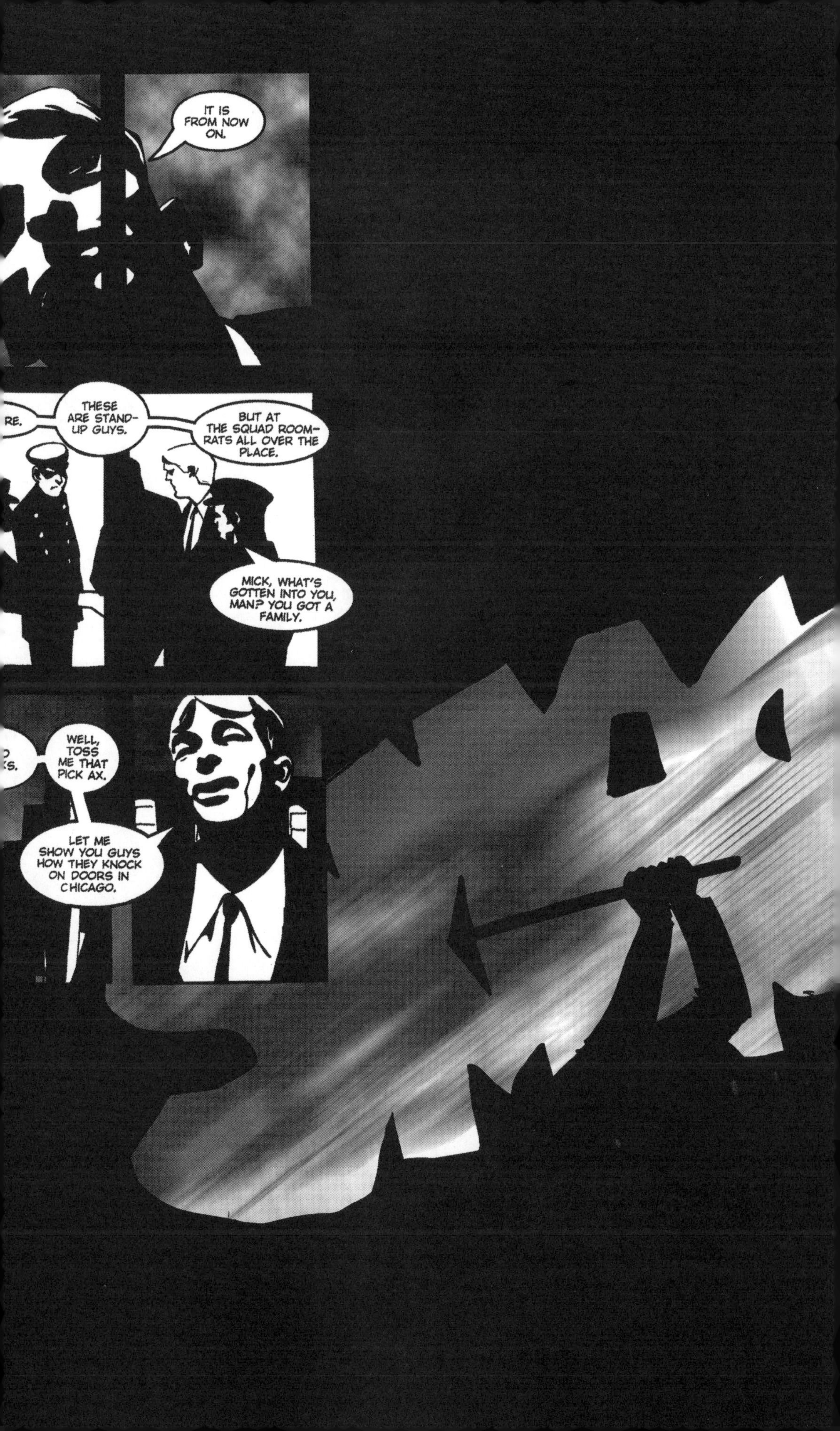
IT IS FROM NOW ON.
THESE ARE STAND-UP GUYS.
BUT AT THE SQUAD ROOM-RATS ALL OVER THE PLACE.
MICK, WHAT'S GOTTEN INTO YOU, MAN? YOU GOT A FAMILY.
WELL, TOSS ME THAT PICK AX.
LET ME SHOW YOU GUYS HOW THEY KNOCK ON DOORS IN CHICAGO.

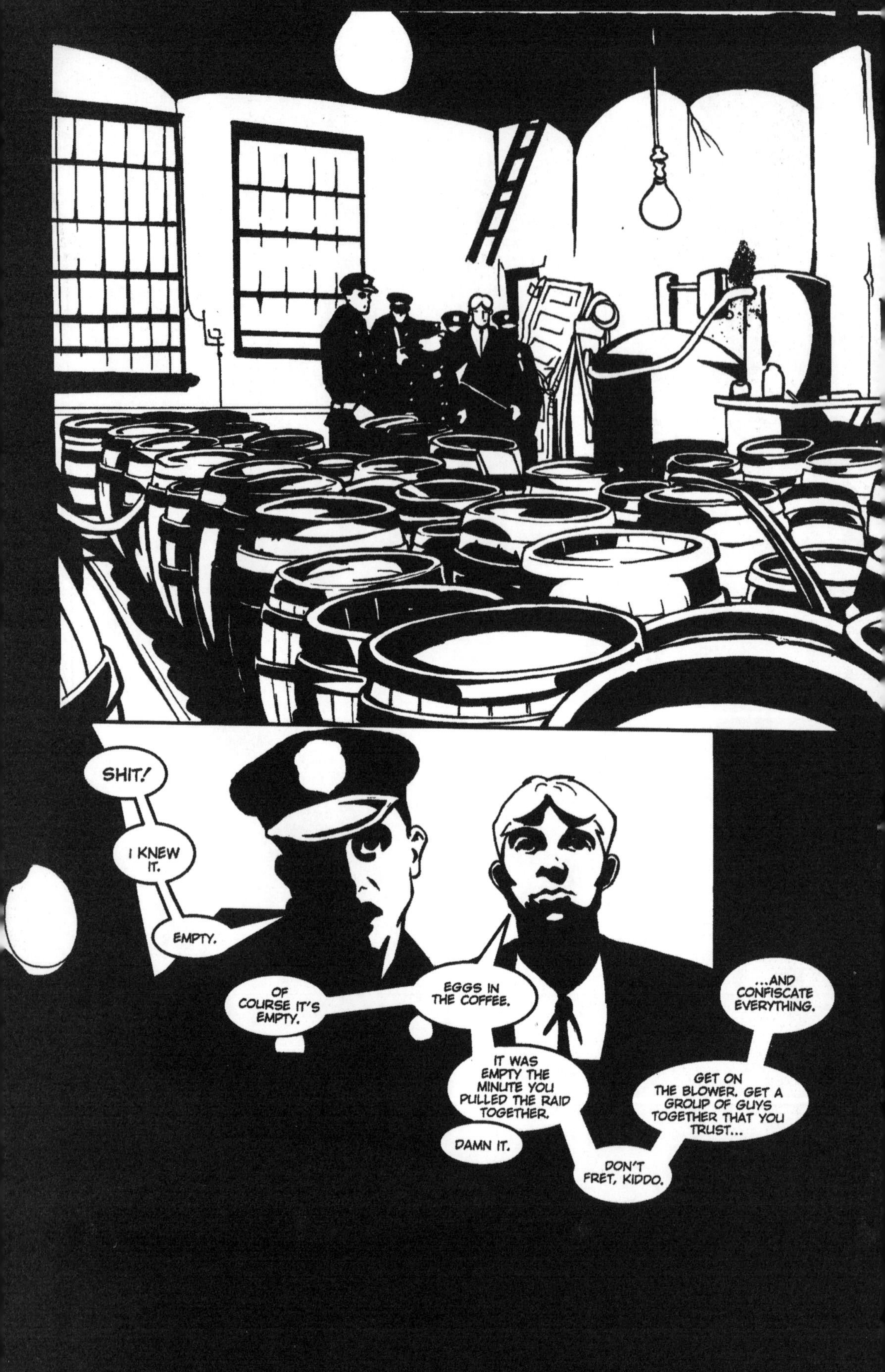
SHIT!
I KNEW IT.
EMPTY.
OF COURSE IT'S EMPTY.
EGGS IN THE COFFEE.
IT WAS EMPTY THE MINUTE YOU PULLED THE RAID TOGETHER.
DAMN IT.
DON'T FRET, KIDDO.
GET ON THE BLOWER. GET A GROUP OF GUYS TOGETHER THAT YOU TRUST...
...AND CONFISCATE EVERYTHING.

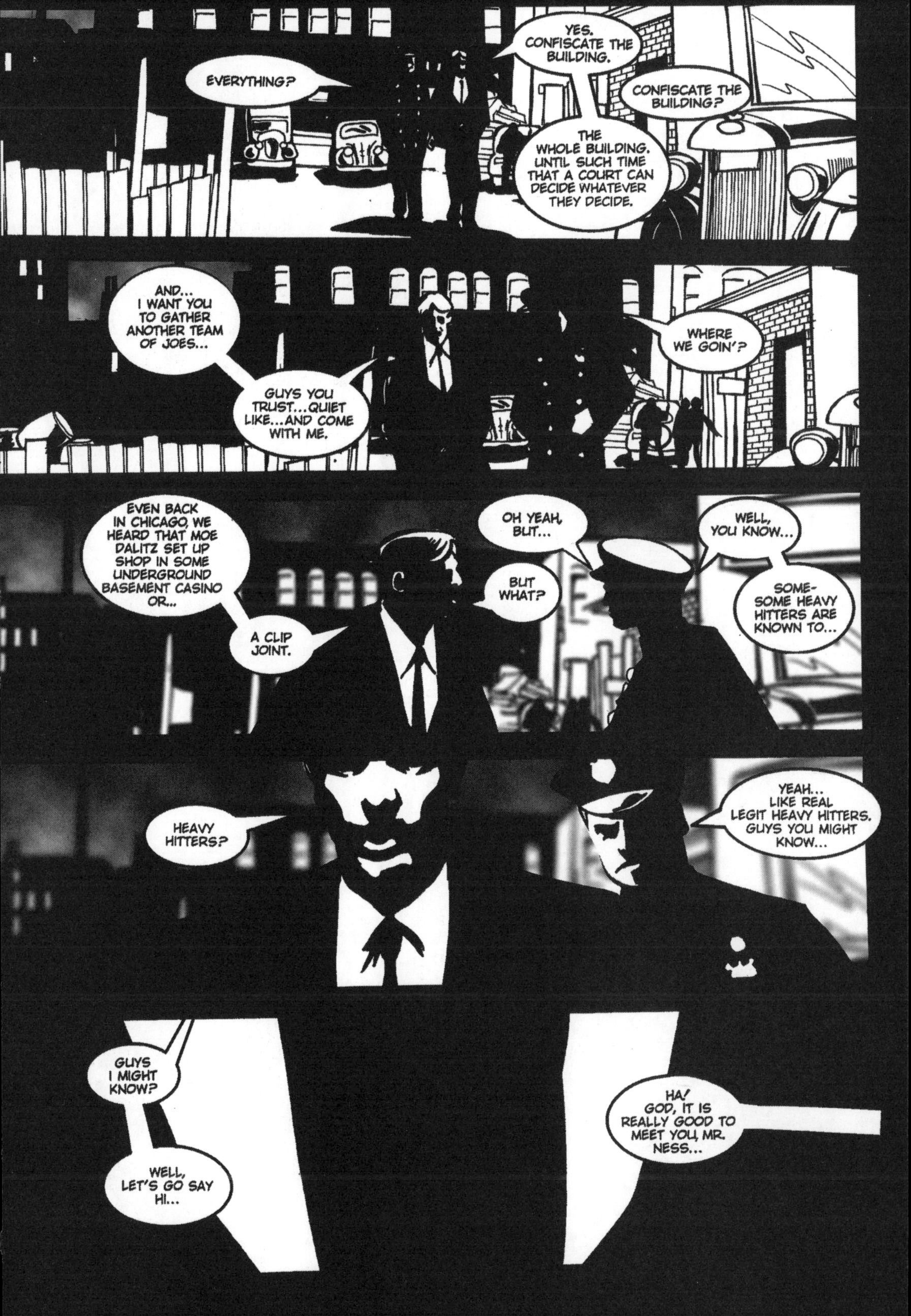
EVERYTHING?
YES. CONFISCATE THE BUILDING.
CONFISCATE THE BUILDING?
THE WHOLE BUILDING. UNTIL SUCH TIME THAT A COURT CAN DECIDE WHATEVER THEY DECIDE.
AND... I WANT YOU TO GATHER ANOTHER TEAM OF JOES...
GUYS YOU TRUST...QUIET LIKE...AND COME WITH ME.
WHERE WE GOIN'?
EVEN BACK IN CHICAGO, WE HEARD THAT MOE DALITZ SET UP SHOP IN SOME UNDERGROUND BASEMENT CASINO OR...
A CLIP JOINT.
OH YEAH, BUT...
BUT WHAT?
WELL, YOU KNOW...
SOME- SOME HEAVY HITTERS ARE KNOWN TO...
HEAVY HITTERS?
YEAH... LIKE REAL LEGIT HEAVY HITTERS. GUYS YOU MIGHT KNOW...
GUYS I MIGHT KNOW?
WELL, LET'S GO SAY HI...
HA! GOD, IT IS REALLY GOOD TO MEET YOU, MR. NESS...

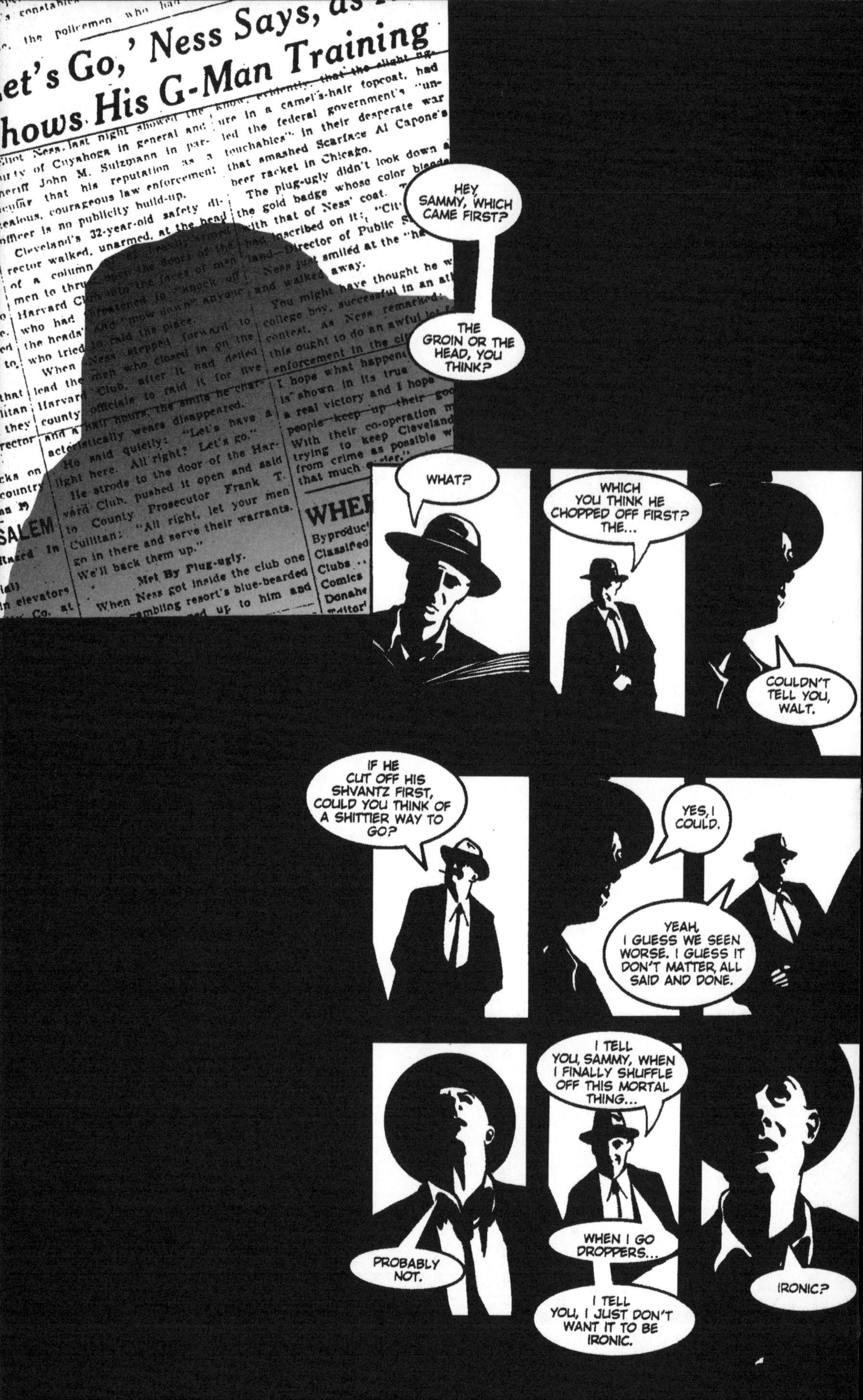
'Let's Go,' Ness Says, as
Shows His G-Man Training
HEY, SAMMY, WHICH CAME FIRST?
THE GROIN OR THE HEAD, YOU THINK?
WHAT?
WHICH YOU THINK HE CHOPPED OFF FIRST? THE...
COULDN'T TELL YOU, WALT.
IF HE CUT OFF HIS SHVANTZ FIRST, COULD YOU THINK OF A SHITTIER WAY TO GO?
YES, I COULD.
YEAH, I GUESS WE SEEN WORSE. I GUESS IT DON'T MATTER, ALL SAID AND DONE.
PROBABLY NOT.
I TELL YOU, SAMMY, WHEN I FINALLY SHUFFLE OFF THIS MORTAL THING...
WHEN I GO DROPPERS...
I TELL YOU, I JUST DON'T WANT IT TO BE IRONIC.
IRONIC?

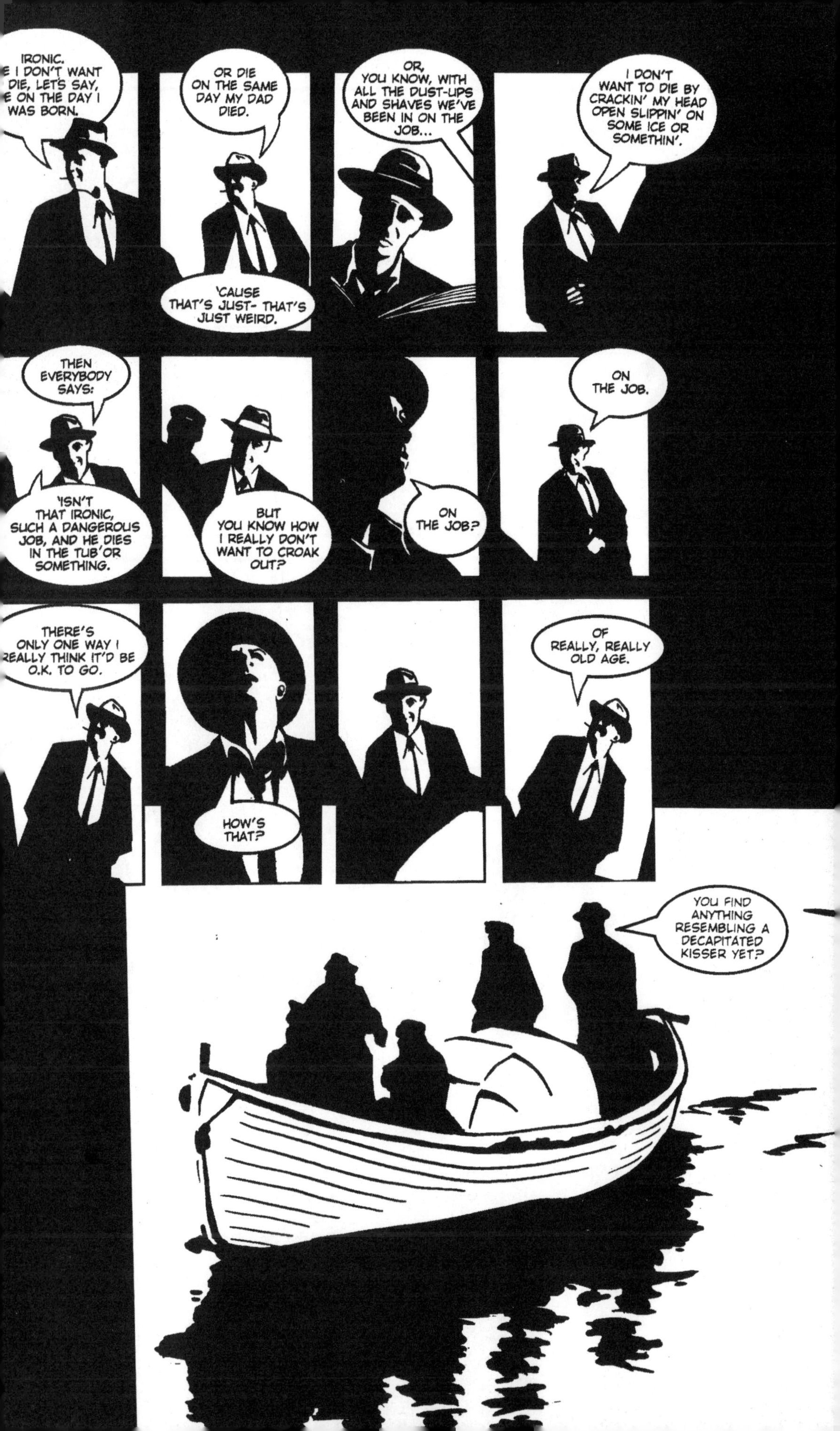
IRONIC.
E I DON'T WANT DIE, LET'S SAY, E ON THE DAY I WAS BORN.
OR DIE ON THE SAME DAY MY DAD DIED.
'CAUSE THAT'S JUST- THAT'S JUST WEIRD.
OR, YOU KNOW, WITH ALL THE DUST-UPS AND SHAVES WE'VE BEEN IN ON THE JOB...
I DON'T WANT TO DIE BY CRACKIN' MY HEAD OPEN SLIPPIN' ON SOME ICE OR SOMETHIN'.
THEN EVERYBODY SAYS:
'ISN'T THAT IRONIC, SUCH A DANGEROUS JOB, AND HE DIES IN THE TUB'OR SOMETHING.
BUT YOU KNOW HOW I REALLY DON'T WANT TO CROAK OUT?
ON THE JOB?
ON THE JOB.
THERE'S ONLY ONE WAY I REALLY THINK IT'D BE O.K. TO GO.
HOW'S THAT?
OF REALLY, REALLY OLD AGE.
YOU FIND ANYTHING RESEMBLING A DECAPITATED KISSER YET?

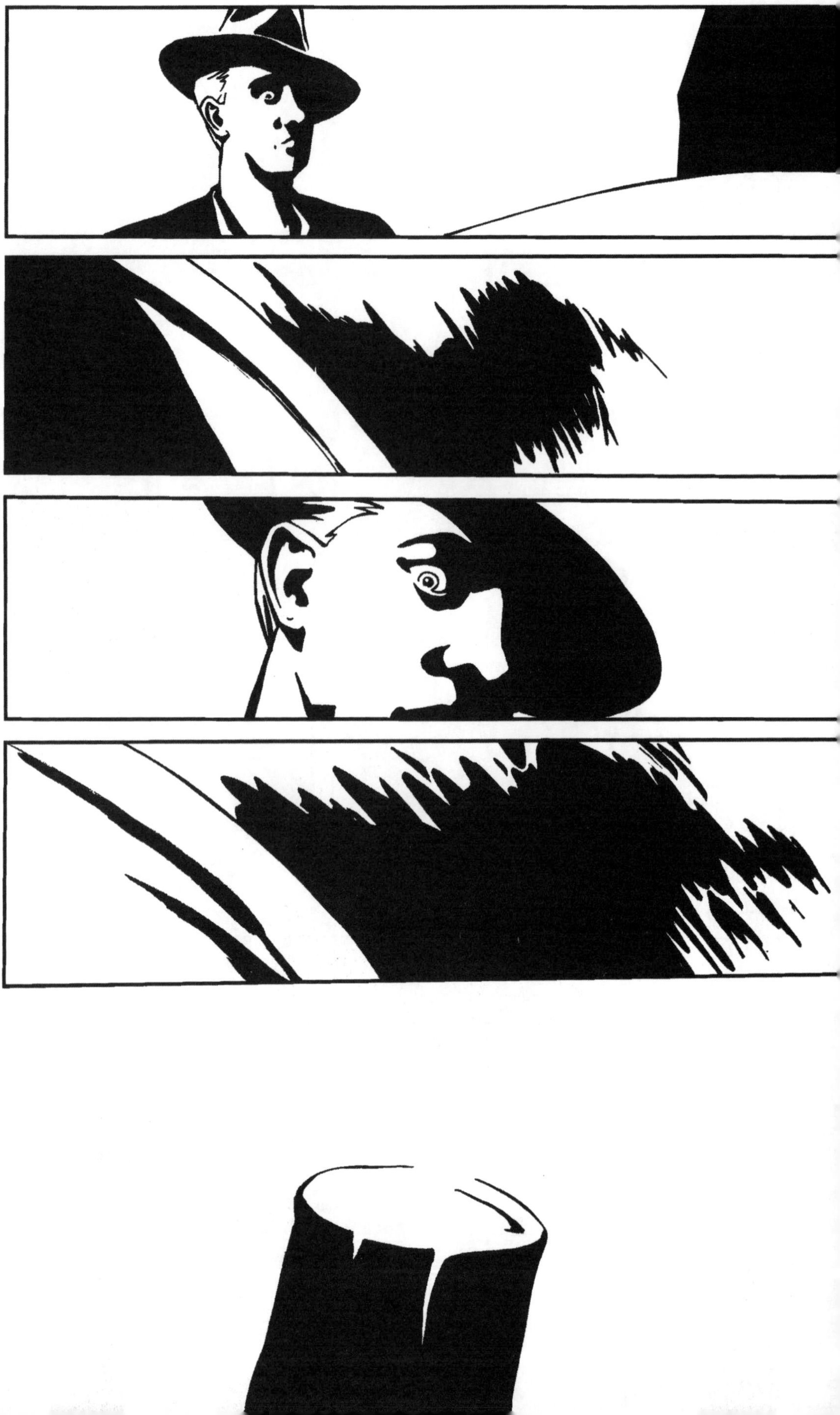

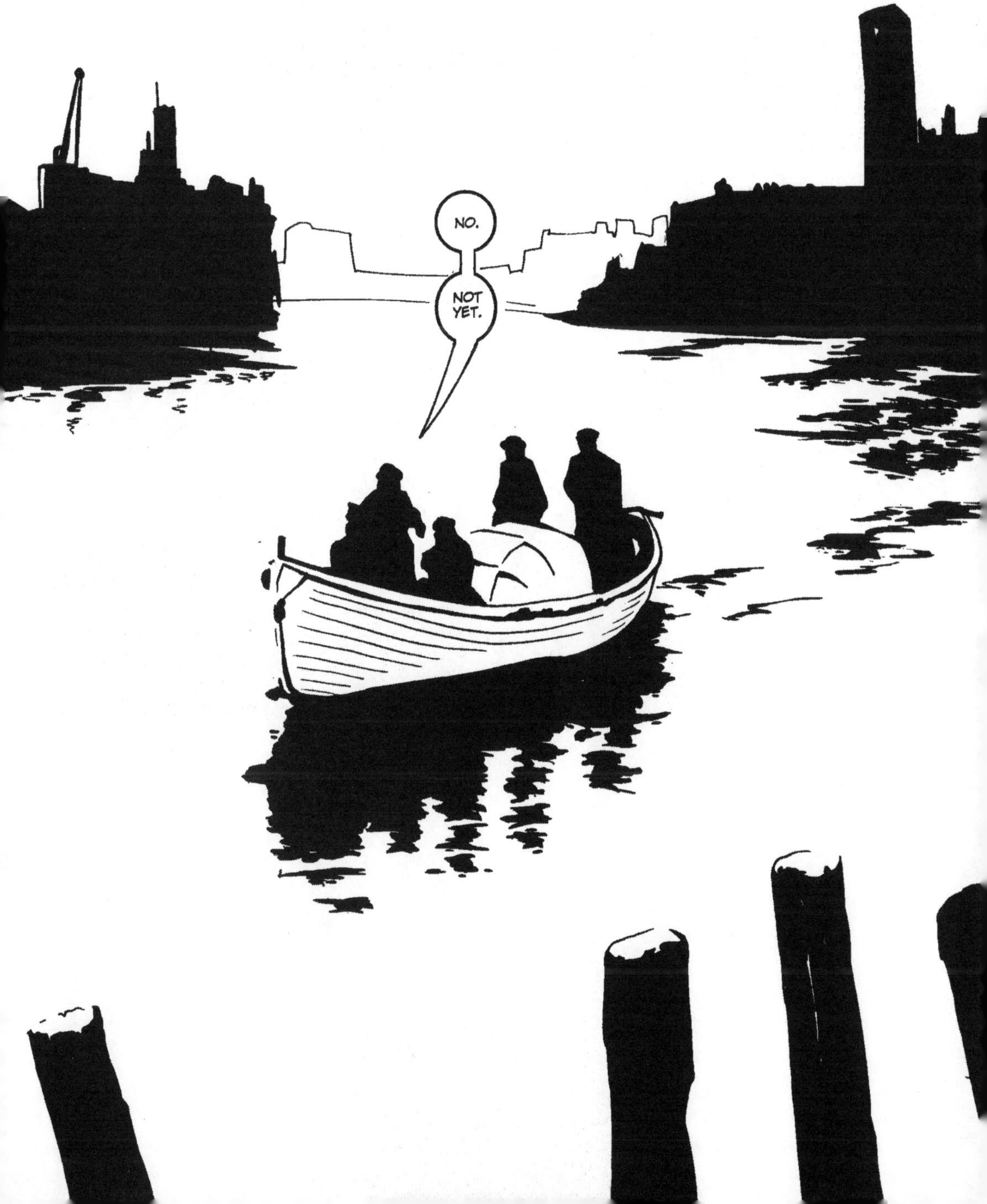
NO.
NOT YET.

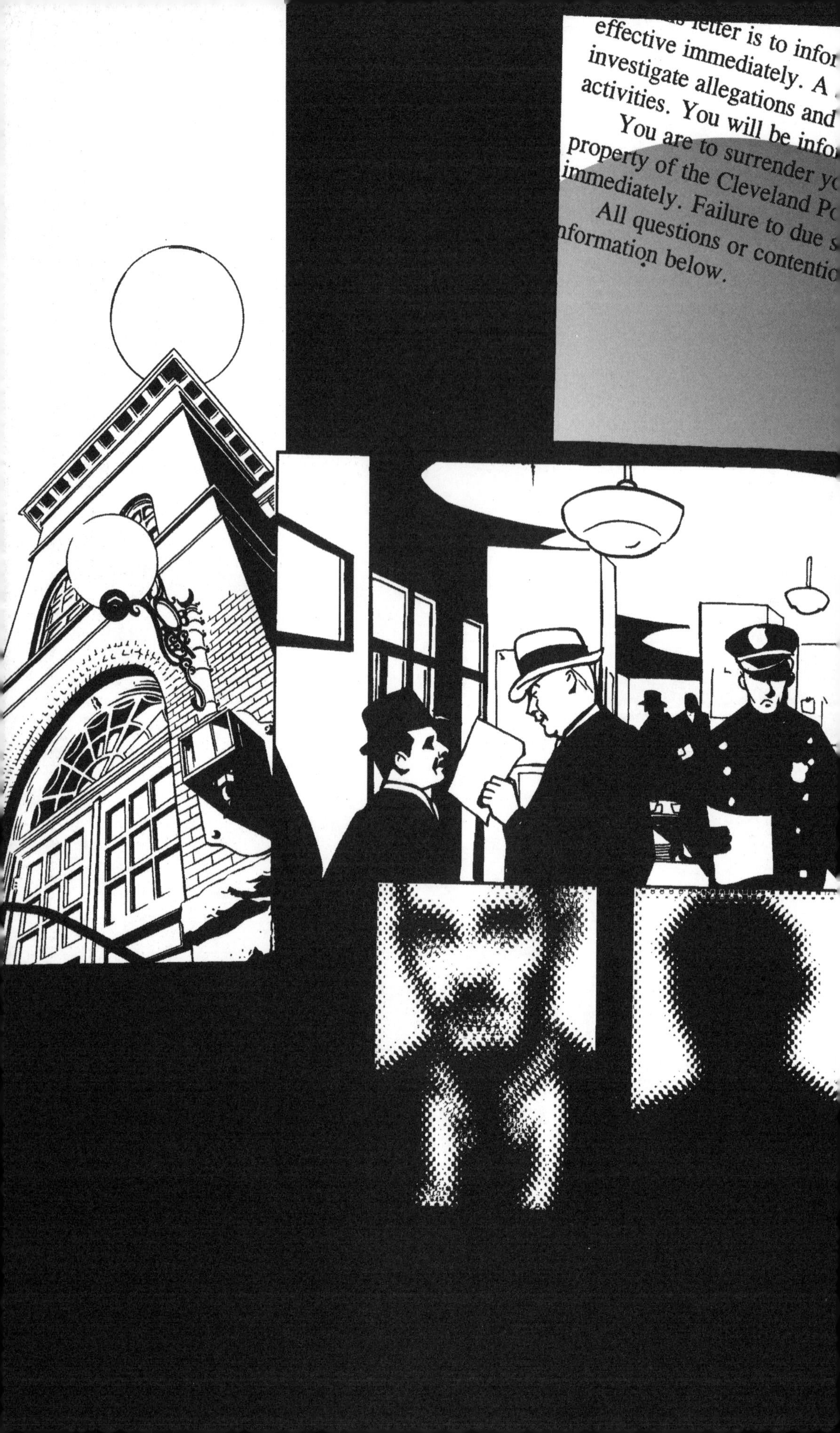

letter is to infor
effective immediately. A
investigate allegations and
activities. You will be infor
You are to surrender yo
property of the Cleveland Po
immediately. Failure to due s
All questions or contentio
nformation below.

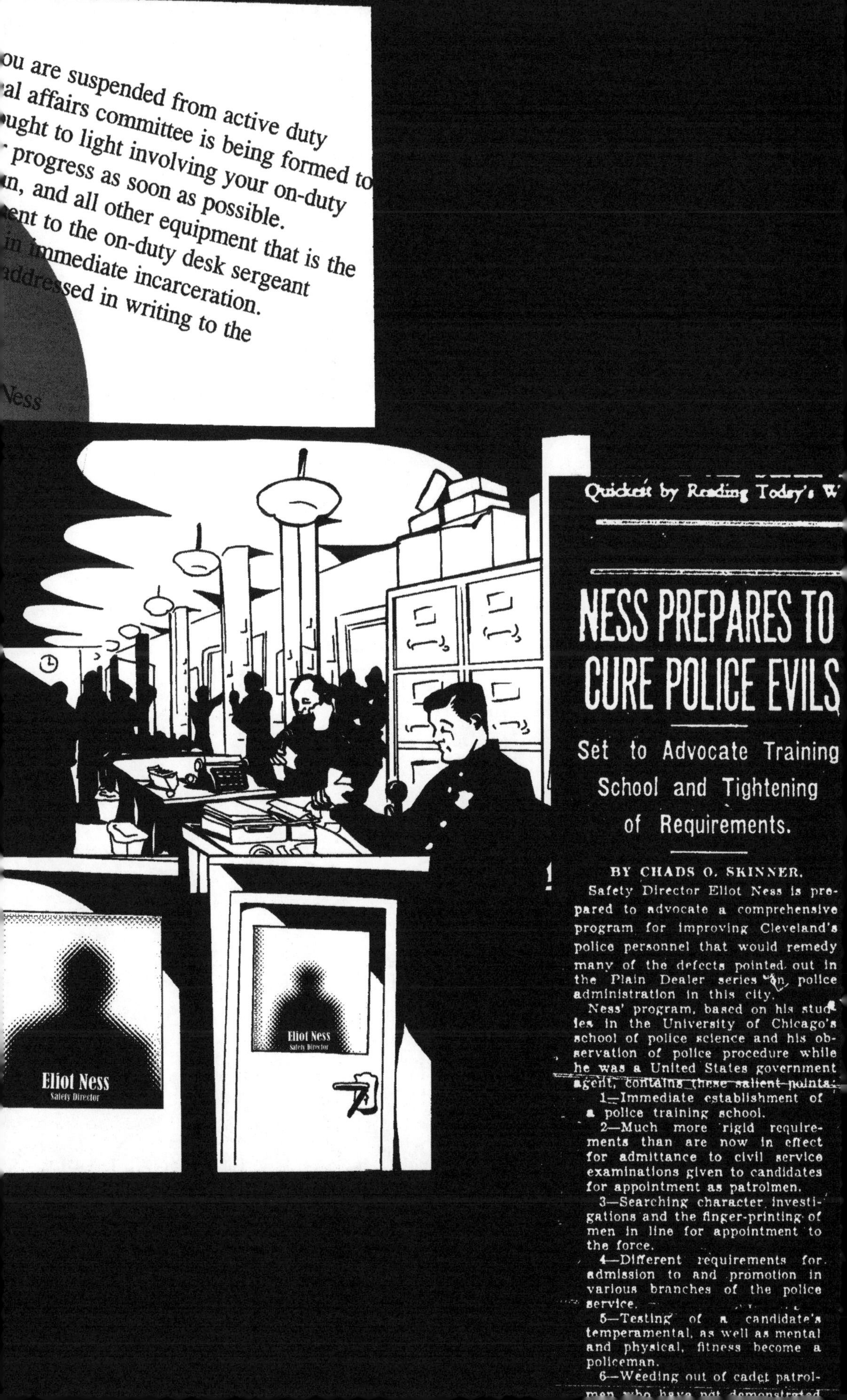
ou are suspended from active duty
al affairs committee is being formed to
ught to light involving your on-duty
progress as soon as possible.
n, and all other equipment that is the
ent to the on-duty desk sergeant
in immediate incarceration.
addressed in writing to the
Ness
Eliot Ness
Safety Director
Eliot Ness
Safety Director
Quickest by Reading Today's W
NESS PREPARES TO CURE POLICE EVILS
Set to Advocate Training School and Tightening of Requirements.
BY CHADS O. SKINNER.
Safety Director Eliot Ness is prepared to advocate a comprehensive program for improving Cleveland's police personnel that would remedy many of the defects pointed out in the Plain Dealer series on police administration in this city.
Ness' program, based on his studies in the University of Chicago's school of police science and his observation of police procedure while he was a United States government agent, contains these salient points:
1—Immediate establishment of a police training school.
2—Much more rigid requirements than are now in effect for admittance to civil service examinations given to candidates for appointment as patrolmen.
3—Searching character investigations and the finger-printing of men in line for appointment to the force.
4—Different requirements for admission to and promotion in various branches of the police service.
5—Testing of a candidate's temperamental, as well as mental and physical, fitness become a policeman.
6—Weeding out of cadet patrol-

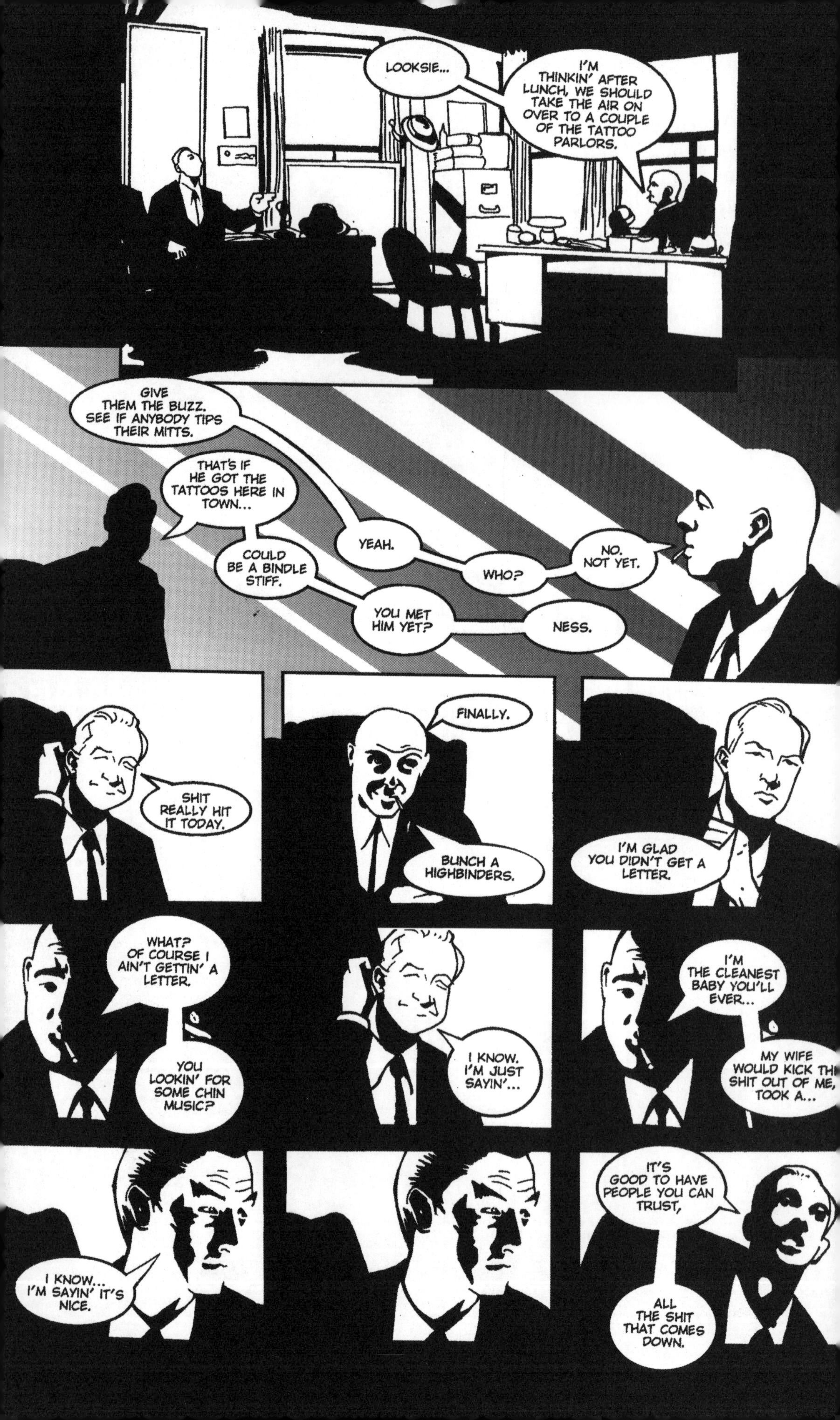
LOOKSIE...
I'M THINKIN' AFTER LUNCH, WE SHOULD TAKE THE AIR ON OVER TO A COUPLE OF THE TATTOO PARLORS.
GIVE THEM THE BUZZ. SEE IF ANYBODY TIPS THEIR MITTS.
THAT'S IF HE GOT THE TATTOOS HERE IN TOWN...
YEAH.
COULD BE A BINDLE STIFF.
WHO?
NO. NOT YET.
YOU MET HIM YET?
NESS.
SHIT REALLY HIT IT TODAY.
FINALLY.
BUNCH A HIGHBINDERS.
I'M GLAD YOU DIDN'T GET A LETTER.
WHAT? OF COURSE I AIN'T GETTIN' A LETTER.
YOU LOOKIN' FOR SOME CHIN MUSIC?
I KNOW. I'M JUST SAYIN'...
I'M THE CLEANEST BABY YOU'LL EVER...
MY WIFE WOULD KICK TH SHIT OUT OF ME, TOOK A...
I KNOW... I'M SAYIN' IT'S NICE.
IT'S GOOD TO HAVE PEOPLE YOU CAN TRUST,
ALL THE SHIT THAT COMES DOWN.

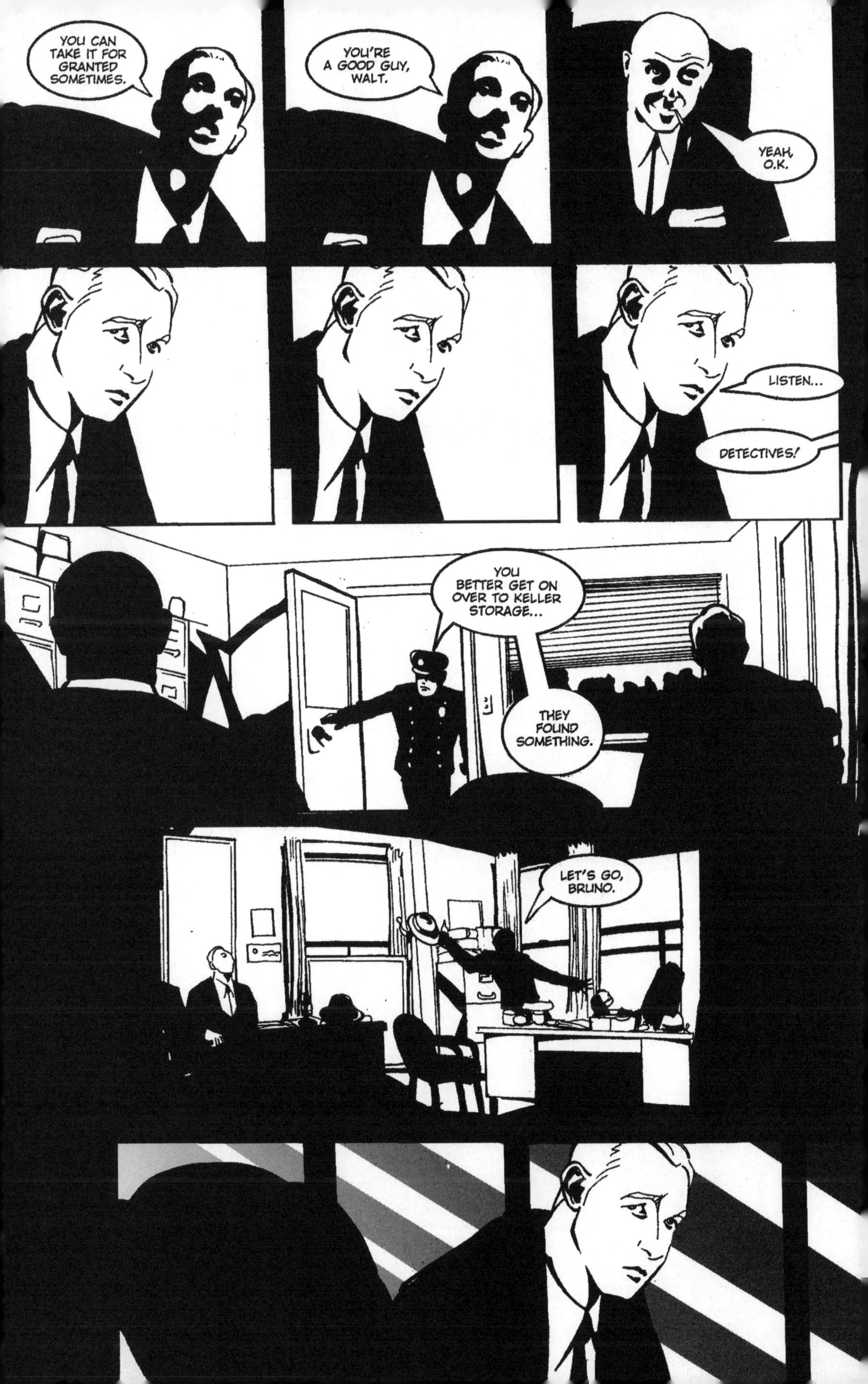
YOU CAN TAKE IT FOR GRANTED SOMETIMES.
YOU'RE A GOOD GUY, WALT.
YEAH, O.K.
LISTEN...
DETECTIVES!
YOU BETTER GET ON OVER TO KELLER STORAGE...
THEY FOUND SOMETHING.
LET'S GO, BRUNO.

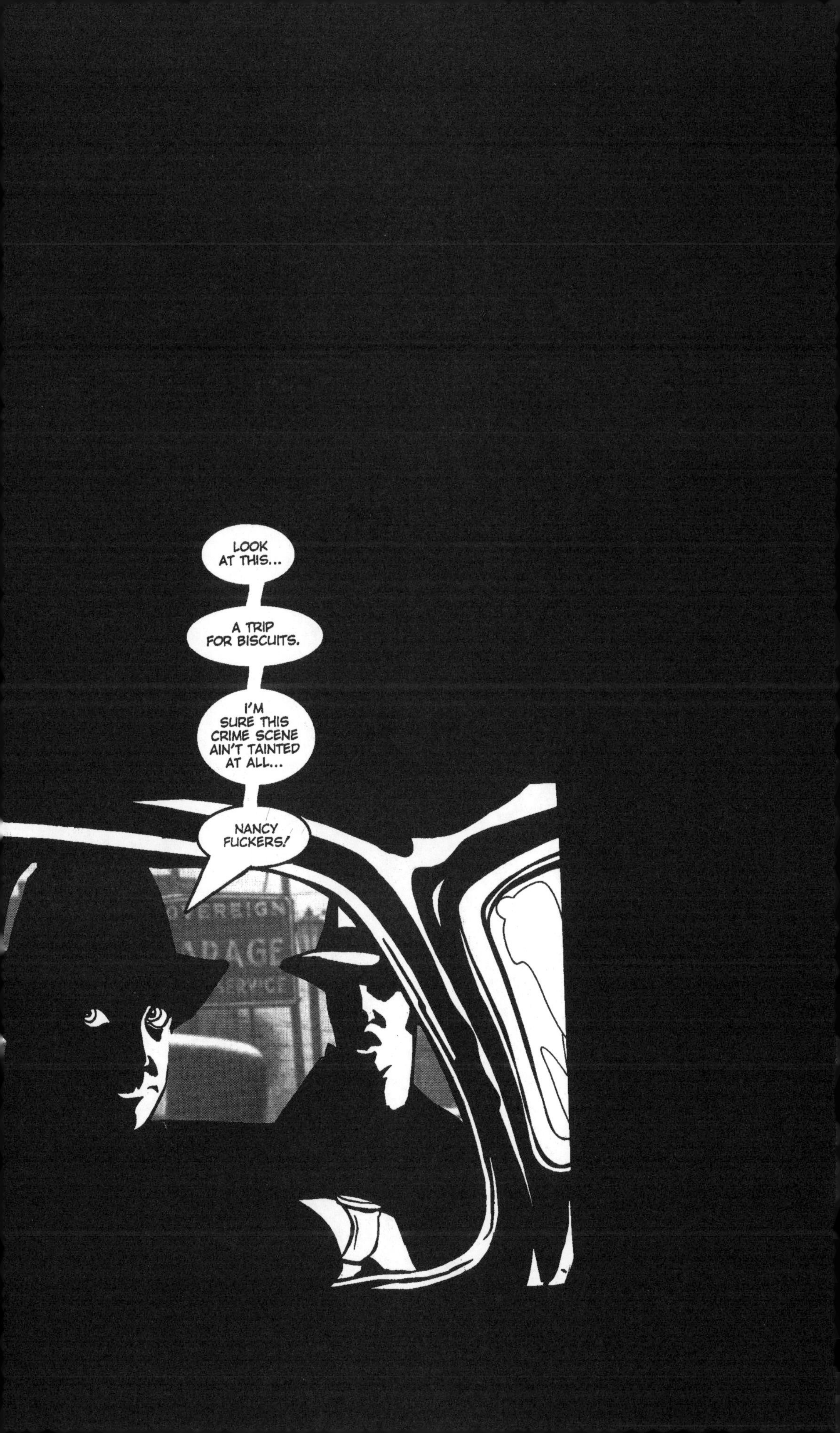
LOOK AT THIS...
A TRIP FOR BISCUITS.
I'M SURE THIS CRIME SCENE AIN'T TAINTED AT ALL...
NANCY FUCKERS!

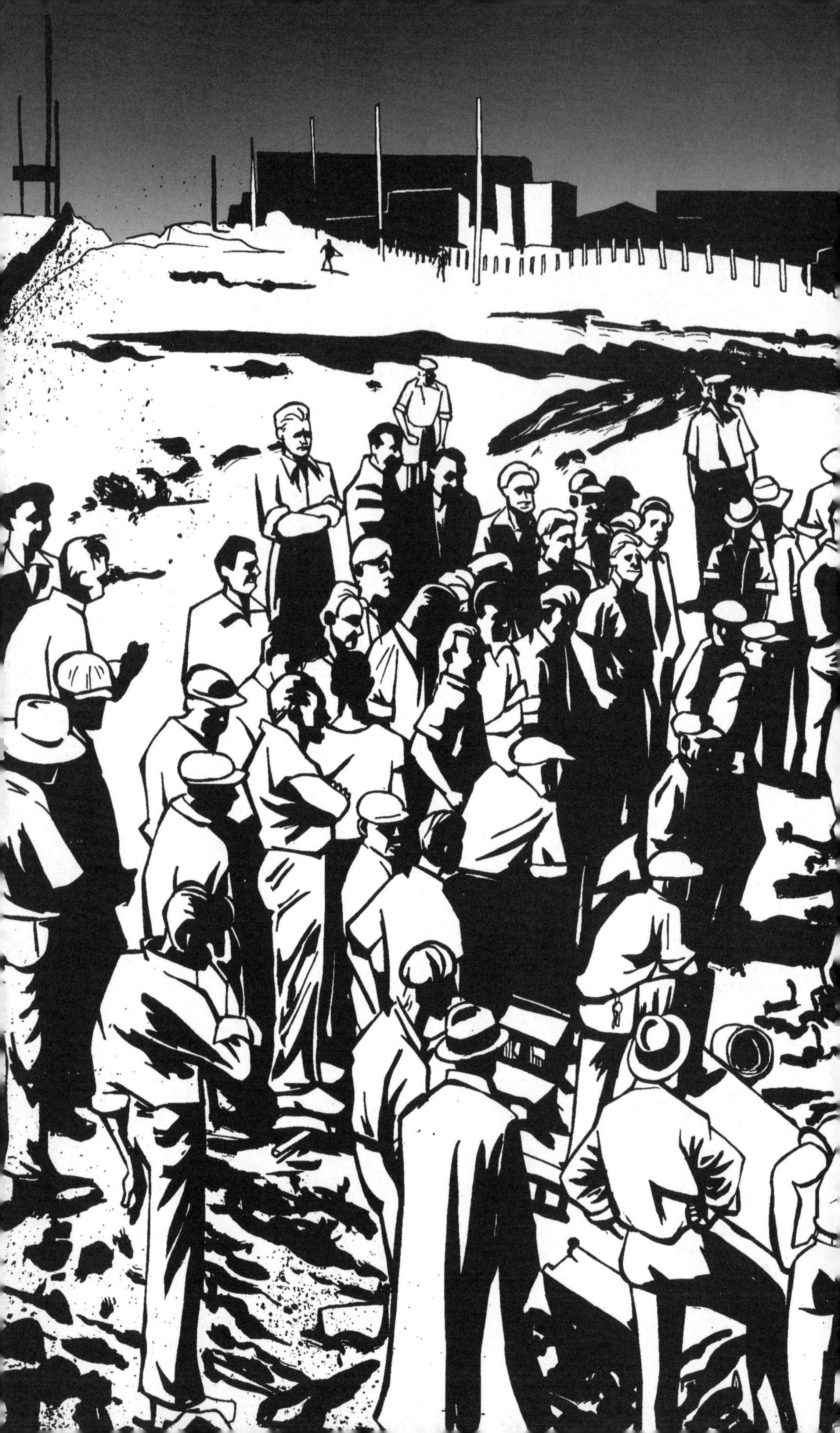

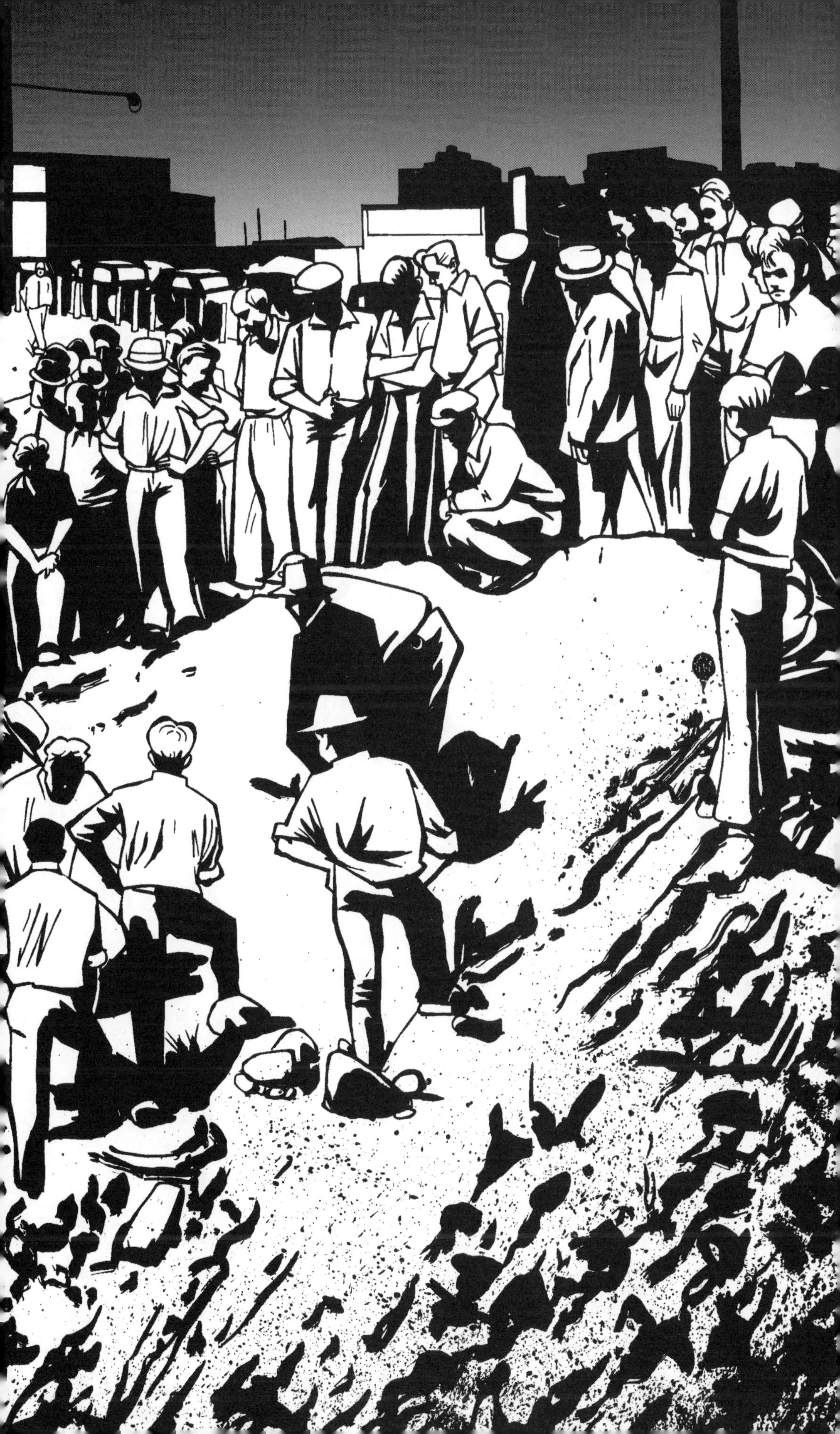

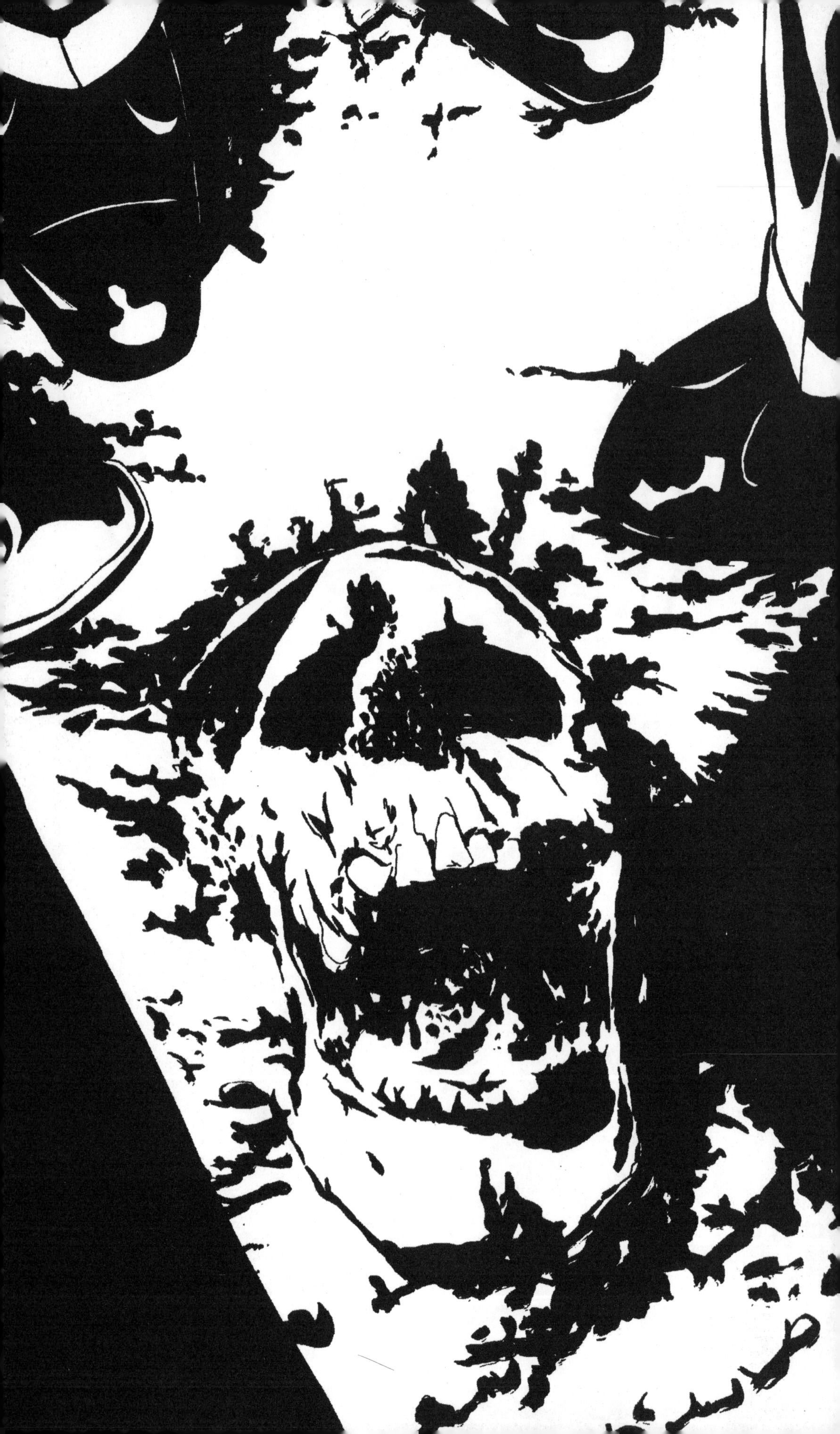

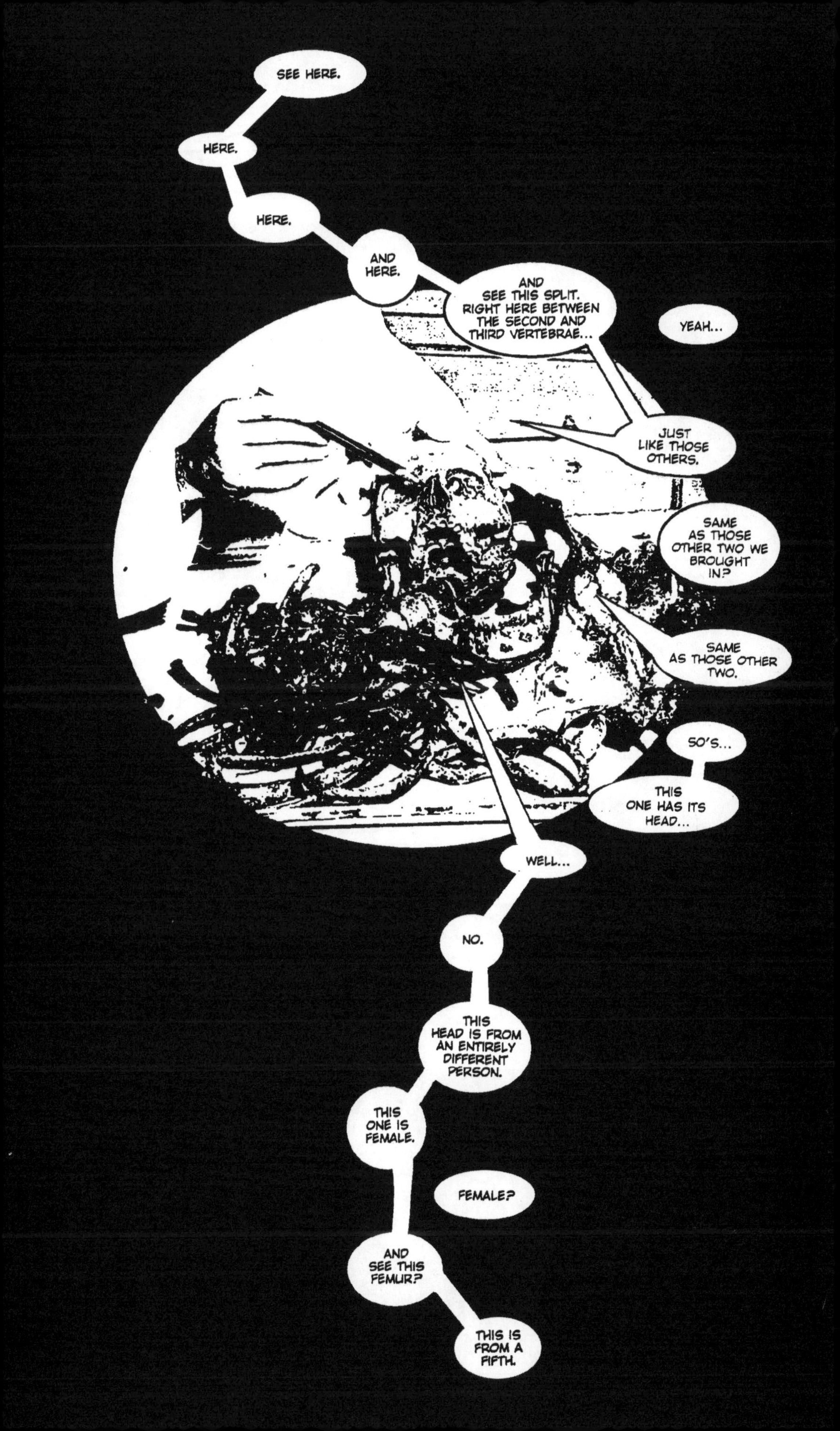
SEE HERE.
HERE.
HERE.
AND HERE.
AND SEE THIS SPLIT. RIGHT HERE BETWEEN THE SECOND AND THIRD VERTEBRAE...
YEAH...
JUST LIKE THOSE OTHERS.
SAME AS THOSE OTHER TWO WE BROUGHT IN?
SAME AS THOSE OTHER TWO.
SO'S...
THIS ONE HAS ITS HEAD...
WELL...
NO.
THIS HEAD IS FROM AN ENTIRELY DIFFERENT PERSON.
THIS ONE IS FEMALE.
FEMALE?
AND SEE THIS FEMUR?
THIS IS FROM A FIFTH.

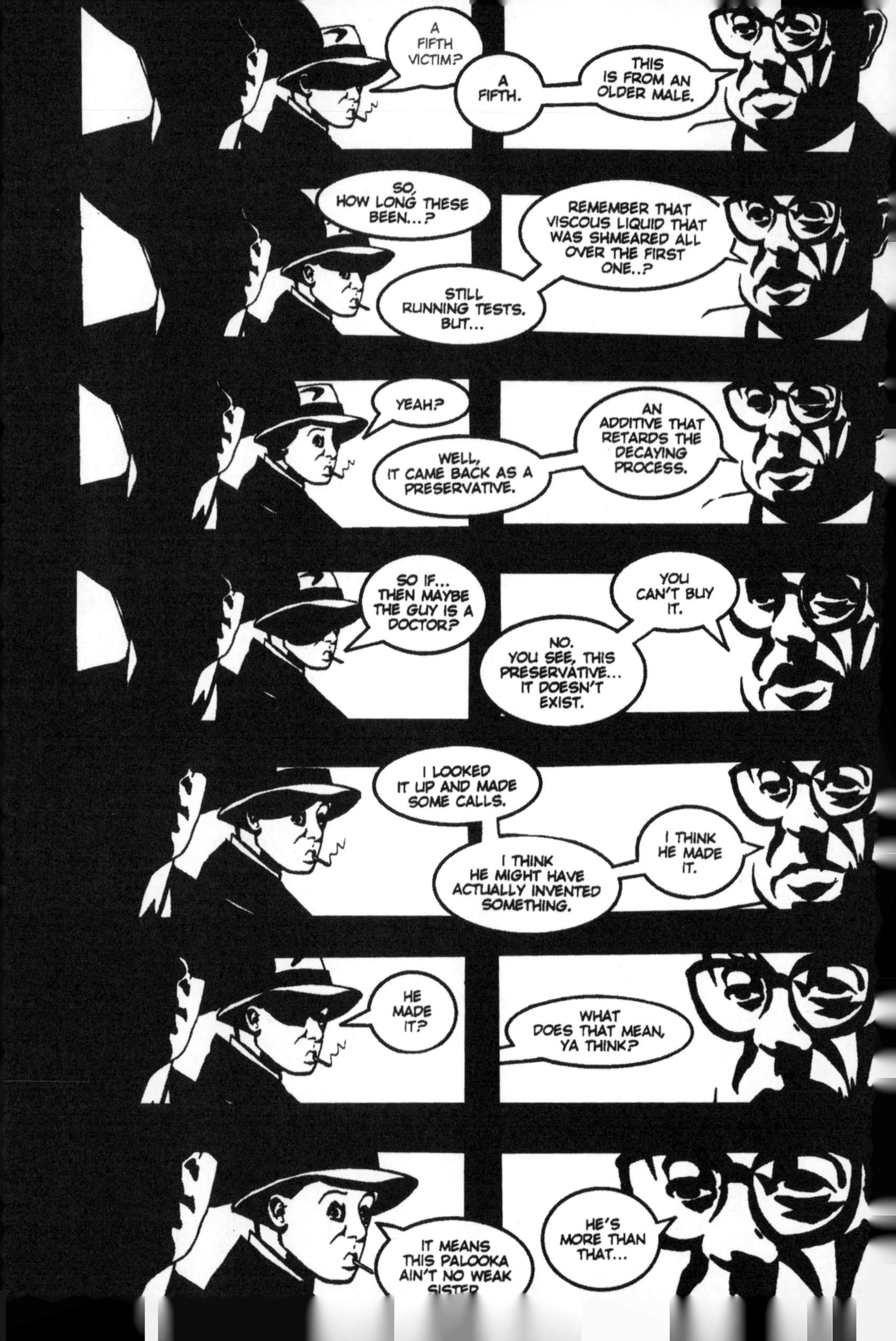
A FIFTH VICTIM?
A FIFTH.
THIS IS FROM AN OLDER MALE.
SO, HOW LONG THESE BEEN...?
STILL RUNNING TESTS. BUT...
REMEMBER THAT VISCOUS LIQUID THAT WAS SHMEARED ALL OVER THE FIRST ONE..?
YEAH?
WELL, IT CAME BACK AS A PRESERVATIVE.
AN ADDITIVE THAT RETARDS THE DECAYING PROCESS.
SO IF... THEN MAYBE THE GUY IS A DOCTOR?
NO. YOU SEE, THIS PRESERVATIVE... IT DOESN'T EXIST.
YOU CAN'T BUY IT.
I LOOKED IT UP AND MADE SOME CALLS.
I THINK HE MIGHT HAVE ACTUALLY INVENTED SOMETHING.
I THINK HE MADE IT.
HE MADE IT?
WHAT DOES THAT MEAN, YA THINK?
IT MEANS THIS PALOOKA AIN'T NO WEAK SISTER.
HE'S MORE THAN THAT...

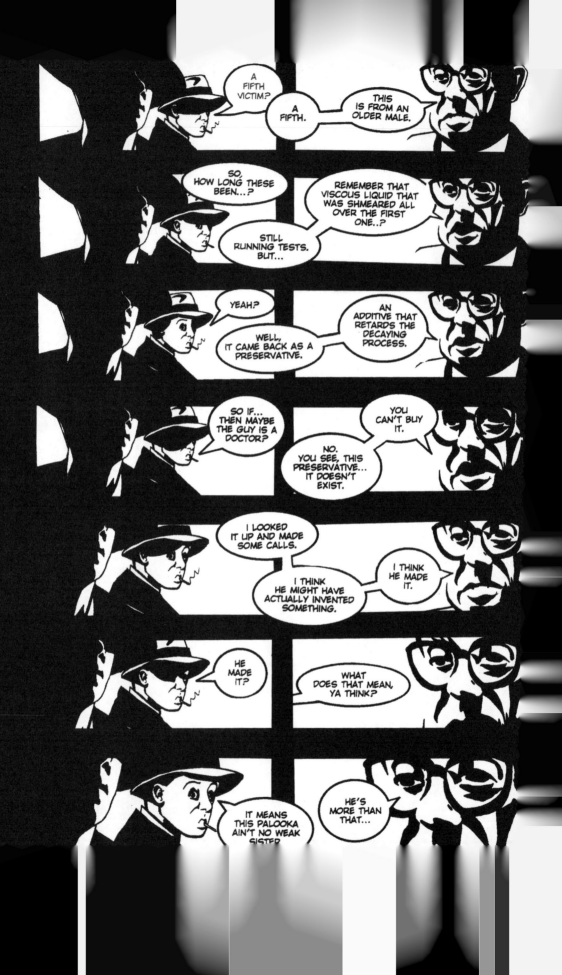

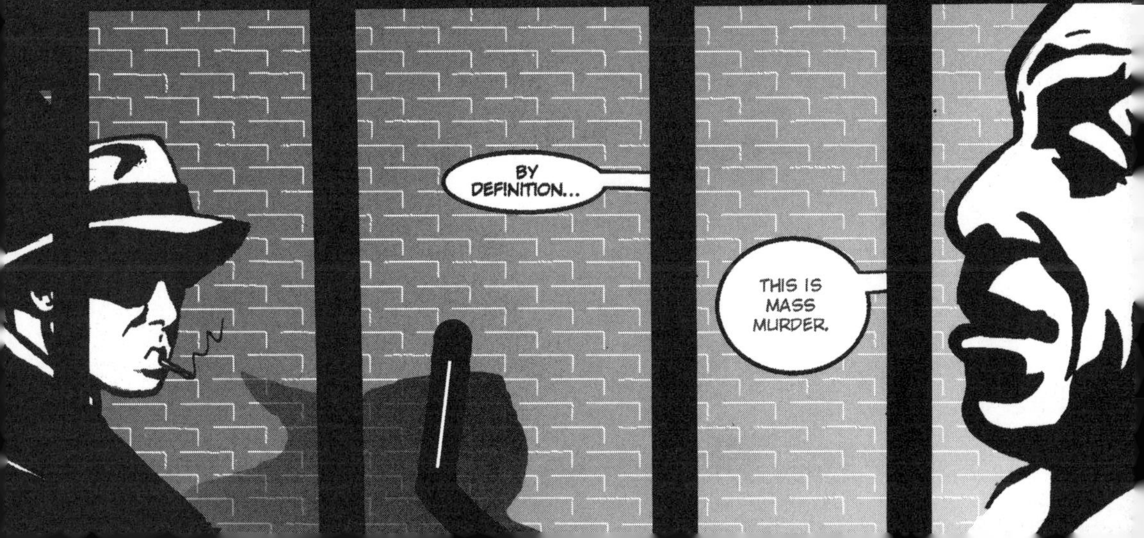
BY DEFINITION...
THIS IS MASS MURDER.

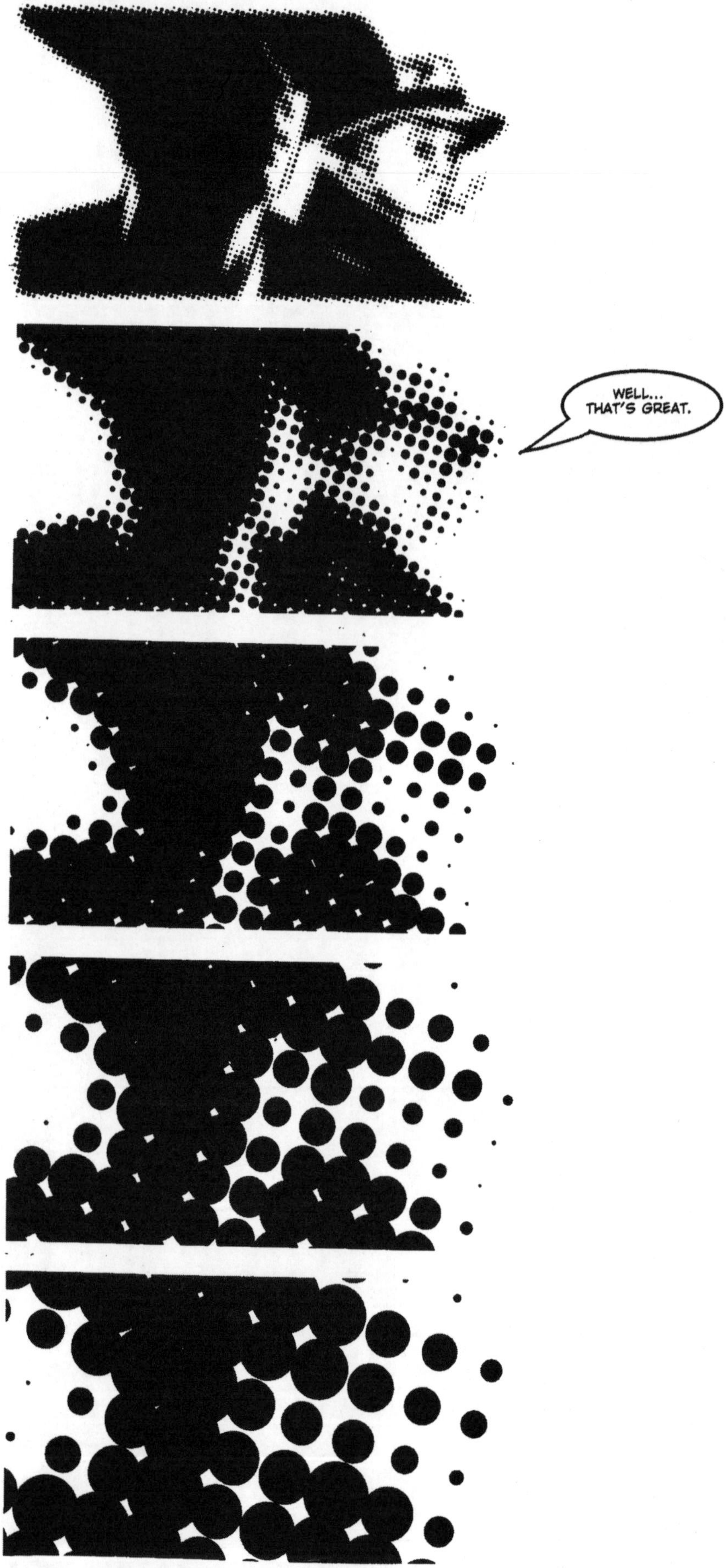
WELL...
THAT'S GREAT.

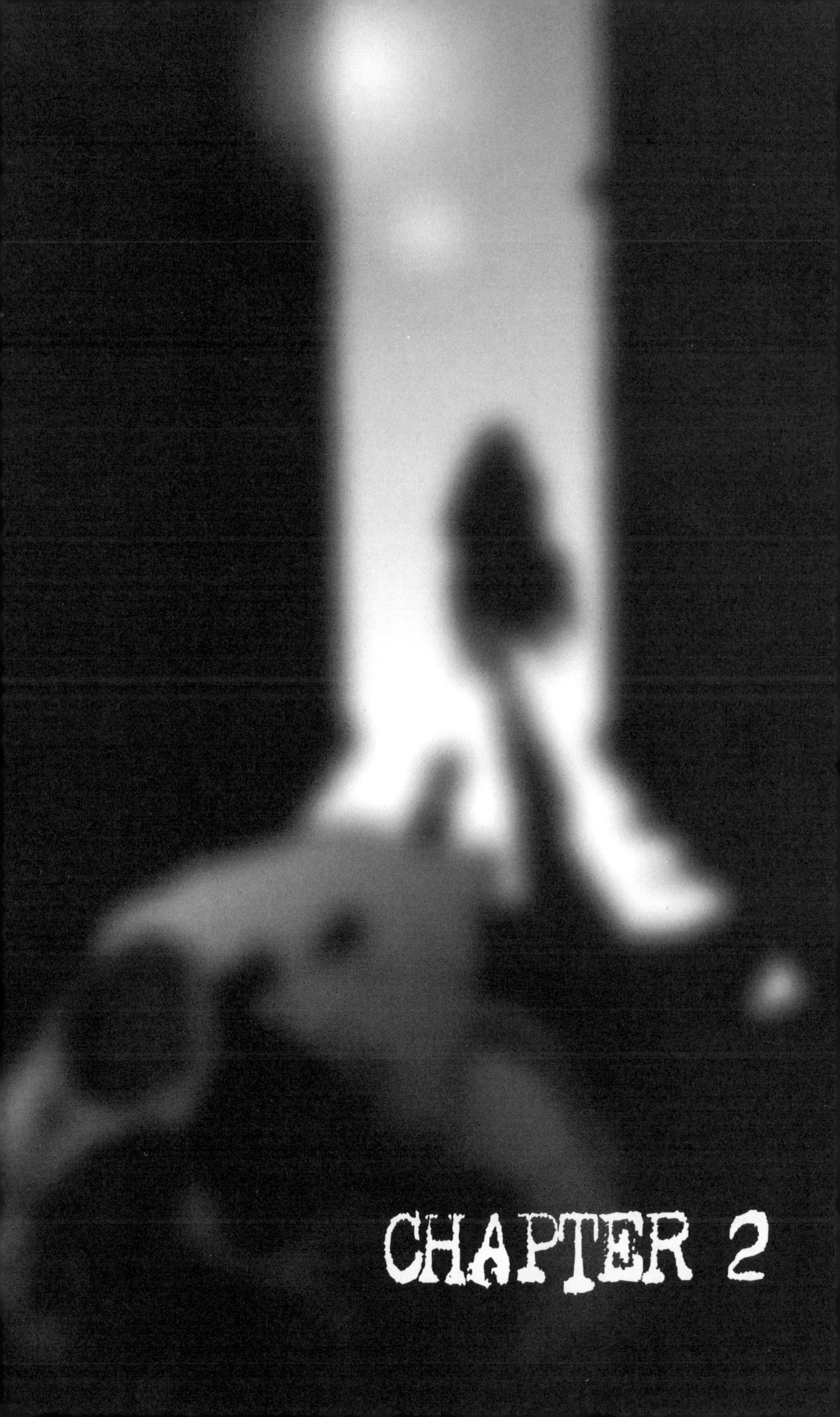

CHAPTER 2

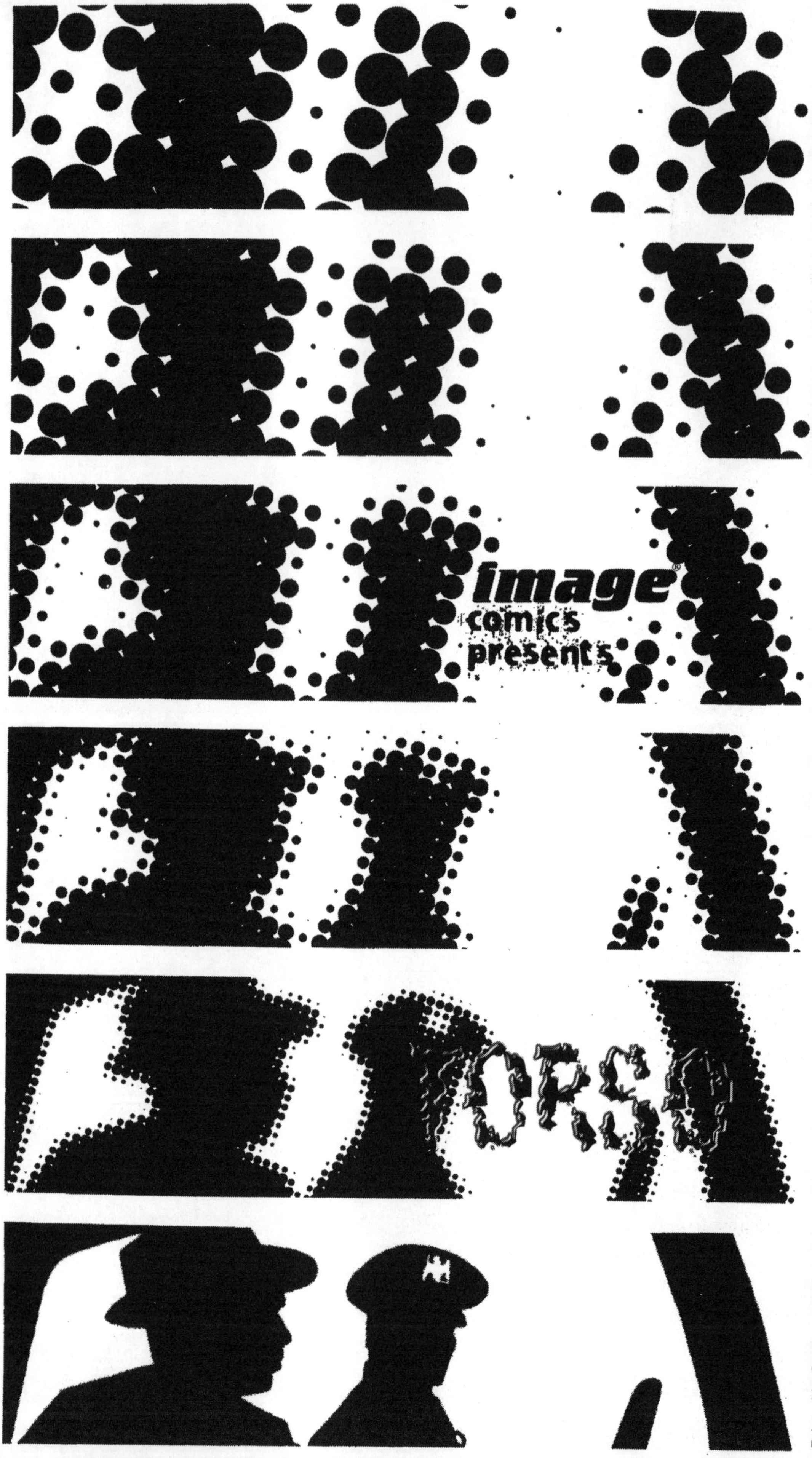
image comics presents

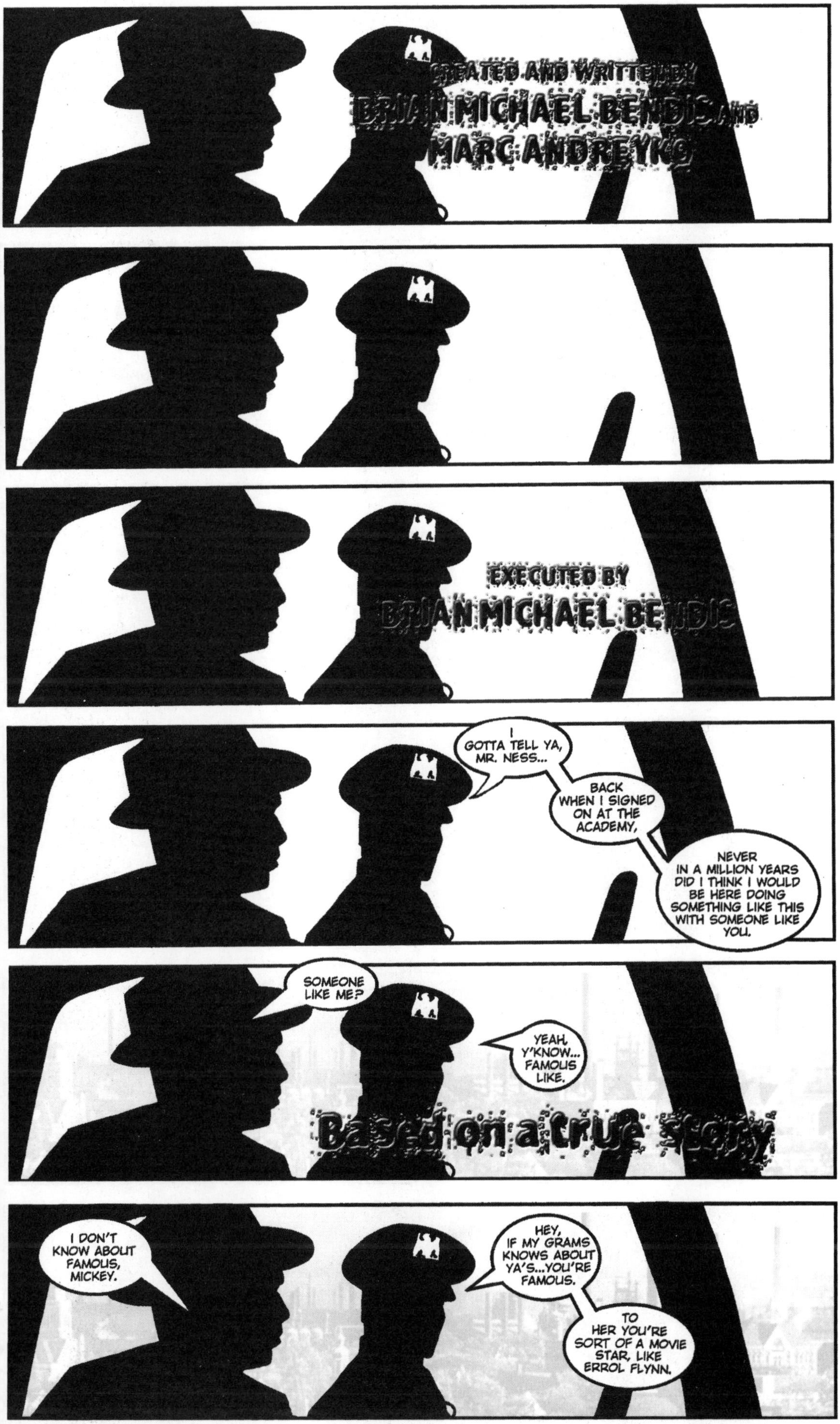
CREATED AND WRITTEN BY
BRIAN MICHAEL BENDIS AND
MARC ANDREYKO
EXECUTED BY
BRIAN MICHAEL BENDIS
I GOTTA TELL YA, MR. NESS...
BACK WHEN I SIGNED ON AT THE ACADEMY,
NEVER IN A MILLION YEARS DID I THINK I WOULD BE HERE DOING SOMETHING LIKE THIS WITH SOMEONE LIKE YOU.
SOMEONE LIKE ME?
YEAH, Y'KNOW... FAMOUS LIKE.
Based on a true story
I DON'T KNOW ABOUT FAMOUS, MICKEY.
HEY, IF MY GRAMS KNOWS ABOUT YA'S...YOU'RE FAMOUS.
TO HER YOU'RE SORT OF A MOVIE STAR, LIKE ERROL FLYNN.

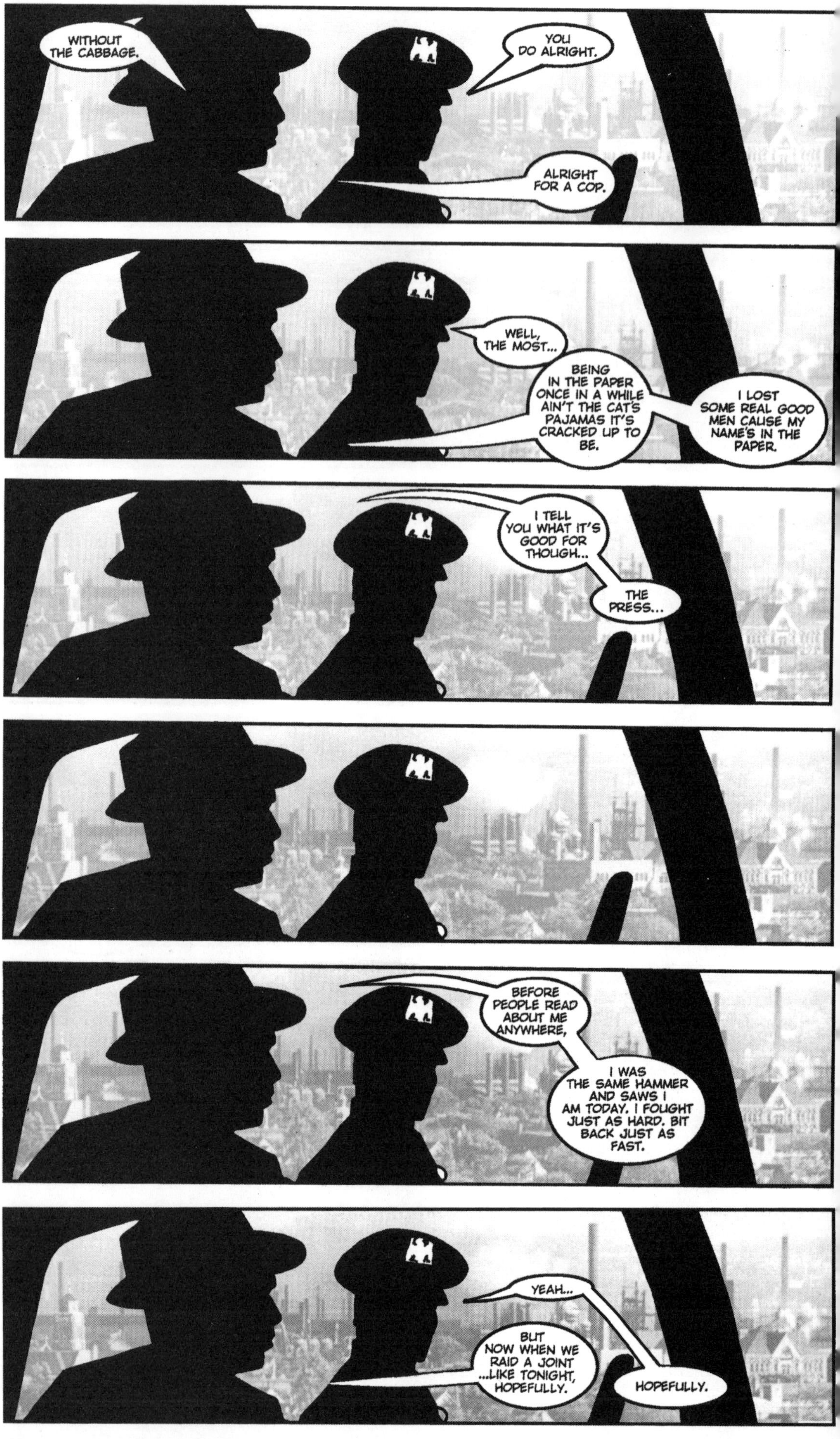
WITHOUT THE CABBAGE.
YOU DO ALRIGHT.
ALRIGHT FOR A COP.
WELL, THE MOST...
BEING IN THE PAPER ONCE IN A WHILE AIN'T THE CAT'S PAJAMAS IT'S CRACKED UP TO BE.
I LOST SOME REAL GOOD MEN CAUSE MY NAME'S IN THE PAPER.
I TELL YOU WHAT IT'S GOOD FOR THOUGH...
THE PRESS...
BEFORE PEOPLE READ ABOUT ME ANYWHERE,
I WAS THE SAME HAMMER AND SAWS I AM TODAY. I FOUGHT JUST AS HARD. BIT BACK JUST AS FAST.
YEAH...
BUT NOW WHEN WE RAID A JOINT ...LIKE TONIGHT, HOPEFULLY.
HOPEFULLY.

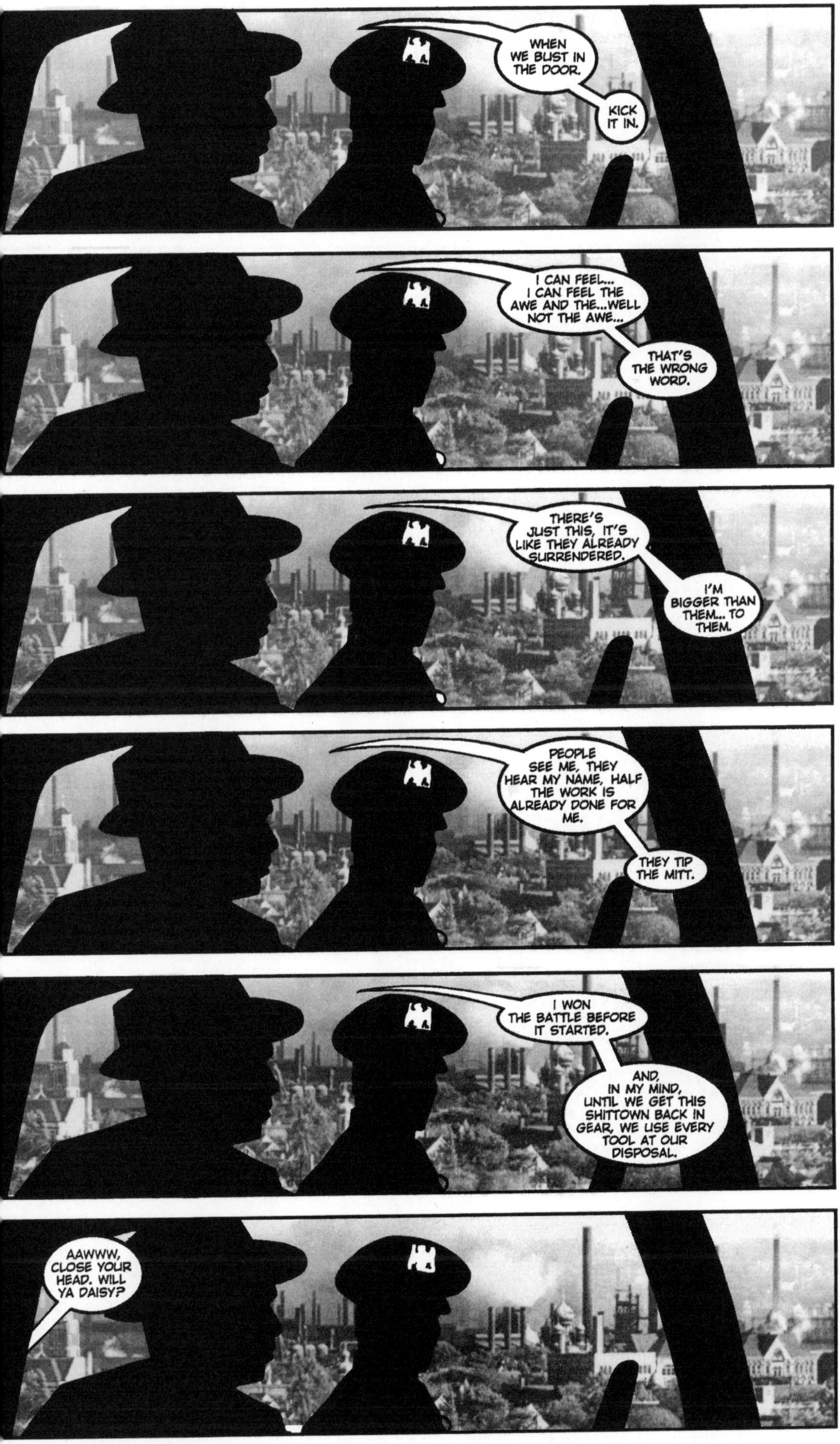
WHEN WE BUST IN THE DOOR.
KICK IT IN.
I CAN FEEL... I CAN FEEL THE AWE AND THE...WELL NOT THE AWE...
THAT'S THE WRONG WORD.
THERE'S JUST THIS, IT'S LIKE THEY ALREADY SURRENDERED.
I'M BIGGER THAN THEM... TO THEM.
PEOPLE SEE ME, THEY HEAR MY NAME, HALF THE WORK IS ALREADY DONE FOR ME.
THEY TIP THE MITT.
I WON THE BATTLE BEFORE IT STARTED.
AND, IN MY MIND, UNTIL WE GET THIS SHITTOWN BACK IN GEAR, WE USE EVERY TOOL AT OUR DISPOSAL.
AAWWW, CLOSE YOUR HEAD. WILL YA DAISY?

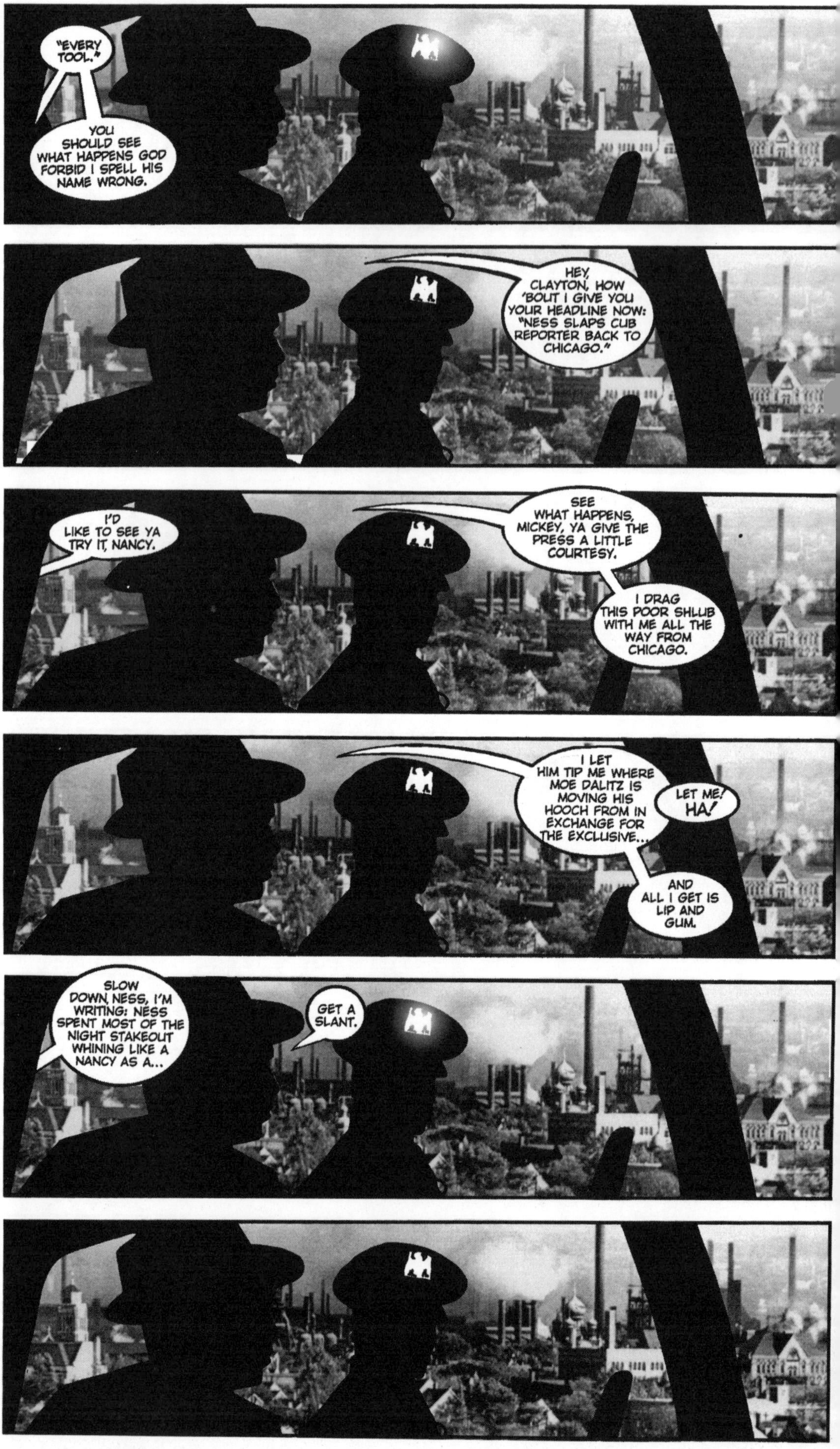
"EVERY TOOL."
YOU SHOULD SEE WHAT HAPPENS GOD FORBID I SPELL HIS NAME WRONG.
HEY, CLAYTON, HOW 'BOUT I GIVE YOU YOUR HEADLINE NOW: "NESS SLAPS CUB REPORTER BACK TO CHICAGO."
I'D LIKE TO SEE YA TRY IT, NANCY.
SEE WHAT HAPPENS, MICKEY, YA GIVE THE PRESS A LITTLE COURTESY.
I DRAG THIS POOR SHLUB WITH ME ALL THE WAY FROM CHICAGO.
I LET HIM TIP ME WHERE MOE DALITZ IS MOVING HIS HOOCH FROM IN EXCHANGE FOR THE EXCLUSIVE...
LET ME! HA!
AND ALL I GET IS LIP AND GUM.
SLOW DOWN, NESS, I'M WRITING: NESS SPENT MOST OF THE NIGHT STAKEOUT WHINING LIKE A NANCY AS A...
GET A SLANT.

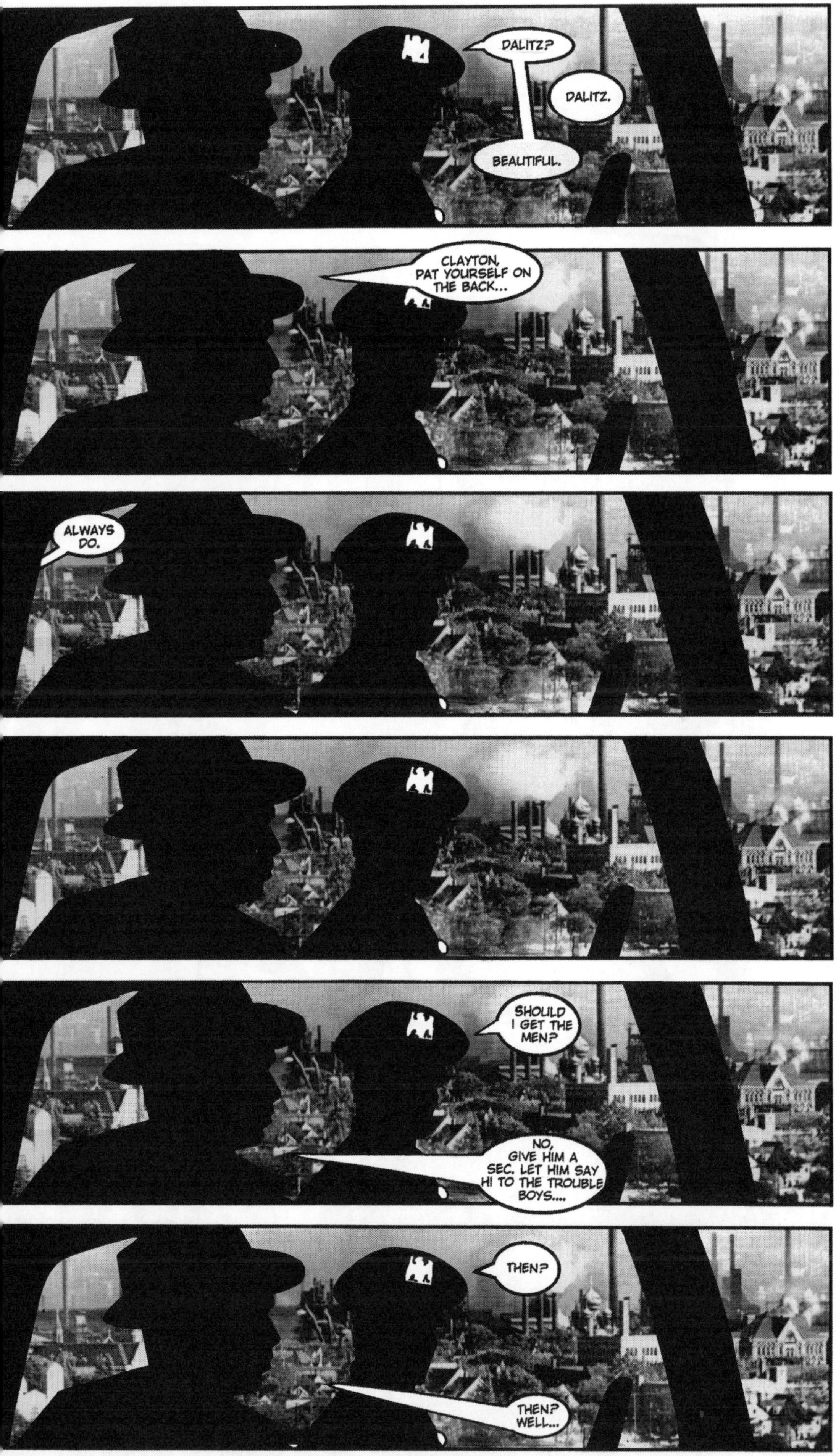
DALITZ?
DALITZ.
BEAUTIFUL.
CLAYTON, PAT YOURSELF ON THE BACK...
ALWAYS DO.
SHOULD I GET THE MEN?
NO, GIVE HIM A SEC. LET HIM SAY HI TO THE TROUBLE BOYS....
THEN?
THEN? WELL...

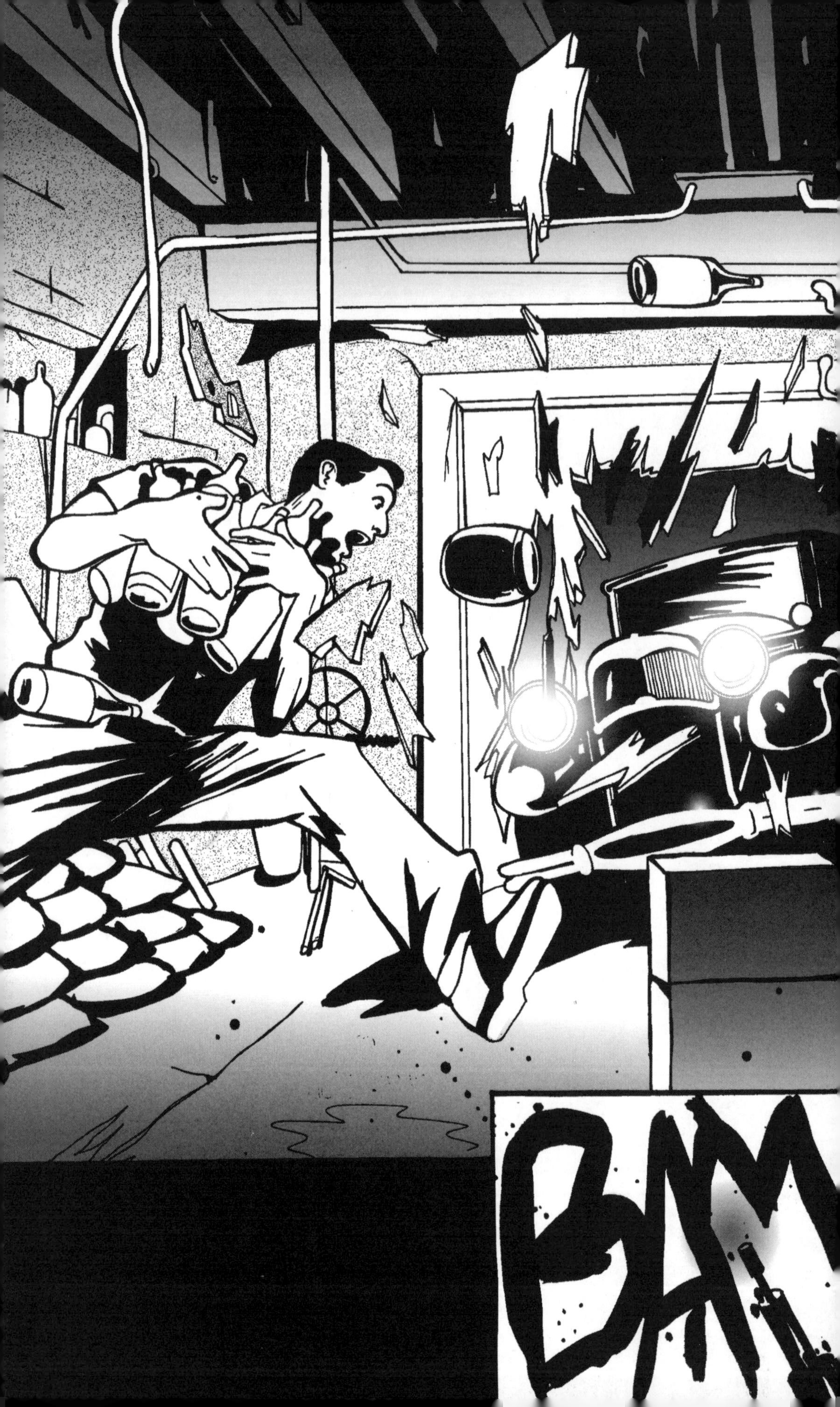
BAM

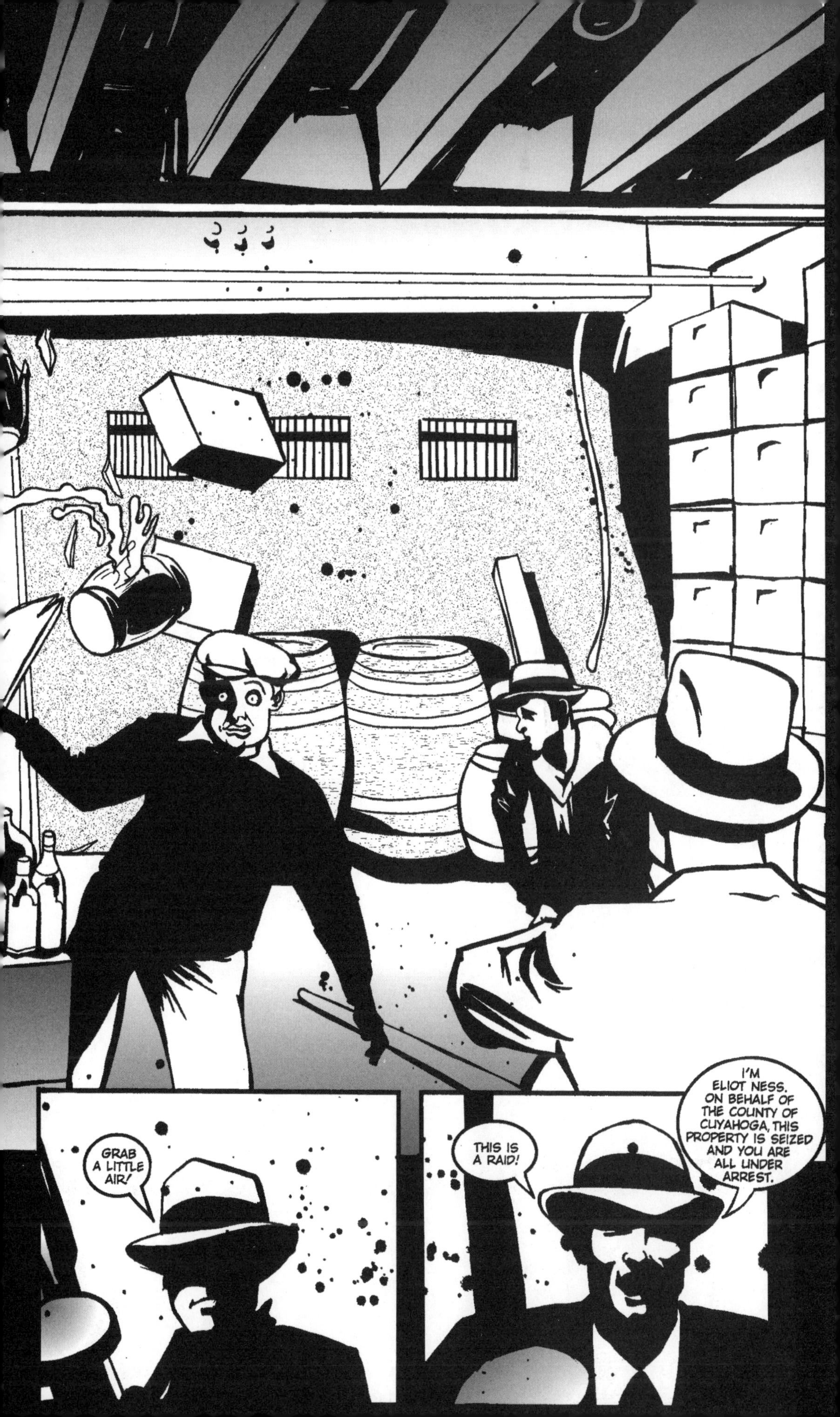
GRAB A LITTLE AIR!
THIS IS A RAID!
I'M ELIOT NESS. ON BEHALF OF THE COUNTY OF CUYAHOGA, THIS PROPERTY IS SEIZED AND YOU ARE ALL UNDER ARREST.

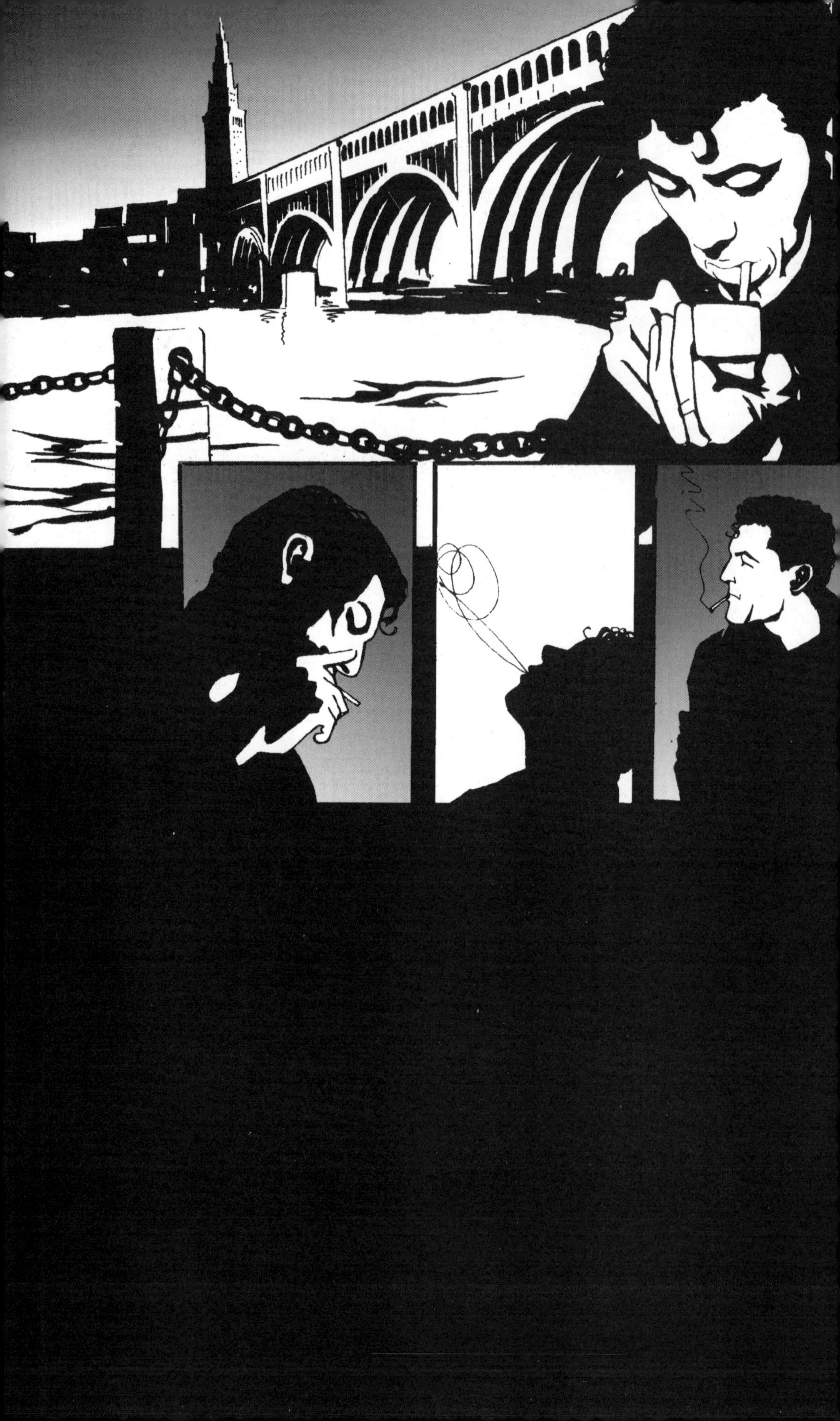

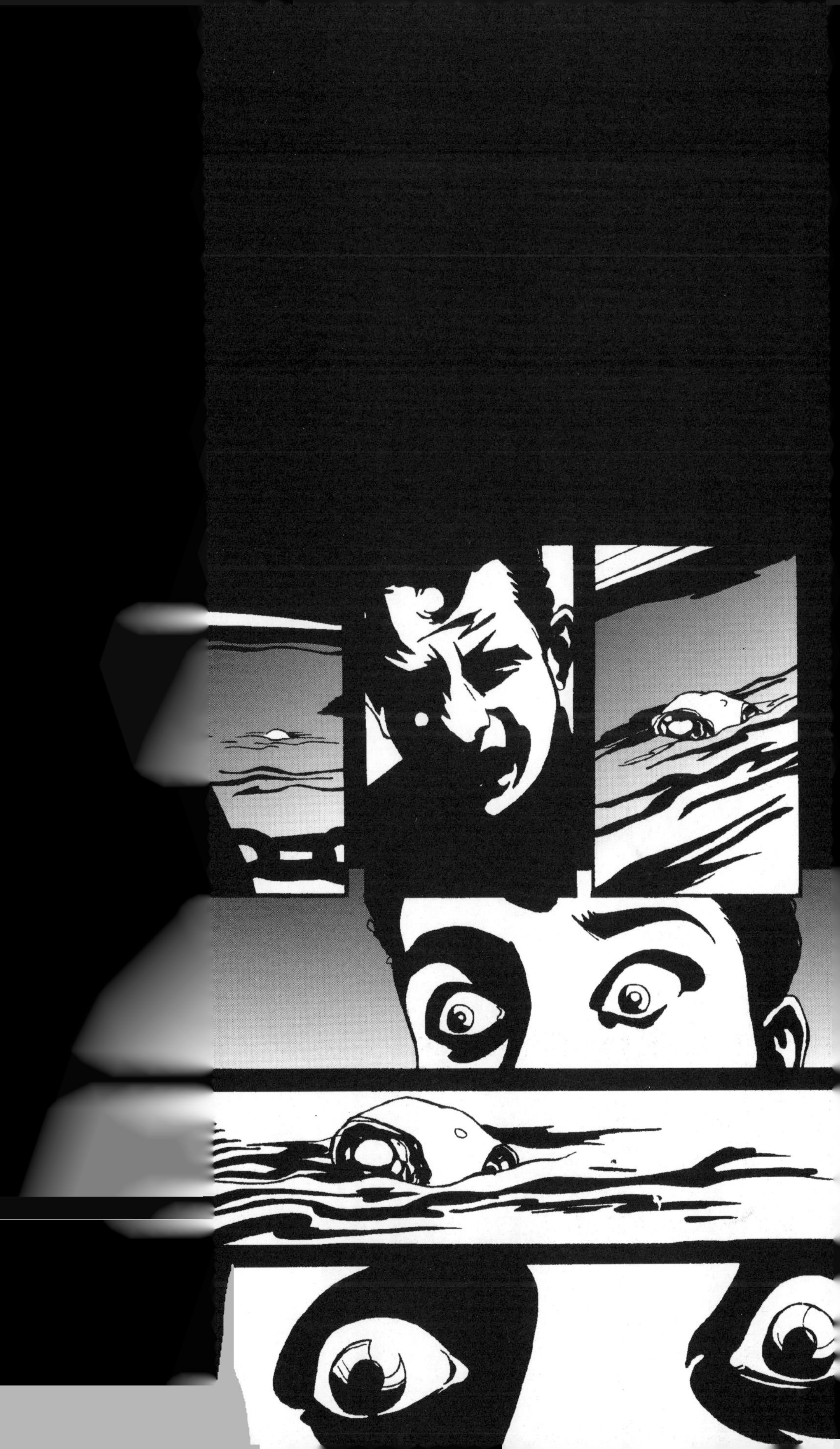

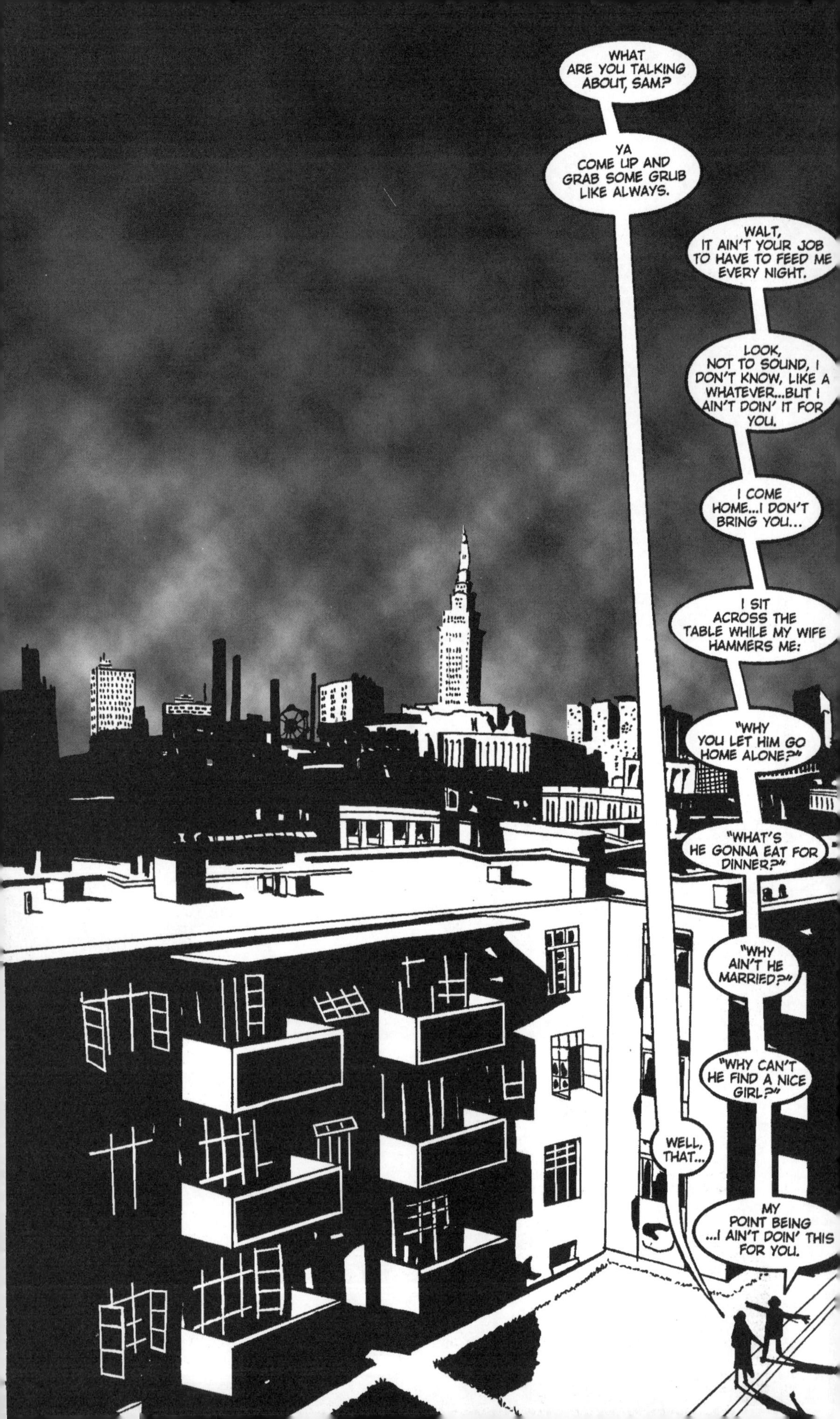
WHAT ARE YOU TALKING ABOUT, SAM?
YA COME UP AND GRAB SOME GRUB LIKE ALWAYS.
WALT, IT AIN'T YOUR JOB TO HAVE TO FEED ME EVERY NIGHT.
LOOK, NOT TO SOUND, I DON'T KNOW, LIKE A WHATEVER...BUT I AIN'T DOIN' IT FOR YOU.
I COME HOME...I DON'T BRING YOU...
I SIT ACROSS THE TABLE WHILE MY WIFE HAMMERS ME:
"WHY YOU LET HIM GO HOME ALONE?"
"WHAT'S HE GONNA EAT FOR DINNER?"
"WHY AIN'T HE MARRIED?"
"WHY CAN'T HE FIND A NICE GIRL?"
WELL, THAT...
MY POINT BEING ...I AIN'T DOIN' THIS FOR YOU.

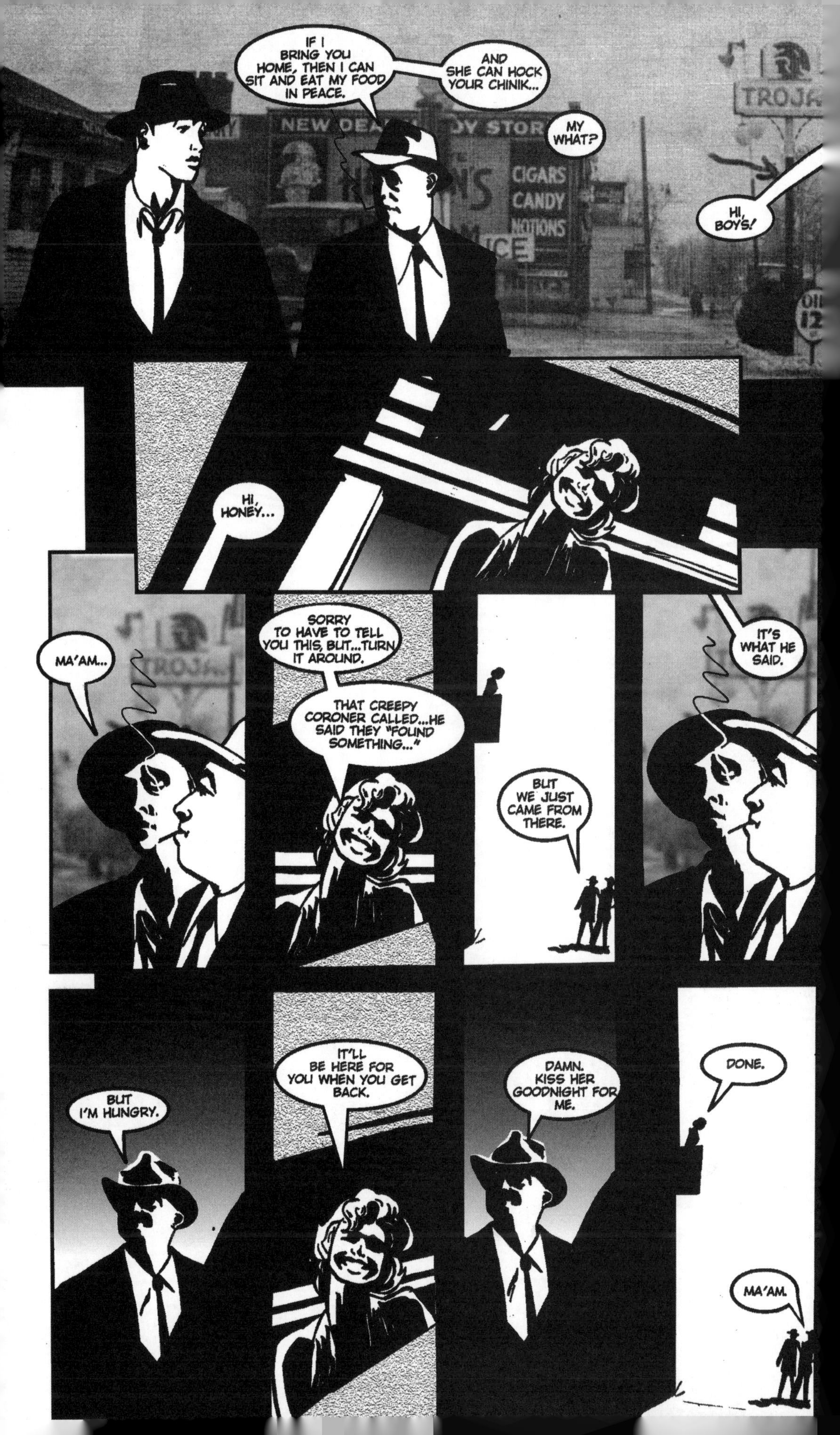
IF I BRING YOU HOME, THEN I CAN SIT AND EAT MY FOOD IN PEACE.
AND SHE CAN HOCK YOUR CHINIK...
MY WHAT?
HI, BOYS!
NEW DEAL
CIGARS
CANDY
NOTIONS
TROJA
HI, HONEY...
MA'AM...
SORRY TO HAVE TO TELL YOU THIS, BUT...TURN IT AROUND.
THAT CREEPY CORONER CALLED...HE SAID THEY "FOUND SOMETHING..."
BUT WE JUST CAME FROM THERE.
IT'S WHAT HE SAID.
BUT I'M HUNGRY.
IT'LL BE HERE FOR YOU WHEN YOU GET BACK.
DAMN. KISS HER GOODNIGHT FOR ME.
DONE.
MA'AM.

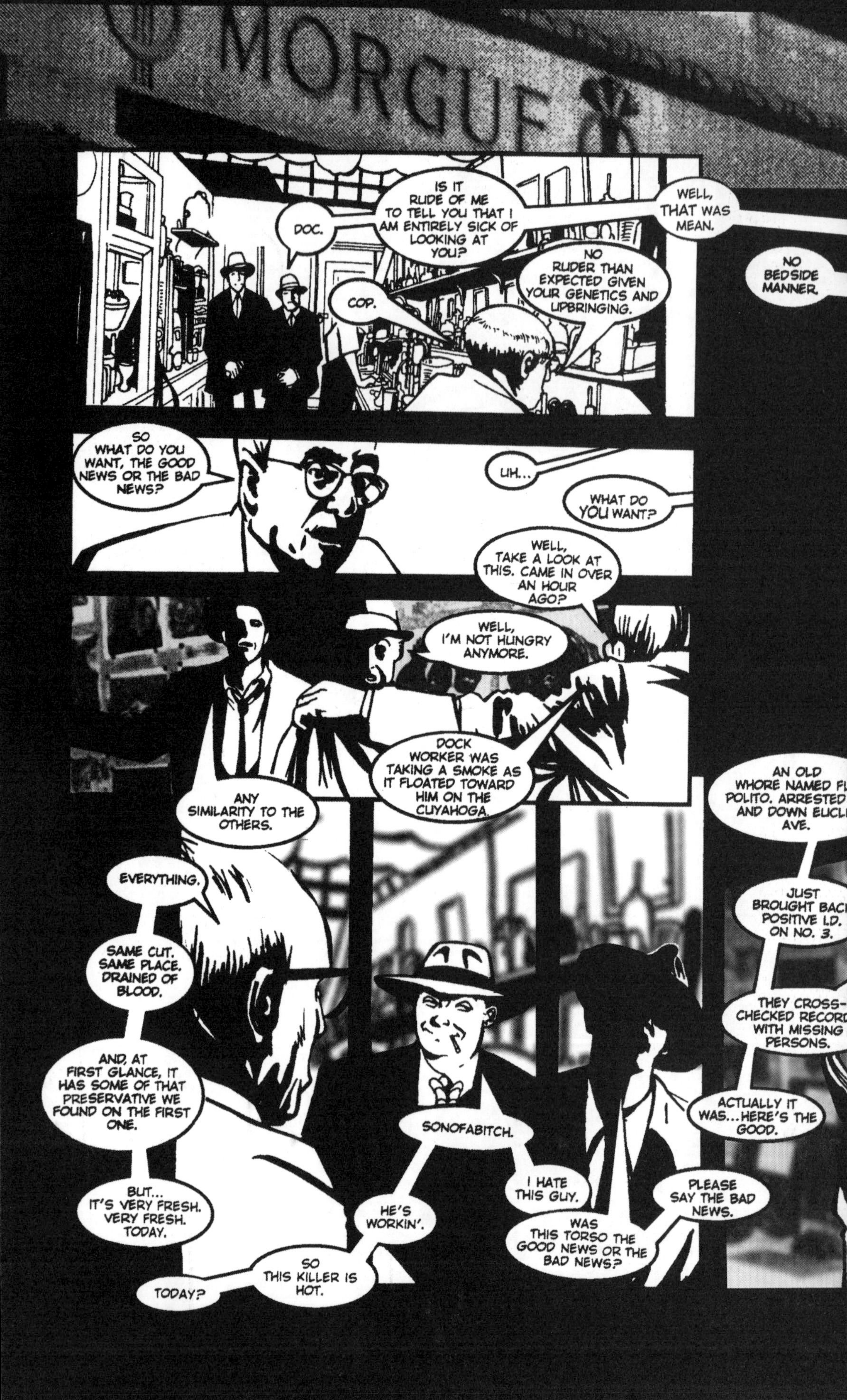
MORGUE
DOC.
IS IT RUDE OF ME TO TELL YOU THAT I AM ENTIRELY SICK OF LOOKING AT YOU?
WELL, THAT WAS MEAN.
NO BEDSIDE MANNER.
COP.
NO RUDER THAN EXPECTED GIVEN YOUR GENETICS AND UPBRINGING.
SO WHAT DO YOU WANT, THE GOOD NEWS OR THE BAD NEWS?
UH...
WHAT DO YOU WANT?
WELL, TAKE A LOOK AT THIS. CAME IN OVER AN HOUR AGO?
WELL, I'M NOT HUNGRY ANYMORE.
DOCK WORKER WAS TAKING A SMOKE AS IT FLOATED TOWARD HIM ON THE CUYAHOGA.
ANY SIMILARITY TO THE OTHERS.
EVERYTHING.
SAME CUT. SAME PLACE. DRAINED OF BLOOD.
AND, AT FIRST GLANCE, IT HAS SOME OF THAT PRESERVATIVE WE FOUND ON THE FIRST ONE.
BUT... IT'S VERY FRESH. VERY FRESH. TODAY.
TODAY?
SO THIS KILLER IS HOT.
HE'S WORKIN'.
SONOFABITCH.
I HATE THIS GUY.
WAS THIS TORSO THE GOOD NEWS OR THE BAD NEWS?
PLEASE SAY THE BAD NEWS.
ACTUALLY IT WAS...HERE'S THE GOOD.
THEY CROSS-CHECKED RECORD WITH MISSING PERSONS.
JUST BROUGHT BAC POSITIVE I.D. ON NO. 3.
AN OLD WHORE NAMED F POLITO. ARRESTED AND DOWN EUCL AVE.

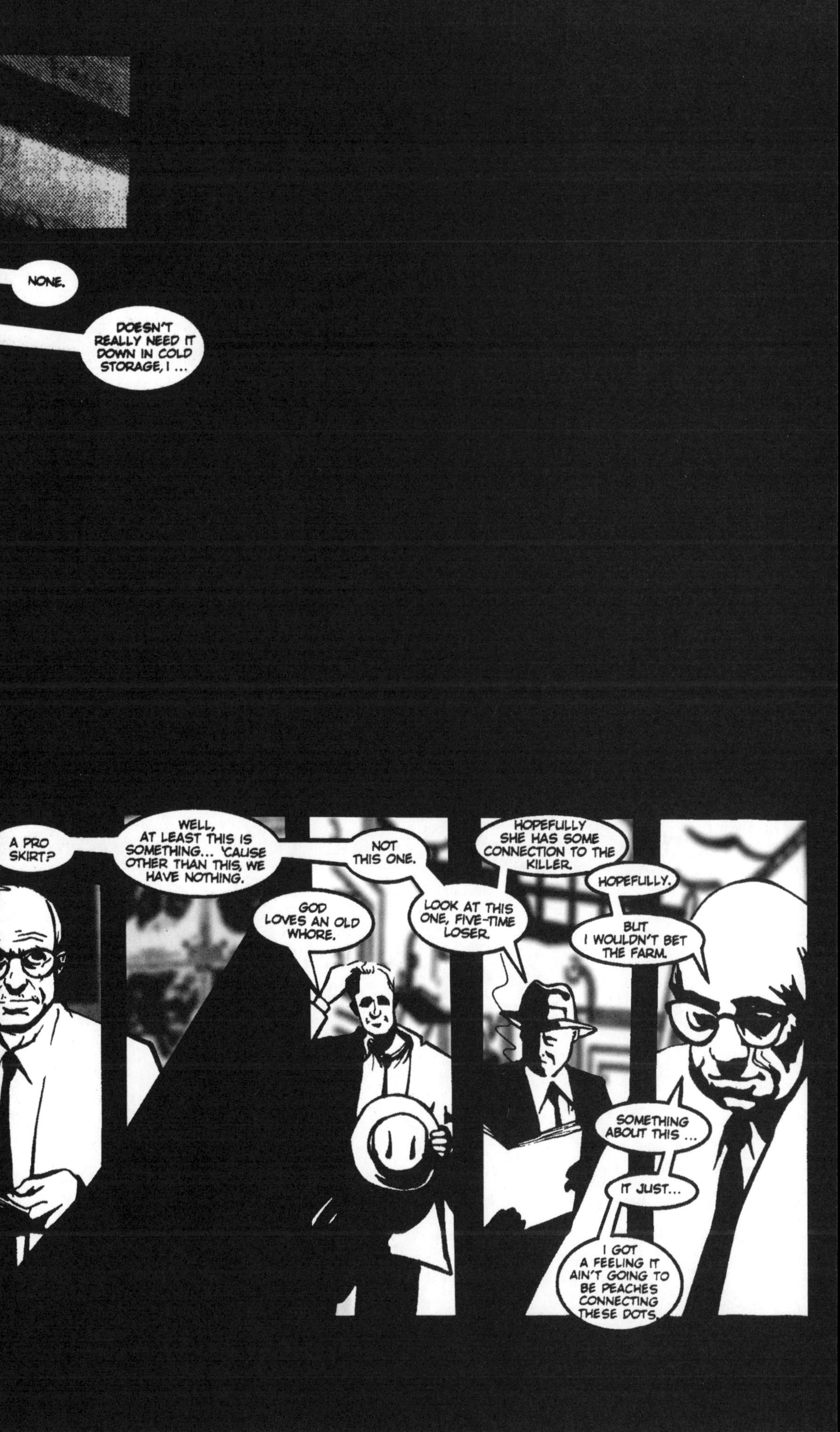
NONE.
DOESN'T REALLY NEED IT DOWN IN COLD STORAGE, I ...
A PRO SKIRT?
WELL, AT LEAST THIS IS SOMETHING... 'CAUSE OTHER THAN THIS, WE HAVE NOTHING.
NOT THIS ONE.
GOD LOVES AN OLD WHORE.
LOOK AT THIS ONE, FIVE-TIME LOSER.
HOPEFULLY SHE HAS SOME CONNECTION TO THE KILLER.
HOPEFULLY.
BUT I WOULDN'T BET THE FARM.
SOMETHING ABOUT THIS ...
IT JUST...
I GOT A FEELING IT AIN'T GOING TO BE PEACHES CONNECTING THESE DOTS.

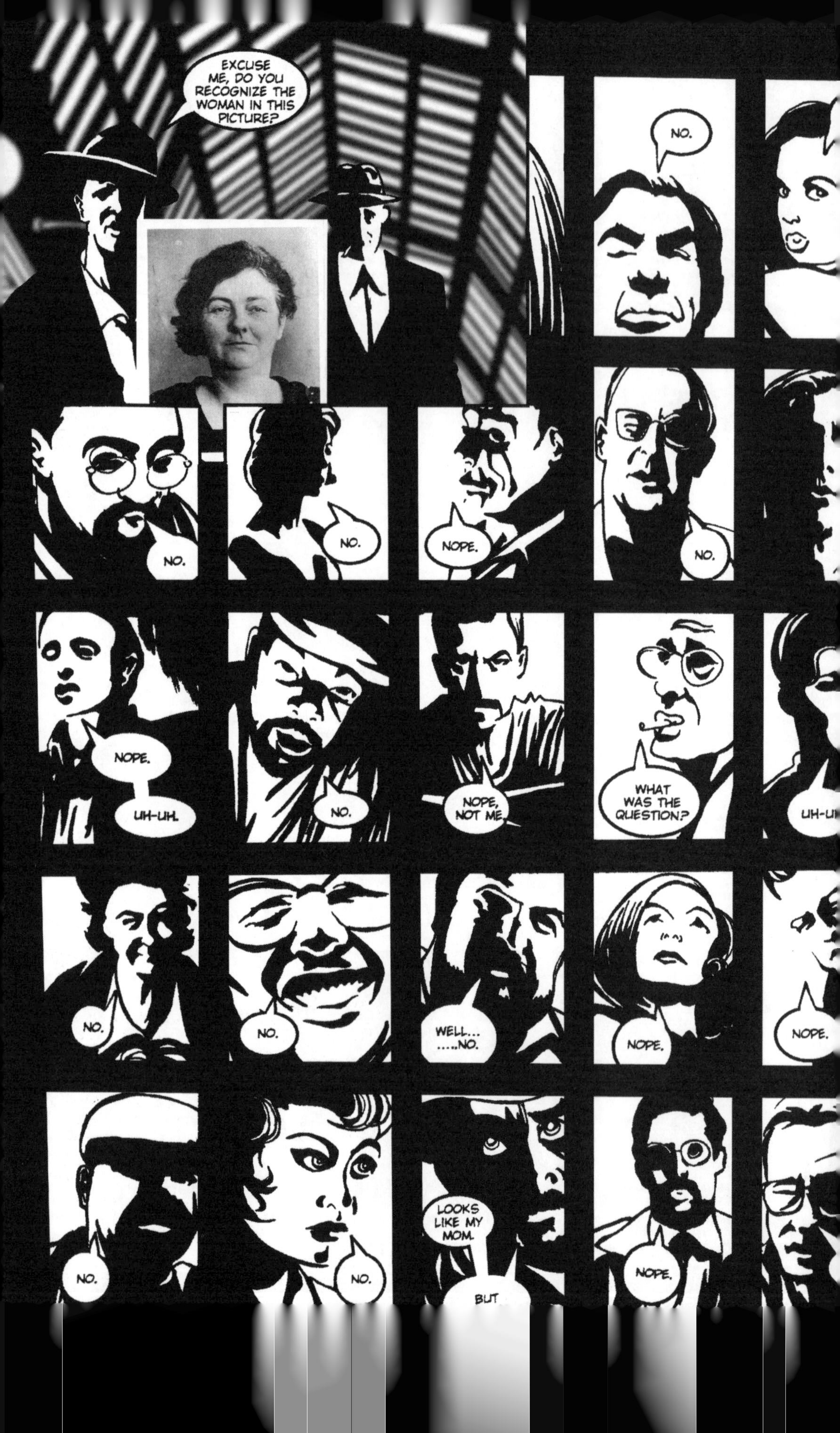

EXCUSE ME, DO YOU RECOGNIZE THE WOMAN IN THIS PICTURE?
NO.
NO.
NO.
NOPE.
NO.
NOPE.
UH-UH.
NO.
NOPE, NOT ME.
WHAT WAS THE QUESTION?
NO.
NO.
WELL... ....NO.
NOPE.
NOPE.
NO.
NO.
LOOKS LIKE MY MOM.
BUT
NOPE.

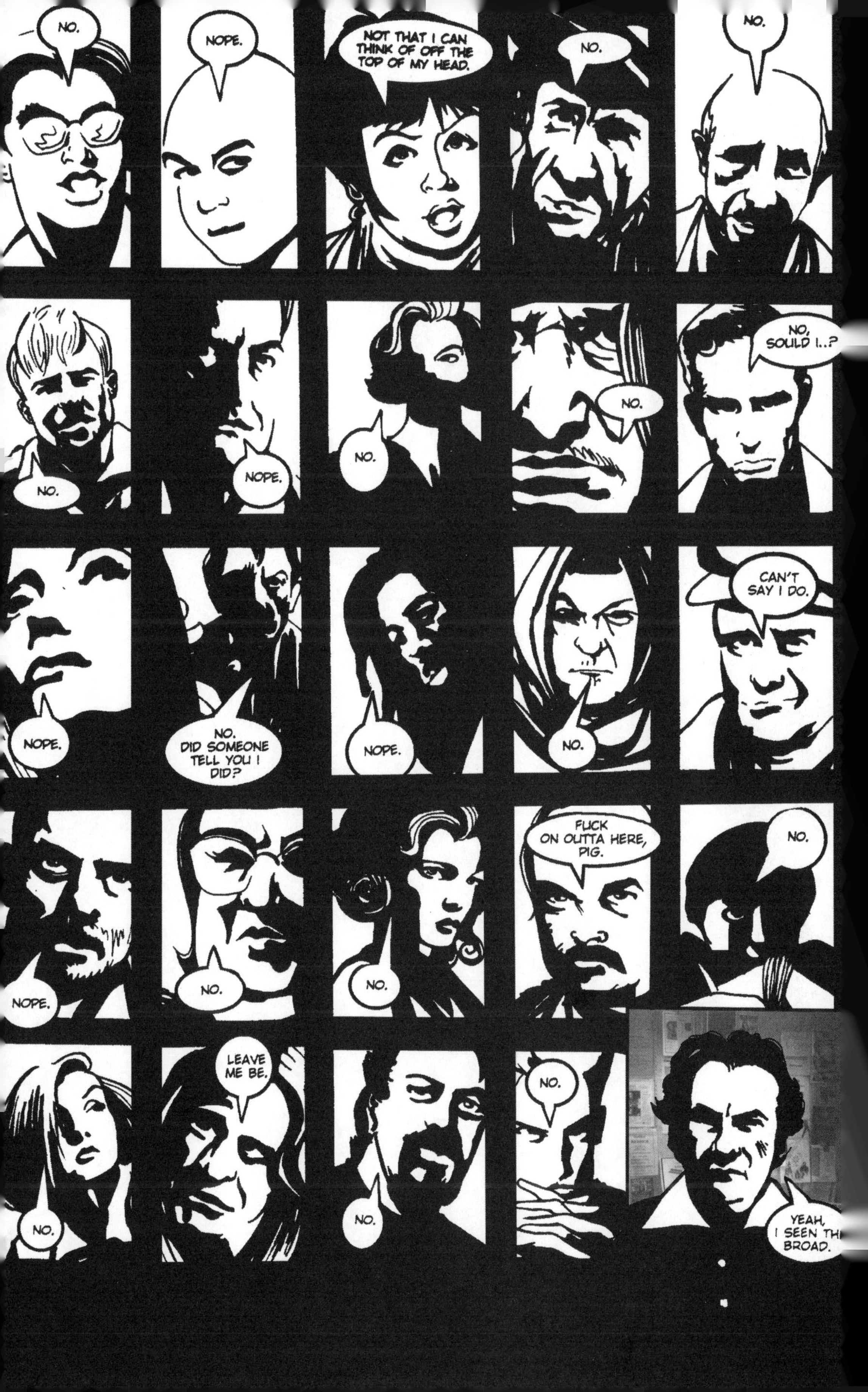
NO.
NOPE.
NOT THAT I CAN THINK OF OFF THE TOP OF MY HEAD.
NO.
NO.
NO.
NOPE.
NO.
NO.
NO, SOULD I..?
NOPE.
NO. DID SOMEONE TELL YOU I DID?
NOPE.
NO.
CAN'T SAY I DO.
NOPE.
NO.
NO.
FUCK ON OUTTA HERE, PIG.
NO.
NO.
LEAVE ME BE.
NO.
NO.
YEAH, I SEEN TH BROAD.

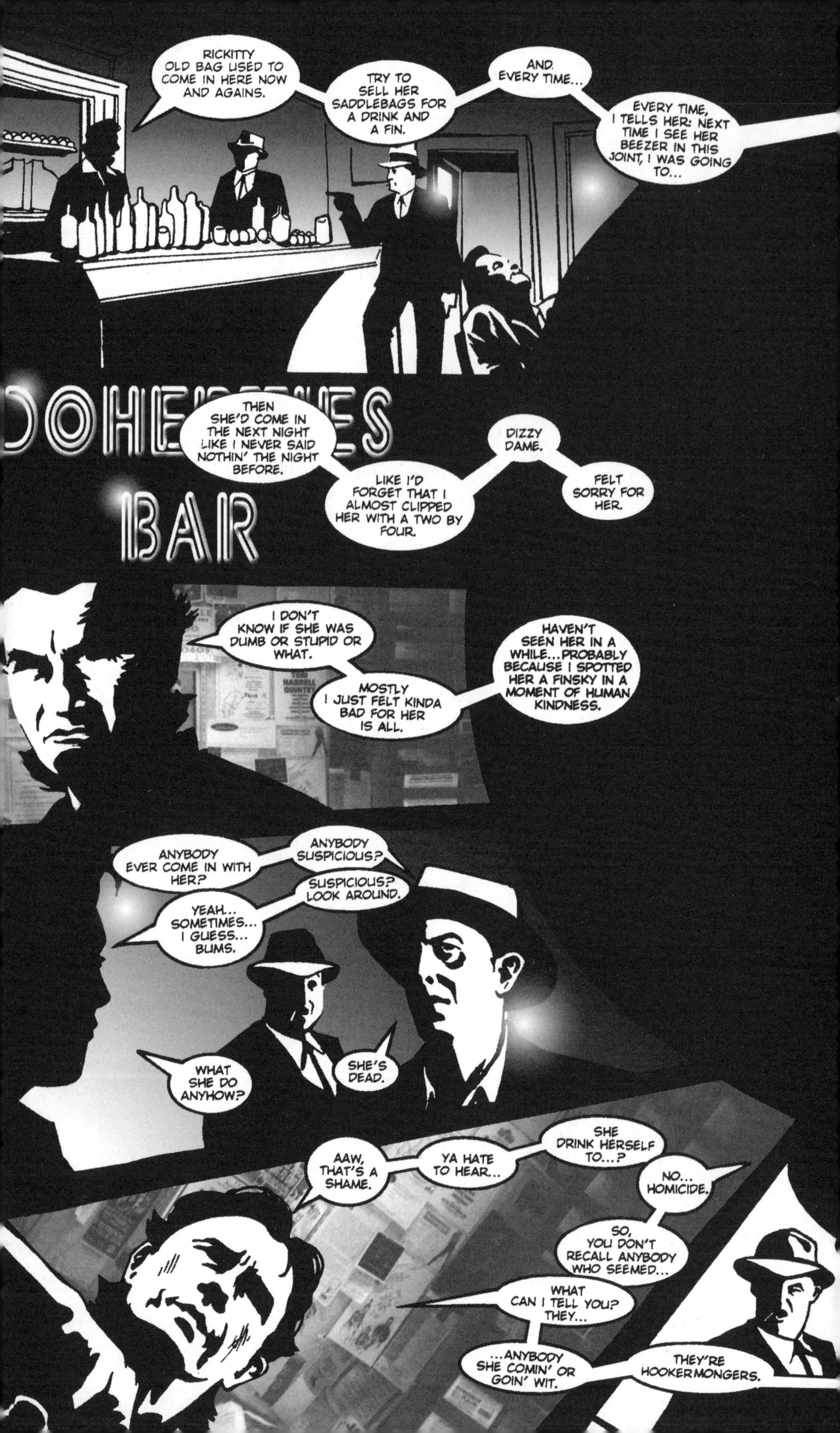
RICKITTY OLD BAG USED TO COME IN HERE NOW AND AGAINS.
TRY TO SELL HER SADDLEBAGS FOR A DRINK AND A FIN.
AND. EVERY TIME...
EVERY TIME, I TELLS HER: NEXT TIME I SEE HER BEEZER IN THIS JOINT, I WAS GOING TO...
BAR
THEN SHE'D COME IN THE NEXT NIGHT LIKE I NEVER SAID NOTHIN' THE NIGHT BEFORE.
LIKE I'D FORGET THAT I ALMOST CLIPPED HER WITH A TWO BY FOUR.
DIZZY DAME.
FELT SORRY FOR HER.
I DON'T KNOW IF SHE WAS DUMB OR STUPID OR WHAT.
MOSTLY I JUST FELT KINDA BAD FOR HER IS ALL.
HAVEN'T SEEN HER IN A WHILE...PROBABLY BECAUSE I SPOTTED HER A FINSKY IN A MOMENT OF HUMAN KINDNESS.
ANYBODY EVER COME IN WITH HER?
ANYBODY SUSPICIOUS?
SUSPICIOUS? LOOK AROUND.
YEAH... SOMETIMES... I GUESS... BUMS.
WHAT SHE DO ANYHOW?
SHE'S DEAD.
AAW, THAT'S A SHAME.
YA HATE TO HEAR...
SHE DRINK HERSELF TO...?
NO... HOMICIDE.
SO, YOU DON'T RECALL ANYBODY WHO SEEMED...
WHAT CAN I TELL YOU? THEY...
...ANYBODY SHE COMIN' OR GOIN' WIT.
THEY'RE HOOKERMONGERS.

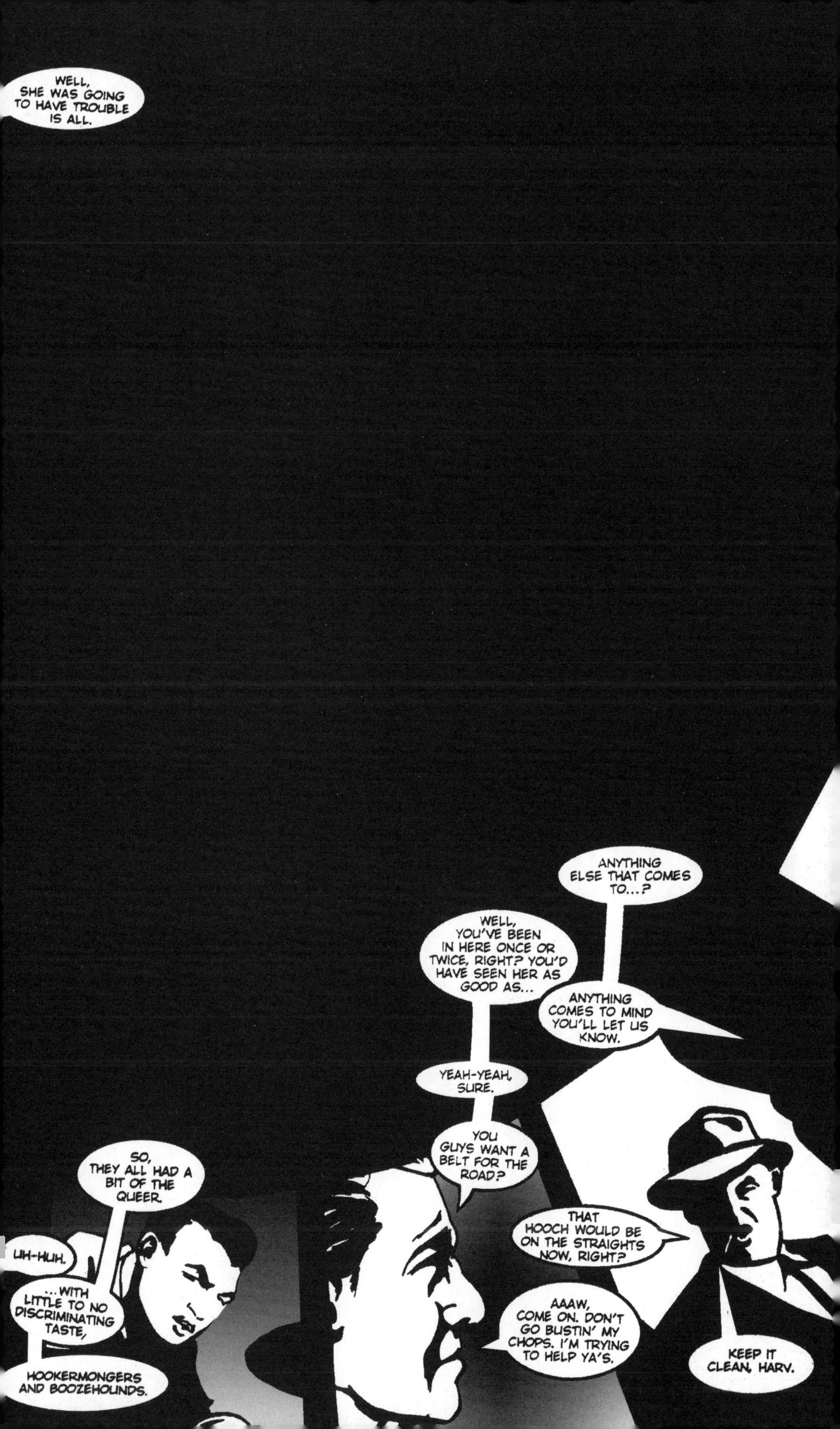
WELL, SHE WAS GOING TO HAVE TROUBLE IS ALL.
ANYTHING ELSE THAT COMES TO...?
WELL, YOU'VE BEEN IN HERE ONCE OR TWICE, RIGHT? YOU'D HAVE SEEN HER AS GOOD AS...
ANYTHING COMES TO MIND YOU'LL LET US KNOW.
YEAH-YEAH, SURE.
YOU GUYS WANT A BELT FOR THE ROAD?
SO, THEY ALL HAD A BIT OF THE QUEER.
UH-HUH.
...WITH LITTLE TO NO DISCRIMINATING TASTE,
HOOKERMONGERS AND BOOZEHOUNDS.
THAT HOOCH WOULD BE ON THE STRAIGHTS NOW, RIGHT?
AAAW, COME ON. DON'T GO BUSTIN' MY CHOPS. I'M TRYING TO HELP YA'S.
KEEP IT CLEAN, HARV.

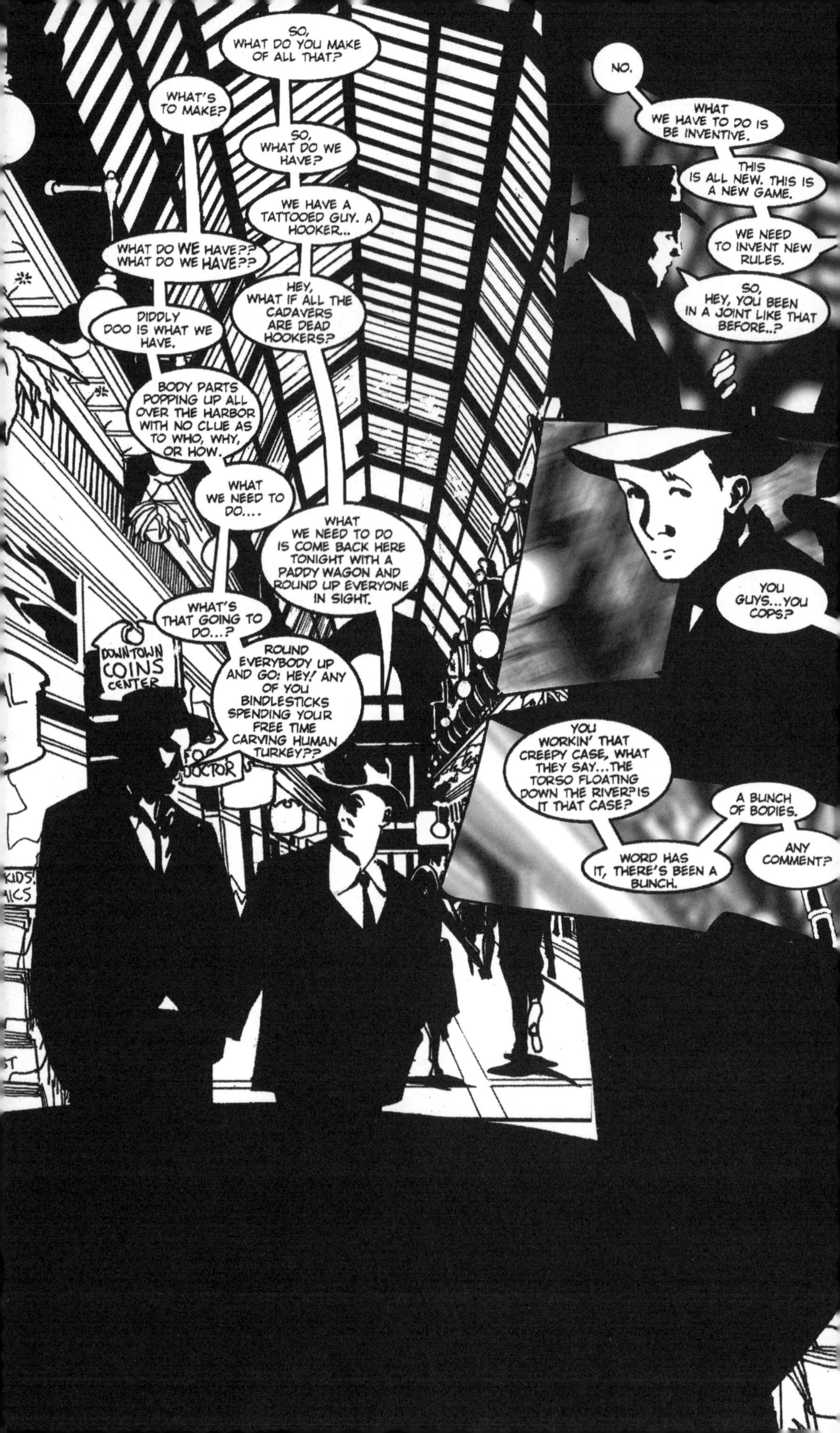
SO, WHAT DO YOU MAKE OF ALL THAT?
WHAT'S TO MAKE?
SO, WHAT DO WE HAVE?
WE HAVE A TATTOOED GUY. A HOOKER...
WHAT DO WE HAVE?? WHAT DO WE HAVE??
HEY, WHAT IF ALL THE CADAVERS ARE DEAD HOOKERS?
DIDDLY DOO IS WHAT WE HAVE.
BODY PARTS POPPING UP ALL OVER THE HARBOR WITH NO CLUE AS TO WHO, WHY, OR HOW.
WHAT WE NEED TO DO....
WHAT WE NEED TO DO IS COME BACK HERE TONIGHT WITH A PADDY WAGON AND ROUND UP EVERYONE IN SIGHT.
WHAT'S THAT GOING TO DO...?
ROUND EVERYBODY UP AND GO: HEY! ANY OF YOU BINDLESTICKS SPENDING YOUR FREE TIME CARVING HUMAN TURKEY??
DOWNTOWN COINS CENTER
FOOT DOCTOR
NO.
WHAT WE HAVE TO DO IS BE INVENTIVE.
THIS IS ALL NEW. THIS IS A NEW GAME.
WE NEED TO INVENT NEW RULES.
SO, HEY, YOU BEEN IN A JOINT LIKE THAT BEFORE..?
YOU GUYS...YOU COPS?
YOU WORKIN' THAT CREEPY CASE, WHAT THEY SAY...THE TORSO FLOATING DOWN THE RIVER? IS IT THAT CASE?
WORD HAS IT, THERE'S BEEN A BUNCH.
A BUNCH OF BODIES.
ANY COMMENT?

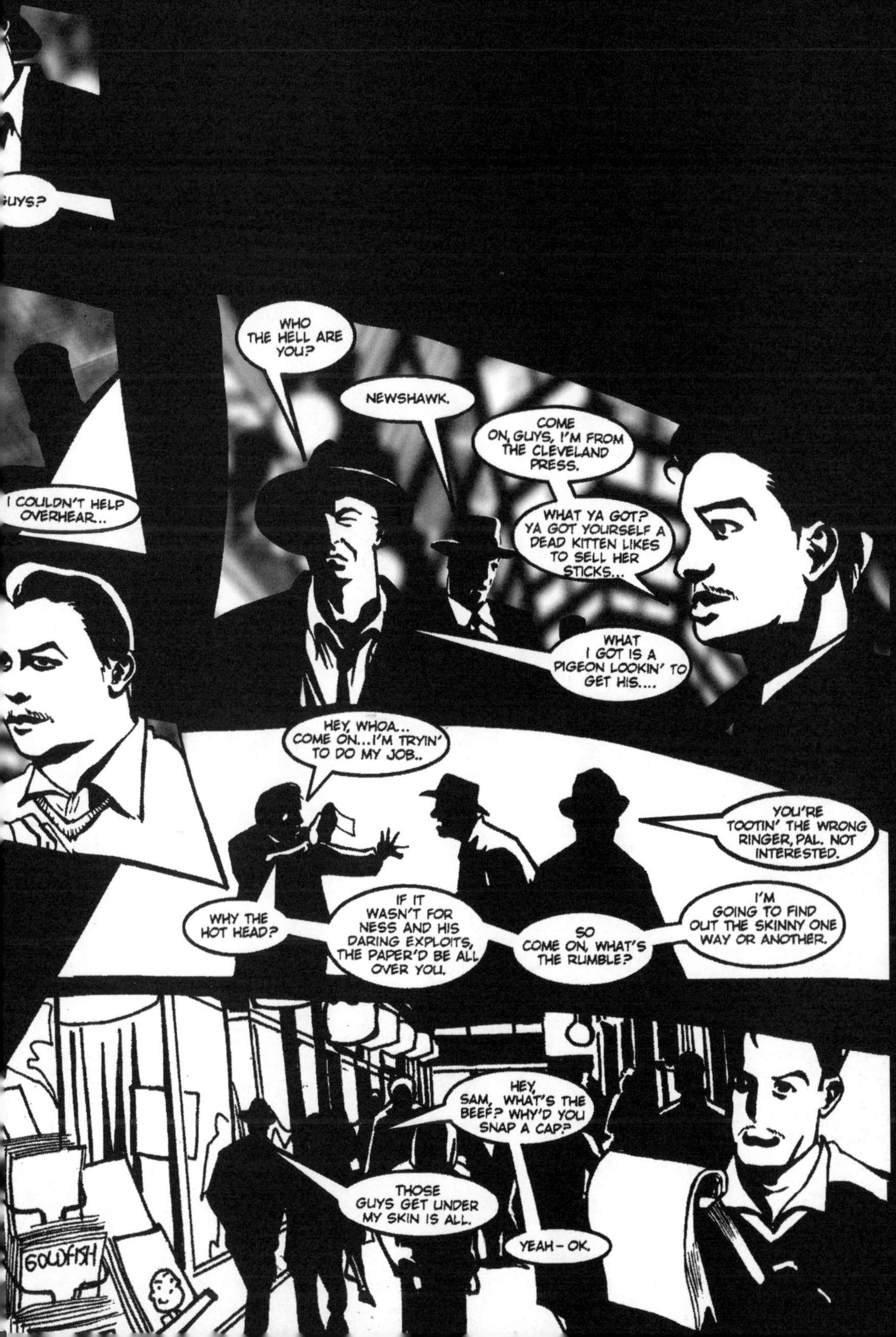

GUYS?
I COULDN'T HELP OVERHEAR...
WHO THE HELL ARE YOU?
NEWSHAWK.
COME ON, GUYS, I'M FROM THE CLEVELAND PRESS.
WHAT YA GOT? YA GOT YOURSELF A DEAD KITTEN LIKES TO SELL HER STICKS...
WHAT I GOT IS A PIGEON LOOKIN' TO GET HIS....
HEY, WHOA... COME ON...I'M TRYIN' TO DO MY JOB..
YOU'RE TOOTIN' THE WRONG RINGER, PAL. NOT INTERESTED.
WHY THE HOT HEAD?
IF IT WASN'T FOR NESS AND HIS DARING EXPLOITS, THE PAPER'D BE ALL OVER YOU.
SO COME ON, WHAT'S THE RUMBLE?
I'M GOING TO FIND OUT THE SKINNY ONE WAY OR ANOTHER.
HEY, SAM, WHAT'S THE BEEF? WHY'D YOU SNAP A CAP?
THOSE GUYS GET UNDER MY SKIN IS ALL.
YEAH - OK.
GOLDFISH

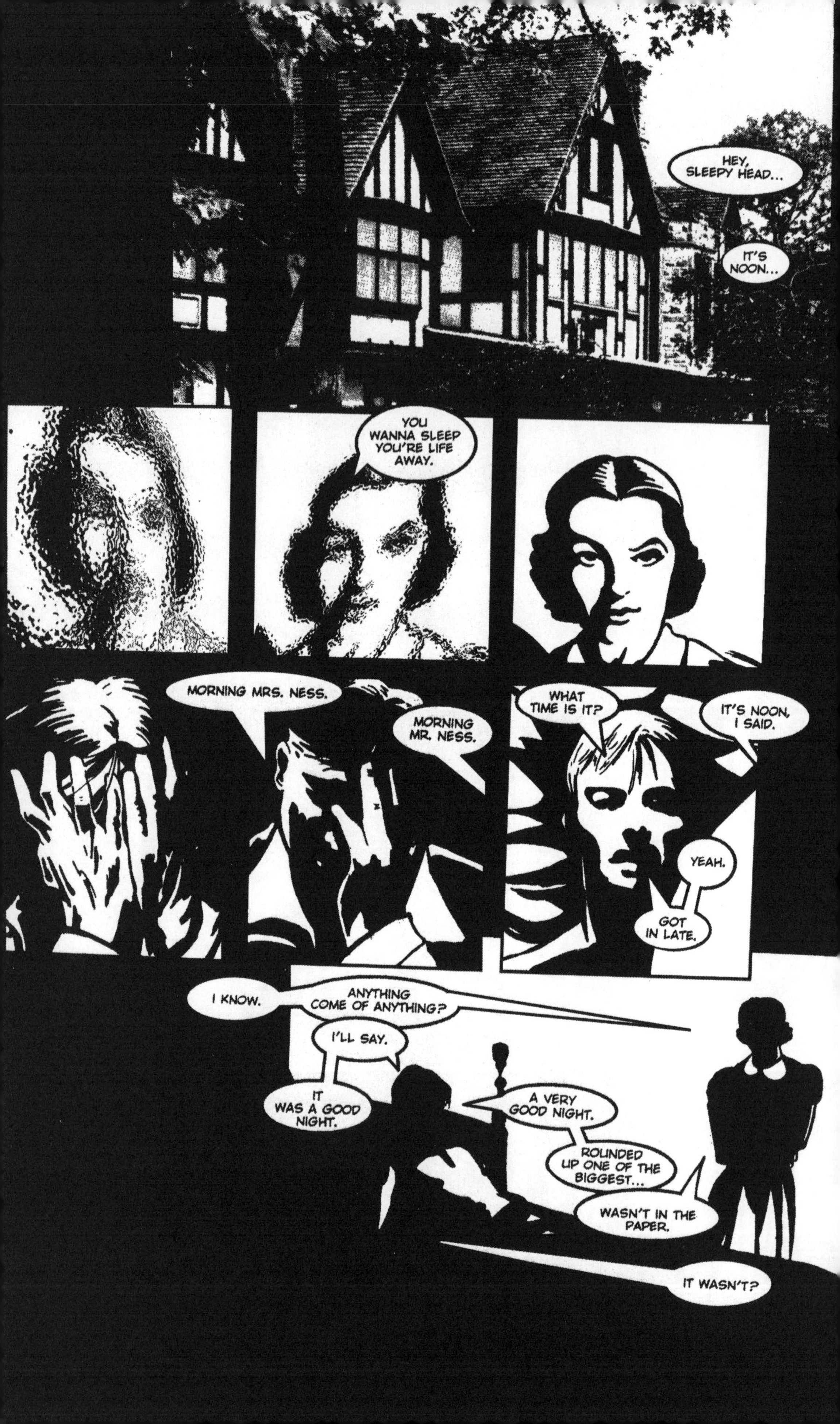

HEY, SLEEPY HEAD...
IT'S NOON...
YOU WANNA SLEEP YOU'RE LIFE AWAY.
MORNING MRS. NESS.
MORNING MR. NESS.
WHAT TIME IS IT?
IT'S NOON, I SAID.
YEAH.
GOT IN LATE.
I KNOW.
ANYTHING COME OF ANYTHING?
I'LL SAY.
IT WAS A GOOD NIGHT.
A VERY GOOD NIGHT.
ROUNDED UP ONE OF THE BIGGEST...
WASN'T IN THE PAPER.
IT WASN'T?

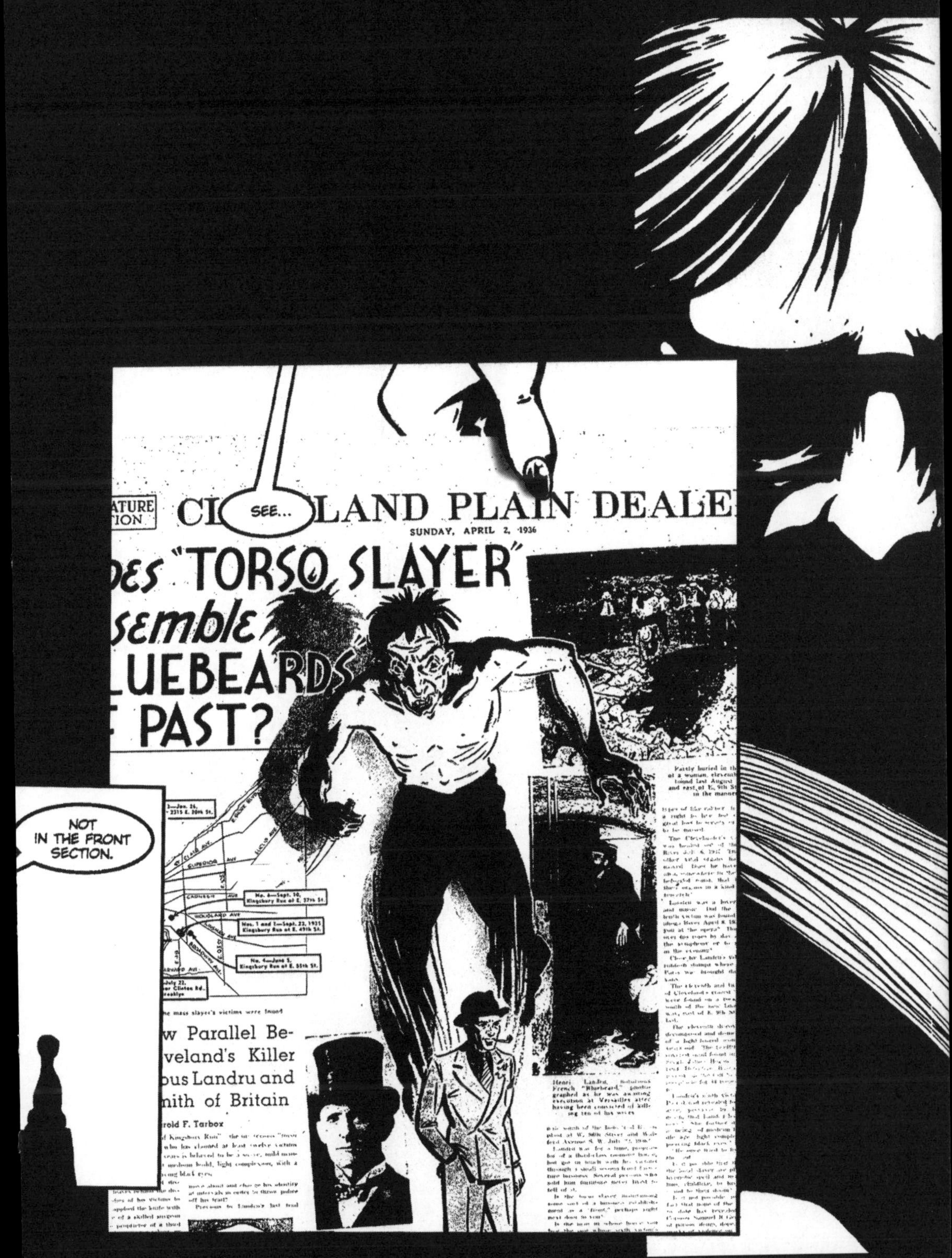
SEE...
NOT IN THE FRONT SECTION.
ATURE
TION
CL LAND PLAIN DEALE
SUNDAY, APRIL 2, 1936
DES "TORSO SLAYER"
semble
LUEBEARDS
F PAST?
w Parallel Be-
veland's Killer
ous Landru and
mith of Britain
rold F. Tarbox
he mass slayer's victims were found
Henri Landru, notorious French "Bluebeard," photographed as he was awaiting execution at Versailles after having been convicted of killing ten of his wives

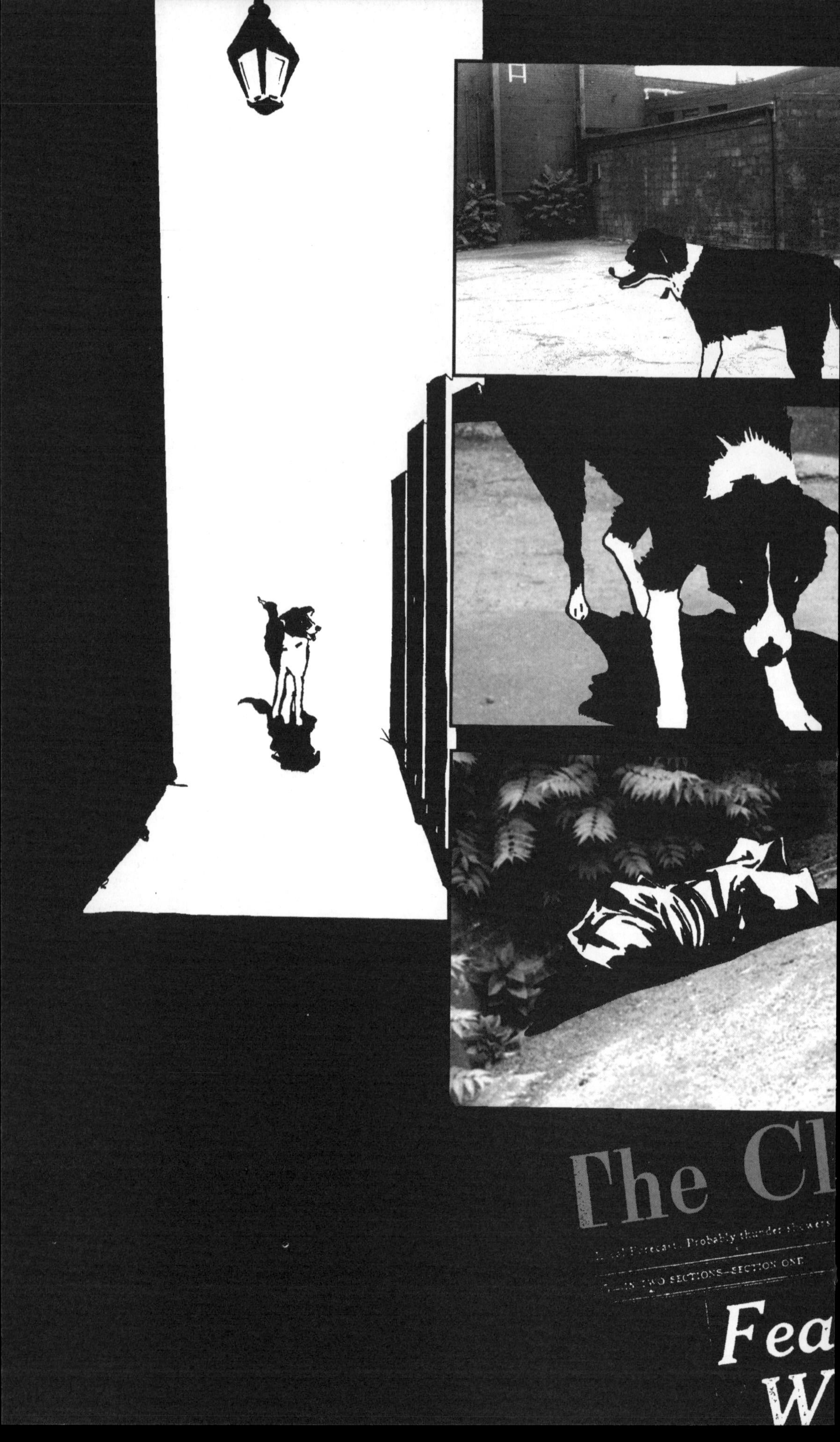
The Cl
Probably thunder showers
SECTIONS—SECTION ONE
Fea
W

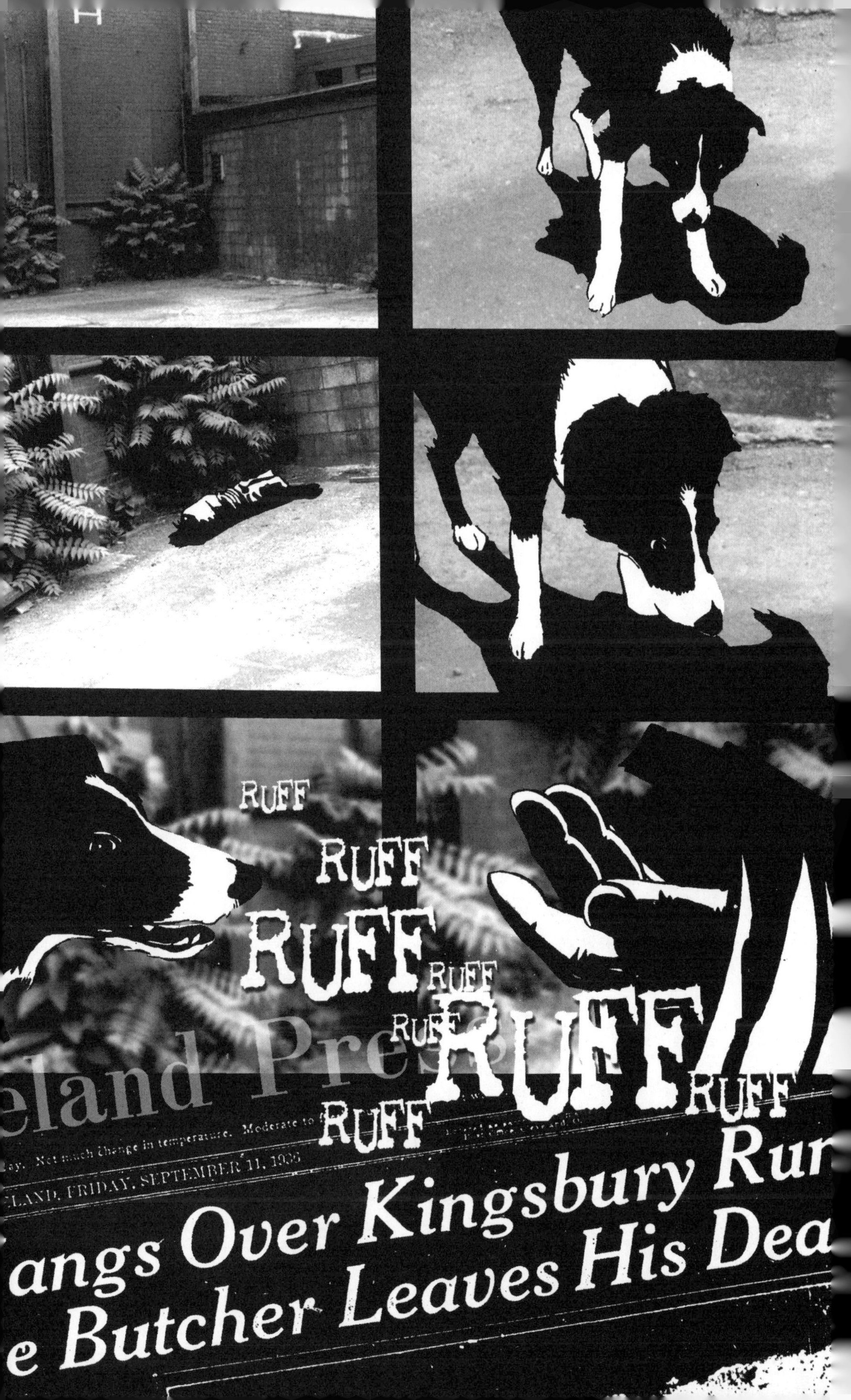
RUFF
RUFF
RUFF
RUFF
RUFF
RUFF
RUFF
RUFF
eland Press
ay. Not much change in temperature. Moderate to
LAND, FRIDAY, SEPTEMBER 11, 1936
angs Over Kingsbury Run
e Butcher Leaves His Dea

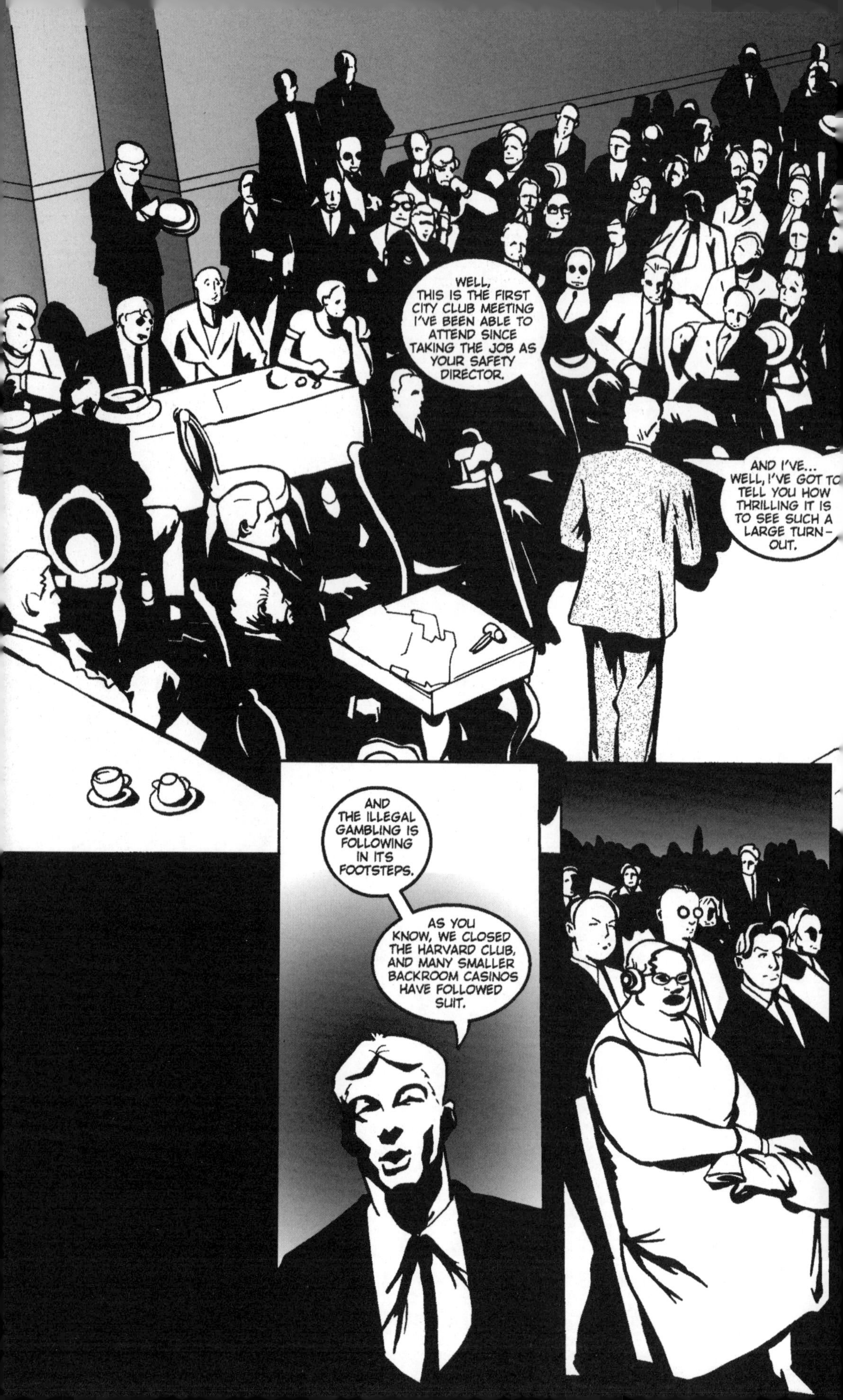

WELL, THIS IS THE FIRST CITY CLUB MEETING I'VE BEEN ABLE TO ATTEND SINCE TAKING THE JOB AS YOUR SAFETY DIRECTOR.
AND I'VE... WELL, I'VE GOT TO TELL YOU HOW THRILLING IT IS TO SEE SUCH A LARGE TURN-OUT.
AND THE ILLEGAL GAMBLING IS FOLLOWING IN ITS FOOTSTEPS.
AS YOU KNOW, WE CLOSED THE HARVARD CLUB, AND MANY SMALLER BACKROOM CASINOS HAVE FOLLOWED SUIT.

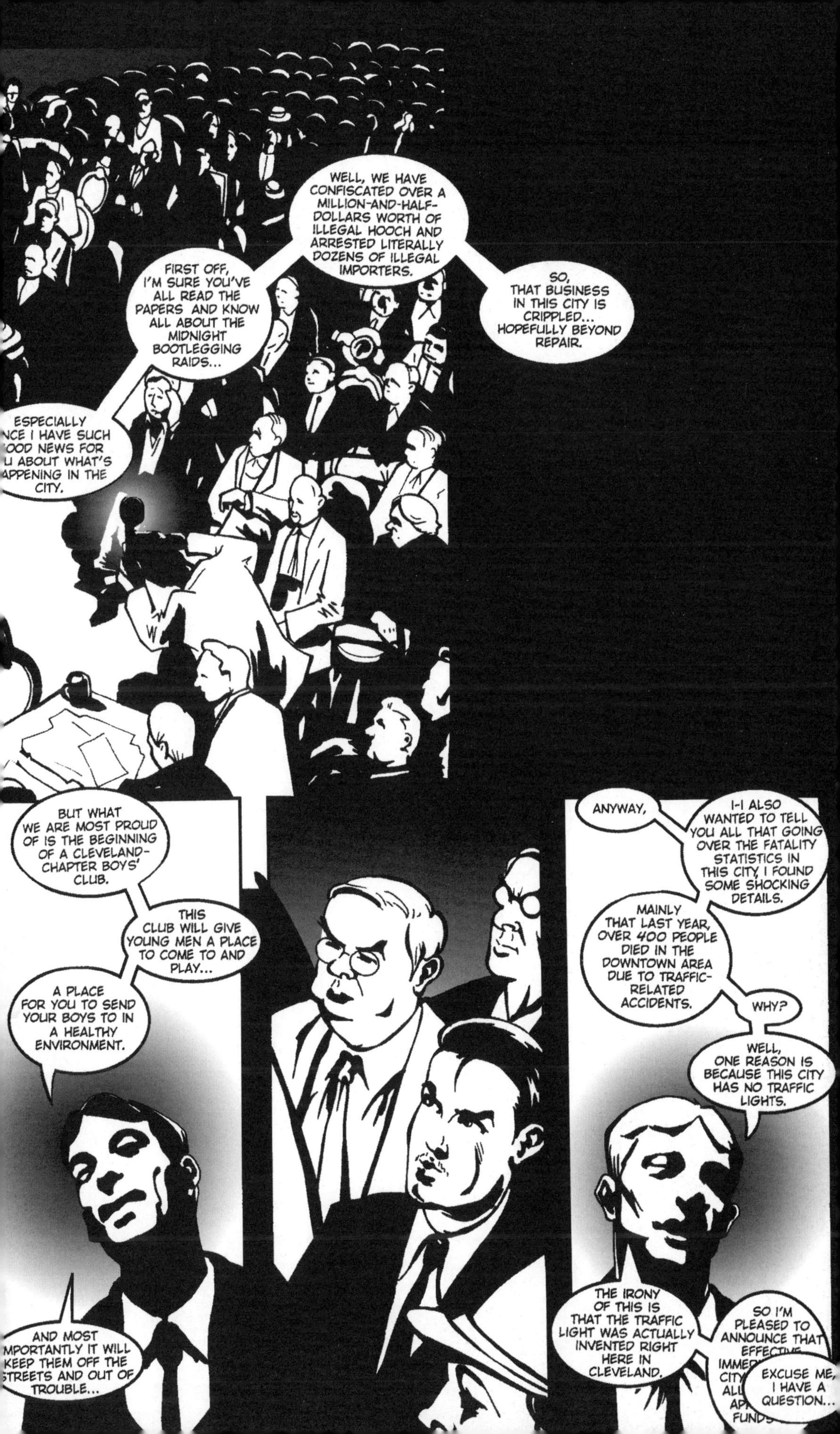
FIRST OFF, I'M SURE YOU'VE ALL READ THE PAPERS AND KNOW ALL ABOUT THE MIDNIGHT BOOTLEGGING RAIDS...
ESPECIALLY NCE I HAVE SUCH OOD NEWS FOR U ABOUT WHAT'S APPENING IN THE CITY.
WELL, WE HAVE CONFISCATED OVER A MILLION-AND-HALF-DOLLARS WORTH OF ILLEGAL HOOCH AND ARRESTED LITERALLY DOZENS OF ILLEGAL IMPORTERS.
SO, THAT BUSINESS IN THIS CITY IS CRIPPLED... HOPEFULLY BEYOND REPAIR.
BUT WHAT WE ARE MOST PROUD OF IS THE BEGINNING OF A CLEVELAND-CHAPTER BOYS' CLUB.
THIS CLUB WILL GIVE YOUNG MEN A PLACE TO COME TO AND PLAY...
A PLACE FOR YOU TO SEND YOUR BOYS TO IN A HEALTHY ENVIRONMENT.
AND MOST MPORTANTLY IT WILL KEEP THEM OFF THE STREETS AND OUT OF TROUBLE...
ANYWAY,
I-I ALSO WANTED TO TELL YOU ALL THAT GOING OVER THE FATALITY STATISTICS IN THIS CITY, I FOUND SOME SHOCKING DETAILS.
MAINLY THAT LAST YEAR, OVER 400 PEOPLE DIED IN THE DOWNTOWN AREA DUE TO TRAFFIC-RELATED ACCIDENTS.
WHY?
WELL, ONE REASON IS BECAUSE THIS CITY HAS NO TRAFFIC LIGHTS.
THE IRONY OF THIS IS THAT THE TRAFFIC LIGHT WAS ACTUALLY INVENTED RIGHT HERE IN CLEVELAND.
SO I'M PLEASED TO ANNOUNCE THAT
EXCUSE ME, I HAVE A QUESTION...

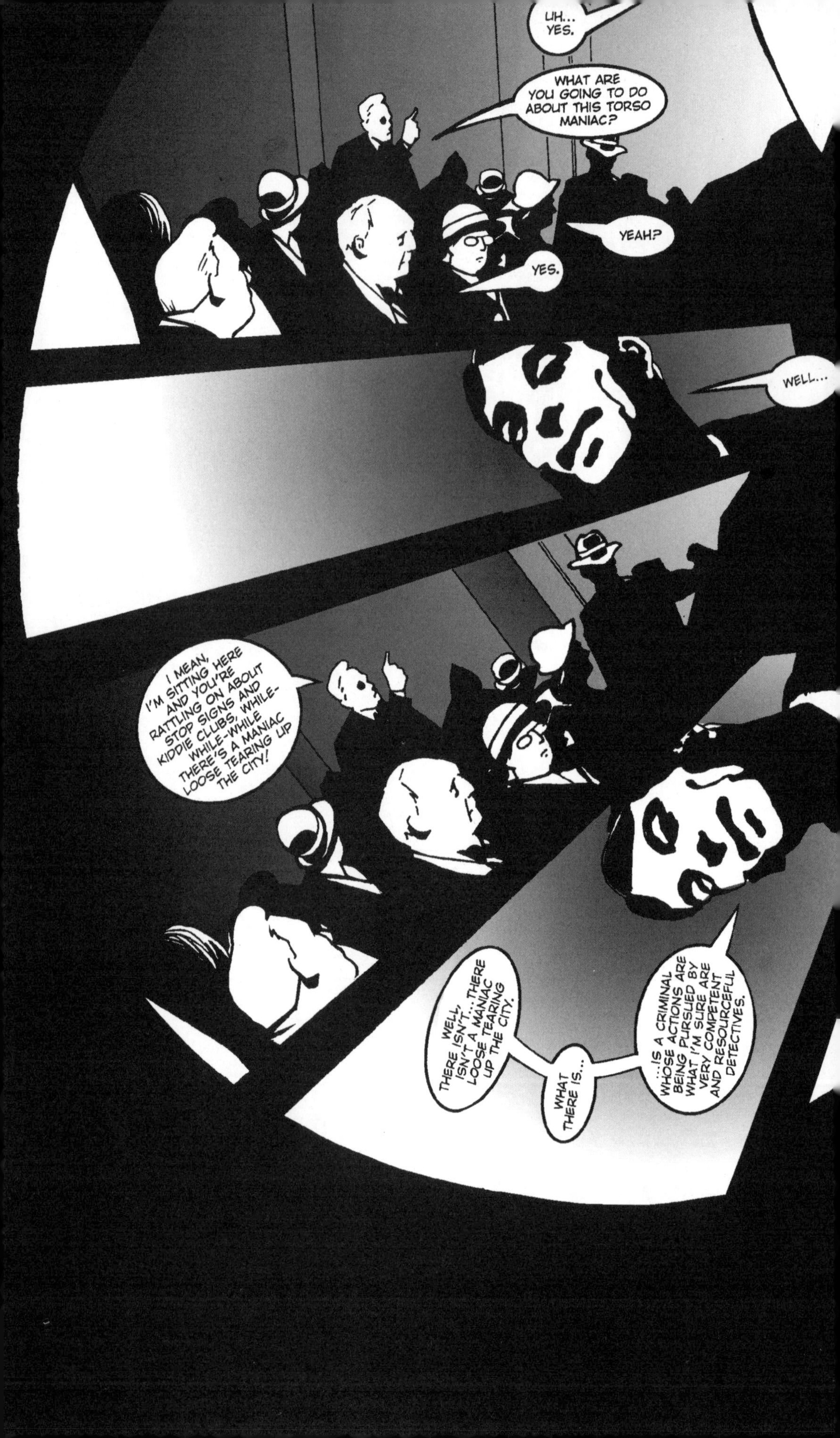
UH... YES.
WHAT ARE YOU GOING TO DO ABOUT THIS TORSO MANIAC?
YEAH?
YES.
WELL...
I MEAN, I'M SITTING HERE AND YOU'RE RATTLING ON ABOUT STOP SIGNS AND KIDDIE CLUBS, WHILE-WHILE-WHILE THERE'S A MANIAC LOOSE TEARING UP THE CITY!
WELL, THERE ISN'T... THERE ISN'T A MANIAC LOOSE TEARING UP THE CITY.
WHAT THERE IS...
...IS A CRIMINAL WHOSE ACTIONS ARE BEING PURSUED BY WHAT I'M SURE ARE VERY COMPETENT AND RESOURCEFUL DETECTIVES.

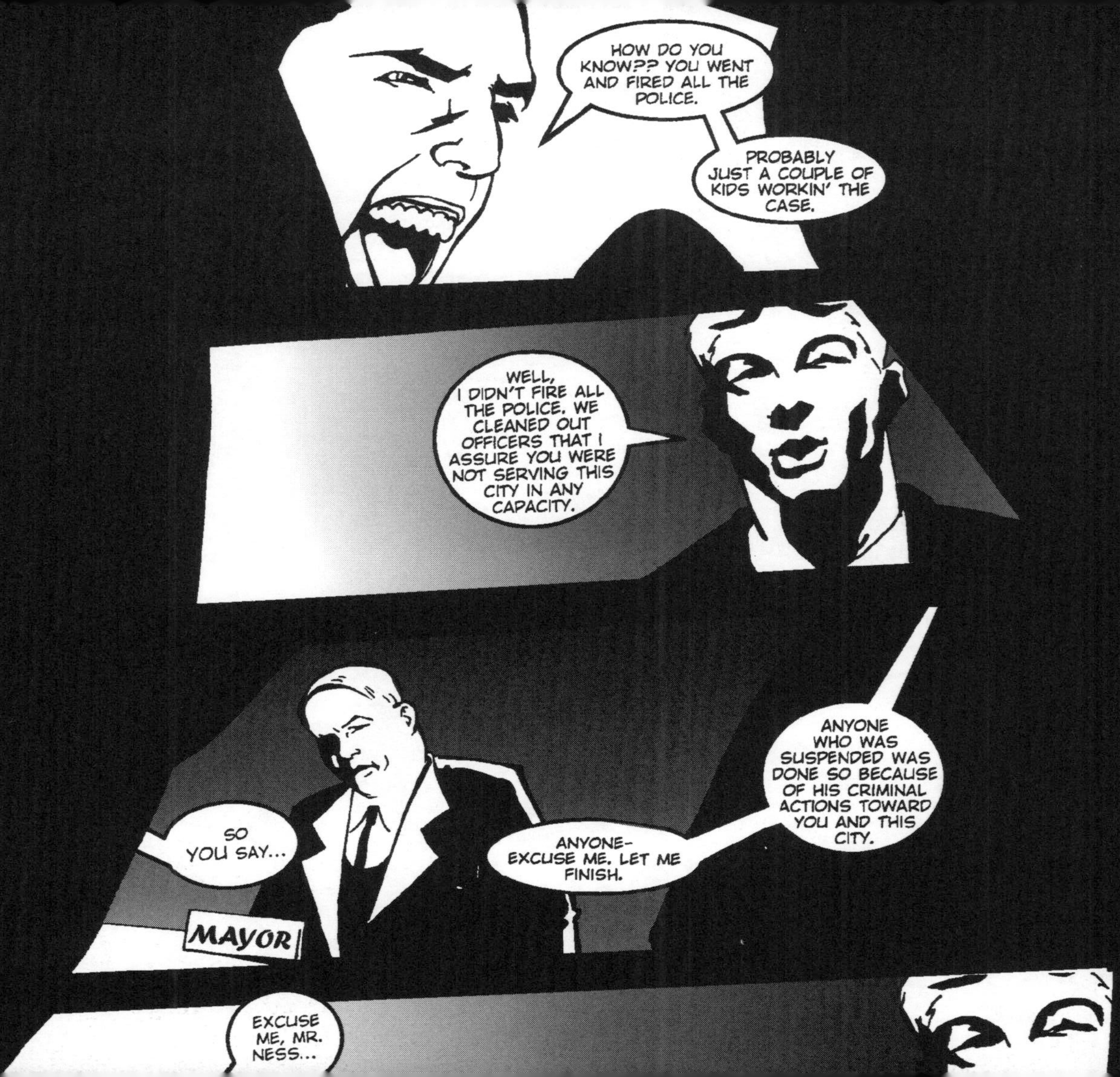
HOW DO YOU KNOW?? YOU WENT AND FIRED ALL THE POLICE.
PROBABLY JUST A COUPLE OF KIDS WORKIN' THE CASE.
WELL, I DIDN'T FIRE ALL THE POLICE. WE CLEANED OUT OFFICERS THAT I ASSURE YOU WERE NOT SERVING THIS CITY IN ANY CAPACITY.
SO YOU SAY...
ANYONE- EXCUSE ME. LET ME FINISH.
ANYONE WHO WAS SUSPENDED WAS DONE SO BECAUSE OF HIS CRIMINAL ACTIONS TOWARD YOU AND THIS CITY.
MAYOR
EXCUSE ME, MR. NESS...

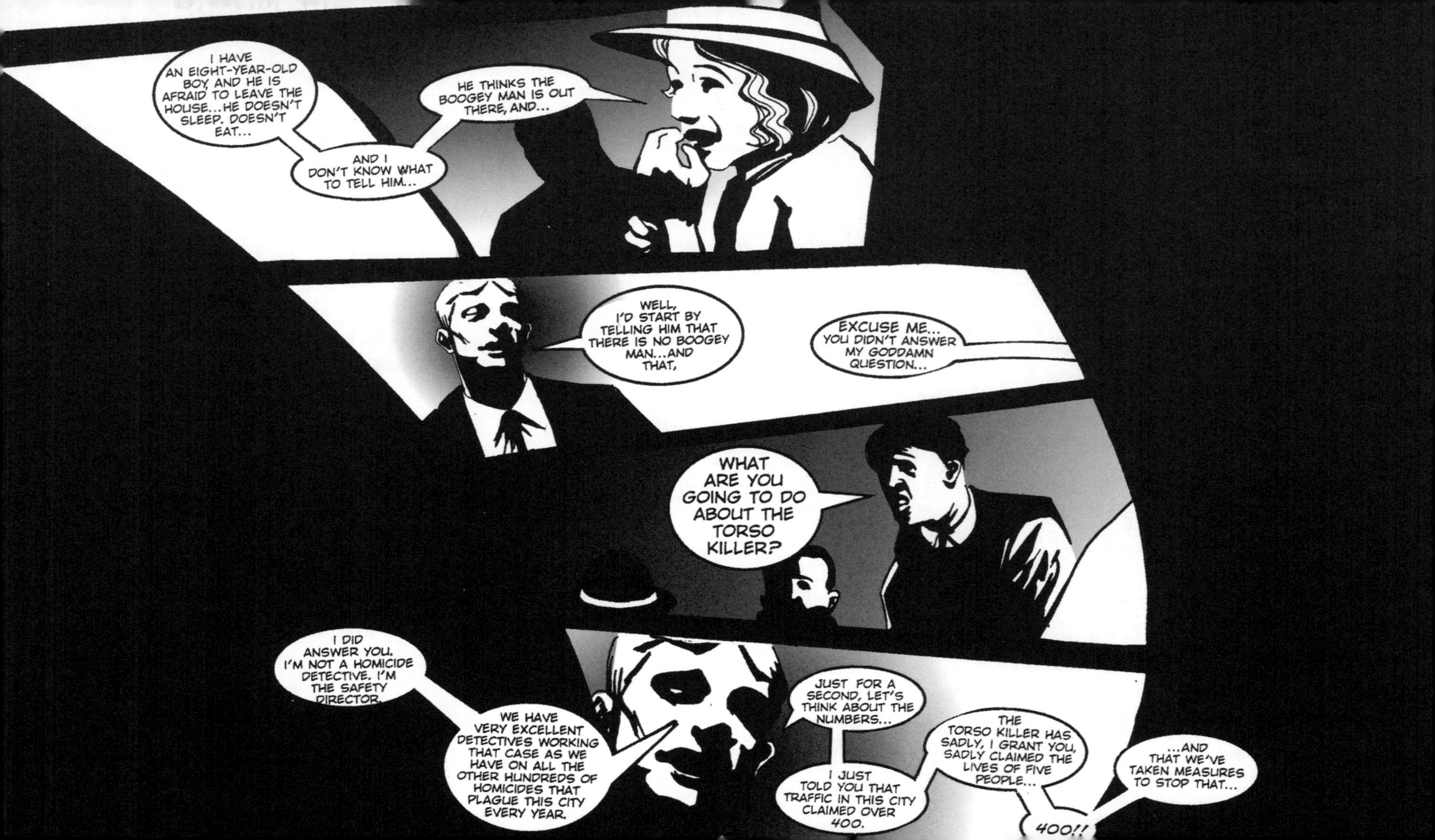
I HAVE AN EIGHT-YEAR-OLD BOY, AND HE IS AFRAID TO LEAVE THE HOUSE...HE DOESN'T SLEEP. DOESN'T EAT...
AND I DON'T KNOW WHAT TO TELL HIM...
HE THINKS THE BOOGEY MAN IS OUT THERE, AND...
WELL, I'D START BY TELLING HIM THAT THERE IS NO BOOGEY MAN...AND THAT,
EXCUSE ME... YOU DIDN'T ANSWER MY GODDAMN QUESTION...
WHAT ARE YOU GOING TO DO ABOUT THE TORSO KILLER?
I DID ANSWER YOU. I'M NOT A HOMICIDE DETECTIVE. I'M THE SAFETY DIRECTOR.
WE HAVE VERY EXCELLENT DETECTIVES WORKING THAT CASE AS WE HAVE ON ALL THE OTHER HUNDREDS OF HOMICIDES THAT PLAGUE THIS CITY EVERY YEAR.
JUST FOR A SECOND, LET'S THINK ABOUT THE NUMBERS...
I JUST TOLD YOU THAT TRAFFIC IN THIS CITY CLAIMED OVER 400.
THE TORSO KILLER HAS SADLY, I GRANT YOU, SADLY CLAIMED THE LIVES OF FIVE PEOPLE...
400!!
...AND THAT WE'VE TAKEN MEASURES TO STOP THAT...

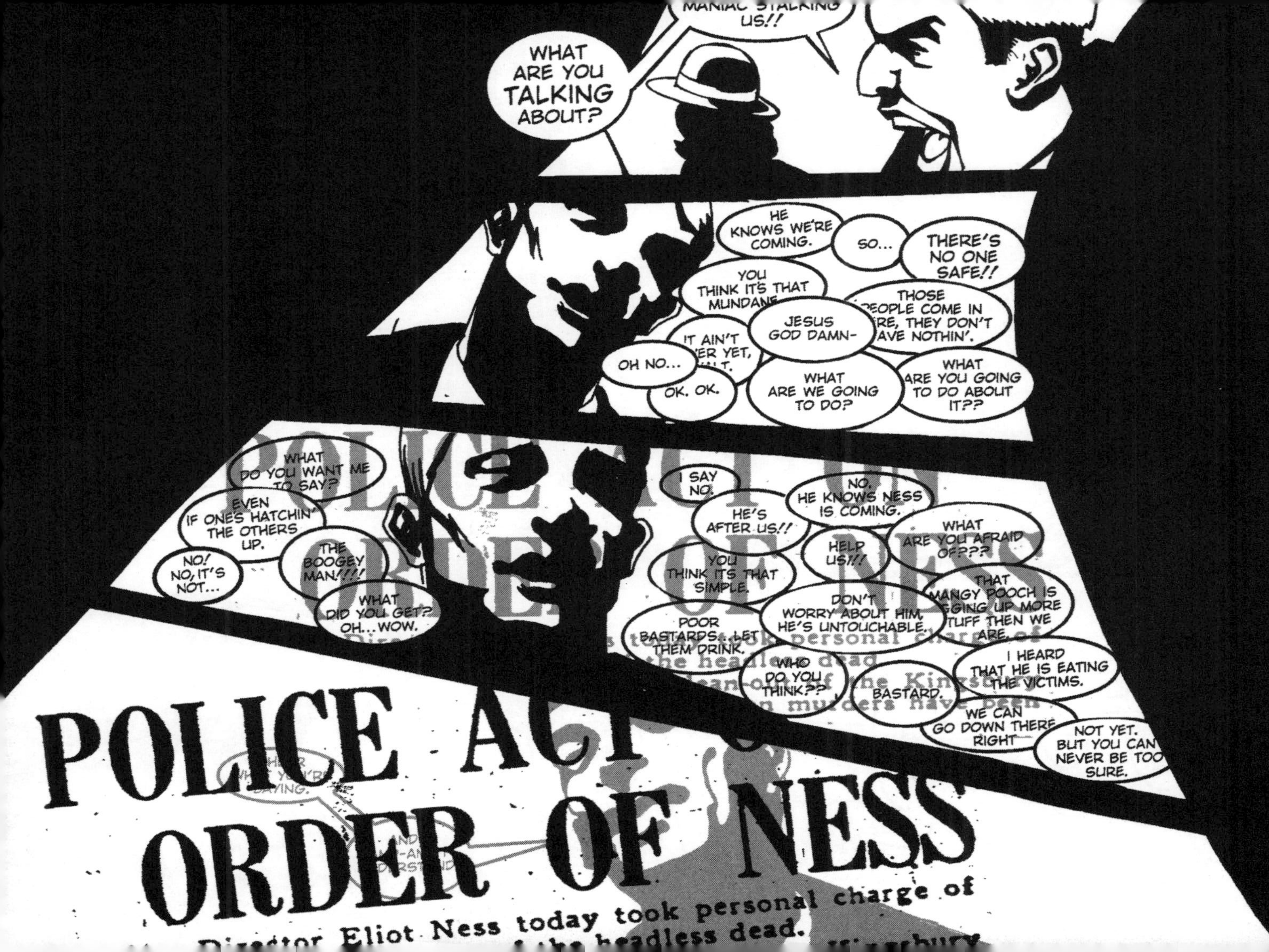
WHAT ARE YOU TALKING ABOUT?
HE KNOWS WE'RE COMING.
SO...
THERE'S NO ONE SAFE!!
JESUS GOD DAMN-
OH NO...
OK. OK.
WHAT ARE WE GOING TO DO?
WHAT ARE YOU GOING TO DO ABOUT IT??
WHAT DO YOU WANT ME TO SAY?
EVEN IF ONE'S HATCHIN' THE OTHERS UP.
NO! NO, IT'S NOT...
THE BOOGEY MAN!!!!
WHAT DID YOU GET? OH...WOW.
I SAY NO.
HE'S AFTER US!!
NO. HE KNOWS NESS IS COMING.
HELP US!!!
WHAT ARE YOU AFRAID OF???
YOU THINK IT'S THAT SIMPLE.
DON'T WORRY ABOUT HIM. HE'S UNTOUCHABLE.
POOR BASTARDS...LET THEM DRINK.
WHO DO YOU THINK??
BASTARD.
I HEARD THAT HE IS EATING THE VICTIMS.
WE CAN GO DOWN THERE RIGHT
NOT YET. BUT YOU CAN NEVER BE TOO SURE.
POLICE ACT
ORDER OF NESS
Director Eliot Ness today took personal charge of
the headless dead.

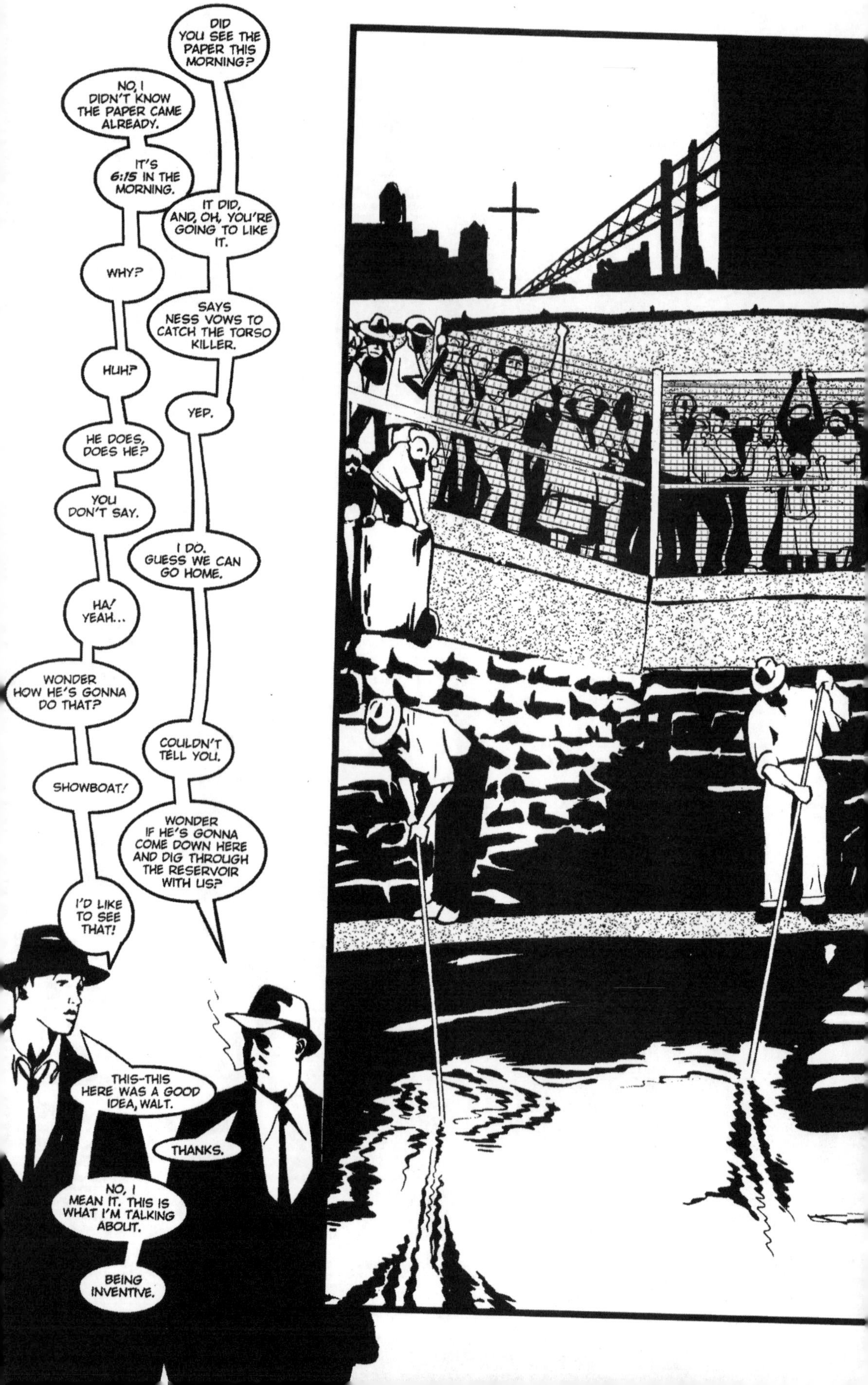
DID YOU SEE THE PAPER THIS MORNING?
NO, I DIDN'T KNOW THE PAPER CAME ALREADY.
IT'S 6:15 IN THE MORNING.
IT DID, AND, OH, YOU'RE GOING TO LIKE IT.
WHY?
SAYS NESS VOWS TO CATCH THE TORSO KILLER.
HUH?
YEP.
HE DOES, DOES HE?
YOU DON'T SAY.
I DO. GUESS WE CAN GO HOME.
HA! YEAH...
WONDER HOW HE'S GONNA DO THAT?
COULDN'T TELL YOU.
SHOWBOAT!
WONDER IF HE'S GONNA COME DOWN HERE AND DIG THROUGH THE RESERVOIR WITH US?
I'D LIKE TO SEE THAT!
THIS-THIS HERE WAS A GOOD IDEA, WALT.
THANKS.
NO, I MEAN IT. THIS IS WHAT I'M TALKING ABOUT.
BEING INVENTIVE.

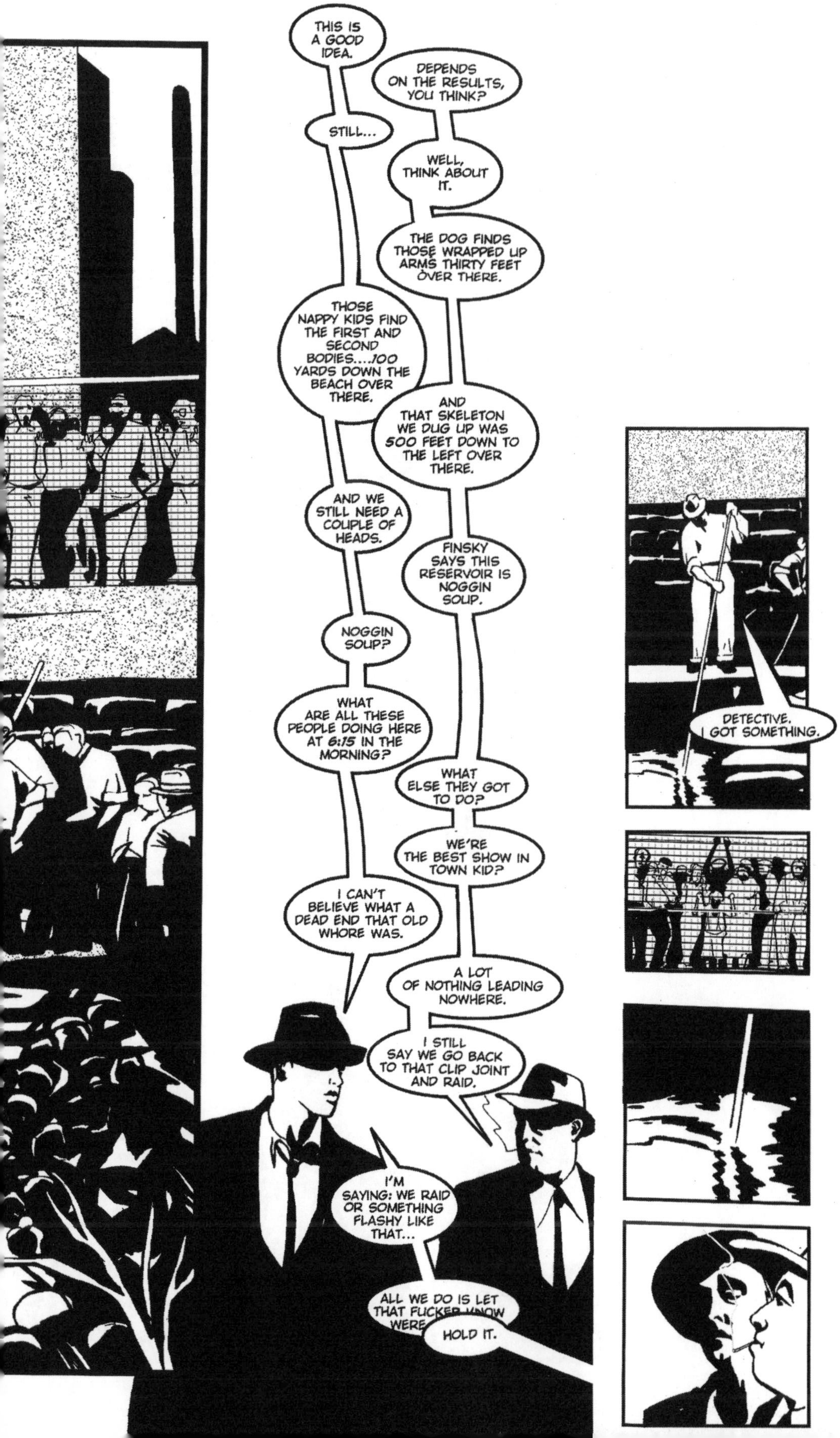
THIS IS A GOOD IDEA.
DEPENDS ON THE RESULTS, YOU THINK?
STILL...
WELL, THINK ABOUT IT.
THE DOG FINDS THOSE WRAPPED UP ARMS THIRTY FEET OVER THERE.
THOSE NAPPY KIDS FIND THE FIRST AND SECOND BODIES....100 YARDS DOWN THE BEACH OVER THERE.
AND THAT SKELETON WE DUG UP WAS 500 FEET DOWN TO THE LEFT OVER THERE.
AND WE STILL NEED A COUPLE OF HEADS.
FINSKY SAYS THIS RESERVOIR IS NOGGIN SOUP.
NOGGIN SOUP?
WHAT ARE ALL THESE PEOPLE DOING HERE AT 6:15 IN THE MORNING?
WHAT ELSE THEY GOT TO DO?
WE'RE THE BEST SHOW IN TOWN KID?
I CAN'T BELIEVE WHAT A DEAD END THAT OLD WHORE WAS.
A LOT OF NOTHING LEADING NOWHERE.
I STILL SAY WE GO BACK TO THAT CLIP JOINT AND RAID.
I'M SAYING: WE RAID OR SOMETHING FLASHY LIKE THAT...
ALL WE DO IS LET THAT FUCK WERE
HOLD IT.
DETECTIVE. I GOT SOMETHING.

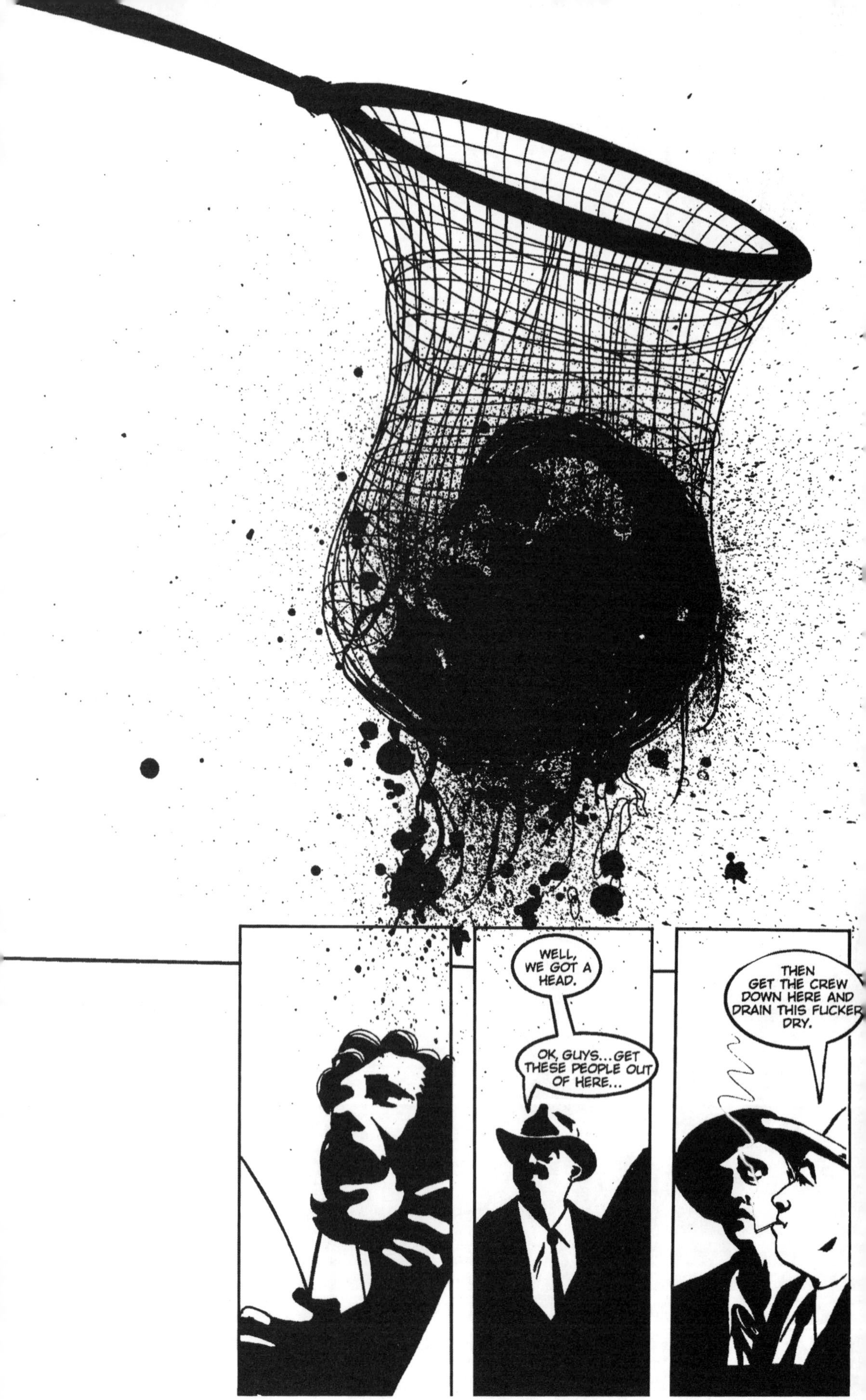
WELL, WE GOT A HEAD.
OK, GUYS...GET THESE PEOPLE OUT OF HERE...
THEN GET THE CREW DOWN HERE AND DRAIN THIS FLICKER DRY.

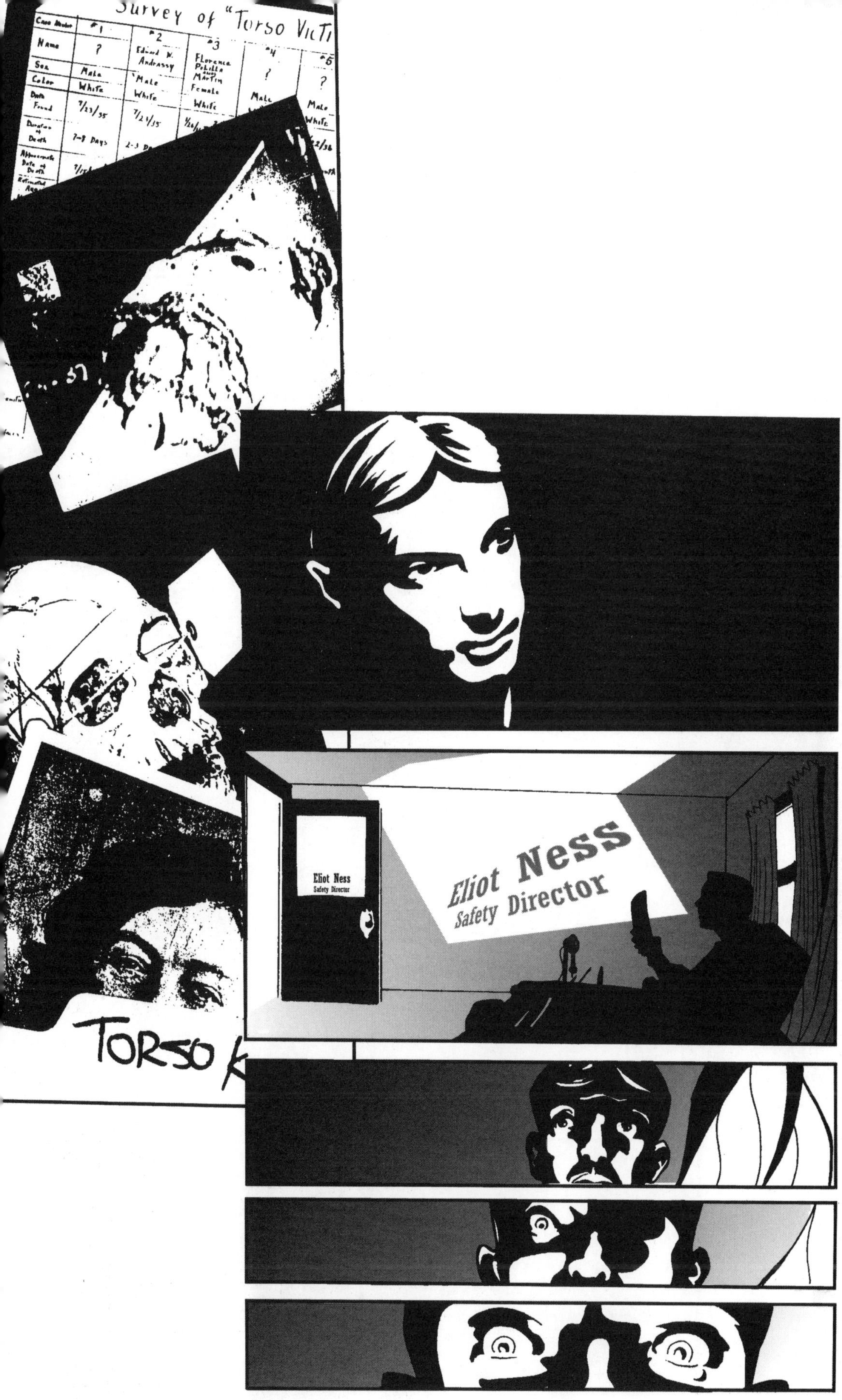

Survey of "Torso Victi
Name
Sex
Color
Date Found
Duration of Death
Approximate Date of Death
#1
?
Male
White
7/23/35
7-8 Days
#2
Edward W. Andrassy
Male
White
7/24/35
#3
Florence Polillo
Martin
Female
White
#4
?
Male
#5
?
Male
White
Eliot Ness
Safety Director
Eliot Ness
Safety Director
TORSO K

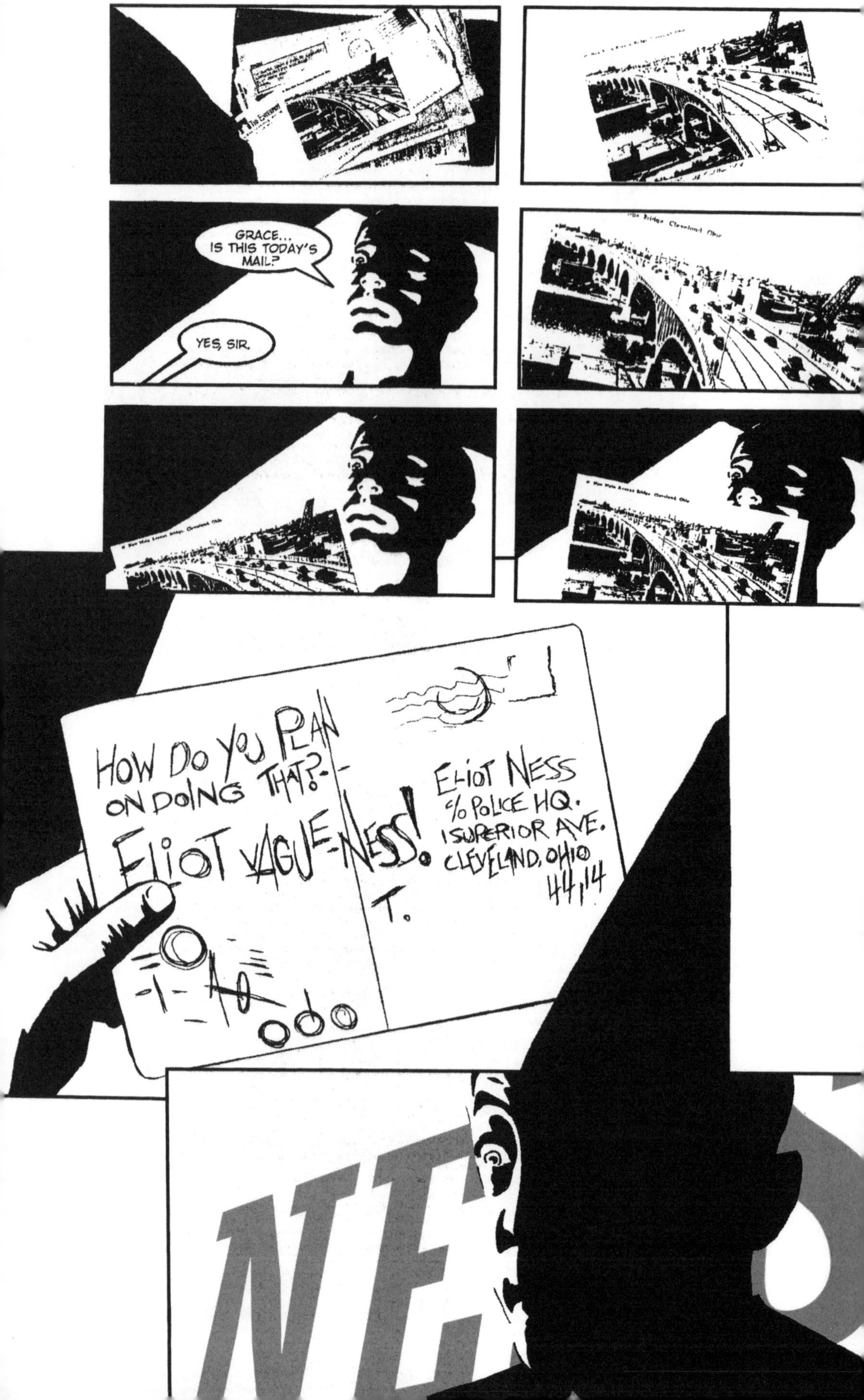
GRACE... IS THIS TODAY'S MAIL?
YES, SIR.
HOW DO YOU PLAN ON DOING THAT?- ELIOT VAGUE-NESS!
ELIOT NESS
% POLICE HQ.
1 SUPERIOR AVE.
CLEVELAND, OHIO
44,14
T.

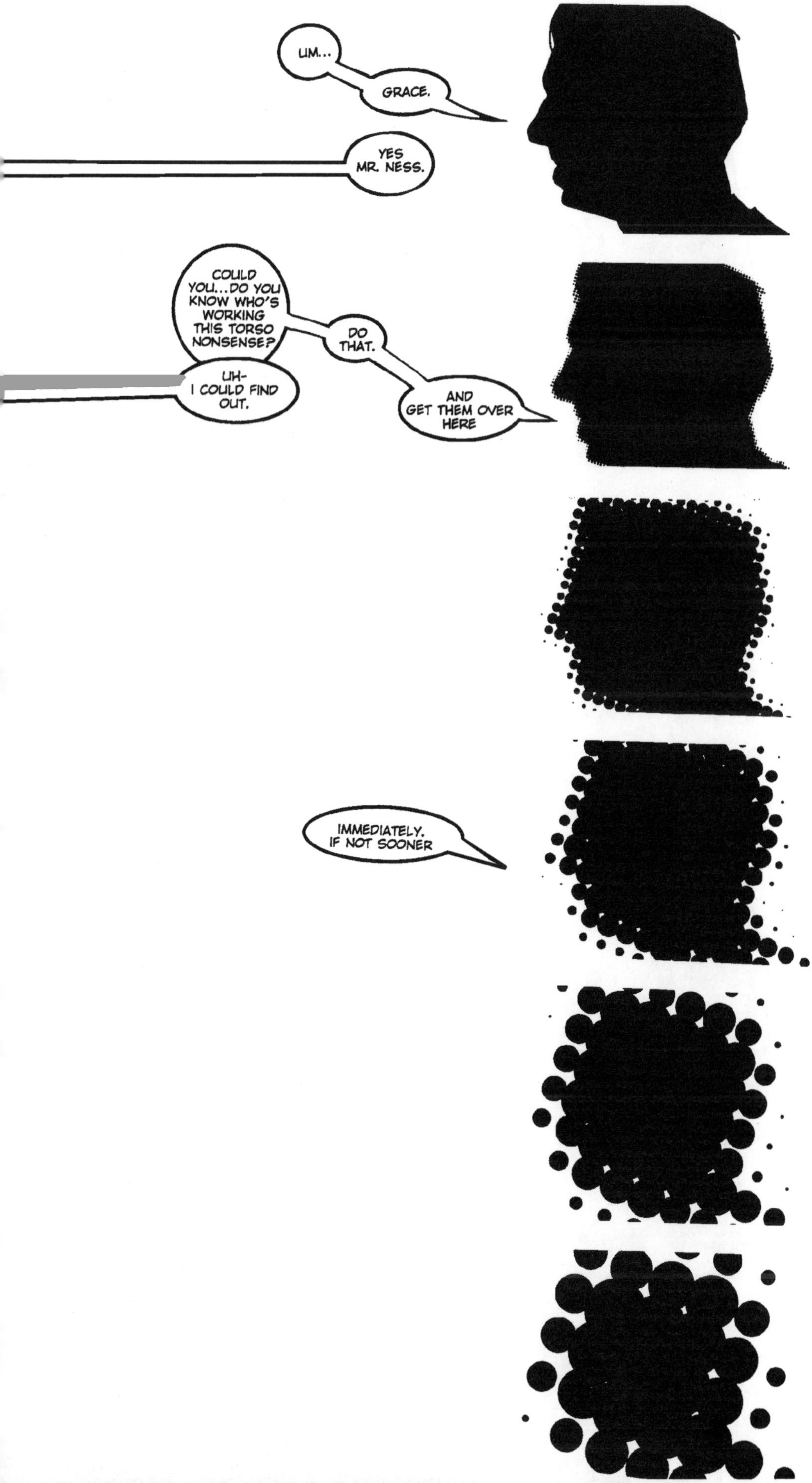
UM...
GRACE.
YES MR. NESS.
COULD YOU...DO YOU KNOW WHO'S WORKING THIS TORSO NONSENSE?
DO THAT.
UH- I COULD FIND OUT.
AND GET THEM OVER HERE
IMMEDIATELY. IF NOT SOONER

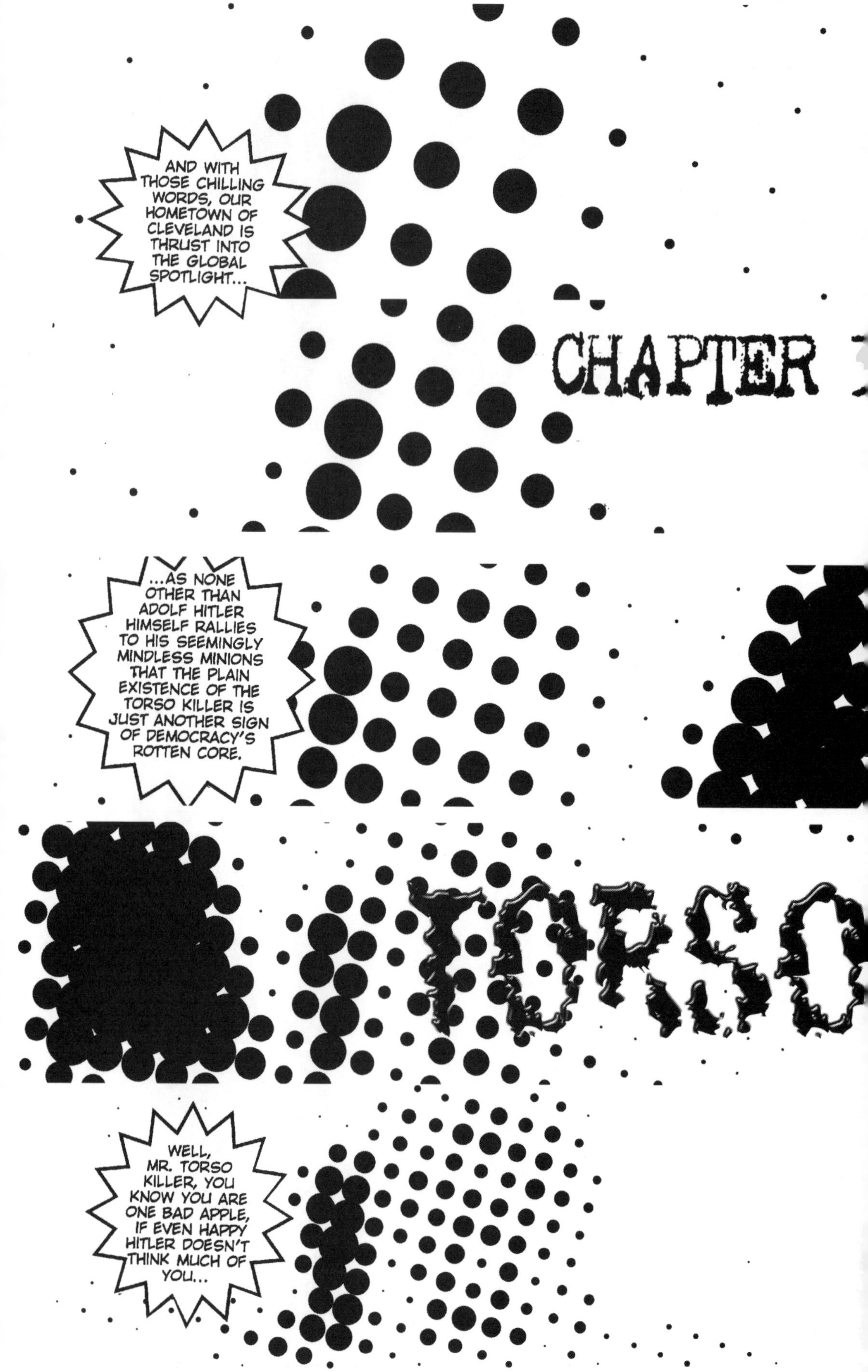
AND WITH THOSE CHILLING WORDS, OUR HOMETOWN OF CLEVELAND IS THRUST INTO THE GLOBAL SPOTLIGHT...
CHAPTER
...AS NONE OTHER THAN ADOLF HITLER HIMSELF RALLIES TO HIS SEEMINGLY MINDLESS MINIONS THAT THE PLAIN EXISTENCE OF THE TORSO KILLER IS JUST ANOTHER SIGN OF DEMOCRACY'S ROTTEN CORE.
TORSO
WELL, MR. TORSO KILLER, YOU KNOW YOU ARE ONE BAD APPLE, IF EVEN HAPPY HITLER DOESN'T THINK MUCH OF YOU...

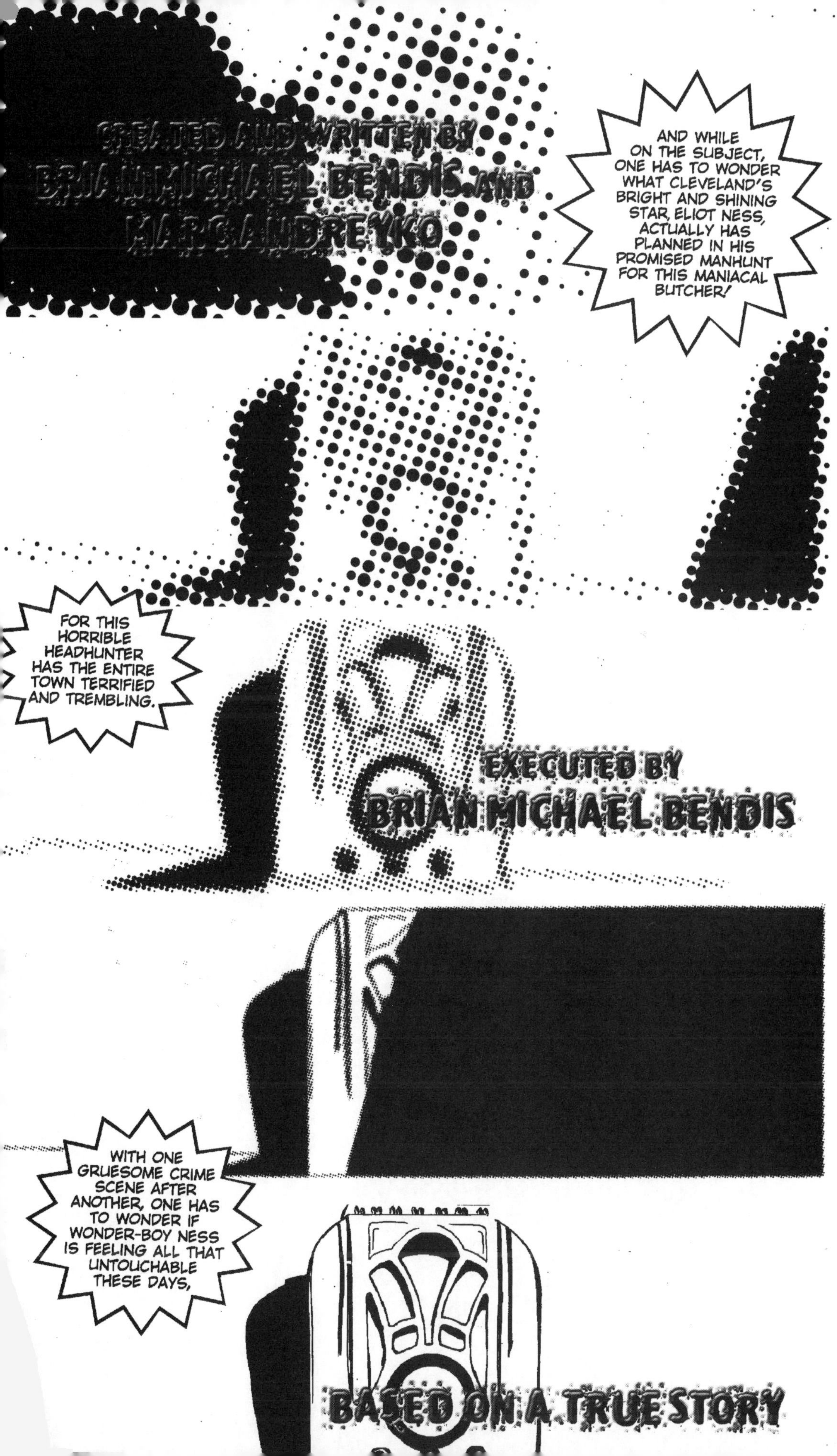
CREATED AND WRITTEN BY
BRIAN MICHAEL BENDIS AND
MARC ANDREYKO
AND WHILE ON THE SUBJECT, ONE HAS TO WONDER WHAT CLEVELAND'S BRIGHT AND SHINING STAR, ELIOT NESS, ACTUALLY HAS PLANNED IN HIS PROMISED MANHUNT FOR THIS MANIACAL BUTCHER!
FOR THIS HORRIBLE HEADHUNTER HAS THE ENTIRE TOWN TERRIFIED AND TREMBLING.
EXECUTED BY
BRIAN MICHAEL BENDIS
WITH ONE GRUESOME CRIME SCENE AFTER ANOTHER, ONE HAS TO WONDER IF WONDER-BOY NESS IS FEELING ALL THAT UNTOUCHABLE THESE DAYS,
BASED ON A TRUE STORY

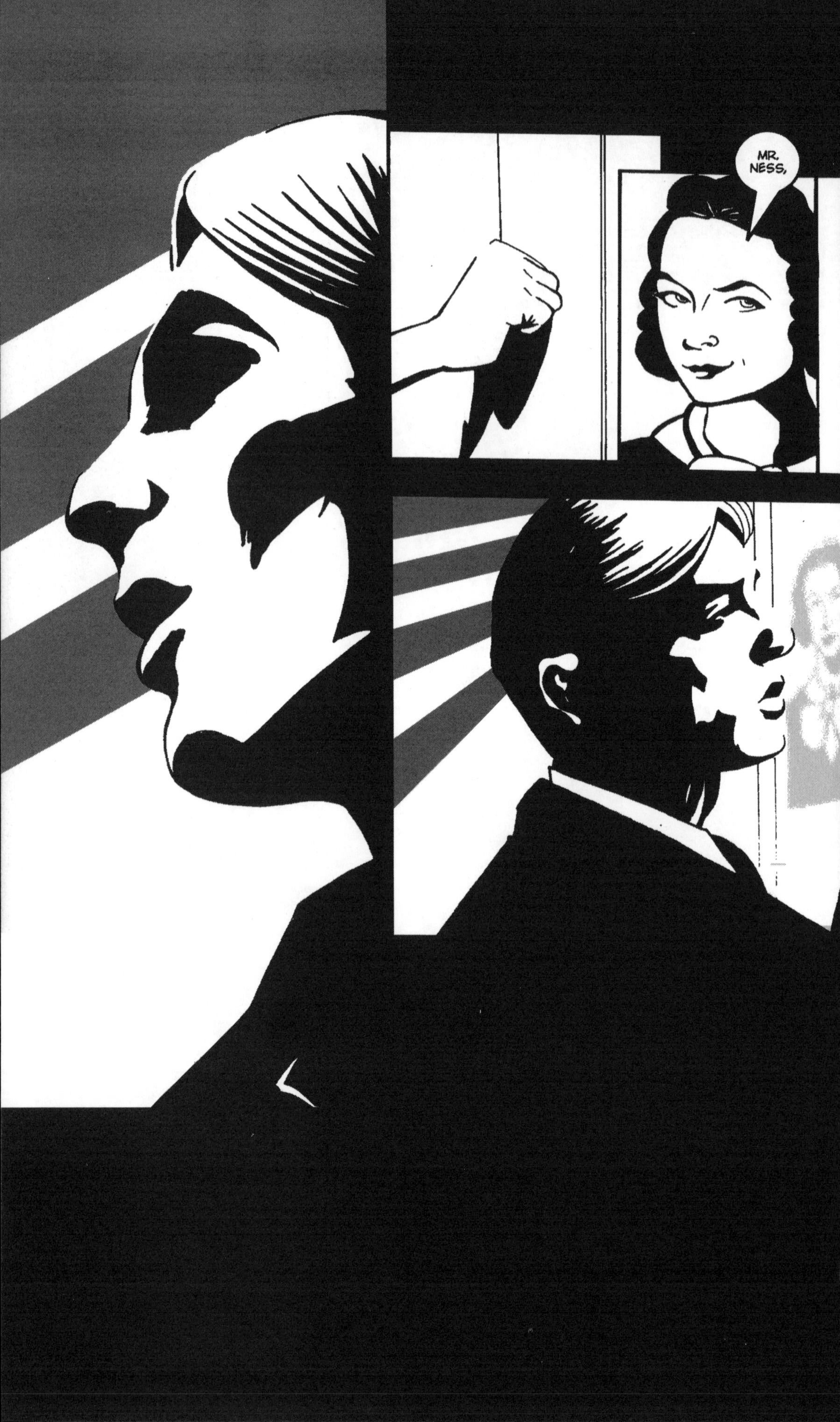
MR. NESS,

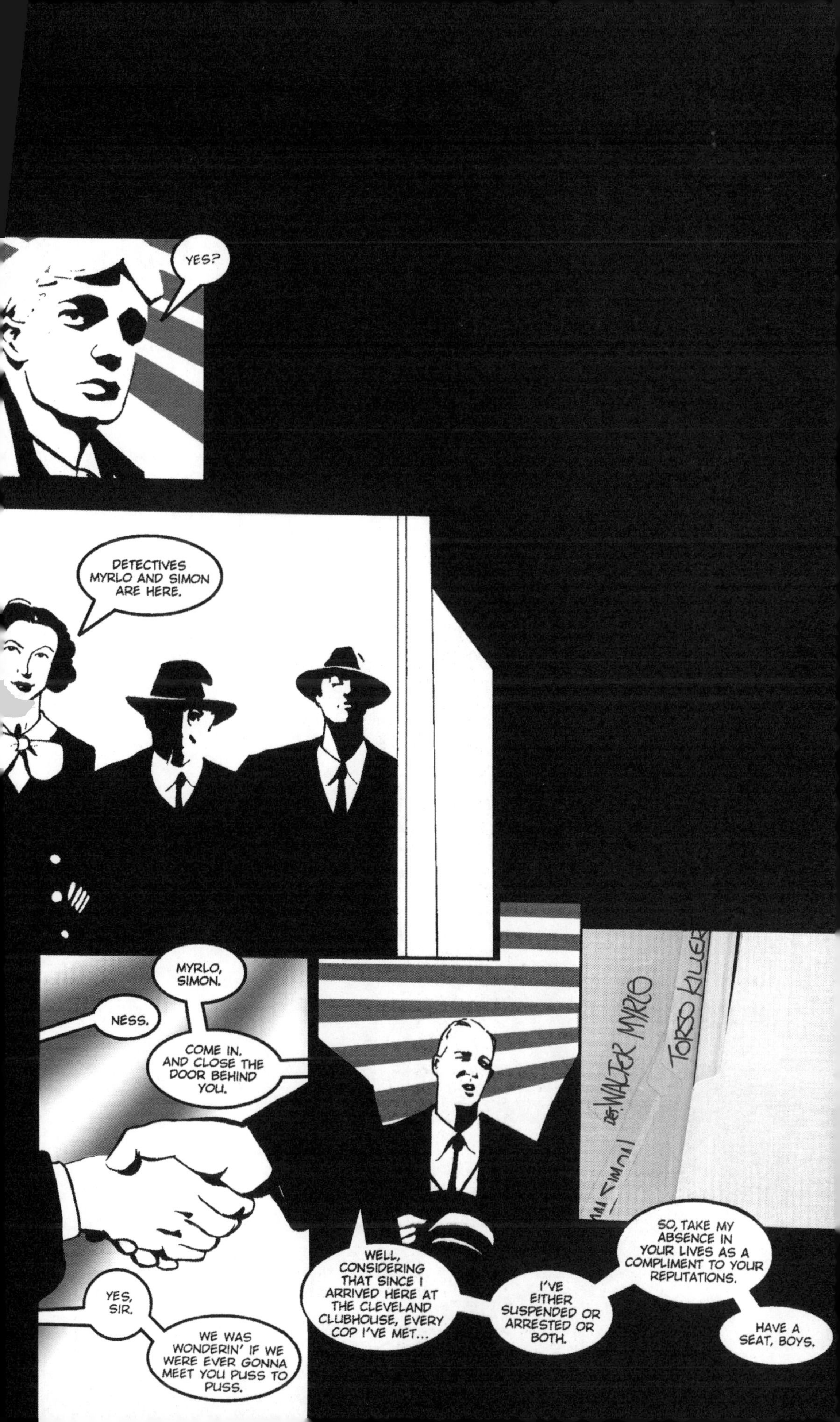
YES?
DETECTIVES MYRLO AND SIMON ARE HERE.
MYRLO, SIMON.
NESS.
COME IN. AND CLOSE THE DOOR BEHIND YOU.
YES, SIR.
WE WAS WONDERIN' IF WE WERE EVER GONNA MEET YOU PUSS TO PUSS.
DET. WALTER MYRLO
TORSO KILLER
WELL, CONSIDERING THAT SINCE I ARRIVED HERE AT THE CLEVELAND CLUBHOUSE, EVERY COP I'VE MET...
I'VE EITHER SUSPENDED OR ARRESTED OR BOTH.
SO, TAKE MY ABSENCE IN YOUR LIVES AS A COMPLIMENT TO YOUR REPUTATIONS.
HAVE A SEAT, BOYS.

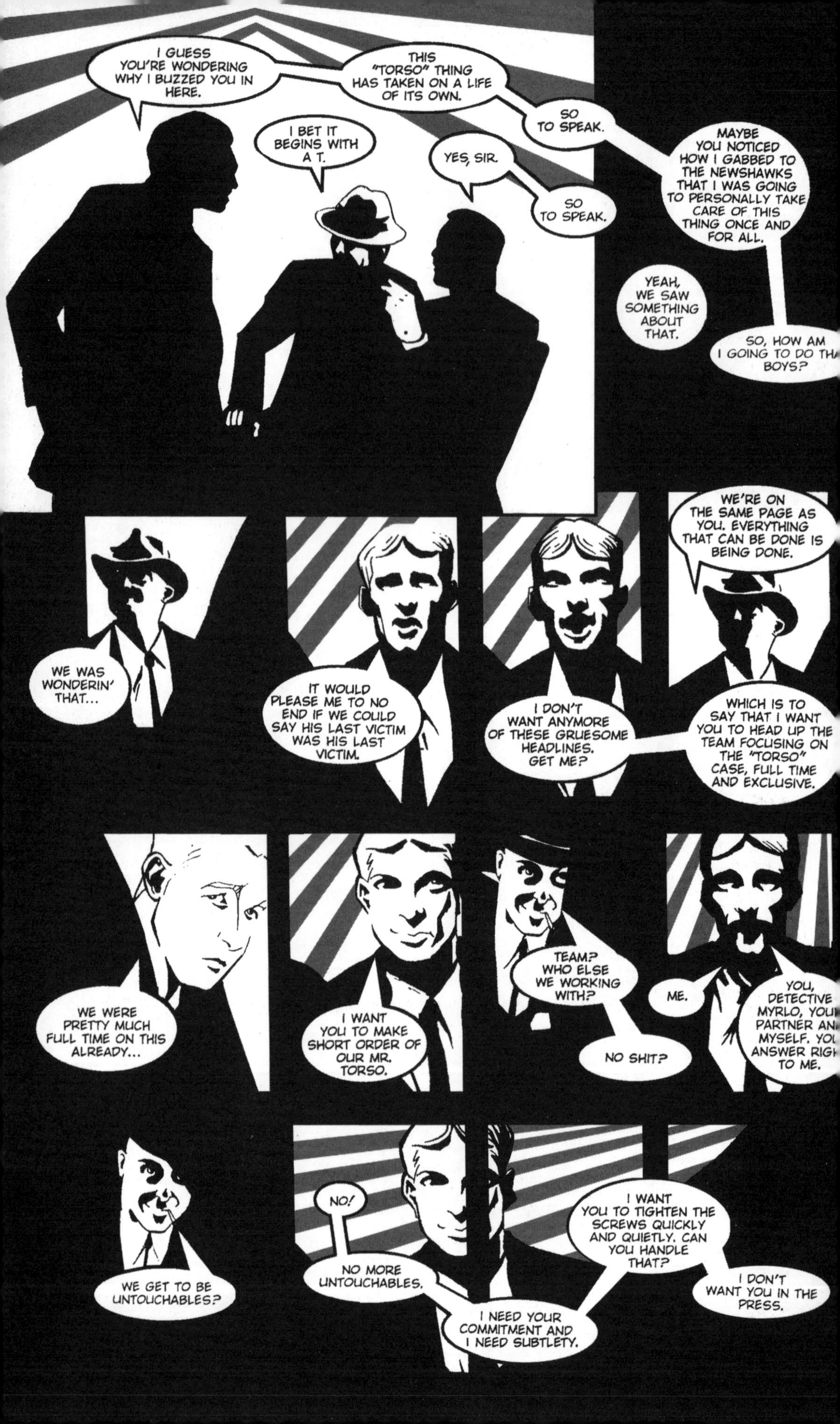
I GUESS YOU'RE WONDERING WHY I BUZZED YOU IN HERE.
THIS "TORSO" THING HAS TAKEN ON A LIFE OF ITS OWN.
SO TO SPEAK.
I BET IT BEGINS WITH A T.
YES, SIR.
SO TO SPEAK.
MAYBE YOU NOTICED HOW I GABBED TO THE NEWSHAWKS THAT I WAS GOING TO PERSONALLY TAKE CARE OF THIS THING ONCE AND FOR ALL.
YEAH, WE SAW SOMETHING ABOUT THAT.
SO, HOW AM I GOING TO DO THA BOYS?
WE WAS WONDERIN' THAT...
IT WOULD PLEASE ME TO NO END IF WE COULD SAY HIS LAST VICTIM WAS HIS LAST VICTIM.
I DON'T WANT ANYMORE OF THESE GRUESOME HEADLINES. GET ME?
WE'RE ON THE SAME PAGE AS YOU. EVERYTHING THAT CAN BE DONE IS BEING DONE.
WHICH IS TO SAY THAT I WANT YOU TO HEAD UP THE TEAM FOCUSING ON THE "TORSO" CASE, FULL TIME AND EXCLUSIVE.
WE WERE PRETTY MUCH FULL TIME ON THIS ALREADY...
I WANT YOU TO MAKE SHORT ORDER OF OUR MR. TORSO.
TEAM? WHO ELSE WE WORKING WITH?
NO SHIT?
ME.
YOU, DETECTIVE MYRLO, YOU PARTNER AN MYSELF. YO ANSWER RIG TO ME.
WE GET TO BE UNTOUCHABLES?
NO!
NO MORE UNTOUCHABLES.
I NEED YOUR COMMITMENT AND I NEED SUBTLETY.
I WANT YOU TO TIGHTEN THE SCREWS QUICKLY AND QUIETLY. CAN YOU HANDLE THAT?
I DON'T WANT YOU IN THE PRESS.

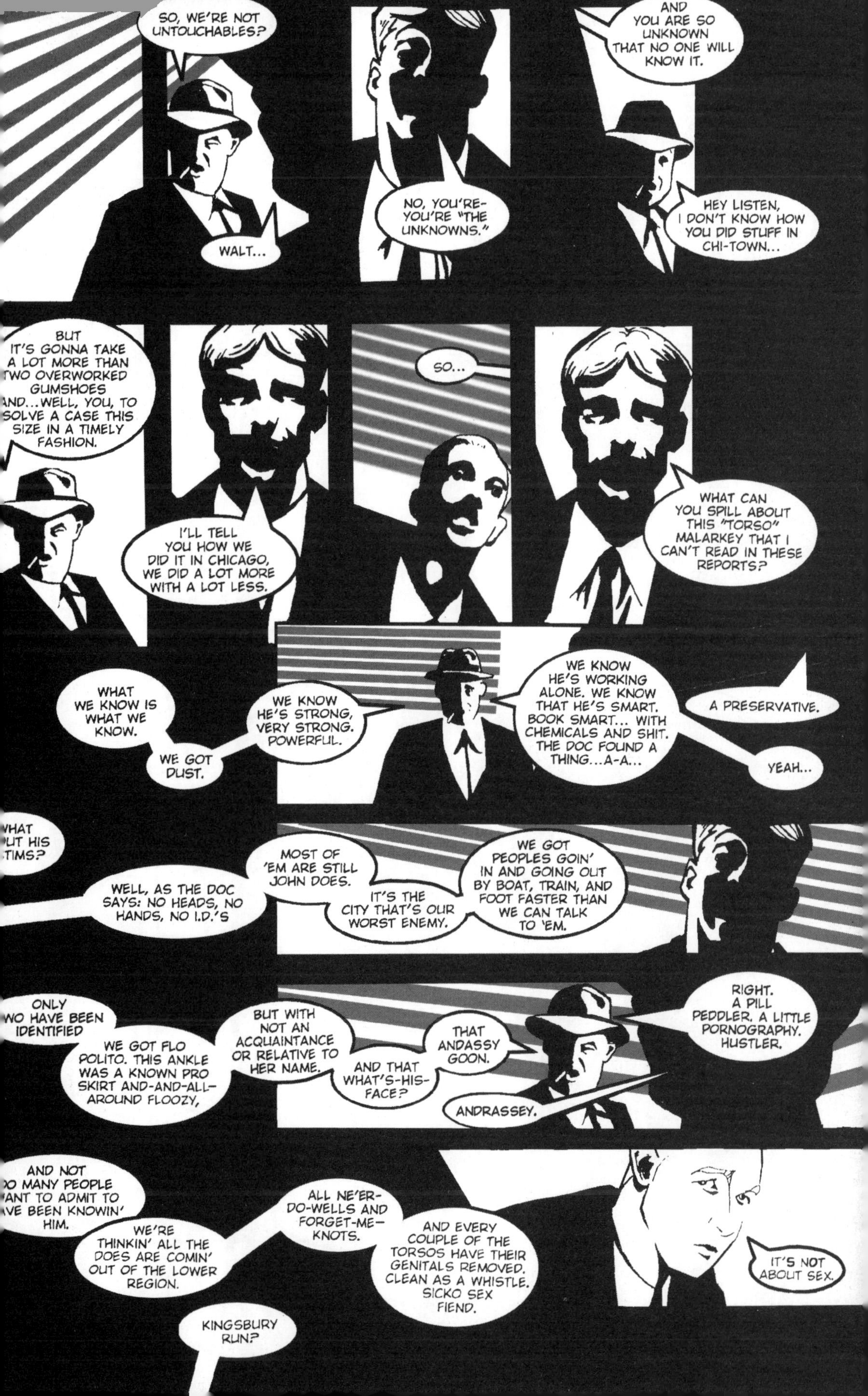
SO, WE'RE NOT UNTOUCHABLES?
WALT...
NO, YOU'RE- YOU'RE "THE UNKNOWNS."
AND YOU ARE SO UNKNOWN THAT NO ONE WILL KNOW IT.
HEY LISTEN, I DON'T KNOW HOW YOU DID STUFF IN CHI-TOWN...
BUT IT'S GONNA TAKE A LOT MORE THAN TWO OVERWORKED GUMSHOES AND...WELL, YOU, TO SOLVE A CASE THIS SIZE IN A TIMELY FASHION.
I'LL TELL YOU HOW WE DID IT IN CHICAGO, WE DID A LOT MORE WITH A LOT LESS.
SO...
WHAT CAN YOU SPILL ABOUT THIS "TORSO" MALARKEY THAT I CAN'T READ IN THESE REPORTS?
WHAT WE KNOW IS WHAT WE KNOW.
WE GOT DUST.
WE KNOW HE'S STRONG, VERY STRONG. POWERFUL.
WE KNOW HE'S WORKING ALONE. WE KNOW THAT HE'S SMART. BOOK SMART... WITH CHEMICALS AND SHIT. THE DOC FOUND A THING...A-A...
A PRESERVATIVE.
YEAH...
WELL, AS THE DOC SAYS: NO HEADS, NO HANDS, NO I.D.'S
MOST OF 'EM ARE STILL JOHN DOES.
IT'S THE CITY THAT'S OUR WORST ENEMY.
WE GOT PEOPLES GOIN' IN AND GOING OUT BY BOAT, TRAIN, AND FOOT FASTER THAN WE CAN TALK TO 'EM.
ONLY WO HAVE BEEN IDENTIFIED
WE GOT FLO POLITO. THIS ANKLE WAS A KNOWN PRO SKIRT AND-AND-ALL-AROUND FLOOZY,
BUT WITH NOT AN ACQUAINTANCE OR RELATIVE TO HER NAME.
AND THAT WHAT'S-HIS-FACE?
THAT ANDASSY GOON.
ANDRASSEY.
RIGHT. A PILL PEDDLER. A LITTLE PORNOGRAPHY. HUSTLER.
AND NOT O MANY PEOPLE ANT TO ADMIT TO VE BEEN KNOWIN' HIM.
ALL NE'ER-DO-WELLS AND FORGET-ME-KNOTS.
WE'RE THINKIN' ALL THE DOES ARE COMIN' OUT OF THE LOWER REGION.
KINGSBURY RUN?
AND EVERY COUPLE OF THE TORSOS HAVE THEIR GENITALS REMOVED. CLEAN AS A WHISTLE. SICKO SEX FIEND.
IT'S NOT ABOUT SEX.

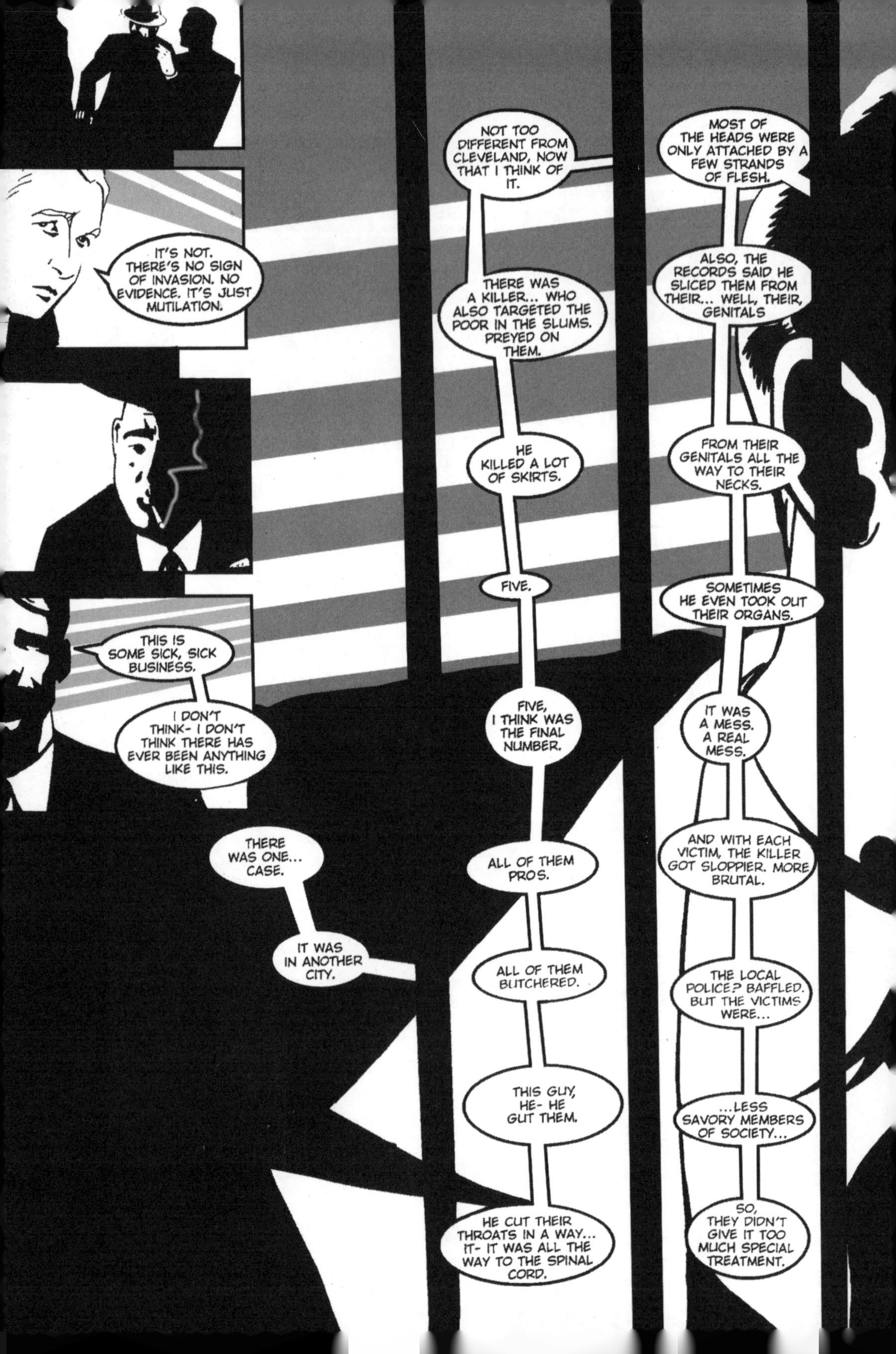
IT'S NOT. THERE'S NO SIGN OF INVASION. NO EVIDENCE. IT'S JUST MUTILATION.
THIS IS SOME SICK, SICK BUSINESS.
I DON'T THINK- I DON'T THINK THERE HAS EVER BEEN ANYTHING LIKE THIS.
THERE WAS ONE... CASE.
IT WAS IN ANOTHER CITY.
NOT TOO DIFFERENT FROM CLEVELAND, NOW THAT I THINK OF IT.
THERE WAS A KILLER... WHO ALSO TARGETED THE POOR IN THE SLUMS. PREYED ON THEM.
HE KILLED A LOT OF SKIRTS.
FIVE.
FIVE, I THINK WAS THE FINAL NUMBER.
ALL OF THEM PROS.
ALL OF THEM BUTCHERED.
THIS GUY, HE- HE GUT THEM.
HE CUT THEIR THROATS IN A WAY... IT- IT WAS ALL THE WAY TO THE SPINAL CORD.
MOST OF THE HEADS WERE ONLY ATTACHED BY A FEW STRANDS OF FLESH.
ALSO, THE RECORDS SAID HE SLICED THEM FROM THEIR... WELL, THEIR, GENITALS
FROM THEIR GENITALS ALL THE WAY TO THEIR NECKS.
SOMETIMES HE EVEN TOOK OUT THEIR ORGANS.
IT WAS A MESS. A REAL MESS.
AND WITH EACH VICTIM, THE KILLER GOT SLOPPIER. MORE BRUTAL.
THE LOCAL POLICE? BAFFLED. BUT THE VICTIMS WERE...
...LESS SAVORY MEMBERS OF SOCIETY...
SO, THEY DIDN'T GIVE IT TOO MUCH SPECIAL TREATMENT.

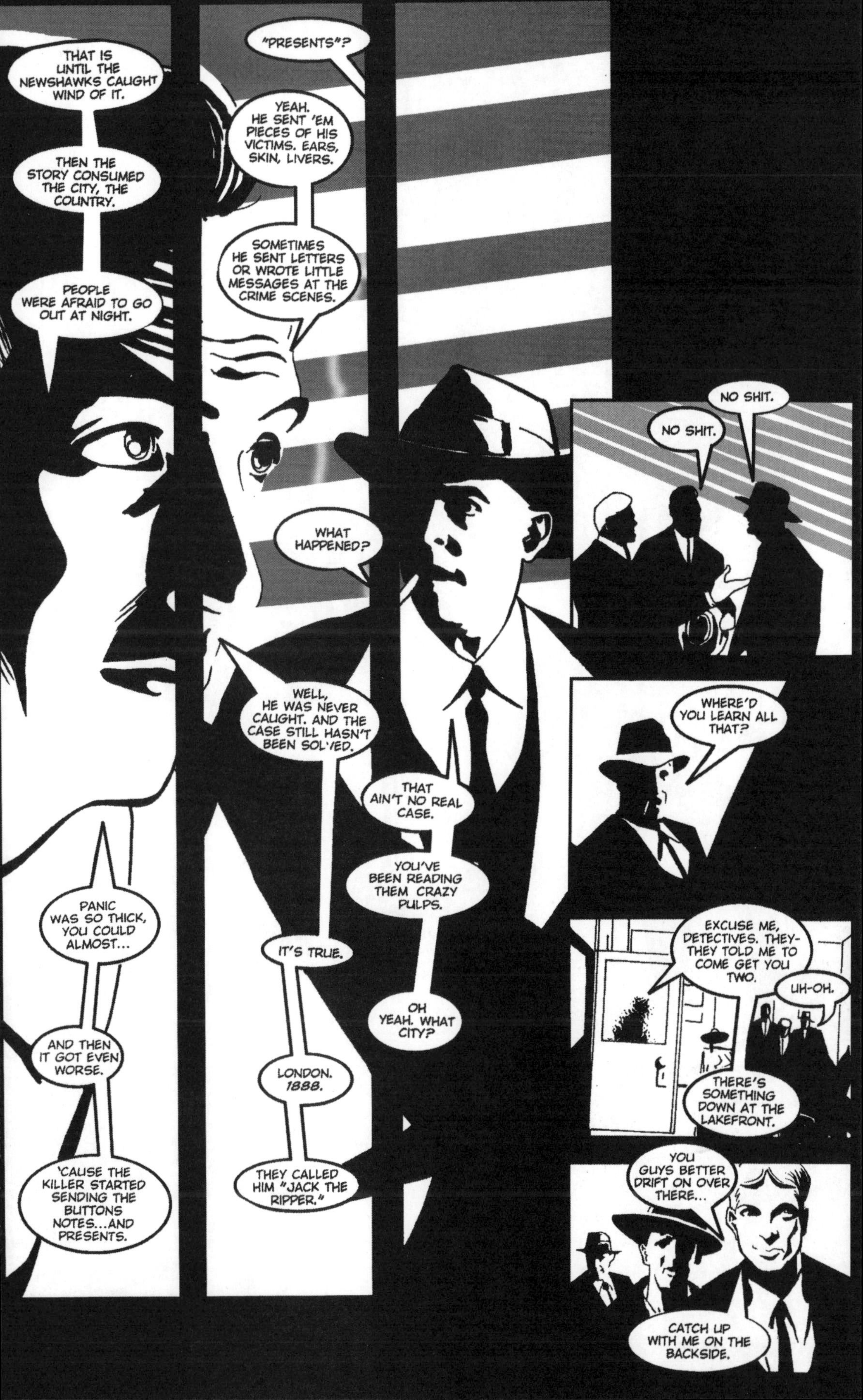
THAT IS UNTIL THE NEWSHAWKS CAUGHT WIND OF IT.
THEN THE STORY CONSUMED THE CITY, THE COUNTRY.
PEOPLE WERE AFRAID TO GO OUT AT NIGHT.
PANIC WAS SO THICK, YOU COULD ALMOST...
AND THEN IT GOT EVEN WORSE.
'CAUSE THE KILLER STARTED SENDING THE BUTTONS NOTES...AND PRESENTS.
"PRESENTS"?
YEAH. HE SENT 'EM PIECES OF HIS VICTIMS. EARS, SKIN, LIVERS.
SOMETIMES HE SENT LETTERS OR WROTE LITTLE MESSAGES AT THE CRIME SCENES.
WHAT HAPPENED?
WELL, HE WAS NEVER CAUGHT. AND THE CASE STILL HASN'T BEEN SOLVED.
THAT AIN'T NO REAL CASE.
YOU'VE BEEN READING THEM CRAZY PULPS.
IT'S TRUE.
OH YEAH. WHAT CITY?
LONDON. *1888.*
THEY CALLED HIM "JACK THE RIPPER."
NO SHIT.
NO SHIT.
WHERE'D YOU LEARN ALL THAT?
EXCUSE ME, DETECTIVES. THEY- THEY TOLD ME TO COME GET YOU TWO.
UH-OH.
THERE'S SOMETHING DOWN AT THE LAKEFRONT.
YOU GUYS BETTER DRIFT ON OVER THERE...
CATCH UP WITH ME ON THE BACKSIDE.

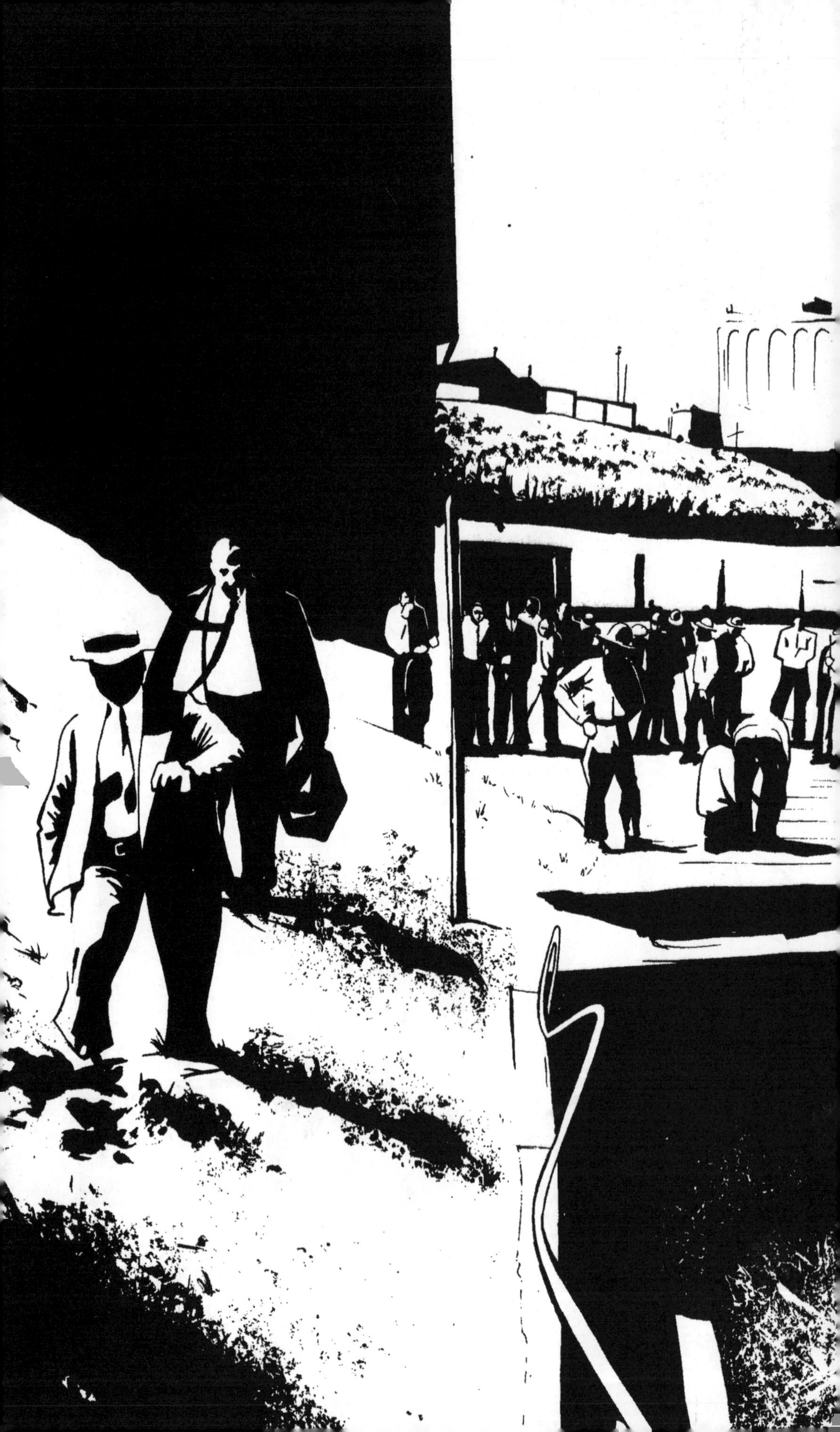

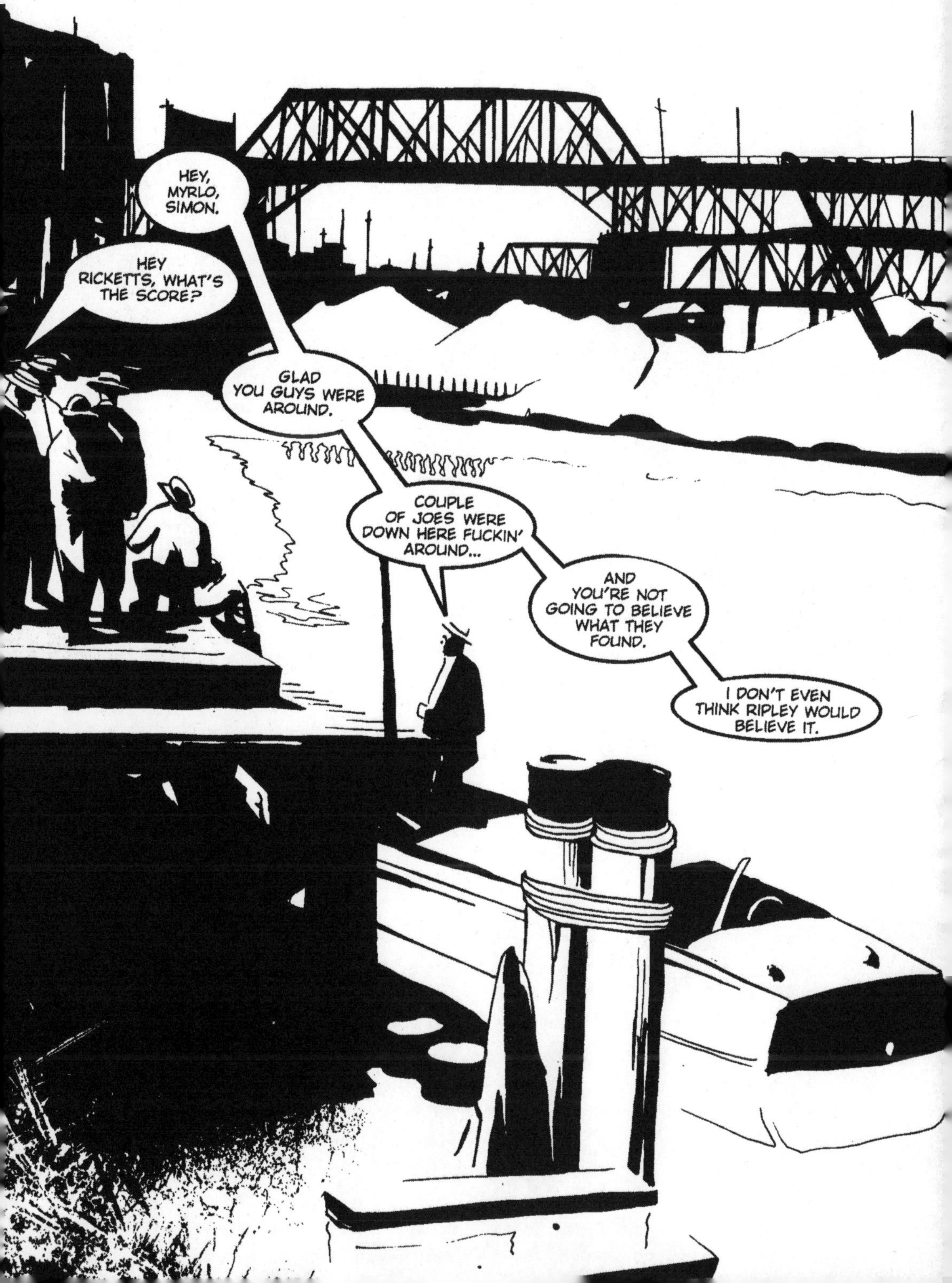
HEY, MYRLO, SIMON.
HEY RICKETTS, WHAT'S THE SCORE?
GLAD YOU GUYS WERE AROUND.
COUPLE OF JOES WERE DOWN HERE FUCKIN' AROUND...
AND YOU'RE NOT GOING TO BELIEVE WHAT THEY FOUND.
I DON'T EVEN THINK RIPLEY WOULD BELIEVE IT.

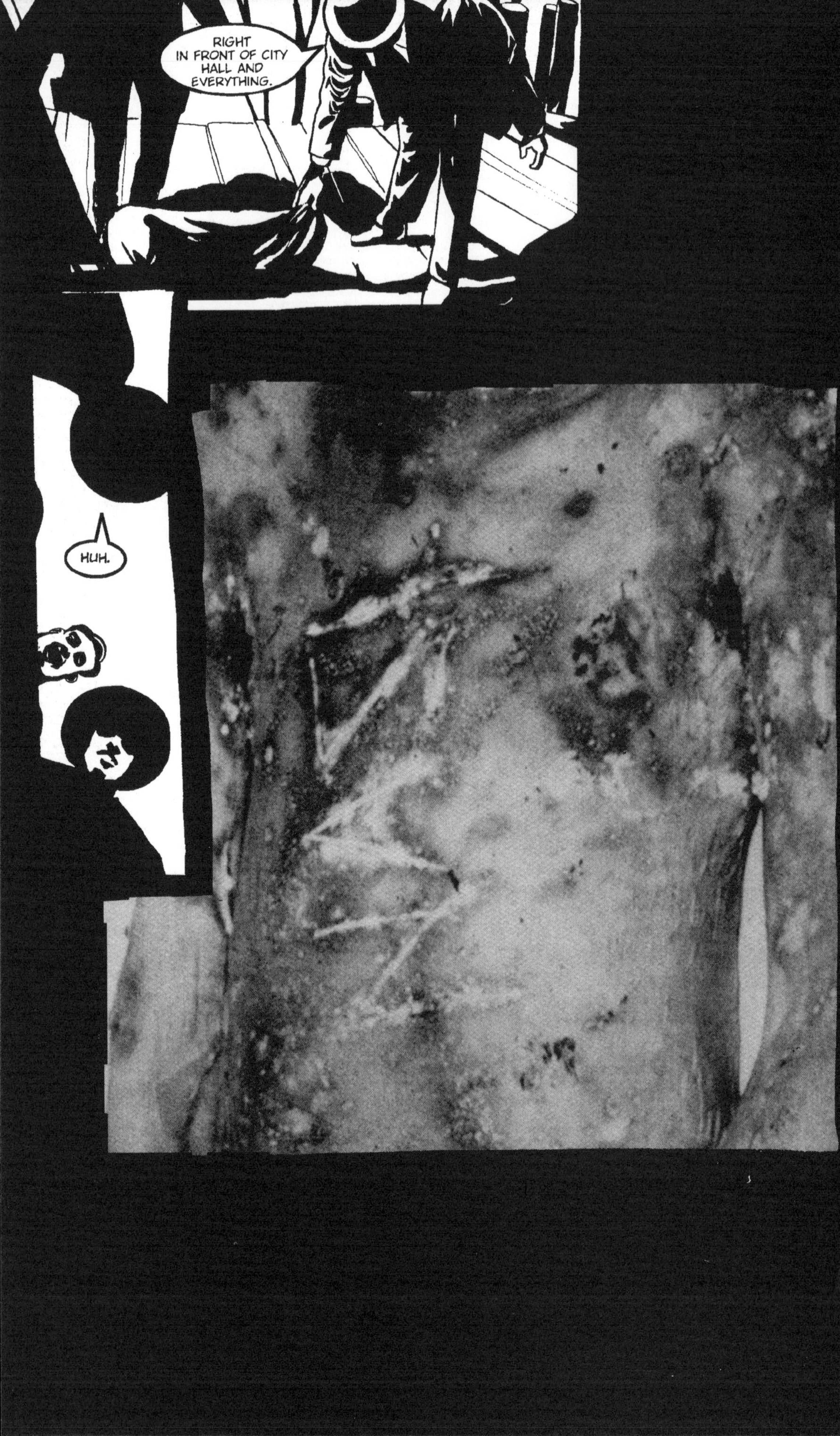
RIGHT IN FRONT OF CITY HALL AND EVERYTHING.
HUH.

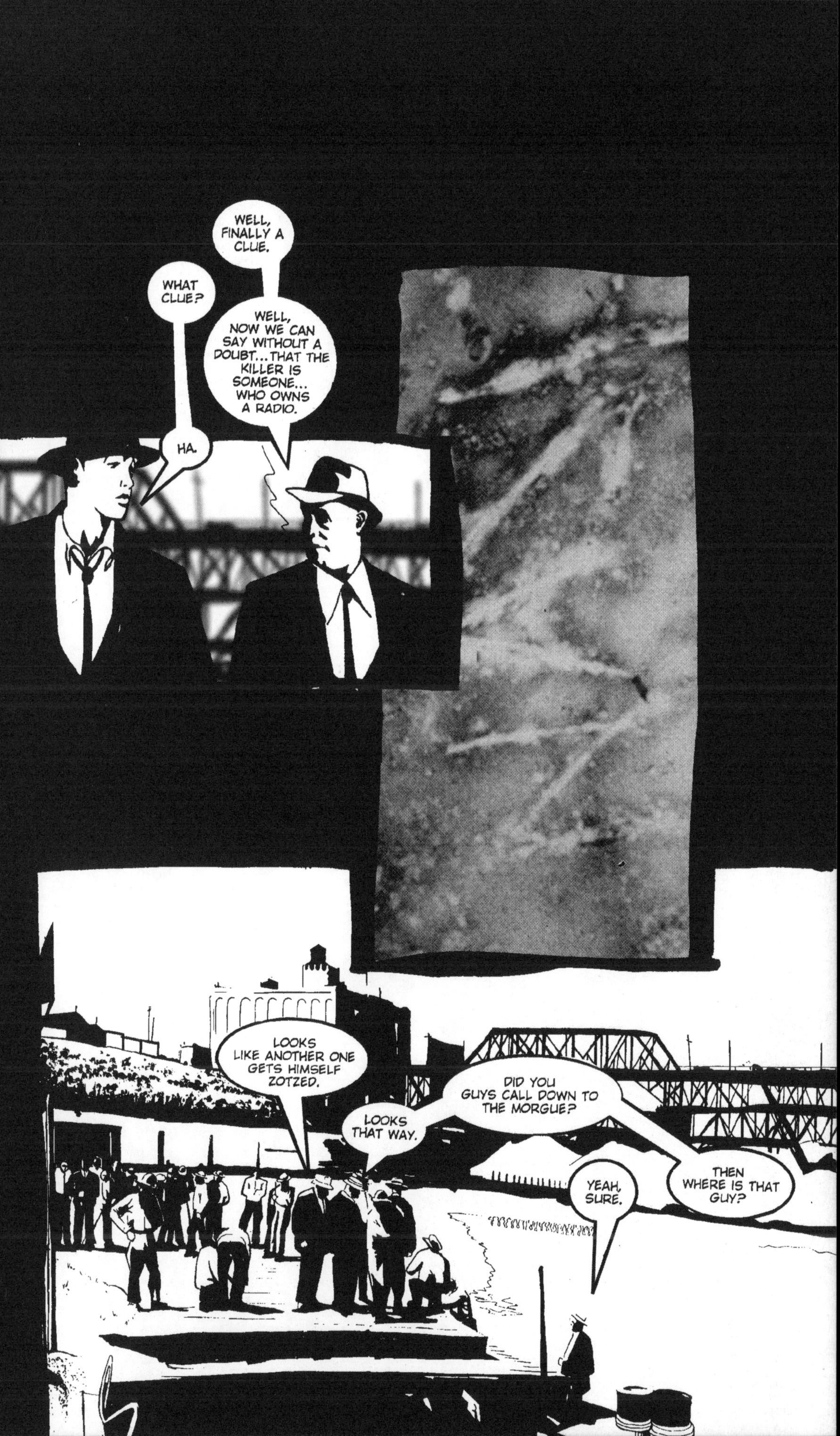
WHAT CLUE?
WELL, FINALLY A CLUE.
WELL, NOW WE CAN SAY WITHOUT A DOUBT...THAT THE KILLER IS SOMEONE... WHO OWNS A RADIO.
HA.
LOOKS LIKE ANOTHER ONE GETS HIMSELF ZOTZED.
LOOKS THAT WAY.
DID YOU GUYS CALL DOWN TO THE MORGUE?
YEAH, SURE.
THEN WHERE IS THAT GUY?

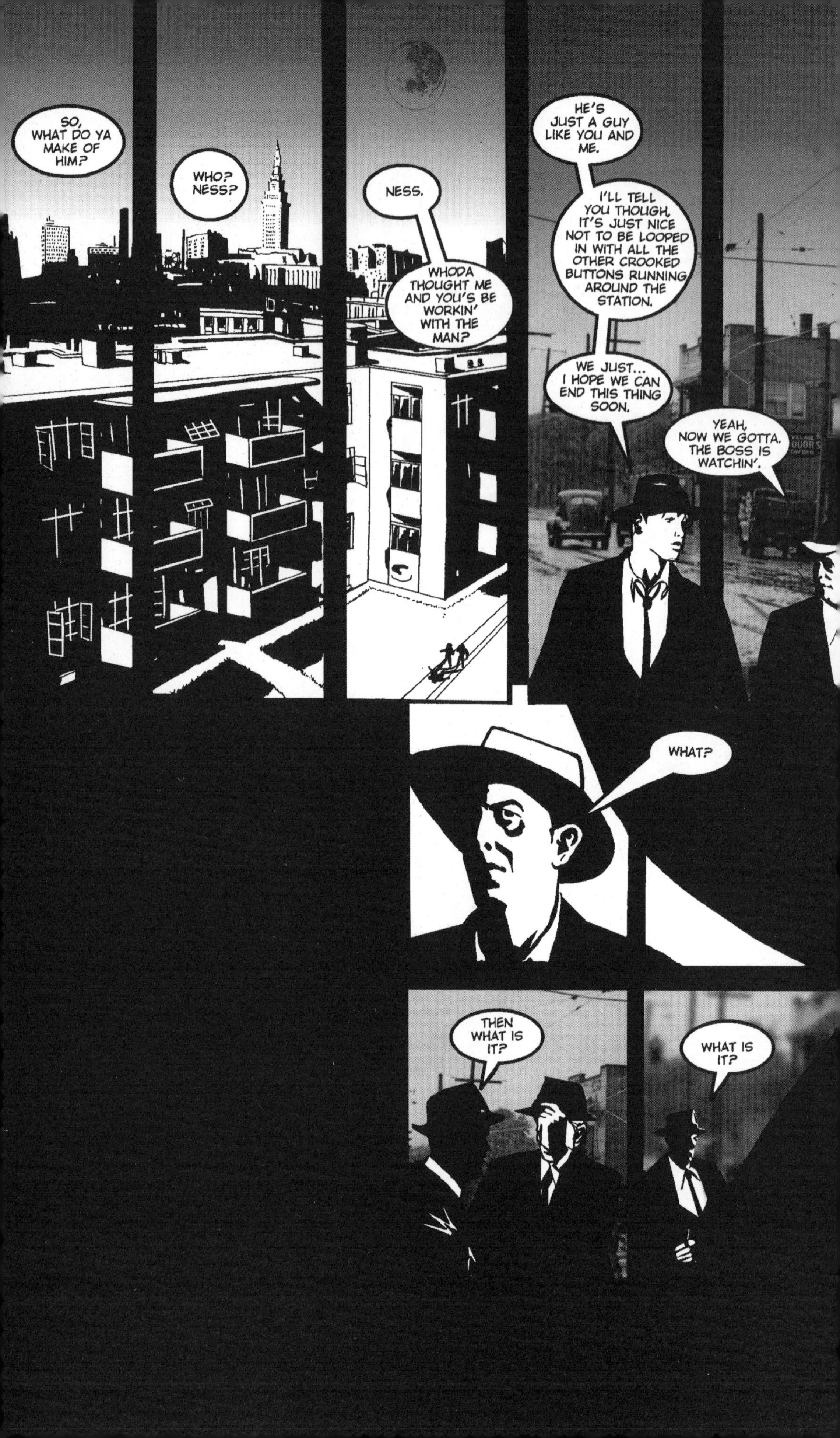
SO, WHAT DO YA MAKE OF HIM?
WHO? NESS?
NESS.
WHODA THOUGHT ME AND YOU'S BE WORKIN' WITH THE MAN?
HE'S JUST A GUY LIKE YOU AND ME.
I'LL TELL YOU THOUGH, IT'S JUST NICE NOT TO BE LOOPED IN WITH ALL THE OTHER CROOKED BUTTONS RUNNING AROUND THE STATION.
WE JUST... I HOPE WE CAN END THIS THING SOON.
YEAH, NOW WE GOTTA. THE BOSS IS WATCHIN'.
WHAT?
THEN WHAT IS IT?
WHAT IS IT?

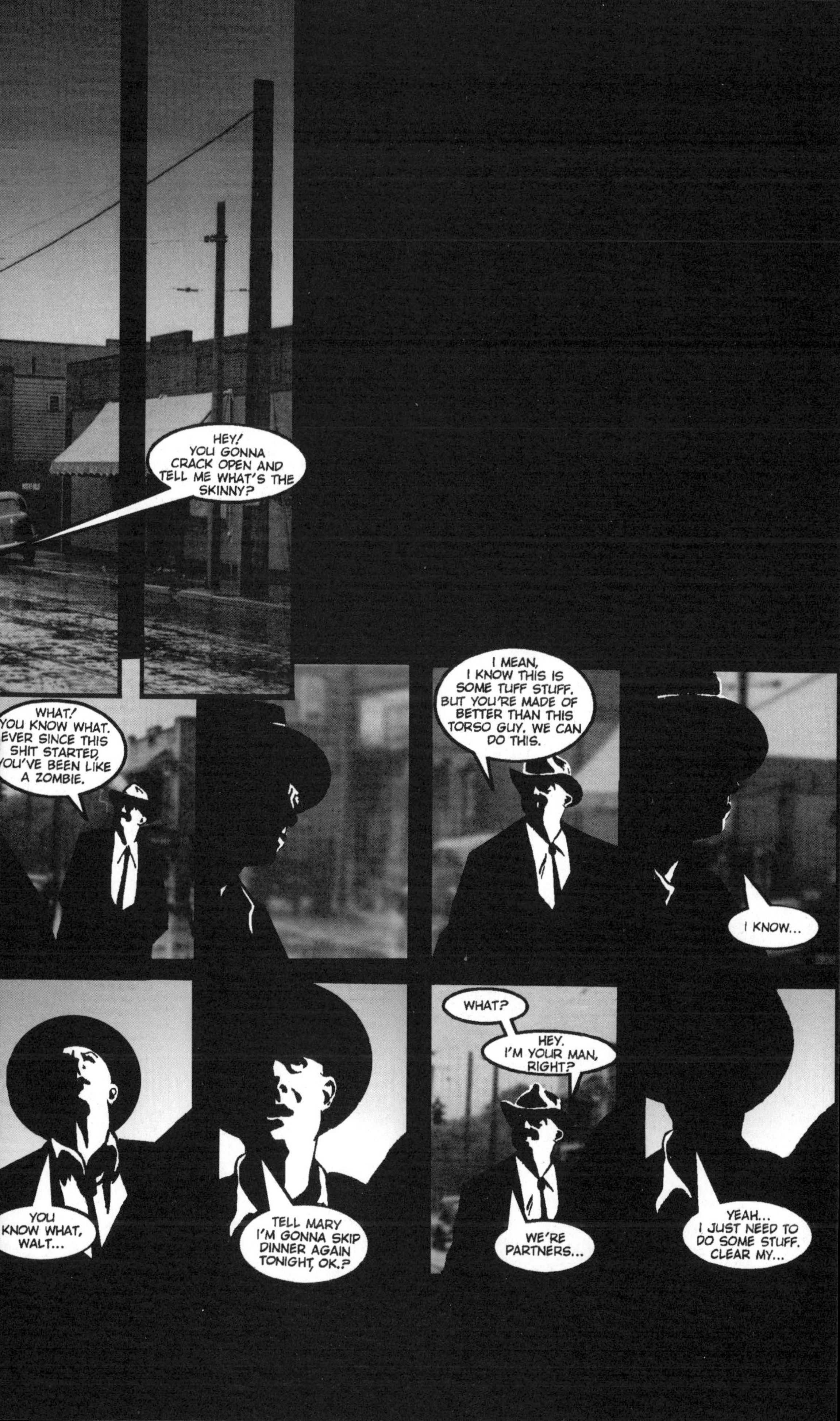
HEY! YOU GONNA CRACK OPEN AND TELL ME WHAT'S THE SKINNY?
WHAT! YOU KNOW WHAT. EVER SINCE THIS SHIT STARTED, YOU'VE BEEN LIKE A ZOMBIE.
I MEAN, I KNOW THIS IS SOME TUFF STUFF. BUT YOU'RE MADE OF BETTER THAN THIS TORSO GUY. WE CAN DO THIS.
I KNOW...
YOU KNOW WHAT, WALT...
TELL MARY I'M GONNA SKIP DINNER AGAIN TONIGHT, OK.?
WHAT?
HEY. I'M YOUR MAN, RIGHT?
WE'RE PARTNERS...
YEAH... I JUST NEED TO DO SOME STUFF. CLEAR MY...

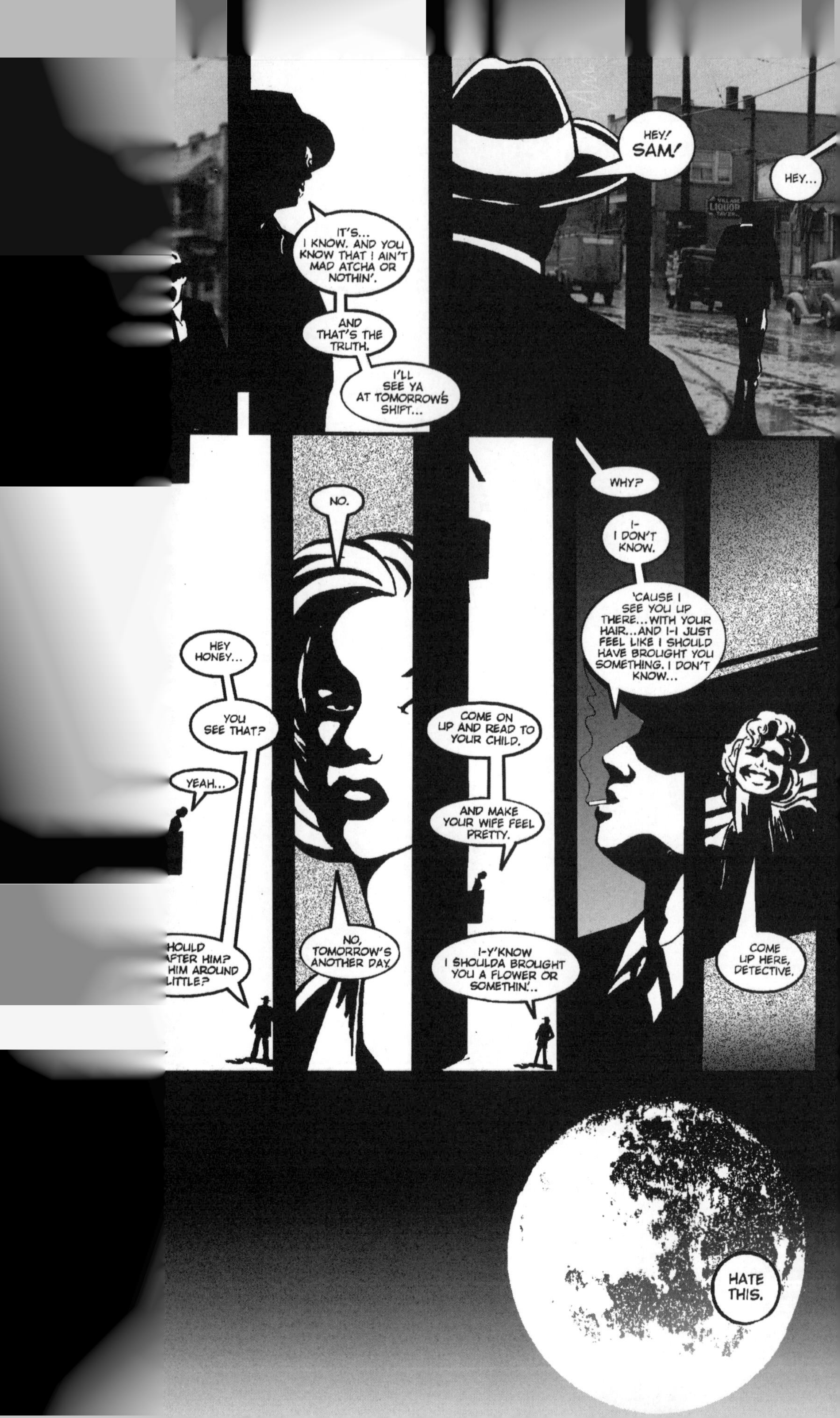
IT'S... I KNOW. AND YOU KNOW THAT I AIN'T MAD ATCHA OR NOTHIN'.
AND THAT'S THE TRUTH.
I'LL SEE YA AT TOMORROW'S SHIFT...
HEY! SAM!
HEY...
LIQUOR
HEY HONEY...
YOU SEE THAT?
YEAH...
HOULD AFTER HIM? HIM AROUND LITTLE?
NO.
NO, TOMORROW'S ANOTHER DAY.
COME ON UP AND READ TO YOUR CHILD.
AND MAKE YOUR WIFE FEEL PRETTY.
I-Y'KNOW I SHOULDA BROUGHT YOU A FLOWER OR SOMETHIN'...
WHY?
I- I DON'T KNOW.
'CAUSE I SEE YOU UP THERE...WITH YOUR HAIR...AND I-I JUST FEEL LIKE I SHOULD HAVE BROUGHT YOU SOMETHING. I DON'T KNOW...
COME UP HERE, DETECTIVE.
HATE THIS.

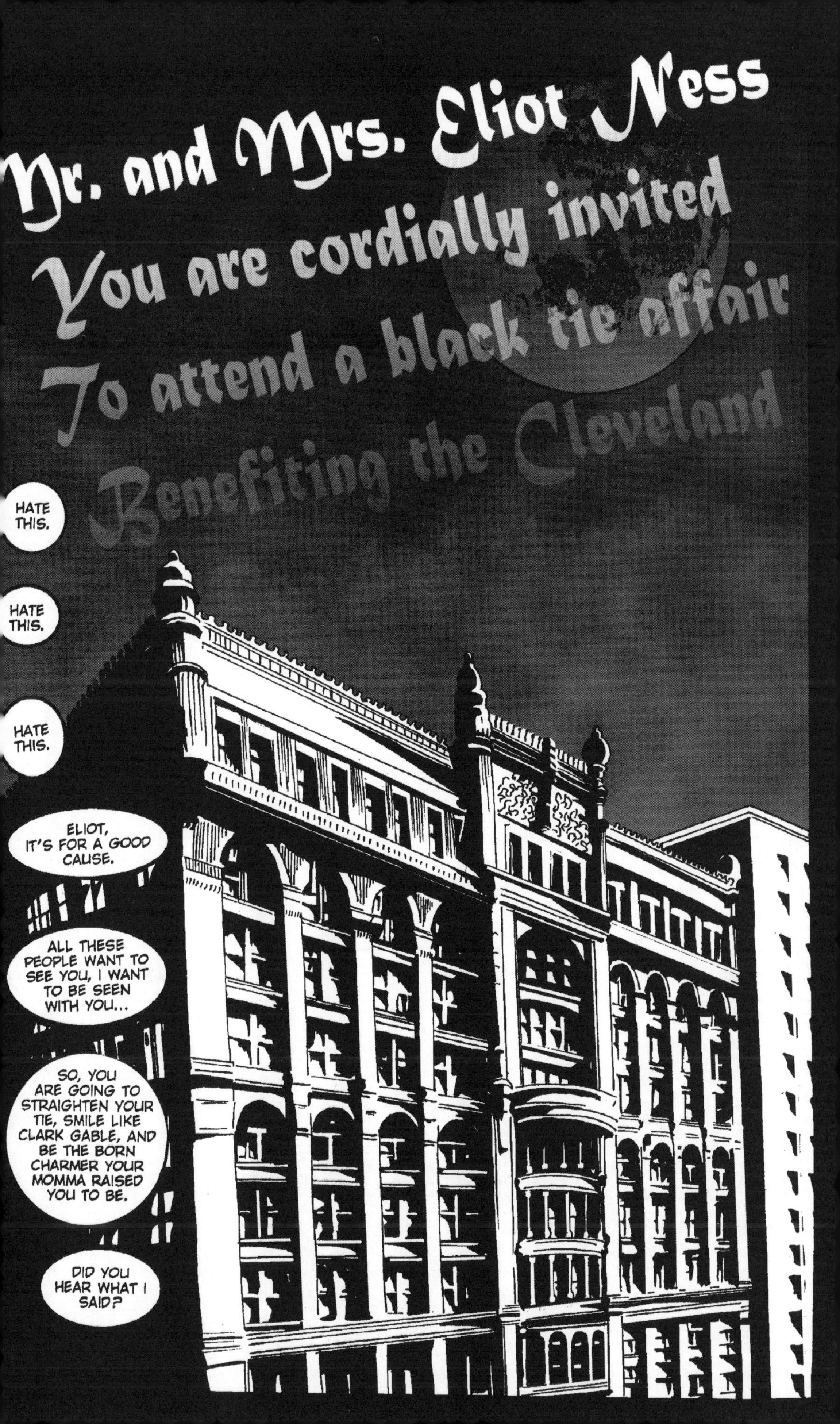
Mr. and Mrs. Eliot Ness
You are cordially invited
To attend a black tie affair
Benefiting the Cleveland
HATE THIS.
HATE THIS.
HATE THIS.
ELIOT, IT'S FOR A GOOD CAUSE.
ALL THESE PEOPLE WANT TO SEE YOU, I WANT TO BE SEEN WITH YOU...
SO, YOU ARE GOING TO STRAIGHTEN YOUR TIE, SMILE LIKE CLARK GABLE, AND BE THE BORN CHARMER YOUR MOMMA RAISED YOU TO BE.
DID YOU HEAR WHAT I SAID?

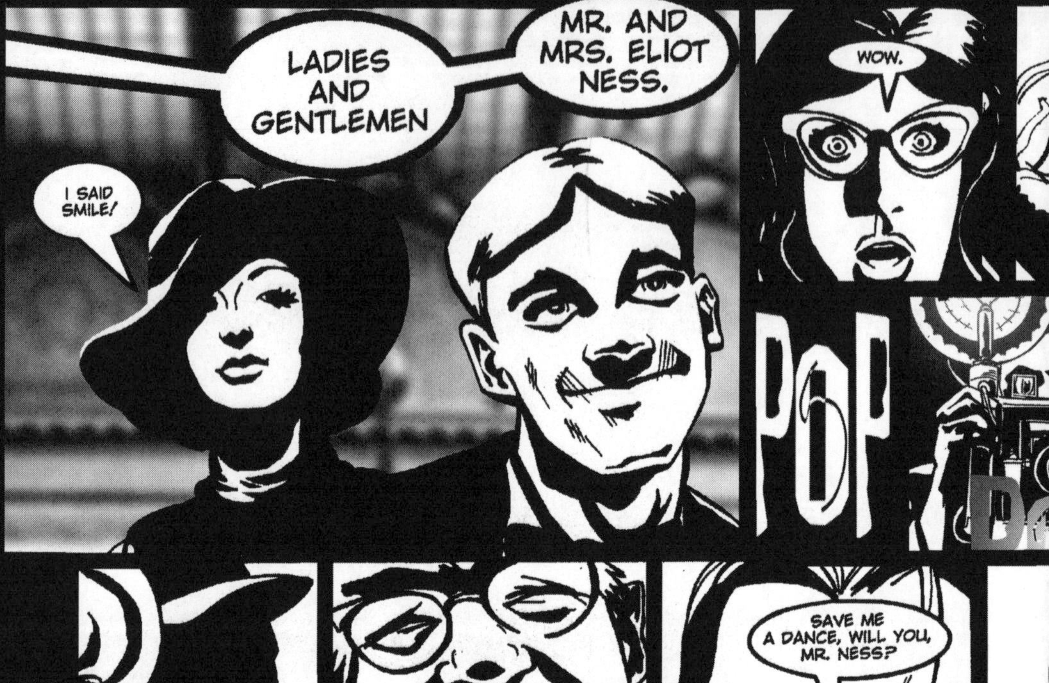
LADIES AND GENTLEMEN
MR. AND MRS. ELIOT NESS.
I SAID SMILE!
WOW.
POP
SAVE ME A DANCE, WILL YOU, MR. NESS?
OOOH. HOW EXCITING.
HEY THERE, NESS OLD BOY.
SENATOR KILLCANON. FIND SOME TIME FOR ME BEFORE THE NIGHT IS OVER.

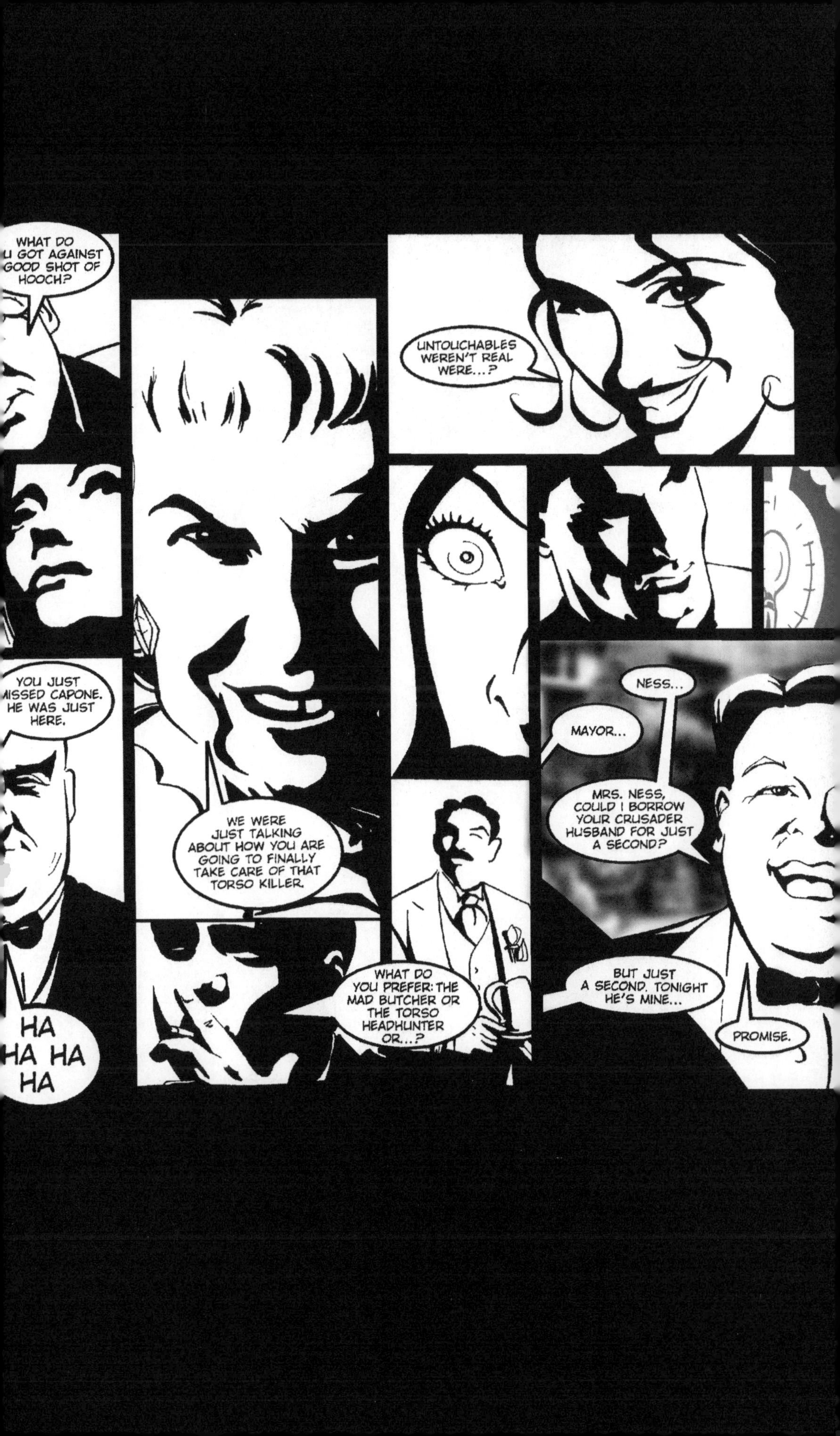
WHAT DO U GOT AGAINST GOOD SHOT OF HOOCH?
YOU JUST MISSED CAPONE. HE WAS JUST HERE.
HA HA HA HA
WE WERE JUST TALKING ABOUT HOW YOU ARE GOING TO FINALLY TAKE CARE OF THAT TORSO KILLER.
WHAT DO YOU PREFER: THE MAD BUTCHER OR THE TORSO HEADHUNTER OR...?
UNTOUCHABLES WEREN'T REAL WERE...?
NESS...
MAYOR...
MRS. NESS, COULD I BORROW YOUR CRUSADER HUSBAND FOR JUST A SECOND?
BUT JUST A SECOND. TONIGHT HE'S MINE...
PROMISE.

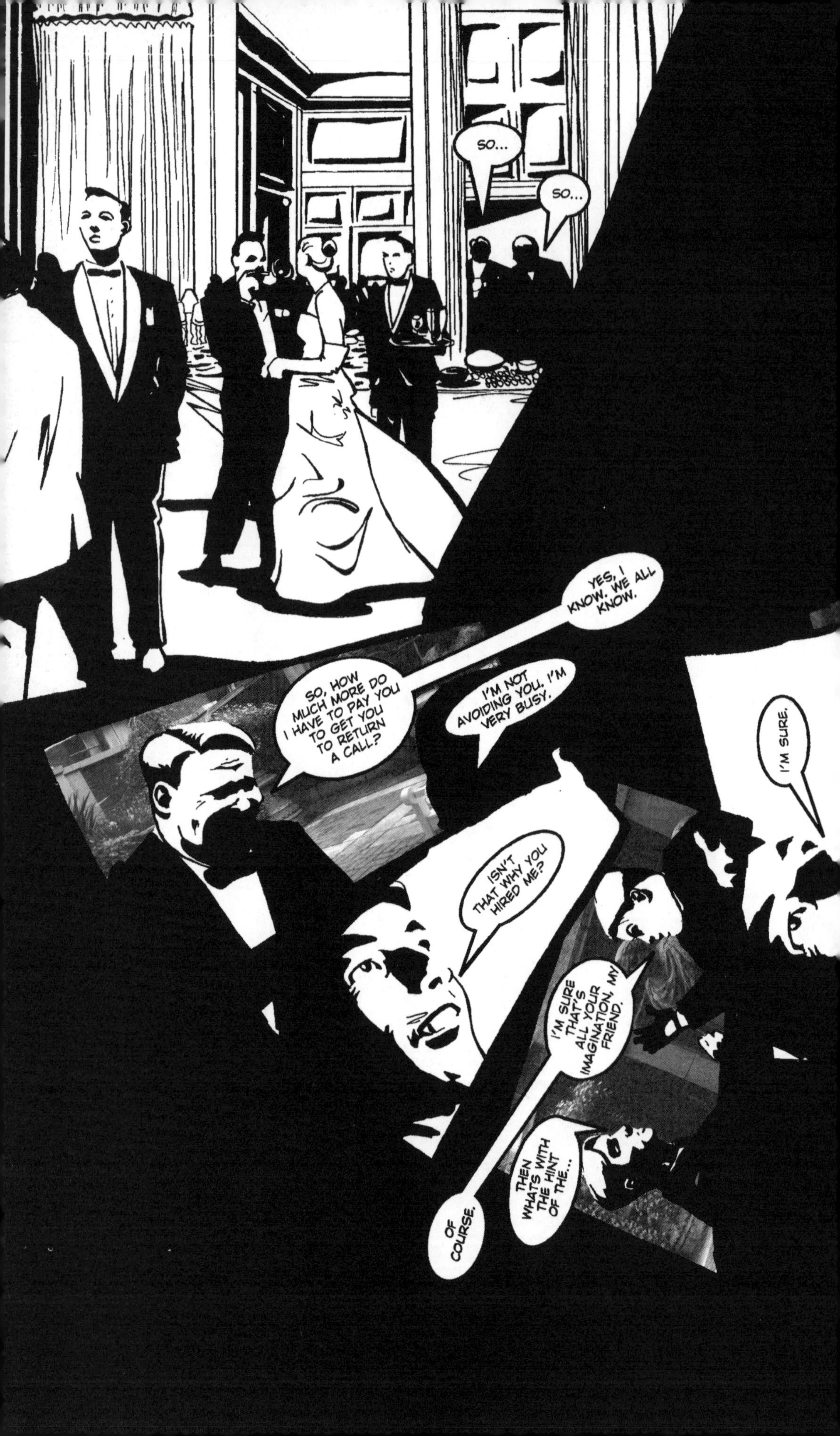
SO...
SO...
SO, HOW MUCH MORE DO I HAVE TO PAY YOU TO GET YOU TO RETURN A CALL?
I'M NOT AVOIDING YOU. I'M VERY BUSY.
YES, I KNOW. WE ALL KNOW.
ISN'T THAT WHY YOU HIRED ME?
I'M SURE.
I'M SURE THAT'S ALL YOUR IMAGINATION, MY FRIEND.
THEN WHATS WITH THE HINT OF THE...
OF COURSE.

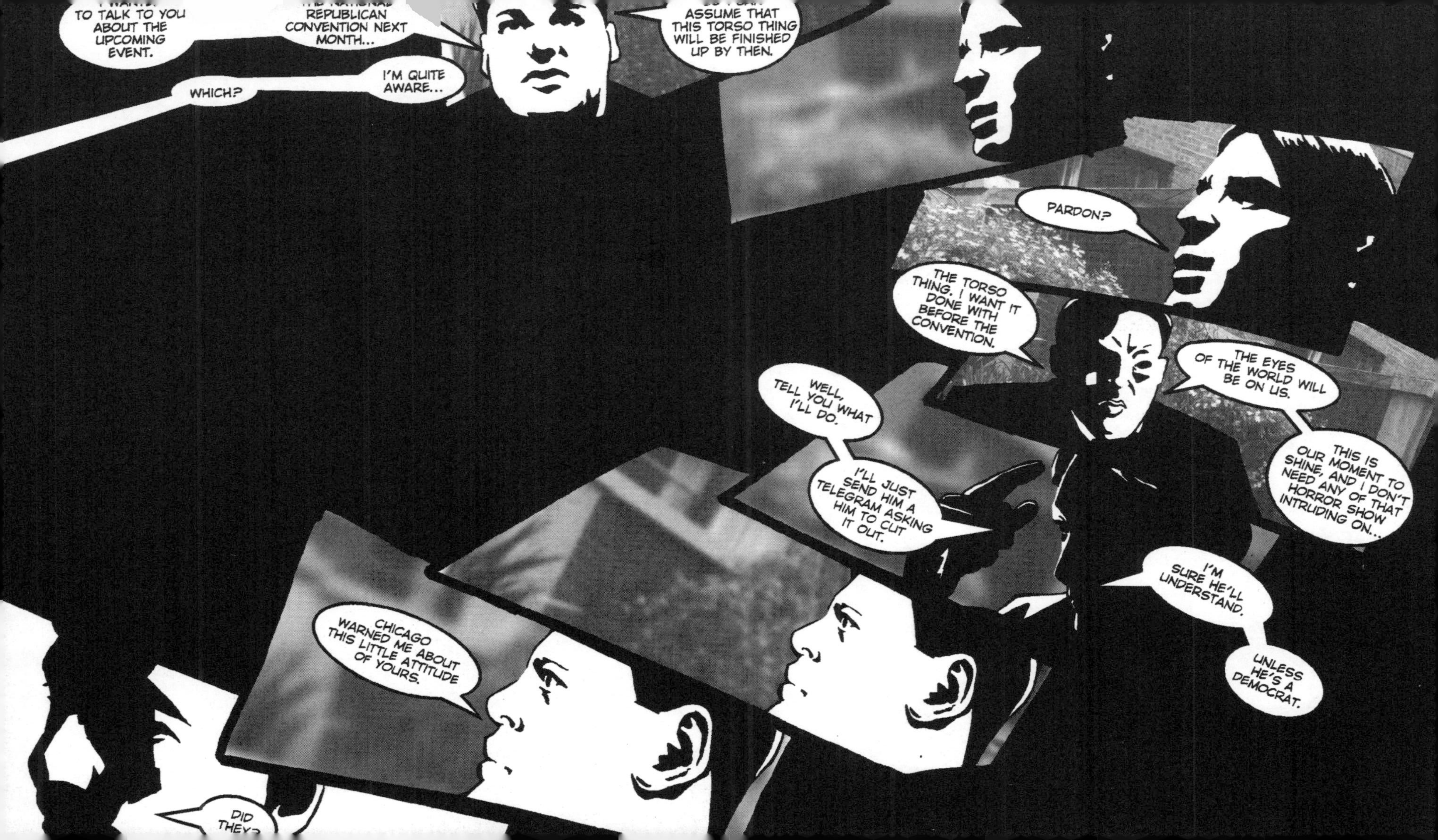
TO TALK TO YOU ABOUT THE UPCOMING EVENT.
WHICH?
REPUBLICAN CONVENTION NEXT MONTH...
I'M QUITE AWARE...
ASSUME THAT THIS TORSO THING WILL BE FINISHED UP BY THEN.
PARDON?
THE TORSO THING. I WANT IT DONE WITH BEFORE THE CONVENTION.
THE EYES OF THE WORLD WILL BE ON US.
THIS IS OUR MOMENT TO SHINE, AND I DON'T NEED ANY OF THAT HORROR SHOW INTRUDING ON...
WELL, TELL YOU WHAT I'LL DO.
I'LL JUST SEND HIM A TELEGRAM ASKING HIM TO CUT IT OUT.
I'M SURE HE'LL UNDERSTAND.
UNLESS HE'S A DEMOCRAT.
CHICAGO WARNED ME ABOUT THIS LITTLE ATTITUDE OF YOURS.
DID

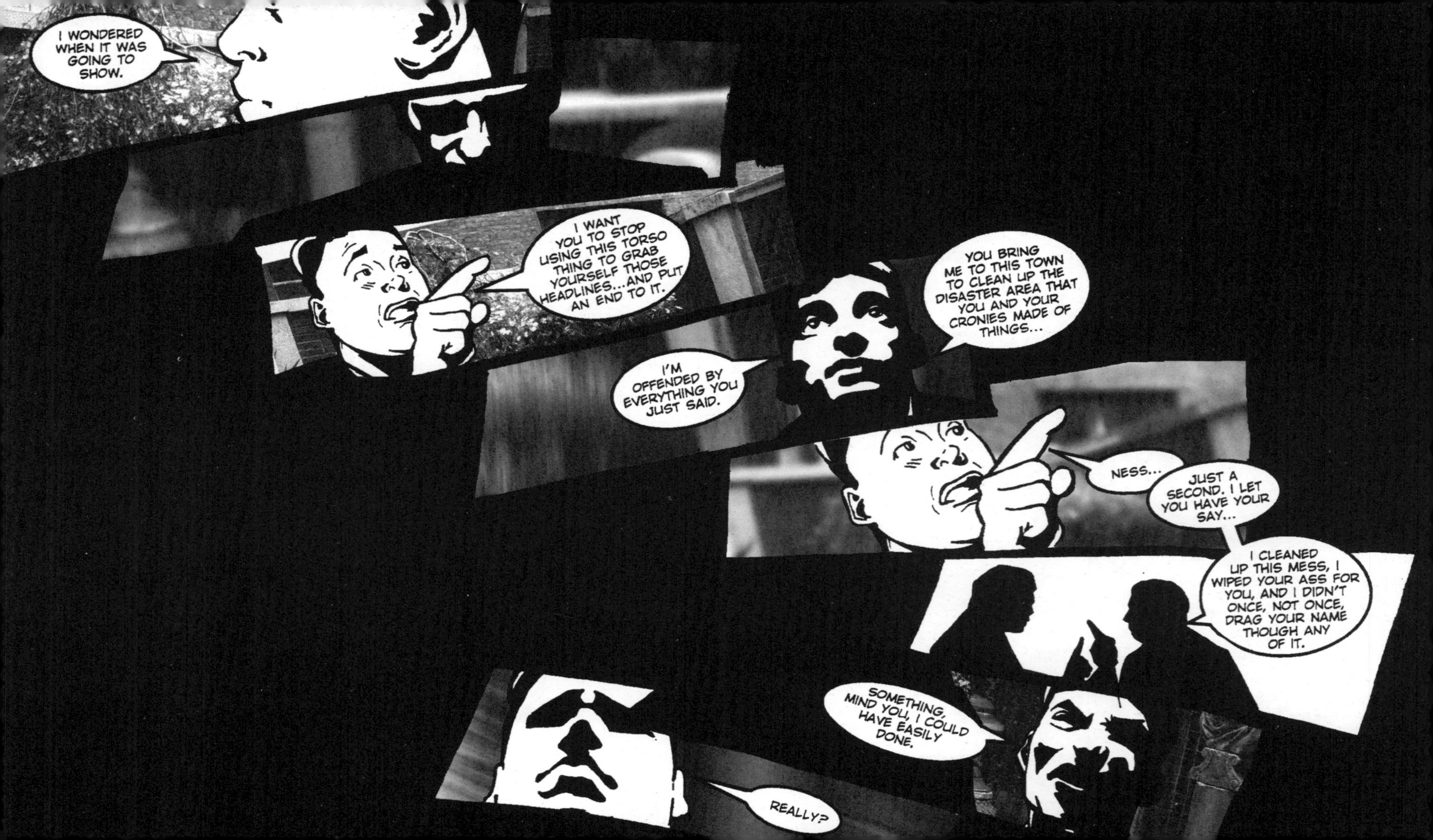
I WONDERED WHEN IT WAS GOING TO SHOW.
I WANT YOU TO STOP USING THIS TORSO THING TO GRAB YOURSELF THOSE HEADLINES...AND PUT AN END TO IT.
YOU BRING ME TO THIS TOWN TO CLEAN UP THE DISASTER AREA THAT YOU AND YOUR CRONIES MADE OF THINGS...
I'M OFFENDED BY EVERYTHING YOU JUST SAID.
NESS...
JUST A SECOND. I LET YOU HAVE YOUR SAY...
I CLEANED UP THIS MESS, I WIPED YOUR ASS FOR YOU, AND I DIDN'T ONCE, NOT ONCE, DRAG YOUR NAME THOUGH ANY OF IT.
SOMETHING, MIND YOU, I COULD HAVE EASILY DONE.
REALLY?

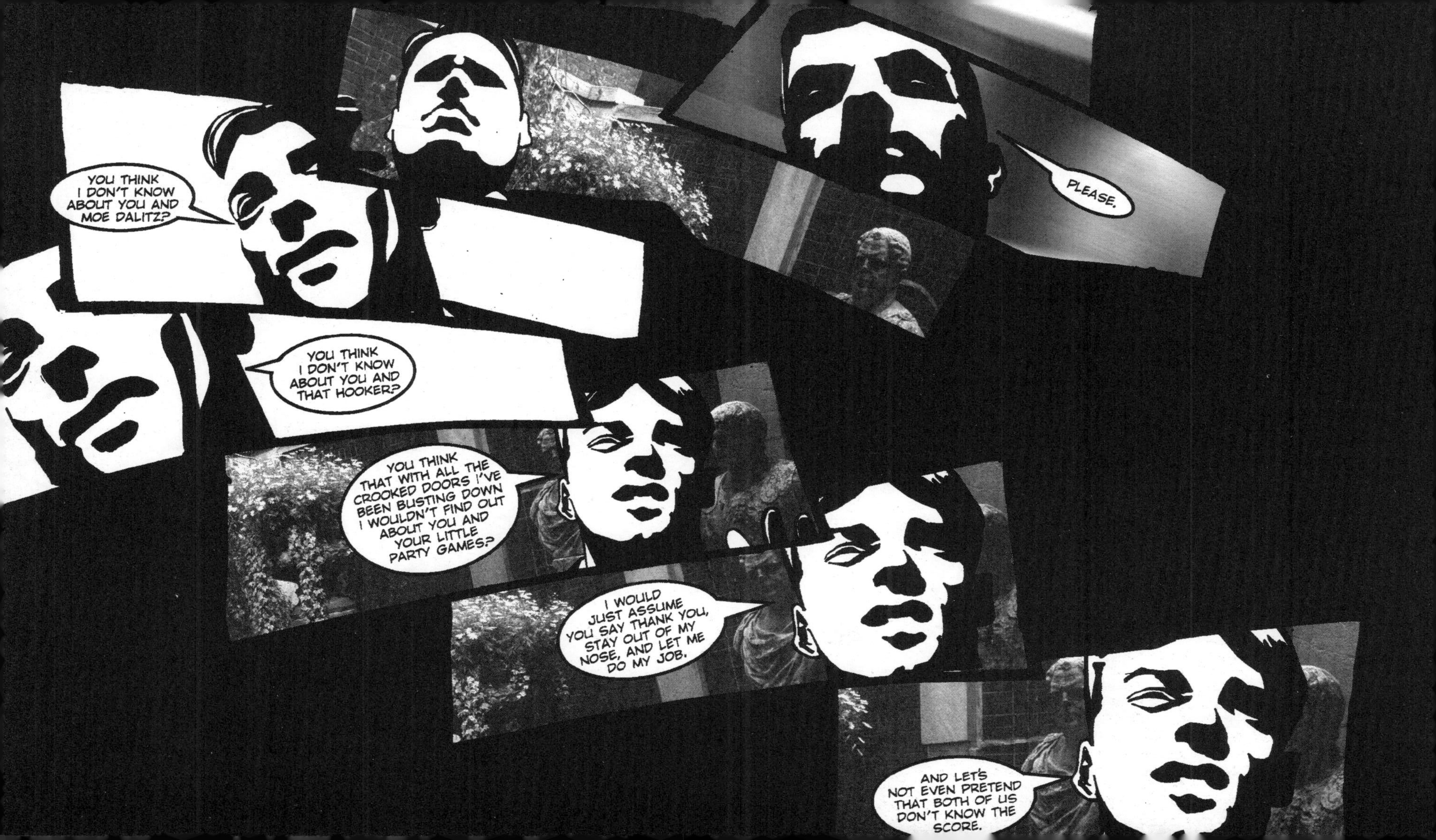
YOU THINK I DON'T KNOW ABOUT YOU AND MOE DALITZ?
PLEASE.
YOU THINK I DON'T KNOW ABOUT YOU AND THAT HOOKER?
YOU THINK THAT WITH ALL THE CROOKED DOORS I'VE BEEN BUSTING DOWN I WOULDN'T FIND OUT ABOUT YOU AND YOUR LITTLE PARTY GAMES?
I WOULD JUST ASSUME YOU SAY THANK YOU, STAY OUT OF MY NOSE, AND LET ME DO MY JOB.
AND LET'S NOT EVEN PRETEND THAT BOTH OF US DON'T KNOW THE SCORE.

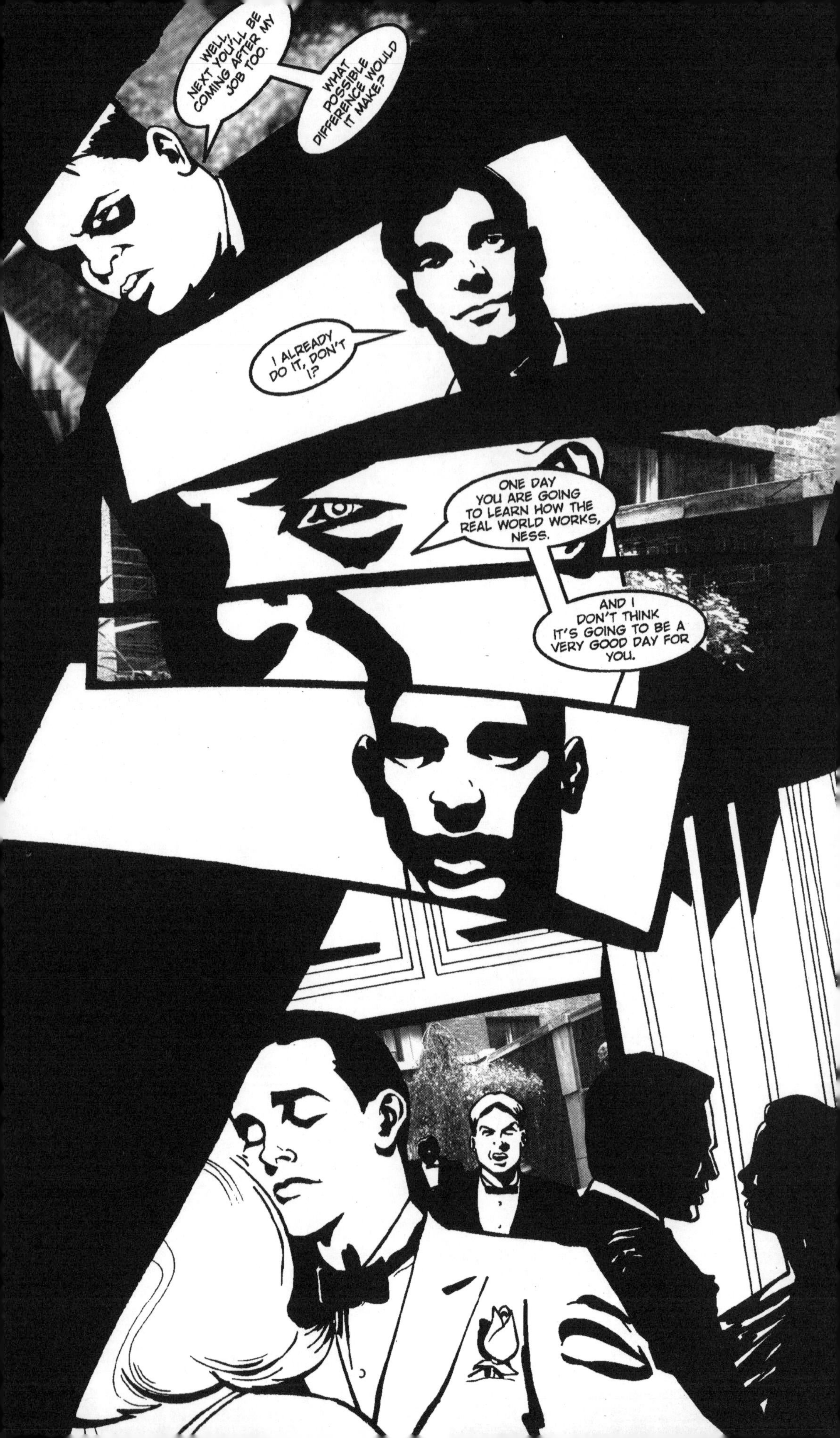
WELL, NEXT YOU'LL BE COMING AFTER MY JOB TOO.
WHAT POSSIBLE DIFFERENCE WOULD IT MAKE?
I ALREADY DO IT, DON'T I?
ONE DAY YOU ARE GOING TO LEARN HOW THE REAL WORLD WORKS, NESS.
AND I DON'T THINK IT'S GOING TO BE A VERY GOOD DAY FOR YOU.

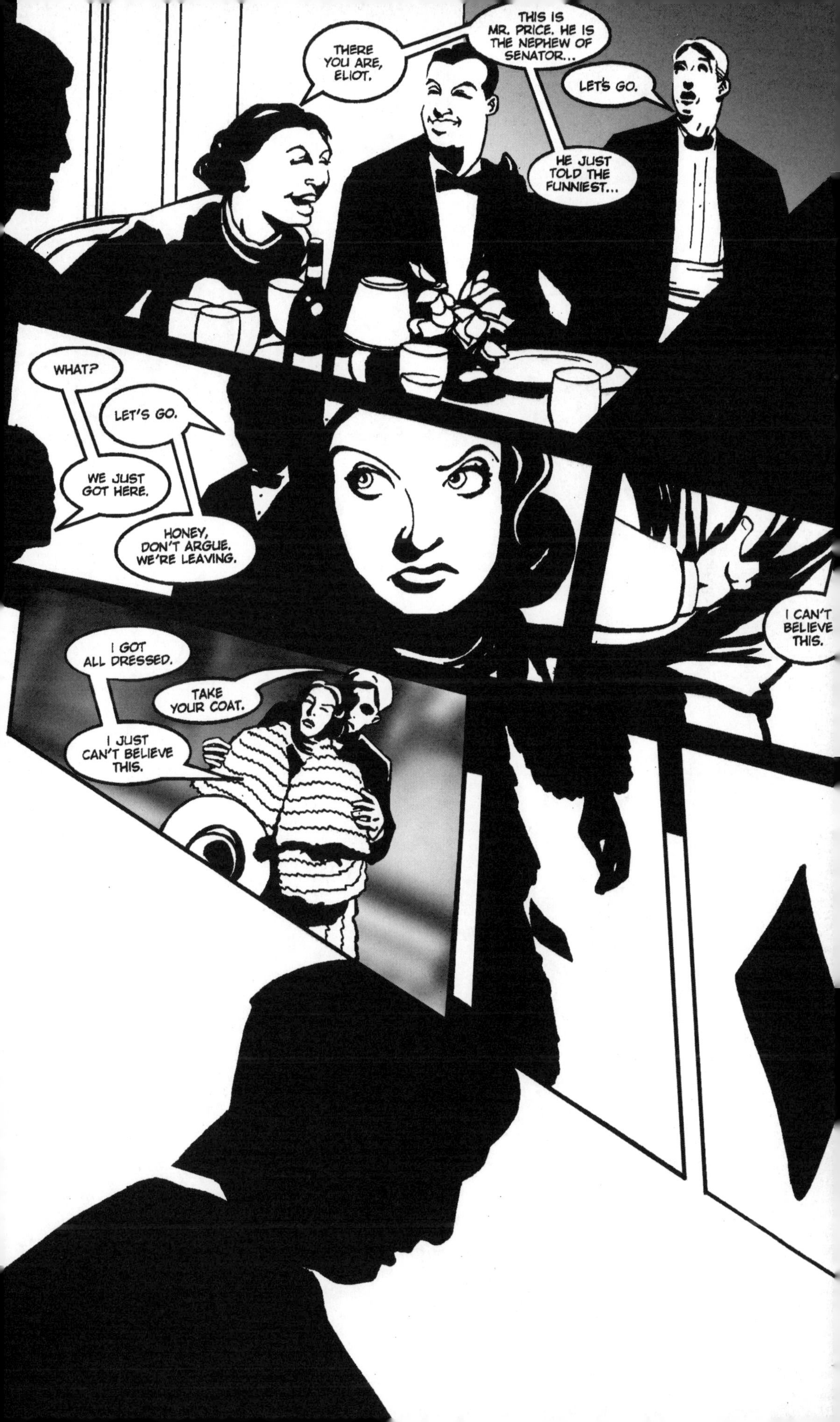
THERE YOU ARE, ELIOT.
THIS IS MR. PRICE. HE IS THE NEPHEW OF SENATOR...
LET'S GO.
HE JUST TOLD THE FUNNIEST...
WHAT?
LET'S GO.
WE JUST GOT HERE.
HONEY, DON'T ARGUE. WE'RE LEAVING.
I CAN'T BELIEVE THIS.
I GOT ALL DRESSED.
TAKE YOUR COAT.
I JUST CAN'T BELIEVE THIS.

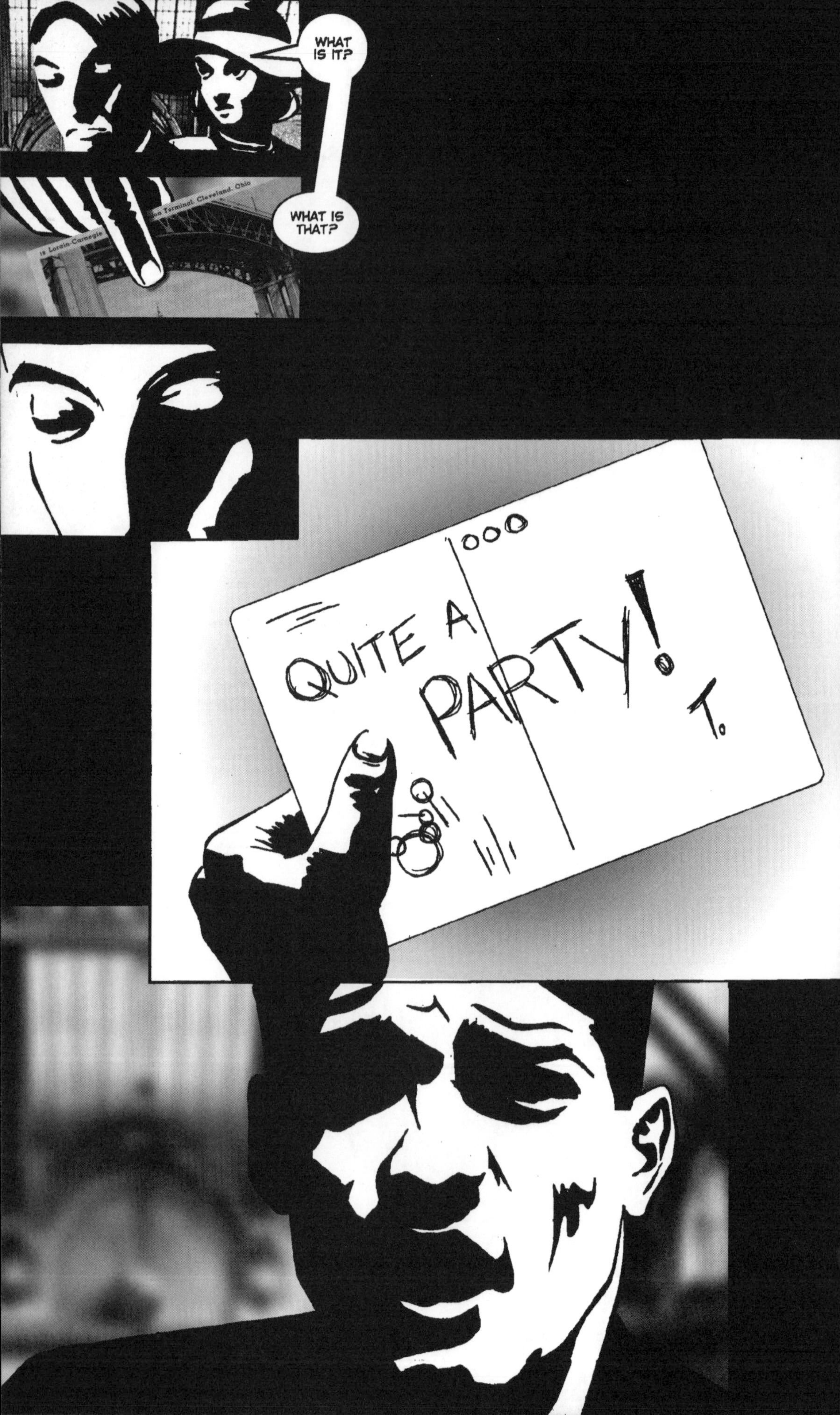
WHAT IS IT?
WHAT IS THAT?
Lorain-Carnegie
Terminal, Cleveland, Ohio
QUITE A PARTY!
T.

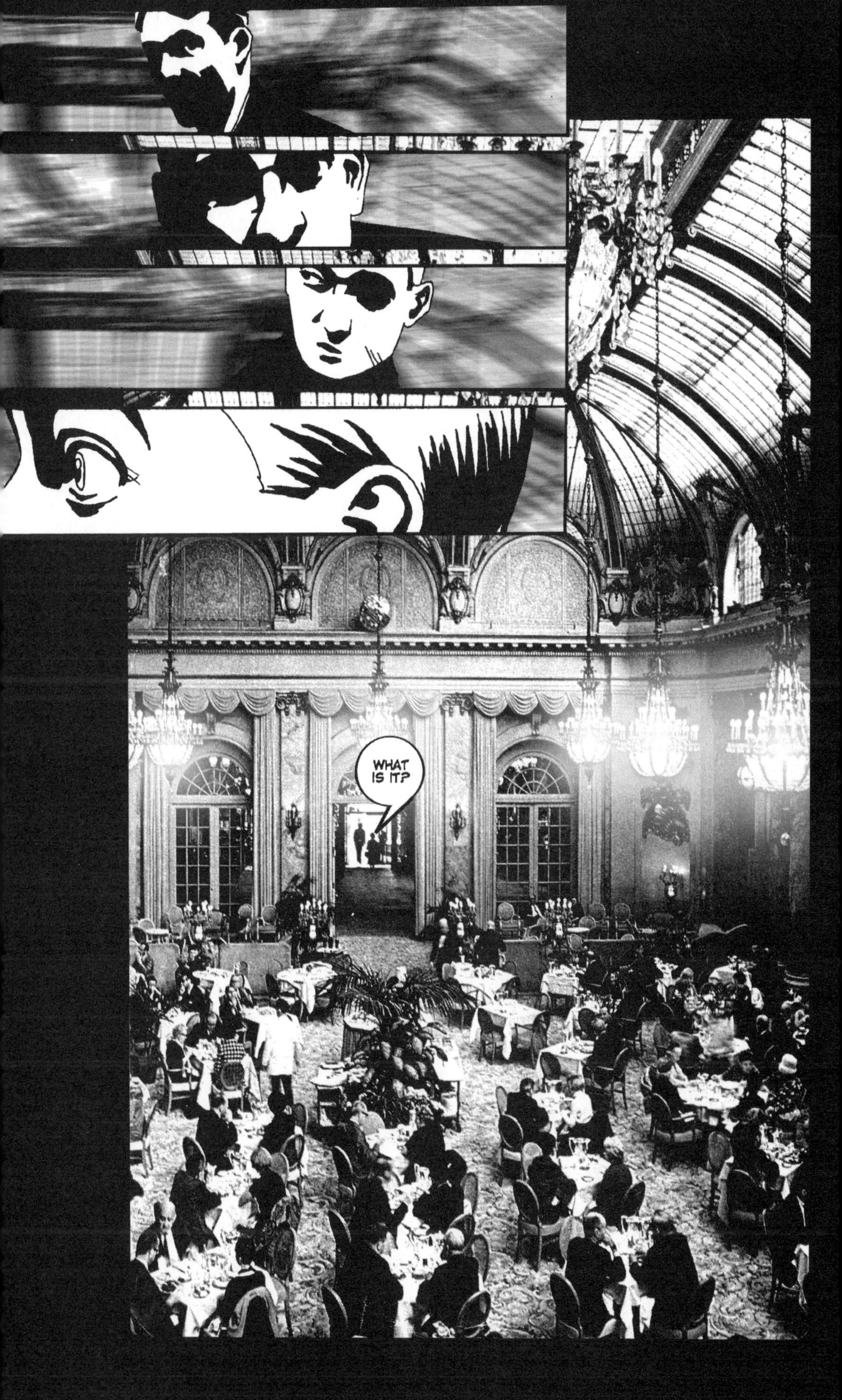
WHAT IS IT?

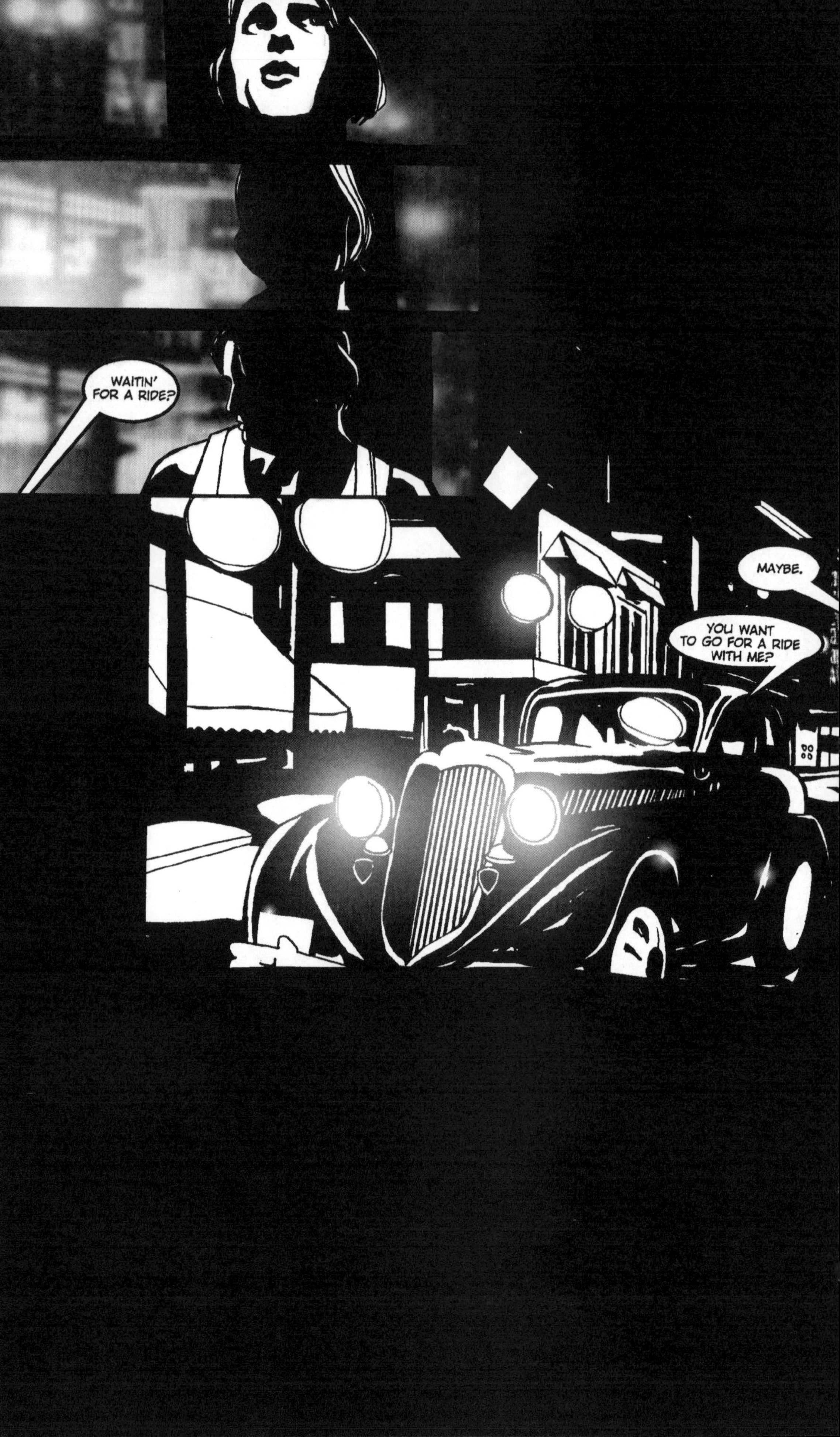
WAITIN' FOR A RIDE?
MAYBE.
YOU WANT TO GO FOR A RIDE WITH ME?

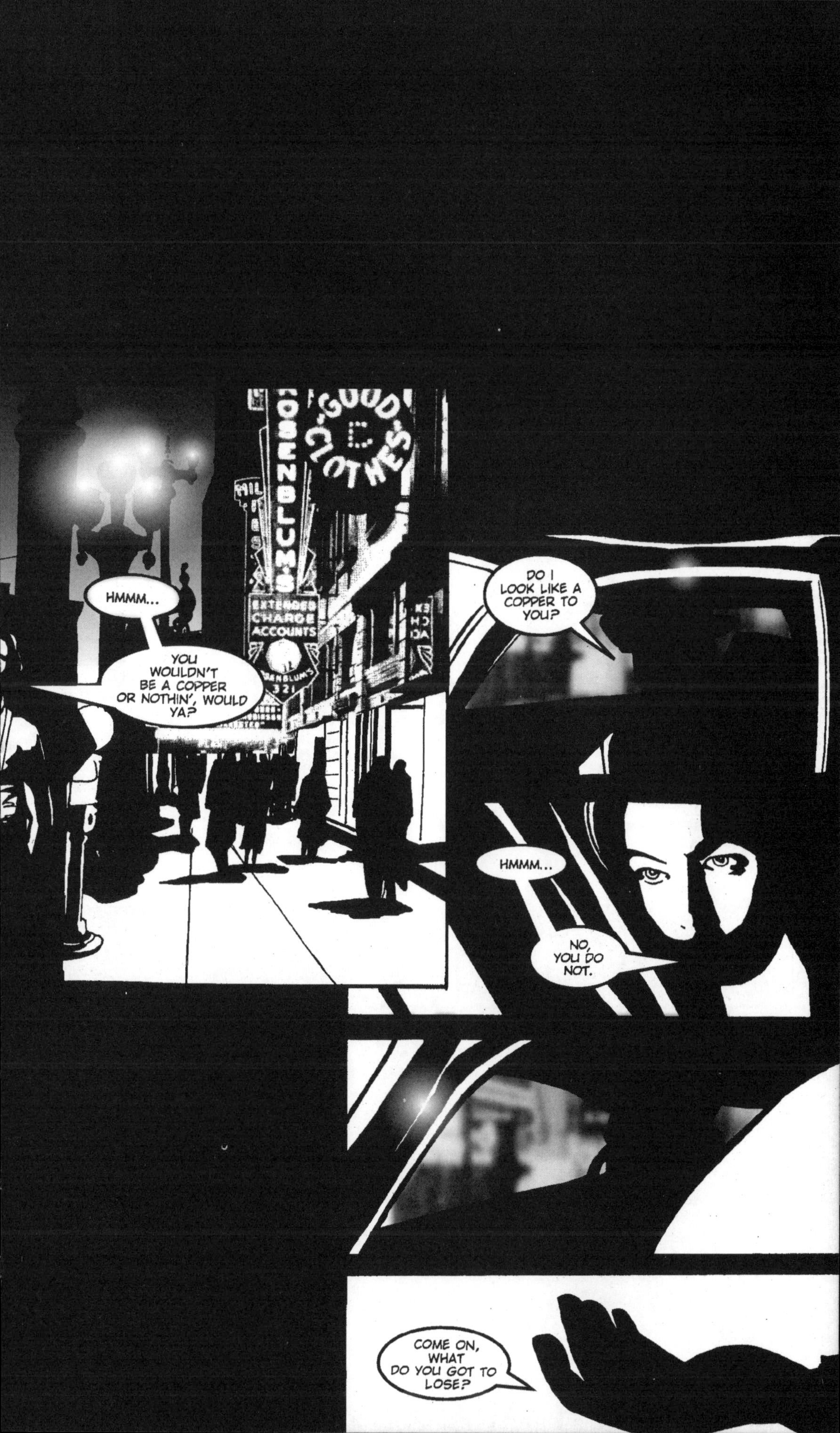
GOOD CLOTHES
ROSENBLUM'S
EXTENDED CHARGE ACCOUNTS
321
HMMM...
YOU WOULDN'T BE A COPPER OR NOTHIN', WOULD YA?
DO I LOOK LIKE A COPPER TO YOU?
HMMM...
NO, YOU DO NOT.
COME ON, WHAT DO YOU GOT TO LOSE?

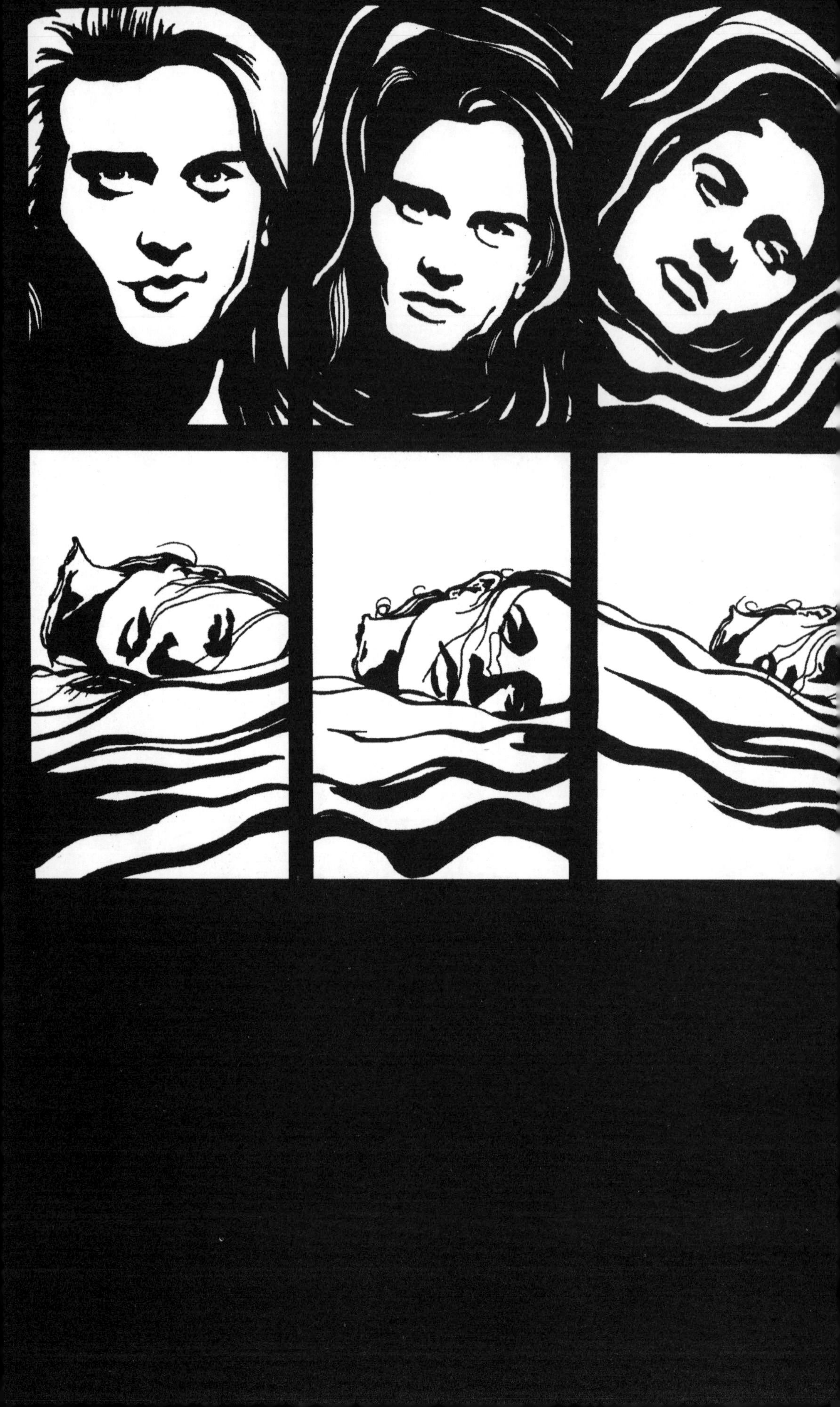

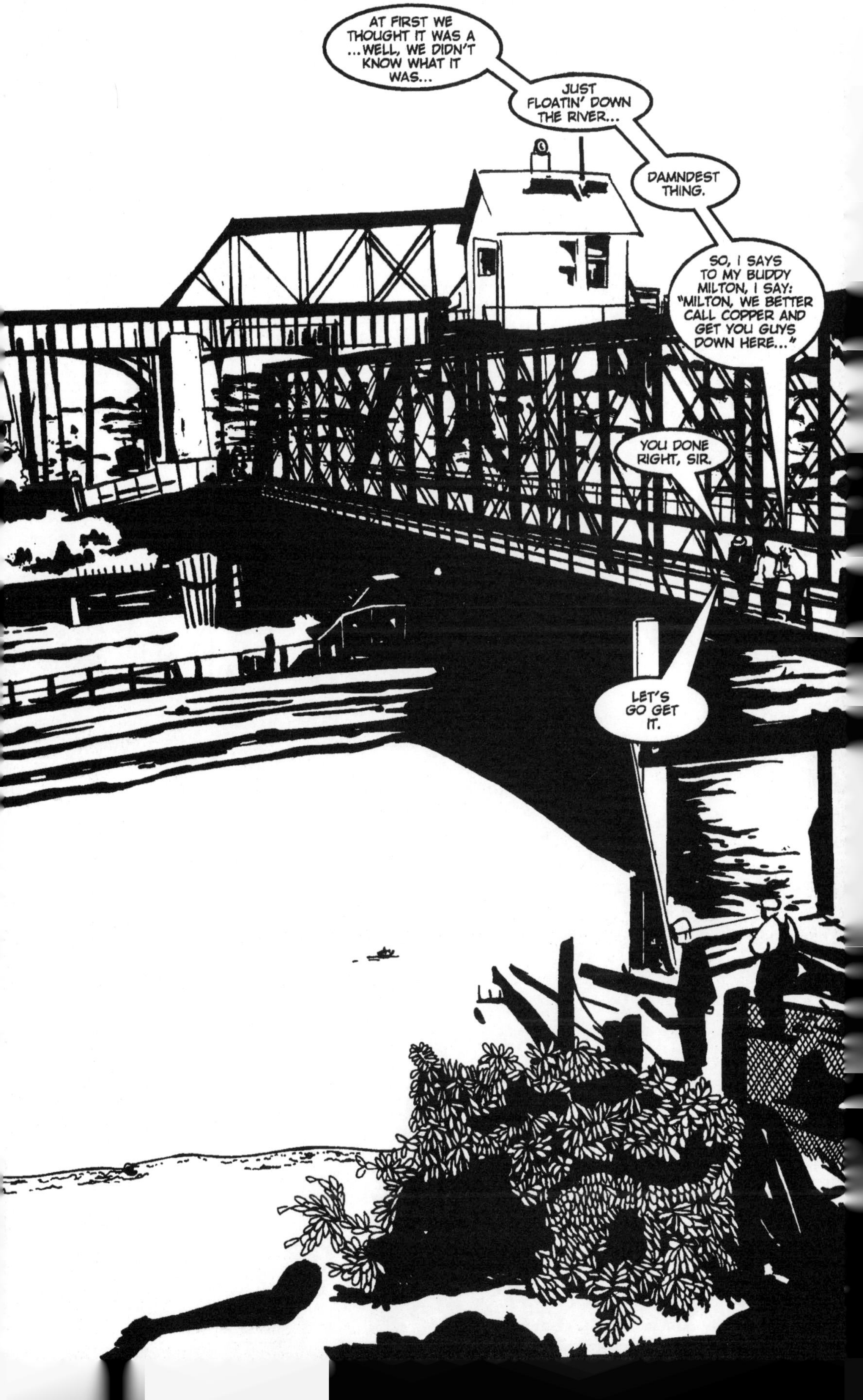
AT FIRST WE THOUGHT IT WAS A ...WELL, WE DIDN'T KNOW WHAT IT WAS...
JUST FLOATIN' DOWN THE RIVER...
DAMNDEST THING.
SO, I SAYS TO MY BUDDY MILTON, I SAY: "MILTON, WE BETTER CALL COPPER AND GET YOU GUYS DOWN HERE..."
YOU DONE RIGHT, SIR.
LET'S GO GET IT.

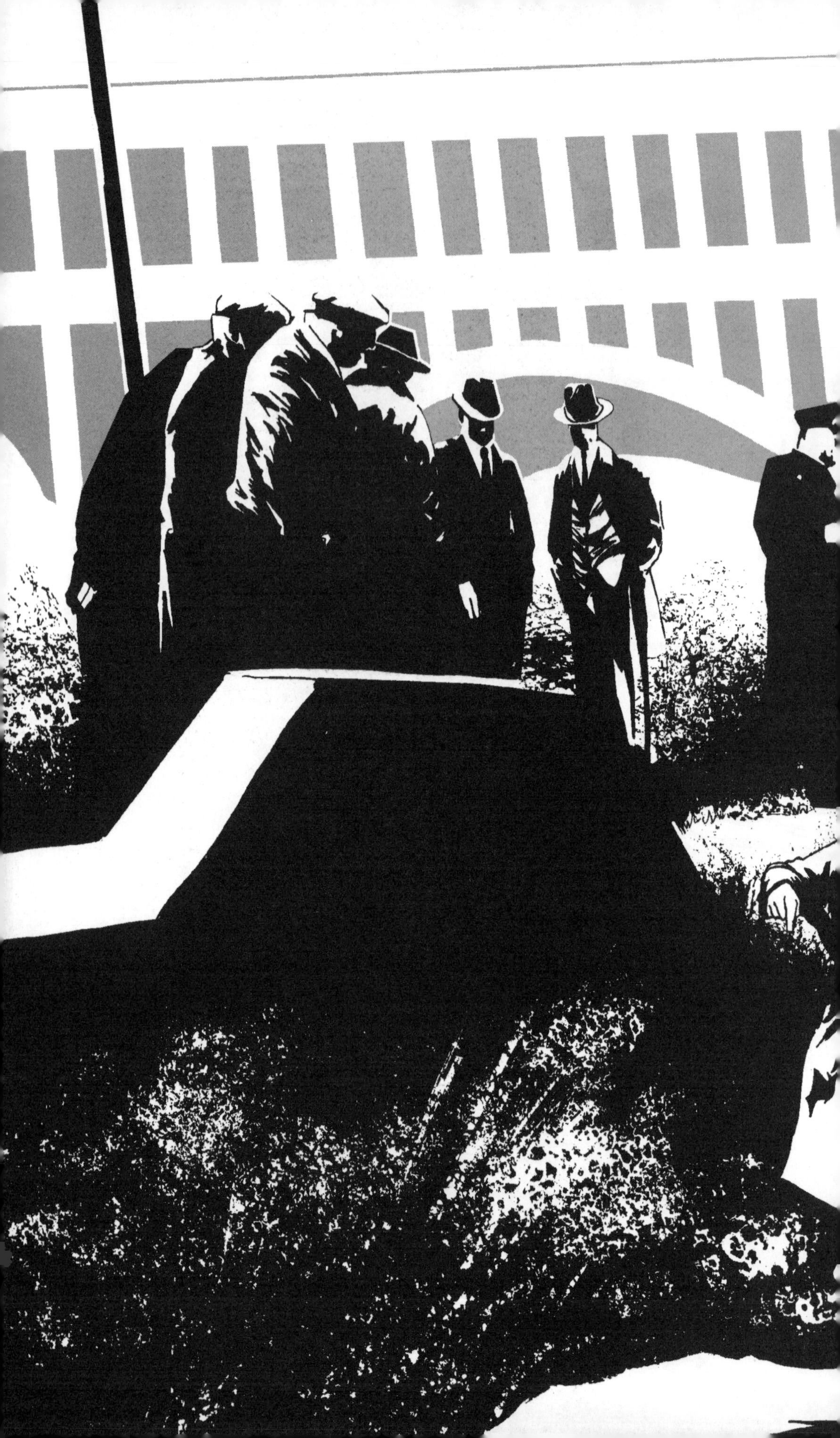

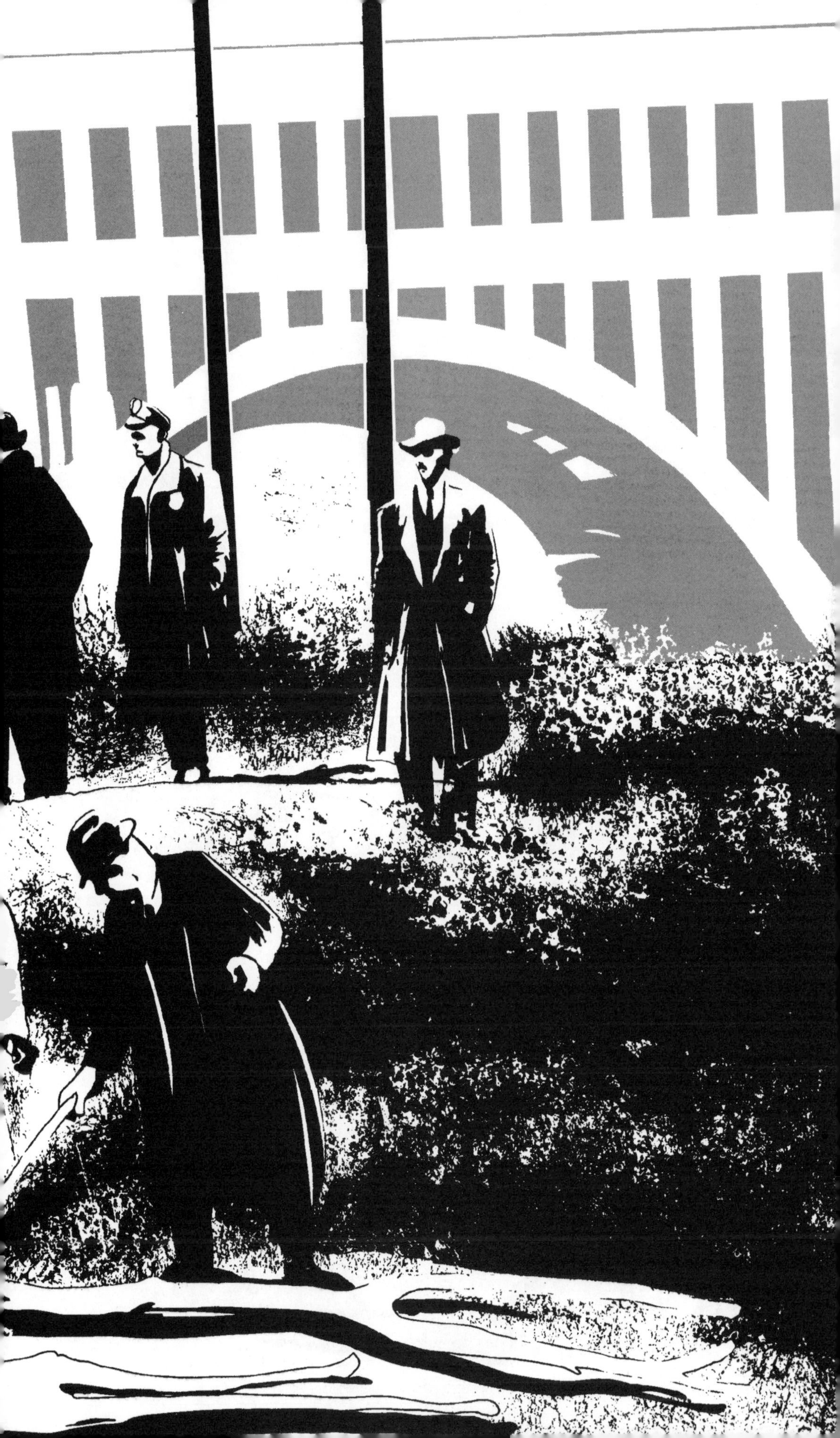

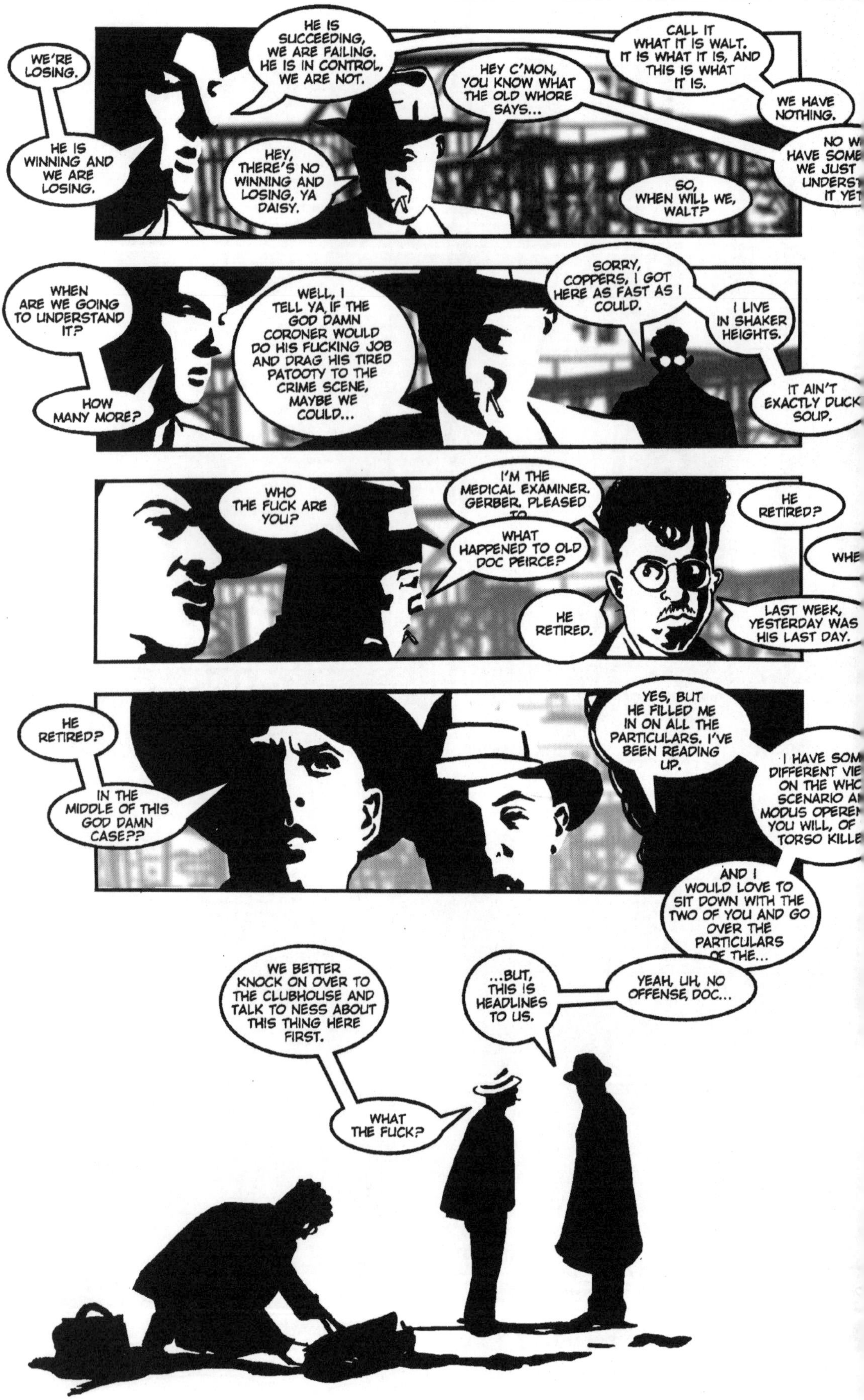
WE'RE LOSING.
HE IS WINNING AND WE ARE LOSING.
HE IS SUCCEEDING, WE ARE FAILING. HE IS IN CONTROL, WE ARE NOT.
HEY, THERE'S NO WINNING AND LOSING, YA DAISY.
HEY C'MON, YOU KNOW WHAT THE OLD WHORE SAYS...
CALL IT WHAT IT IS WALT. IT IS WHAT IT IS, AND THIS IS WHAT IT IS.
WE HAVE NOTHING.
NO W HAVE SOME WE JUST UNDERST IT YET
SO, WHEN WILL WE, WALT?
WHEN ARE WE GOING TO UNDERSTAND IT?
HOW MANY MORE?
WELL, I TELL YA, IF THE GOD DAMN CORONER WOULD DO HIS FUCKING JOB AND DRAG HIS TIRED PATOOTY TO THE CRIME SCENE, MAYBE WE COULD...
SORRY, COPPERS, I GOT HERE AS FAST AS I COULD.
I LIVE IN SHAKER HEIGHTS.
IT AIN'T EXACTLY DUCK SOUP.
WHO THE FUCK ARE YOU?
I'M THE MEDICAL EXAMINER. GERBER. PLEASED TO
WHAT HAPPENED TO OLD DOC PEIRCE?
HE RETIRED.
HE RETIRED?
WHE
LAST WEEK, YESTERDAY WAS HIS LAST DAY.
HE RETIRED?
IN THE MIDDLE OF THIS GOD DAMN CASE??
YES, BUT HE FILLED ME IN ON ALL THE PARTICULARS. I'VE BEEN READING UP.
I HAVE SOM DIFFERENT VIE ON THE WHO SCENARIO A MODUS OPERE YOU WILL, OF TORSO KILLE
AND I WOULD LOVE TO SIT DOWN WITH THE TWO OF YOU AND GO OVER THE PARTICULARS OF THE...
YEAH, UH, NO OFFENSE, DOC...
...BUT, THIS IS HEADLINES TO US.
WE BETTER KNOCK ON OVER TO THE CLUBHOUSE AND TALK TO NESS ABOUT THIS THING HERE FIRST.
WHAT THE FUCK?

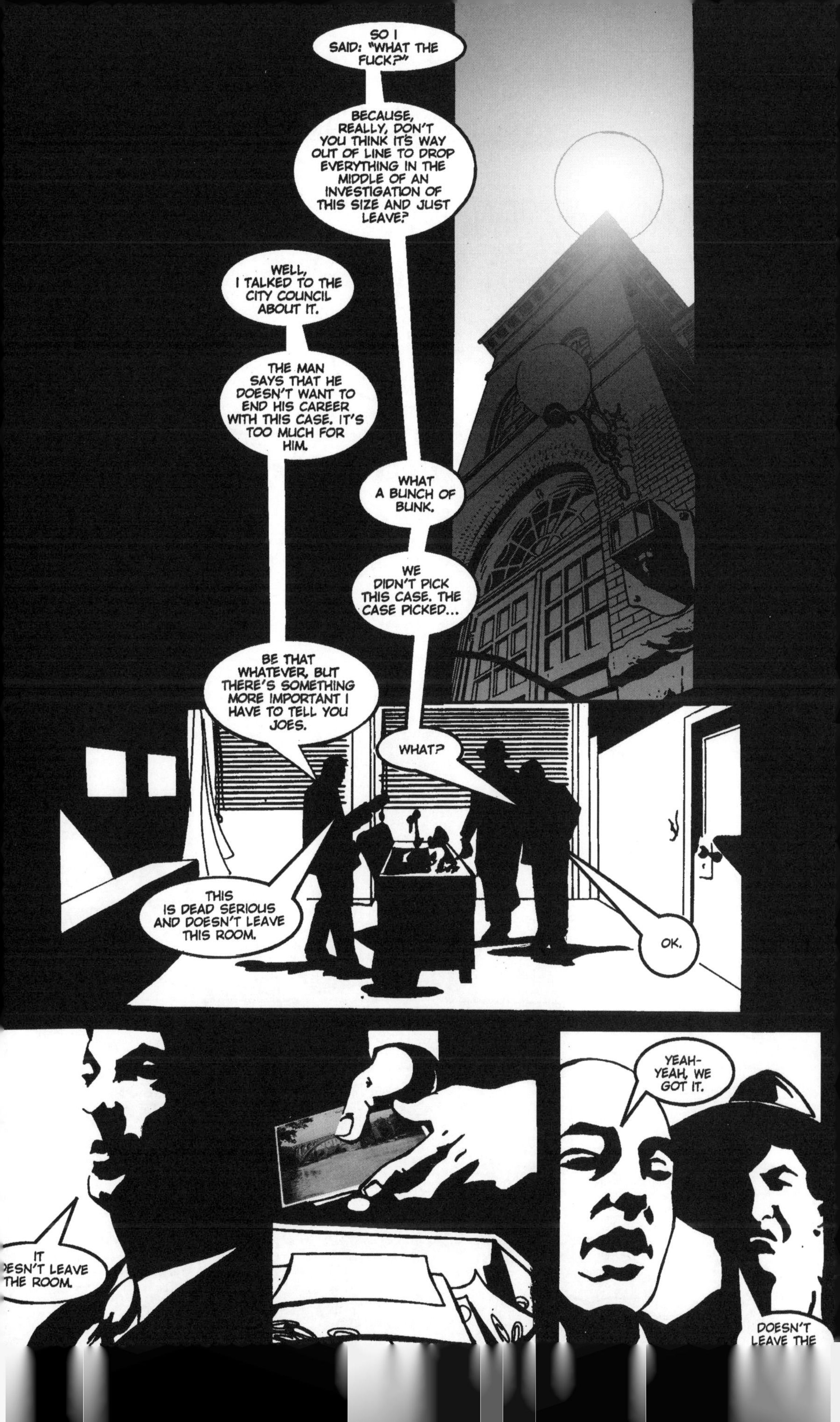
SO I SAID: "WHAT THE FUCK?"
BECAUSE, REALLY, DON'T YOU THINK IT'S WAY OUT OF LINE TO DROP EVERYTHING IN THE MIDDLE OF AN INVESTIGATION OF THIS SIZE AND JUST LEAVE?
WELL, I TALKED TO THE CITY COUNCIL ABOUT IT.
THE MAN SAYS THAT HE DOESN'T WANT TO END HIS CAREER WITH THIS CASE. IT'S TOO MUCH FOR HIM.
WHAT A BUNCH OF BUNK.
WE DIDN'T PICK THIS CASE. THE CASE PICKED...
BE THAT WHATEVER, BUT THERE'S SOMETHING MORE IMPORTANT I HAVE TO TELL YOU JOES.
WHAT?
THIS IS DEAD SERIOUS AND DOESN'T LEAVE THIS ROOM.
OK.
IT OESN'T LEAVE THE ROOM.
YEAH-YEAH, WE GOT IT.
DOESN'T LEAVE THE

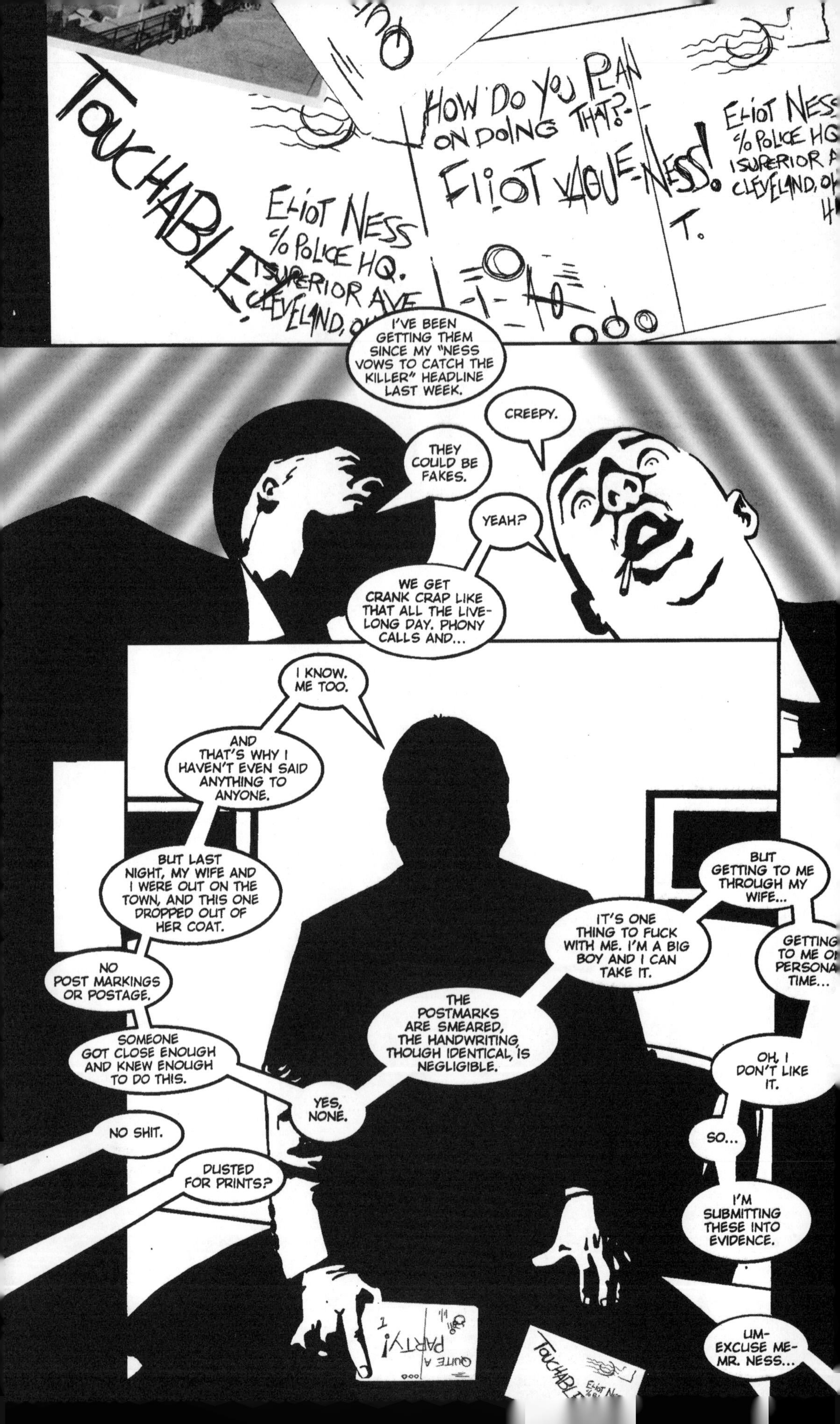
TOUCHABLE!
ELIOT NESS
% POLICE HQ.
1 SUPERIOR AVE
CLEVELAND, O
HOW DO YOU PLAN ON DOING THAT?
ELIOT "LOVE"-NESS!
T.
ELIOT NESS
% POLICE HQ
1 SUPERIOR A
CLEVELAND, O
I'VE BEEN GETTING THEM SINCE MY "NESS VOWS TO CATCH THE KILLER" HEADLINE LAST WEEK.
CREEPY.
THEY COULD BE FAKES.
YEAH?
WE GET CRANK CRAP LIKE THAT ALL THE LIVE-LONG DAY. PHONY CALLS AND...
I KNOW. ME TOO.
AND THAT'S WHY I HAVEN'T EVEN SAID ANYTHING TO ANYONE.
BUT LAST NIGHT, MY WIFE AND I WERE OUT ON THE TOWN, AND THIS ONE DROPPED OUT OF HER COAT.
NO POST MARKINGS OR POSTAGE.
SOMEONE GOT CLOSE ENOUGH AND KNEW ENOUGH TO DO THIS.
NO SHIT.
DUSTED FOR PRINTS?
YES, NONE.
THE POSTMARKS ARE SMEARED, THE HANDWRITING, THOUGH IDENTICAL, IS NEGLIGIBLE.
IT'S ONE THING TO FUCK WITH ME. I'M A BIG BOY AND I CAN TAKE IT.
BUT GETTING TO ME THROUGH MY WIFE...
GETTING TO ME O PERSONA TIME...
OH, I DON'T LIKE IT.
SO...
I'M SUBMITTING THESE INTO EVIDENCE.
QUITE A PARTY!
T
TOUCHABL
UM- EXCUSE ME- MR. NESS...

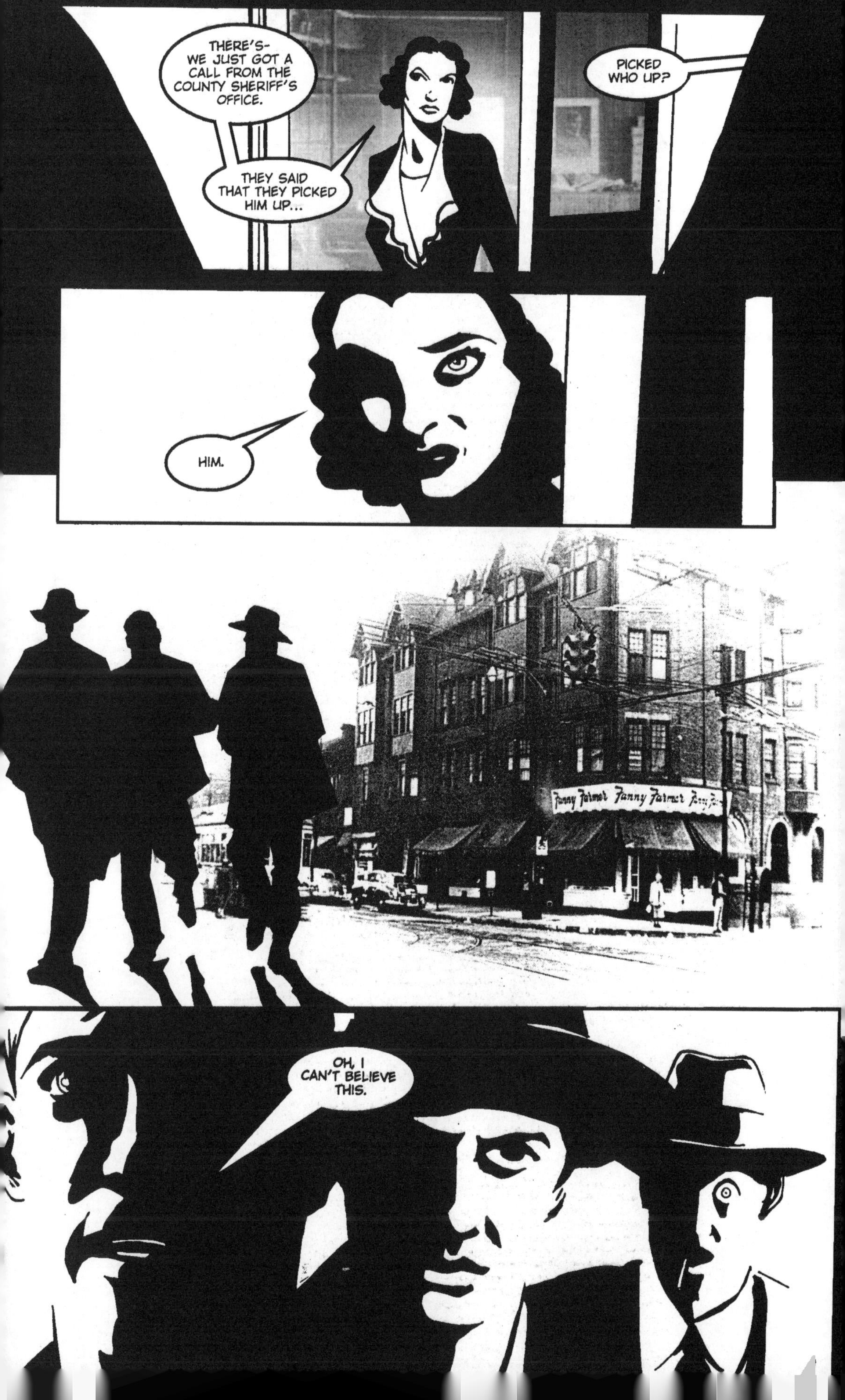
THERE'S- WE JUST GOT A CALL FROM THE COUNTY SHERIFF'S OFFICE.
THEY SAID THAT THEY PICKED HIM UP...
PICKED WHO UP?
HIM.
Fanny Farmer Fanny Farmer
OH, I CAN'T BELIEVE THIS.

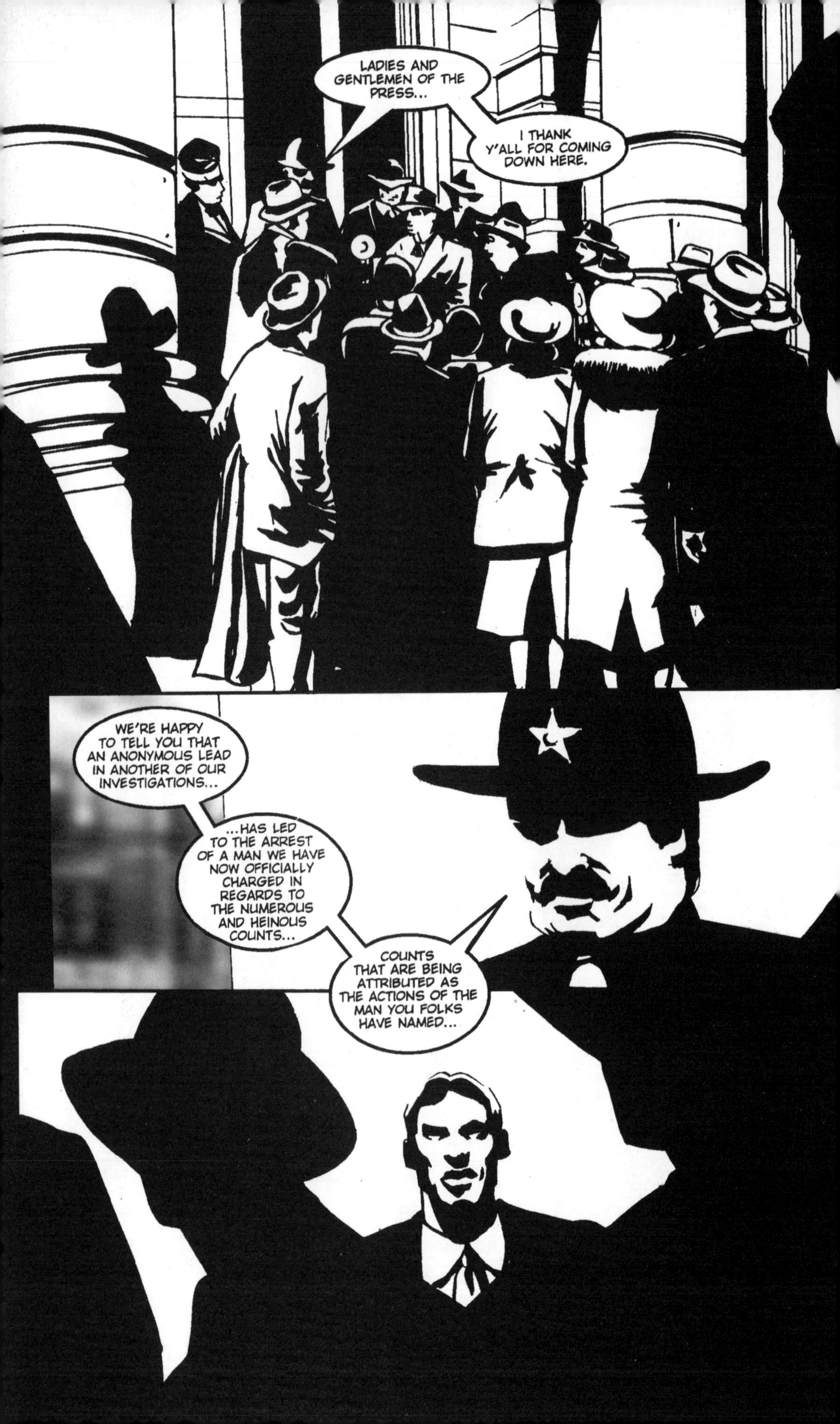
LADIES AND GENTLEMEN OF THE PRESS...
I THANK Y'ALL FOR COMING DOWN HERE.
WE'RE HAPPY TO TELL YOU THAT AN ANONYMOUS LEAD IN ANOTHER OF OUR INVESTIGATIONS...
...HAS LED TO THE ARREST OF A MAN WE HAVE NOW OFFICIALLY CHARGED IN REGARDS TO THE NUMEROUS AND HEINOUS COUNTS...
COUNTS THAT ARE BEING ATTRIBUTED AS THE ACTIONS OF THE MAN YOU FOLKS HAVE NAMED...

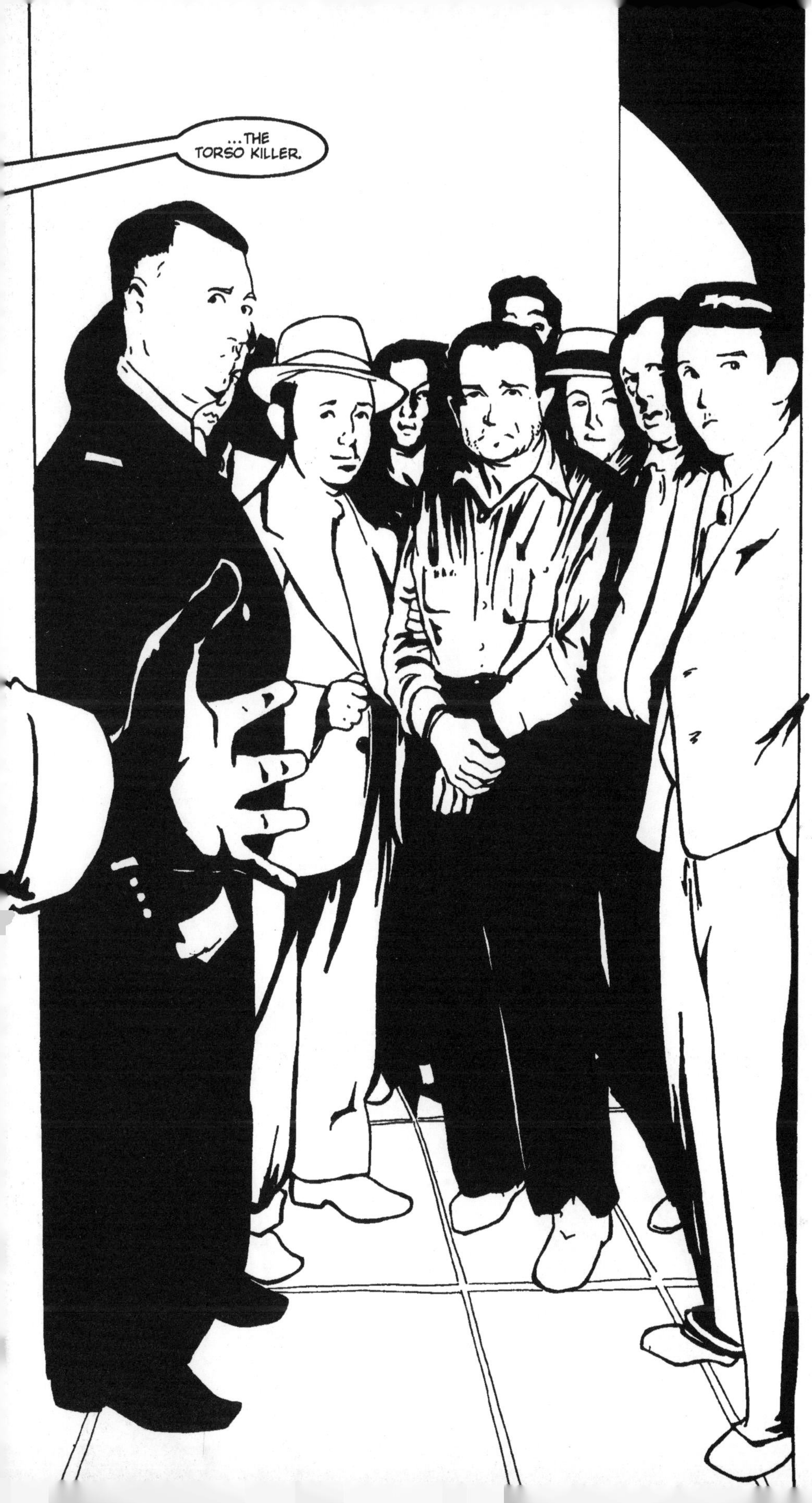
...THE TORSO KILLER.

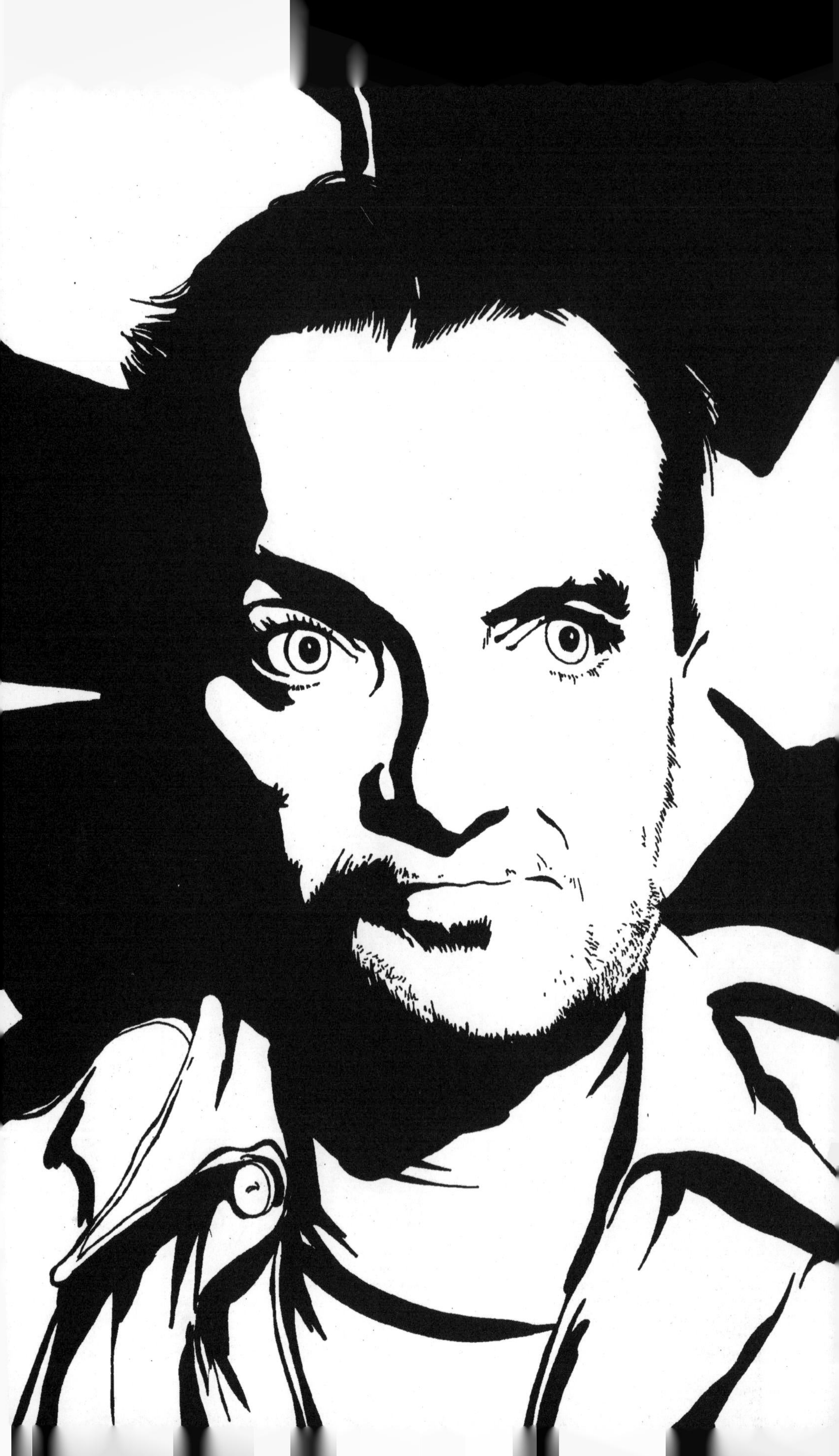

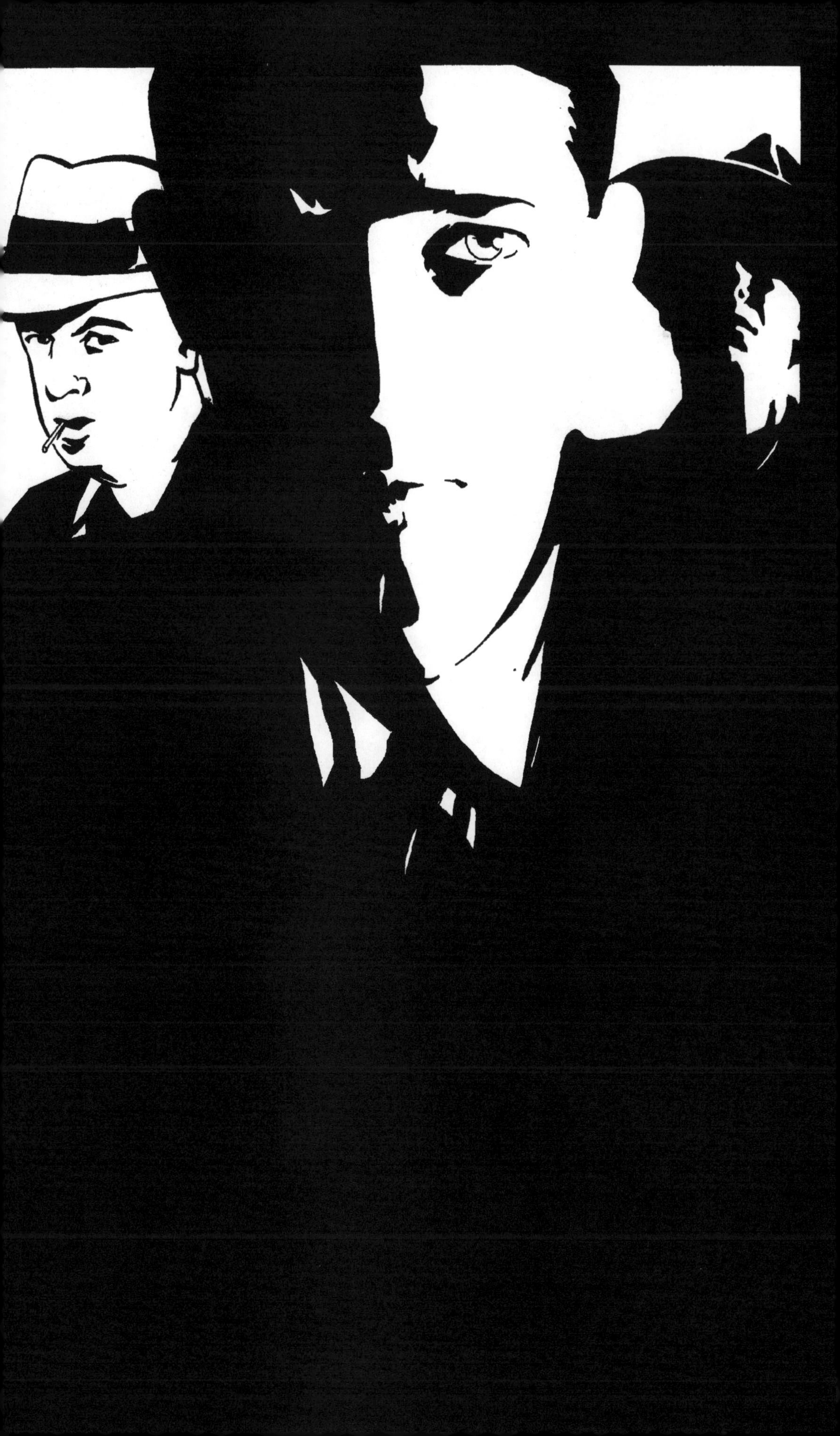

CHAPTER 4

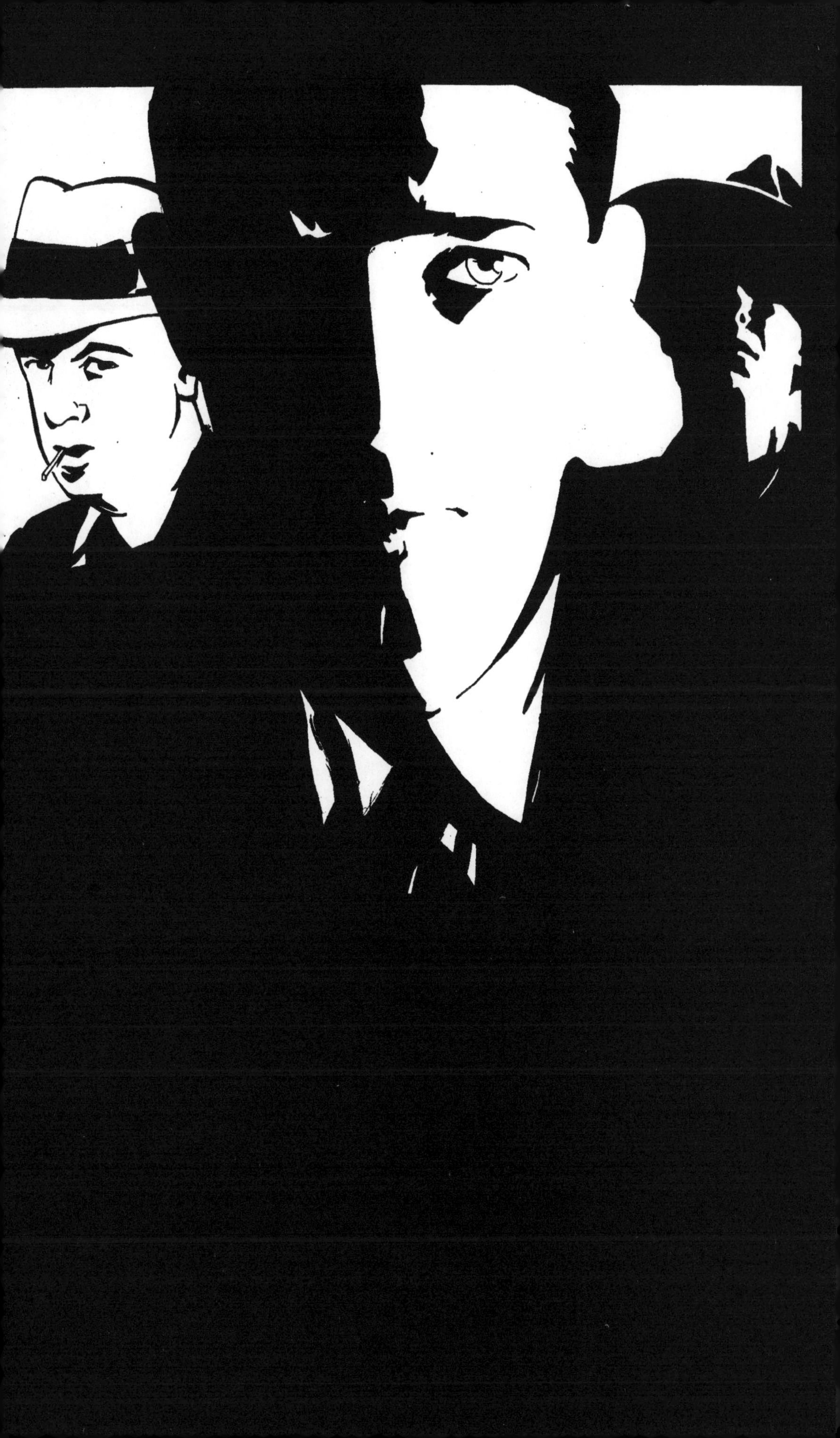

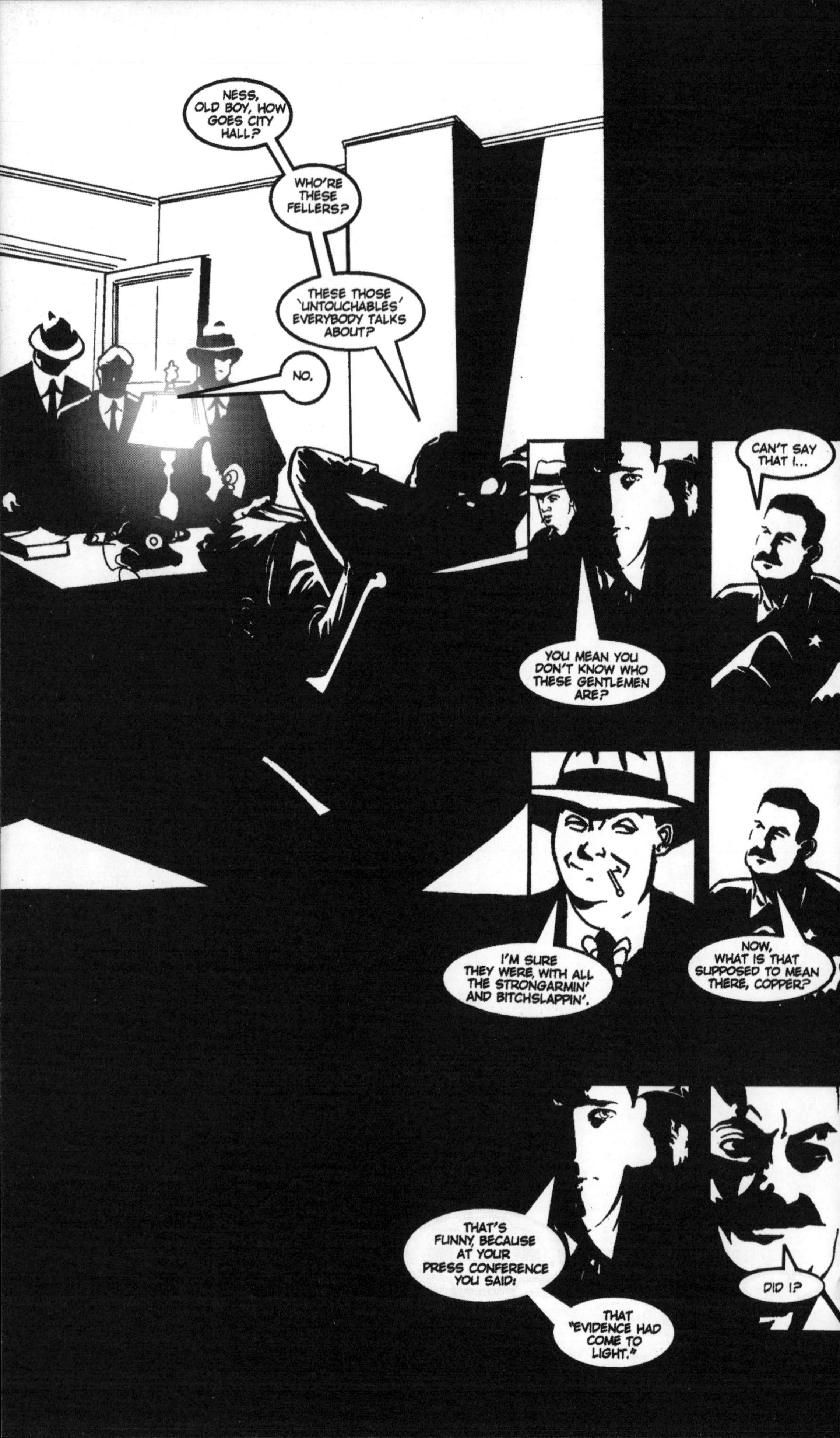
NESS, OLD BOY, HOW GOES CITY HALL?
WHO'RE THESE FELLERS?
THESE THOSE 'UNTOUCHABLES' EVERYBODY TALKS ABOUT?
NO.
CAN'T SAY THAT I...
YOU MEAN YOU DON'T KNOW WHO THESE GENTLEMEN ARE?
I'M SURE THEY WERE, WITH ALL THE STRONGARMIN' AND BITCHSLAPPIN'.
NOW, WHAT IS THAT SUPPOSED TO MEAN THERE, COPPER?
THAT'S FUNNY, BECAUSE AT YOUR PRESS CONFERENCE YOU SAID:
THAT "EVIDENCE HAD COME TO LIGHT."
DID I?

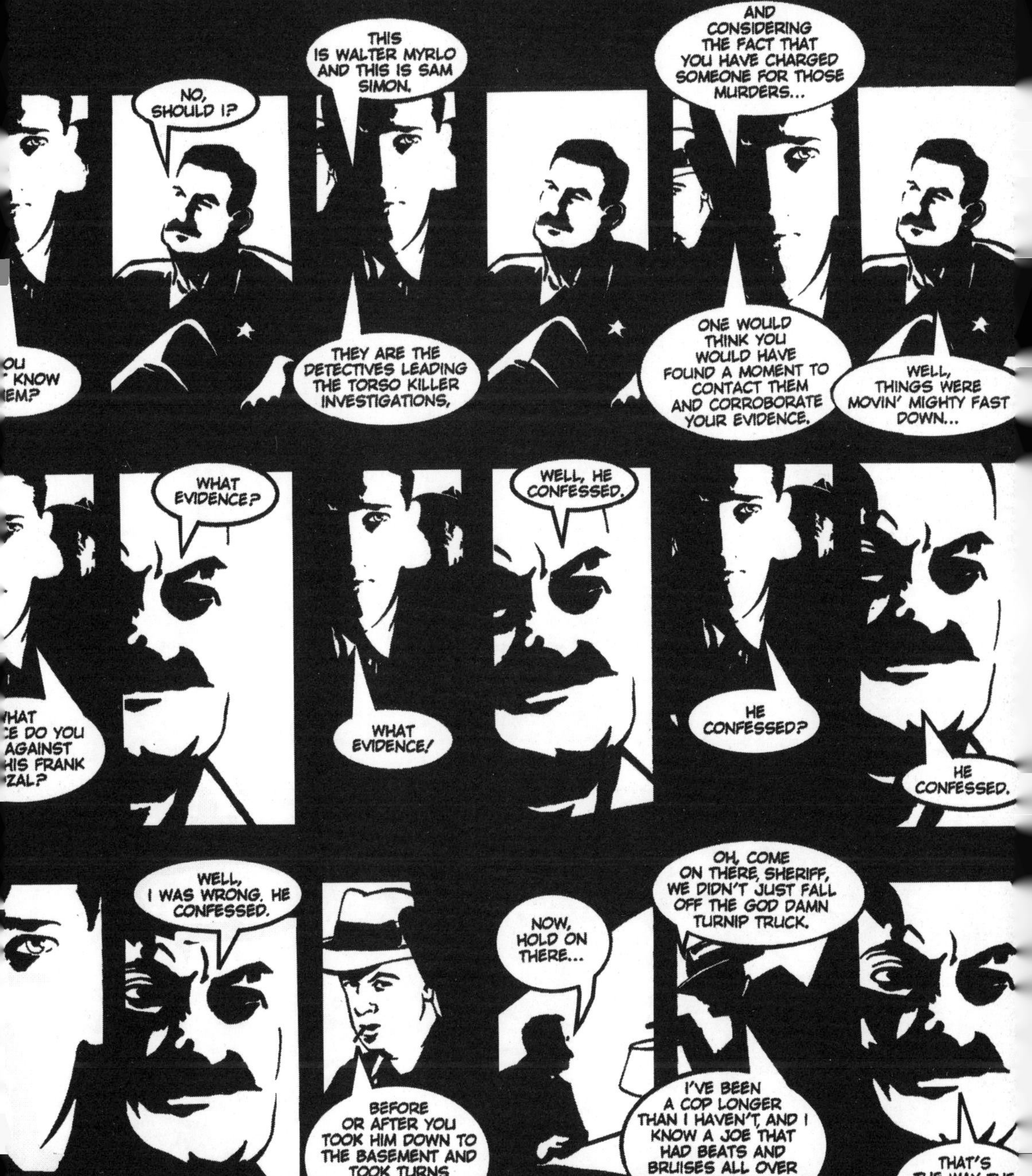

OU ' KNOW EM?
NO, SHOULD I?
THIS IS WALTER MYRLO AND THIS IS SAM SIMON.
THEY ARE THE DETECTIVES LEADING THE TORSO KILLER INVESTIGATIONS,
AND CONSIDERING THE FACT THAT YOU HAVE CHARGED SOMEONE FOR THOSE MURDERS...
ONE WOULD THINK YOU WOULD HAVE FOUND A MOMENT TO CONTACT THEM AND CORROBORATE YOUR EVIDENCE.
WELL, THINGS WERE MOVIN' MIGHTY FAST DOWN...
HAT E DO YOU AGAINST HIS FRANK ZAL?
WHAT EVIDENCE?
WHAT EVIDENCE!
WELL, HE CONFESSED.
HE CONFESSED?
HE CONFESSED.
WELL, I WAS WRONG. HE CONFESSED.
BEFORE OR AFTER YOU TOOK HIM DOWN TO THE BASEMENT AND TOOK TURNS POUNDIN' HIS MELON?
NOW, HOLD ON THERE...
OH, COME ON THERE, SHERIFF, WE DIDN'T JUST FALL OFF THE GOD DAMN TURNIP TRUCK.
I'VE BEEN A COP LONGER THAN I HAVEN'T, AND I KNOW A JOE THAT HAD BEATS AND BRUISES ALL OVER HIM WHEN I SEES IT.
THAT'S THE WAY THE GUY CAME IN HERE...

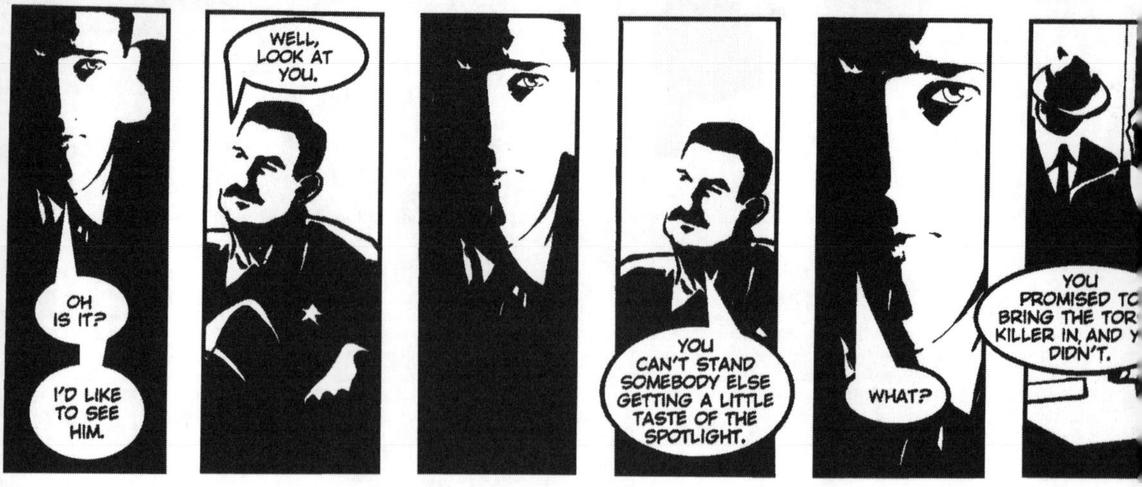
OH IS IT?
I'D LIKE TO SEE HIM.
WELL, LOOK AT YOU.
YOU CAN'T STAND SOMEBODY ELSE GETTING A LITTLE TASTE OF THE SPOTLIGHT.
WHAT?
YOU PROMISED TO BRING THE TOR KILLER IN, AND Y DIDN'T.

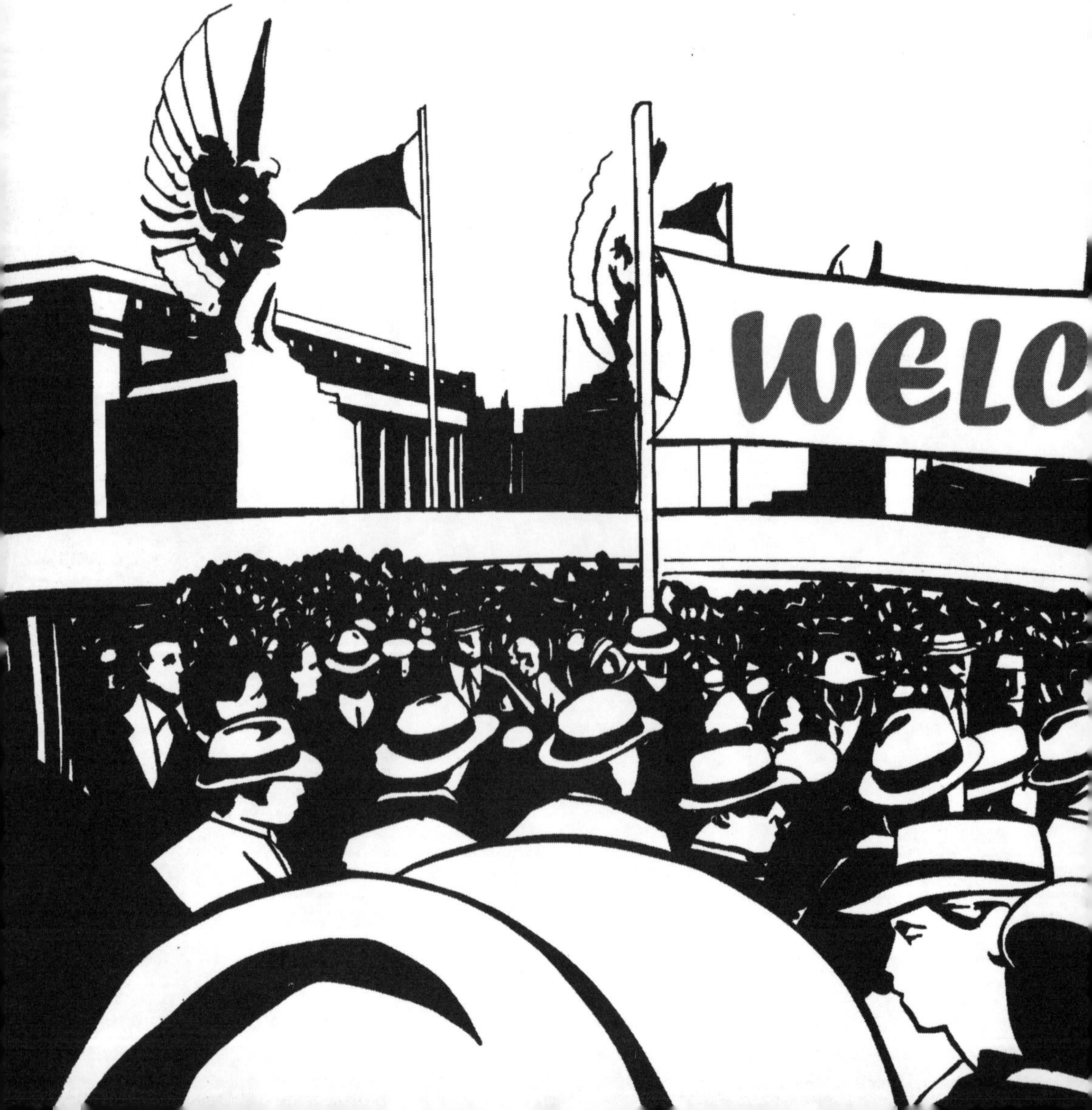
WELC

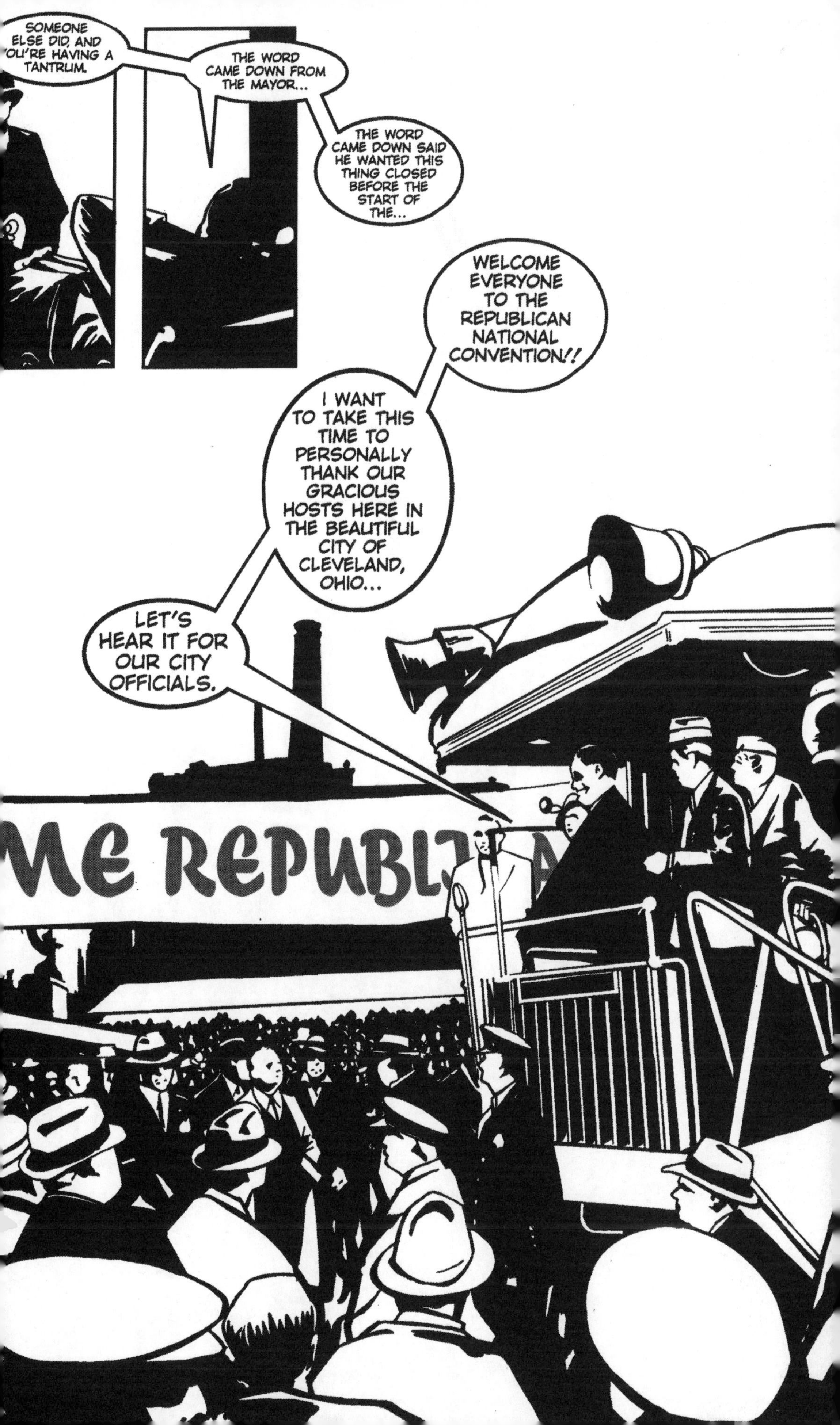
SOMEONE ELSE DID, AND YOU'RE HAVING A TANTRUM.
THE WORD CAME DOWN FROM THE MAYOR...
THE WORD CAME DOWN SAID HE WANTED THIS THING CLOSED BEFORE THE START OF THE...
WELCOME EVERYONE TO THE REPUBLICAN NATIONAL CONVENTION!!
I WANT TO TAKE THIS TIME TO PERSONALLY THANK OUR GRACIOUS HOSTS HERE IN THE BEAUTIFUL CITY OF CLEVELAND, OHIO...
LET'S HEAR IT FOR OUR CITY OFFICIALS.
ME REPUBLI

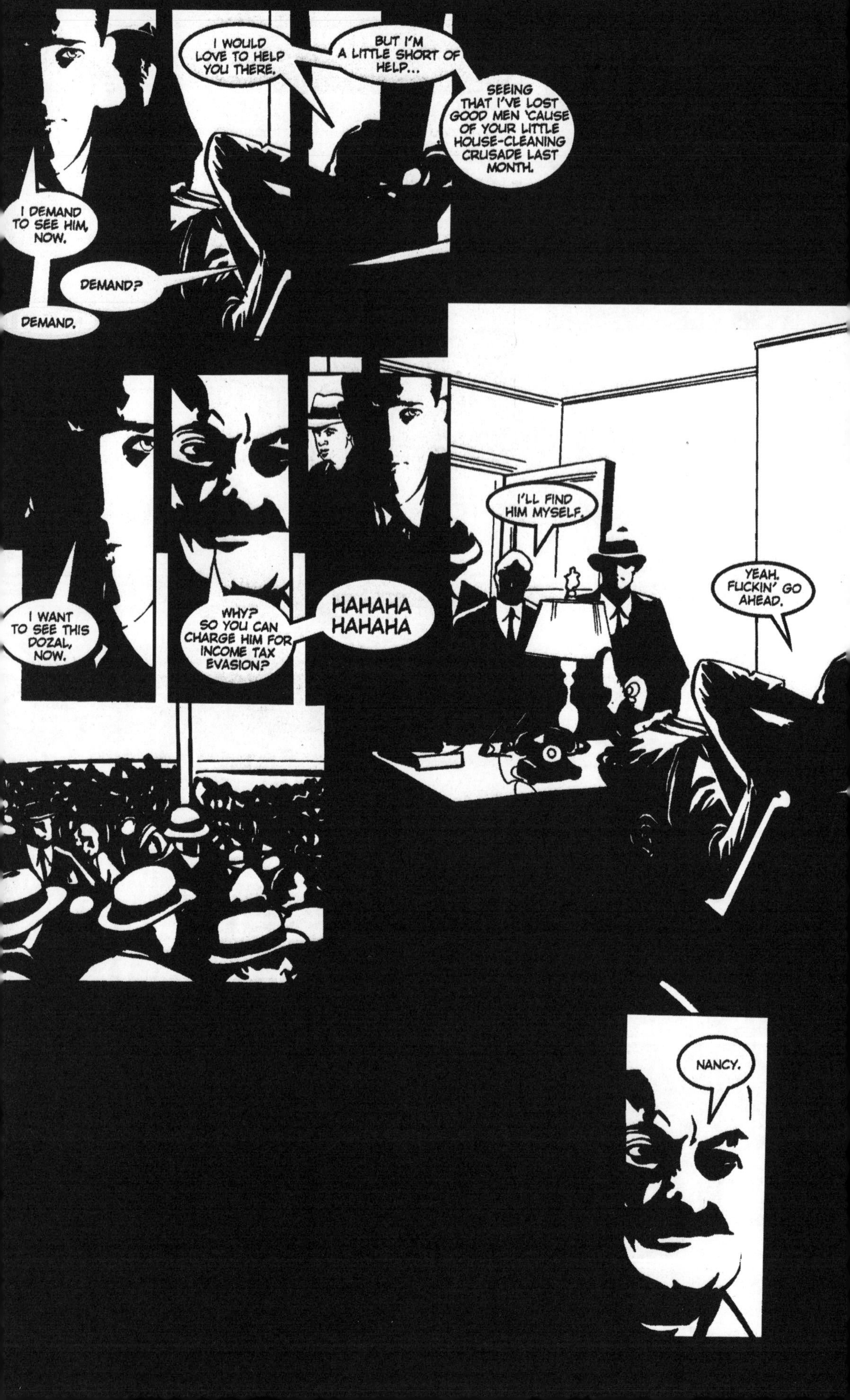
I WOULD LOVE TO HELP YOU THERE.
BUT I'M A LITTLE SHORT OF HELP...
SEEING THAT I'VE LOST GOOD MEN 'CAUSE OF YOUR LITTLE HOUSE-CLEANING CRUSADE LAST MONTH.
I DEMAND TO SEE HIM, NOW.
DEMAND?
DEMAND.
I WANT TO SEE THIS DOZAL, NOW.
WHY? SO YOU CAN CHARGE HIM FOR INCOME TAX EVASION?
HAHAHA HAHAHA
I'LL FIND HIM MYSELF.
YEAH. FUCKIN' GO AHEAD.
NANCY.

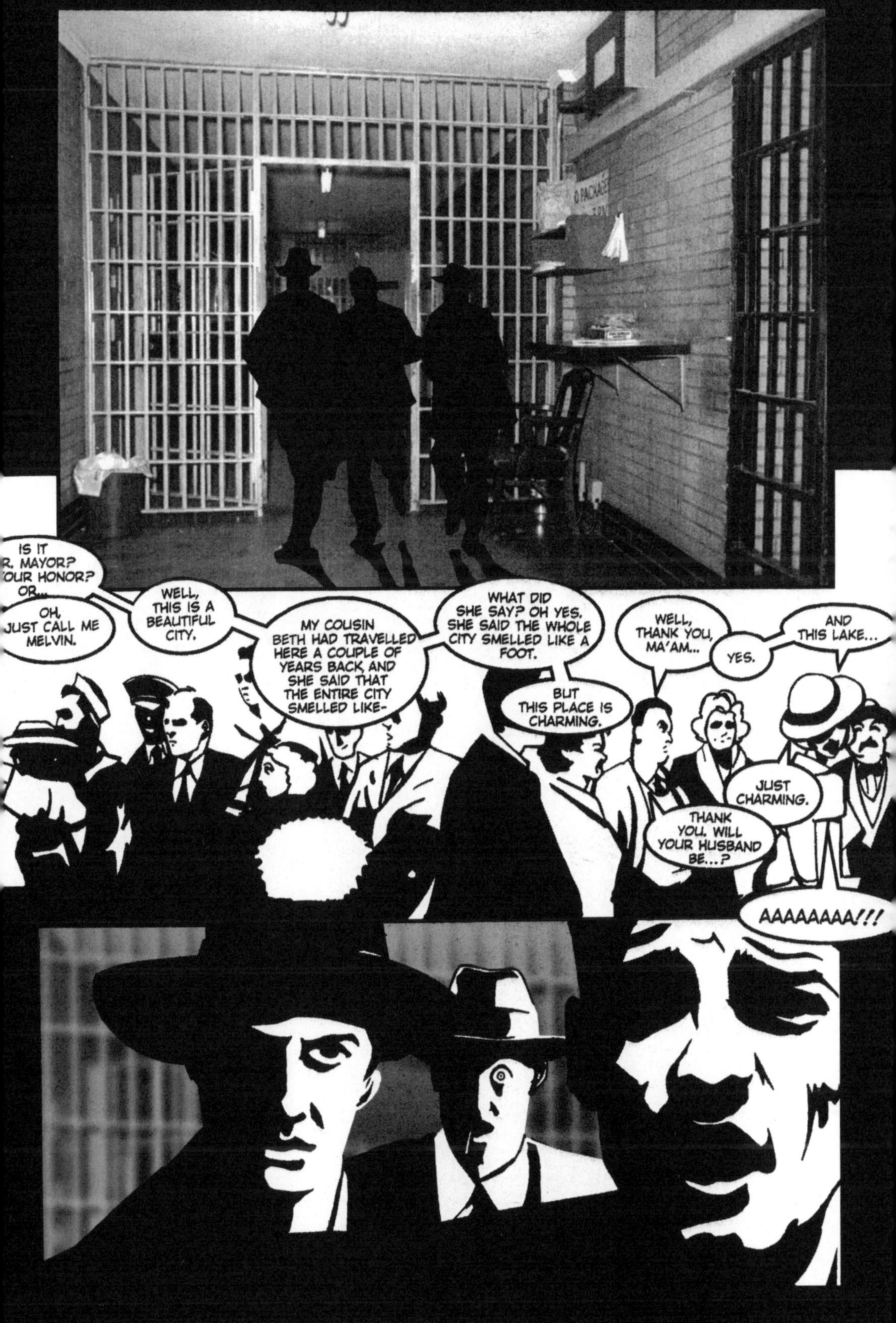

IS IT R. MAYOR? OUR HONOR? OR...
OH, JUST CALL ME MELVIN.
WELL, THIS IS A BEAUTIFUL CITY.
MY COUSIN BETH HAD TRAVELLED HERE A COUPLE OF YEARS BACK, AND SHE SAID THAT THE ENTIRE CITY SMELLED LIKE-
WHAT DID SHE SAY? OH YES. SHE SAID THE WHOLE CITY SMELLED LIKE A FOOT.
BUT THIS PLACE IS CHARMING.
WELL, THANK YOU, MA'AM...
YES.
AND THIS LAKE...
JUST CHARMING.
THANK YOU. WILL YOUR HUSBAND BE...?
AAAAAAAA!!!

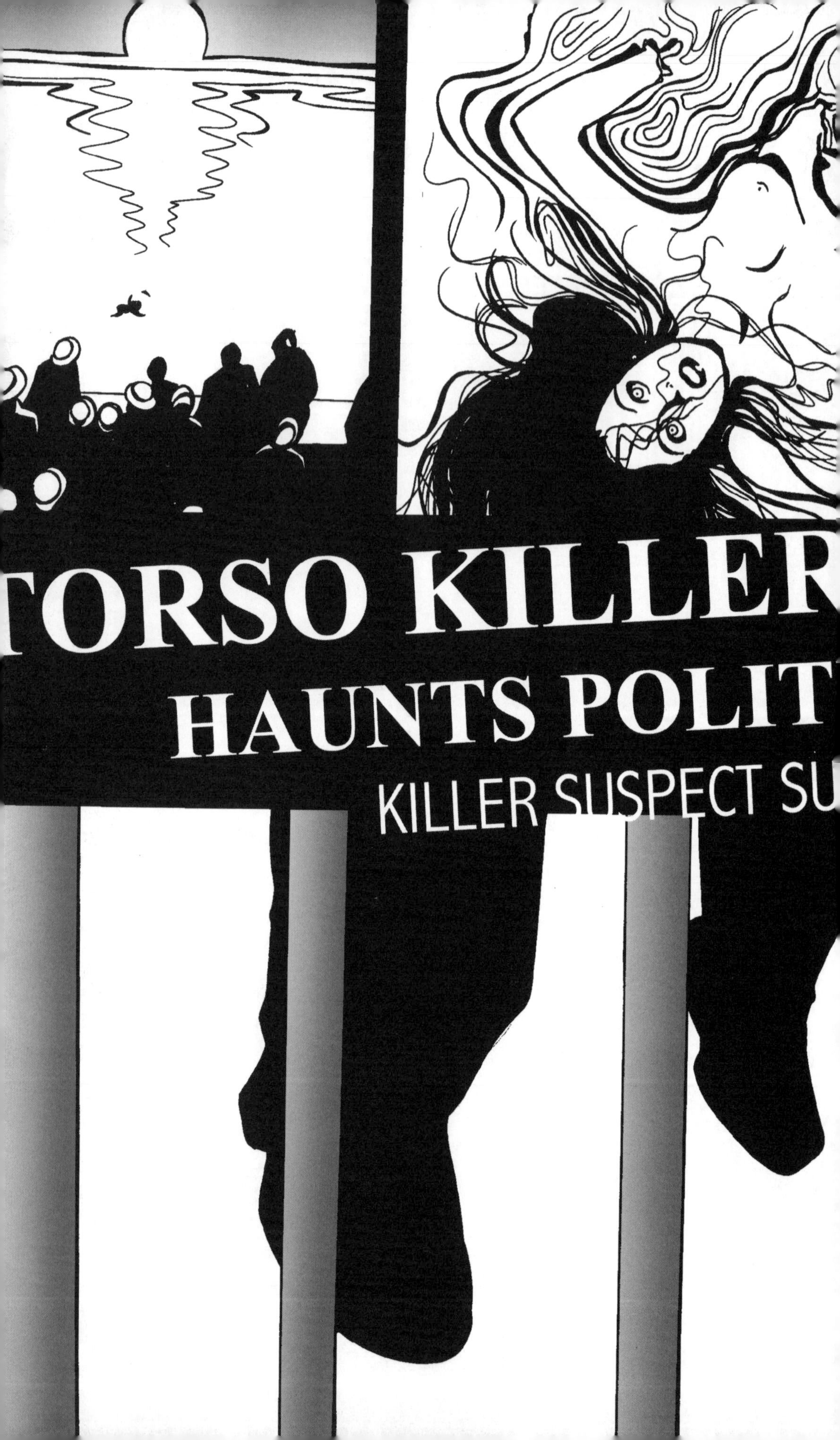
TORSO KILLER
HAUNTS POLIT
KILLER SUSPECT SU

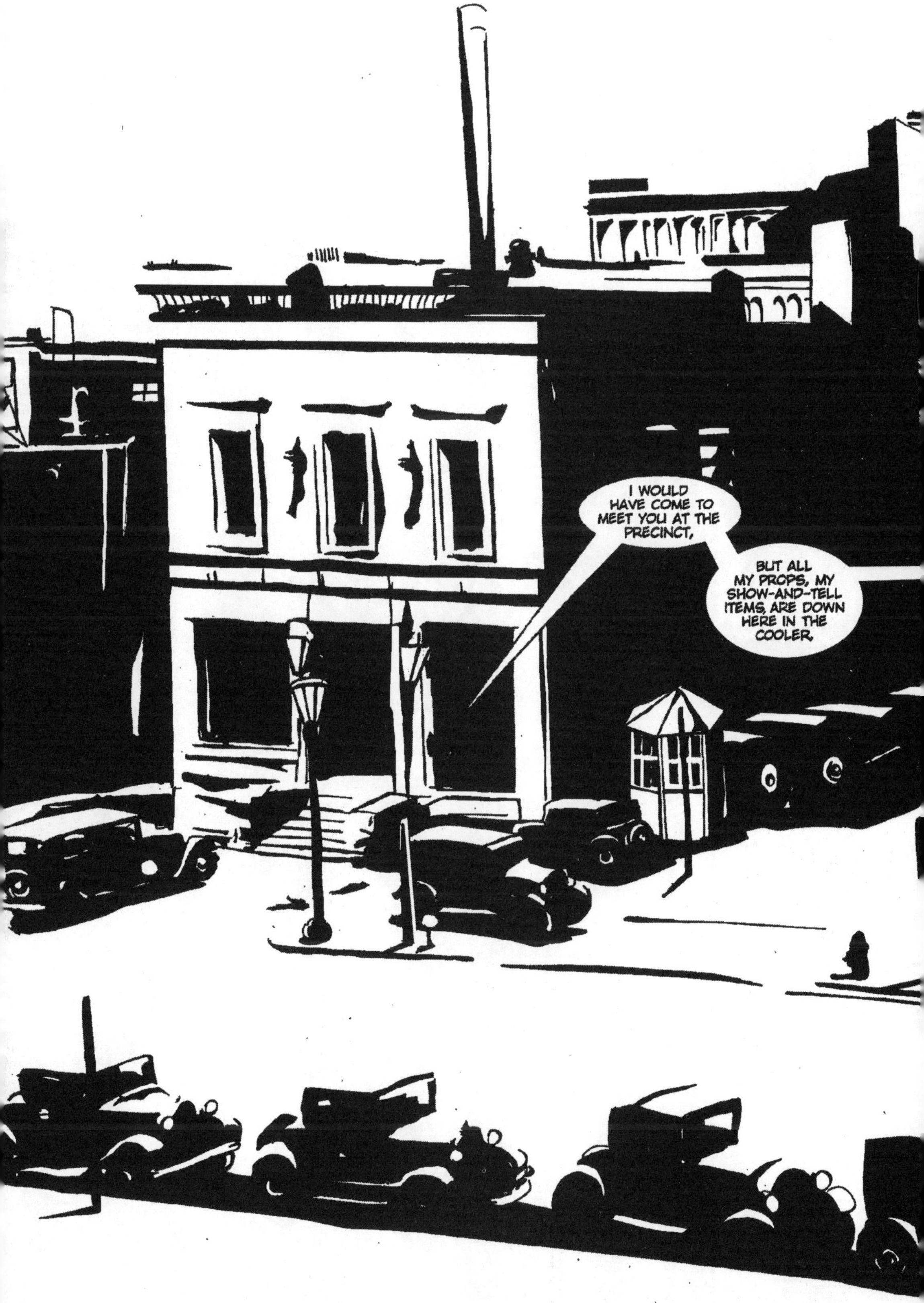
I WOULD HAVE COME TO MEET YOU AT THE PRECINCT,
BUT ALL MY PROPS, MY SHOW-AND-TELL ITEMS, ARE DOWN HERE IN THE COOLER.

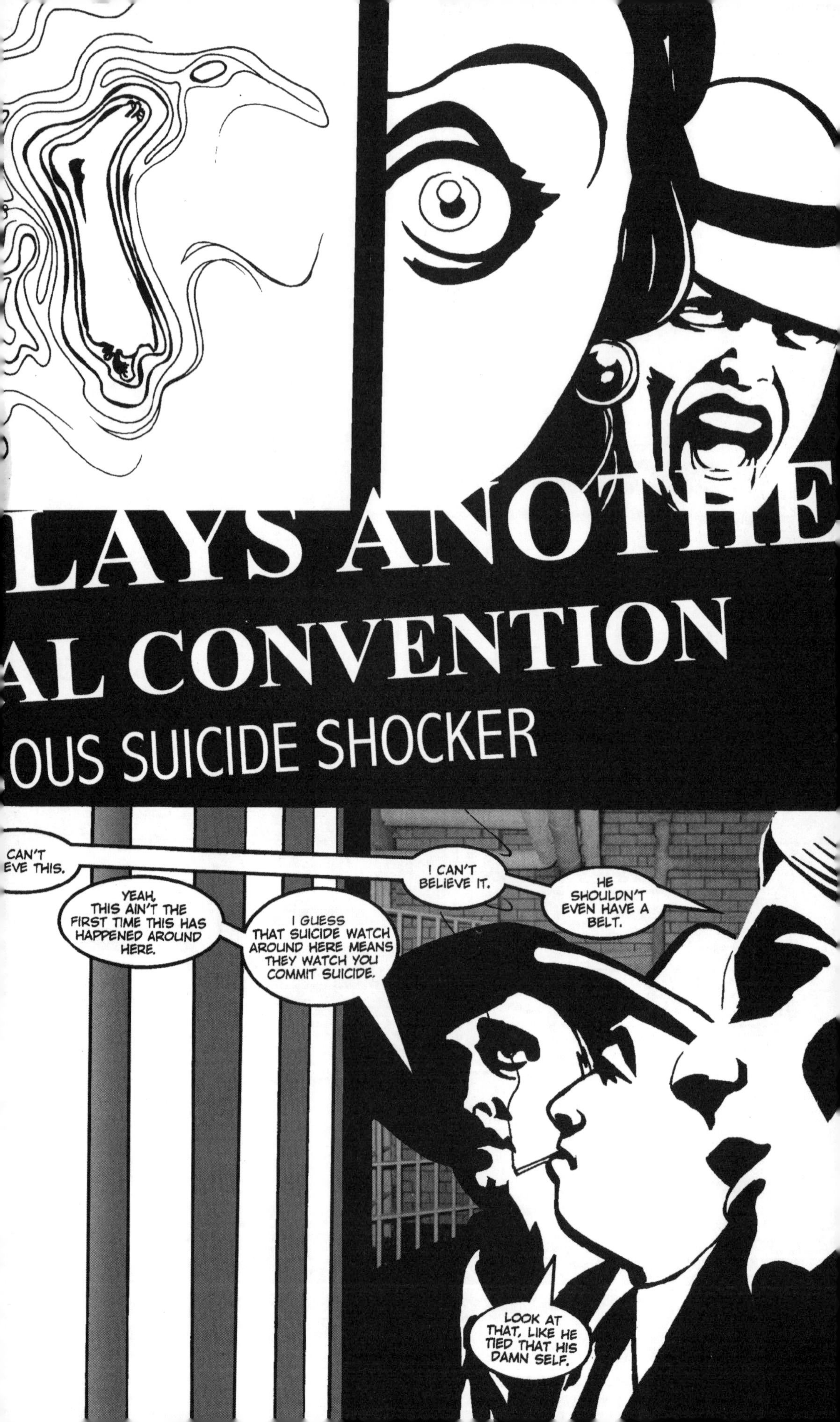
LAYS ANOTHE
AL CONVENTION
OUS SUICIDE SHOCKER
CAN'T
EVE THIS.
YEAH, THIS AIN'T THE FIRST TIME THIS HAS HAPPENED AROUND HERE.
I GUESS THAT SUICIDE WATCH AROUND HERE MEANS THEY WATCH YOU COMMIT SUICIDE.
I CAN'T BELIEVE IT.
HE SHOULDN'T EVEN HAVE A BELT.
LOOK AT THAT, LIKE HE TIED THAT HIS DAMN SELF.

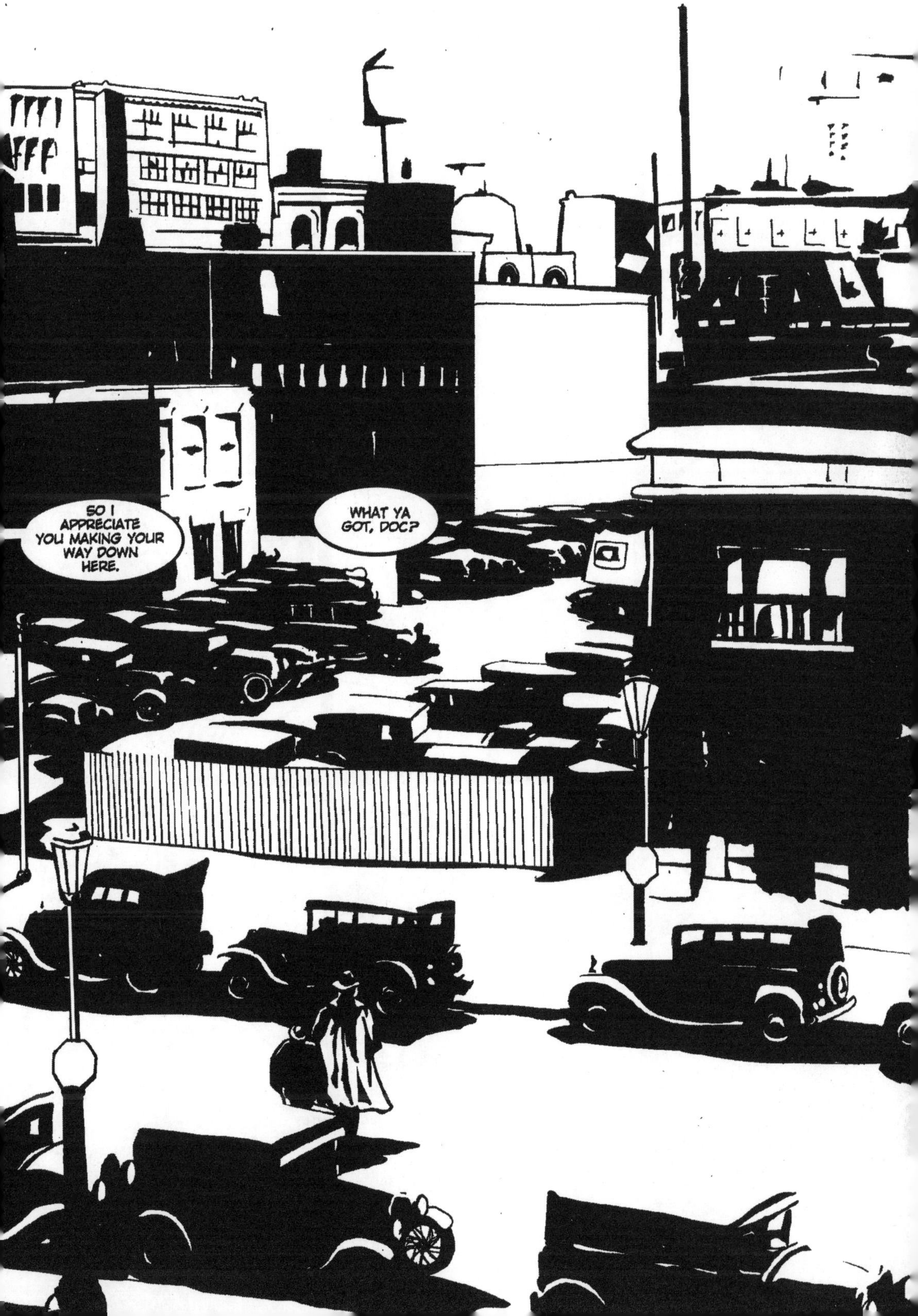
SO I APPRECIATE YOU MAKING YOUR WAY DOWN HERE.
WHAT YA GOT, DOC?

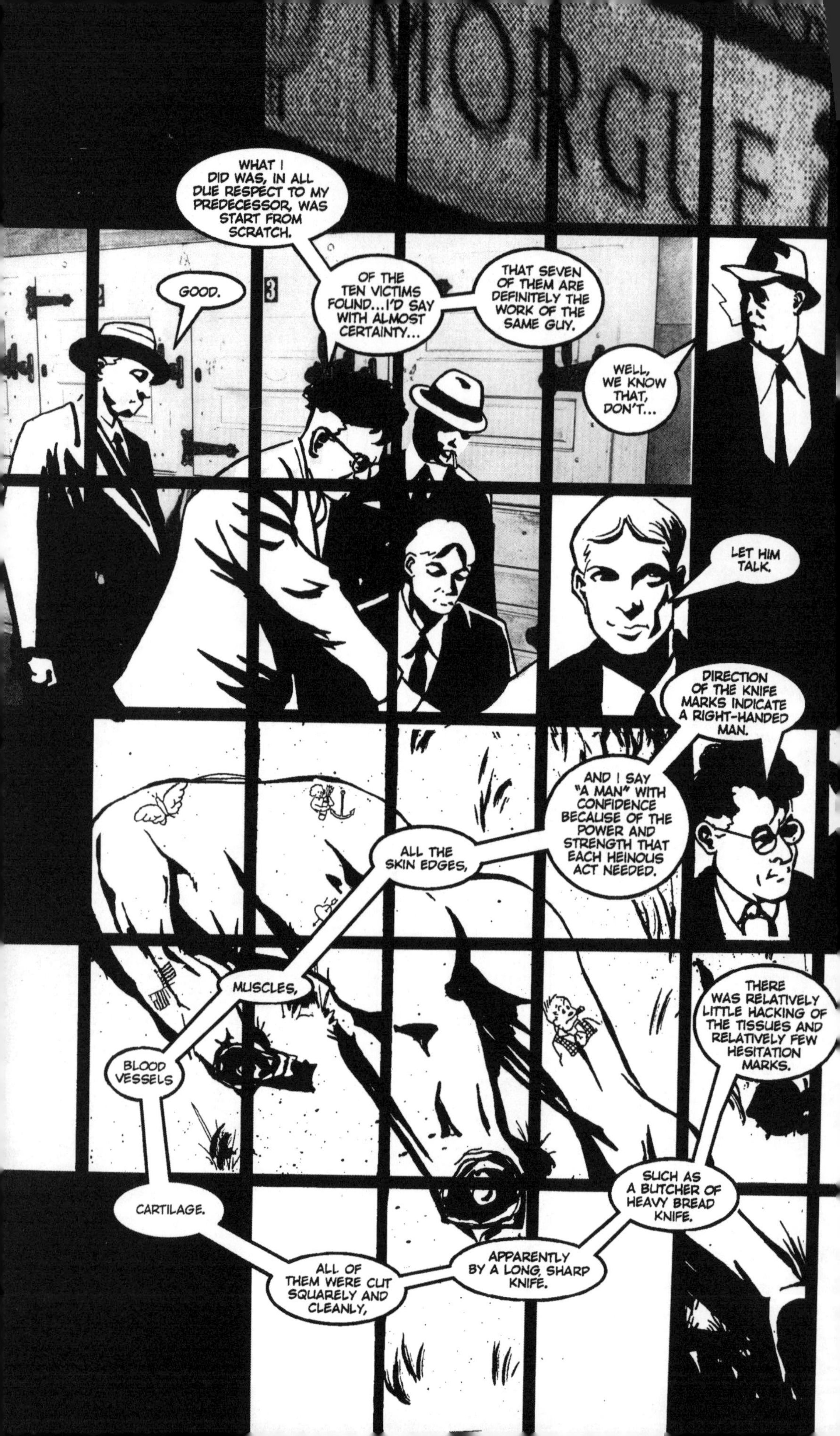
MORGUE
WHAT I DID WAS, IN ALL DUE RESPECT TO MY PREDECESSOR, WAS START FROM SCRATCH.
GOOD.
OF THE TEN VICTIMS FOUND...I'D SAY WITH ALMOST CERTAINTY...
THAT SEVEN OF THEM ARE DEFINITELY THE WORK OF THE SAME GUY.
WELL, WE KNOW THAT, DON'T...
LET HIM TALK.
DIRECTION OF THE KNIFE MARKS INDICATE A RIGHT-HANDED MAN.
AND I SAY "A MAN" WITH CONFIDENCE BECAUSE OF THE POWER AND STRENGTH THAT EACH HEINOUS ACT NEEDED.
ALL THE SKIN EDGES,
MUSCLES,
BLOOD VESSELS
CARTILAGE.
ALL OF THEM WERE CUT SQUARELY AND CLEANLY,
APPARENTLY BY A LONG, SHARP KNIFE.
SUCH AS A BUTCHER OF HEAVY BREAD KNIFE.
THERE WAS RELATIVELY LITTLE HACKING OF THE TISSUES AND RELATIVELY FEW HESITATION MARKS.

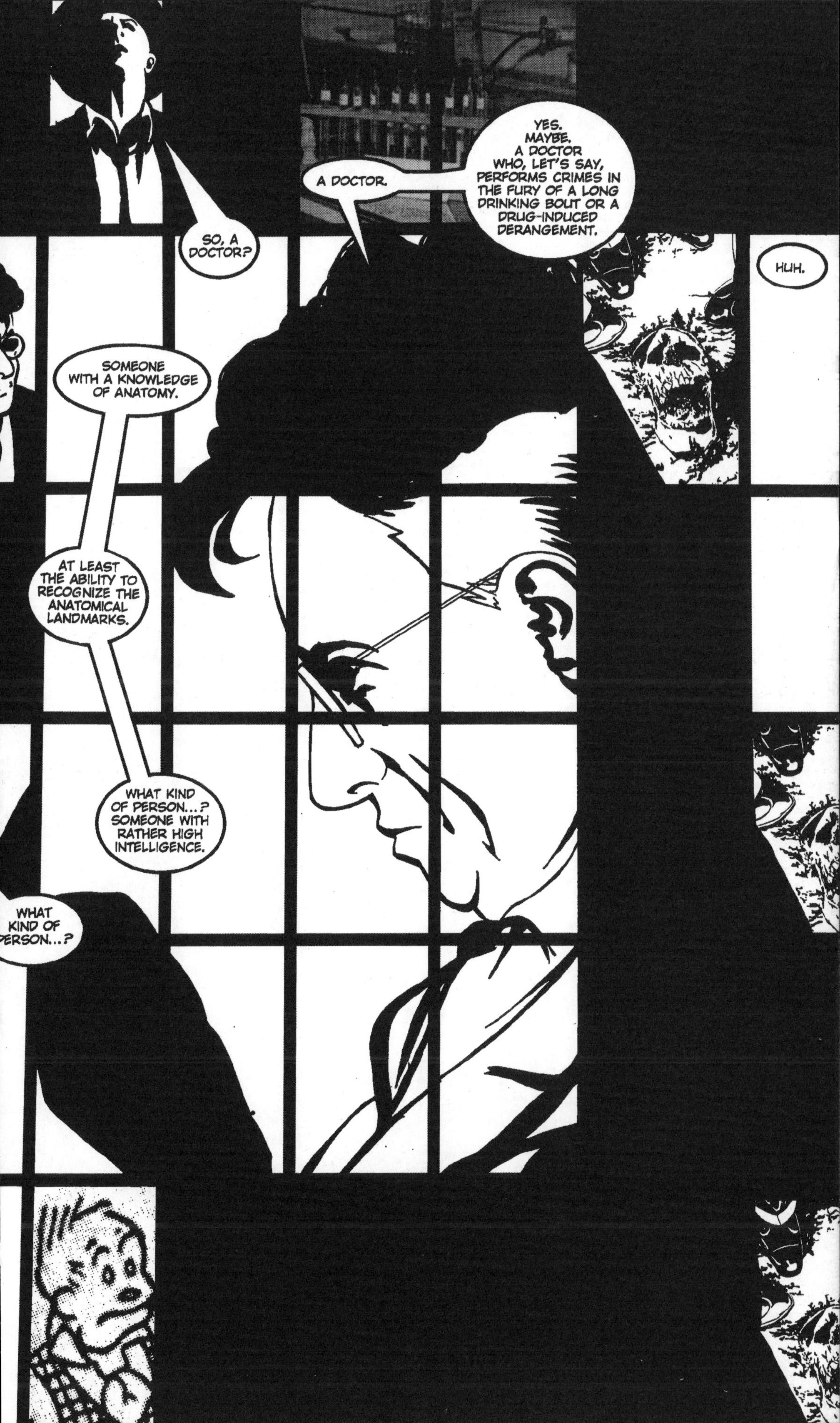
SO, A DOCTOR?
A DOCTOR.
YES. MAYBE. A DOCTOR WHO, LET'S SAY, PERFORMS CRIMES IN THE FURY OF A LONG DRINKING BOUT OR A DRUG-INDUCED DERANGEMENT.
HUH.
SOMEONE WITH A KNOWLEDGE OF ANATOMY.
AT LEAST THE ABILITY TO RECOGNIZE THE ANATOMICAL LANDMARKS.
WHAT KIND OF PERSON...? SOMEONE WITH RATHER HIGH INTELLIGENCE.
WHAT KIND OF PERSON...?

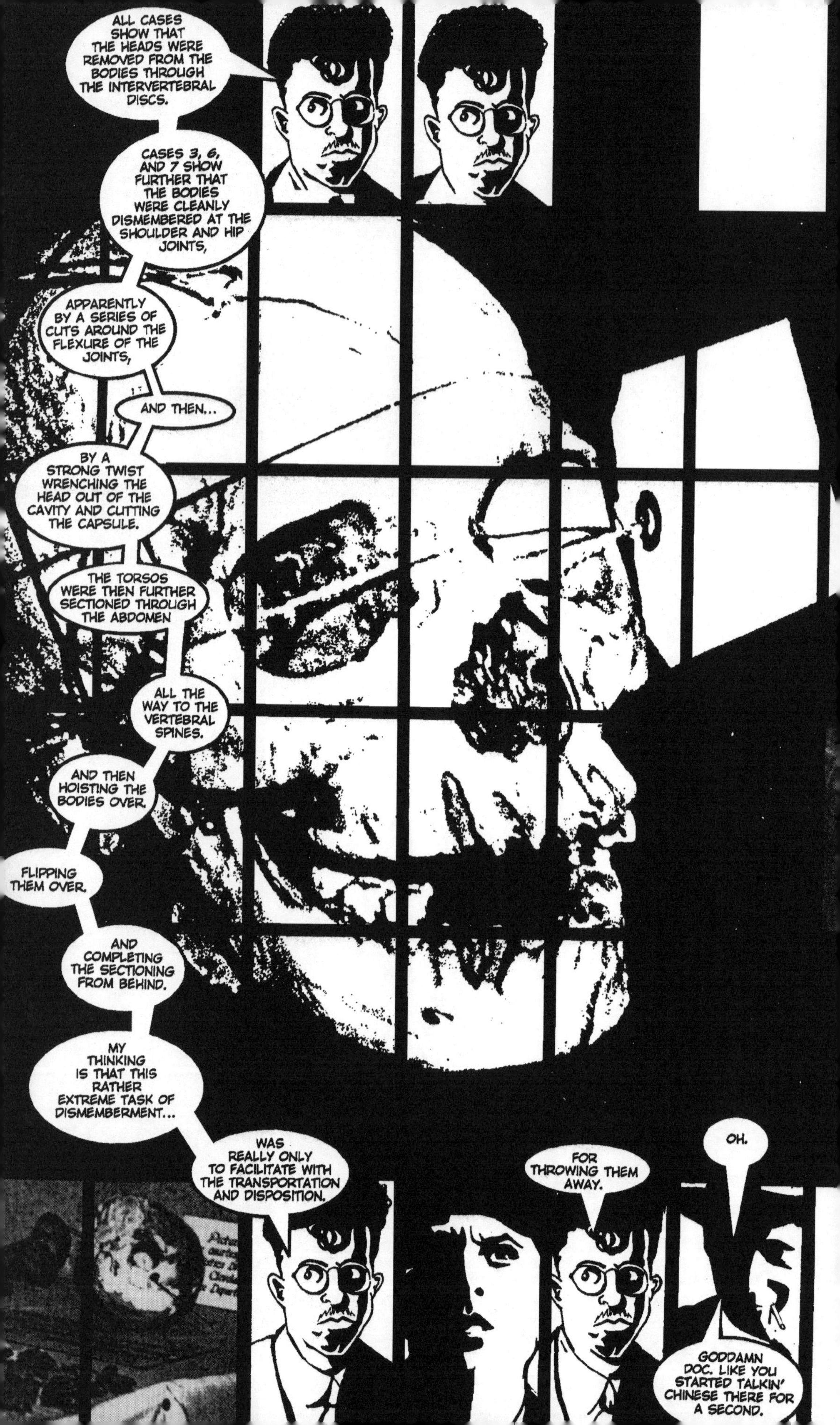
ALL CASES SHOW THAT THE HEADS WERE REMOVED FROM THE BODIES THROUGH THE INTERVERTEBRAL DISCS.
CASES 3, 6, AND 7 SHOW FURTHER THAT THE BODIES WERE CLEANLY DISMEMBERED AT THE SHOULDER AND HIP JOINTS,
APPARENTLY BY A SERIES OF CUTS AROUND THE FLEXURE OF THE JOINTS,
AND THEN...
BY A STRONG TWIST WRENCHING THE HEAD OUT OF THE CAVITY AND CUTTING THE CAPSULE.
THE TORSOS WERE THEN FURTHER SECTIONED THROUGH THE ABDOMEN
ALL THE WAY TO THE VERTEBRAL SPINES.
AND THEN HOISTING THE BODIES OVER.
FLIPPING THEM OVER.
AND COMPLETING THE SECTIONING FROM BEHIND.
MY THINKING IS THAT THIS RATHER EXTREME TASK OF DISMEMBERMENT...
WAS REALLY ONLY TO FACILITATE WITH THE TRANSPORTATION AND DISPOSITION.
FOR THROWING THEM AWAY.
OH.
GODDAMN DOC. LIKE YOU STARTED TALKIN' CHINESE THERE FOR A SECOND.

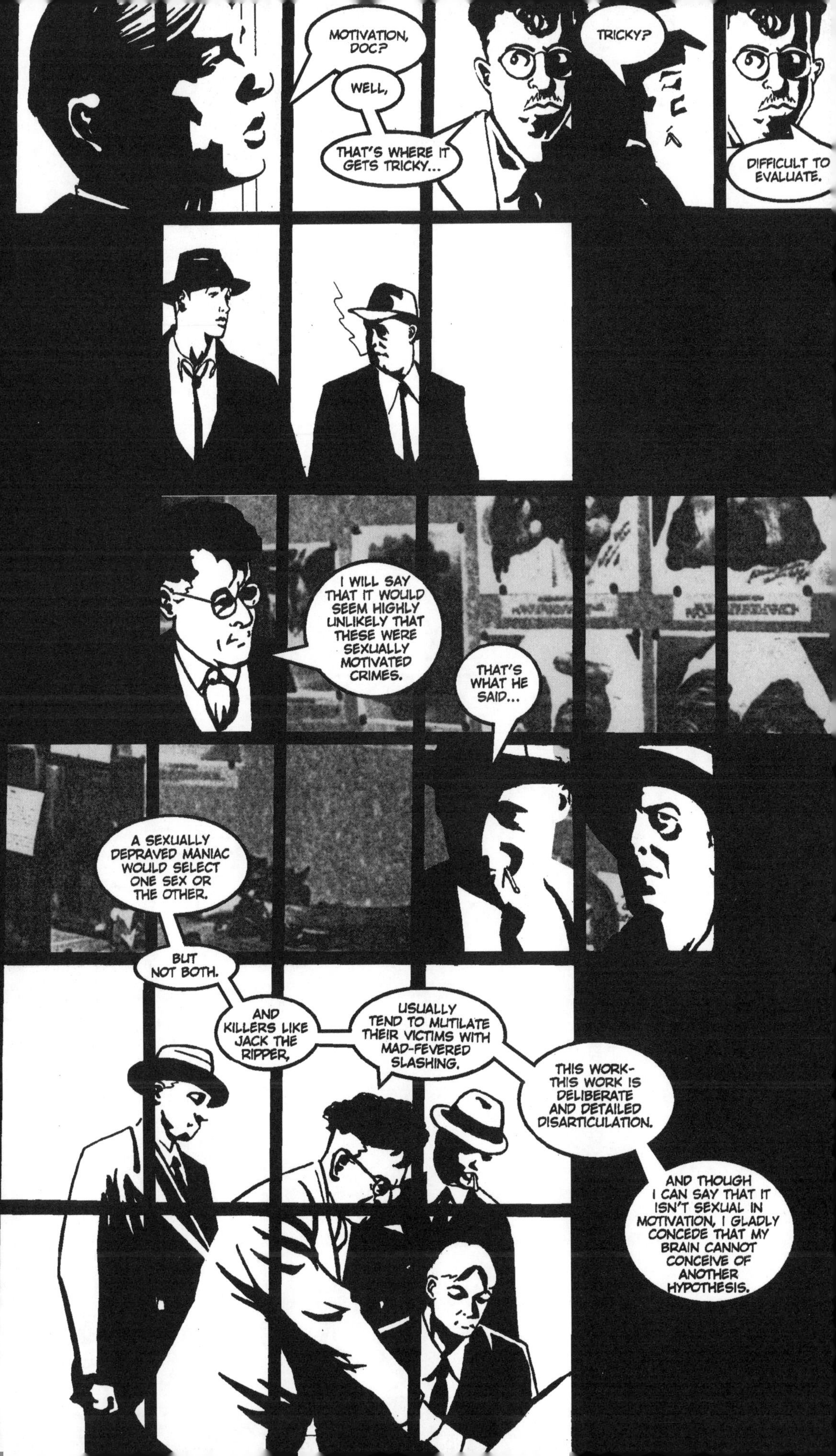
MOTIVATION, DOC?
WELL,
THAT'S WHERE IT GETS TRICKY...
TRICKY?
DIFFICULT TO EVALUATE.
I WILL SAY THAT IT WOULD SEEM HIGHLY UNLIKELY THAT THESE WERE SEXUALLY MOTIVATED CRIMES.
THAT'S WHAT HE SAID...
A SEXUALLY DEPRAVED MANIAC WOULD SELECT ONE SEX OR THE OTHER.
BUT NOT BOTH.
AND KILLERS LIKE JACK THE RIPPER,
USUALLY TEND TO MUTILATE THEIR VICTIMS WITH MAD-FEVERED SLASHING.
THIS WORK- THIS WORK IS DELIBERATE AND DETAILED DISARTICULATION.
AND THOUGH I CAN SAY THAT IT ISN'T SEXUAL IN MOTIVATION, I GLADLY CONCEDE THAT MY BRAIN CANNOT CONCEIVE OF ANOTHER HYPOTHESIS.

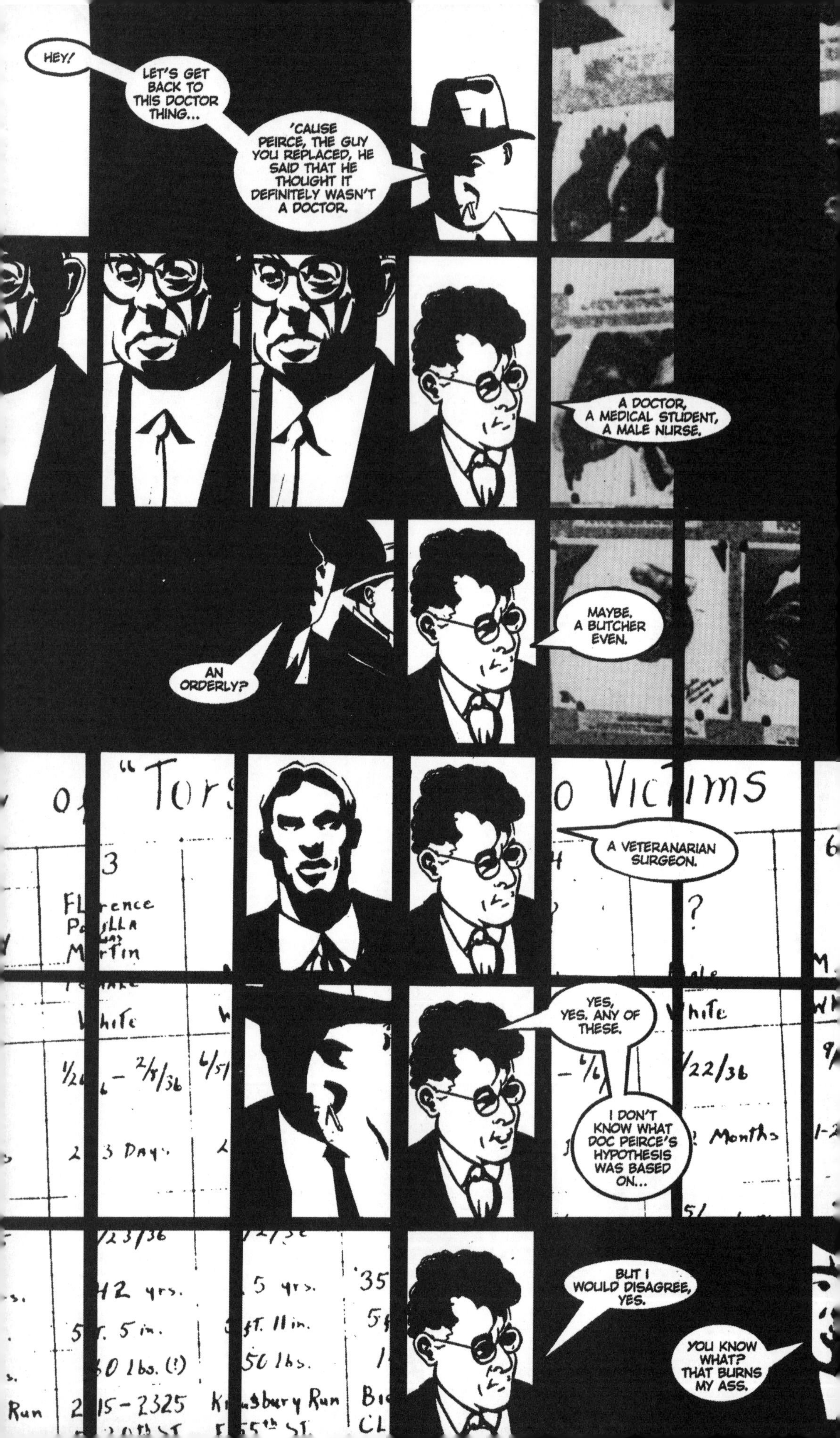
HEY!
LET'S GET BACK TO THIS DOCTOR THING...
'CAUSE PEIRCE, THE GUY YOU REPLACED, HE SAID THAT HE THOUGHT IT DEFINITELY WASN'T A DOCTOR.
A DOCTOR, A MEDICAL STUDENT, A MALE NURSE.
AN ORDERLY?
MAYBE. A BUTCHER EVEN.
A VETERANARIAN SURGEON.
YES, YES. ANY OF THESE.
I DON'T KNOW WHAT DOC PEIRCE'S HYPOTHESIS WAS BASED ON...
BUT I WOULD DISAGREE, YES.
YOU KNOW WHAT? THAT BURNS MY ASS.

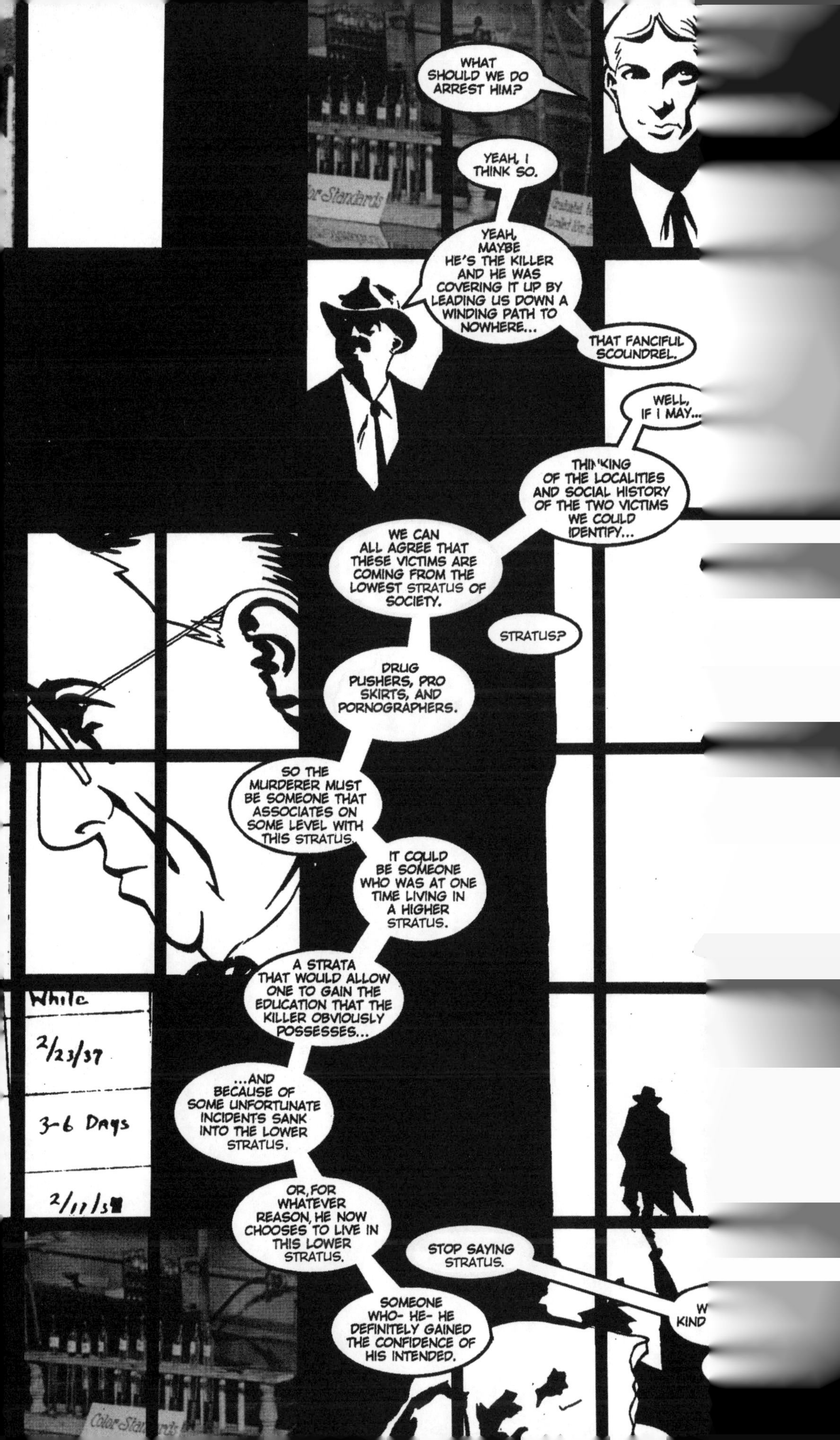
WHAT SHOULD WE DO ARREST HIM?
YEAH, I THINK SO.
YEAH, MAYBE HE'S THE KILLER AND HE WAS COVERING IT UP BY LEADING US DOWN A WINDING PATH TO NOWHERE...
THAT FANCIFUL SCOUNDREL.
WELL, IF I MAY...
THINKING OF THE LOCALITIES AND SOCIAL HISTORY OF THE TWO VICTIMS WE COULD IDENTIFY...
WE CAN ALL AGREE THAT THESE VICTIMS ARE COMING FROM THE LOWEST STRATUS OF SOCIETY.
STRATUS?
DRUG PUSHERS, PRO SKIRTS, AND PORNOGRAPHERS.
SO THE MURDERER MUST BE SOMEONE THAT ASSOCIATES ON SOME LEVEL WITH THIS STRATUS.
IT COULD BE SOMEONE WHO WAS AT ONE TIME LIVING IN A HIGHER STRATUS.
A STRATA THAT WOULD ALLOW ONE TO GAIN THE EDUCATION THAT THE KILLER OBVIOUSLY POSSESSES...
...AND BECAUSE OF SOME UNFORTUNATE INCIDENTS SANK INTO THE LOWER STRATUS.
OR, FOR WHATEVER REASON, HE NOW CHOOSES TO LIVE IN THIS LOWER STRATUS.
STOP SAYING STRATUS.
SOMEONE WHO- HE- HE DEFINITELY GAINED THE CONFIDENCE OF HIS INTENDED.
White
2/23/37
3-6 Days

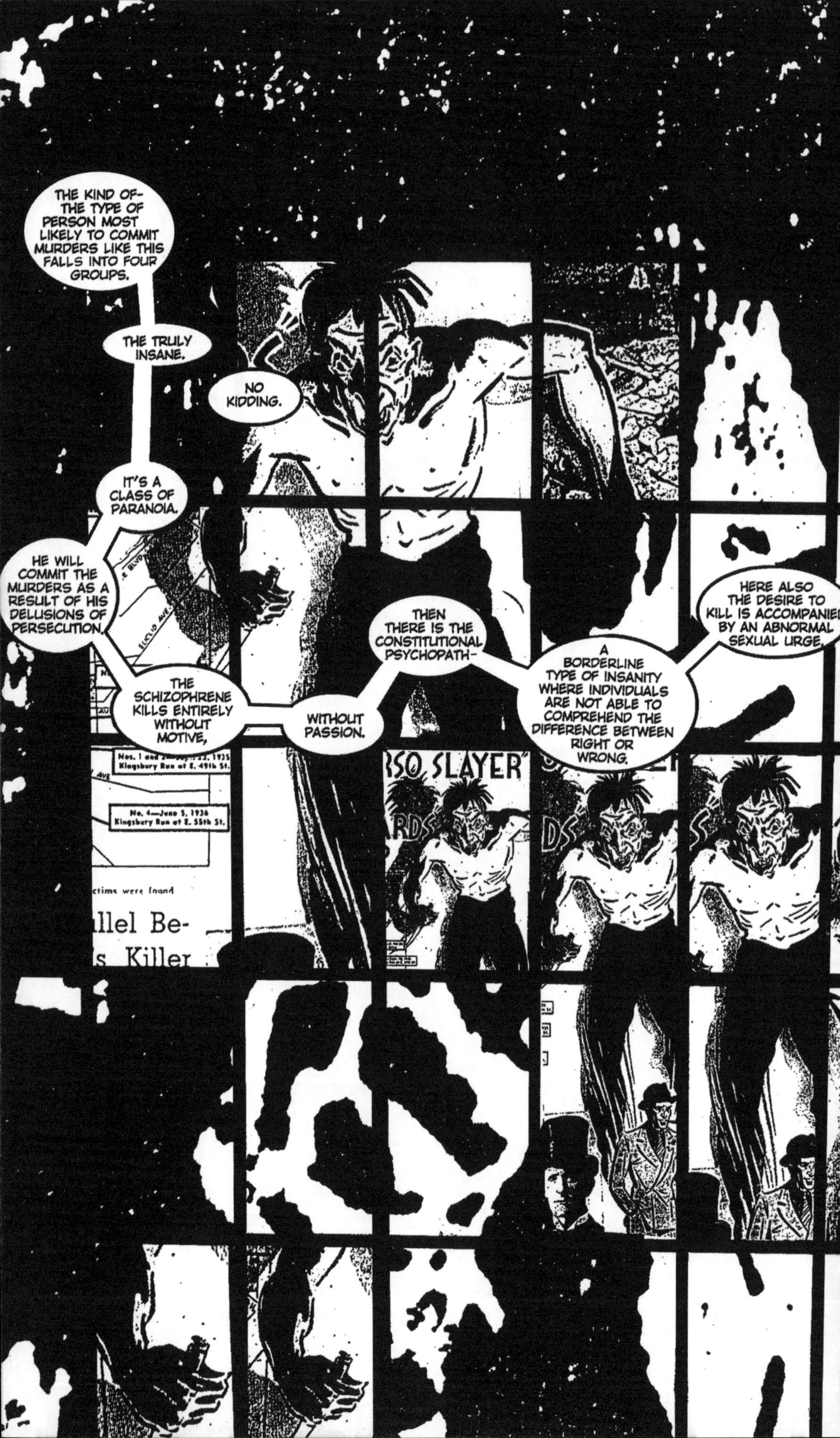
THE KIND OF- THE TYPE OF PERSON MOST LIKELY TO COMMIT MURDERS LIKE THIS FALLS INTO FOUR GROUPS.
THE TRULY INSANE.
NO KIDDING.
IT'S A CLASS OF PARANOIA.
HE WILL COMMIT THE MURDERS AS A RESULT OF HIS DELUSIONS OF PERSECUTION.
THE SCHIZOPHRENE KILLS ENTIRELY WITHOUT MOTIVE,
WITHOUT PASSION.
THEN THERE IS THE CONSTITUTIONAL PSYCHOPATH-
A BORDERLINE TYPE OF INSANITY WHERE INDIVIDUALS ARE NOT ABLE TO COMPREHEND THE DIFFERENCE BETWEEN RIGHT OR WRONG.
HERE ALSO THE DESIRE TO KILL IS ACCOMPANIED BY AN ABNORMAL SEXUAL URGE.
EUCLID AVE
Kingsbury Run at E. 49th St.
No. 4—June 5, 1936
Kingsbury Run at E. 55th St.
ctims were found
ullel Be-
s Killer
SO SLAYER"

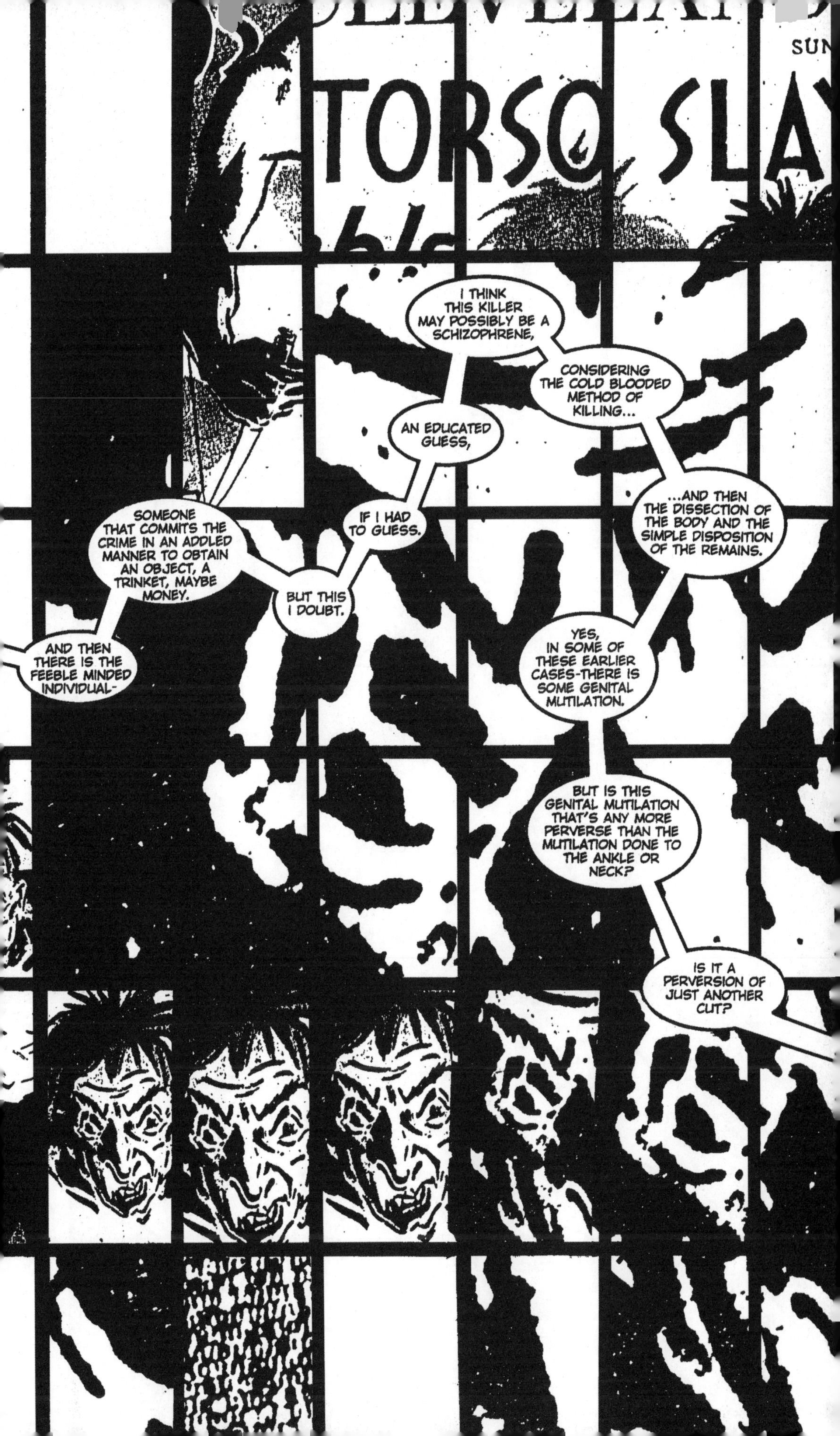
SUN
TORSO
I THINK THIS KILLER MAY POSSIBLY BE A SCHIZOPHRENE,
CONSIDERING THE COLD BLOODED METHOD OF KILLING...
...AND THEN THE DISSECTION OF THE BODY AND THE SIMPLE DISPOSITION OF THE REMAINS.
YES, IN SOME OF THESE EARLIER CASES-THERE IS SOME GENITAL MUTILATION.
BUT IS THIS GENITAL MUTILATION THAT'S ANY MORE PERVERSE THAN THE MUTILATION DONE TO THE ANKLE OR NECK?
IS IT A PERVERSION OF JUST ANOTHER CUT?
AN EDUCATED GUESS,
IF I HAD TO GUESS.
BUT THIS I DOUBT.
SOMEONE THAT COMMITS THE CRIME IN AN ADDLED MANNER TO OBTAIN AN OBJECT, A TRINKET, MAYBE MONEY.
AND THEN THERE IS THE FEEBLE MINDED INDIVIDUAL-

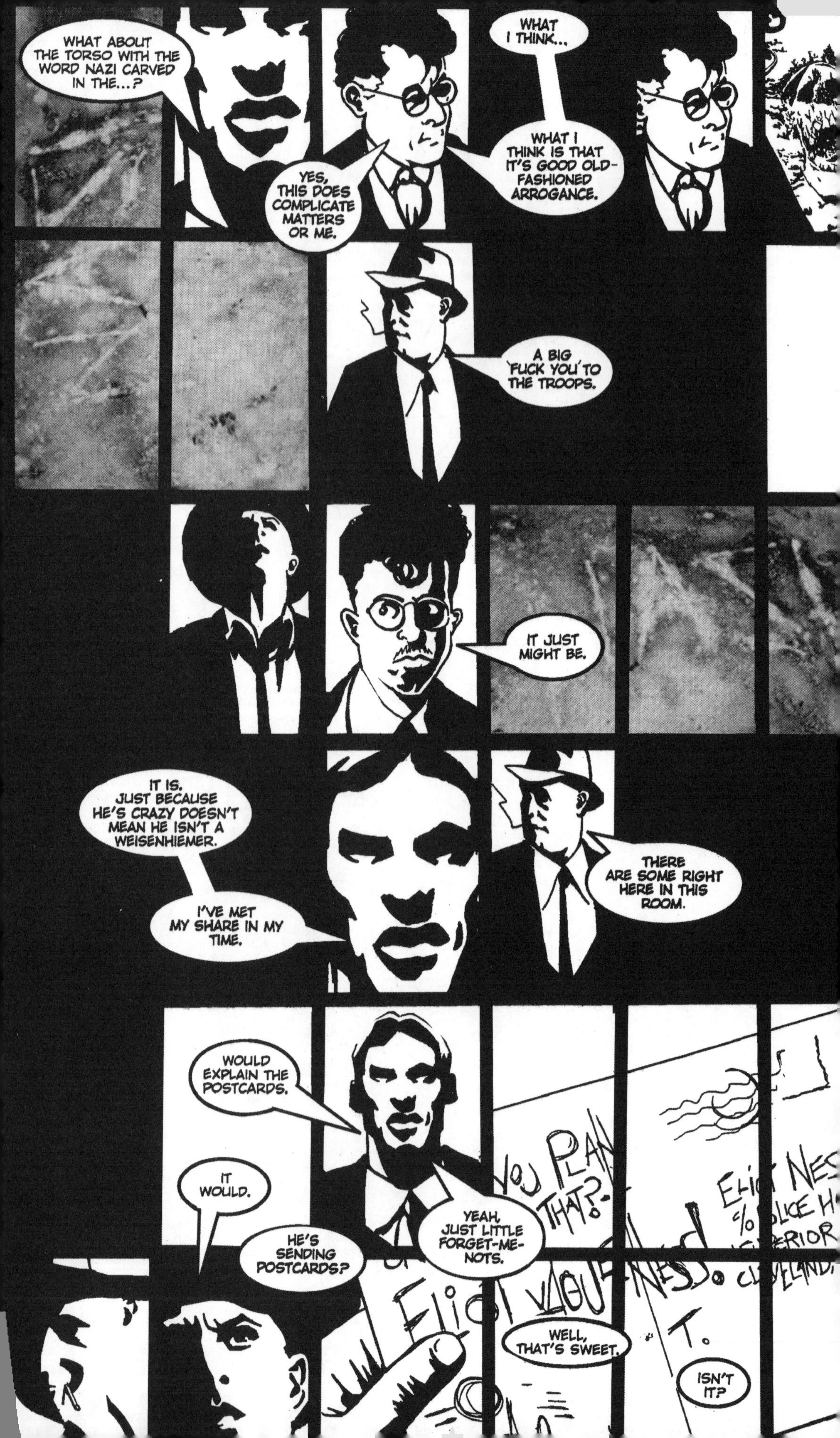
WHAT ABOUT THE TORSO WITH THE WORD NAZI CARVED IN THE...?
YES, THIS DOES COMPLICATE MATTERS OR ME.
WHAT I THINK...
WHAT I THINK IS THAT IT'S GOOD OLD-FASHIONED ARROGANCE.
A BIG 'FUCK YOU' TO THE TROOPS.
IT JUST MIGHT BE.
IT IS. JUST BECAUSE HE'S CRAZY DOESN'T MEAN HE ISN'T A WEISENHIEMER.
I'VE MET MY SHARE IN MY TIME.
THERE ARE SOME RIGHT HERE IN THIS ROOM.
WOULD EXPLAIN THE POSTCARDS.
IT WOULD.
HE'S SENDING POSTCARDS?
YEAH, JUST LITTLE FORGET-ME-NOTS.
YOU PLAN THAT?
WELL, THAT'S SWEET.
ISN'T IT?

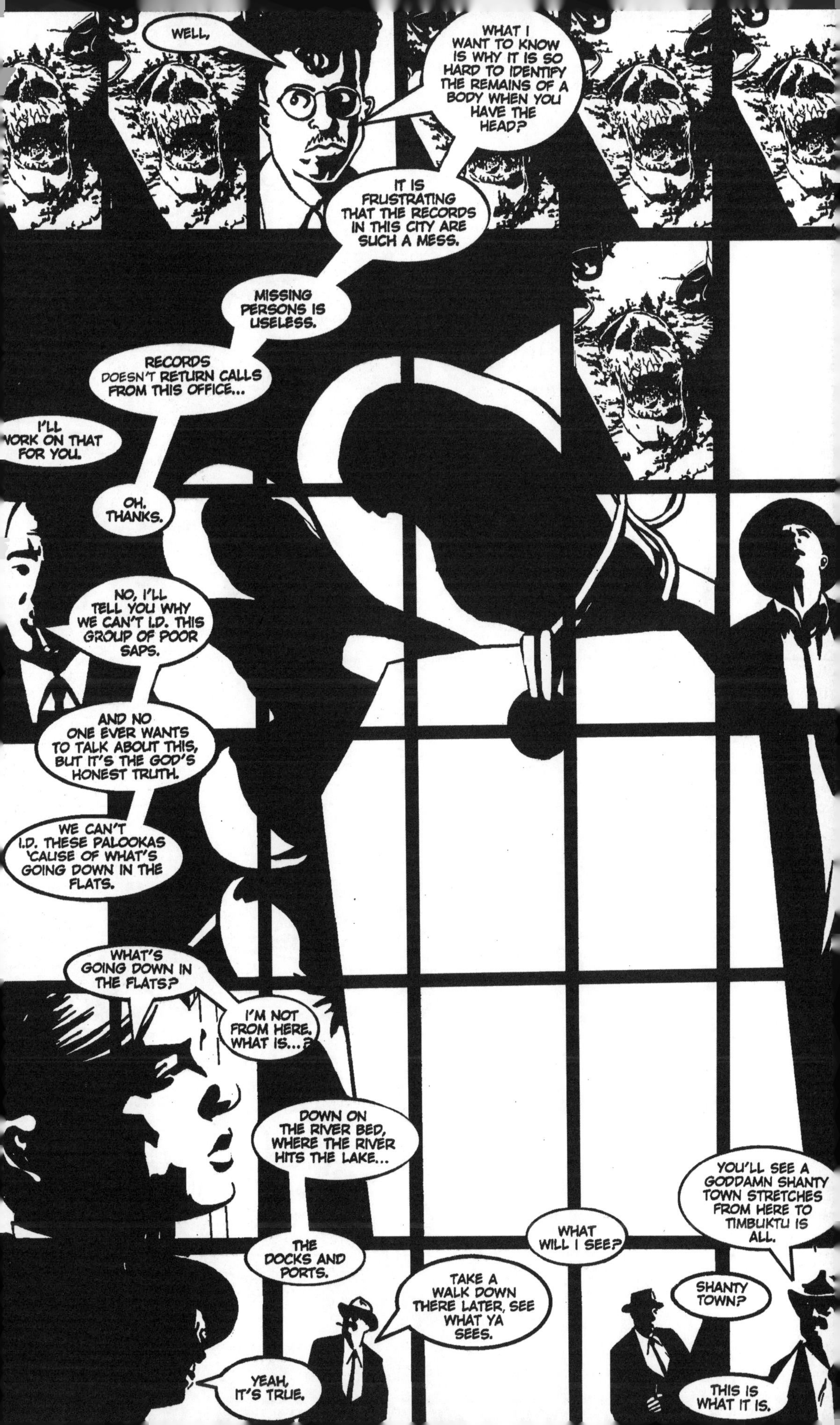
WELL,
WHAT I WANT TO KNOW IS WHY IT IS SO HARD TO IDENTIFY THE REMAINS OF A BODY WHEN YOU HAVE THE HEAD?
IT IS FRUSTRATING THAT THE RECORDS IN THIS CITY ARE SUCH A MESS.
MISSING PERSONS IS USELESS.
RECORDS DOESN'T RETURN CALLS FROM THIS OFFICE...
I'LL WORK ON THAT FOR YOU.
OH. THANKS.
NO, I'LL TELL YOU WHY WE CAN'T I.D. THIS GROUP OF POOR SAPS.
AND NO ONE EVER WANTS TO TALK ABOUT THIS, BUT IT'S THE GOD'S HONEST TRUTH.
WE CAN'T I.D. THESE PALOOKAS 'CAUSE OF WHAT'S GOING DOWN IN THE FLATS.
WHAT'S GOING DOWN IN THE FLATS?
I'M NOT FROM HERE. WHAT IS...?
DOWN ON THE RIVER BED, WHERE THE RIVER HITS THE LAKE...
THE DOCKS AND PORTS.
YEAH, IT'S TRUE.
TAKE A WALK DOWN THERE LATER, SEE WHAT YA SEES.
WHAT WILL I SEE?
YOU'LL SEE A GODDAMN SHANTY TOWN STRETCHES FROM HERE TO TIMBUKTU IS ALL.
SHANTY TOWN?
THIS IS WHAT IT IS.

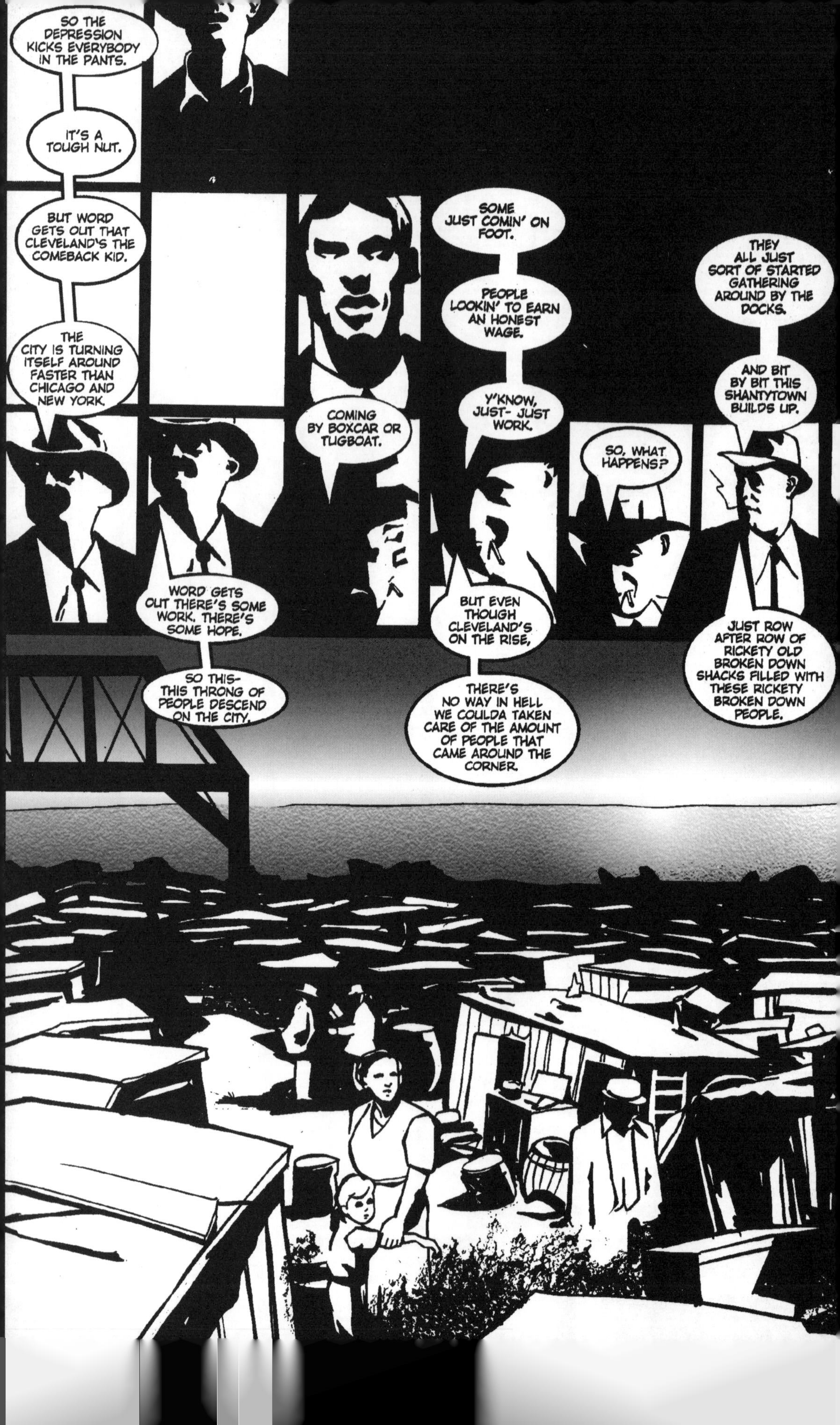

SO THE DEPRESSION KICKS EVERYBODY IN THE PANTS.
IT'S A TOUGH NUT.
BUT WORD GETS OUT THAT CLEVELAND'S THE COMEBACK KID.
THE CITY IS TURNING ITSELF AROUND FASTER THAN CHICAGO AND NEW YORK.
WORD GETS OUT THERE'S SOME WORK. THERE'S SOME HOPE.
SO THIS- THIS THRONG OF PEOPLE DESCEND ON THE CITY.
COMING BY BOXCAR OR TUGBOAT.
SOME JUST COMIN' ON FOOT.
PEOPLE LOOKIN' TO EARN AN HONEST WAGE.
Y'KNOW, JUST- JUST WORK.
BUT EVEN THOUGH CLEVELAND'S ON THE RISE,
THERE'S NO WAY IN HELL WE COULDA TAKEN CARE OF THE AMOUNT OF PEOPLE THAT CAME AROUND THE CORNER.
SO, WHAT HAPPENS?
THEY ALL JUST SORT OF STARTED GATHERING AROUND BY THE DOCKS.
AND BIT BY BIT THIS SHANTYTOWN BUILDS UP.
JUST ROW AFTER ROW OF RICKETY OLD BROKEN DOWN SHACKS FILLED WITH THESE RICKETY BROKEN DOWN PEOPLE.

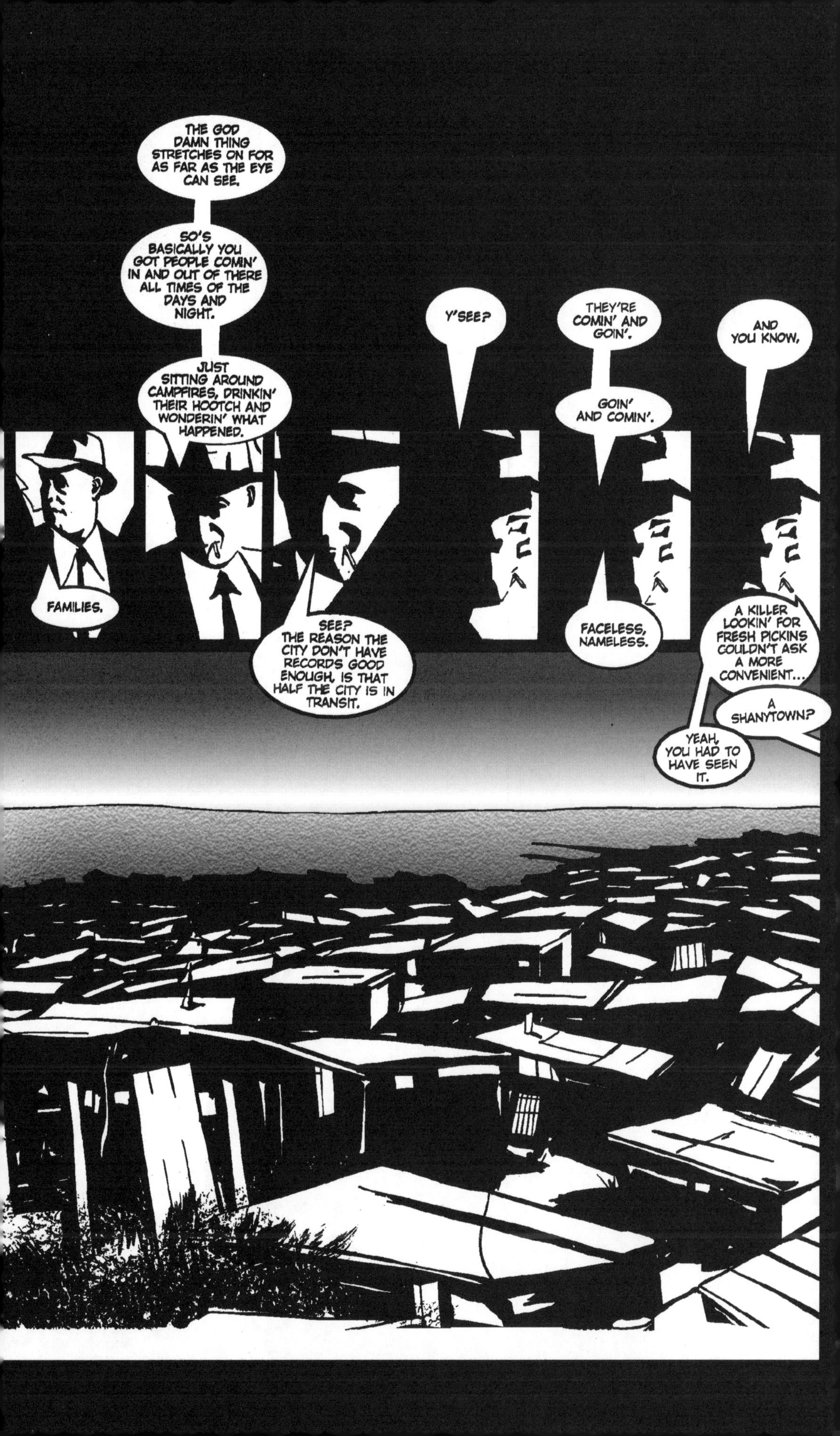
THE GOD DAMN THING STRETCHES ON FOR AS FAR AS THE EYE CAN SEE.
SO'S BASICALLY YOU GOT PEOPLE COMIN' IN AND OUT OF THERE ALL TIMES OF THE DAYS AND NIGHT.
JUST SITTING AROUND CAMPFIRES, DRINKIN' THEIR HOOTCH AND WONDERIN' WHAT HAPPENED.
FAMILIES.
SEE? THE REASON THE CITY DON'T HAVE RECORDS GOOD ENOUGH, IS THAT HALF THE CITY IS IN TRANSIT.
Y'SEE?
THEY'RE COMIN' AND GOIN'.
GOIN' AND COMIN'.
FACELESS, NAMELESS.
AND YOU KNOW,
A KILLER LOOKIN' FOR FRESH PICKINS COULDN'T ASK A MORE CONVENIENT...
A SHANYTOWN?
YEAH, YOU HAD TO HAVE SEEN IT.

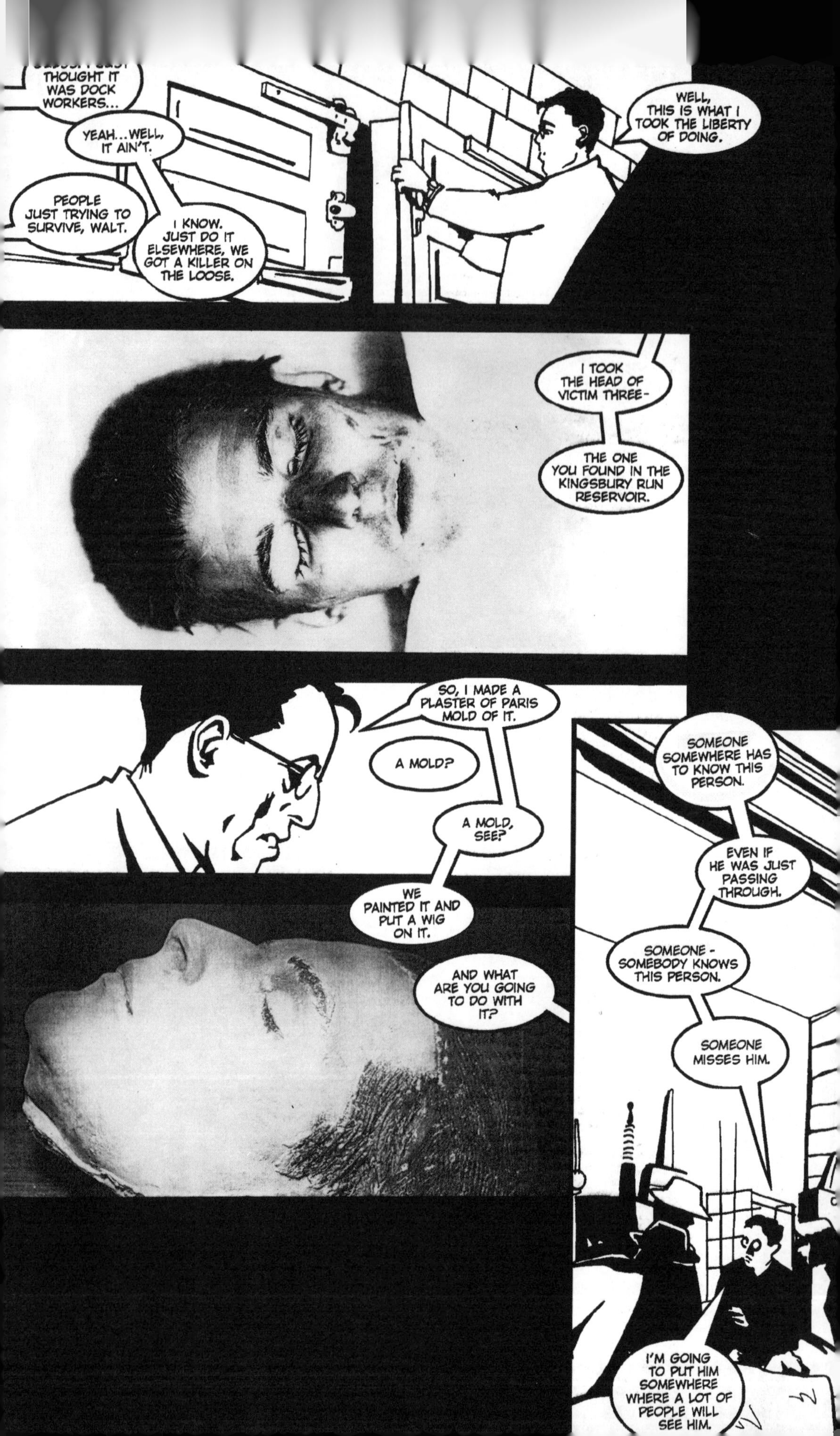
THOUGHT IT WAS DOCK WORKERS...
YEAH...WELL, IT AIN'T.
PEOPLE JUST TRYING TO SURVIVE, WALT.
I KNOW. JUST DO IT ELSEWHERE, WE GOT A KILLER ON THE LOOSE.
WELL, THIS IS WHAT I TOOK THE LIBERTY OF DOING.
I TOOK THE HEAD OF VICTIM THREE-
THE ONE YOU FOUND IN THE KINGSBURY RUN RESERVOIR.
SO, I MADE A PLASTER OF PARIS MOLD OF IT.
A MOLD?
A MOLD, SEE?
WE PAINTED IT AND PUT A WIG ON IT.
AND WHAT ARE YOU GOING TO DO WITH IT?
SOMEONE SOMEWHERE HAS TO KNOW THIS PERSON.
EVEN IF HE WAS JUST PASSING THROUGH.
SOMEONE - SOMEBODY KNOWS THIS PERSON.
SOMEONE MISSES HIM.
I'M GOING TO PUT HIM SOMEWHERE WHERE A LOT OF PEOPLE WILL SEE HIM.

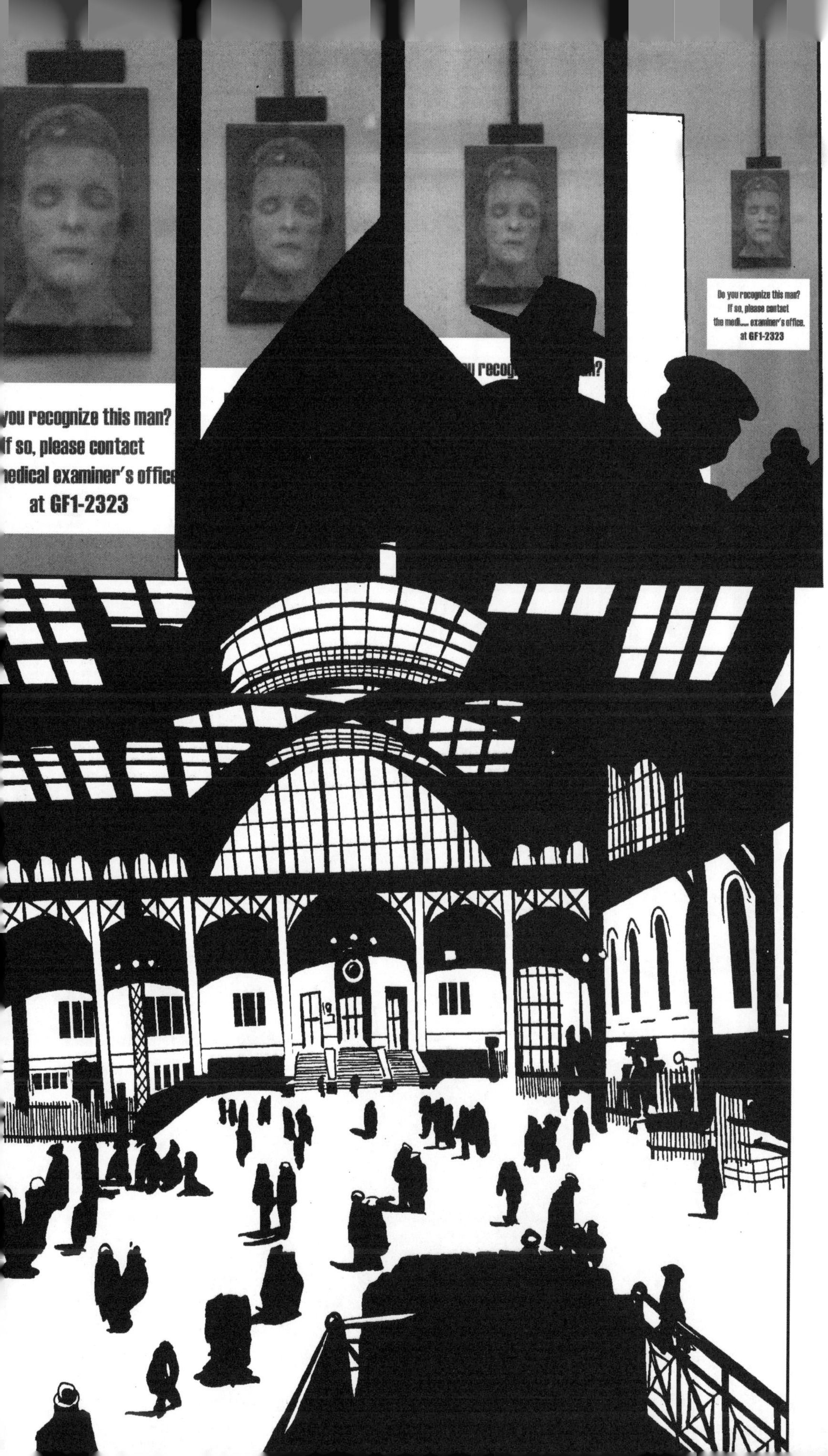
you recognize this man?
f so, please contact
nedical examiner's offic
at GF1-2323
Do you recognize this man?
If so, please contact
the medi.... examiner's office.
at GF1-2323

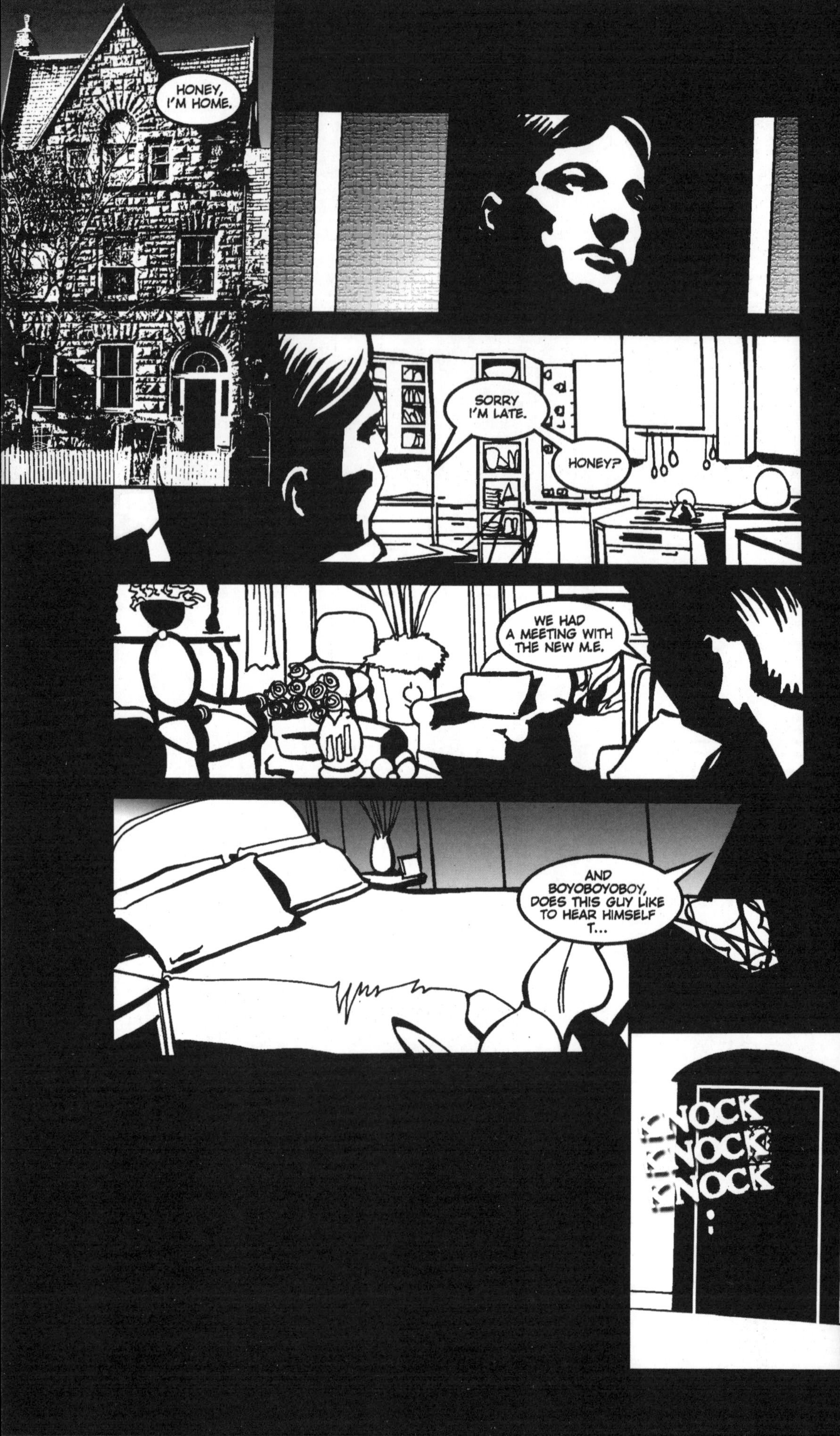
HONEY, I'M HOME.
SORRY I'M LATE.
HONEY?
WE HAD A MEETING WITH THE NEW M.E.
AND BOYOBOYOYOBOY, DOES THIS GUY LIKE TO HEAR HIMSELF T...
KNOCK
KNOCK
KNOCK

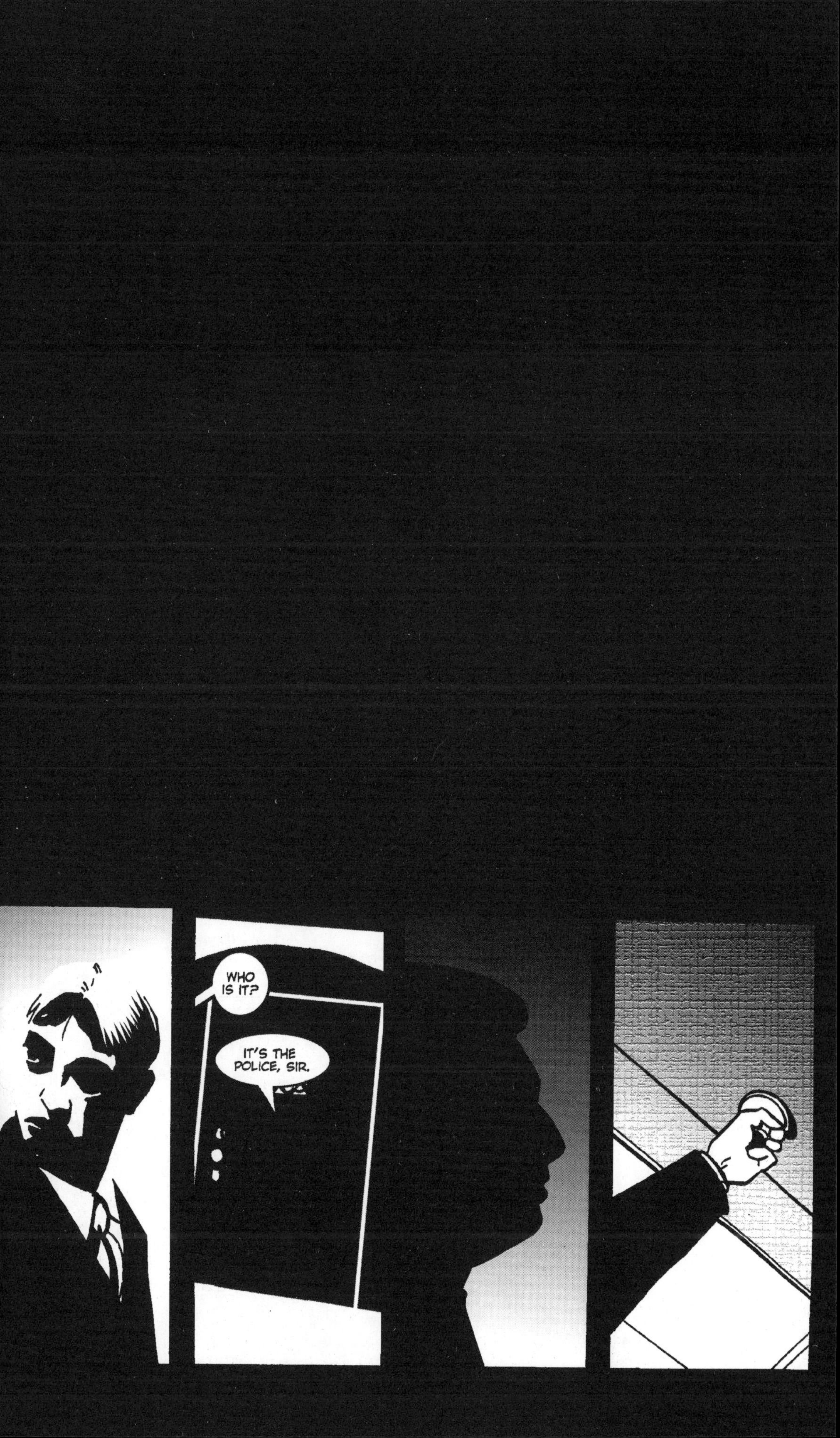
WHO IS IT?
IT'S THE POLICE, SIR.

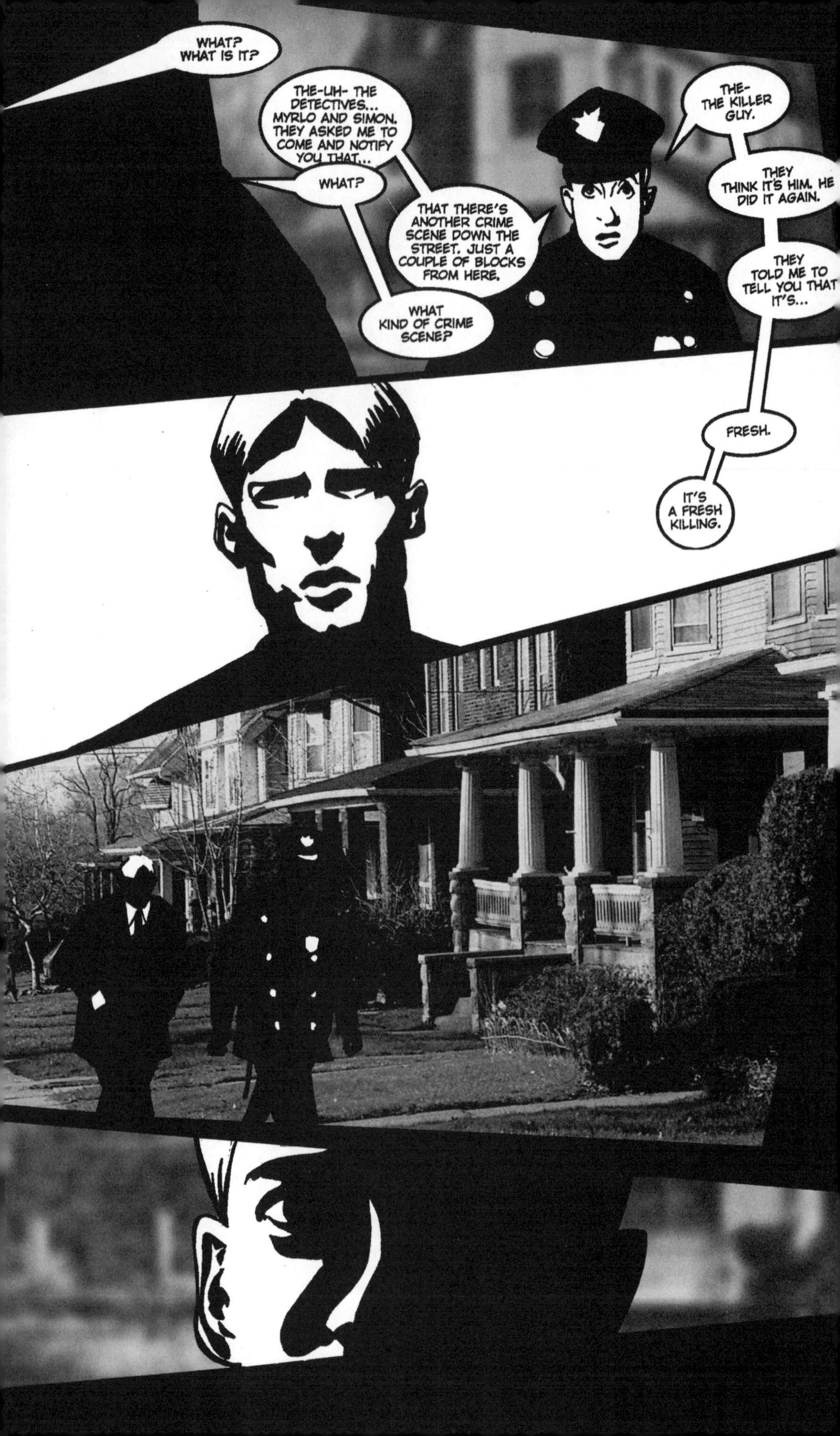
WHAT? WHAT IS IT?
THE-UH- THE DETECTIVES... MYRLO AND SIMON. THEY ASKED ME TO COME AND NOTIFY YOU THAT...
WHAT?
THAT THERE'S ANOTHER CRIME SCENE DOWN THE STREET. JUST A COUPLE OF BLOCKS FROM HERE.
WHAT KIND OF CRIME SCENE?
THE- THE KILLER GUY.
THEY THINK IT'S HIM. HE DID IT AGAIN.
THEY TOLD ME TO TELL YOU THAT IT'S...
FRESH.
IT'S A FRESH KILLING.

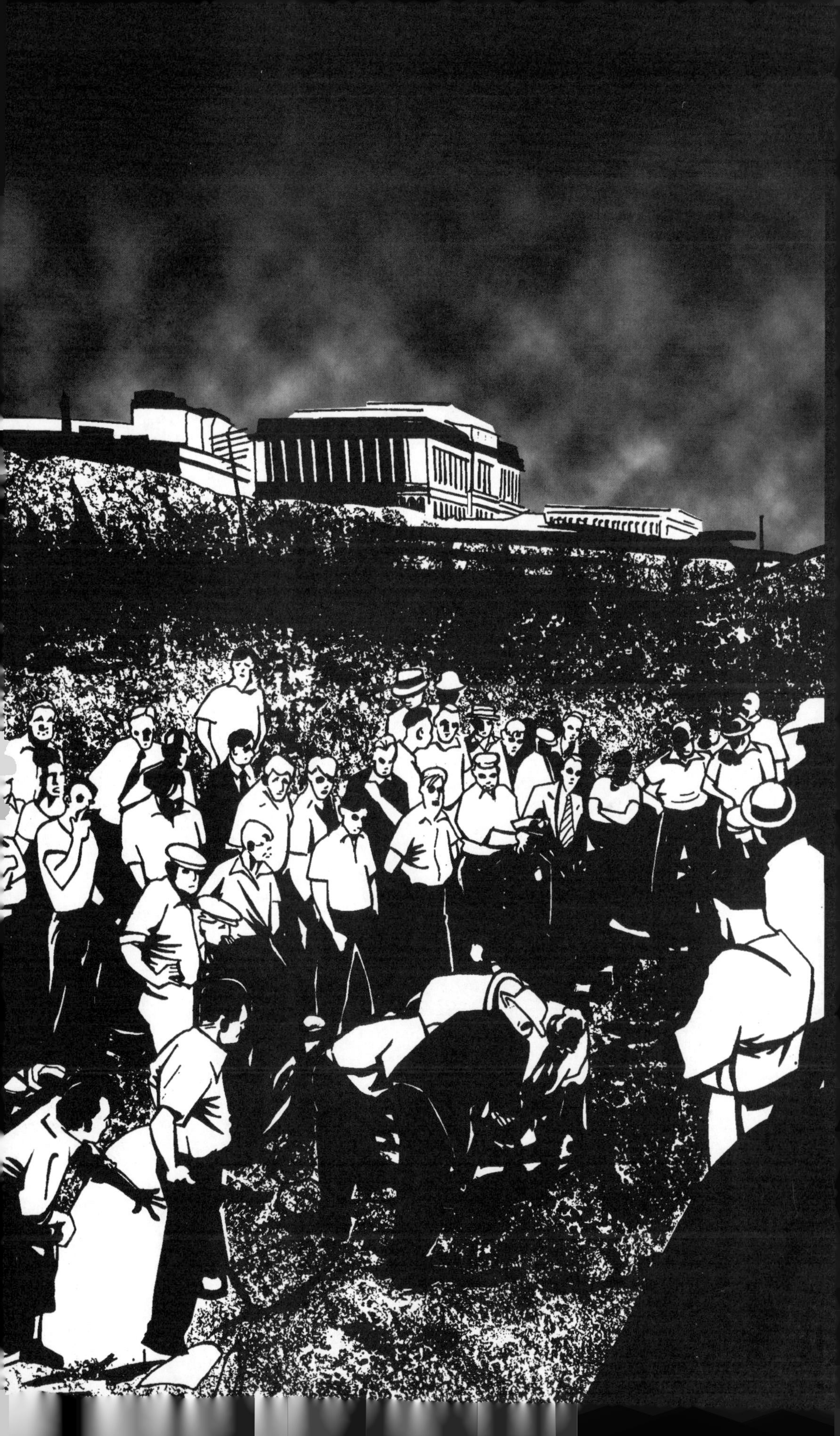

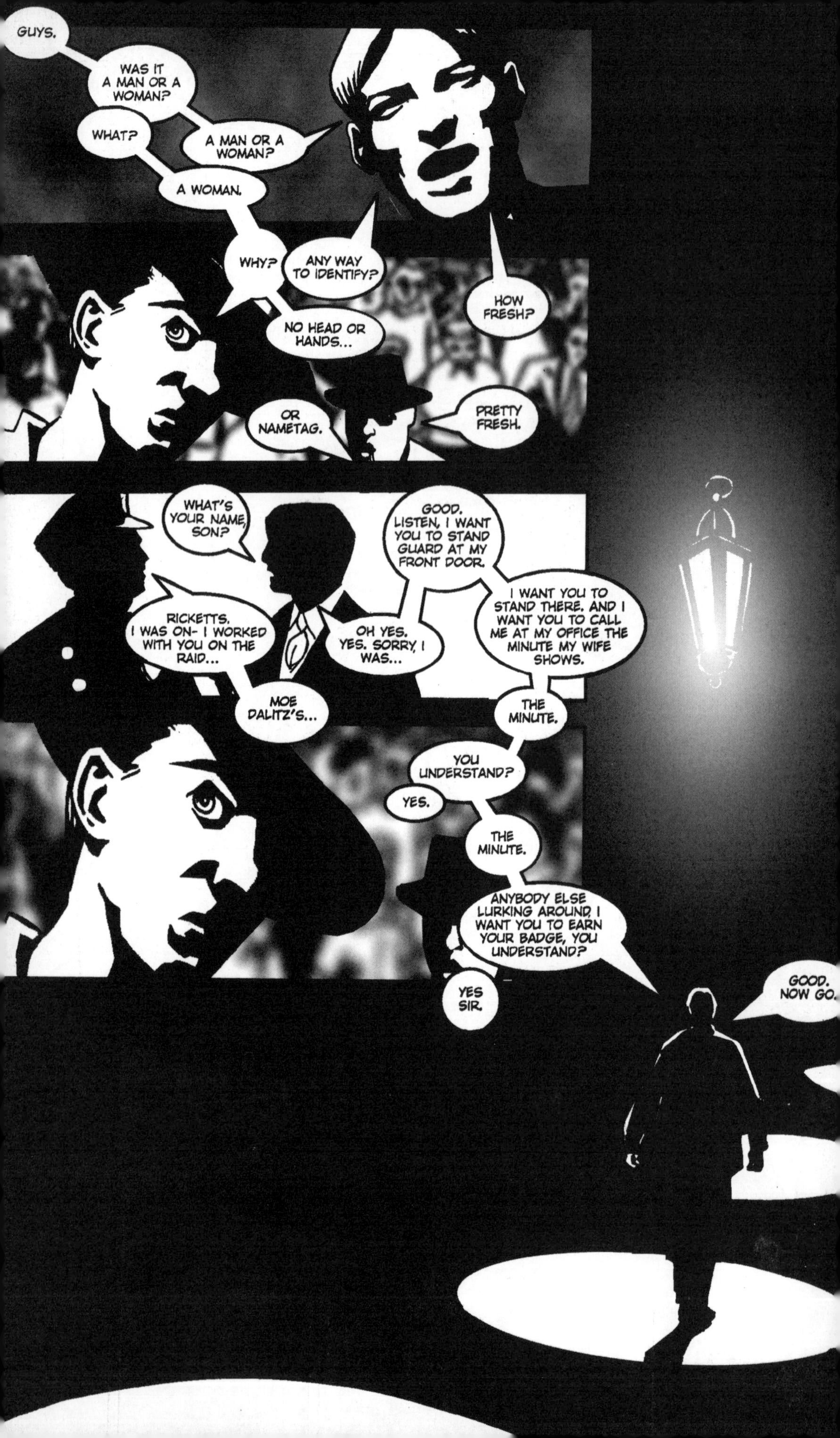
GUYS.
WAS IT A MAN OR A WOMAN?
WHAT?
A MAN OR A WOMAN?
A WOMAN.
WHY?
ANY WAY TO IDENTIFY?
NO HEAD OR HANDS...
HOW FRESH?
OR NAMETAG.
PRETTY FRESH.
WHAT'S YOUR NAME, SON?
RICKETTS. I WAS ON- I WORKED WITH YOU ON THE RAID...
MOE DALITZ'S...
OH YES. YES. SORRY, I WAS...
GOOD. LISTEN, I WANT YOU TO STAND GUARD AT MY FRONT DOOR.
I WANT YOU TO STAND THERE. AND I WANT YOU TO CALL ME AT MY OFFICE THE MINUTE MY WIFE SHOWS.
THE MINUTE.
YOU UNDERSTAND?
YES.
THE MINUTE.
ANYBODY ELSE LURKING AROUND, I WANT YOU TO EARN YOUR BADGE, YOU UNDERSTAND?
YES SIR.
GOOD. NOW GO.

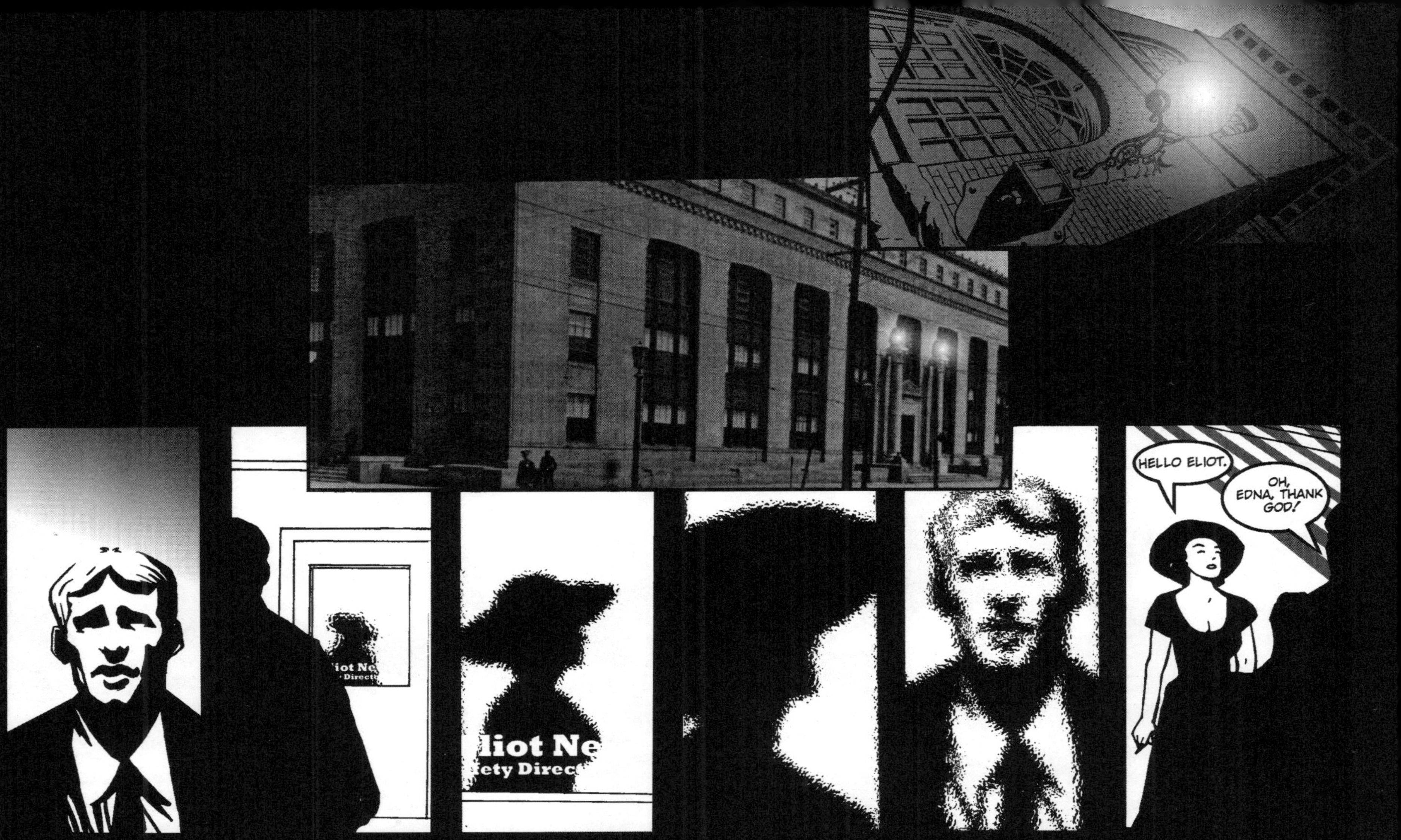
liot Ne
ty Direct
liot Ne
fety Direc
HELLO ELIOT.
OH, EDNA, THANK GOD!

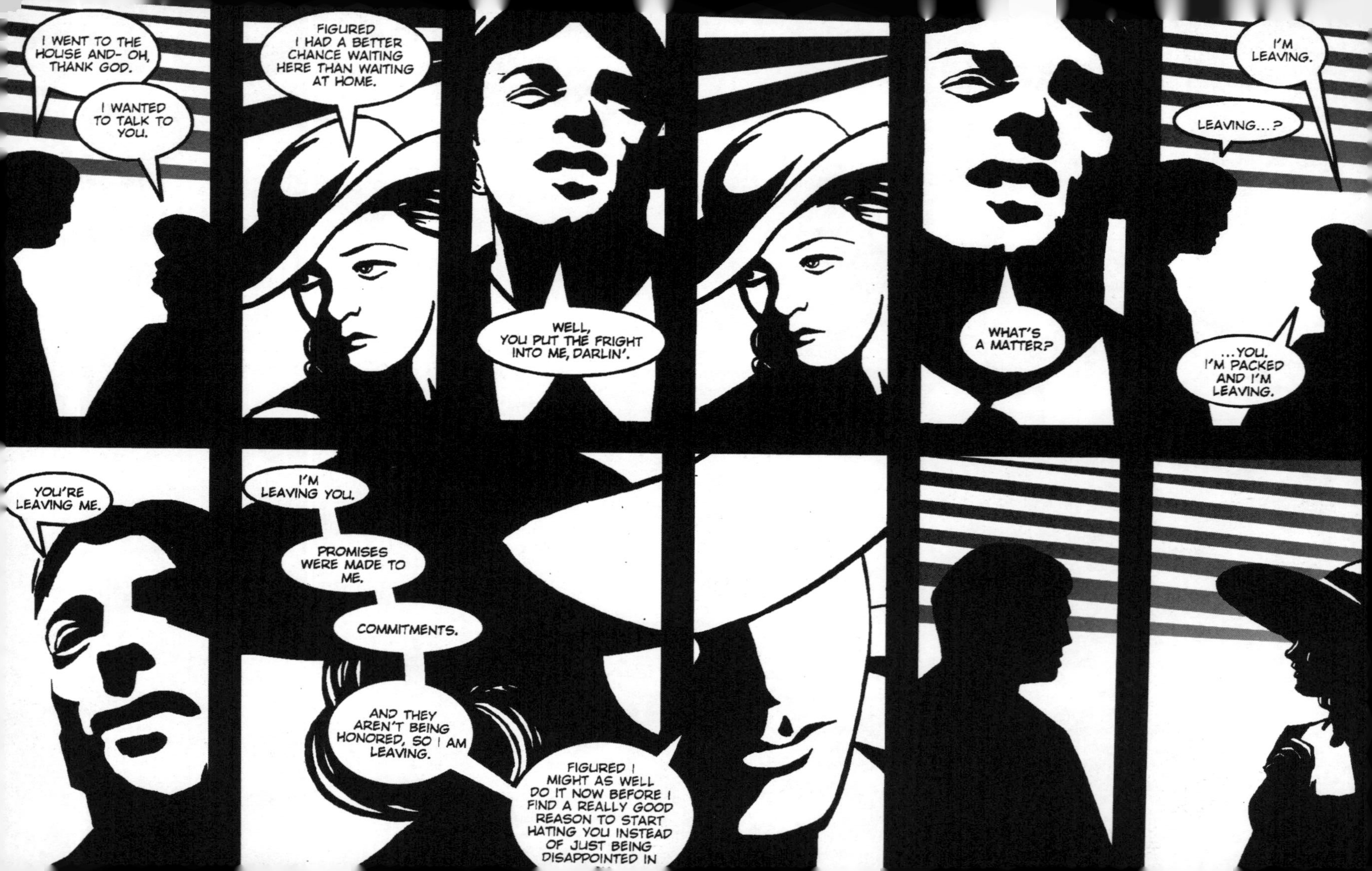
I WENT TO THE HOUSE AND- OH, THANK GOD.
I WANTED TO TALK TO YOU.
FIGURED I HAD A BETTER CHANCE WAITING HERE THAN WAITING AT HOME.
WELL, YOU PUT THE FRIGHT INTO ME, DARLIN'.
WHAT'S A MATTER?
I'M LEAVING.
LEAVING...?
...YOU. I'M PACKED AND I'M LEAVING.
YOU'RE LEAVING ME.
I'M LEAVING YOU.
PROMISES WERE MADE TO ME.
COMMITMENTS.
AND THEY AREN'T BEING HONORED, SO I AM LEAVING.
FIGURED I MIGHT AS WELL DO IT NOW BEFORE I FIND A REALLY GOOD REASON TO START HATING YOU INSTEAD OF JUST BEING DISAPPOINTED IN

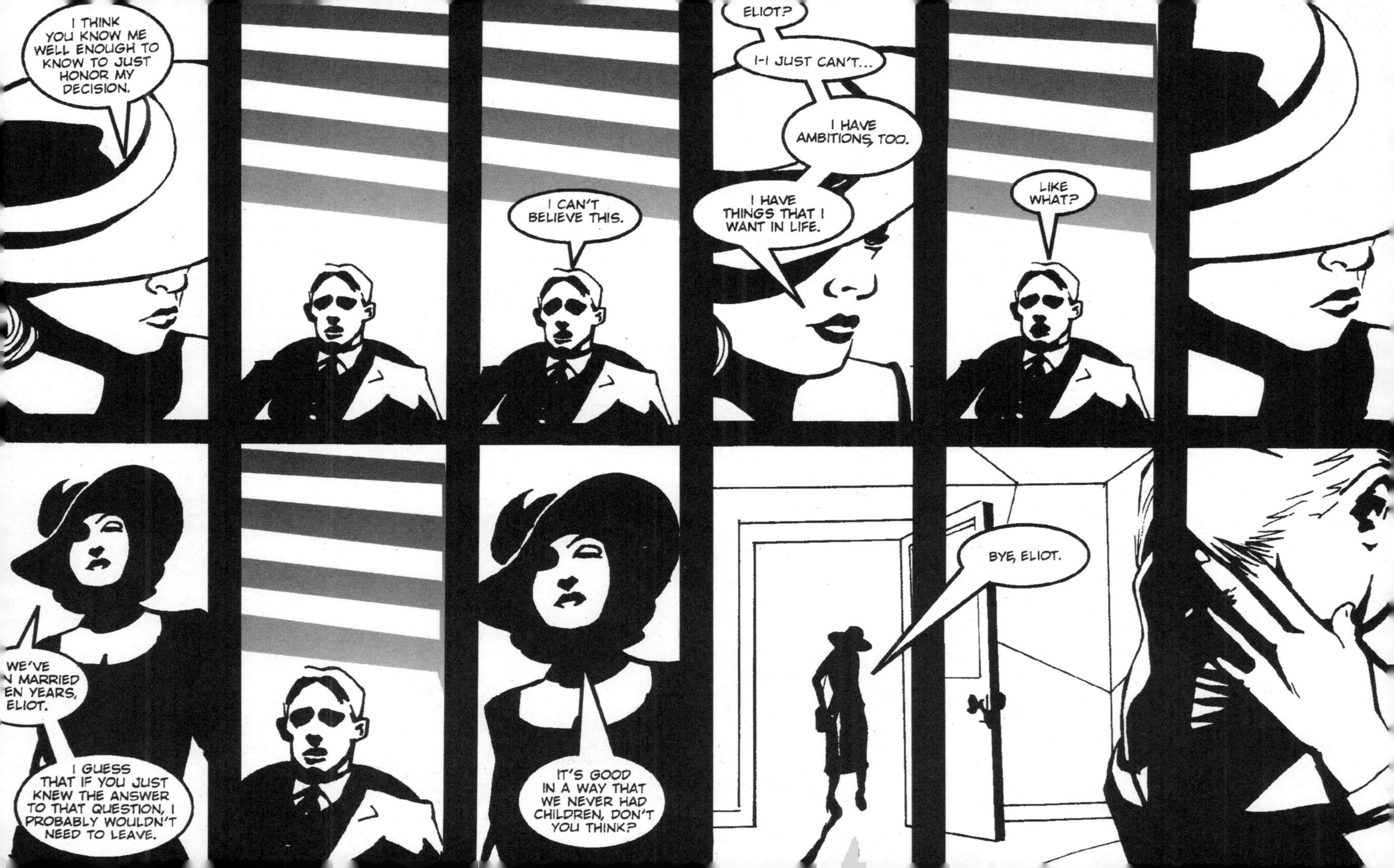
I THINK YOU KNOW ME WELL ENOUGH TO KNOW TO JUST HONOR MY DECISION.
I CAN'T BELIEVE THIS.
ELIOT?
I-I JUST CAN'T...
I HAVE AMBITIONS, TOO.
I HAVE THINGS THAT I WANT IN LIFE.
LIKE WHAT?
WE'VE
MARRIED
EN YEARS,
ELIOT.
I GUESS THAT IF YOU JUST KNEW THE ANSWER TO THAT QUESTION, I PROBABLY WOULDN'T NEED TO LEAVE.
IT'S GOOD IN A WAY THAT WE NEVER HAD CHILDREN, DON'T YOU THINK?
BYE, ELIOT.

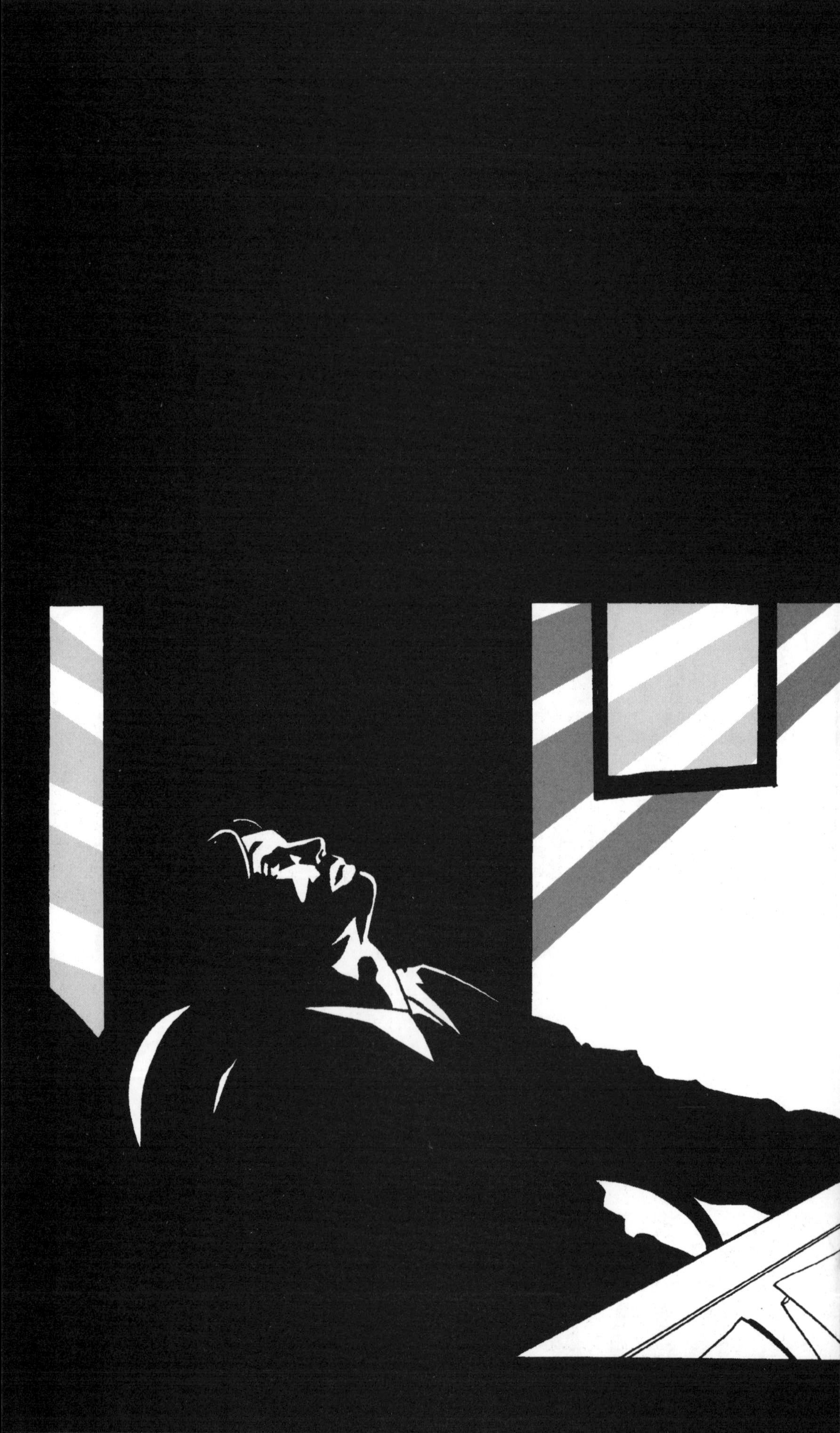

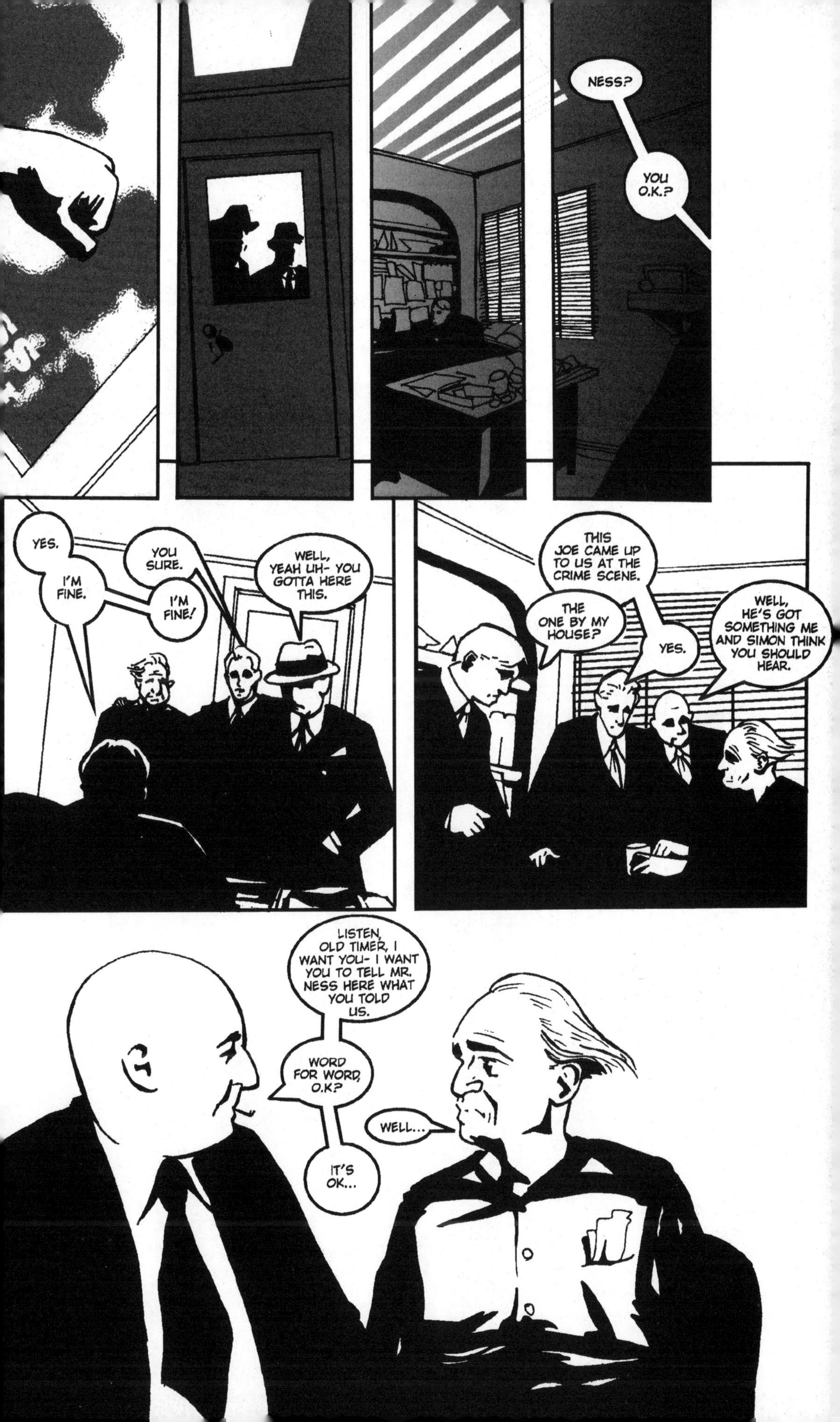
NESS?
YOU O.K.?
YES.
I'M FINE.
YOU SURE.
I'M FINE!
WELL, YEAH UH- YOU GOTTA HERE THIS.
THIS JOE CAME UP TO US AT THE CRIME SCENE.
THE ONE BY MY HOUSE?
YES.
WELL, HE'S GOT SOMETHING ME AND SIMON THINK YOU SHOULD HEAR.
LISTEN, OLD TIMER, I WANT YOU- I WANT YOU TO TELL MR. NESS HERE WHAT YOU TOLD US.
WORD FOR WORD, O.K?
IT'S OK...
WELL...

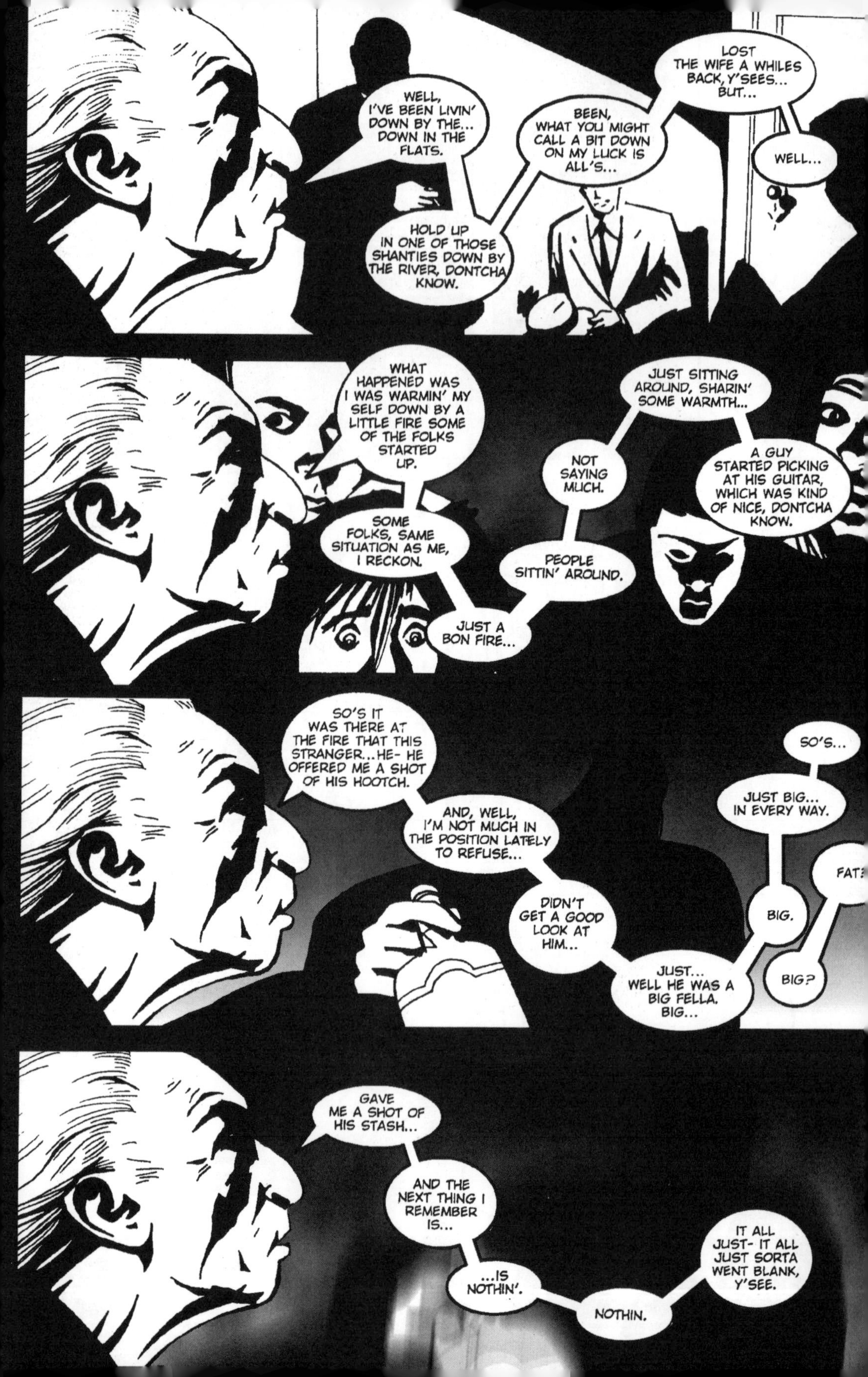
WELL, I'VE BEEN LIVIN' DOWN BY THE... DOWN IN THE FLATS.
HOLD UP IN ONE OF THOSE SHANTIES DOWN BY THE RIVER, DONTCHA KNOW.
BEEN, WHAT YOU MIGHT CALL A BIT DOWN ON MY LUCK IS ALL'S...
LOST THE WIFE A WHILES BACK, Y'SEES... BUT...
WELL...
WHAT HAPPENED WAS I WAS WARMIN' MY SELF DOWN BY A LITTLE FIRE SOME OF THE FOLKS STARTED UP.
SOME FOLKS, SAME SITUATION AS ME, I RECKON.
JUST A BON FIRE...
PEOPLE SITTIN' AROUND.
NOT SAYING MUCH.
JUST SITTING AROUND, SHARIN' SOME WARMTH...
A GUY STARTED PICKING AT HIS GUITAR, WHICH WAS KIND OF NICE, DONTCHA KNOW.
SO'S IT WAS THERE AT THE FIRE THAT THIS STRANGER...HE- HE OFFERED ME A SHOT OF HIS HOOTCH.
AND, WELL, I'M NOT MUCH IN THE POSITION LATELY TO REFUSE...
DIDN'T GET A GOOD LOOK AT HIM...
JUST... WELL HE WAS A BIG FELLA. BIG...
BIG?
BIG.
JUST BIG... IN EVERY WAY.
SO'S...
GAVE ME A SHOT OF HIS STASH...
AND THE NEXT THING I REMEMBER IS...
...IS NOTHIN'.
NOTHIN.
IT ALL JUST- IT ALL JUST SORTA WENT BLANK, Y'SEE.

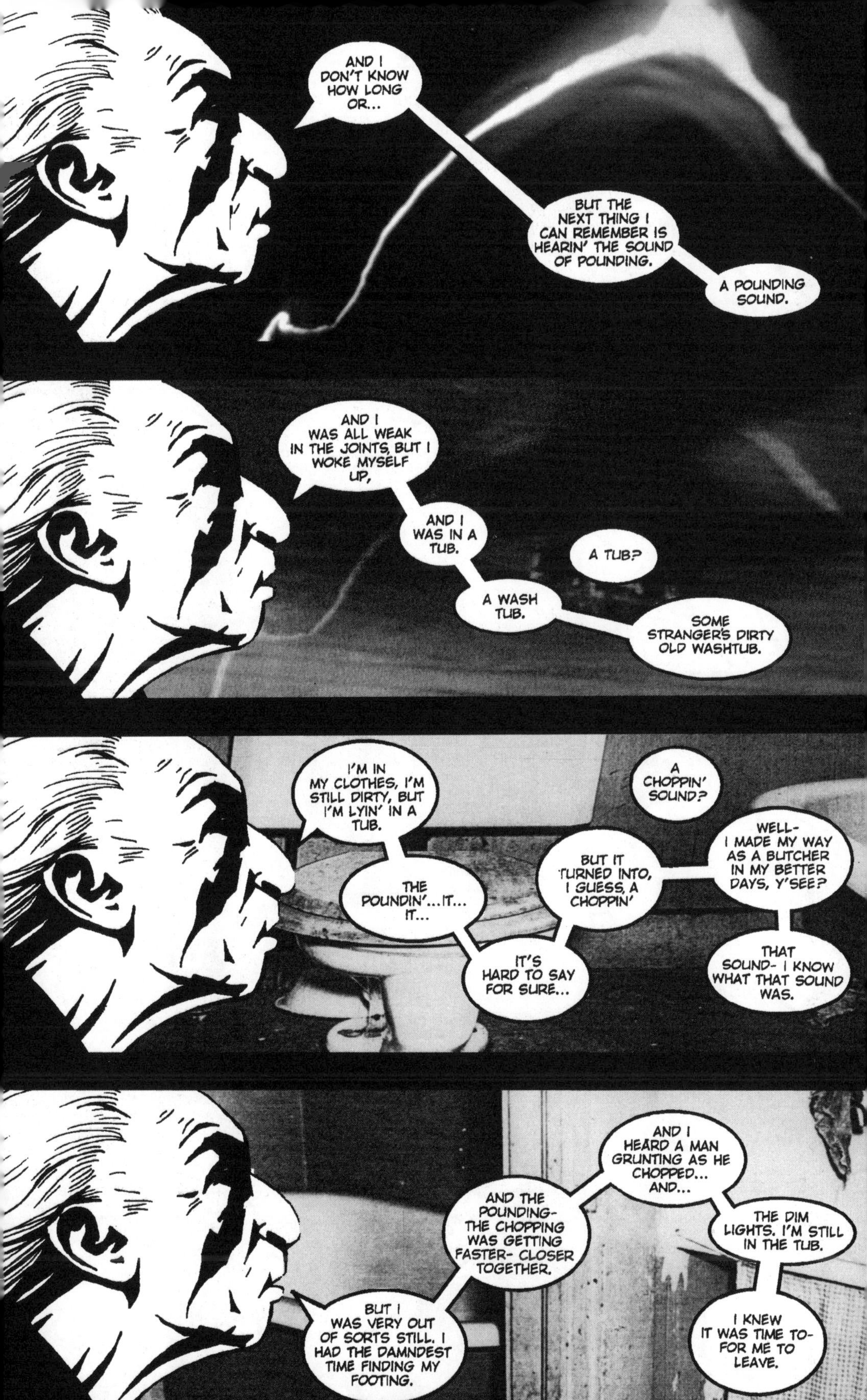
AND I DON'T KNOW HOW LONG OR...
BUT THE NEXT THING I CAN REMEMBER IS HEARIN' THE SOUND OF POUNDING.
A POUNDING SOUND.
AND I WAS ALL WEAK IN THE JOINTS, BUT I WOKE MYSELF UP,
AND I WAS IN A TUB.
A TUB?
A WASH TUB.
SOME STRANGER'S DIRTY OLD WASHTUB.
I'M IN MY CLOTHES, I'M STILL DIRTY, BUT I'M LYIN' IN A TUB.
THE POUNDIN'...IT... IT...
IT'S HARD TO SAY FOR SURE...
BUT IT TURNED INTO, I GUESS, A CHOPPIN'
A CHOPPIN' SOUND?
WELL- I MADE MY WAY AS A BUTCHER IN MY BETTER DAYS, Y'SEE?
THAT SOUND- I KNOW WHAT THAT SOUND WAS.
BUT I WAS VERY OUT OF SORTS STILL. I HAD THE DAMNDEST TIME FINDING MY FOOTING.
AND THE POUNDING- THE CHOPPING WAS GETTING FASTER- CLOSER TOGETHER.
AND I HEARD A MAN GRUNTING AS HE CHOPPED... AND...
THE DIM LIGHTS. I'M STILL IN THE TUB.
I KNEW IT WAS TIME TO- FOR ME TO LEAVE.

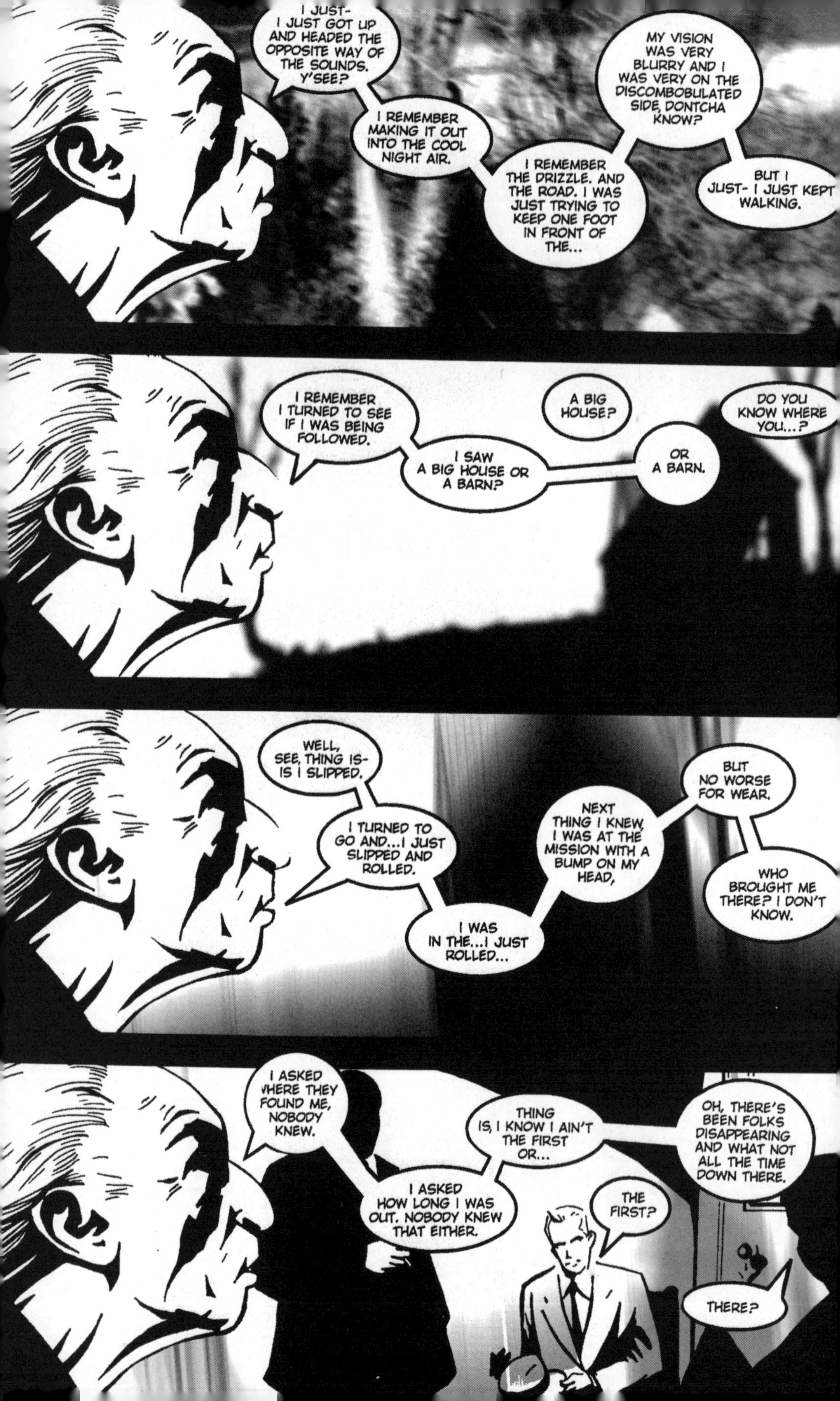
I JUST- I JUST GOT UP AND HEADED THE OPPOSITE WAY OF THE SOUNDS. Y'SEE?
I REMEMBER MAKING IT OUT INTO THE COOL NIGHT AIR.
I REMEMBER THE DRIZZLE. AND THE ROAD. I WAS JUST TRYING TO KEEP ONE FOOT IN FRONT OF THE...
MY VISION WAS VERY BLURRY AND I WAS VERY ON THE DISCOMBOBULATED SIDE, DONTCHA KNOW?
BUT I JUST- I JUST KEPT WALKING.
I REMEMBER I TURNED TO SEE IF I WAS BEING FOLLOWED.
I SAW A BIG HOUSE OR A BARN?
A BIG HOUSE?
OR A BARN.
DO YOU KNOW WHERE YOU...?
WELL, SEE, THING IS- IS I SLIPPED.
I TURNED TO GO AND...I JUST SLIPPED AND ROLLED.
I WAS IN THE...I JUST ROLLED...
NEXT THING I KNEW, I WAS AT THE MISSION WITH A BUMP ON MY HEAD,
BUT NO WORSE FOR WEAR.
WHO BROUGHT ME THERE? I DON'T KNOW.
I ASKED WHERE THEY FOUND ME, NOBODY KNEW.
I ASKED HOW LONG I WAS OUT. NOBODY KNEW THAT EITHER.
THING IS, I KNOW I AIN'T THE FIRST OR...
THE FIRST?
OH, THERE'S BEEN FOLKS DISAPPEARING AND WHAT NOT ALL THE TIME DOWN THERE.
THERE?

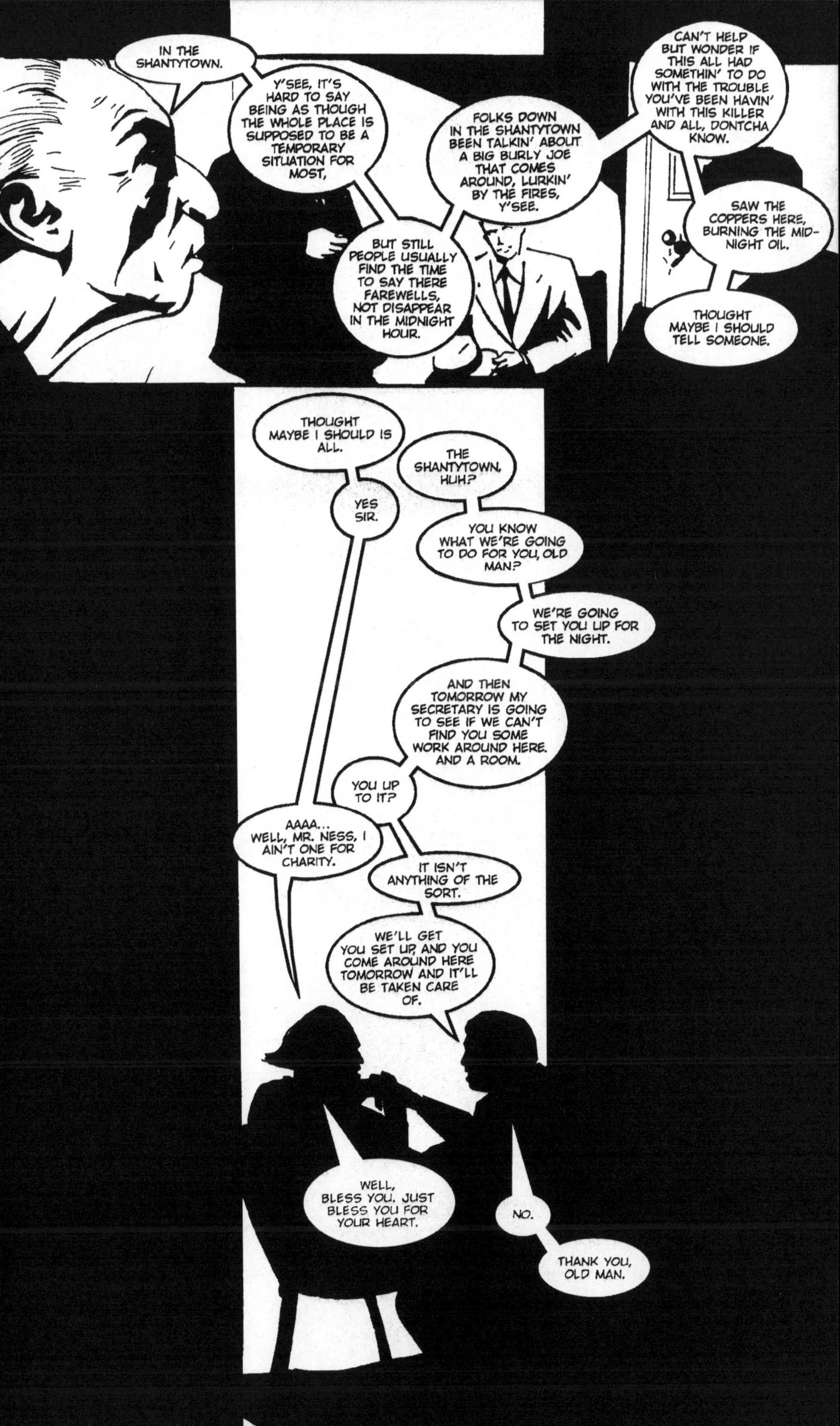
IN THE SHANTYTOWN.
Y'SEE, IT'S HARD TO SAY BEING AS THOUGH THE WHOLE PLACE IS SUPPOSED TO BE A TEMPORARY SITUATION FOR MOST,
BUT STILL PEOPLE USUALLY FIND THE TIME TO SAY THERE FAREWELLS, NOT DISAPPEAR IN THE MIDNIGHT HOUR.
FOLKS DOWN IN THE SHANTYTOWN BEEN TALKIN' ABOUT A BIG BURLY JOE THAT COMES AROUND, LURKIN' BY THE FIRES, Y'SEE.
CAN'T HELP BUT WONDER IF THIS ALL HAD SOMETHIN' TO DO WITH THE TROUBLE YOU'VE BEEN HAVIN' WITH THIS KILLER AND ALL, DONTCHA KNOW.
SAW THE COPPERS HERE, BURNING THE MID-NIGHT OIL.
THOUGHT MAYBE I SHOULD TELL SOMEONE.
THOUGHT MAYBE I SHOULD IS ALL.
THE SHANTYTOWN, HUH?
YES SIR.
YOU KNOW WHAT WE'RE GOING TO DO FOR YOU, OLD MAN?
WE'RE GOING TO SET YOU UP FOR THE NIGHT.
AND THEN TOMORROW MY SECRETARY IS GOING TO SEE IF WE CAN'T FIND YOU SOME WORK AROUND HERE. AND A ROOM.
YOU UP TO IT?
AAAA... WELL, MR. NESS, I AIN'T ONE FOR CHARITY.
IT ISN'T ANYTHING OF THE SORT.
WE'LL GET YOU SET UP, AND YOU COME AROUND HERE TOMORROW AND IT'LL BE TAKEN CARE OF.
WELL, BLESS YOU. JUST BLESS YOU FOR YOUR HEART.
NO.
THANK YOU, OLD MAN.

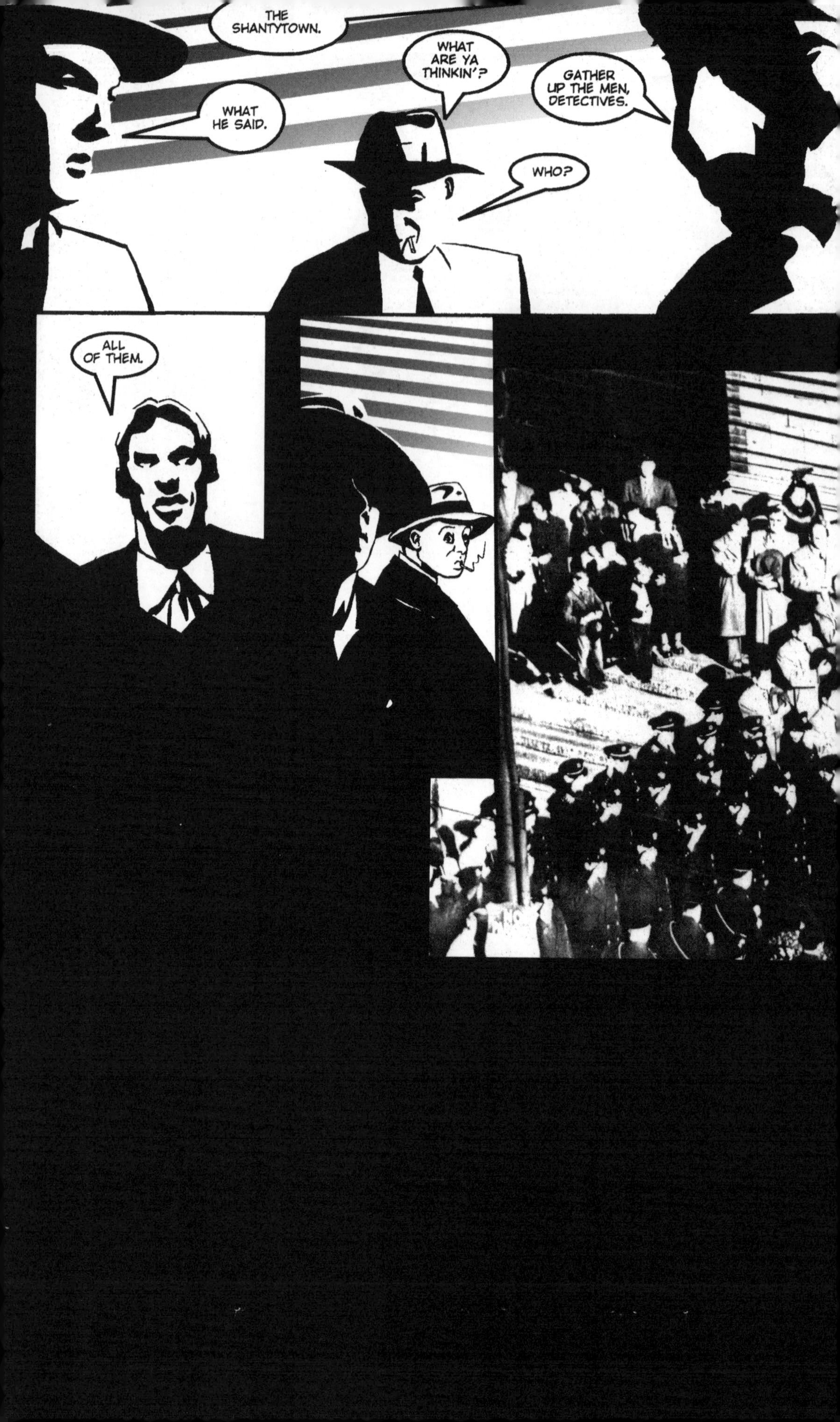
WHAT ARE YA THINKIN'?
THE SHANTYTOWN.
WHAT HE SAID.
GATHER UP THE MEN, DETECTIVES.
WHO?
ALL OF THEM.

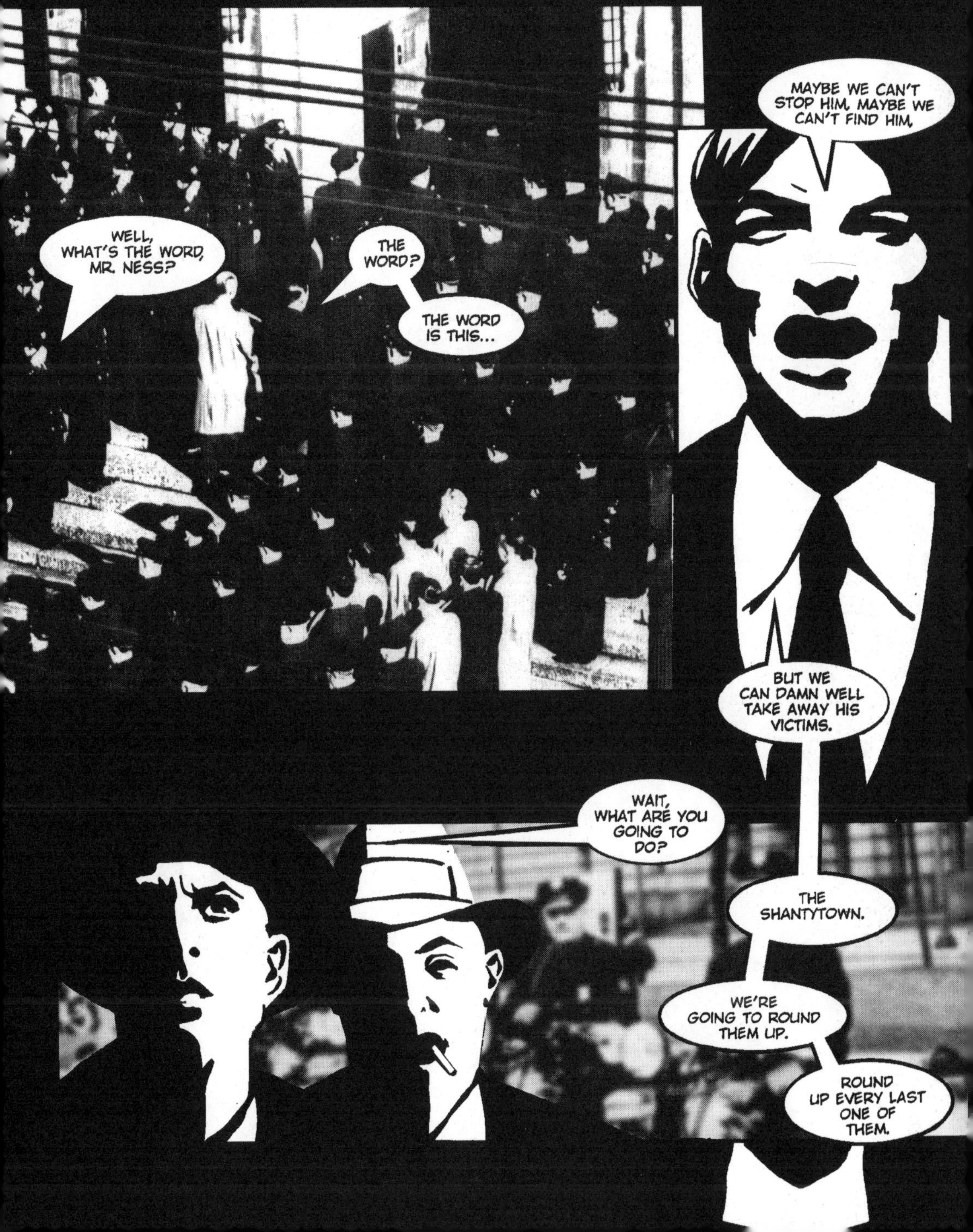
WELL, WHAT'S THE WORD, MR. NESS?
THE WORD?
THE WORD IS THIS...
MAYBE WE CAN'T STOP HIM, MAYBE WE CAN'T FIND HIM,
BUT WE CAN DAMN WELL TAKE AWAY HIS VICTIMS.
WAIT, WHAT ARE YOU GOING TO DO?
THE SHANTYTOWN.
WE'RE GOING TO ROUND THEM UP.
ROUND UP EVERY LAST ONE OF THEM.

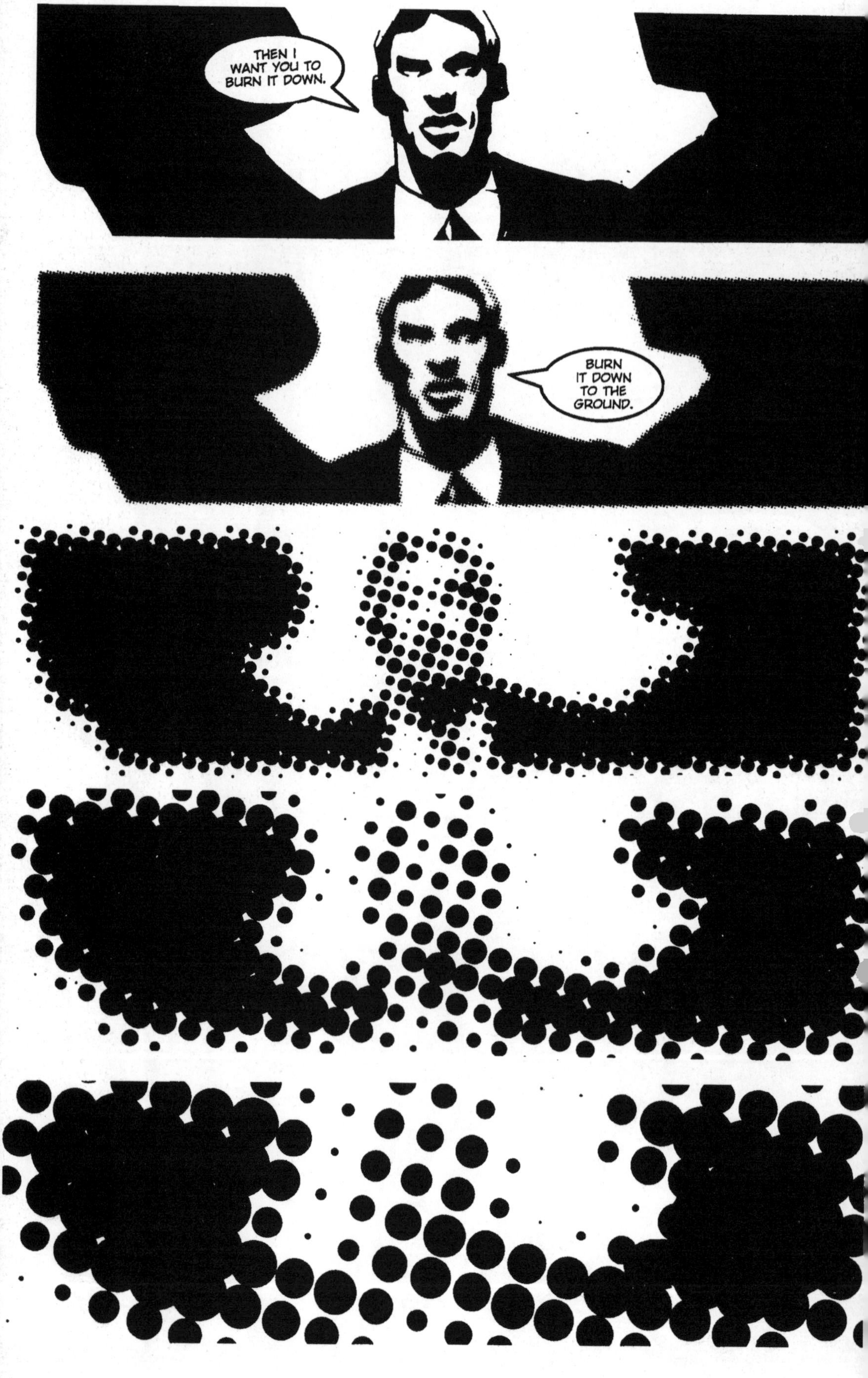
THEN I WANT YOU TO BURN IT DOWN.
BURN IT DOWN TO THE GROUND.

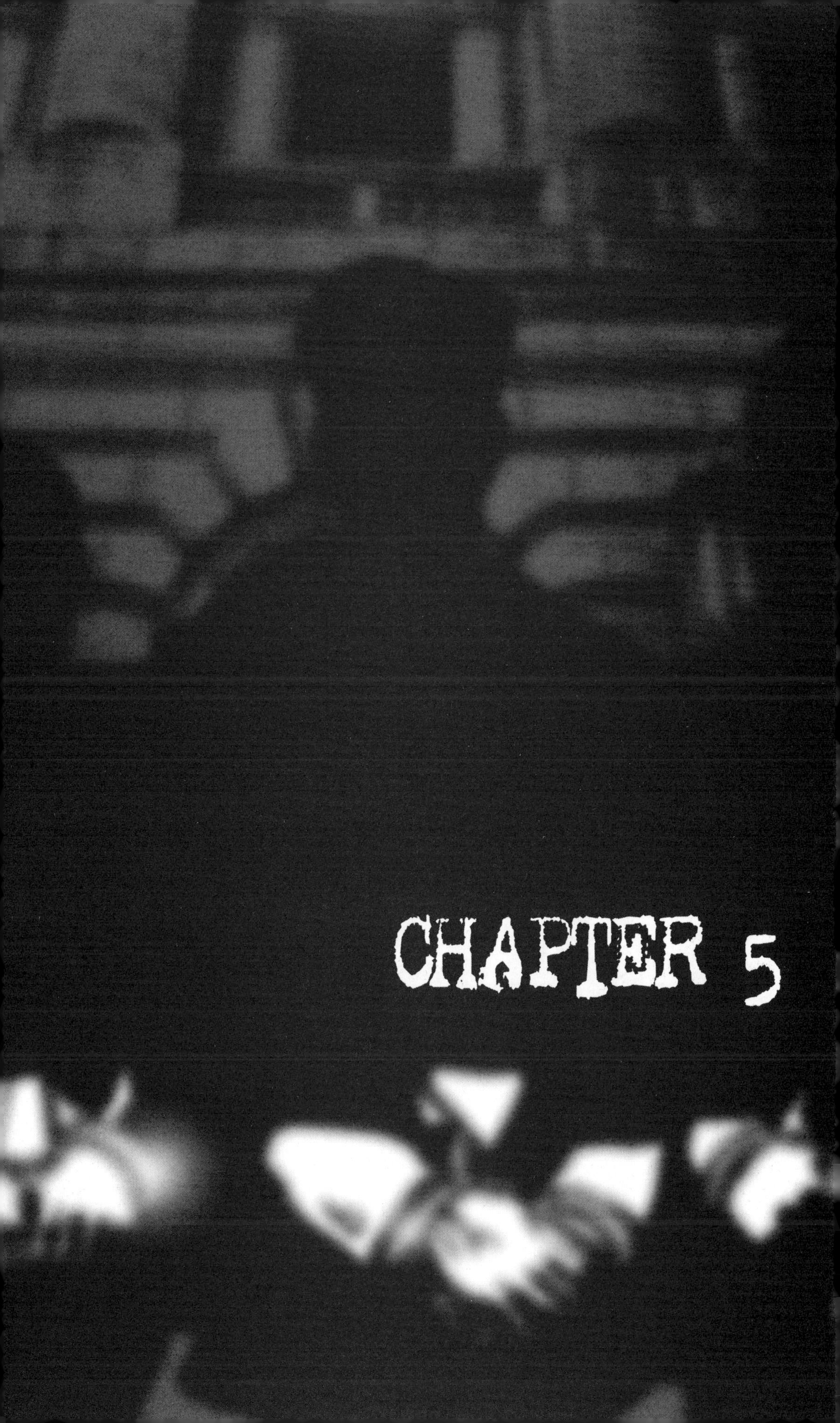

CHAPTER 5

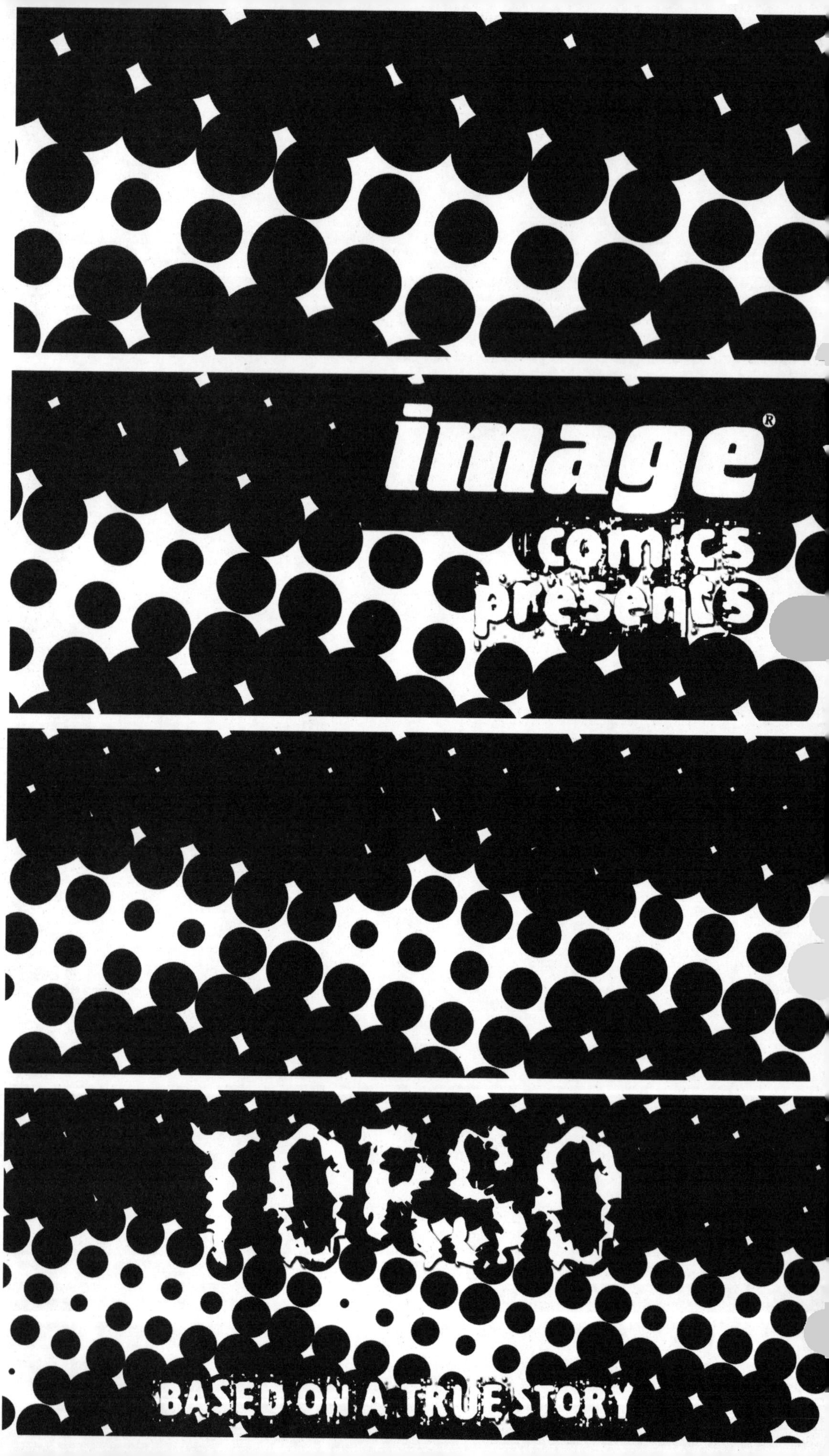
image®
comics presents
TORSO
BASED ON A TRUE STORY

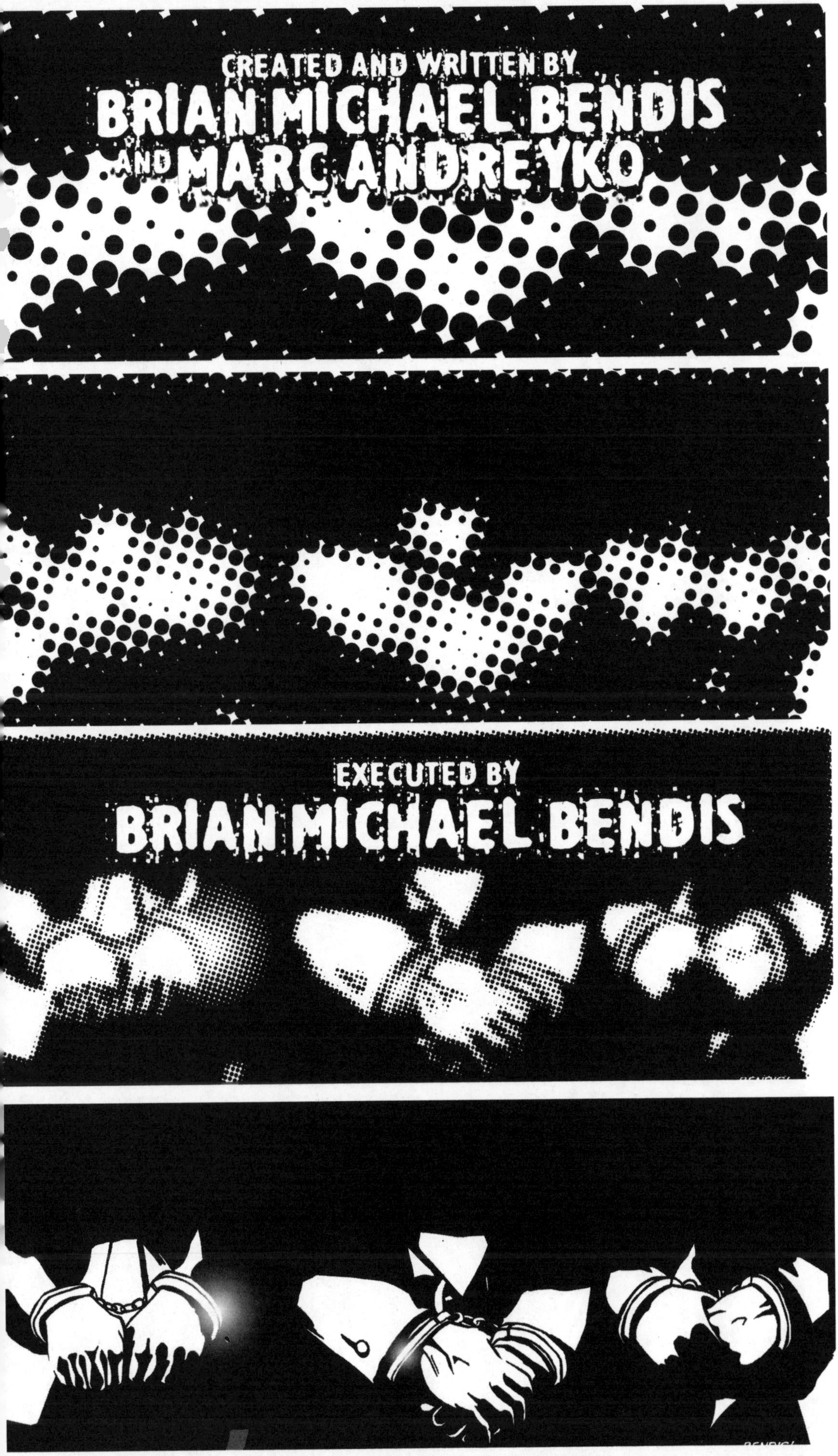
CREATED AND WRITTEN BY
BRIAN MICHAEL BENDIS
AND MARC ANDREYKO
EXECUTED BY
BRIAN MICHAEL BENDIS

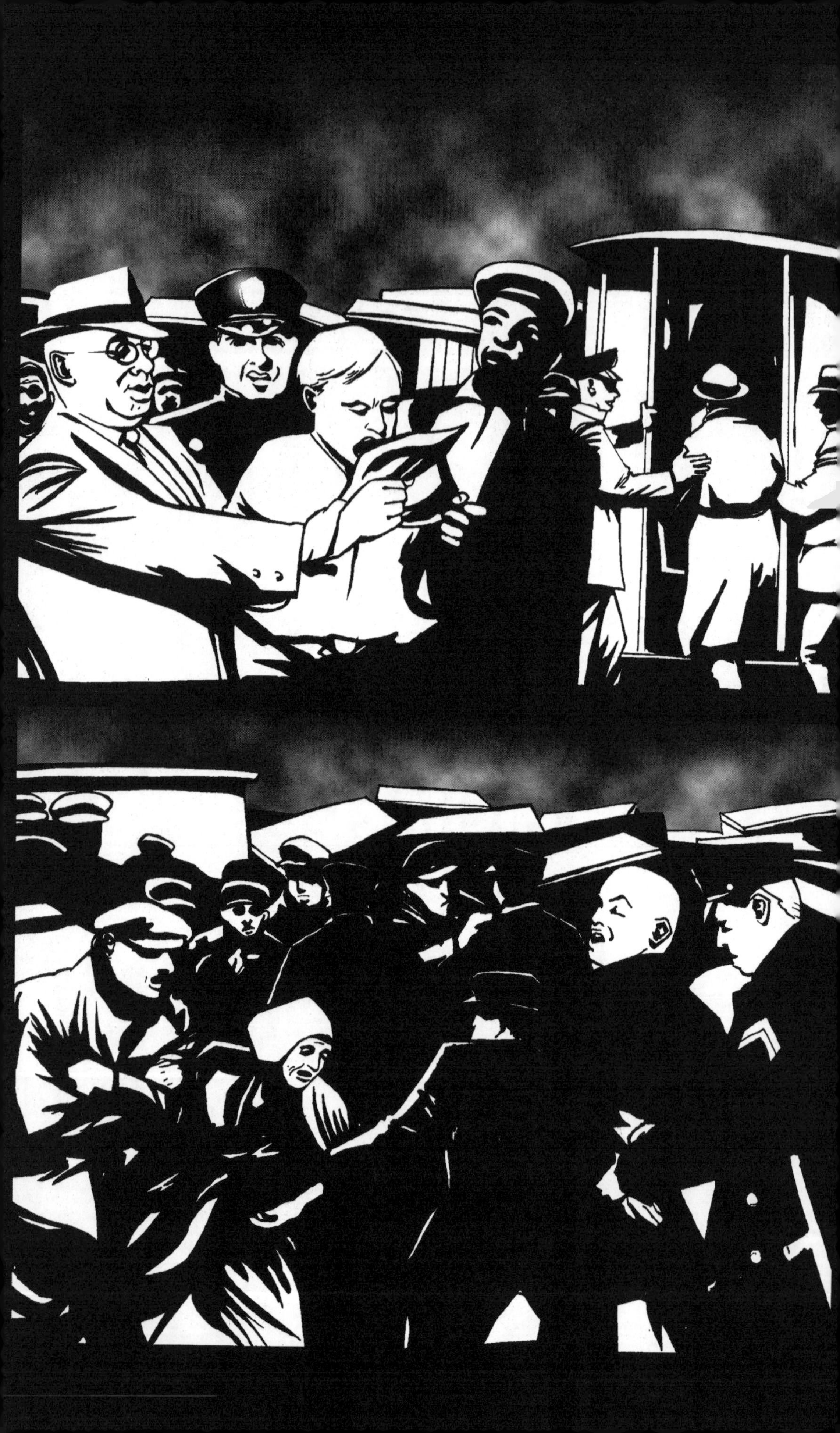

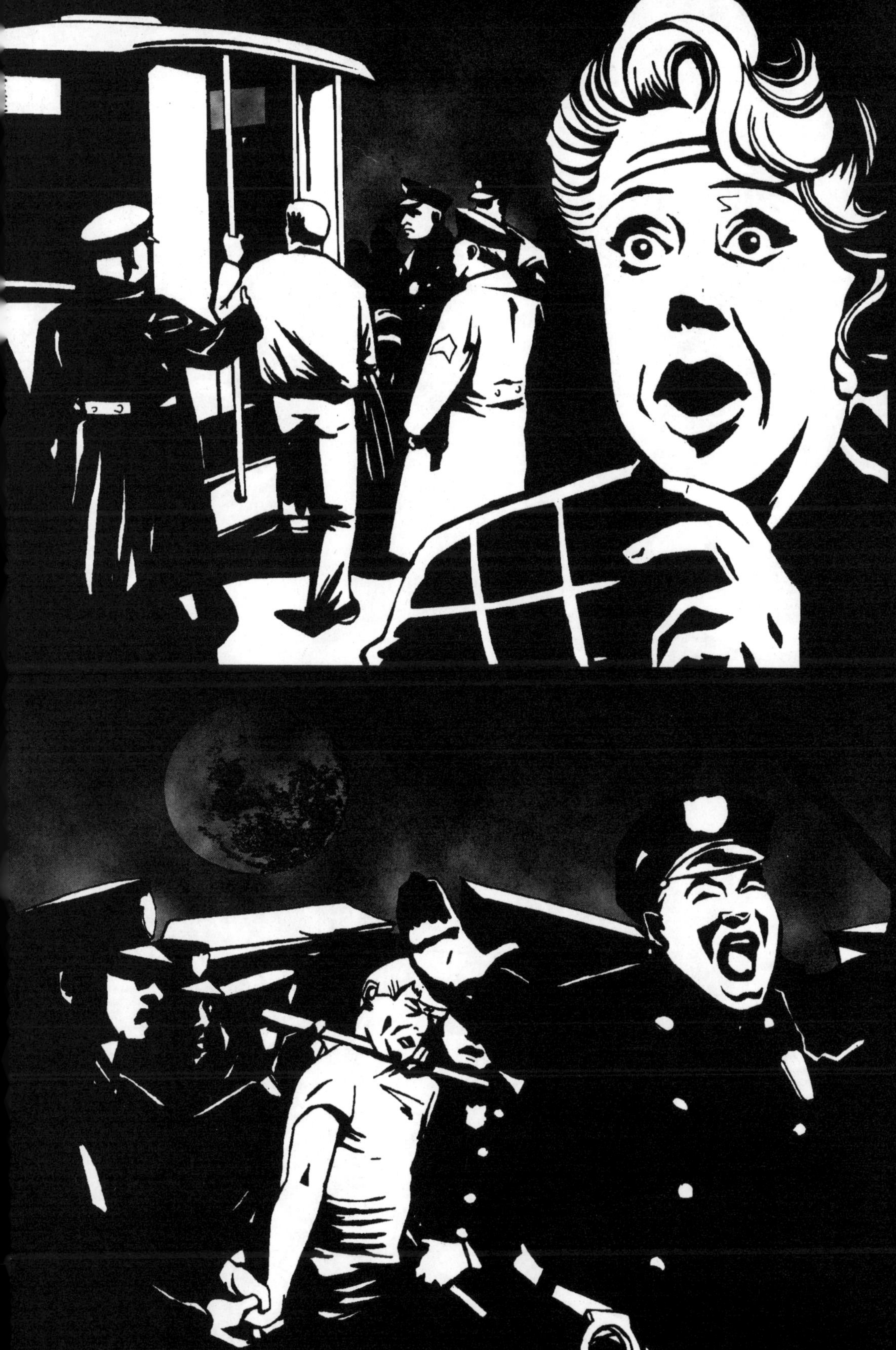

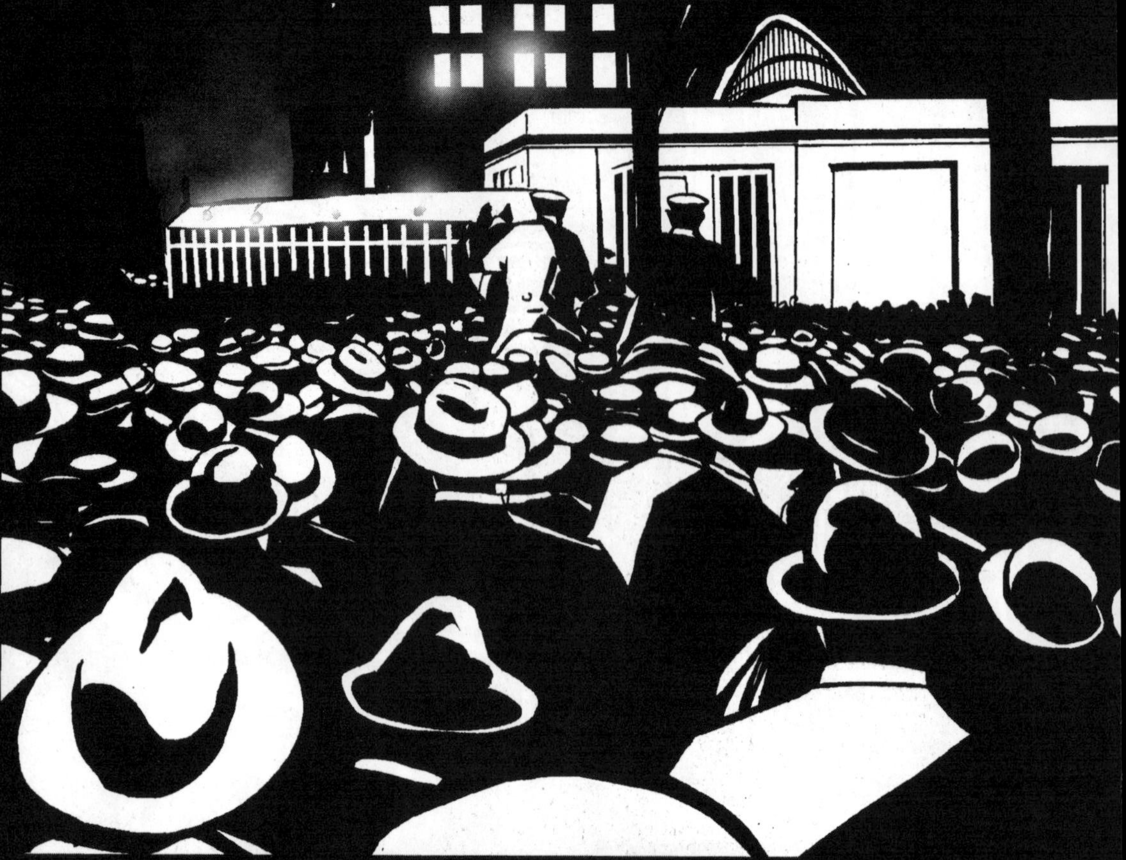

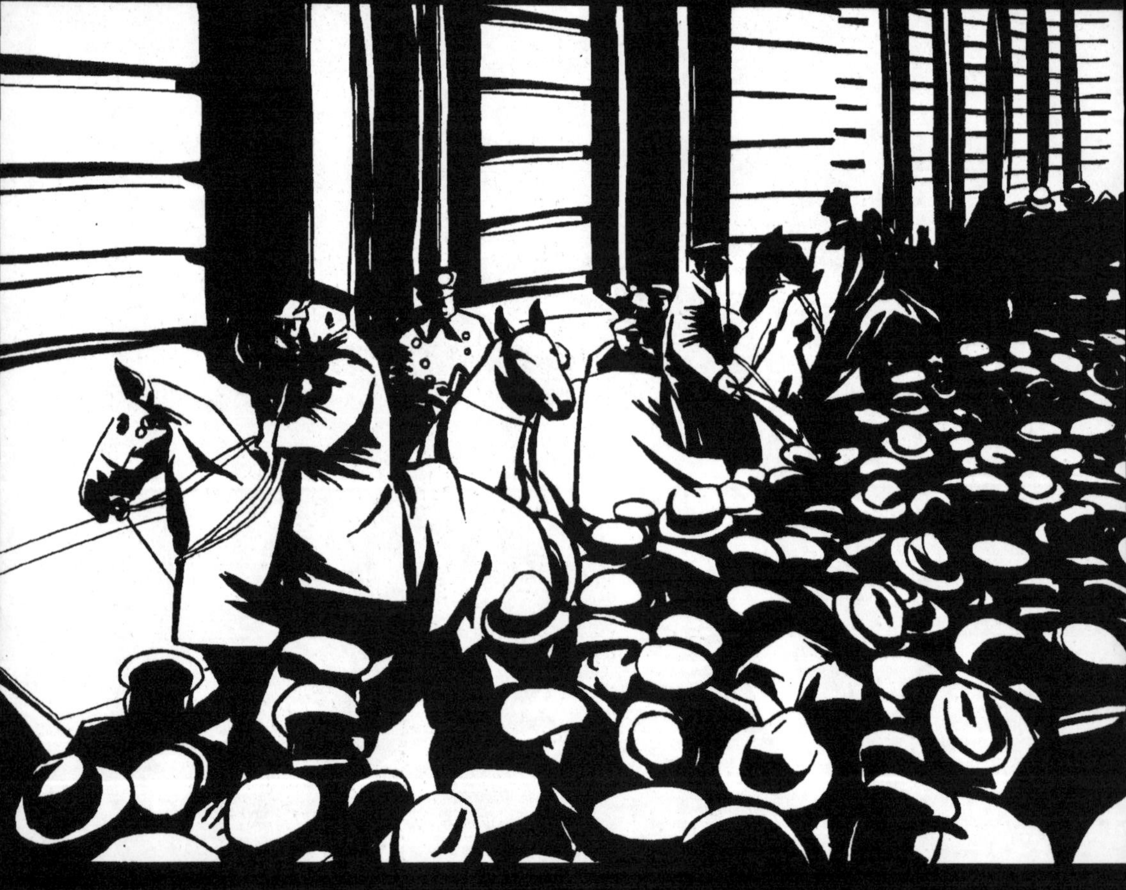

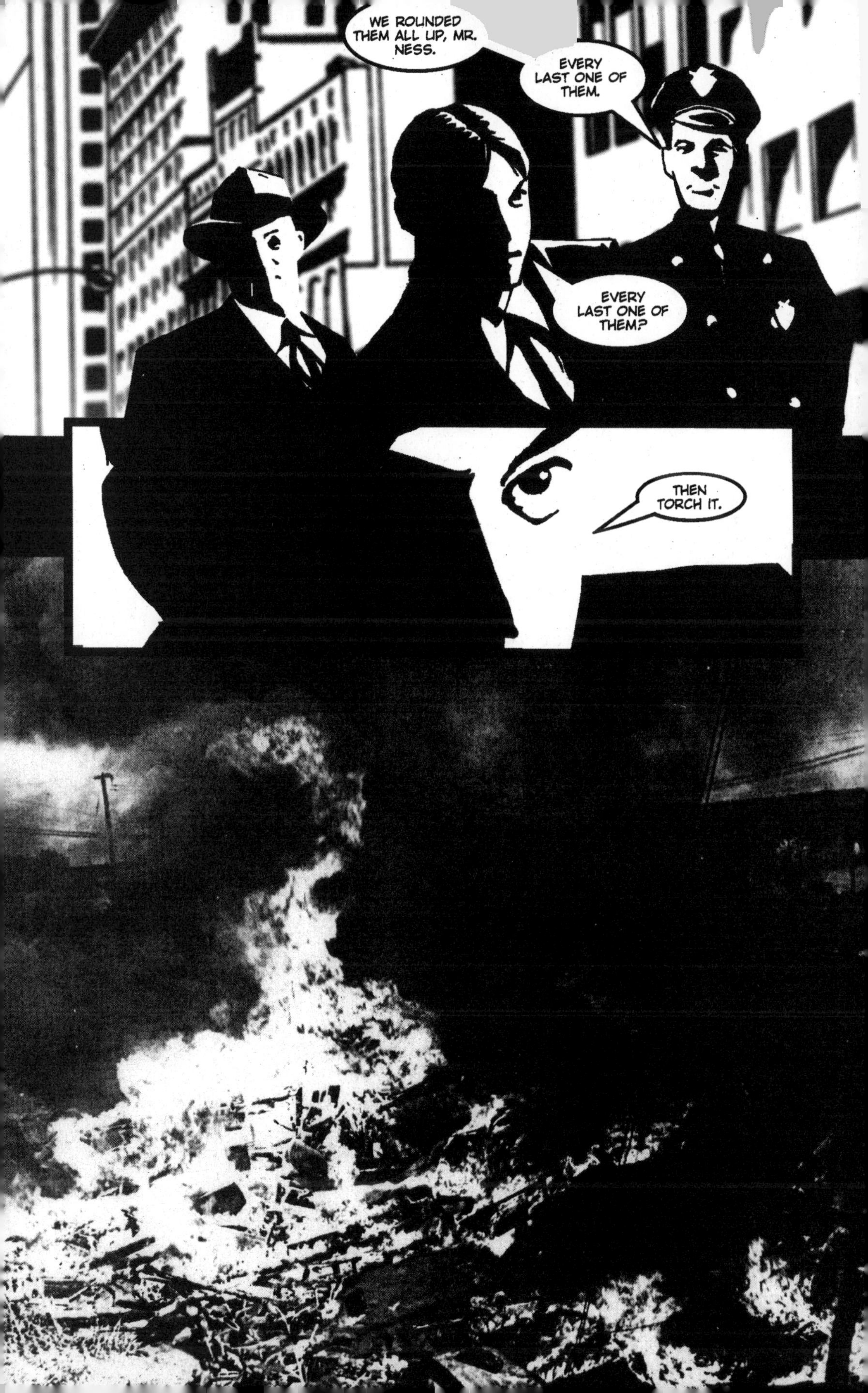
WE ROUNDED THEM ALL UP, MR. NESS.
EVERY LAST ONE OF THEM.
EVERY LAST ONE OF THEM?
THEN TORCH IT.

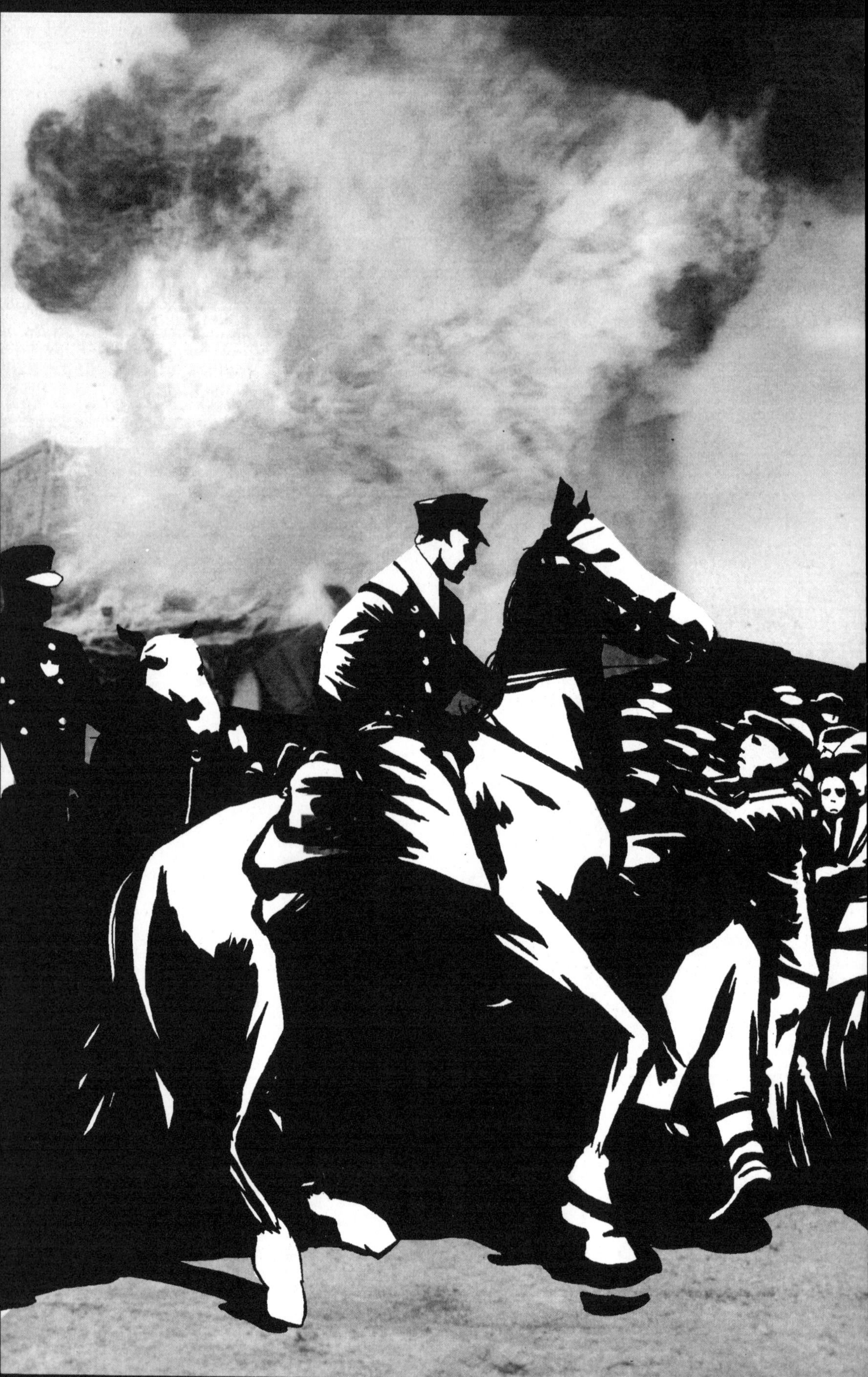

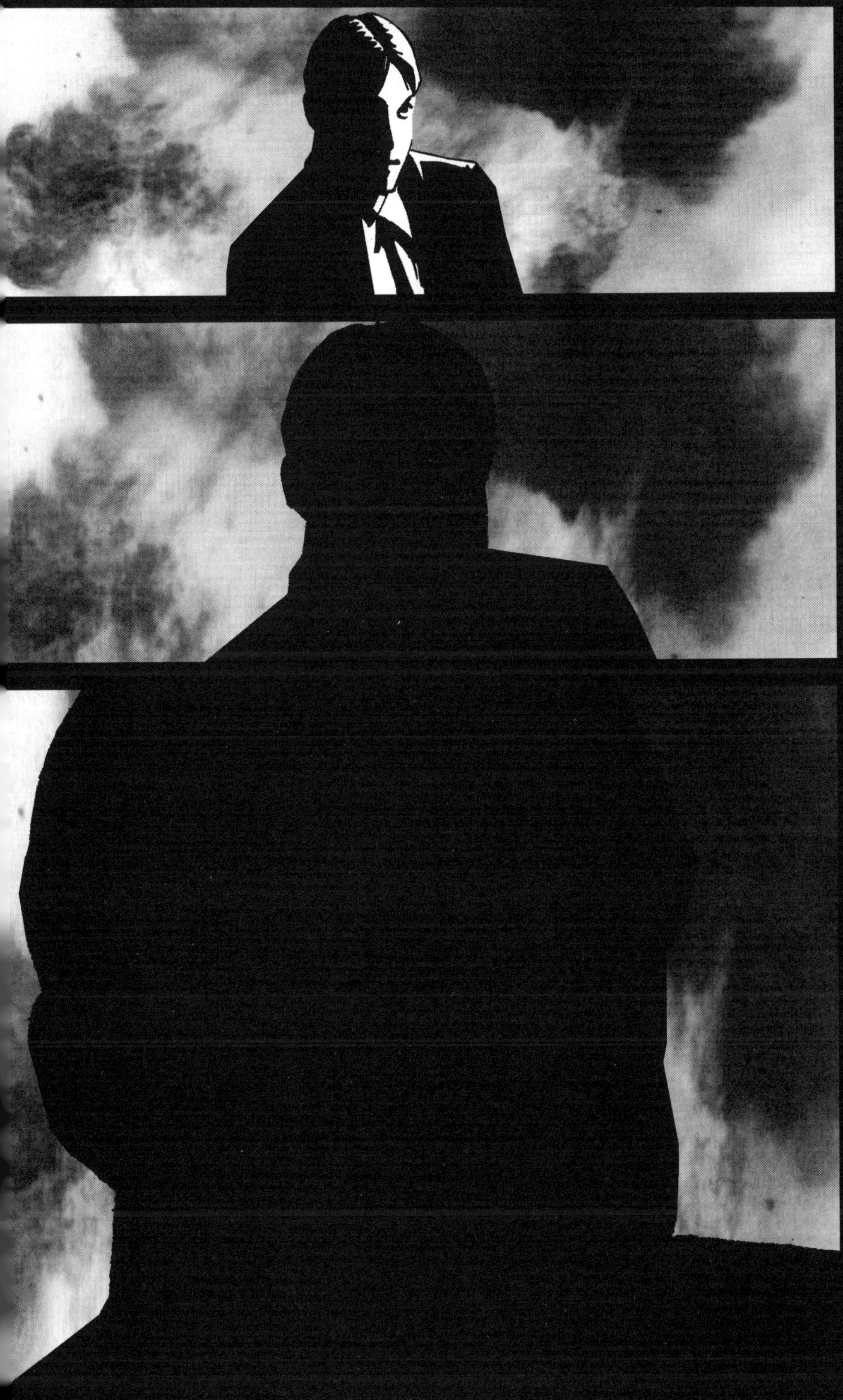

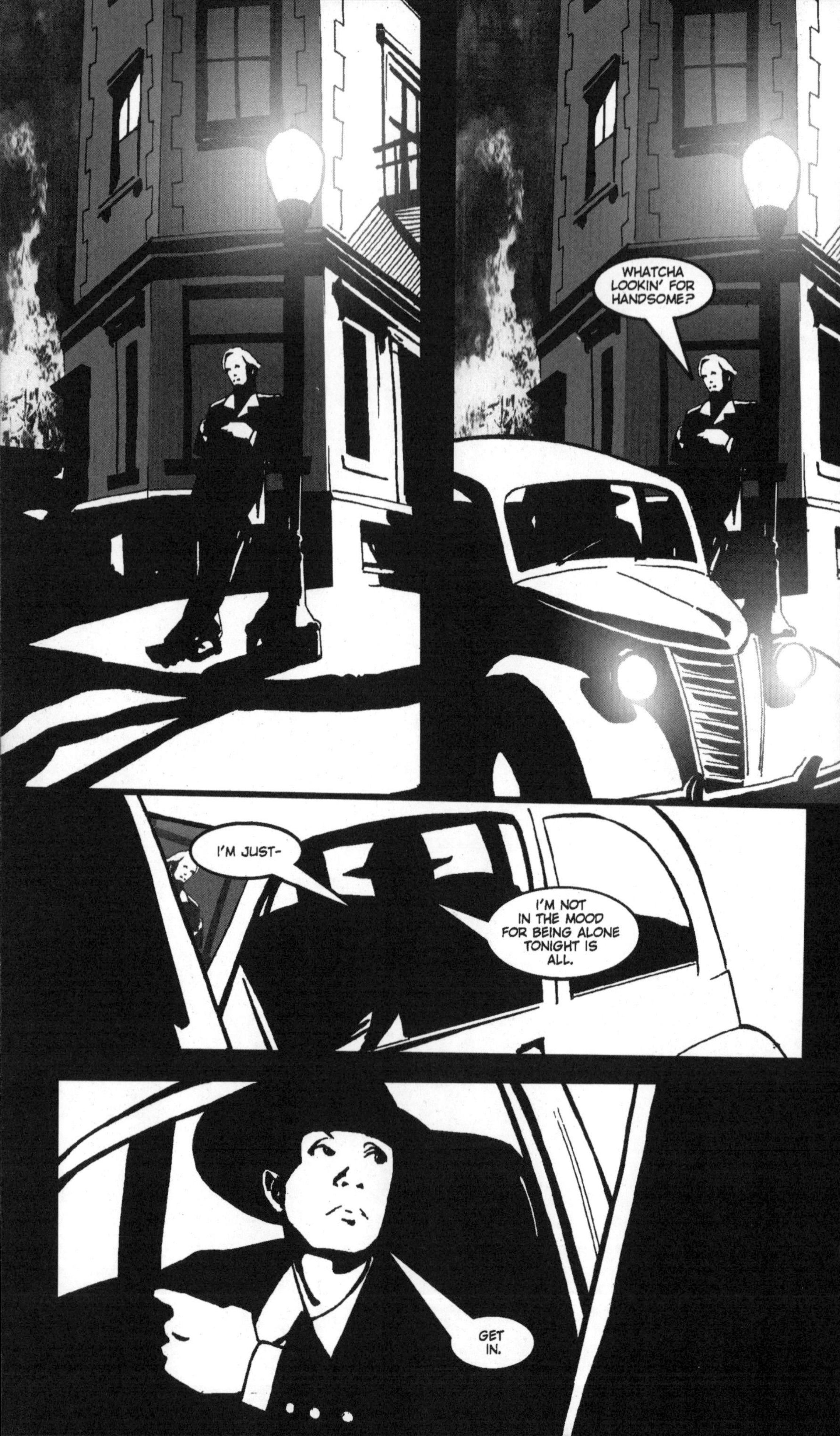
WHATCHA LOOKIN' FOR HANDSOME?
I'M JUST-
I'M NOT IN THE MOOD FOR BEING ALONE TONIGHT IS ALL.
GET IN.

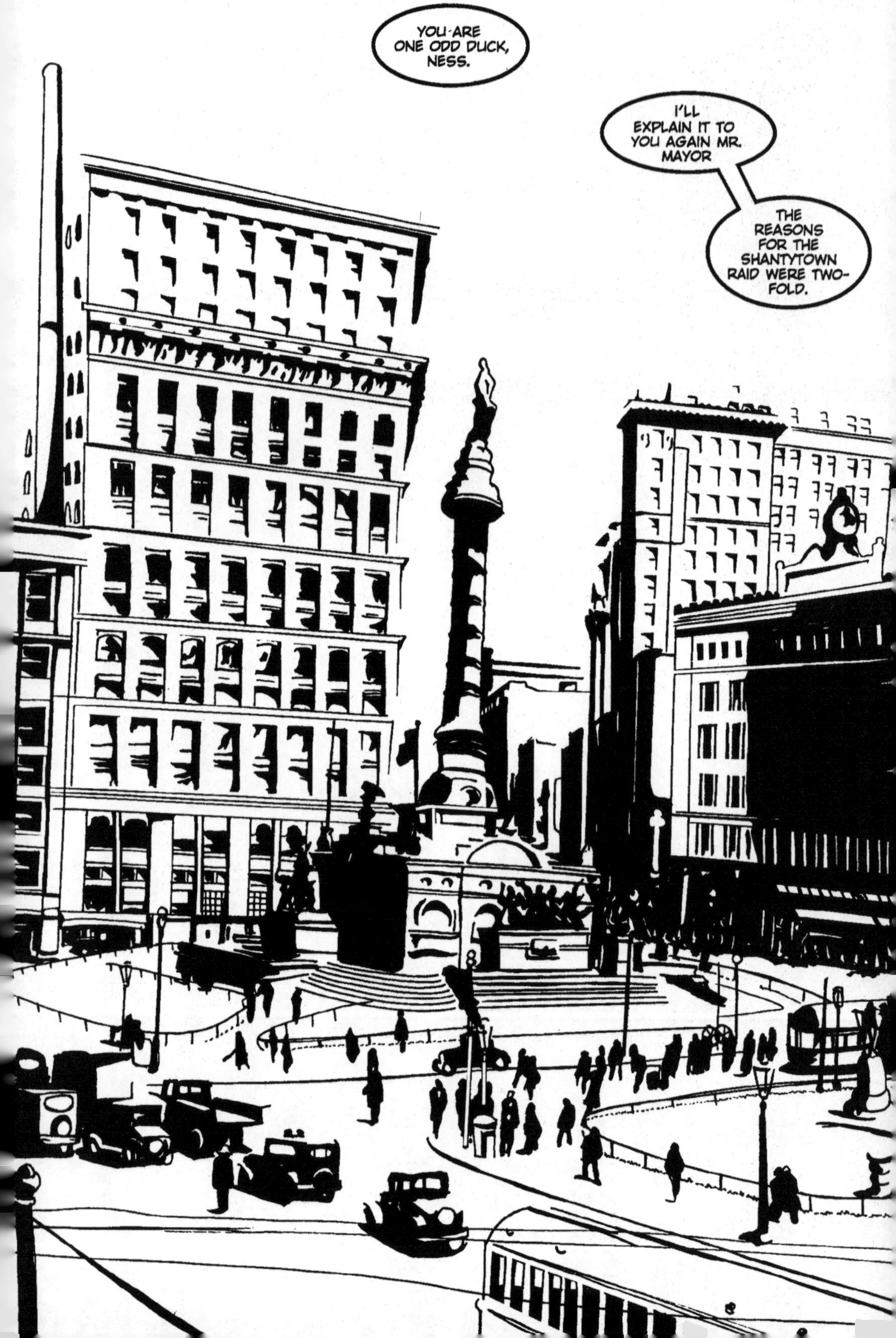
YOU ARE ONE ODD DUCK, NESS.
I'LL EXPLAIN IT TO YOU AGAIN MR. MAYOR
THE REASONS FOR THE SHANTYTOWN RAID WERE TWO-FOLD.

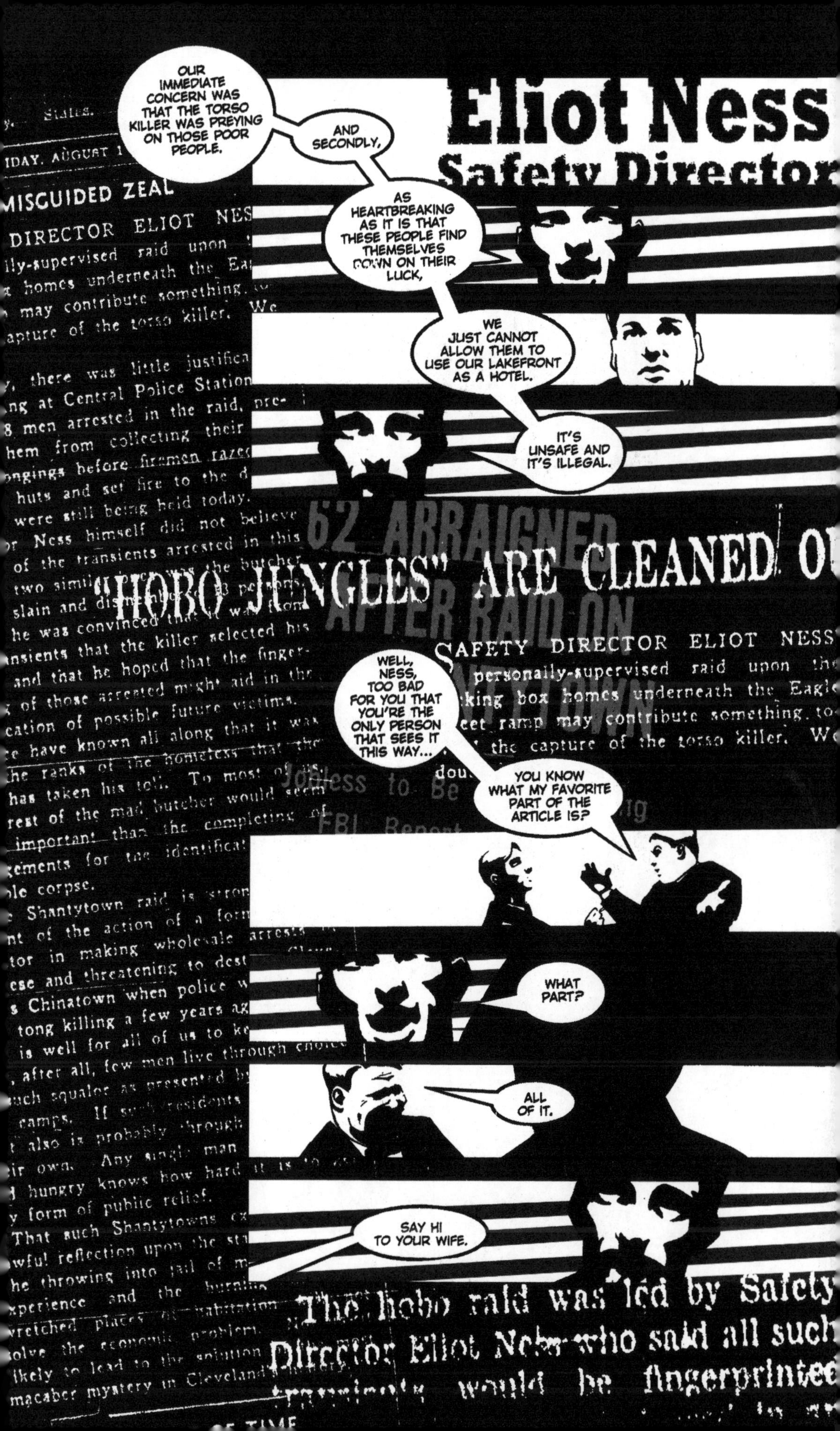
OUR IMMEDIATE CONCERN WAS THAT THE TORSO KILLER WAS PREYING ON THOSE POOR PEOPLE.
AND SECONDLY,
Eliot Ness
MISGUIDED ZEAL
AS HEARTBREAKING AS IT IS THAT THESE PEOPLE FIND THEMSELVES DOWN ON THEIR LUCK,
WE JUST CANNOT ALLOW THEM TO USE OUR LAKEFRONT AS A HOTEL.
IT'S UNSAFE AND IT'S ILLEGAL.
62 ARRAIGNED AFTER RAID ON
"HOBO JUNGLES" ARE CLEANED OU
SAFETY DIRECTOR ELIOT NESS
WELL, NESS, TOO BAD FOR YOU THAT YOU'RE THE ONLY PERSON THAT SEES IT THIS WAY...
YOU KNOW WHAT MY FAVORITE PART OF THE ARTICLE IS?
WHAT PART?
ALL OF IT.
SAY HI TO YOUR WIFE.
The hobo raid was led by Safety
Director Eliot Ness who said all such
would be fingerprinted

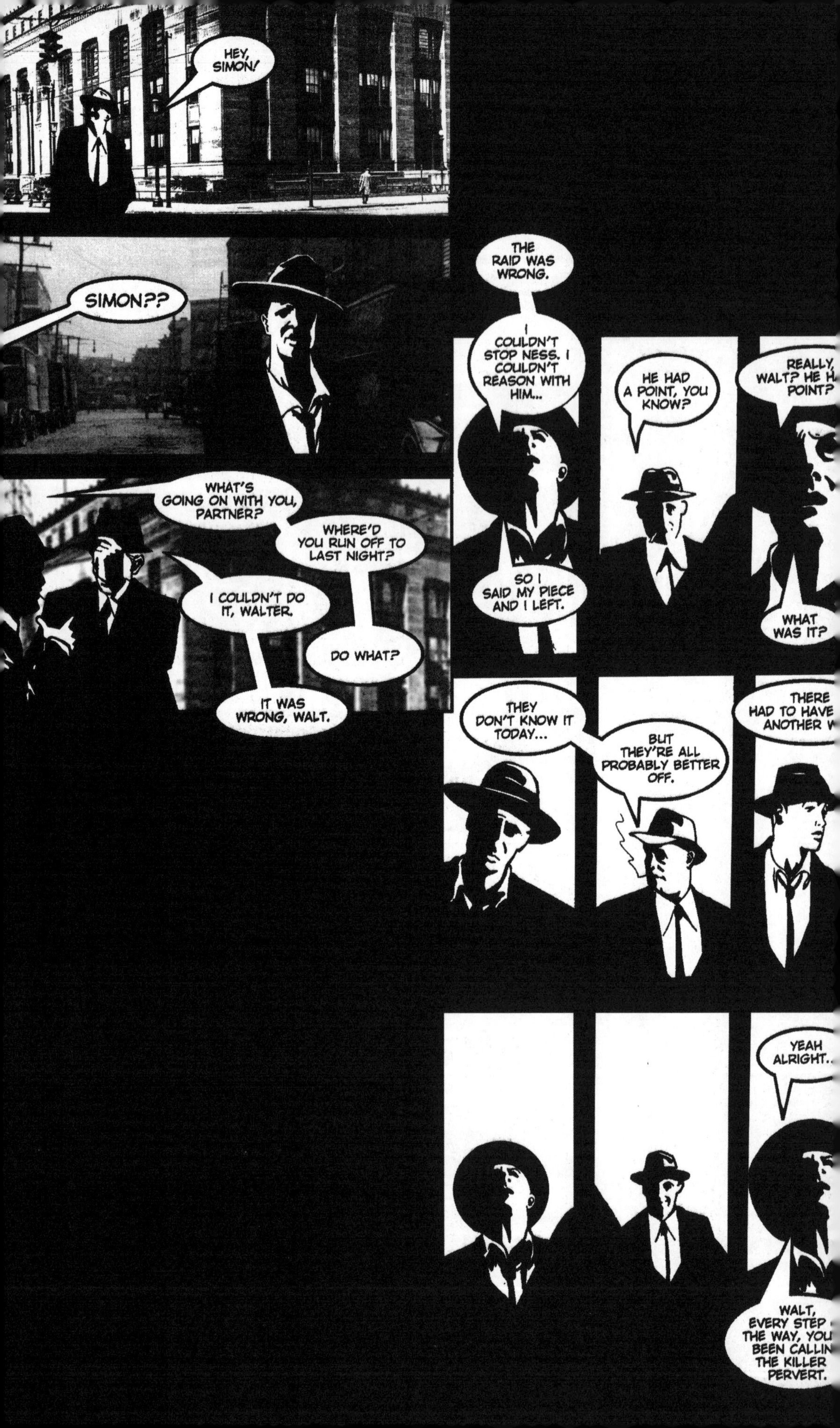
HEY, SIMON!
SIMON??
WHAT'S GOING ON WITH YOU, PARTNER?
WHERE'D YOU RUN OFF TO LAST NIGHT?
I COULDN'T DO IT, WALTER.
DO WHAT?
IT WAS WRONG, WALT.
THE RAID WAS WRONG.
I COULDN'T STOP NESS. I COULDN'T REASON WITH HIM...
SO I SAID MY PIECE AND I LEFT.
HE HAD A POINT, YOU KNOW?
REALLY, WALT? HE H POINT?
WHAT WAS IT?
THEY DON'T KNOW IT TODAY...
BUT THEY'RE ALL PROBABLY BETTER OFF.
THERE HAD TO HAVE ANOTHER
YEAH ALRIGHT..
WALT, EVERY STEP THE WAY, YOU BEEN CALLIN THE KILLER PERVERT.

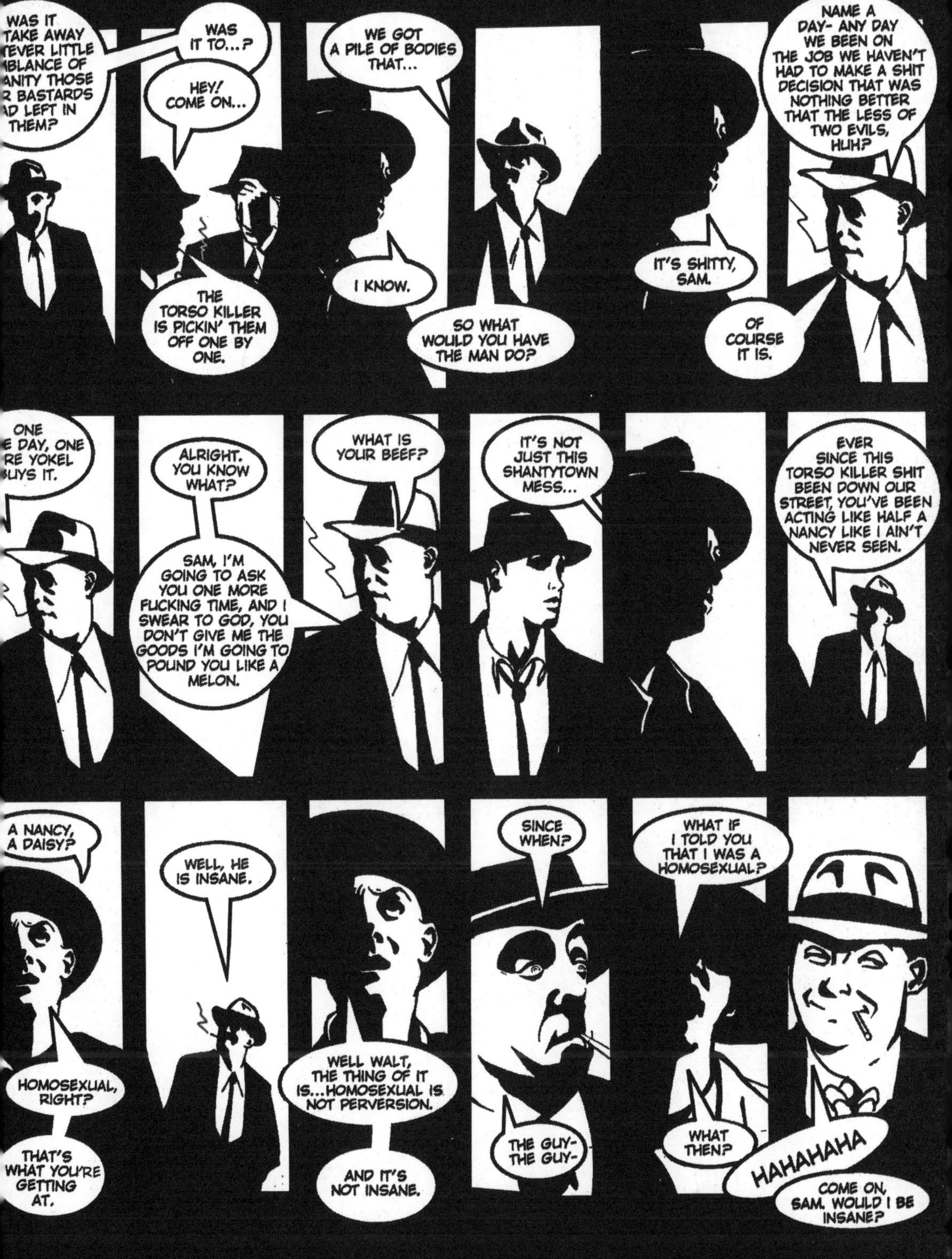
WAS IT TAKE AWAY TEVER LITTLE MBLANCE OF ANITY THOSE R BASTARDS AD LEFT IN THEM?
WAS IT TO...?
HEY! COME ON...
THE TORSO KILLER IS PICKIN' THEM OFF ONE BY ONE.
WE GOT A PILE OF BODIES THAT...
I KNOW.
SO WHAT WOULD YOU HAVE THE MAN DO?
IT'S SHITTY, SAM.
NAME A DAY- ANY DAY WE BEEN ON THE JOB WE HAVEN'T HAD TO MAKE A SHIT DECISION THAT WAS NOTHING BETTER THAT THE LESS OF TWO EVILS, HUH?
OF COURSE IT IS.
ONE E DAY, ONE RE YOKEL BUYS IT.
ALRIGHT. YOU KNOW WHAT?
SAM, I'M GOING TO ASK YOU ONE MORE FUCKING TIME, AND I SWEAR TO GOD, YOU DON'T GIVE ME THE GOODS I'M GOING TO POUND YOU LIKE A MELON.
WHAT IS YOUR BEEF?
IT'S NOT JUST THIS SHANTYTOWN MESS...
EVER SINCE THIS TORSO KILLER SHIT BEEN DOWN OUR STREET, YOU'VE BEEN ACTING LIKE HALF A NANCY LIKE I AIN'T NEVER SEEN.
A NANCY, A DAISY?
HOMOSEXUAL, RIGHT?
THAT'S WHAT YOU'RE GETTING AT.
WELL, HE IS INSANE.
WELL WALT, THE THING OF IT IS...HOMOSEXUAL IS NOT PERVERSION.
AND IT'S NOT INSANE.
SINCE WHEN?
THE GUY- THE GUY-
WHAT IF I TOLD YOU THAT I WAS A HOMOSEXUAL?
WHAT THEN?
HAHAHAHA
COME ON, SAM. WOULD I BE INSANE?

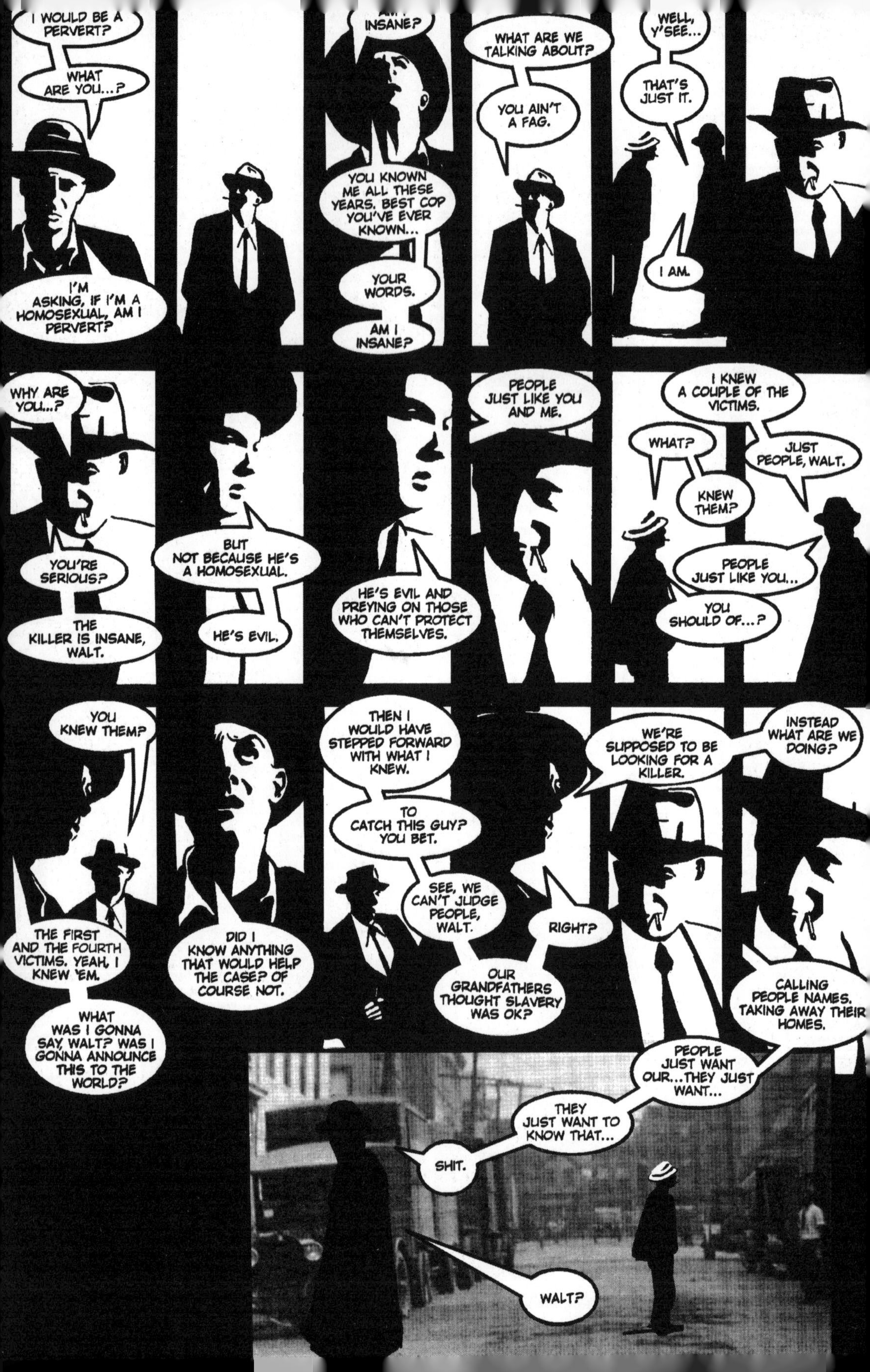
I WOULD BE A PERVERT?
WHAT ARE YOU...?
I'M ASKING, IF I'M A HOMOSEXUAL, AM I PERVERT?
INSANE?
YOU KNOWN ME ALL THESE YEARS. BEST COP YOU'VE EVER KNOWN...
YOUR WORDS.
AM I INSANE?
WHAT ARE WE TALKING ABOUT?
YOU AIN'T A FAG.
WELL, Y'SEE...
THAT'S JUST IT.
I AM.
WHY ARE YOU...?
YOU'RE SERIOUS?
THE KILLER IS INSANE, WALT.
BUT NOT BECAUSE HE'S A HOMOSEXUAL.
HE'S EVIL.
HE'S EVIL AND PREYING ON THOSE WHO CAN'T PROTECT THEMSELVES.
PEOPLE JUST LIKE YOU AND ME.
I KNEW A COUPLE OF THE VICTIMS.
WHAT?
KNEW THEM?
JUST PEOPLE, WALT.
PEOPLE JUST LIKE YOU...
YOU SHOULD OF...?
YOU KNEW THEM?
THE FIRST AND THE FOURTH VICTIMS. YEAH, I KNEW 'EM.
WHAT WAS I GONNA SAY, WALT? WAS I GONNA ANNOUNCE THIS TO THE WORLD?
DID I KNOW ANYTHING THAT WOULD HELP THE CASE? OF COURSE NOT.
THEN I WOULD HAVE STEPPED FORWARD WITH WHAT I KNEW.
TO CATCH THIS GUY? YOU BET.
SEE, WE CAN'T JUDGE PEOPLE, WALT.
RIGHT?
OUR GRANDFATHERS THOUGHT SLAVERY WAS OK?
WE'RE SUPPOSED TO BE LOOKING FOR A KILLER.
INSTEAD WHAT ARE WE DOING?
CALLING PEOPLE NAMES. TAKING AWAY THEIR HOMES.
PEOPLE JUST WANT OUR...THEY JUST WANT...
THEY JUST WANT TO KNOW THAT...
SHIT.
WALT?

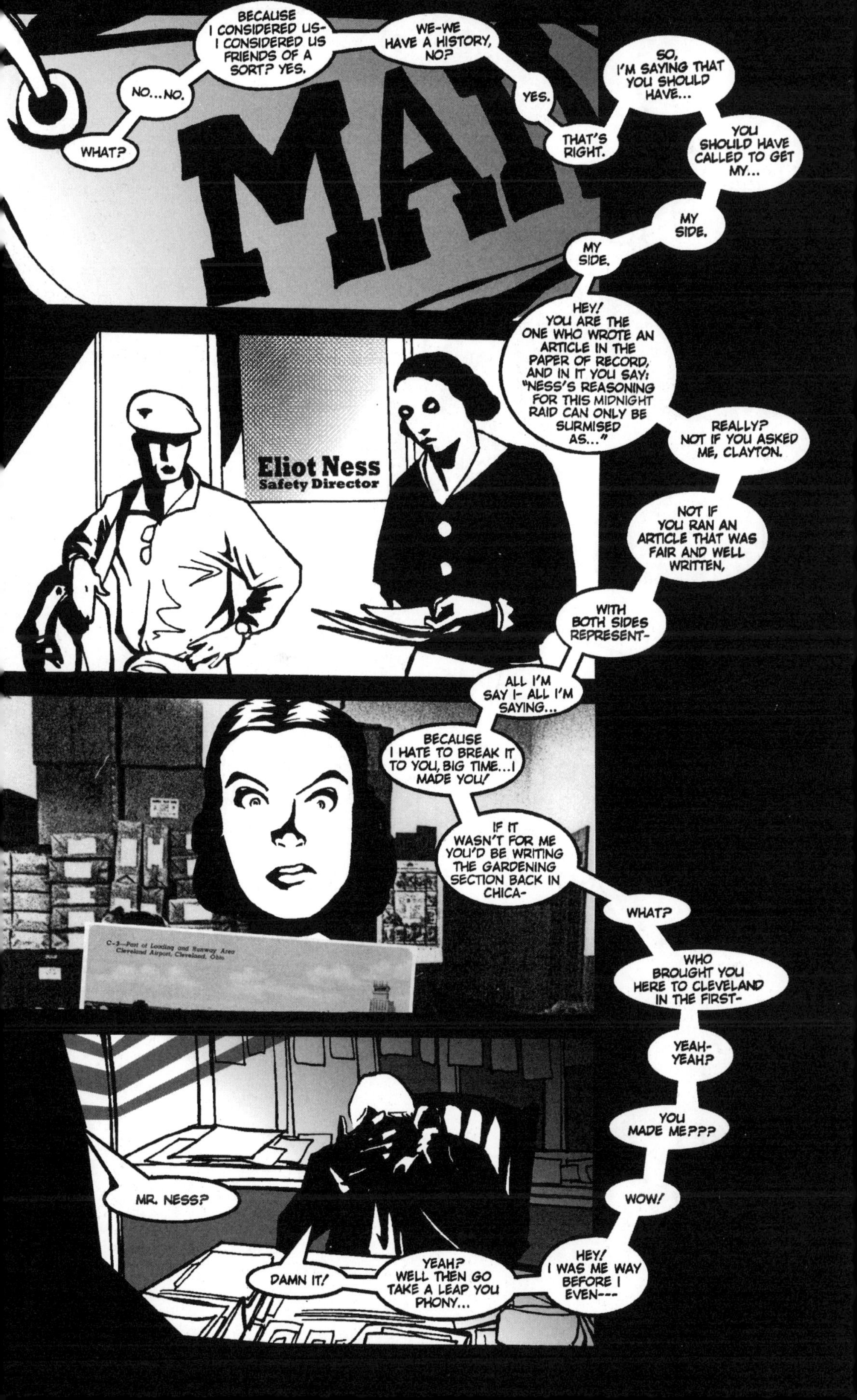
WHAT?
NO...NO.
BECAUSE I CONSIDERED US- I CONSIDERED US FRIENDS OF A SORT? YES.
WE-WE HAVE A HISTORY, NO?
YES.
THAT'S RIGHT.
SO, I'M SAYING THAT YOU SHOULD HAVE...
YOU SHOULD HAVE CALLED TO GET MY...
MY SIDE.
MY SIDE.
HEY! YOU ARE THE ONE WHO WROTE AN ARTICLE IN THE PAPER OF RECORD, AND IN IT YOU SAY: "NESS'S REASONING FOR THIS MIDNIGHT RAID CAN ONLY BE SURMISED AS..."
Eliot Ness
Safety Director
REALLY? NOT IF YOU ASKED ME, CLAYTON.
NOT IF YOU RAN AN ARTICLE THAT WAS FAIR AND WELL WRITTEN,
WITH BOTH SIDES REPRESENT-
ALL I'M SAY I- ALL I'M SAYING...
BECAUSE I HATE TO BREAK IT TO YOU, BIG TIME...I MADE YOU!
IF IT WASN'T FOR ME YOU'D BE WRITING THE GARDENING SECTION BACK IN CHICA-
WHAT?
WHO BROUGHT YOU HERE TO CLEVELAND IN THE FIRST-
YEAH-YEAH?
YOU MADE ME???
WOW!
MR. NESS?
HEY! I WAS ME WAY BEFORE I EVEN---
YEAH? WELL THEN GO TAKE A LEAP YOU PHONY...
DAMN IT!

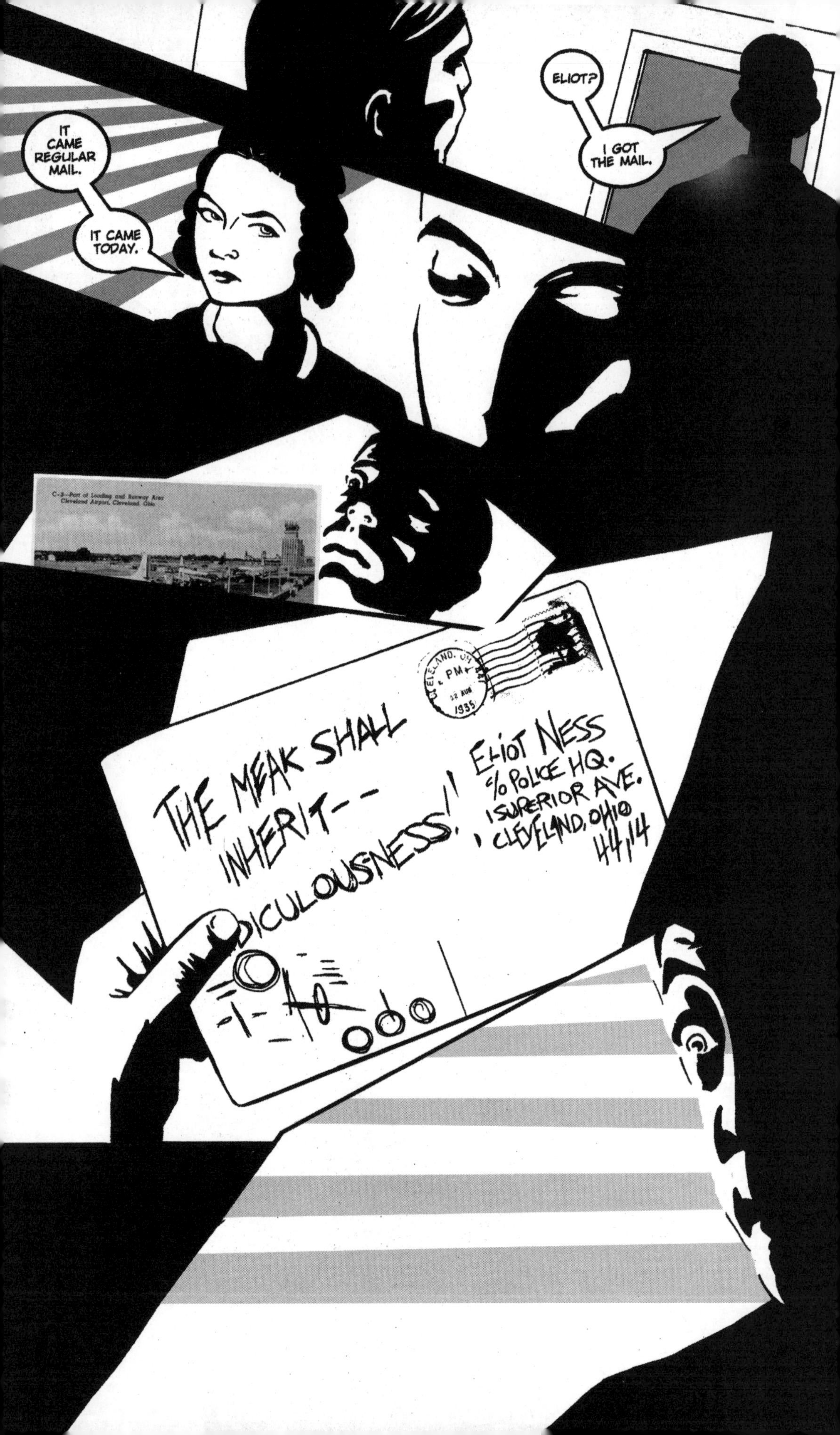

ELIOT?
I GOT THE MAIL.
IT CAME REGULAR MAIL.
IT CAME TODAY.
C-3—Port of Loading and Runway Area Cleveland Airport, Cleveland, Ohio
CLEVELAND, OHIO PM 12 AUG 1935
THE MEAK SHALL INHERIT-- -DICULOUSNESS!
ELIOT NESS
c/o POLICE HQ.
1 SUPERIOR AVE.
CLEVELAND, OHIO
44,14

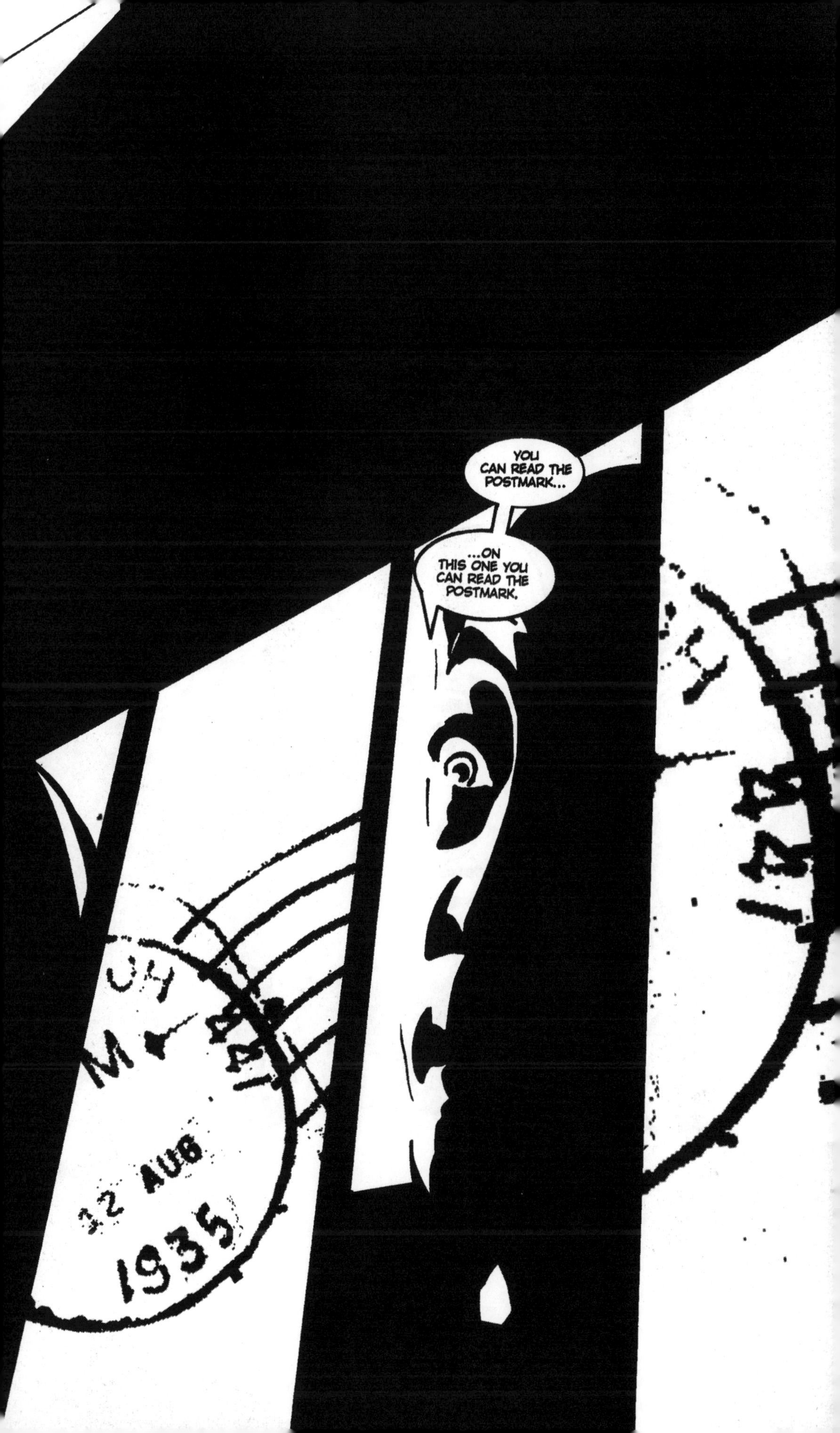

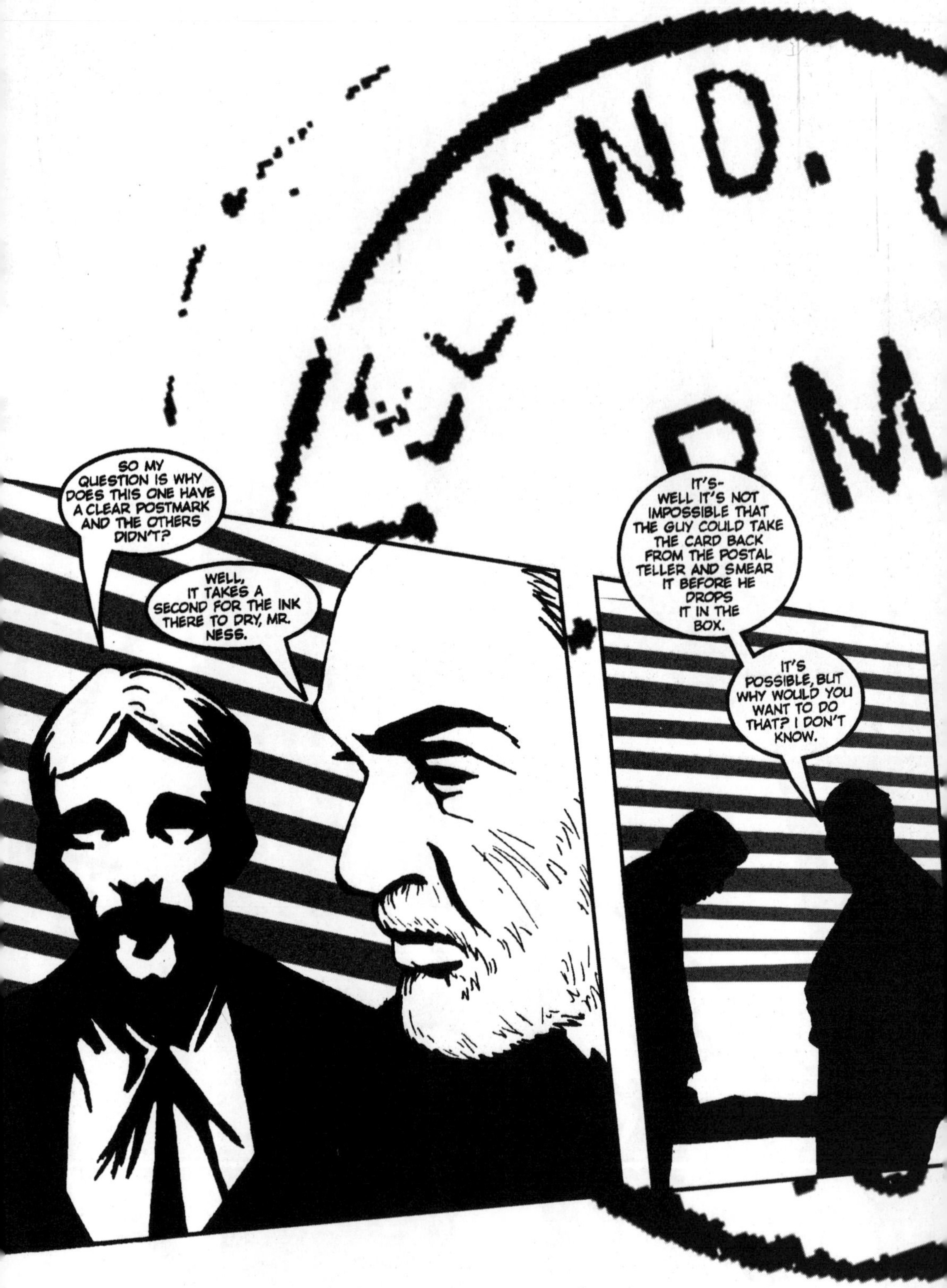

SO MY QUESTION IS WHY DOES THIS ONE HAVE A CLEAR POSTMARK AND THE OTHERS DIDN'T?
WELL, IT TAKES A SECOND FOR THE INK THERE TO DRY, MR. NESS.
IT'S- WELL IT'S NOT IMPOSSIBLE THAT THE GUY COULD TAKE THE CARD BACK FROM THE POSTAL TELLER AND SMEAR IT BEFORE HE DROPS IT IN THE BOX.
IT'S POSSIBLE, BUT WHY WOULD YOU WANT TO DO THAT? I DON'T KNOW.

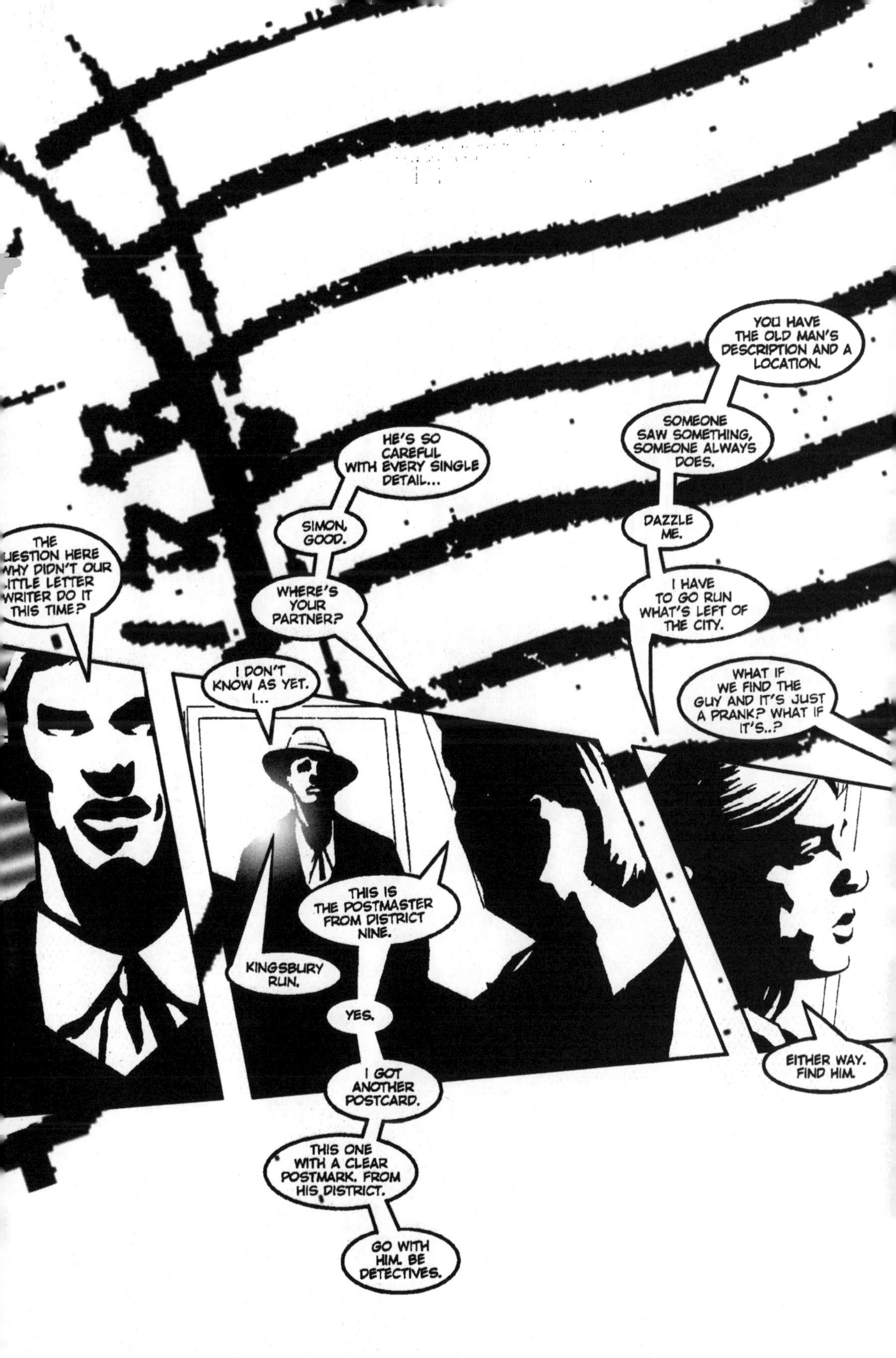
THE
UESTION HERE
WHY DIDN'T OUR
ITTLE LETTER
WRITER DO IT
THIS TIME?
HE'S SO CAREFUL WITH EVERY SINGLE DETAIL...
SIMON, GOOD.
WHERE'S YOUR PARTNER?
YOU HAVE THE OLD MAN'S DESCRIPTION AND A LOCATION.
SOMEONE SAW SOMETHING, SOMEONE ALWAYS DOES.
DAZZLE ME.
I HAVE TO GO RUN WHAT'S LEFT OF THE CITY.
I DON'T KNOW AS YET. I...
WHAT IF WE FIND THE GUY AND IT'S JUST A PRANK? WHAT IF IT'S..?
THIS IS THE POSTMASTER FROM DISTRICT NINE.
KINGSBURY RUN.
YES.
I GOT ANOTHER POSTCARD.
THIS ONE WITH A CLEAR POSTMARK. FROM HIS DISTRICT.
GO WITH HIM. BE DETECTIVES.
EITHER WAY. FIND HIM.

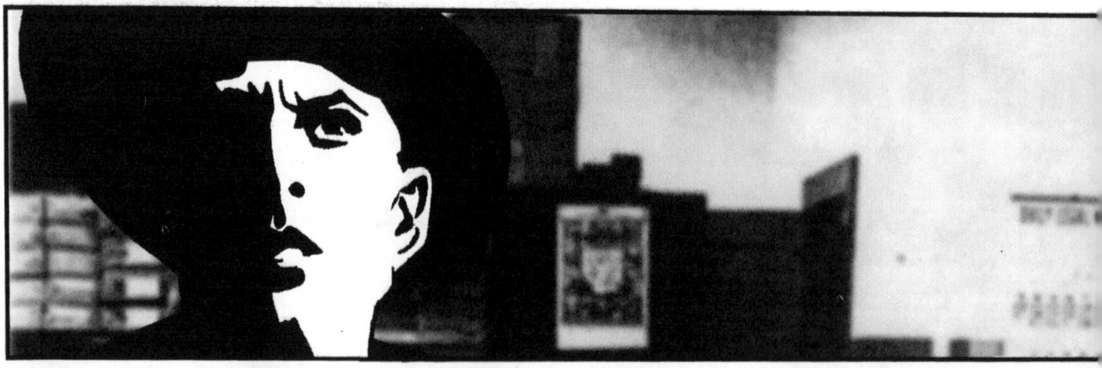

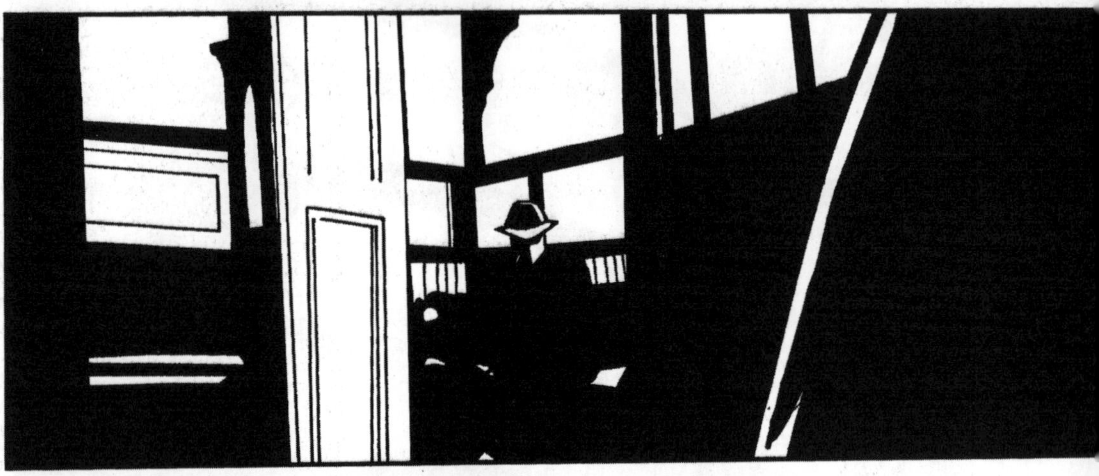

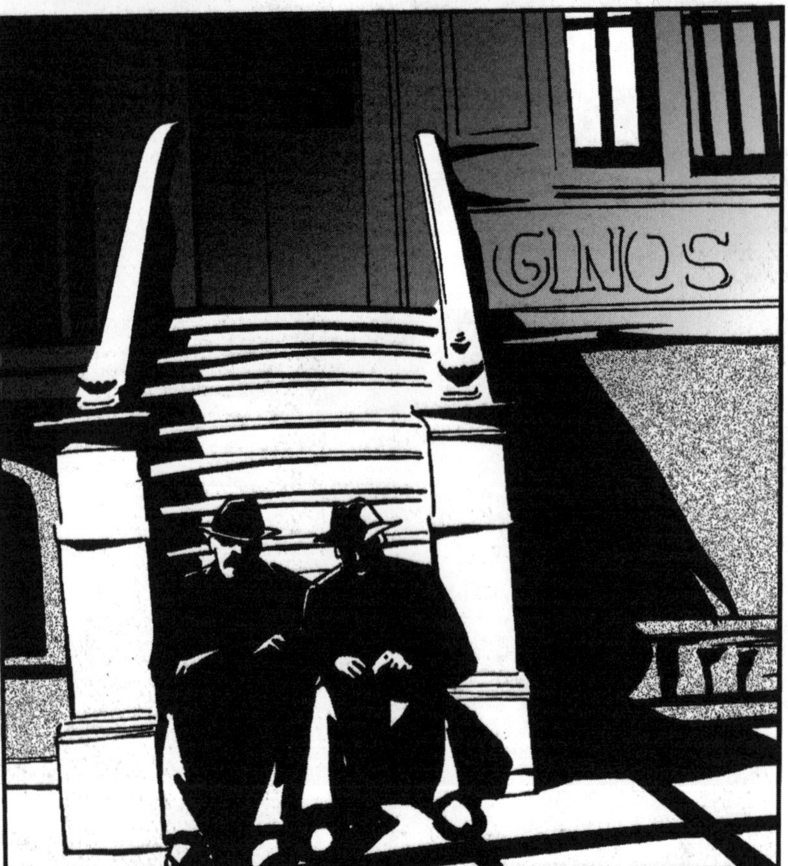
GINOS

MYRLO- SO...

SIMON- SO...

MYRLO- SO, ALL I DID WAS HEAD ON HOME. TALKED TO THE WIFE.

SIMON- WHAT DID SHE HAV TO...?

MYRLO- SEEMS THAT, FROM HER PERSPECTIVE, I AM QU THE ASS. AND IT SEEMS TH THIS IS QUITE OFTEN THAT AM QUITE THE ASS...

SIMON- REALLY?

MYRLO- YES. ALSO SEEMS THAT THIS BIG BOMBSHELL THAT YOU DROPPED ON MY HEAD WAS OF NO SURPRIS TO MY DARLING WIFE AT AL WHO, BY THE WAY, THINKS ARE THE BEE'S KNEES.

SIMON- WELL, THAT'S- THAT'S...

MYRLO- SO, Y'KNOW I'M NO GOING TO TRY TO SIT HERE AND TELL YOU THAT I GET CAUSE I-I-I DON'T.

SIMON- YEAH...

MYRLO- IT'S JUST, WELL, NOT HOW BY BRAIN WORKS

MYRLO- WELL, THIS
MAYBE SILLY BUT... DO YOU
HAVE THE- THE HOT TAMALES
FOR ME?

SIMON- FOR YOU? HA HA
...NO.

MYRLO- NO?

SIMON- NO.

MYRLO- WHY NOT?

SIMON- WHY NOT? BECAUSE I
KNOW YOU. "WHY NOT."

MYRLO- HA HA HA
YEAH, THE MISSUS SAYS THAT
NONE OF THIS IS EASY FOR
YOU AND THAT YOU REALLY
HAD TO HAVE TRUSTED ME TO
HAVE LAID THIS ON...

SIMON- THIS IS TRUE AS WELL.

MYRLO- IT'S JUST A THING
YOU DO.

SIMON- IT'S JUST...WELL,
YEAH.

MYRLO- AIN'T NO BIG DEAL IF
YOU THINK ABOUT IT.

SIMON- THIS IS WHAT I'M
SAYING.

MYRLO- THIS IS THE POINT.

SIMON- YEAH? GOOD.

MYRLO- YEAH. THERE'S
NOTHING ELSE TO THINK 'CEPT
CATCHING THE KILLER.

SIMON- THERE'S NO
OTHER...NO, THAT'S RIGHT.

MYRLO- GOOD.

SIMON- GOOD. YOU'RE
A DAMN GOOD MAN,
WALT. THANK YOU.

MYRLO- YEAH...

SIMON- NO, REALLY. THANK
YOU.

MYRLO- MAYBE WE SHOULD
HEAD ON OVER TO THE HOUSE
AND SEE IF THE WIFE KNOWS
WHO THE KILLER IS...

SIMON- HA HA. DON'T HAVE TO
YET...

MYRLO- WHY'S...?

SIMON- WE GOT OURSELVES A
LEAD.

MYRLO- NO SHIT.

SIMON- NONE.

MYRLO- THEN LET'S HIT THE
BRICKS.

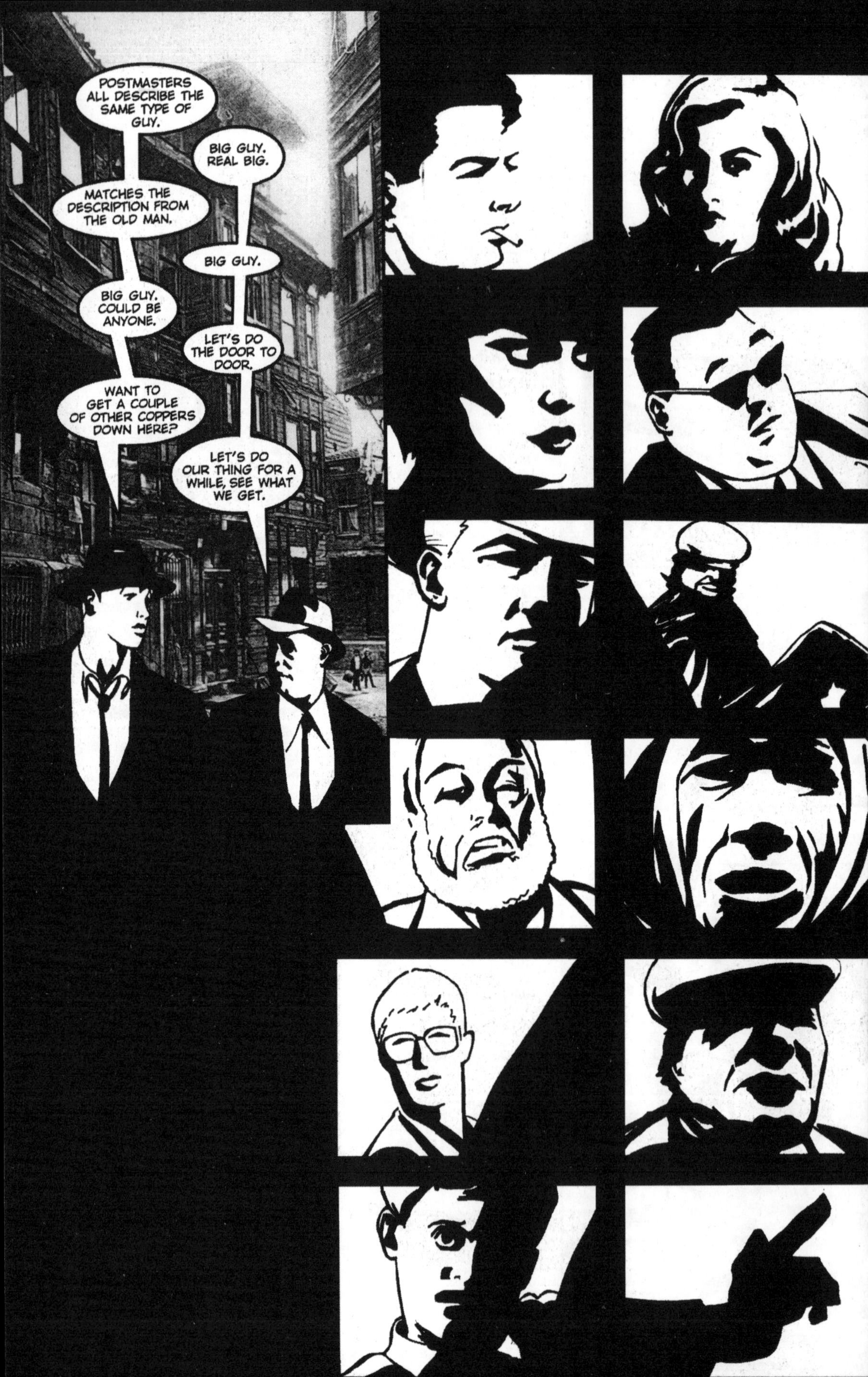
POSTMASTERS ALL DESCRIBE THE SAME TYPE OF GUY.
BIG GUY. REAL BIG.
MATCHES THE DESCRIPTION FROM THE OLD MAN.
BIG GUY.
BIG GUY. COULD BE ANYONE.
LET'S DO THE DOOR TO DOOR.
WANT TO GET A COUPLE OF OTHER COPPERS DOWN HERE?
LET'S DO OUR THING FOR A WHILE, SEE WHAT WE GET.

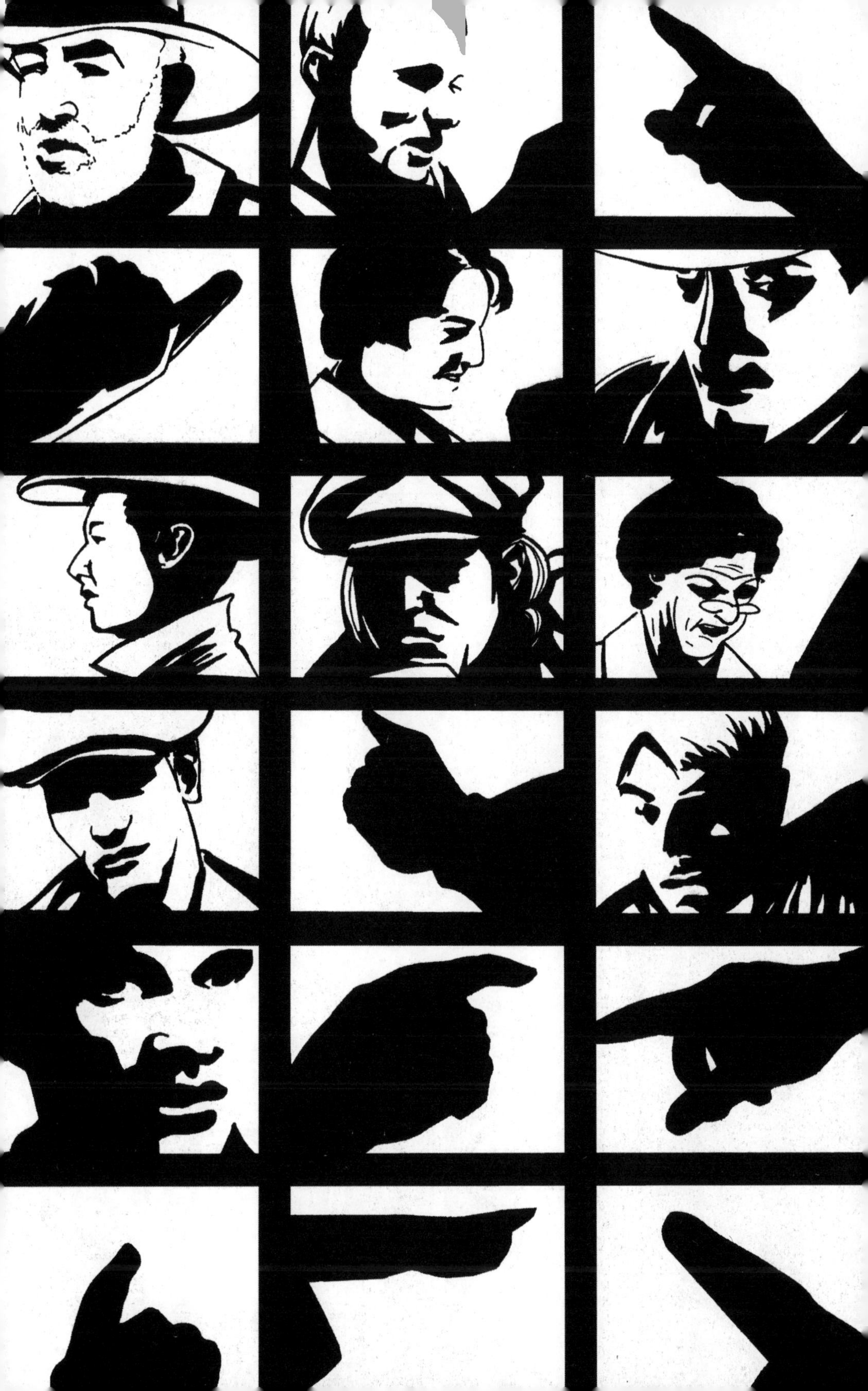

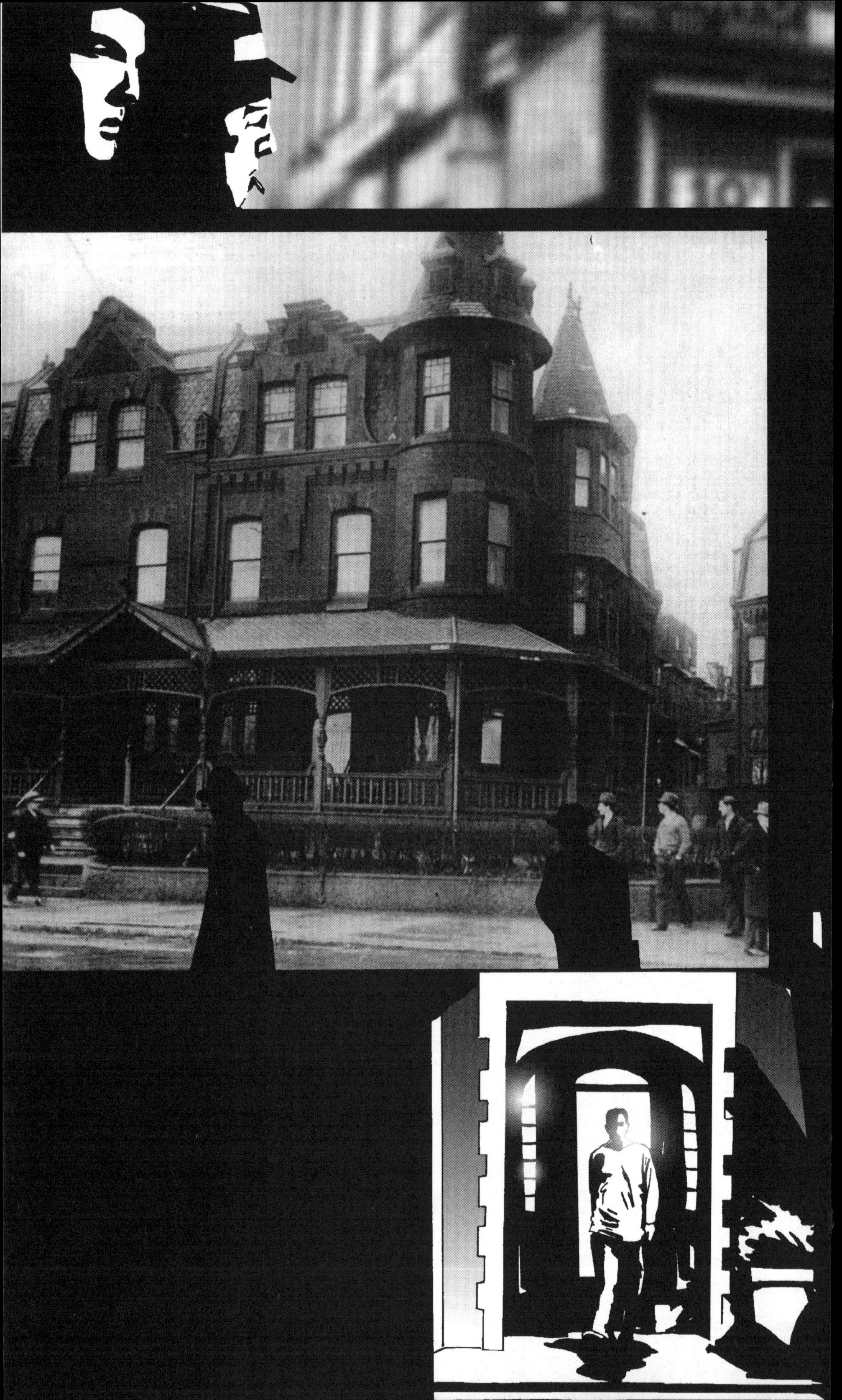

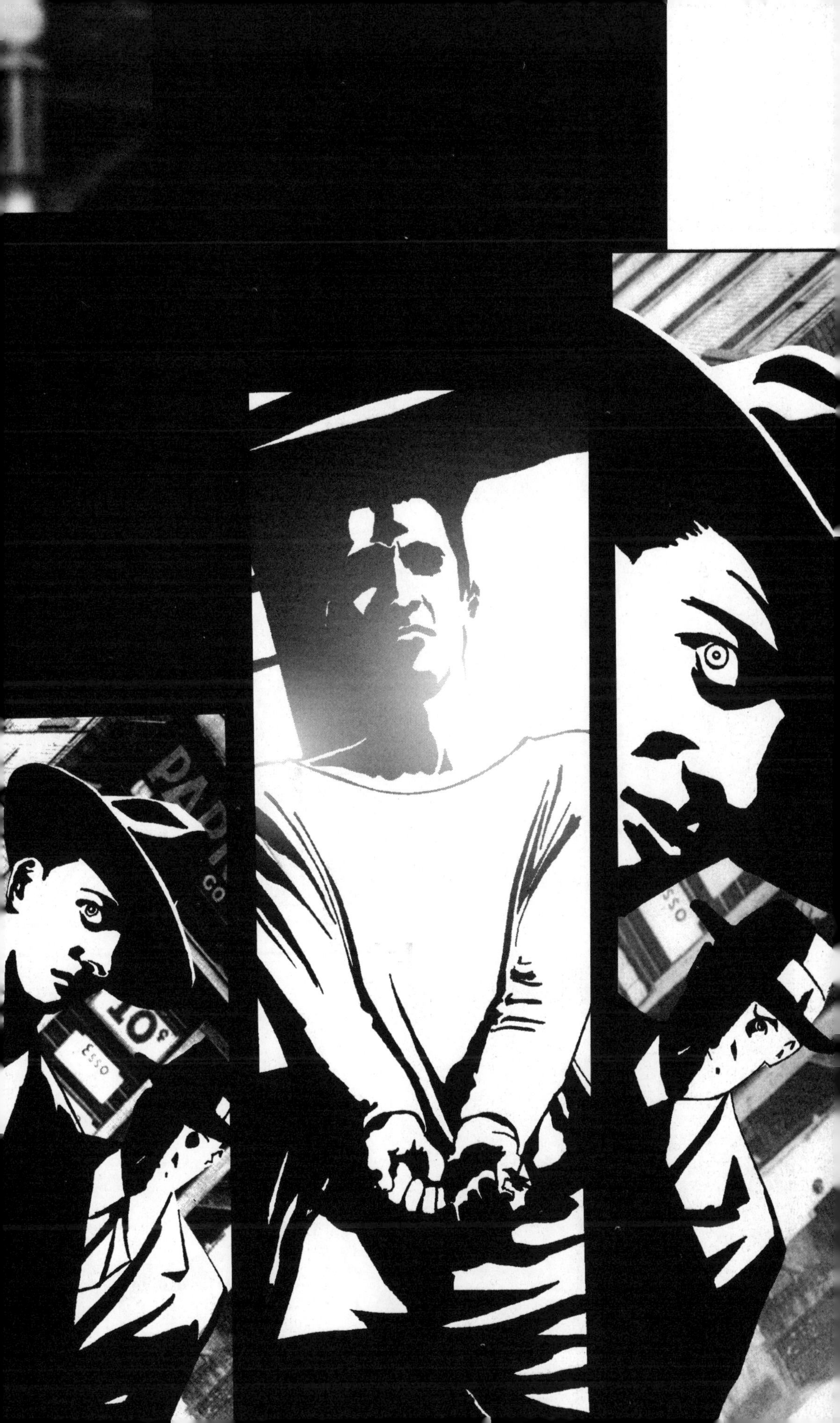
ESSO

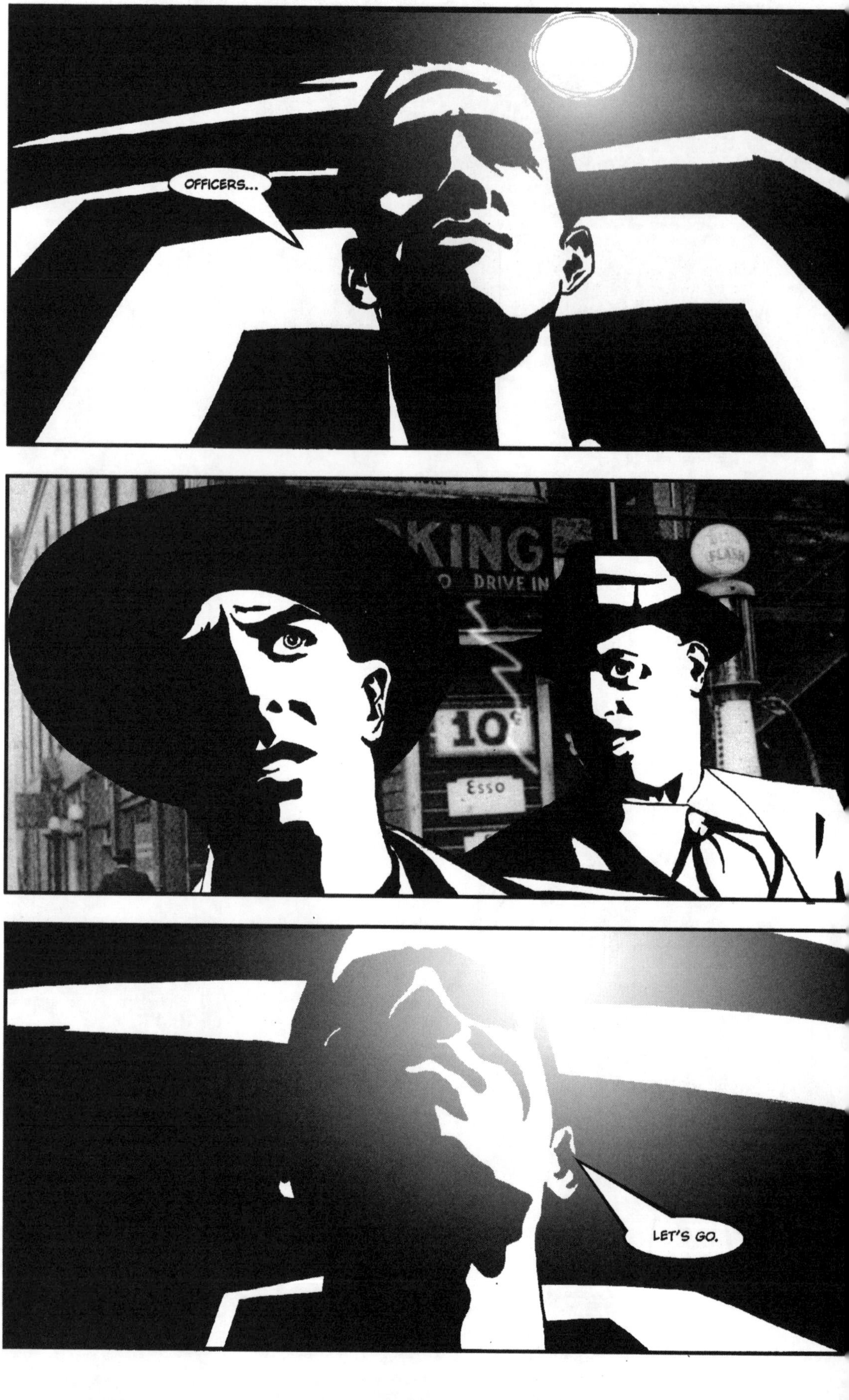
OFFICERS...
KING
DRIVE IN
10¢
Esso
LET'S GO.

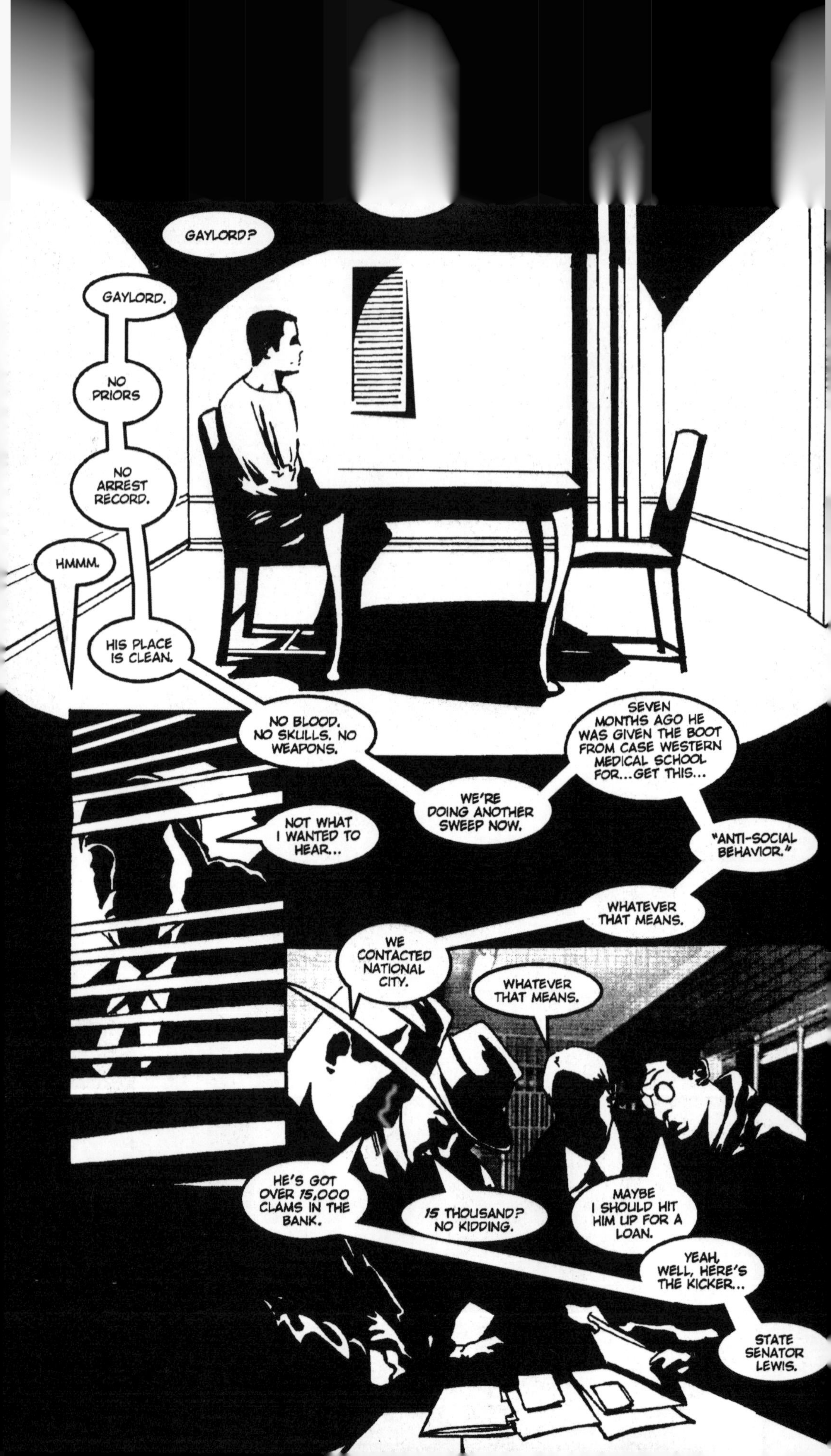
GAYLORD?
GAYLORD.
NO PRIORS
NO ARREST RECORD.
HMMM.
HIS PLACE IS CLEAN.
NO BLOOD. NO SKULLS. NO WEAPONS.
NOT WHAT I WANTED TO HEAR...
WE'RE DOING ANOTHER SWEEP NOW.
SEVEN MONTHS AGO HE WAS GIVEN THE BOOT FROM CASE WESTERN MEDICAL SCHOOL FOR...GET THIS...
"ANTI-SOCIAL BEHAVIOR."
WHATEVER THAT MEANS.
WE CONTACTED NATIONAL CITY.
WHATEVER THAT MEANS.
HE'S GOT OVER 15,000 CLAMS IN THE BANK.
15 THOUSAND? NO KIDDING.
MAYBE I SHOULD HIT HIM UP FOR A LOAN.
YEAH, WELL, HERE'S THE KICKER...
STATE SENATOR LEWIS.

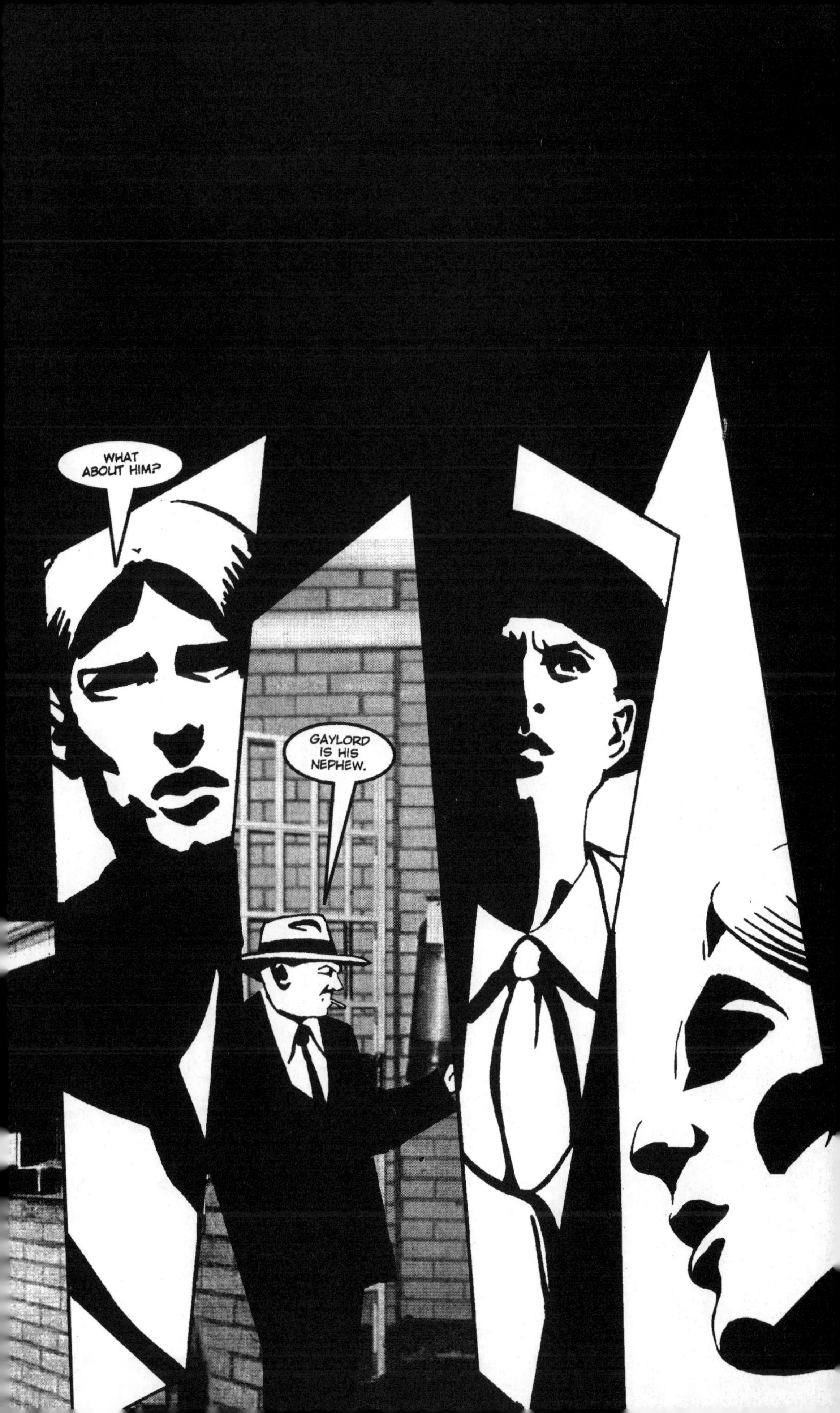
WHAT ABOUT HIM?
GAYLORD IS HIS NEPHEW.

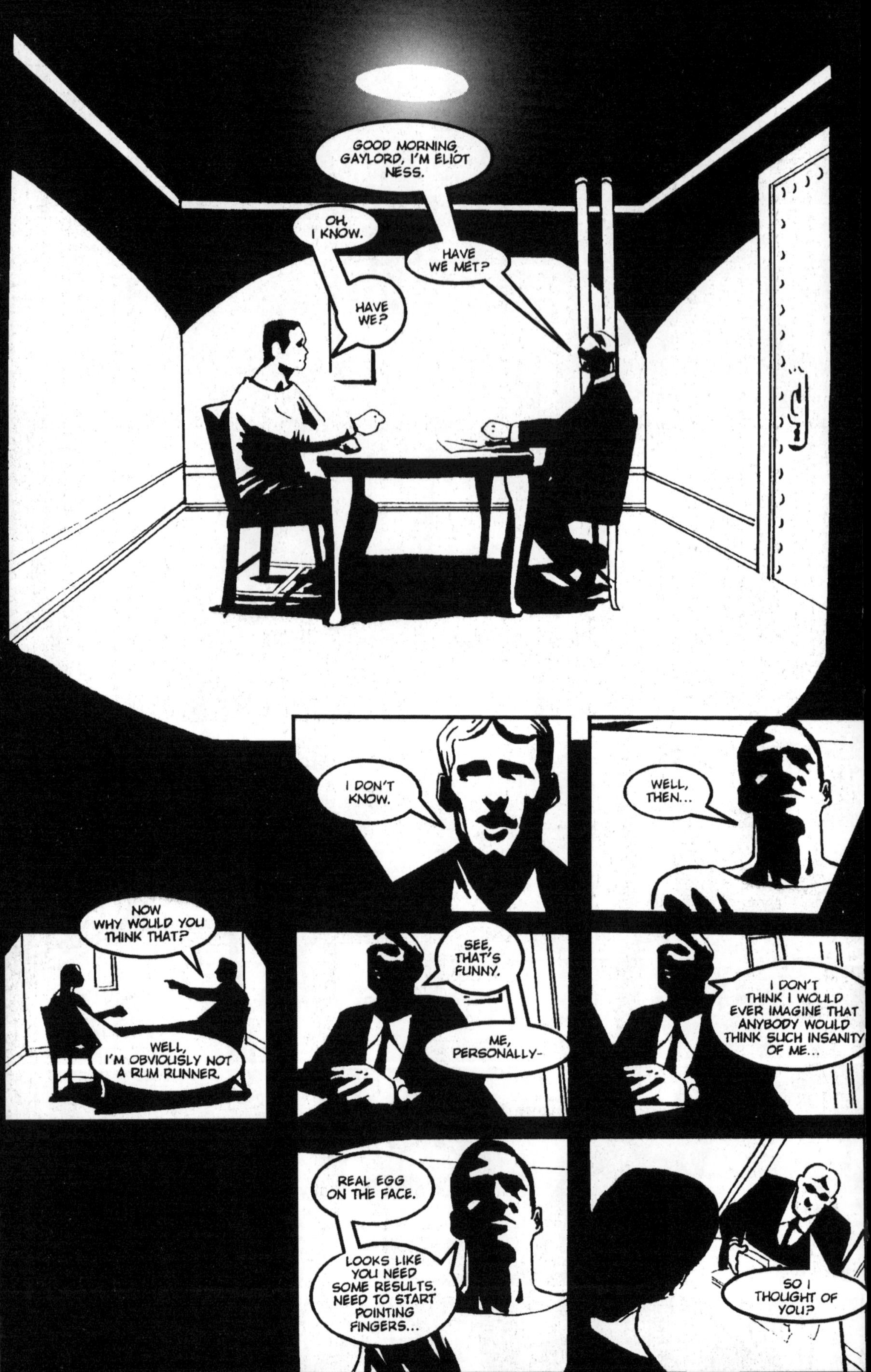
GOOD MORNING, GAYLORD, I'M ELIOT NESS.
OH, I KNOW.
HAVE WE MET?
HAVE WE?
I DON'T KNOW.
WELL, THEN...
NOW WHY WOULD YOU THINK THAT?
WELL, I'M OBVIOUSLY NOT A RUM RUNNER.
SEE, THAT'S FUNNY.
ME, PERSONALLY-
I DON'T THINK I WOULD EVER IMAGINE THAT ANYBODY WOULD THINK SUCH INSANITY OF ME...
REAL EGG ON THE FACE.
LOOKS LIKE YOU NEED SOME RESULTS. NEED TO START POINTING FINGERS...
SO I THOUGHT OF YOU?

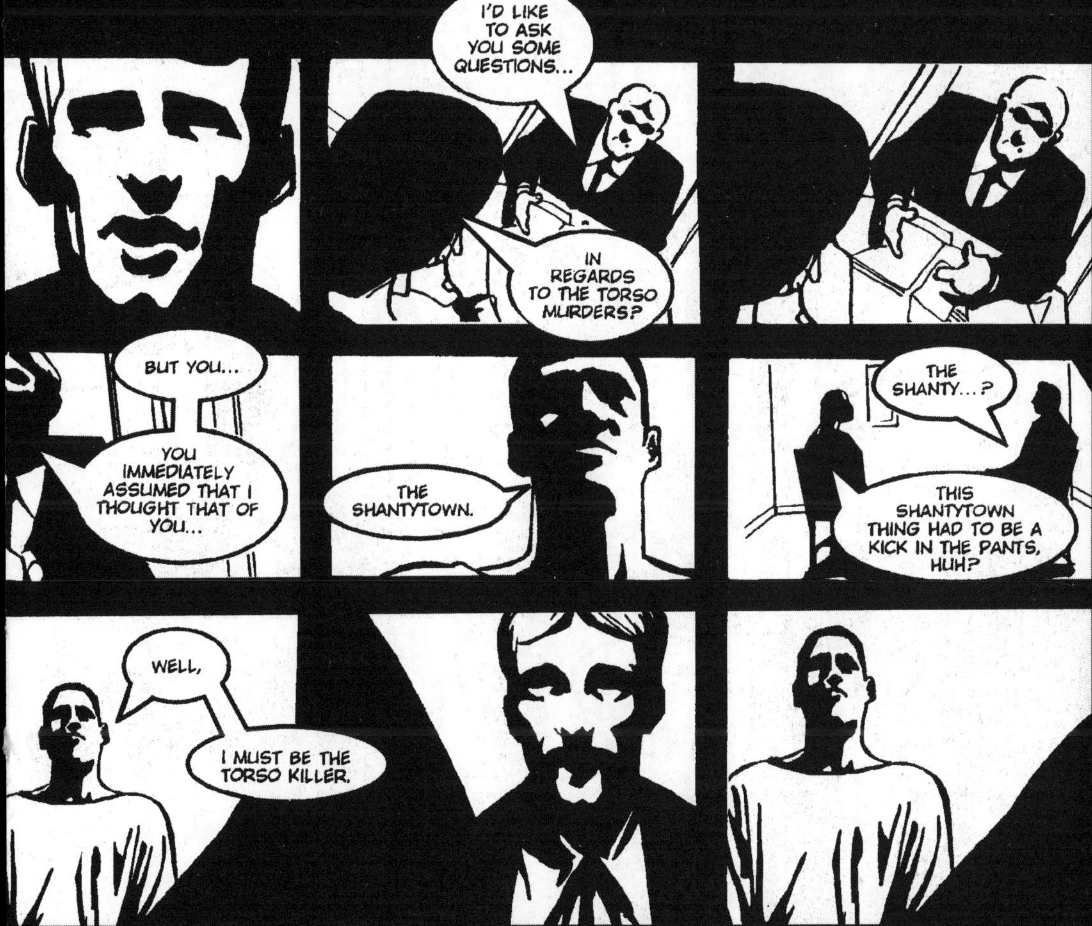
I'D LIKE TO ASK YOU SOME QUESTIONS...
IN REGARDS TO THE TORSO MURDERS?
BUT YOU...
YOU IMMEDIATELY ASSUMED THAT I THOUGHT THAT OF YOU...
THE SHANTYTOWN.
THE SHANTY...?
THIS SHANTYTOWN THING HAD TO BE A KICK IN THE PANTS, HUH?
WELL,
I MUST BE THE TORSO KILLER.

THE ARRESTING OFFICERS SAID THAT YOU GREETED THEM AT THE DOOR READY TO BE CUFFED. READY TO COME DOWN HERE.
WHY?
WHY WHAT?
WHY WOULD AN AMIABLE, LAW-ABIDING CITIZEN SUCH AS YOURSELF BE READY TO BE TAKEN DOWNTOWN?
I SAW THEM ASKING AROUND.
SAW THEM CIRCLING AROUND.
IT INSULTS ME WHEN PEOPLE MAKE ASSUMPTIONS ABOUT MY CHARACTER.
YOU EITHER MEAN TO COMPLIMENT OR PATRONIZE ME BY COMMENTING ON MY INTELLECT.
BUT YOU DO NOT KNOW ME.
SO, EITHER WAY, I FIND YOUR COMMENT INSULTING.
NONE MEANT.
THERE'S JUST AN AIR ABOUT YOU, GAYLORD. IT'S UNDENIABLE.
IS THERE?
YOU WENT TO MEDICAL SCHOOL. NOT EXACTLY A STOOGE FARM.

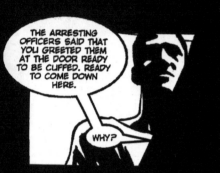

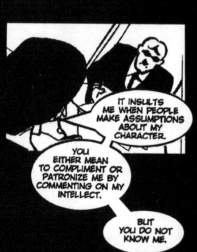

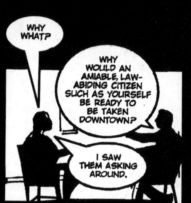

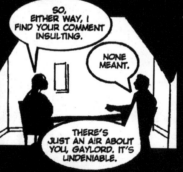

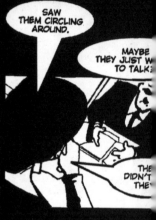

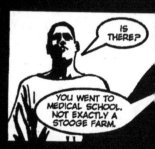

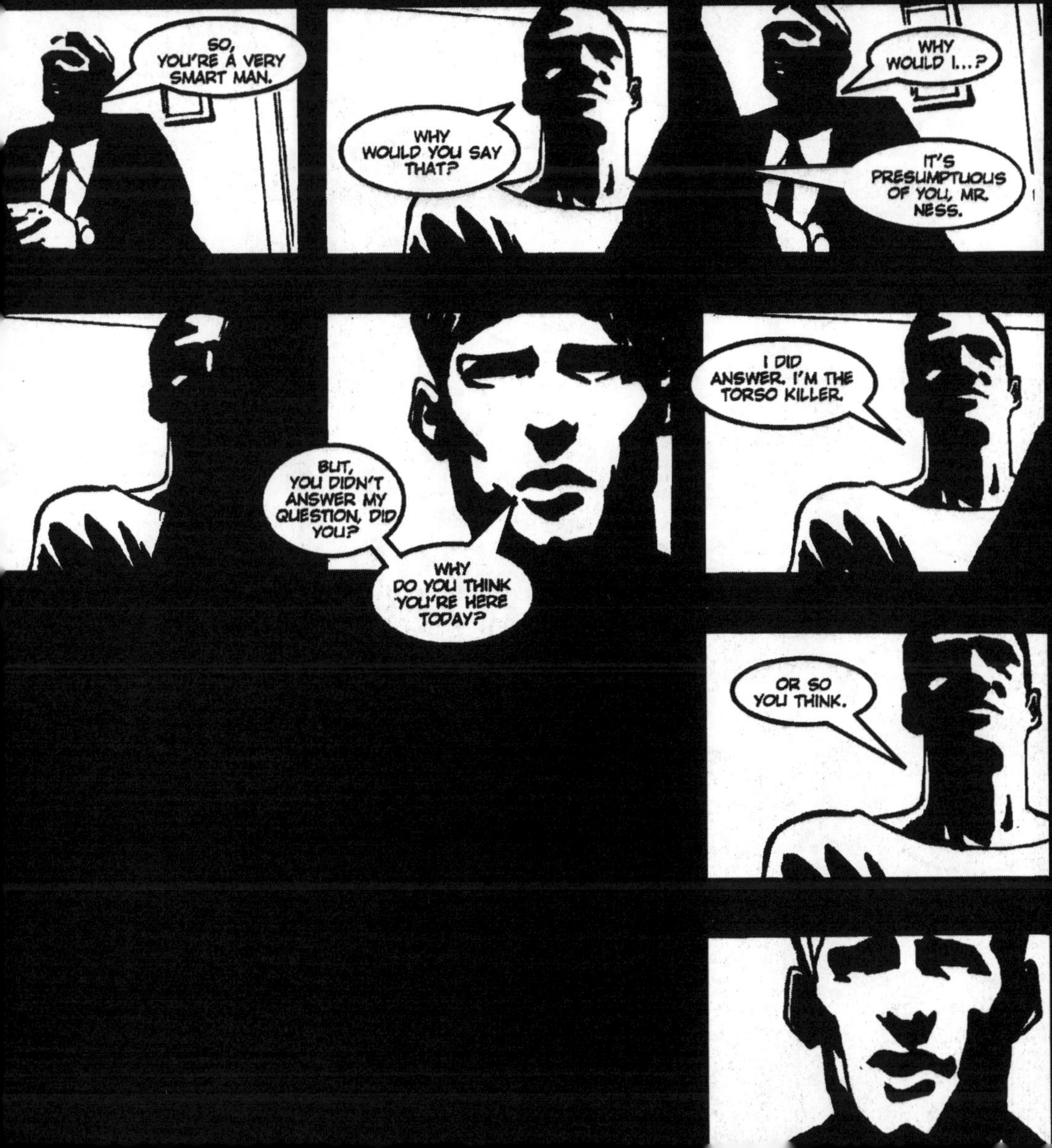
SO, YOU'RE A VERY SMART MAN.
WHY WOULD YOU SAY THAT?
WHY WOULD I...?
IT'S PRESUMPTUOUS OF YOU, MR. NESS.
BUT, YOU DIDN'T ANSWER MY QUESTION, DID YOU?
WHY DO YOU THINK YOU'RE HERE TODAY?
I DID ANSWER. I'M THE TORSO KILLER.
OR SO YOU THINK.

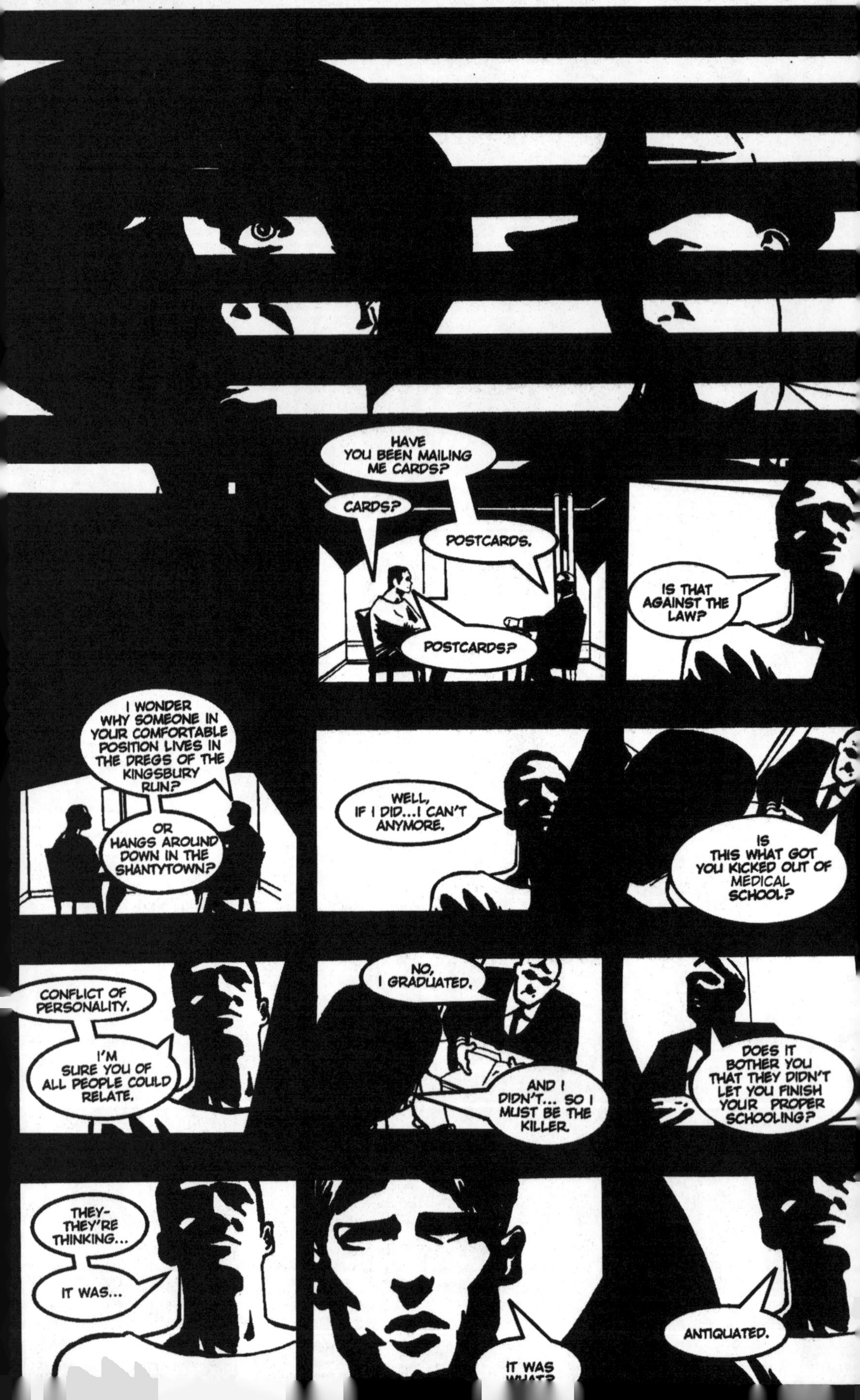
HAVE YOU BEEN MAILING ME CARDS?
CARDS?
POSTCARDS.
POSTCARDS?
IS THAT AGAINST THE LAW?
I WONDER WHY SOMEONE IN YOUR COMFORTABLE POSITION LIVES IN THE DREGS OF THE KINGSBURY RUN?
OR HANGS AROUND DOWN IN THE SHANTYTOWN?
WELL, IF I DID...I CAN'T ANYMORE.
IS THIS WHAT GOT YOU KICKED OUT OF MEDICAL SCHOOL?
CONFLICT OF PERSONALITY.
I'M SURE YOU OF ALL PEOPLE COULD RELATE.
NO, I GRADUATED.
AND I DIDN'T... SO I MUST BE THE KILLER.
DOES IT BOTHER YOU THAT THEY DIDN'T LET YOU FINISH YOUR PROPER SCHOOLING?
THEY- THEY'RE THINKING...
IT WAS...
IT WAS
ANTIQUATED.

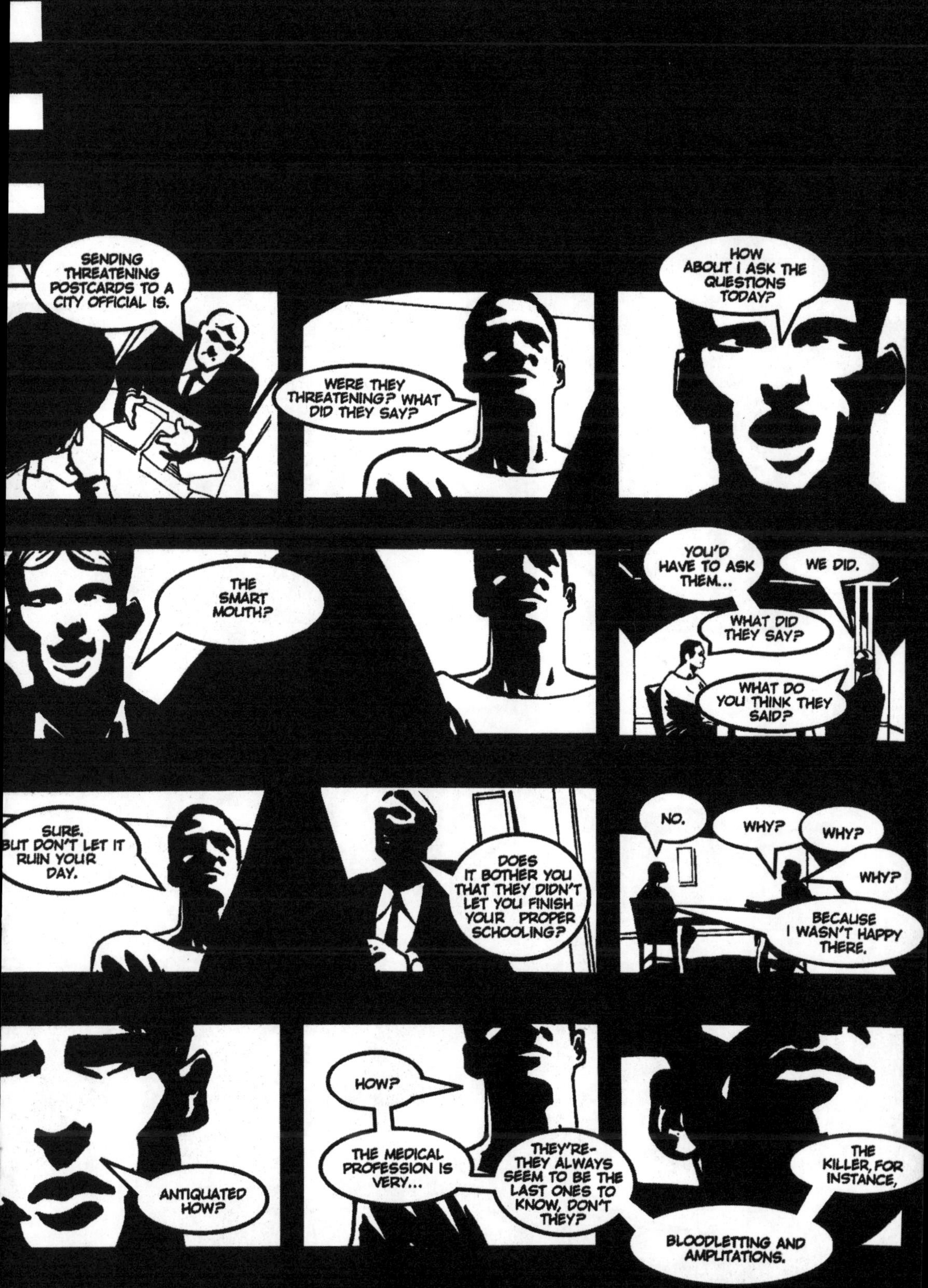
SENDING THREATENING POSTCARDS TO A CITY OFFICIAL IS.
WERE THEY THREATENING? WHAT DID THEY SAY?
HOW ABOUT I ASK THE QUESTIONS TODAY?
THE SMART MOUTH?
YOU'D HAVE TO ASK THEM...
WE DID.
WHAT DID THEY SAY?
WHAT DO YOU THINK THEY SAID?
SURE. BUT DON'T LET IT RUIN YOUR DAY.
DOES IT BOTHER YOU THAT THEY DIDN'T LET YOU FINISH YOUR PROPER SCHOOLING?
NO.
WHY?
WHY?
WHY?
BECAUSE I WASN'T HAPPY THERE.
ANTIQUATED HOW?
HOW?
THE MEDICAL PROFESSION IS VERY...
THEY'RE- THEY ALWAYS SEEM TO BE THE LAST ONES TO KNOW, DON'T THEY?
THE KILLER, FOR INSTANCE,
BLOODLETTING AND AMPUTATIONS.

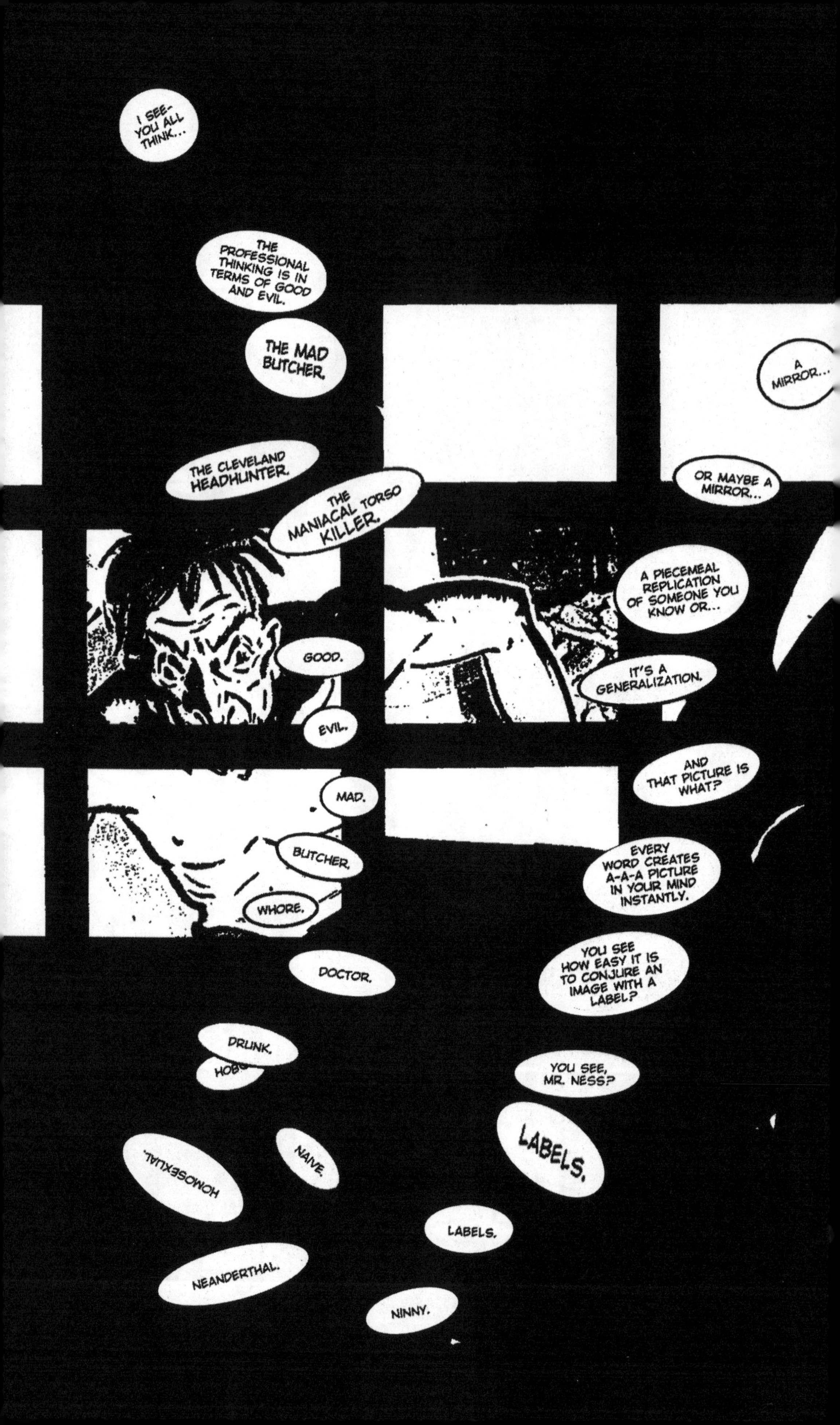
I SEE- YOU ALL THINK...
THE PROFESSIONAL THINKING IS IN TERMS OF GOOD AND EVIL.
THE MAD BUTCHER.
A MIRROR...
THE CLEVELAND HEADHUNTER.
THE MANIACAL TORSO KILLER.
OR MAYBE A MIRROR...
A PIECEMEAL REPLICATION OF SOMEONE YOU KNOW OR...
GOOD.
IT'S A GENERALIZATION.
EVIL.
AND THAT PICTURE IS WHAT?
MAD.
BUTCHER.
EVERY WORD CREATES A-A-A PICTURE IN YOUR MIND INSTANTLY.
WHORE.
DOCTOR.
YOU SEE HOW EASY IT IS TO CONJURE AN IMAGE WITH A LABEL?
DRUNK.
YOU SEE, MR. NESS?
LABELS.
HOMOSEXUAL.
NAIVE.
LABELS.
NEANDERTHAL.
NINNY.

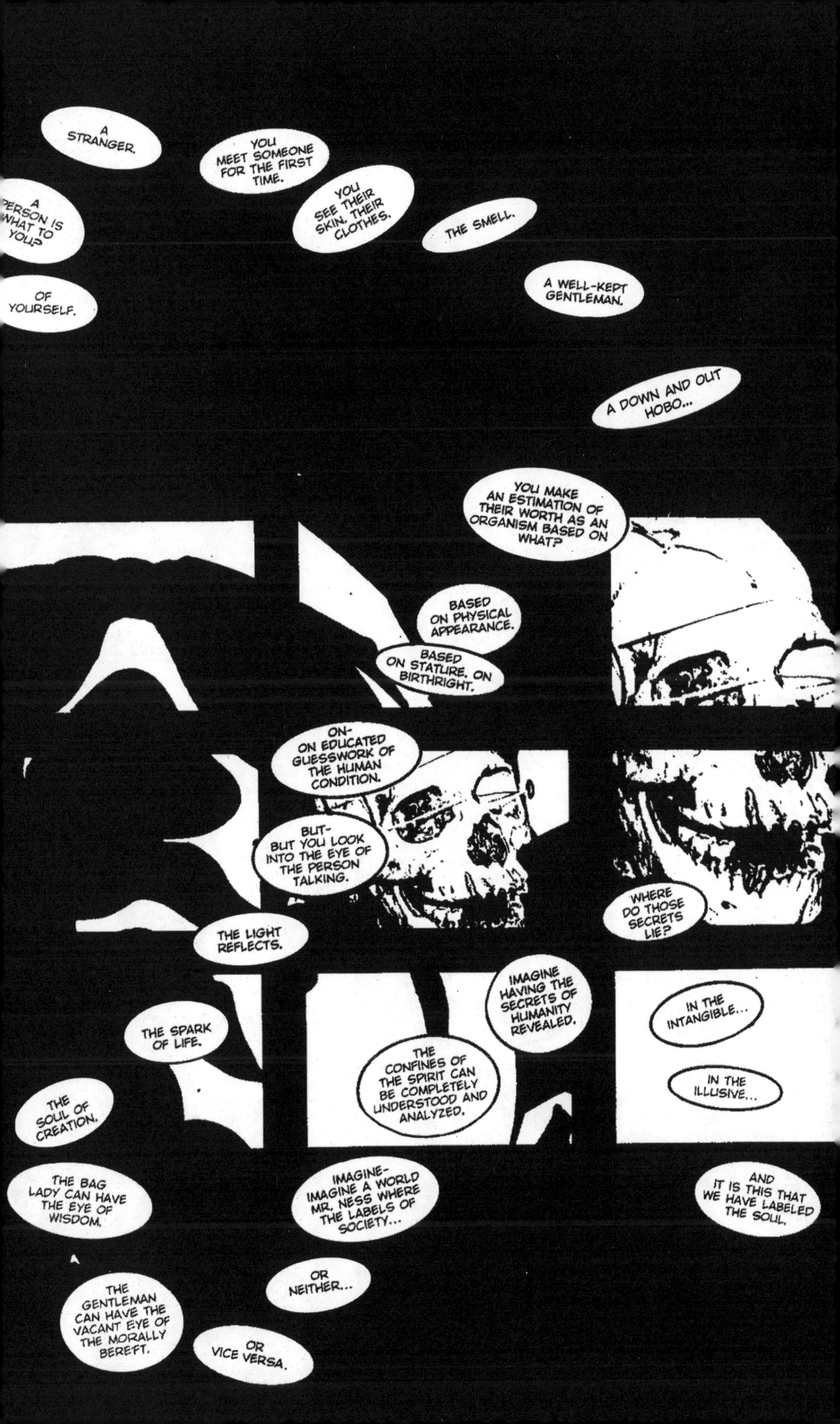

A STRANGER.
YOU MEET SOMEONE FOR THE FIRST TIME.
YOU SEE THEIR SKIN, THEIR CLOTHES.
THE SMELL.
A PERSON IS WHAT TO YOU?
OF YOURSELF.
A WELL-KEPT GENTLEMAN.
A DOWN AND OUT HOBO...
YOU MAKE AN ESTIMATION OF THEIR WORTH AS AN ORGANISM BASED ON WHAT?
BASED ON PHYSICAL APPEARANCE.
BASED ON STATURE, ON BIRTHRIGHT.
ON- ON EDUCATED GUESSWORK OF THE HUMAN CONDITION.
BUT- BUT YOU LOOK INTO THE EYE OF THE PERSON TALKING.
THE LIGHT REFLECTS.
WHERE DO THOSE SECRETS LIE?
THE SPARK OF LIFE.
THE SOUL OF CREATION.
IMAGINE HAVING THE SECRETS OF HUMANITY REVEALED.
THE CONFINES OF THE SPIRIT CAN BE COMPLETELY UNDERSTOOD AND ANALYZED.
IN THE INTANGIBLE...
IN THE ILLUSIVE...
THE BAG LADY CAN HAVE THE EYE OF WISDOM.
THE GENTLEMAN CAN HAVE THE VACANT EYE OF THE MORALLY BEREFT.
OR VICE VERSA.
OR NEITHER...
IMAGINE- IMAGINE A WORLD MR. NESS WHERE THE LABELS OF SOCIETY...
AND IT IS THIS THAT WE HAVE LABELED THE SOUL.

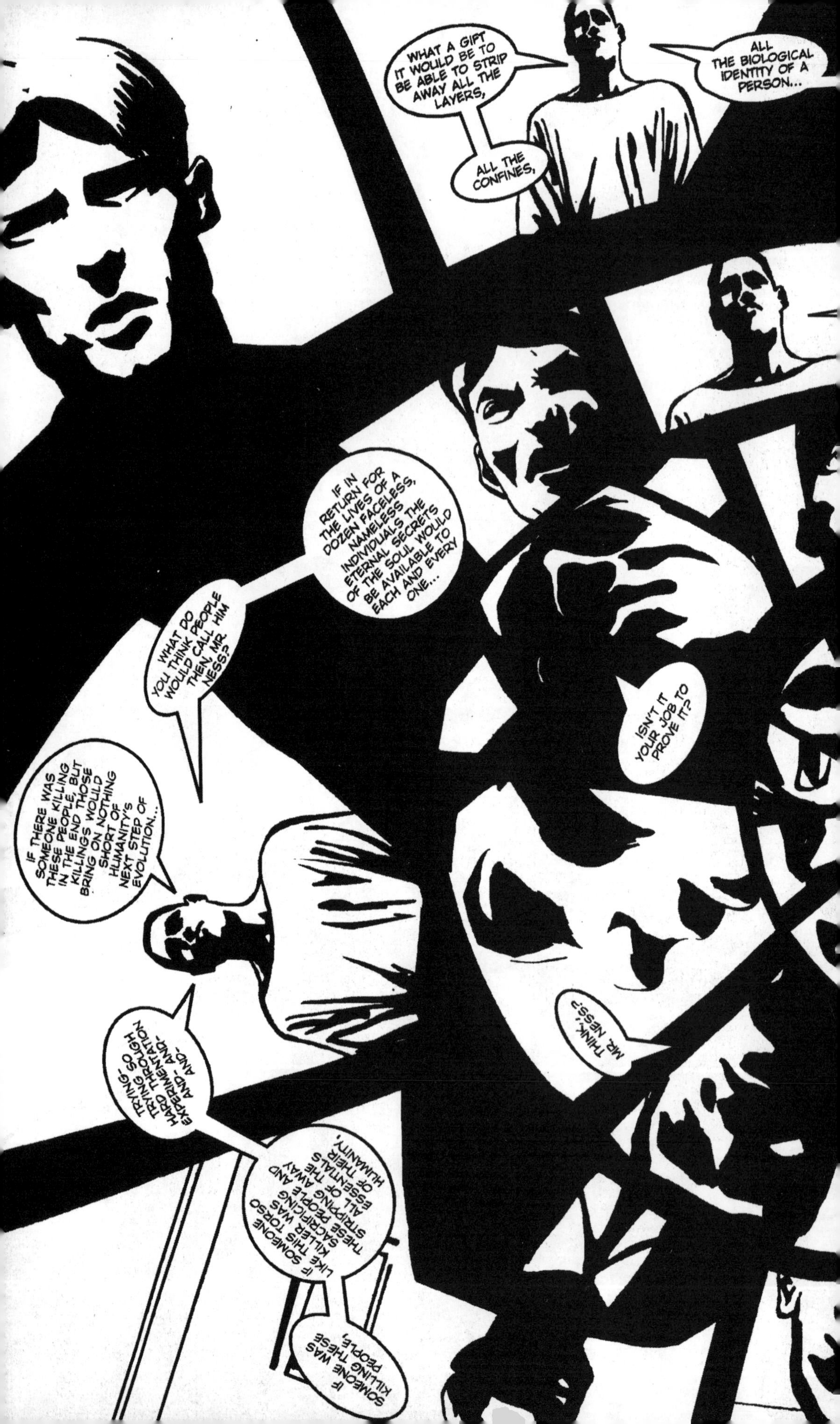

WHAT A GIFT IT WOULD BE TO STRIP AWAY ALL THE LAYERS,
ALL THE CONFINES,
ALL THE BIOLOGICAL IDENTITY OF A PERSON...
IF IN RETURN FOR THE LIVES OF A DOZEN FACELESS, NAMELESS INDIVIDUALS THE ETERNAL SECRETS OF THE SOUL WOULD BE AVAILABLE TO EACH AND EVERY ONE...
WHAT DO YOU THINK PEOPLE WOULD CALL HIM THEN, MR. NESS?
ISN'T IT YOUR JOB TO PROVE IT?
IF THERE WAS SOMEONE KILLING THESE PEOPLE, BUT IN THE END THOSE KILLINGS WOULD BRING ON NOTHING SHORT OF HUMANITY'S NEXT STEP OF EVOLUTION...
THINK, MR. NESS?
TRYING- TRYING SO HARD THROUGH EXPERIMENTATION AND- AND- AND-
IF SOMEONE WAS KILLING THESE PEOPLE,
IF SOMEONE LIKE THIS TORSO KILLER WAS SACRIFICING THESE PEOPLE AND STRIPPING AWAY ALL OF THE ESSENTIALS OF THEIR HUMANITY,

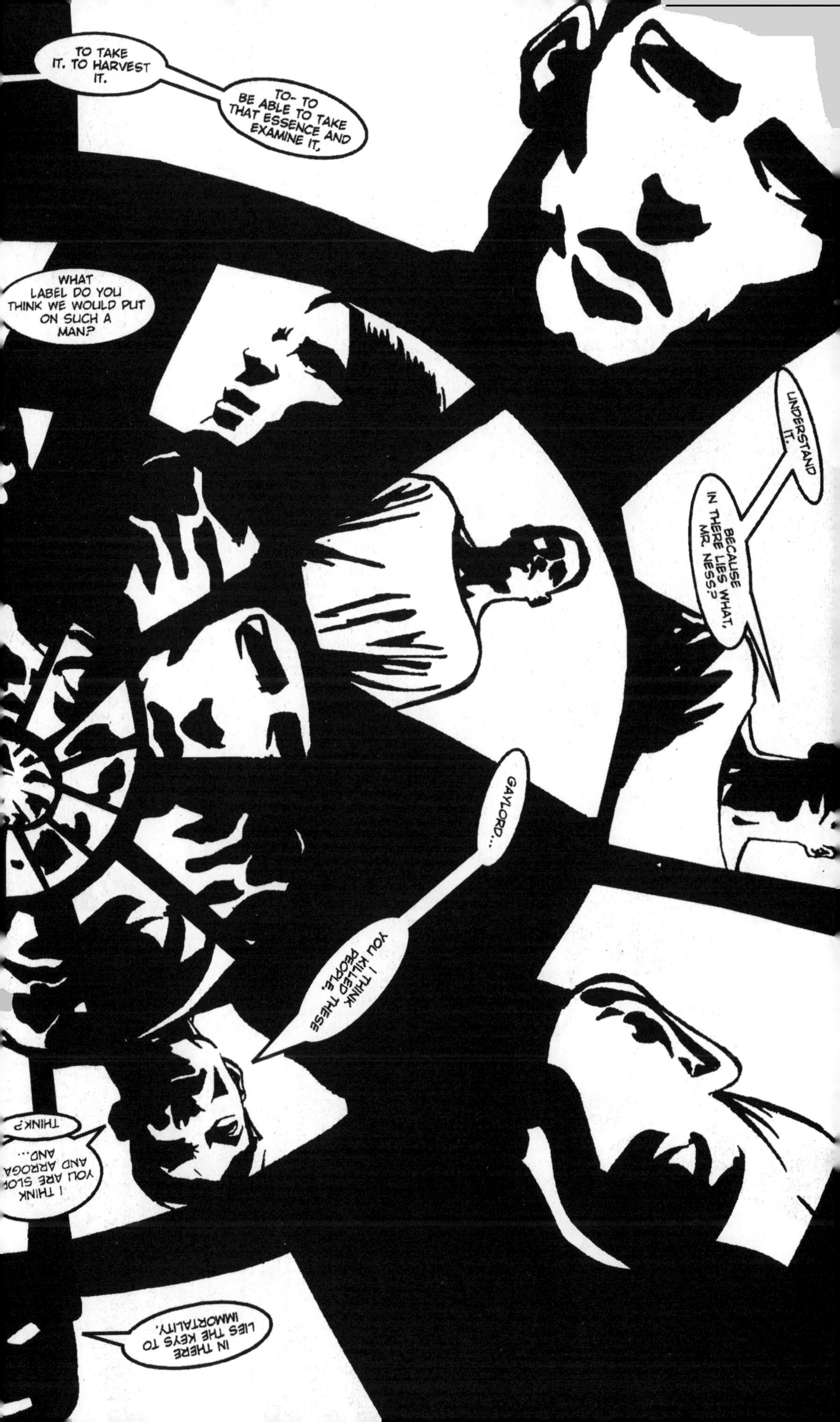
IN THERE LIES THE KEYS TO IMMORTALITY.
BECAUSE IN THERE LIES WHAT, MR. NESS?
UNDERSTAND IT.
TO- TO BE ABLE TO TAKE THAT ESSENCE AND EXAMINE IT.
TO TAKE IT. TO HARVEST IT.
WHAT LABEL DO YOU THINK WE WOULD PUT ON SUCH A MAN?
GAYLORD...
I THINK YOU KILLED THESE PEOPLE.
I THINK YOU ARE SLOP AND ARROGA AND...
THINK?

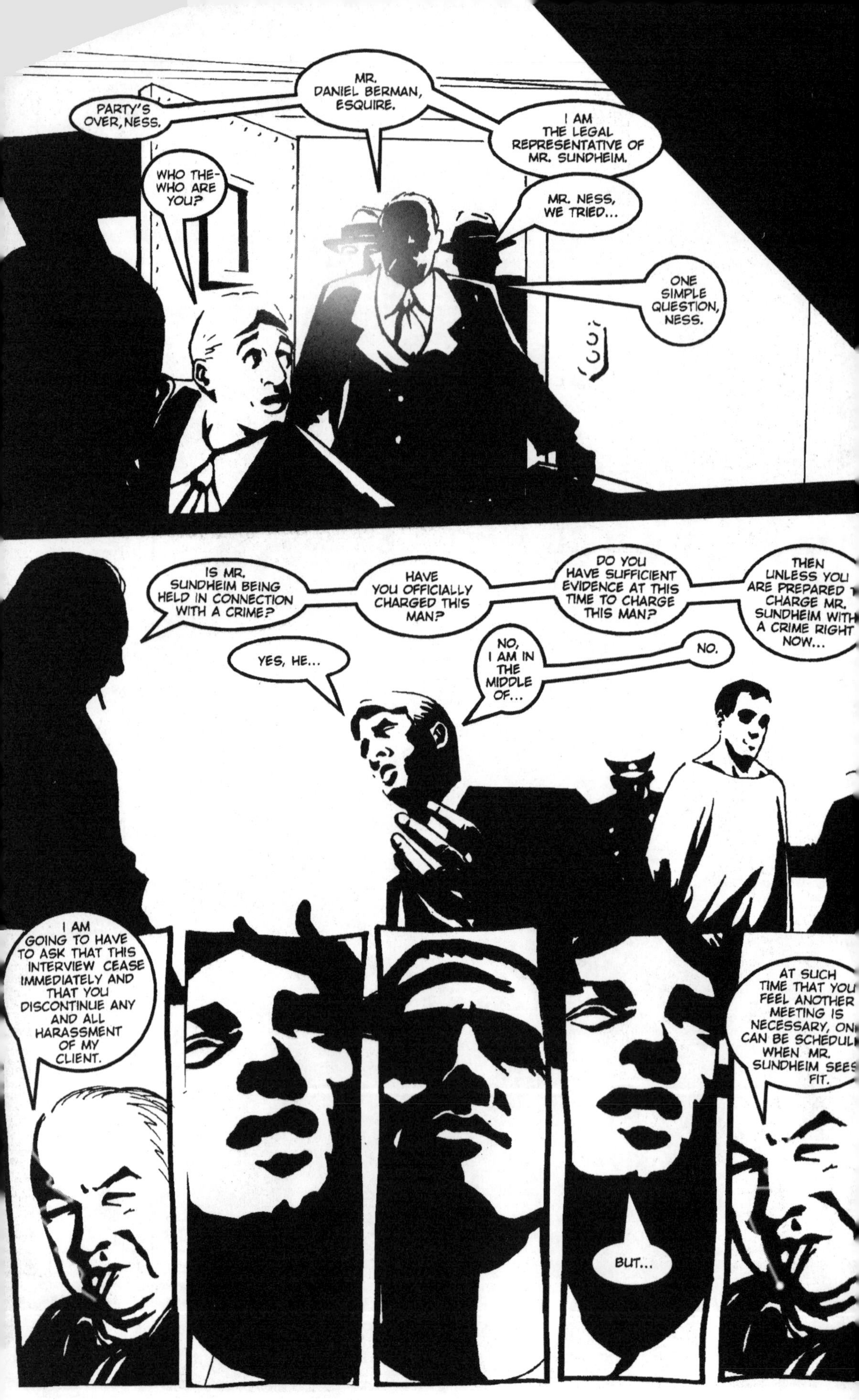
PARTY'S OVER, NESS.
MR. DANIEL BERMAN, ESQUIRE.
I AM THE LEGAL REPRESENTATIVE OF MR. SUNDHEIM.
WHO THE- WHO ARE YOU?
MR. NESS, WE TRIED...
ONE SIMPLE QUESTION, NESS.
IS MR. SUNDHEIM BEING HELD IN CONNECTION WITH A CRIME?
YES, HE...
HAVE YOU OFFICIALLY CHARGED THIS MAN?
NO, I AM IN THE MIDDLE OF...
DO YOU HAVE SUFFICIENT EVIDENCE AT THIS TIME TO CHARGE THIS MAN?
NO.
THEN UNLESS YOU ARE PREPARED CHARGE MR. SUNDHEIM WITH A CRIME RIGHT NOW...
I AM GOING TO HAVE TO ASK THAT THIS INTERVIEW CEASE IMMEDIATELY AND THAT YOU DISCONTINUE ANY AND ALL HARASSMENT OF MY CLIENT.
BUT...
AT SUCH TIME THAT YOU FEEL ANOTHER MEETING IS NECESSARY, ON CAN BE SCHEDUL WHEN MR. SUNDHEIM SEES FIT.

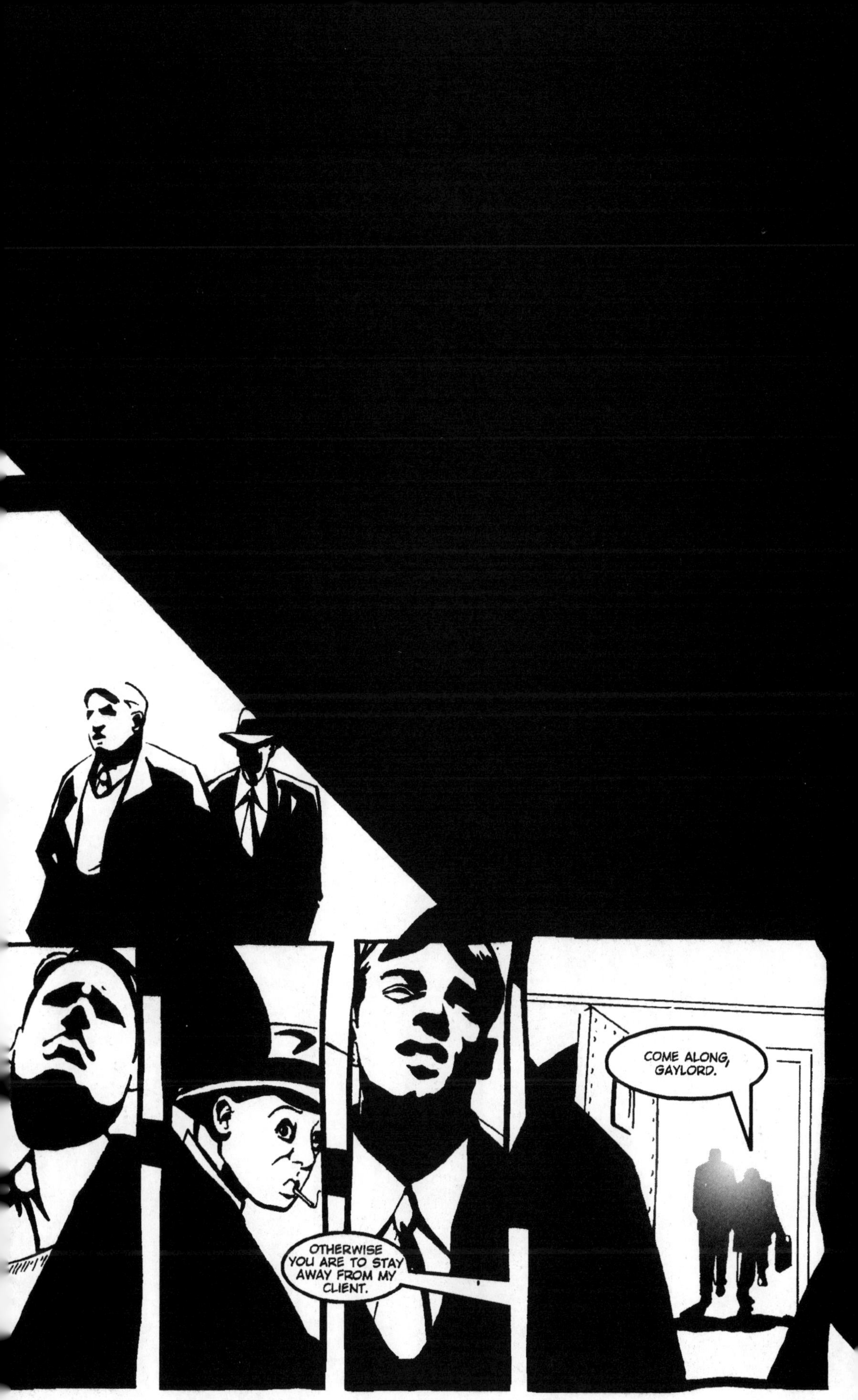
COME ALONG, GAYLORD.
OTHERWISE YOU ARE TO STAY AWAY FROM MY CLIENT.

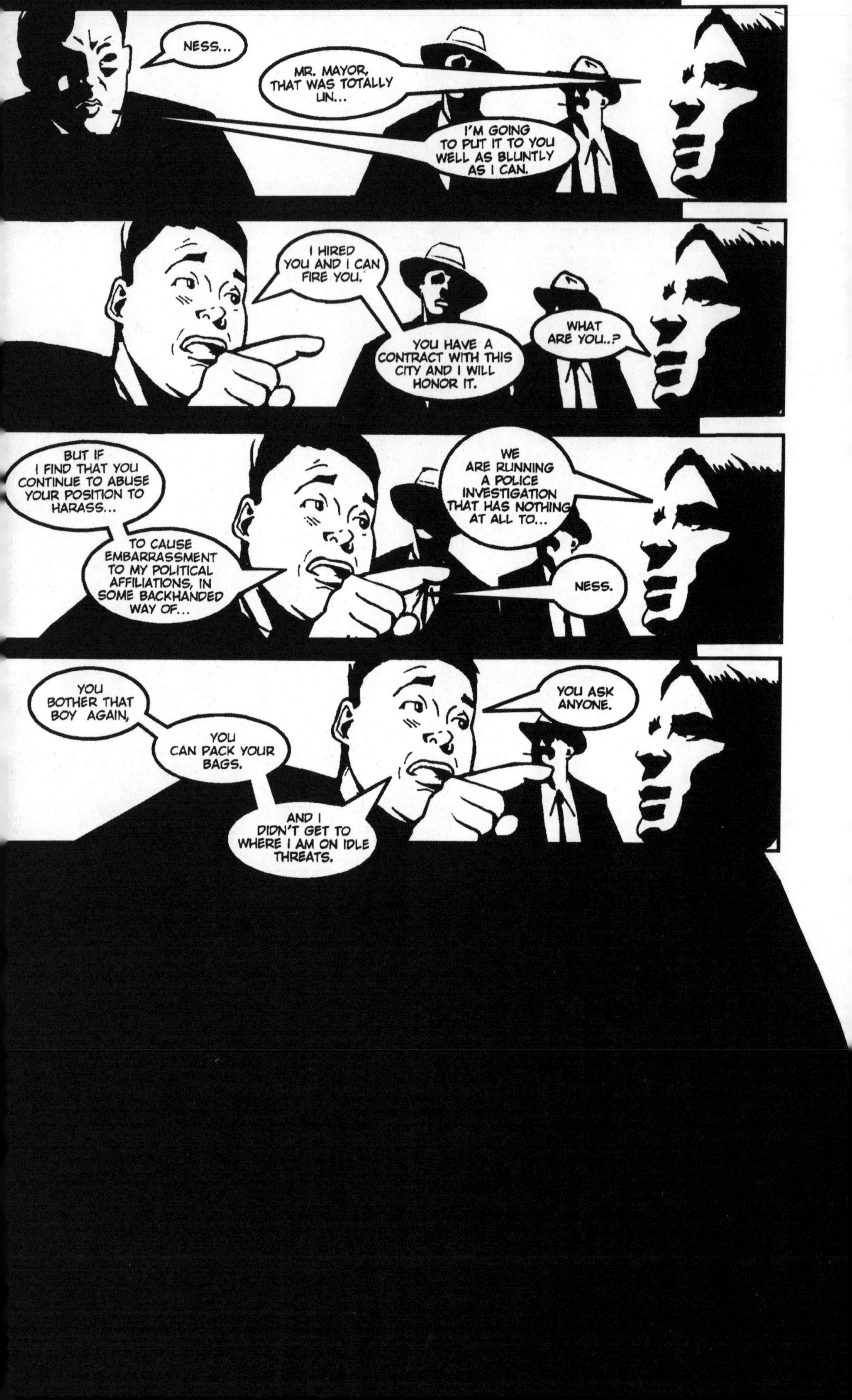
NESS...
MR. MAYOR, THAT WAS TOTALLY UN...
I'M GOING TO PUT IT TO YOU WELL AS BLUNTLY AS I CAN.
I HIRED YOU AND I CAN FIRE YOU.
YOU HAVE A CONTRACT WITH THIS CITY AND I WILL HONOR IT.
WHAT ARE YOU..?
BUT IF I FIND THAT YOU CONTINUE TO ABUSE YOUR POSITION TO HARASS...
TO CAUSE EMBARRASSMENT TO MY POLITICAL AFFILIATIONS, IN SOME BACKHANDED WAY OF...
WE ARE RUNNING A POLICE INVESTIGATION THAT HAS NOTHING AT ALL TO...
NESS.
YOU BOTHER THAT BOY AGAIN,
YOU CAN PACK YOUR BAGS.
AND I DIDN'T GET TO WHERE I AM ON IDLE THREATS.
YOU ASK ANYONE.

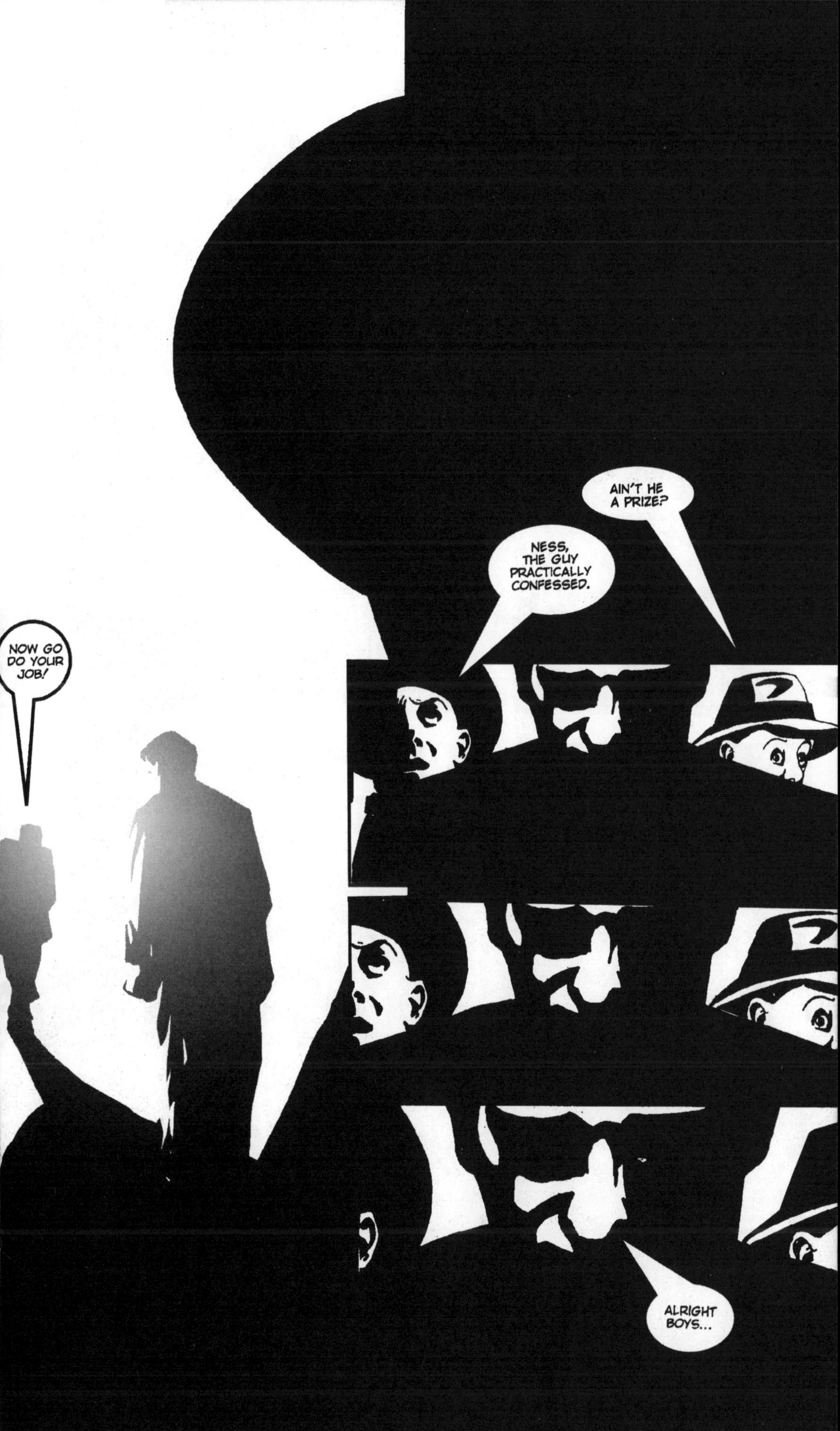
NOW GO DO YOUR JOB!
AIN'T HE A PRIZE?
NESS, THE GUY PRACTICALLY CONFESSED.
ALRIGHT BOYS...

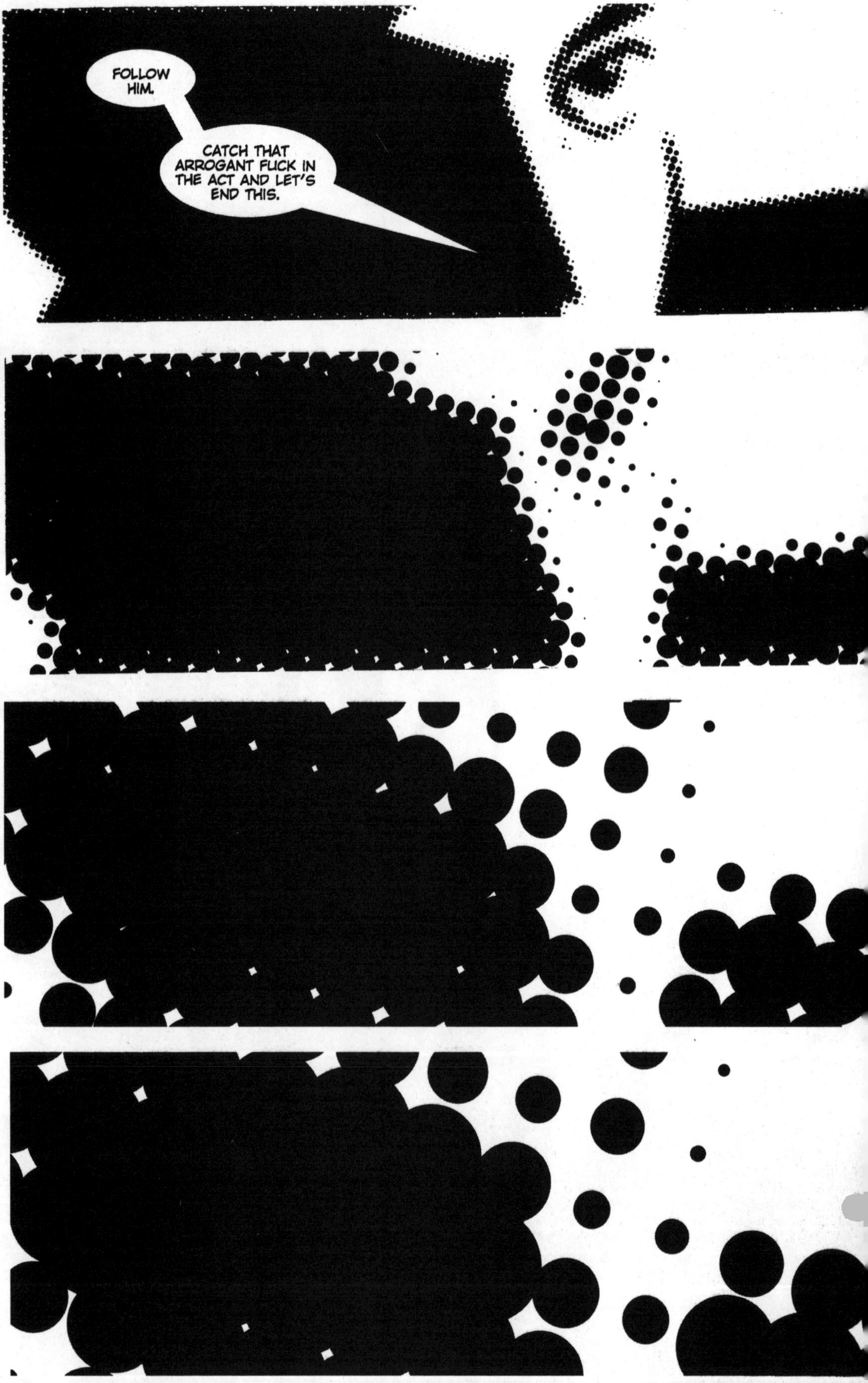
FOLLOW HIM.
CATCH THAT ARROGANT FUCK IN THE ACT AND LET'S END THIS.

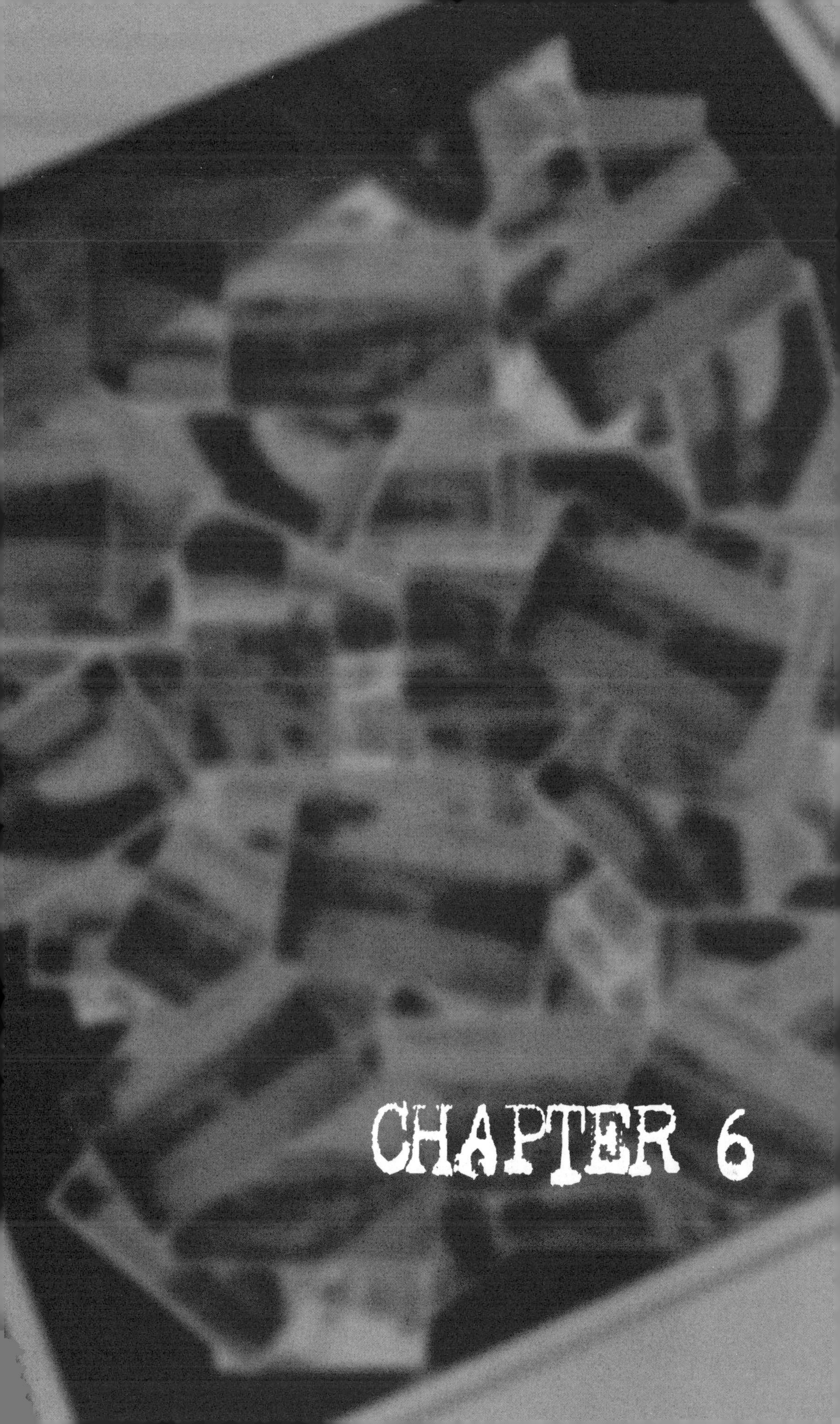

CHAPTER 6

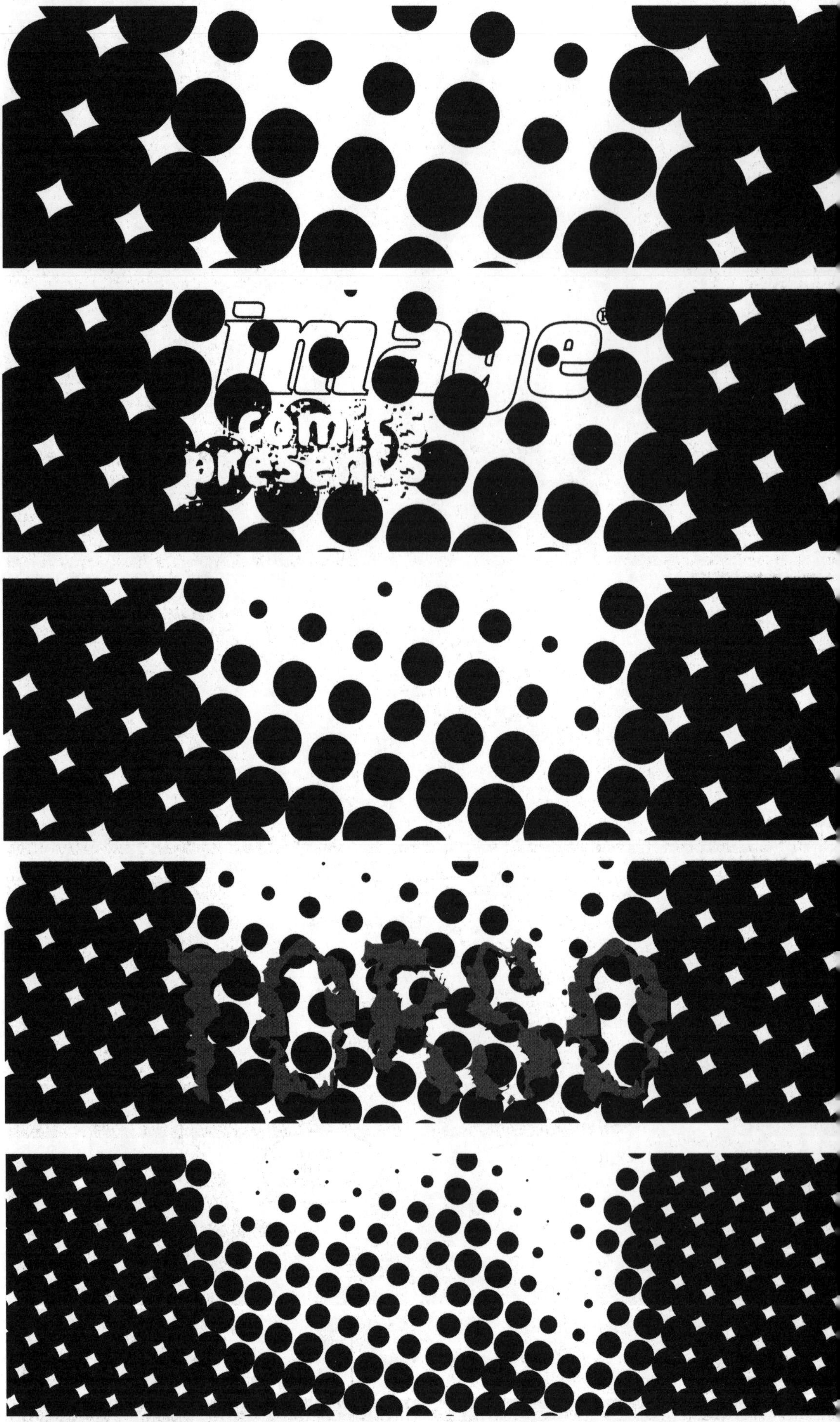
image comics presents
TORSO

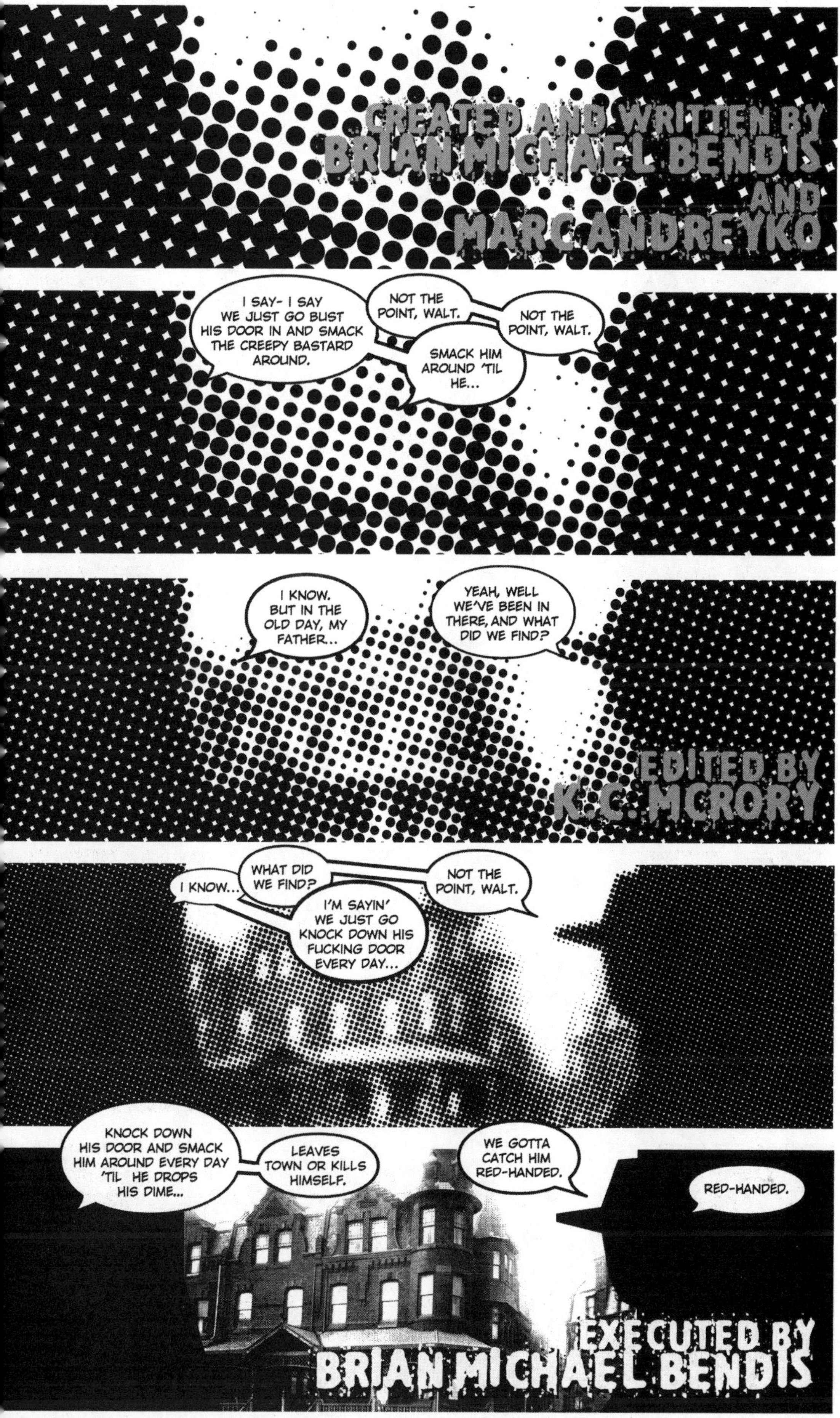
CREATED AND WRITTEN BY
BRIAN MICHAEL BENDIS
AND
MARC ANDREYKO
I SAY- I SAY WE JUST GO BUST HIS DOOR IN AND SMACK THE CREEPY BASTARD AROUND.
NOT THE POINT, WALT.
NOT THE POINT, WALT.
SMACK HIM AROUND 'TIL HE...
I KNOW. BUT IN THE OLD DAY, MY FATHER...
YEAH, WELL WE'VE BEEN IN THERE, AND WHAT DID WE FIND?
EDITED BY
K.C. MCRORY
I KNOW...
WHAT DID WE FIND?
NOT THE POINT, WALT.
I'M SAYIN' WE JUST GO KNOCK DOWN HIS FUCKING DOOR EVERY DAY...
KNOCK DOWN HIS DOOR AND SMACK HIM AROUND EVERY DAY 'TIL HE DROPS HIS DIME...
LEAVES TOWN OR KILLS HIMSELF.
WE GOTTA CATCH HIM RED-HANDED.
RED-HANDED.
EXECUTED BY
BRIAN MICHAEL BENDIS

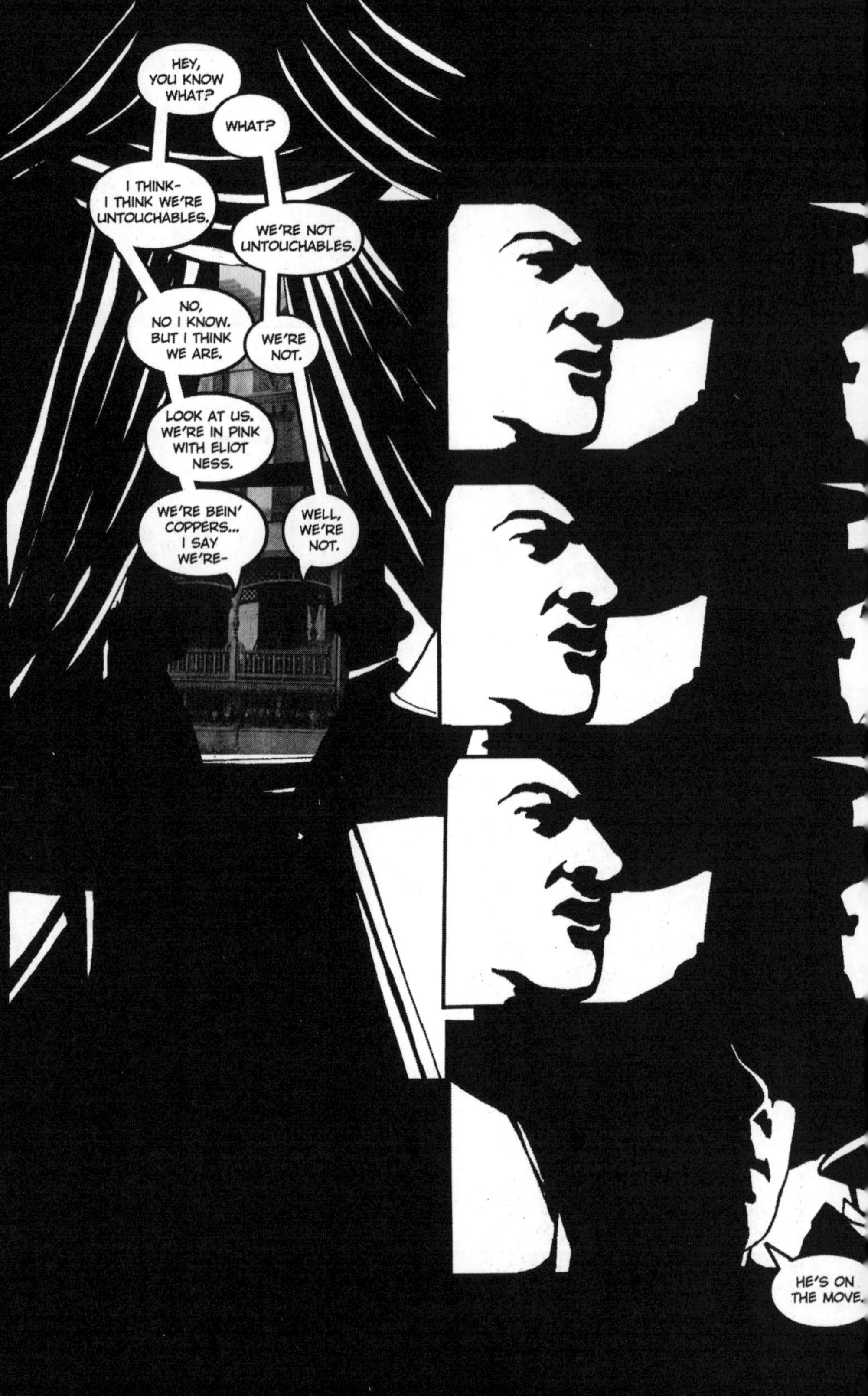
HEY, YOU KNOW WHAT?
WHAT?
I THINK- I THINK WE'RE UNTOUCHABLES.
WE'RE NOT UNTOUCHABLES.
NO, NO I KNOW. BUT I THINK WE ARE.
WE'RE NOT.
LOOK AT US. WE'RE IN PINK WITH ELIOT NESS.
WE'RE BEIN' COPPERS... I SAY WE'RE-
WELL, WE'RE NOT.
HE'S ON THE MOVE.

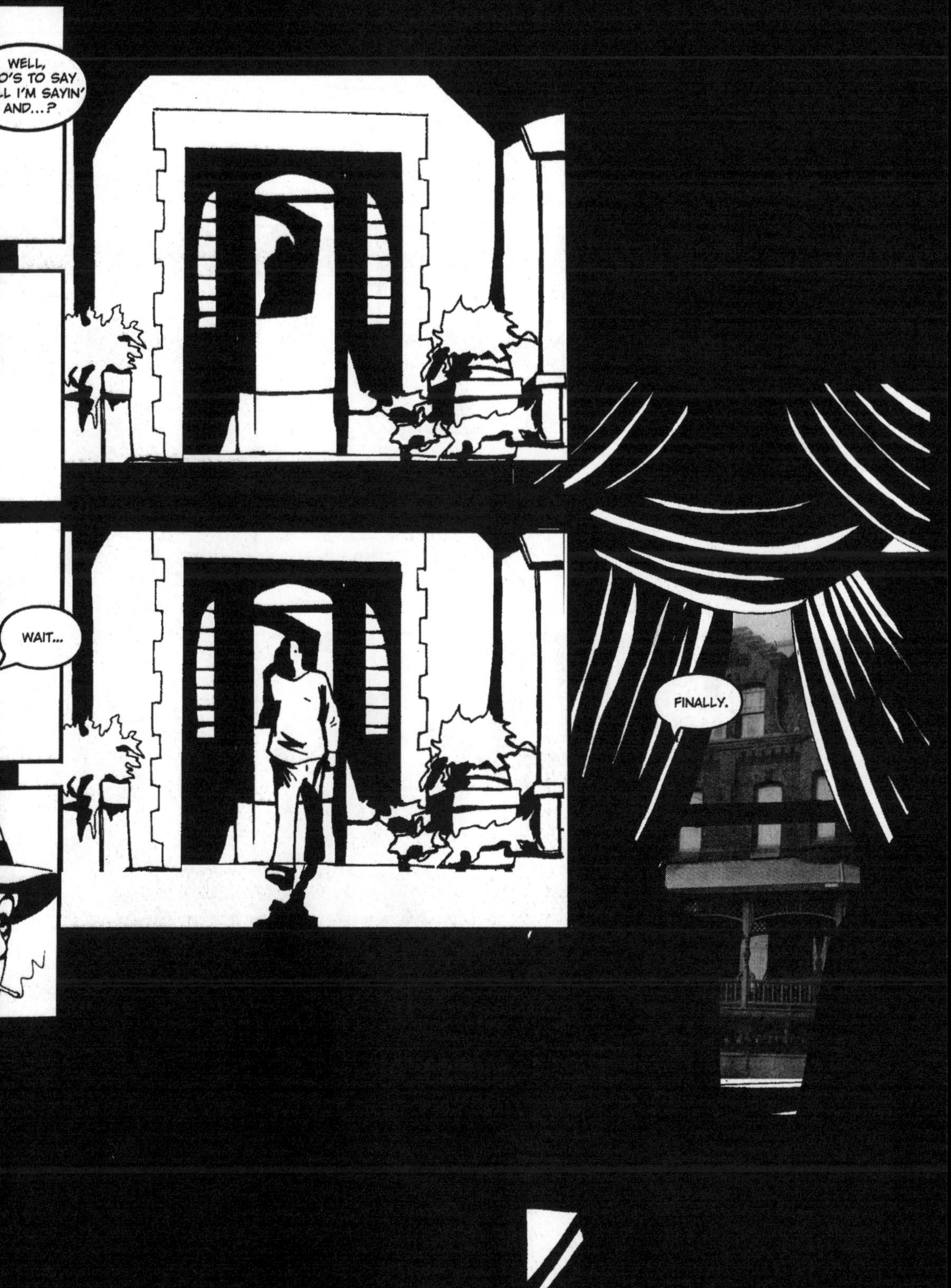
WELL,
O'S TO SAY
L I'M SAYIN'
AND...?
WAIT...
FINALLY.

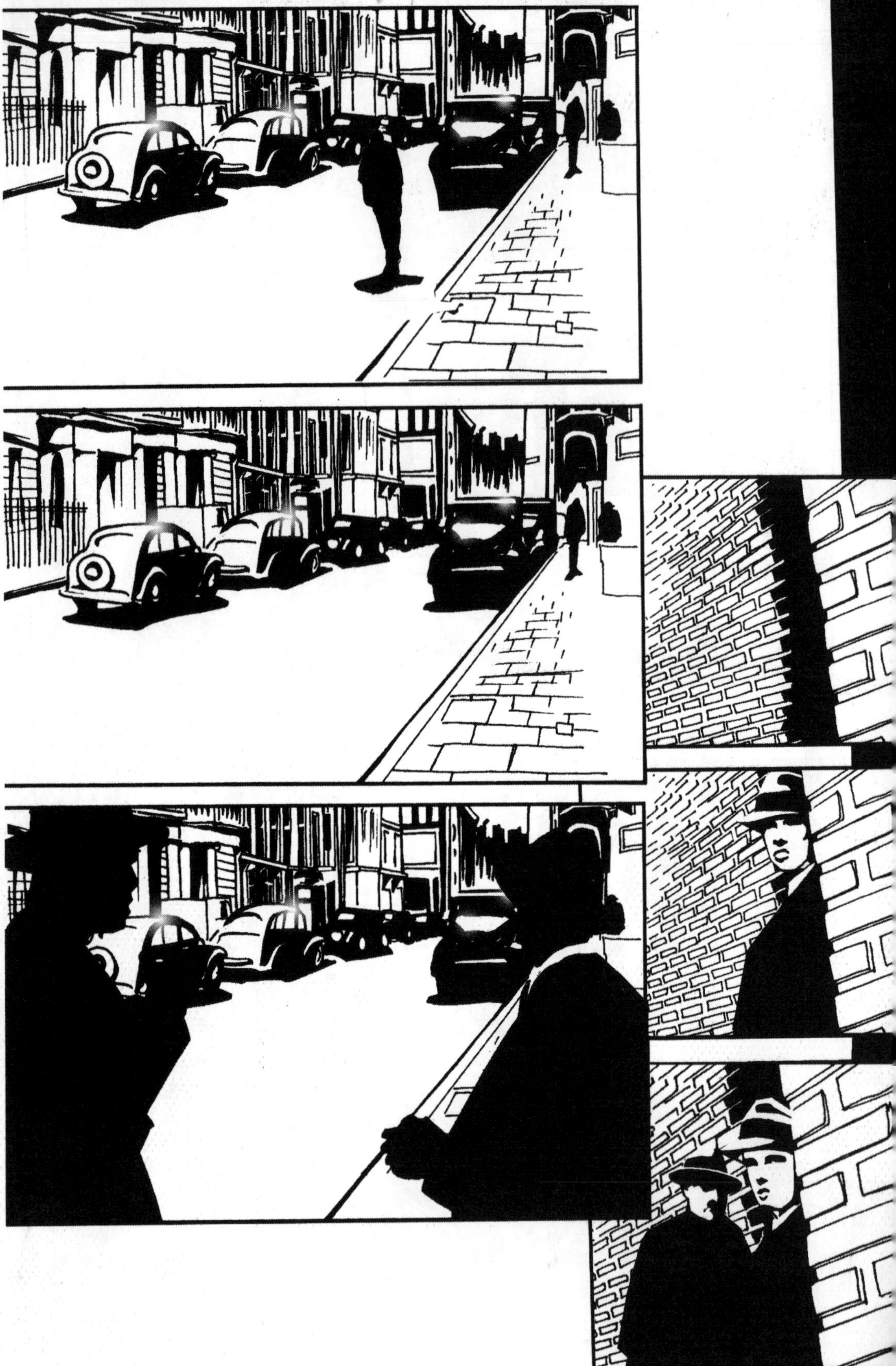

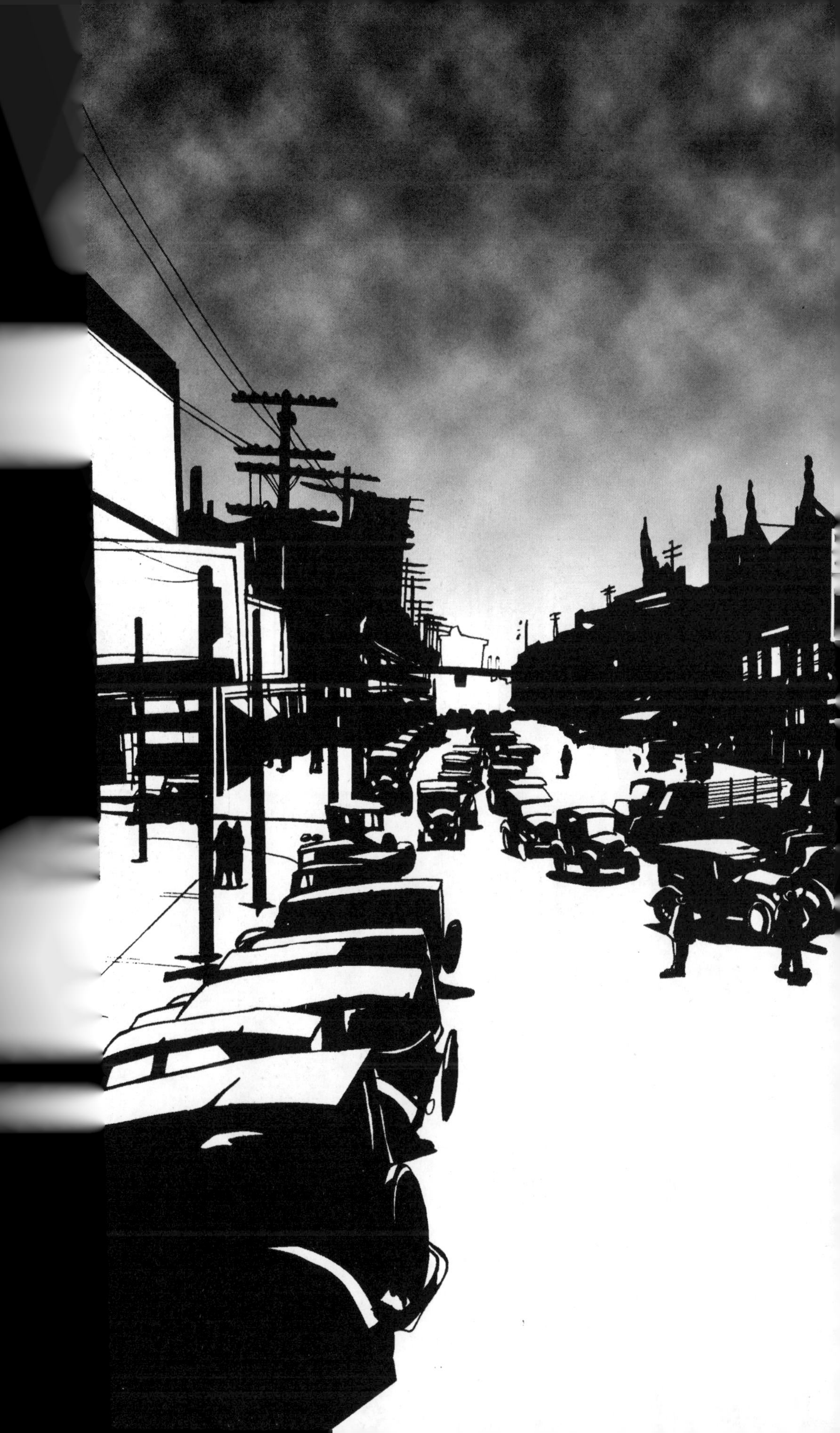

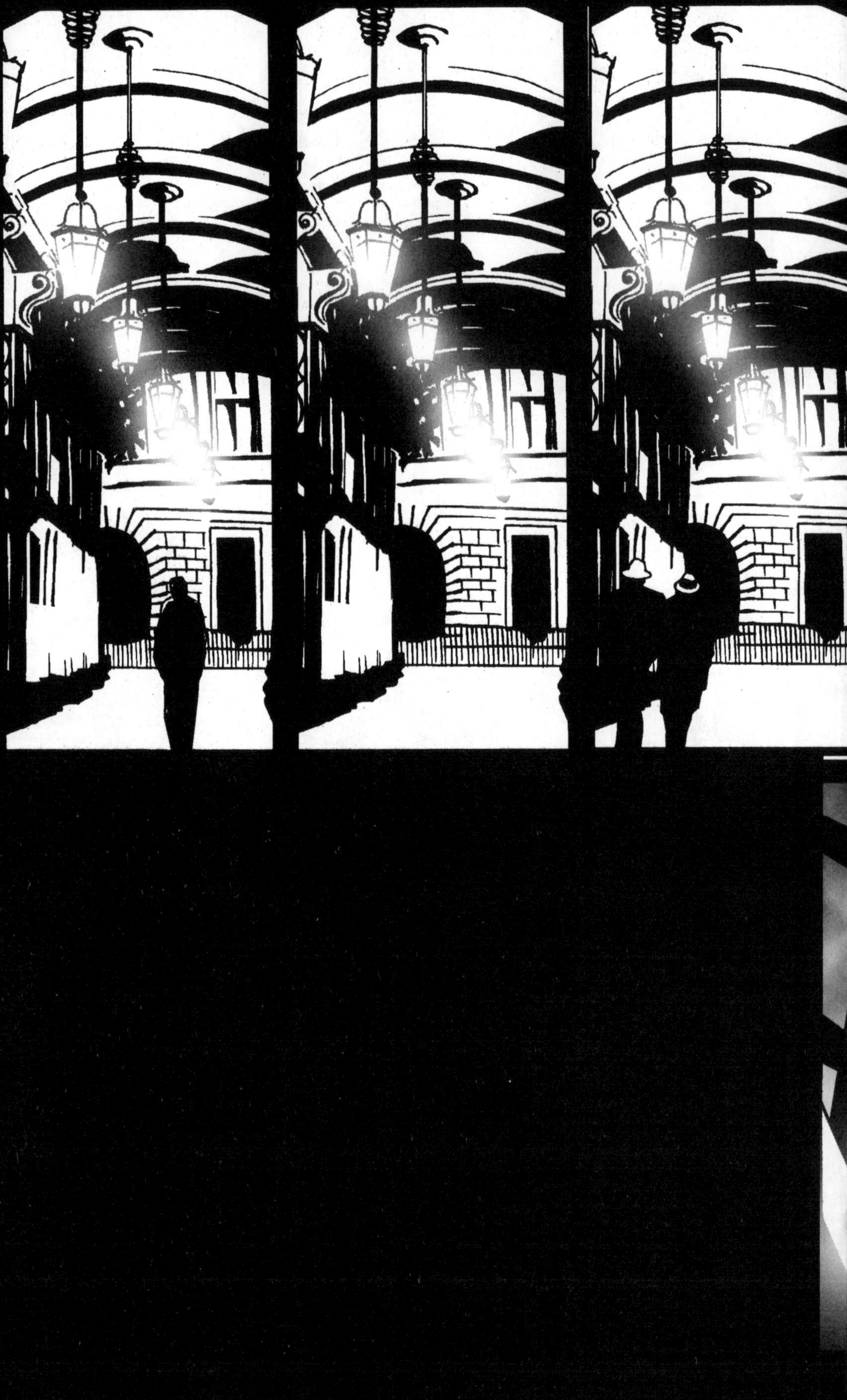

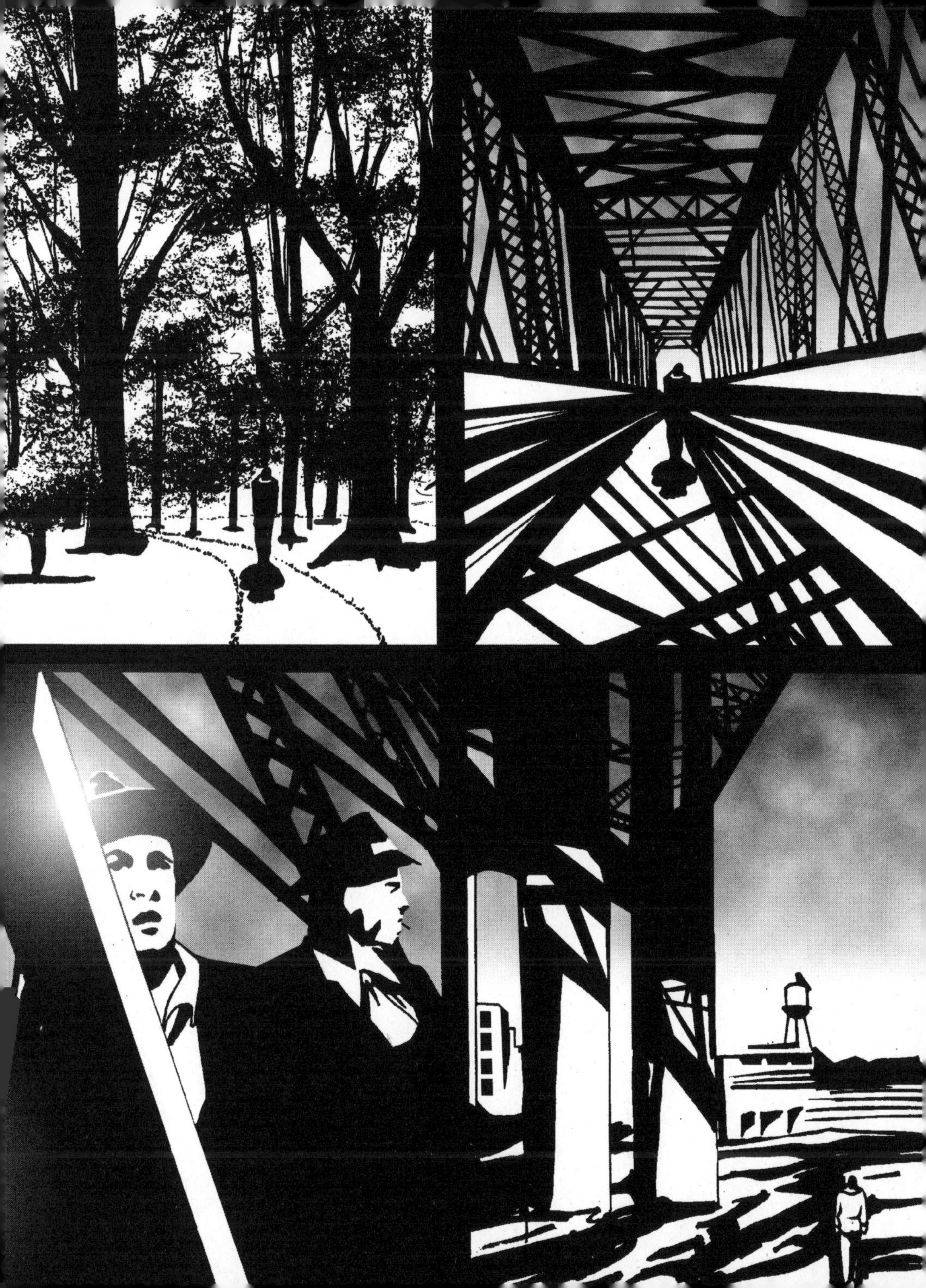

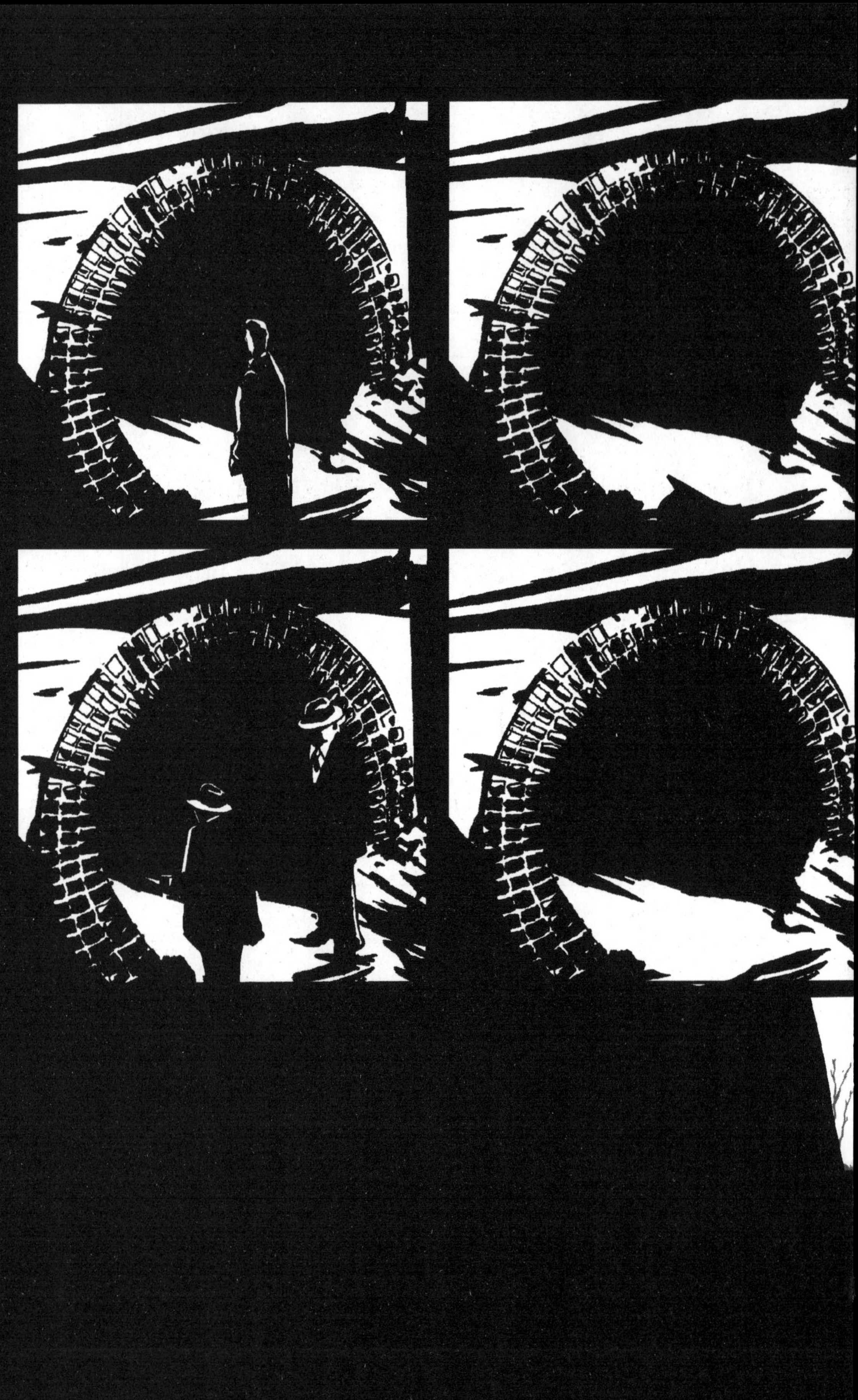

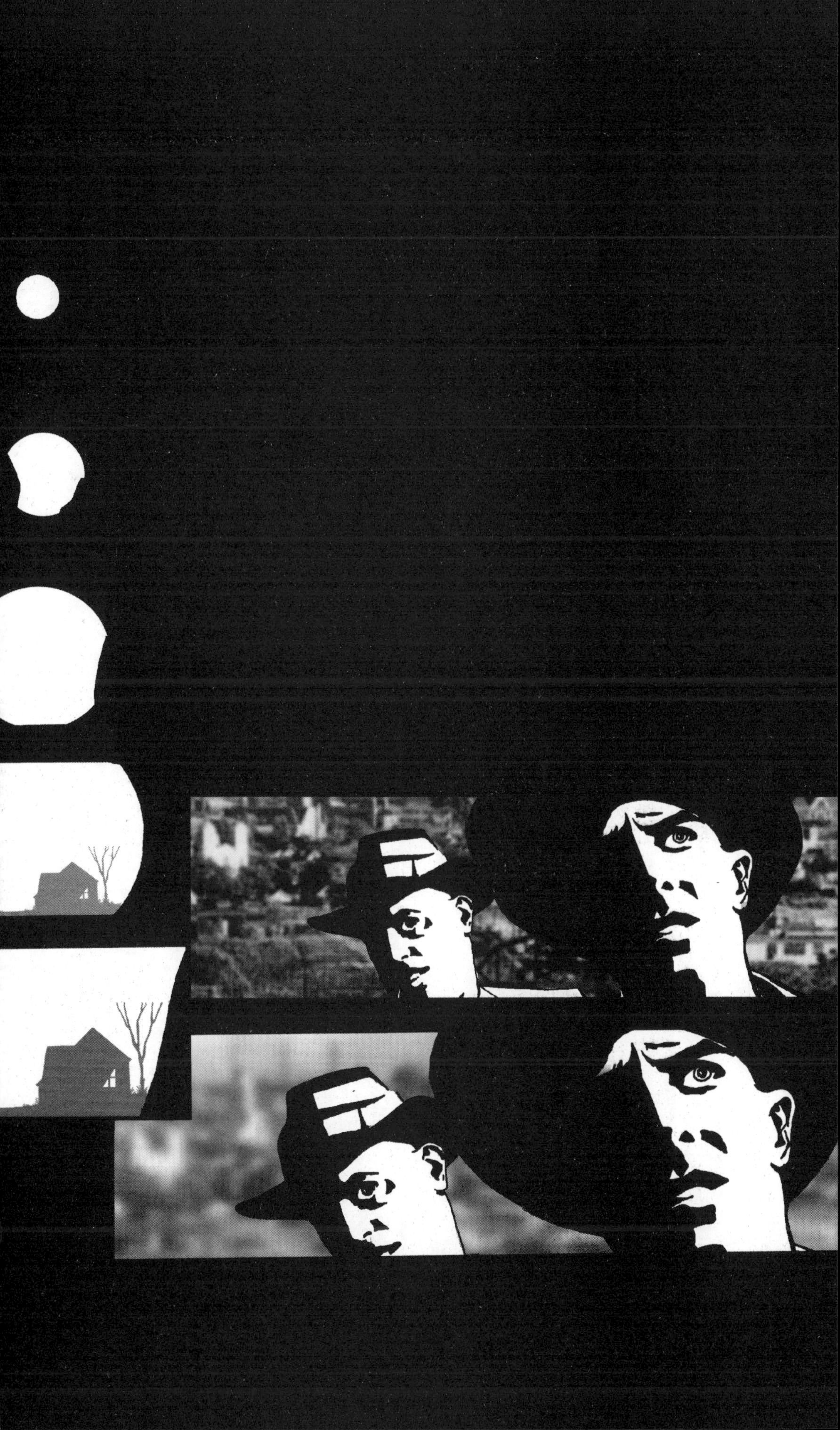

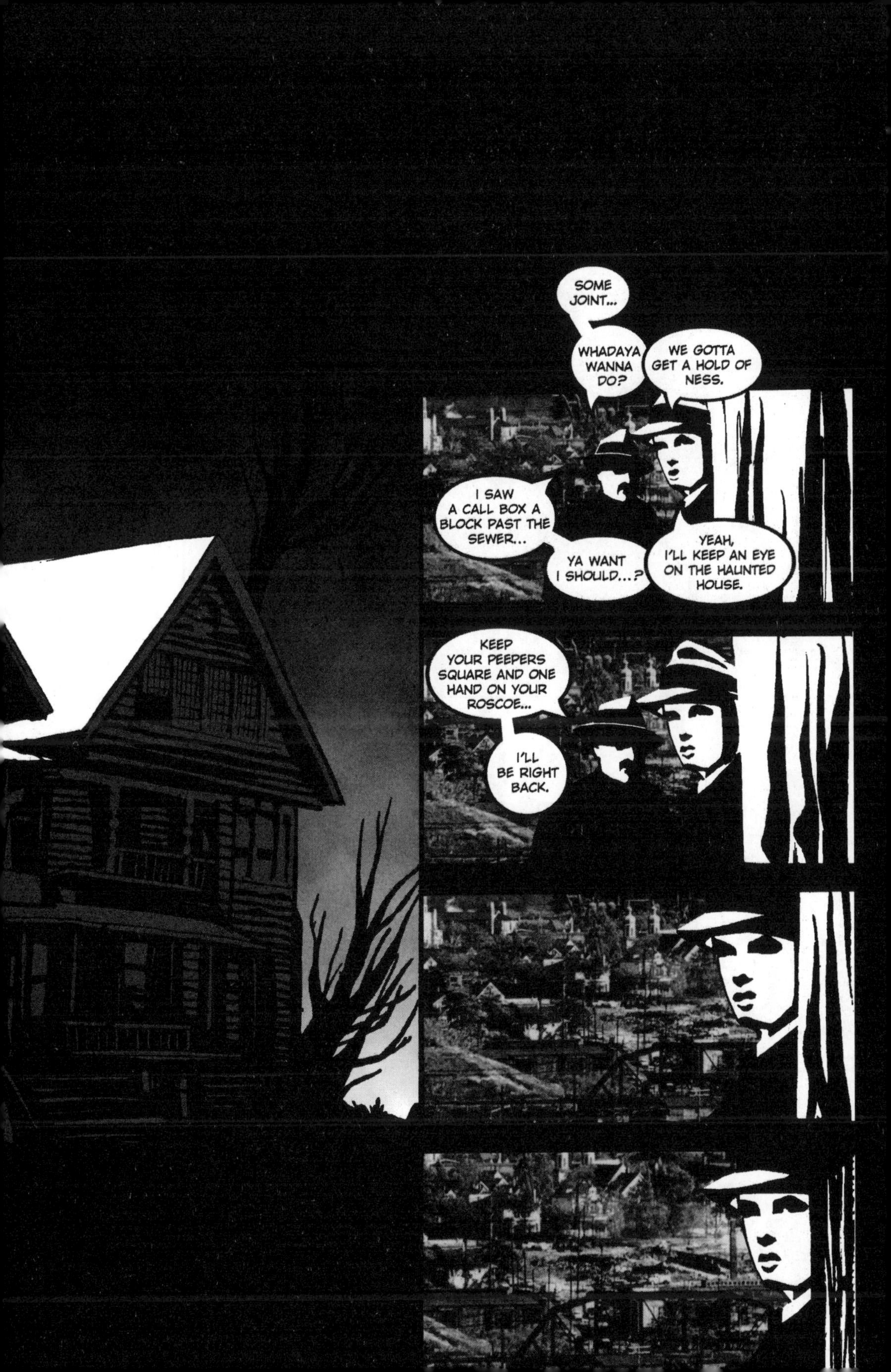
SOME JOINT...
WHADAYA WANNA DO?
WE GOTTA GET A HOLD OF NESS.
I SAW A CALL BOX A BLOCK PAST THE SEWER...
YA WANT I SHOULD...?
YEAH, I'LL KEEP AN EYE ON THE HAUNTED HOUSE.
KEEP YOUR PEEPERS SQUARE AND ONE HAND ON YOUR ROSCOE...
I'LL BE RIGHT BACK.

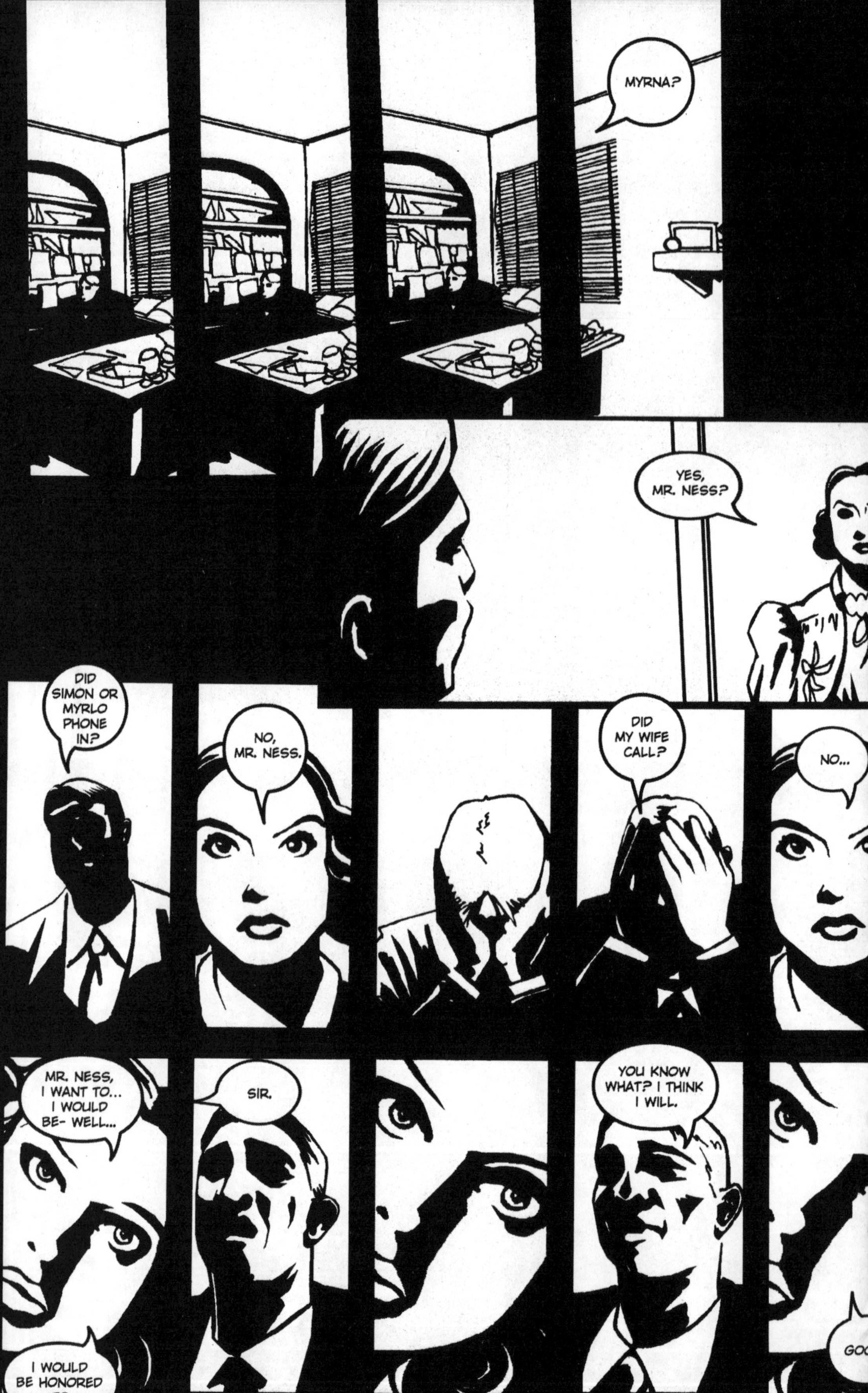
MYRNA?
YES, MR. NESS?
DID SIMON OR MYRLO PHONE IN?
NO, MR. NESS.
DID MY WIFE CALL?
NO...
MR. NESS, I WANT TO... I WOULD BE- WELL...
I WOULD BE HONORED
SIR.
YOU KNOW WHAT? I THINK I WILL.

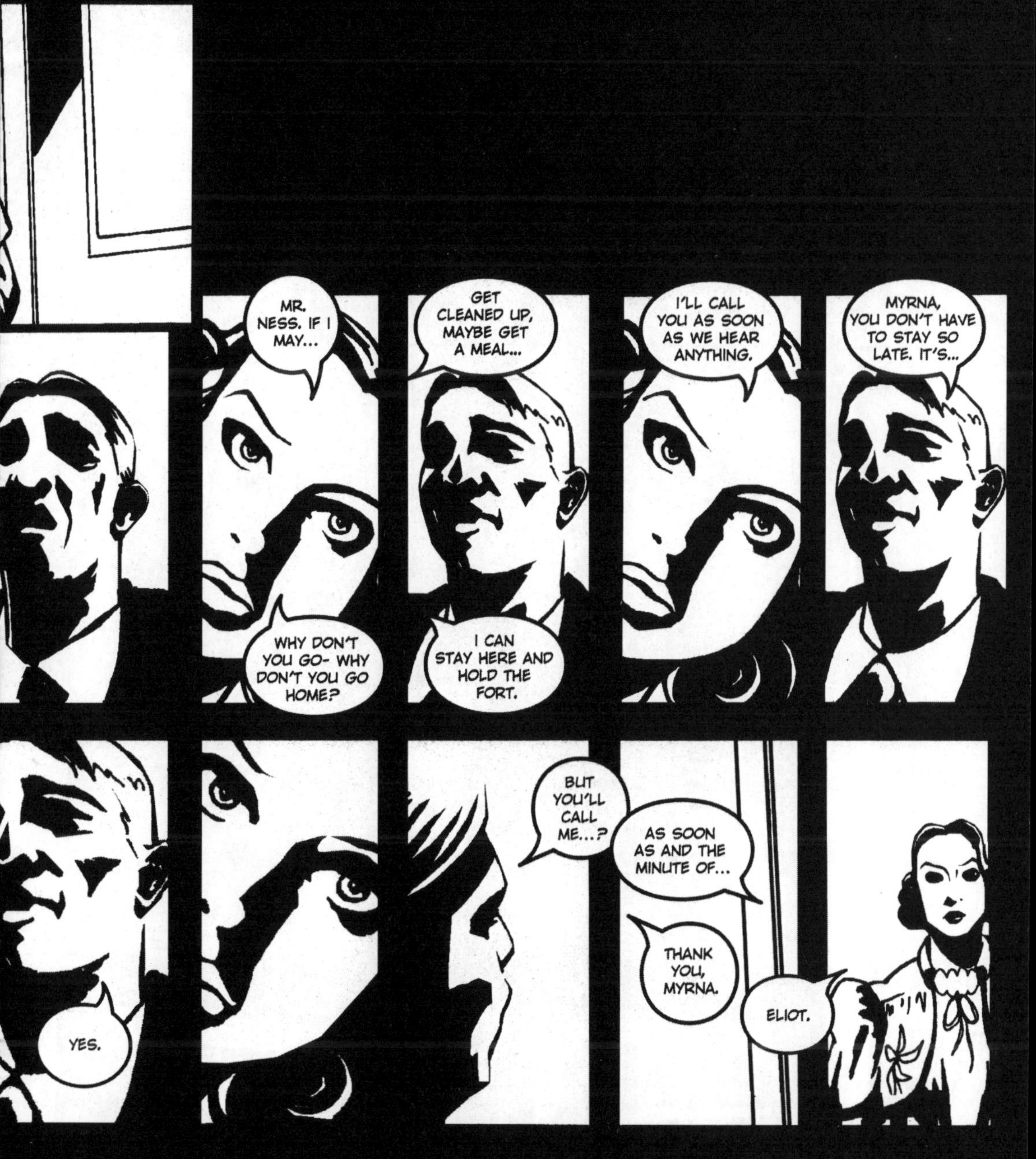
MR. NESS. IF I MAY...
WHY DON'T YOU GO- WHY DON'T YOU GO HOME?
GET CLEANED UP, MAYBE GET A MEAL...
I CAN STAY HERE AND HOLD THE FORT.
I'LL CALL YOU AS SOON AS WE HEAR ANYTHING.
MYRNA, YOU DON'T HAVE TO STAY SO LATE. IT'S...
YES.
BUT YOU'LL CALL ME...?
AS SOON AS AND THE MINUTE OF...
THANK YOU, MYRNA.
ELIOT.

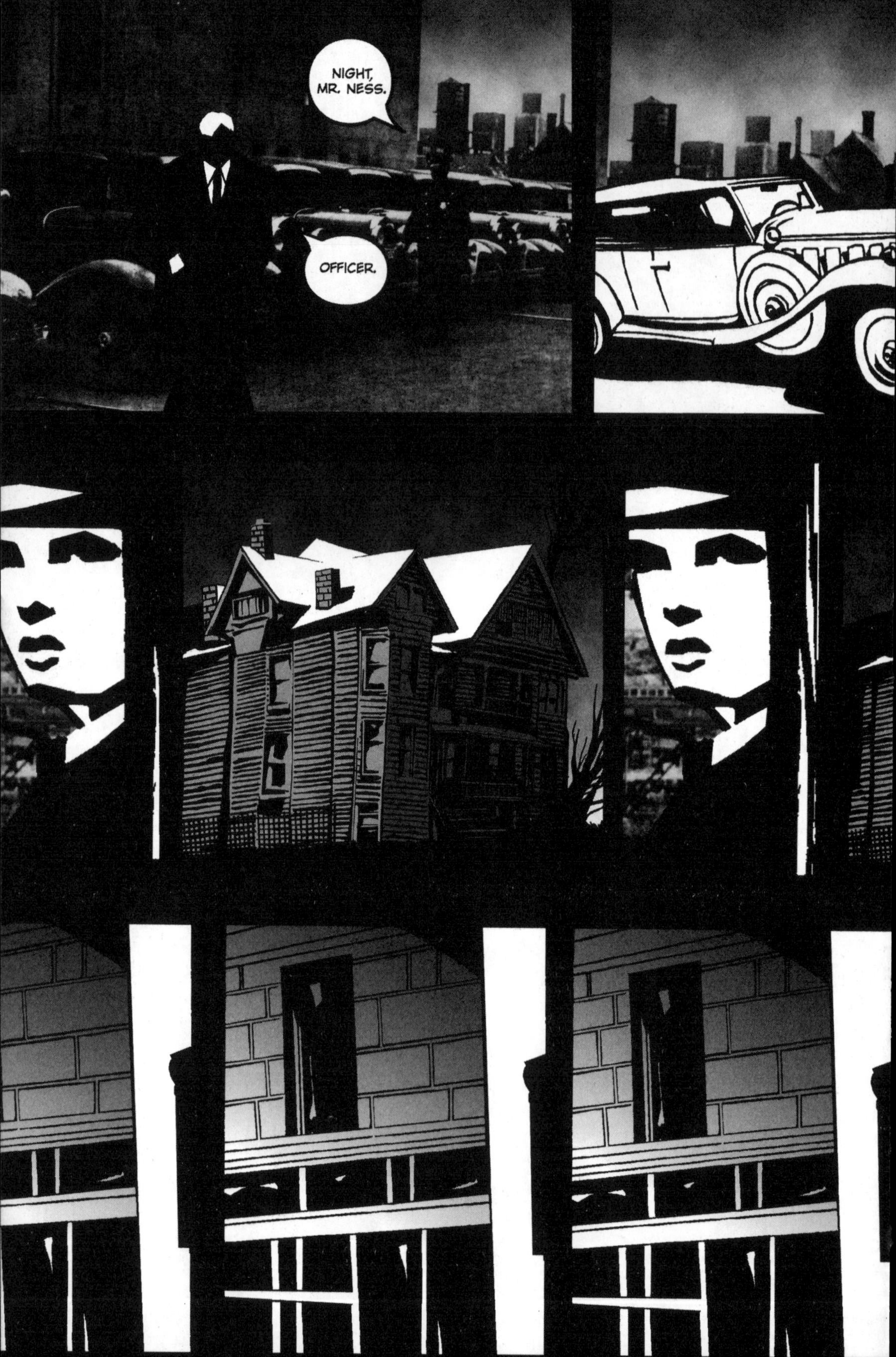
NIGHT, MR. NESS.
OFFICER.

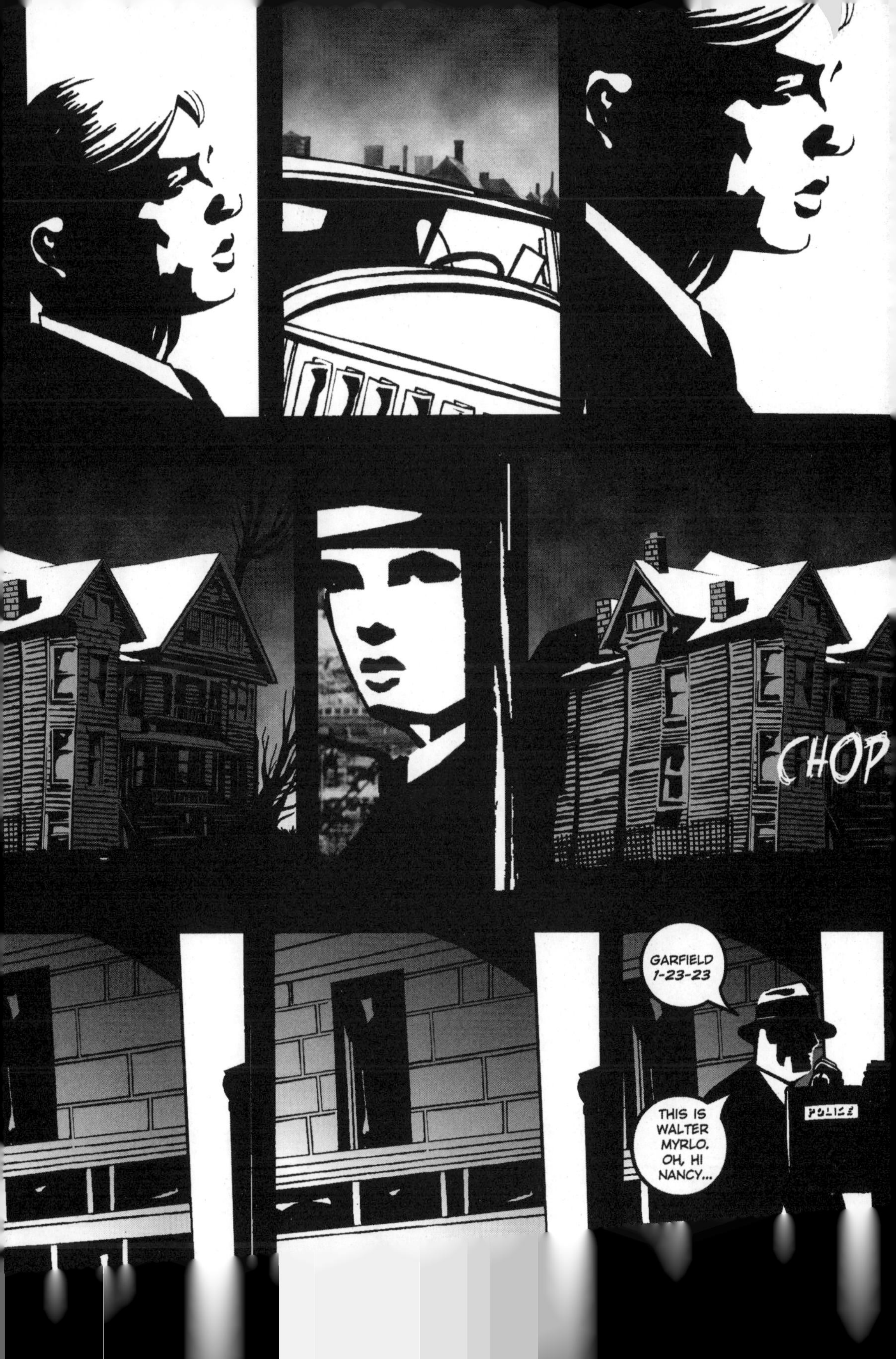
CHOP
GARFIELD 1-23-23
THIS IS WALTER MYRLO. OH, HI NANCY...
POLICE

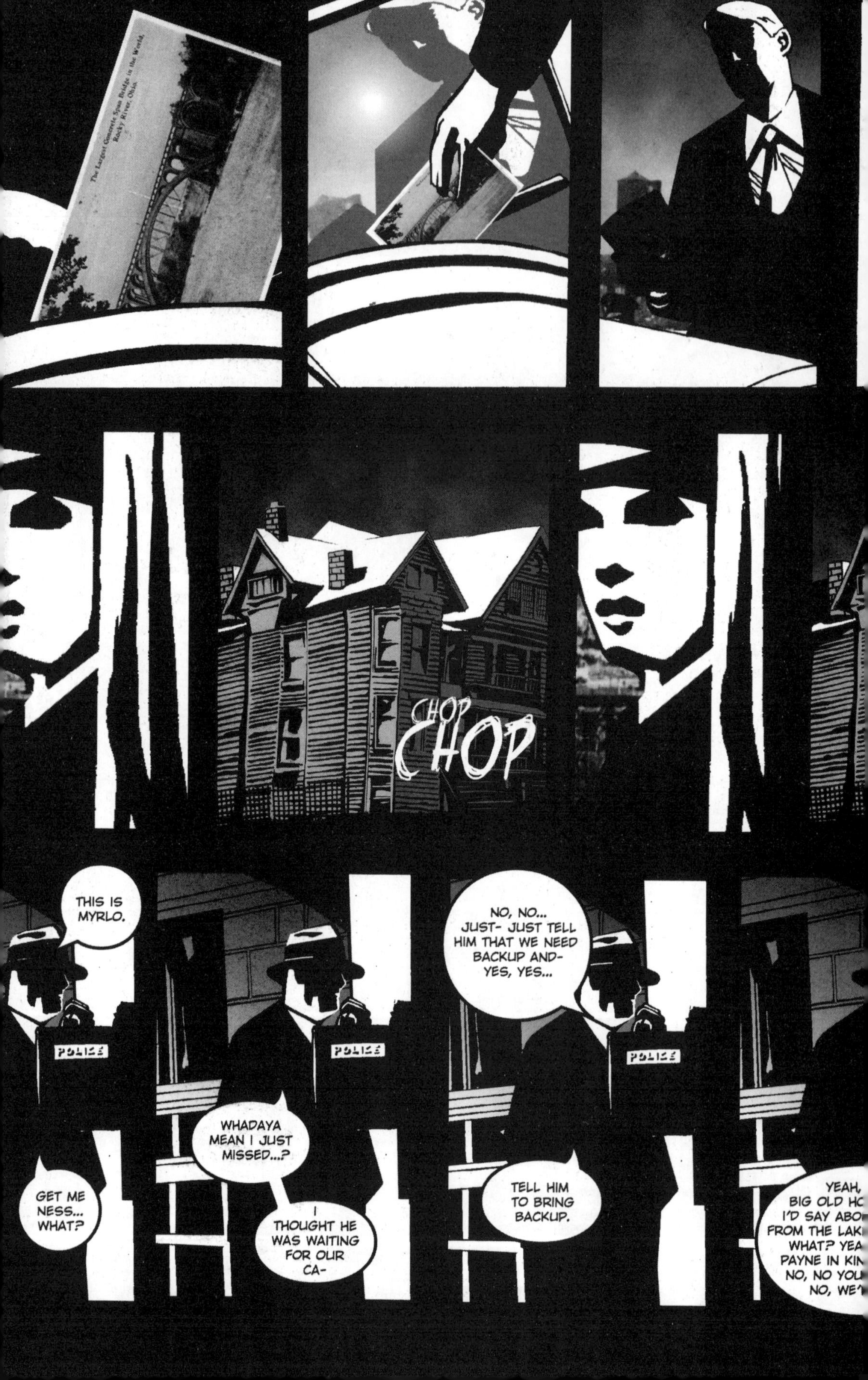
The Largest Concrete Span Bridge in the World.
Rocky River, Ohio.
CHOP
CHOP
THIS IS MYRLO.
GET ME NESS... WHAT?
WHADAYA MEAN I JUST MISSED...?
I THOUGHT HE WAS WAITING FOR OUR CA-
NO, NO... JUST- JUST TELL HIM THAT WE NEED BACKUP AND- YES, YES...
TELL HIM TO BRING BACKUP.
YEAH, BIG OLD HO I'D SAY ABO FROM THE LAK WHAT? YEA PAYNE IN KIN NO, NO YOU NO, WE'

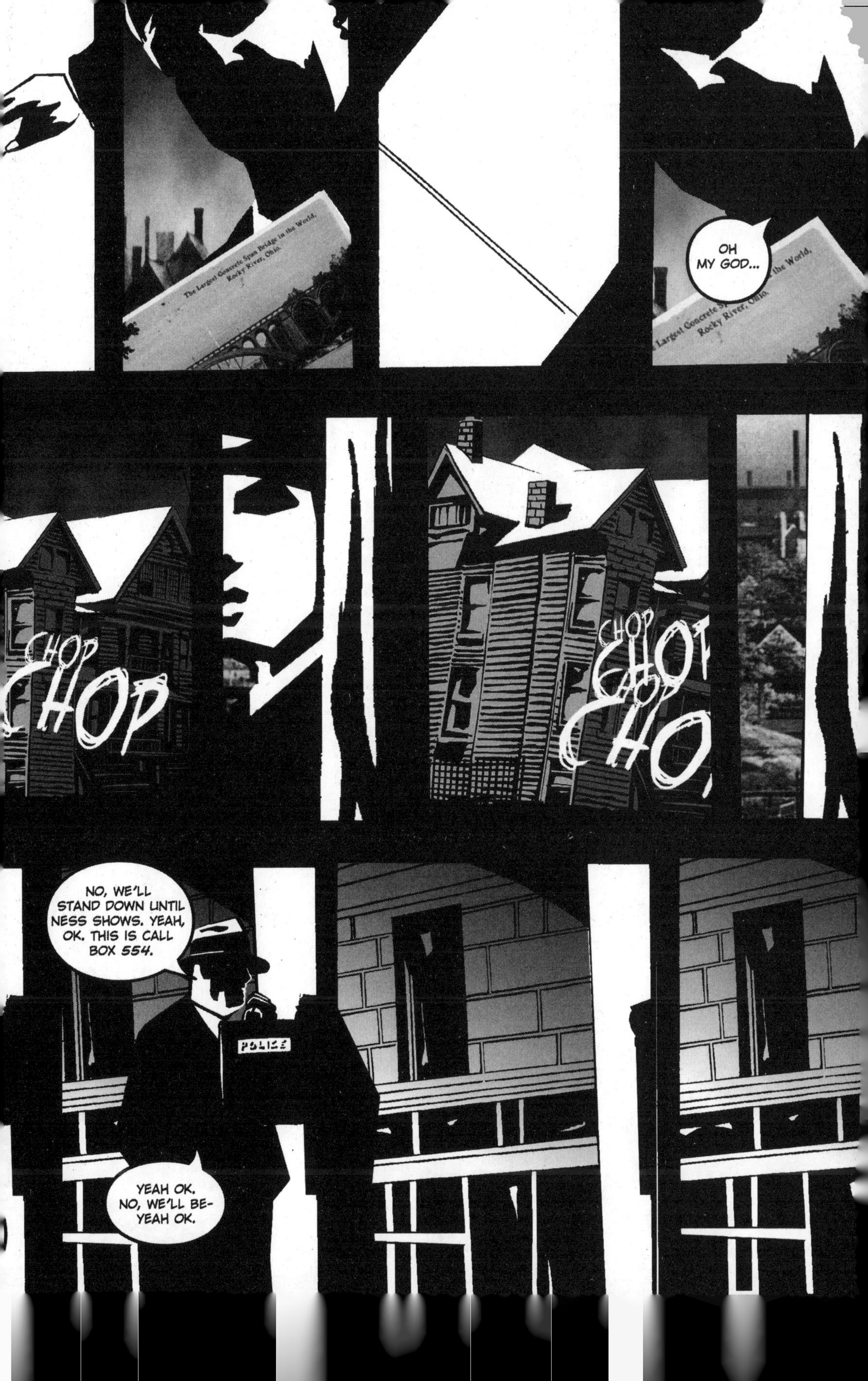
The Largest Concrete Span Bridge in the World,
Rocky River, Ohio.
OH MY GOD...
CHOP
CHOP
CHOP
CHOP
NO, WE'LL STAND DOWN UNTIL NESS SHOWS. YEAH, OK. THIS IS CALL BOX 554.
POLICE
YEAH OK. NO, WE'LL BE- YEAH OK.

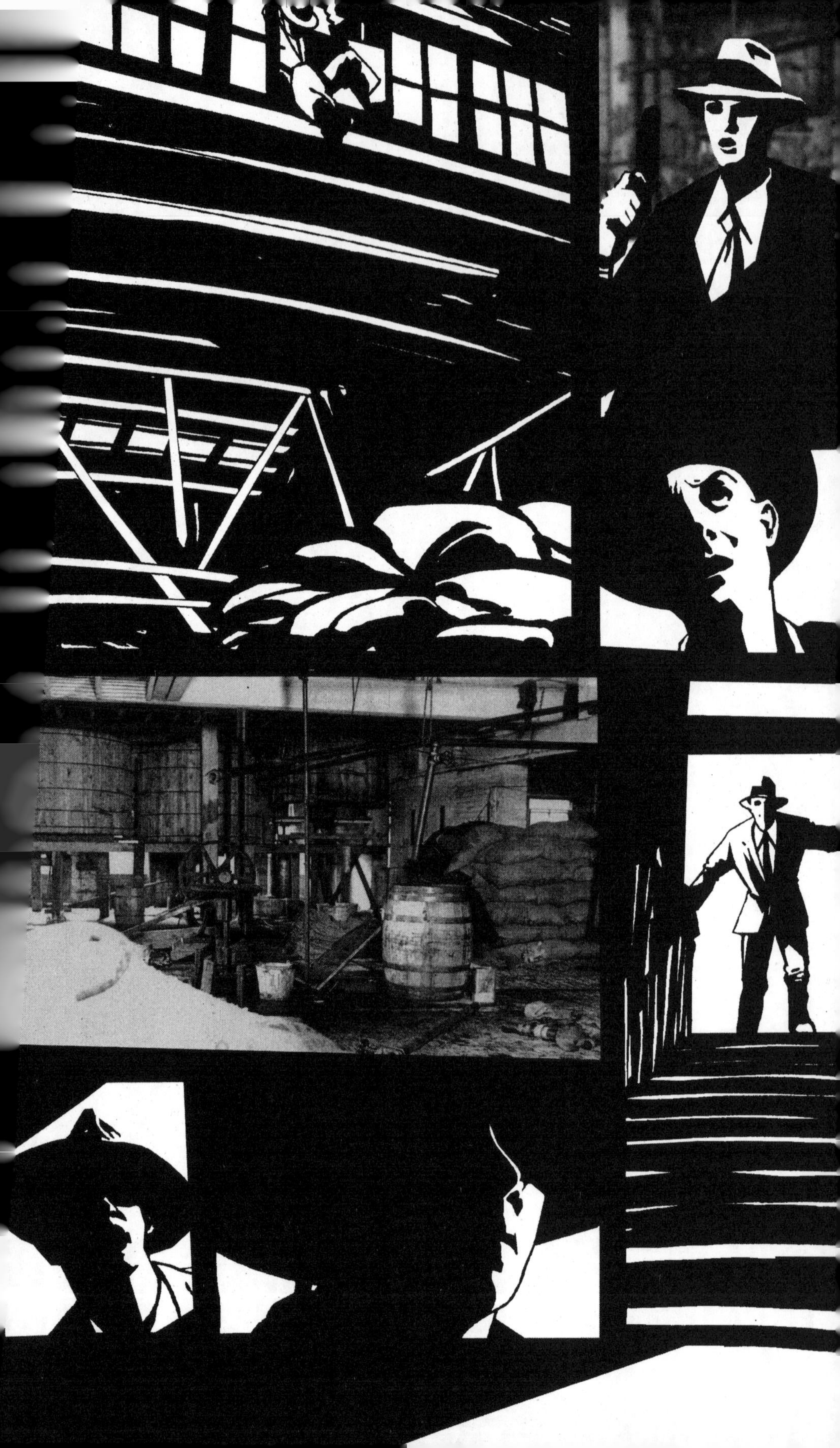

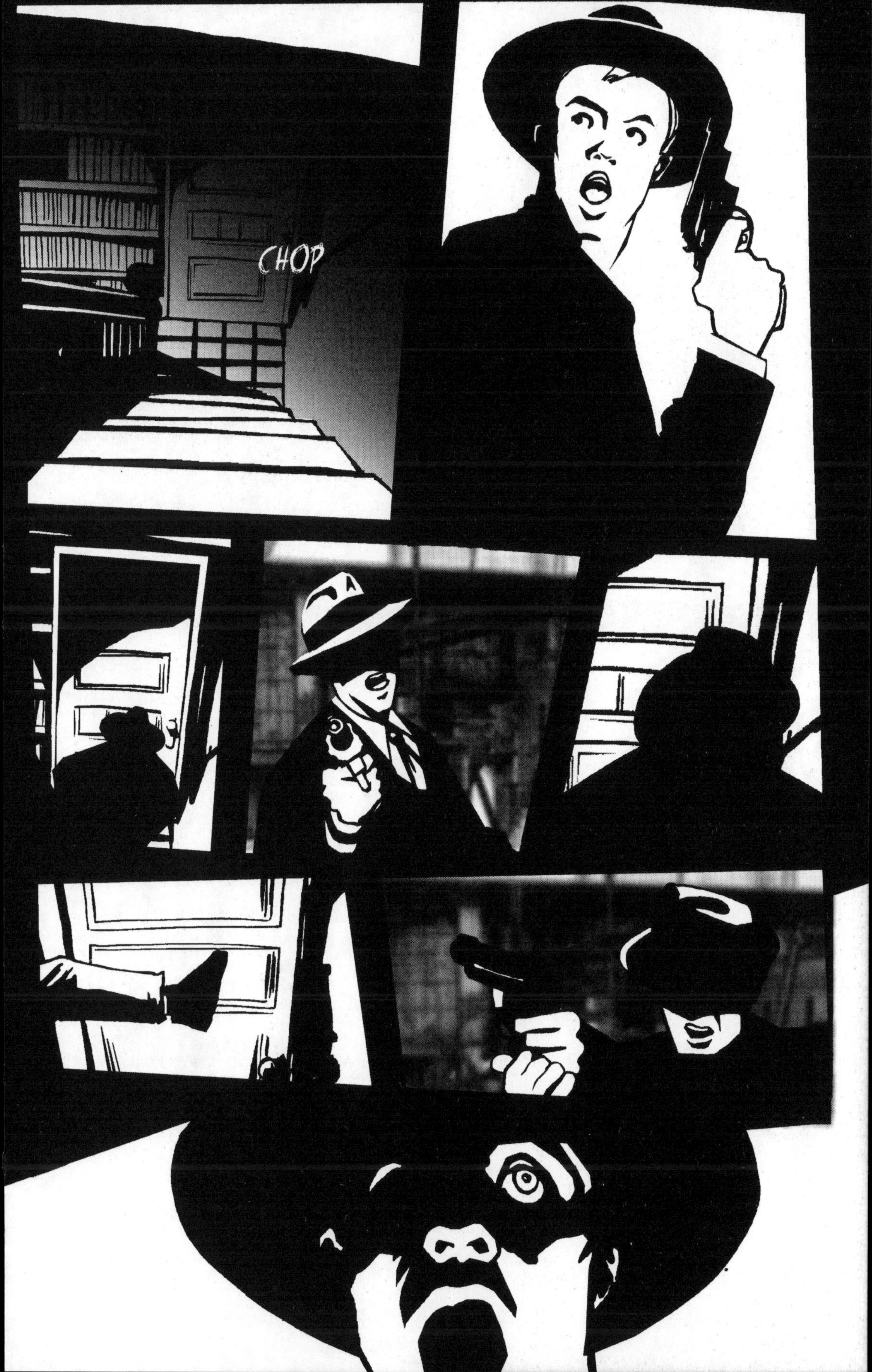
CHOP

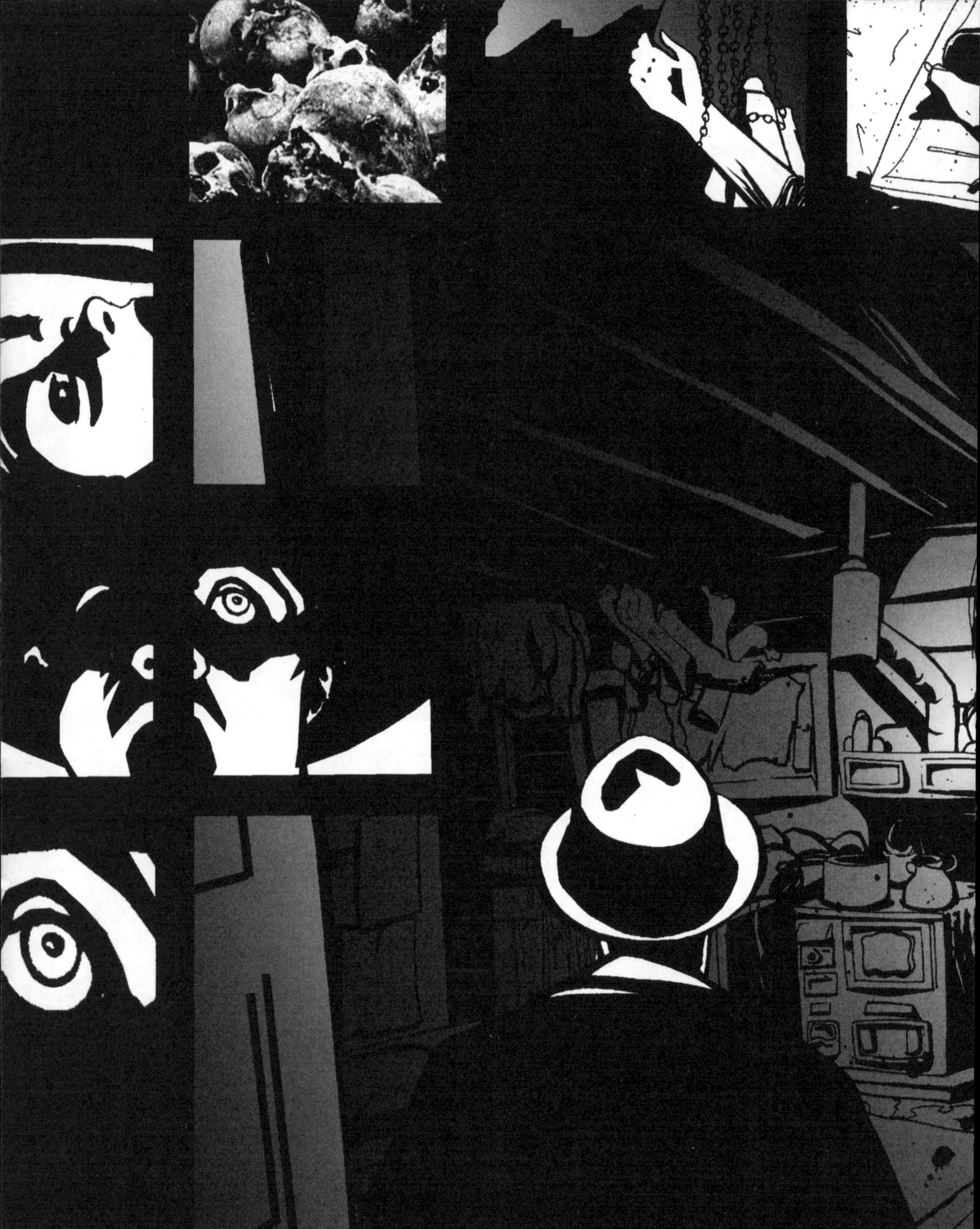

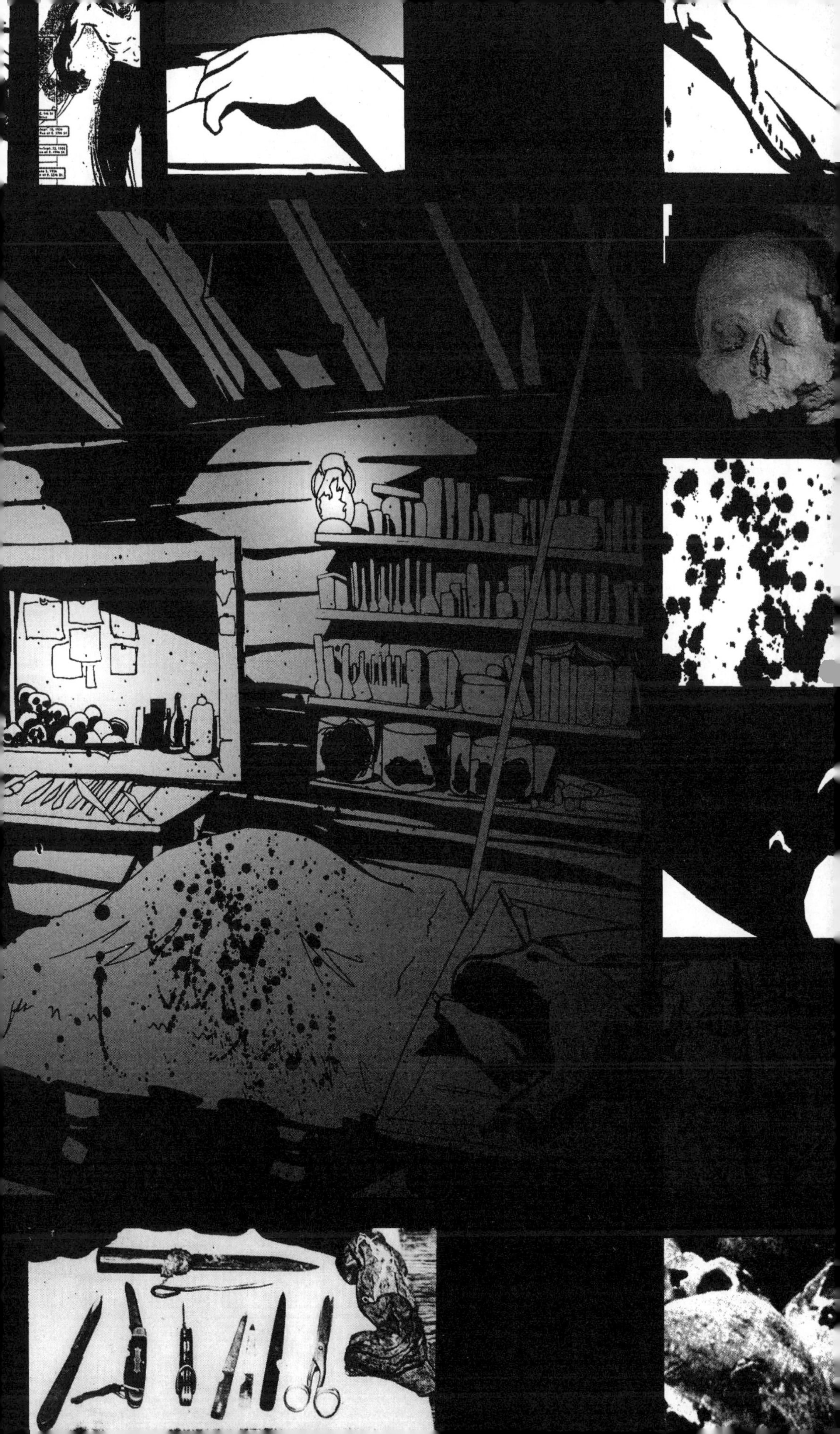

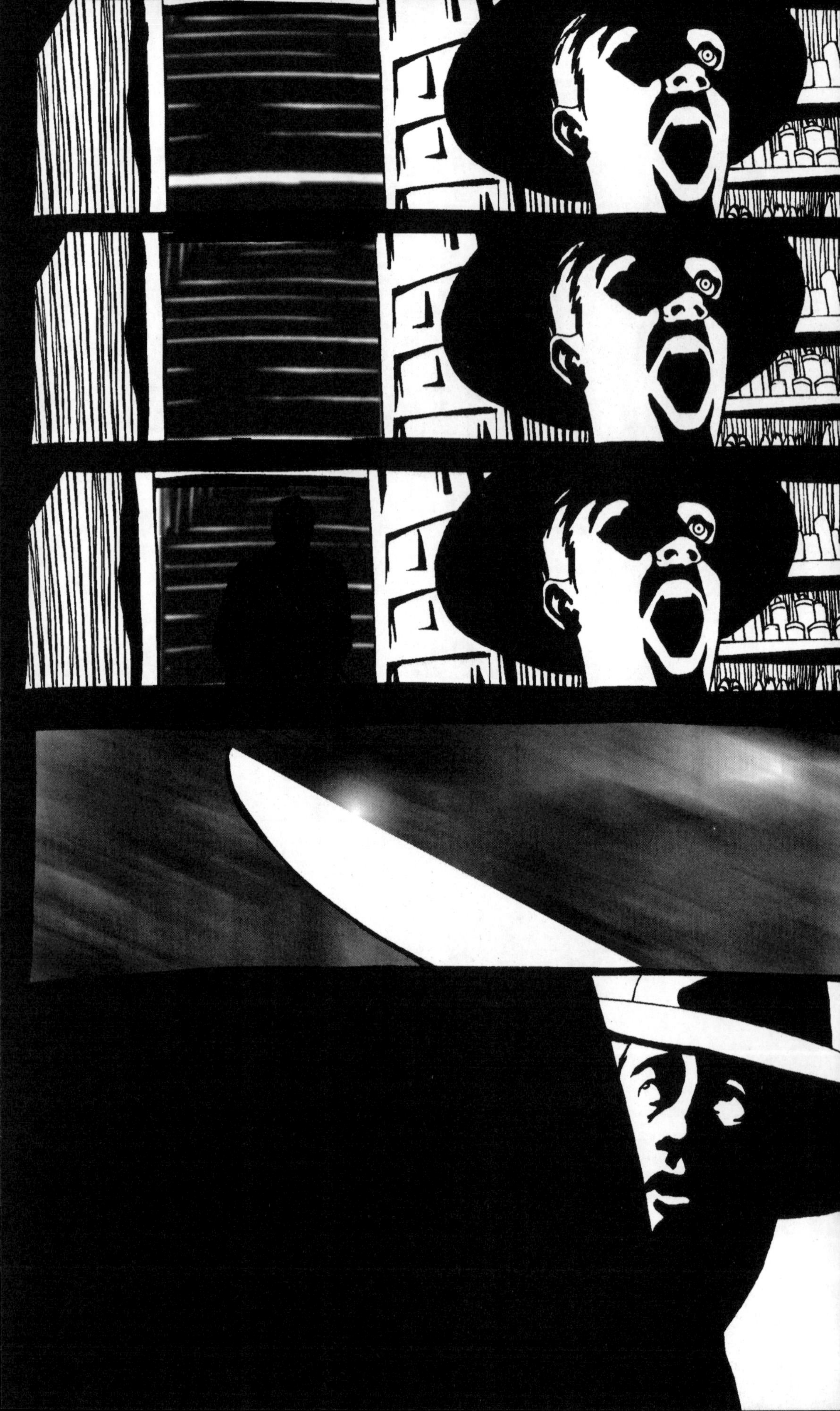

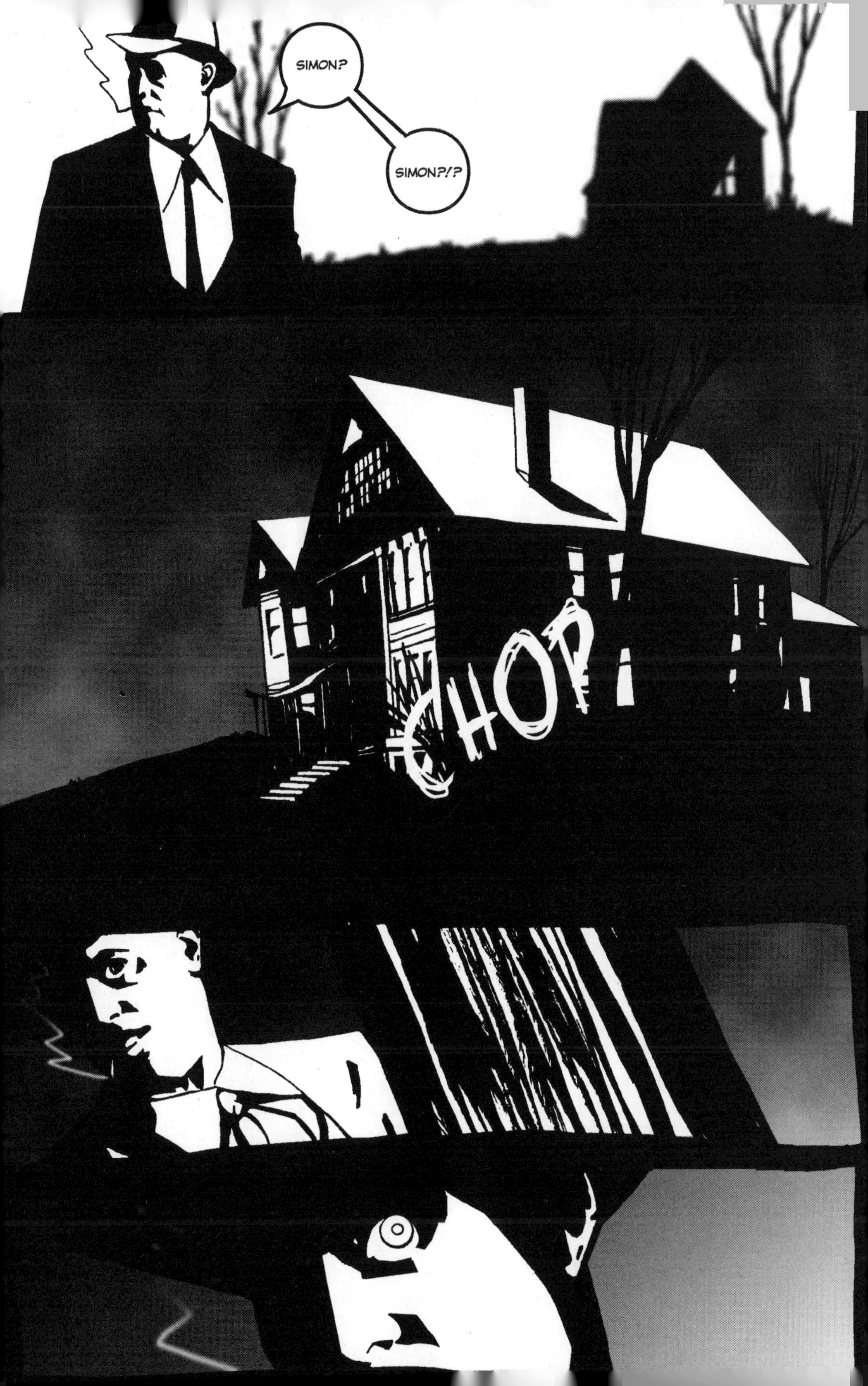
SIMON?
SIMON?!?
CHOP

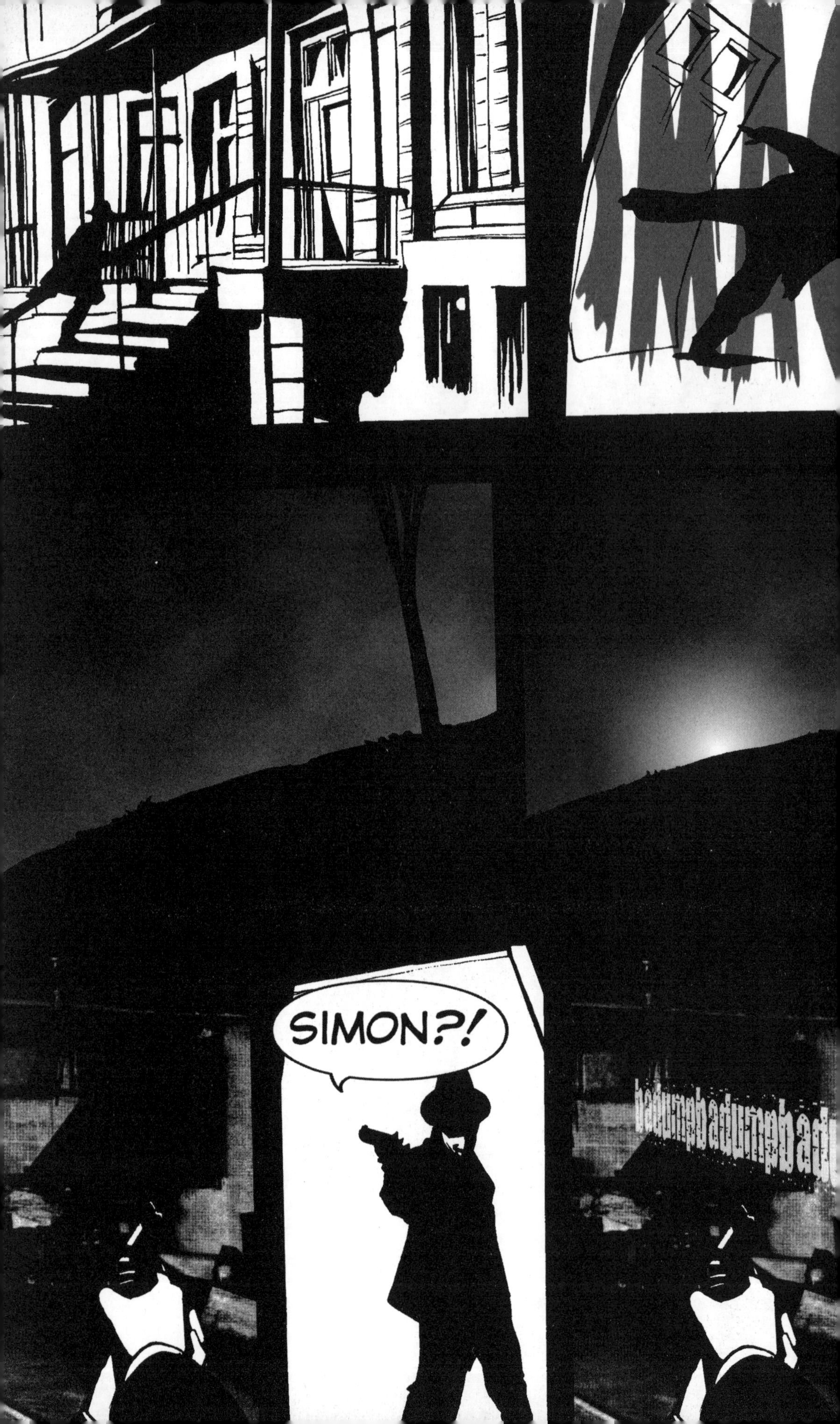
SIMON?!
badumpbadumpbad

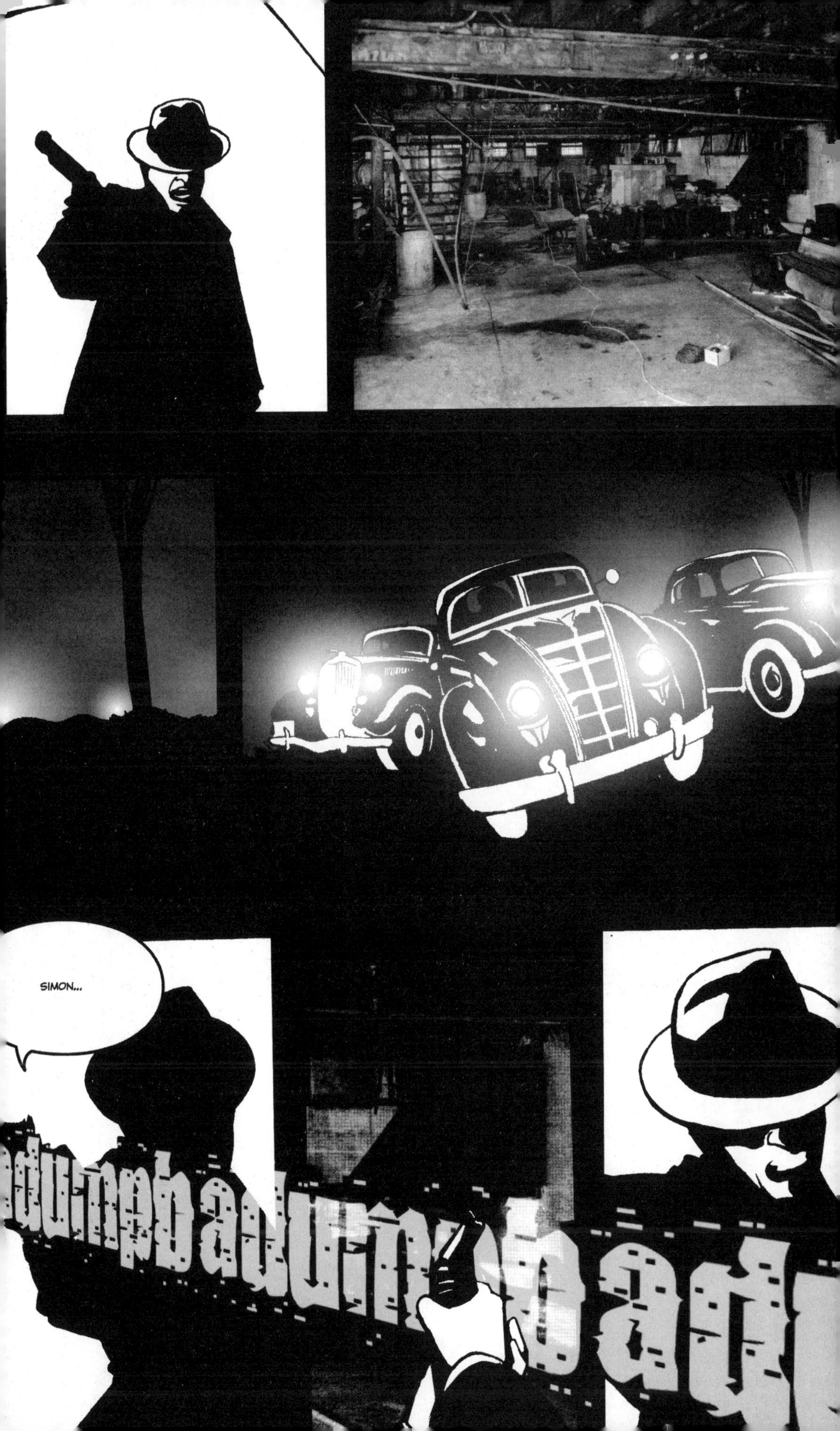
SIMON...

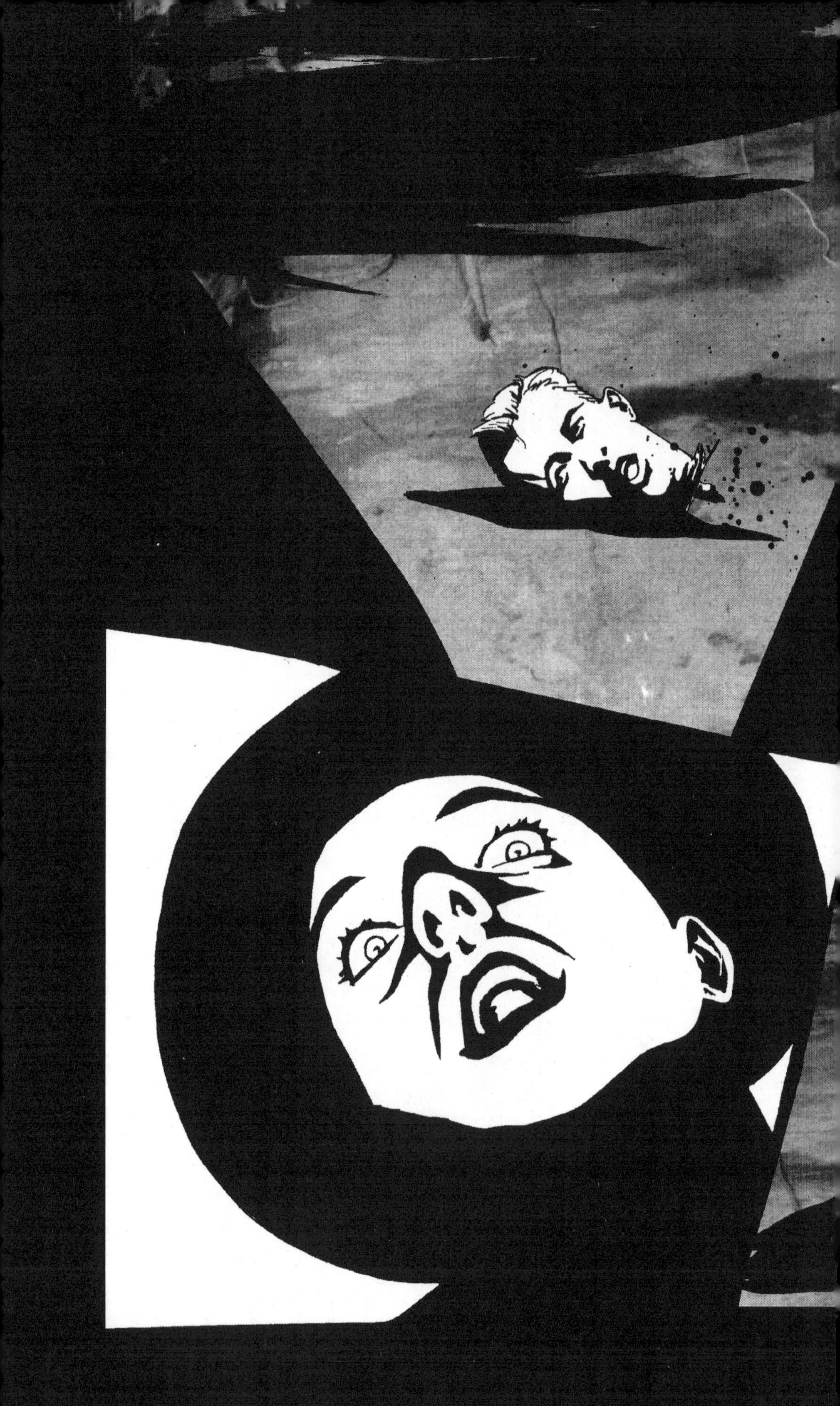

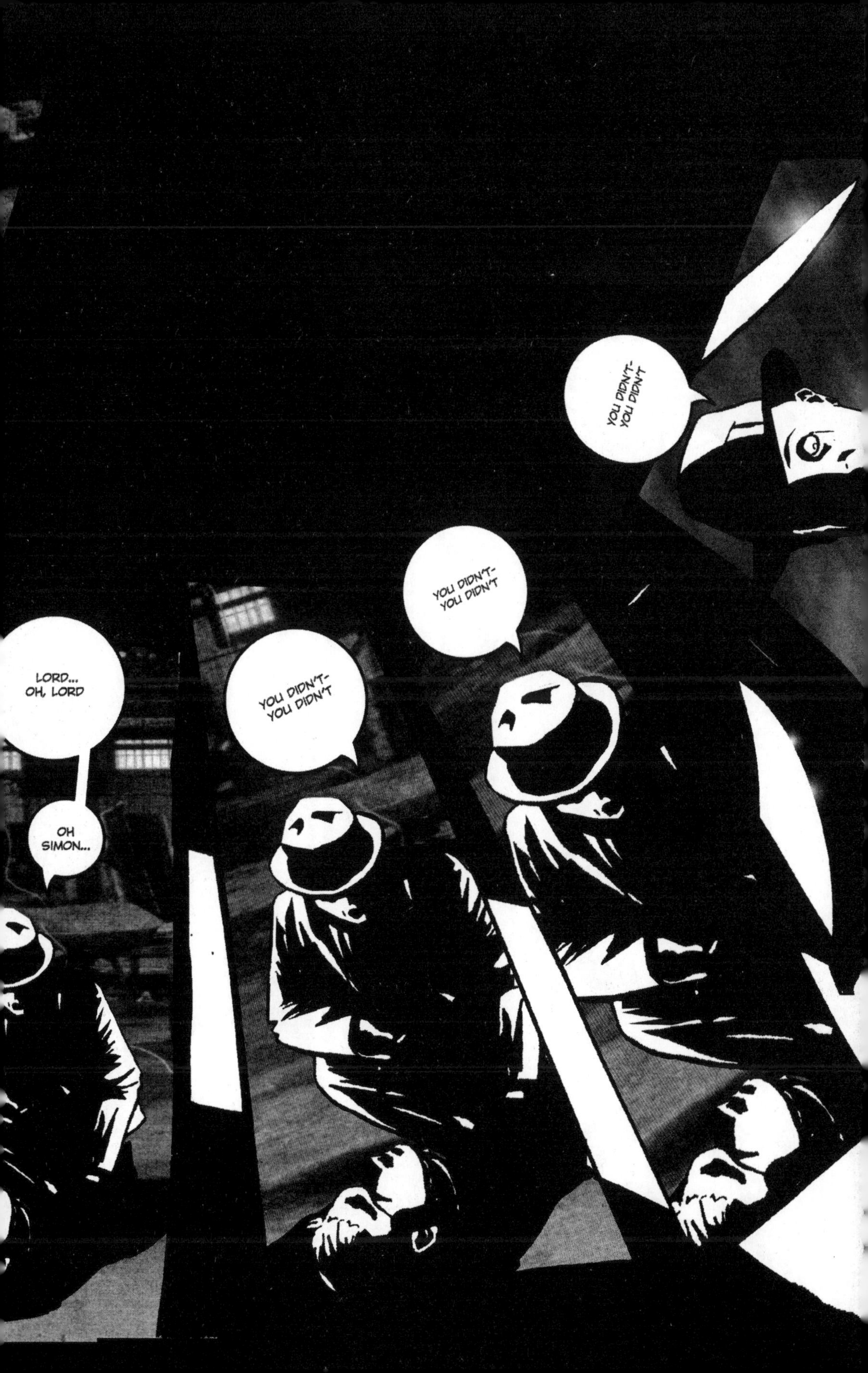
YOU DIDN'T-
YOU DIDN'T
YOU DIDN'T-
YOU DIDN'T
YOU DIDN'T-
YOU DIDN'T
LORD...
OH, LORD
OH
SIMON...

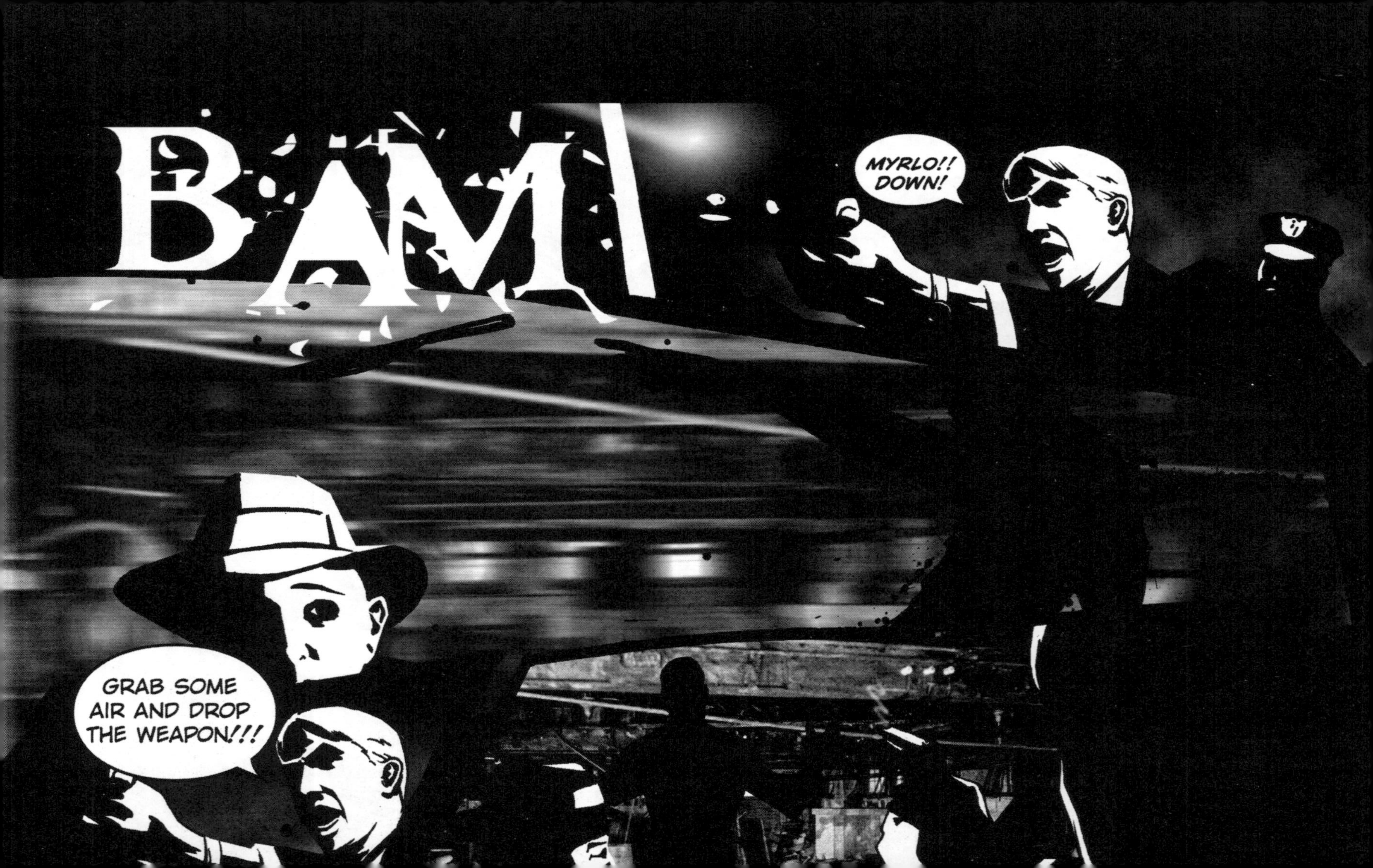
BAM
MYRLO!! DOWN!
GRAB SOME AIR AND DROP THE WEAPON!!!

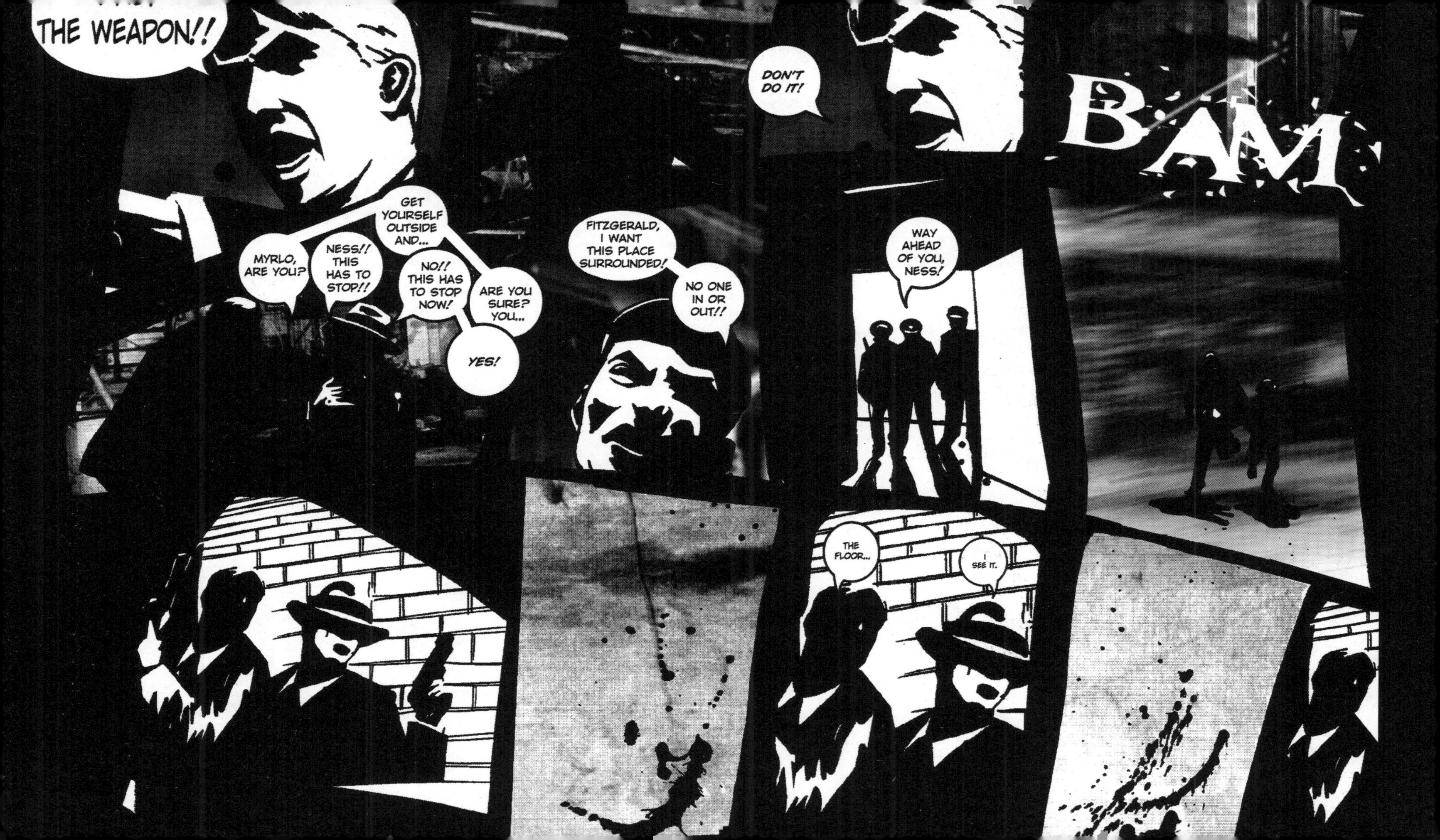
THE WEAPON!!
MYRLO, ARE YOU?
NESS!! THIS HAS TO STOP!!
GET YOURSELF OUTSIDE AND...
NO!! THIS HAS TO STOP NOW!
ARE YOU SURE? YOU...
YES!
FITZGERALD, I WANT THIS PLACE SURROUNDED!
NO ONE IN OR OUT!!
DON'T DO IT!
BAM
WAY AHEAD OF YOU, NESS!
THE FLOOR...
I SEE IT.

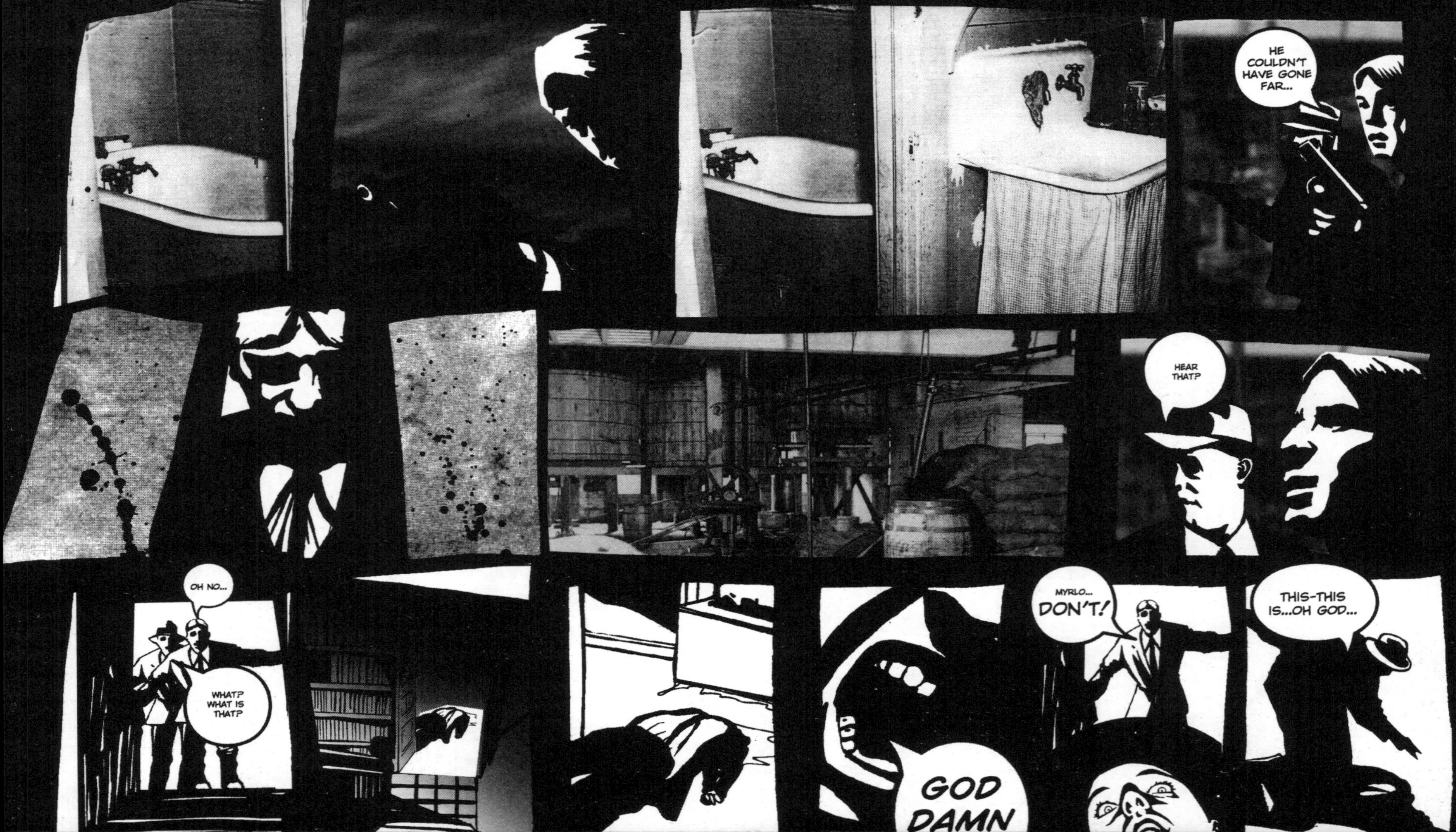
HE COULDN'T HAVE GONE FAR...
HEAR THAT?
OH NO...
WHAT? WHAT IS THAT?
GOD DAMN
MYRLO... DON'T!
THIS-THIS IS...OH GOD...

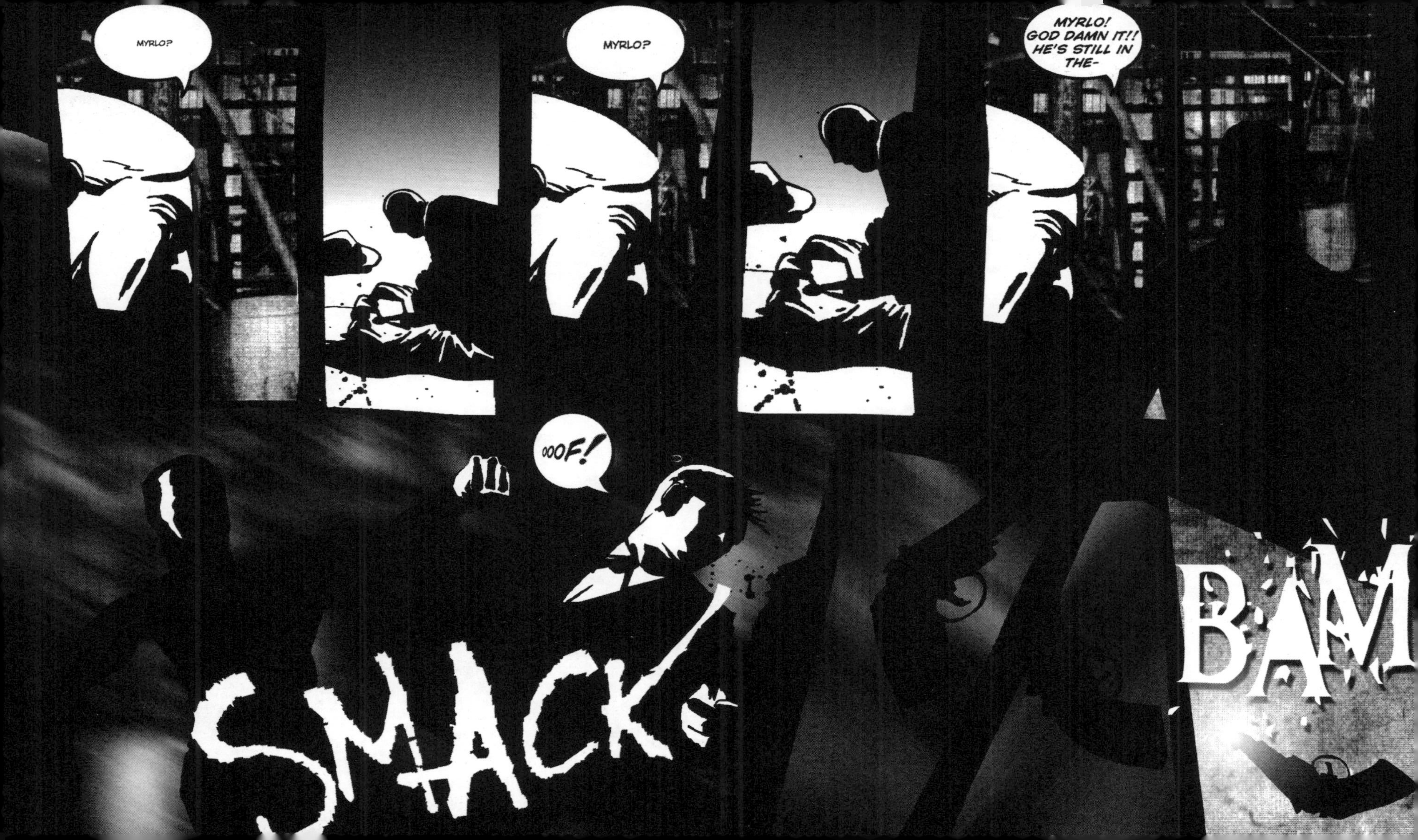
MYRLO?
MYRLO?
MYRLO! GOD DAMN IT!! HE'S STILL IN THE-
OOOF!
SMACK
BAM

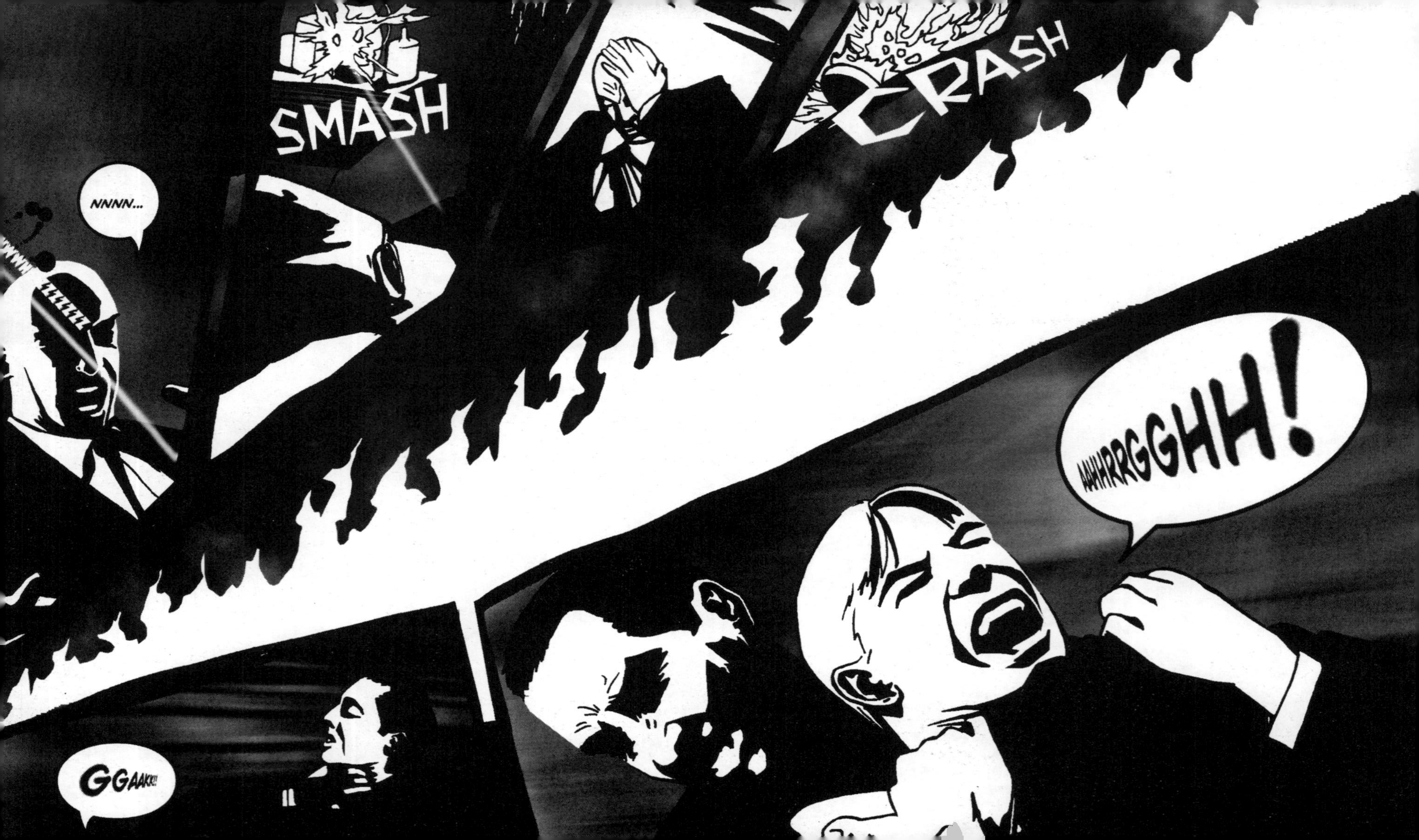
NNNN...
SMASH
CRASH
AAHHRRGGHH!
GGAAKK!!

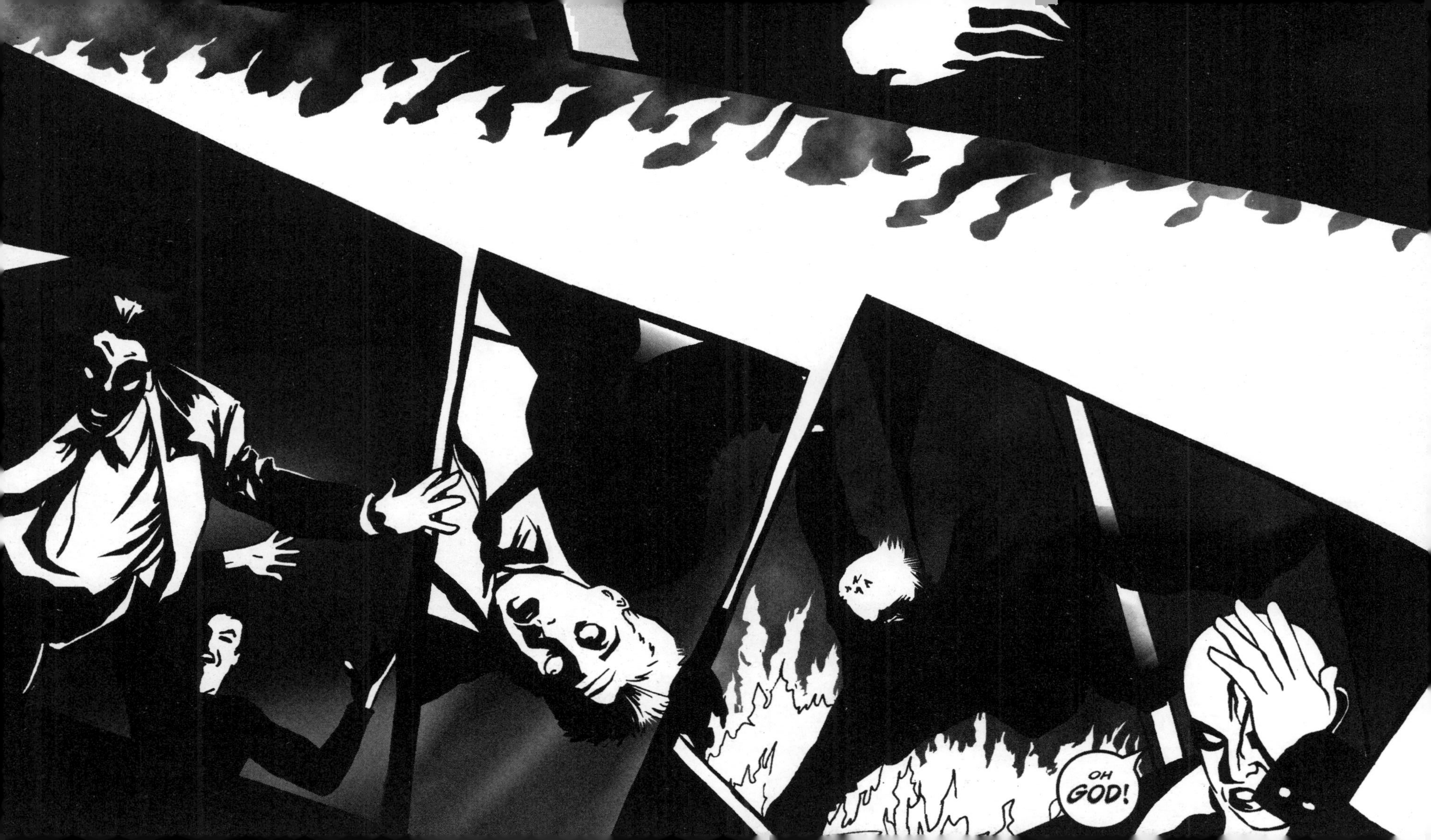
OH GOD!

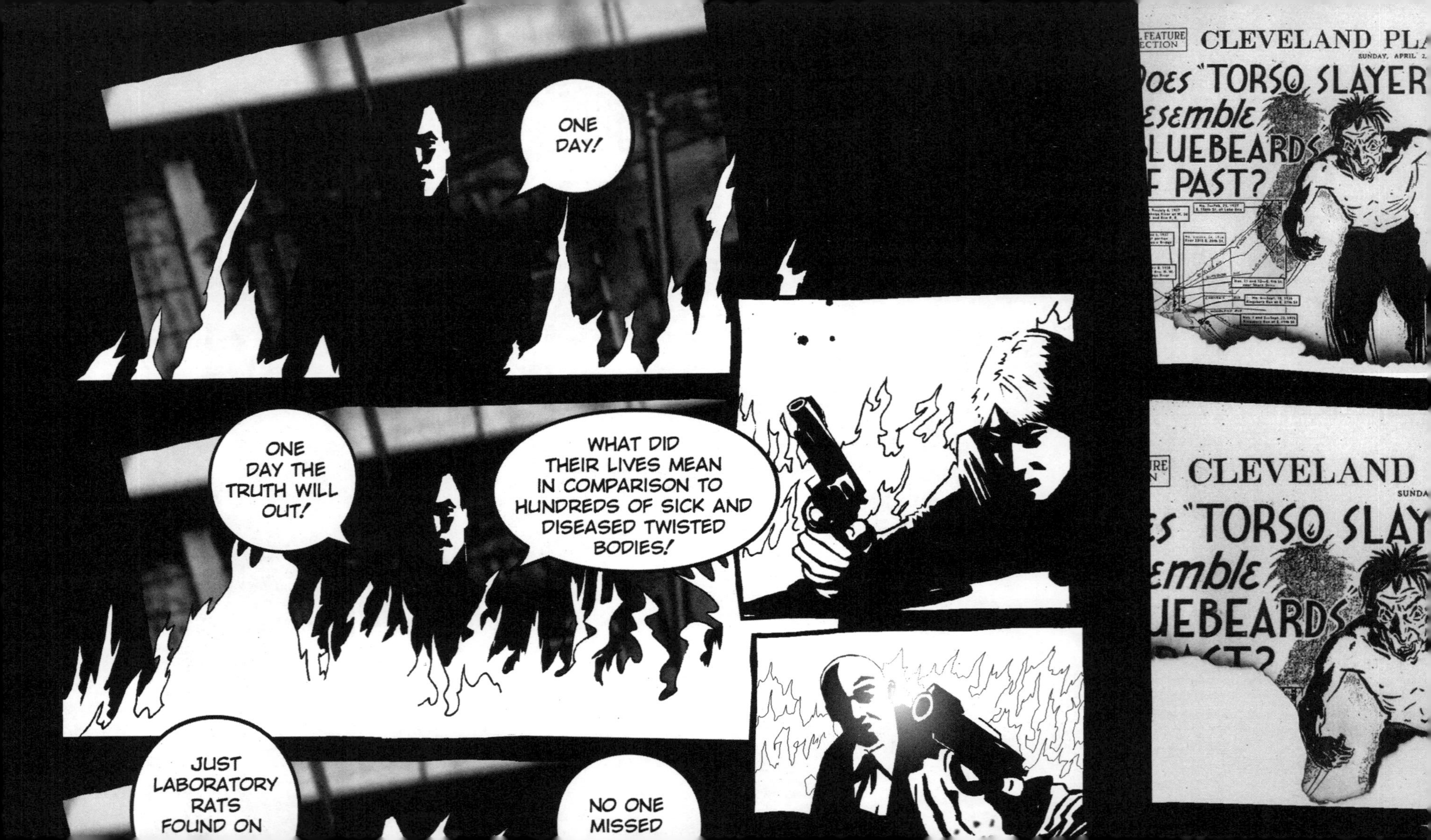
ONE DAY!
ONE DAY THE TRUTH WILL OUT!
WHAT DID THEIR LIVES MEAN IN COMPARISON TO HUNDREDS OF SICK AND DISEASED TWISTED BODIES!
JUST LABORATORY RATS FOUND ON
NO ONE MISSED
CLEVELAND PLA
SUNDAY, APRIL 2,
DOES "TORSO SLAYER
ESEMBLE
LUEBEARDS
F PAST?
CLEVELAND
ES "TORSO SLAY
EMBLE
UEBEARDS

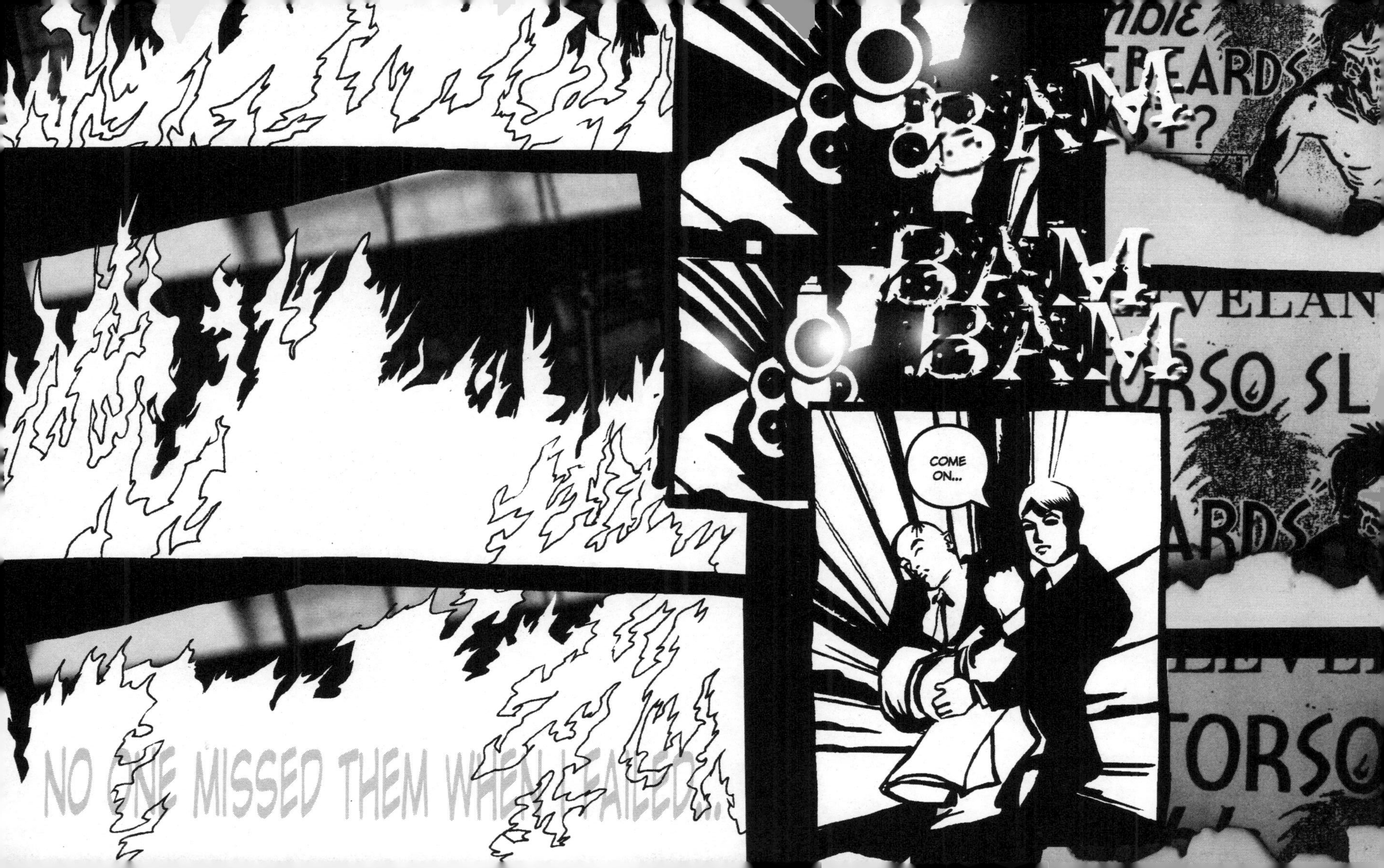

NO ONE MISSED THEM WHEN I FAILED...
BAM
BAM
BAM
COME ON...

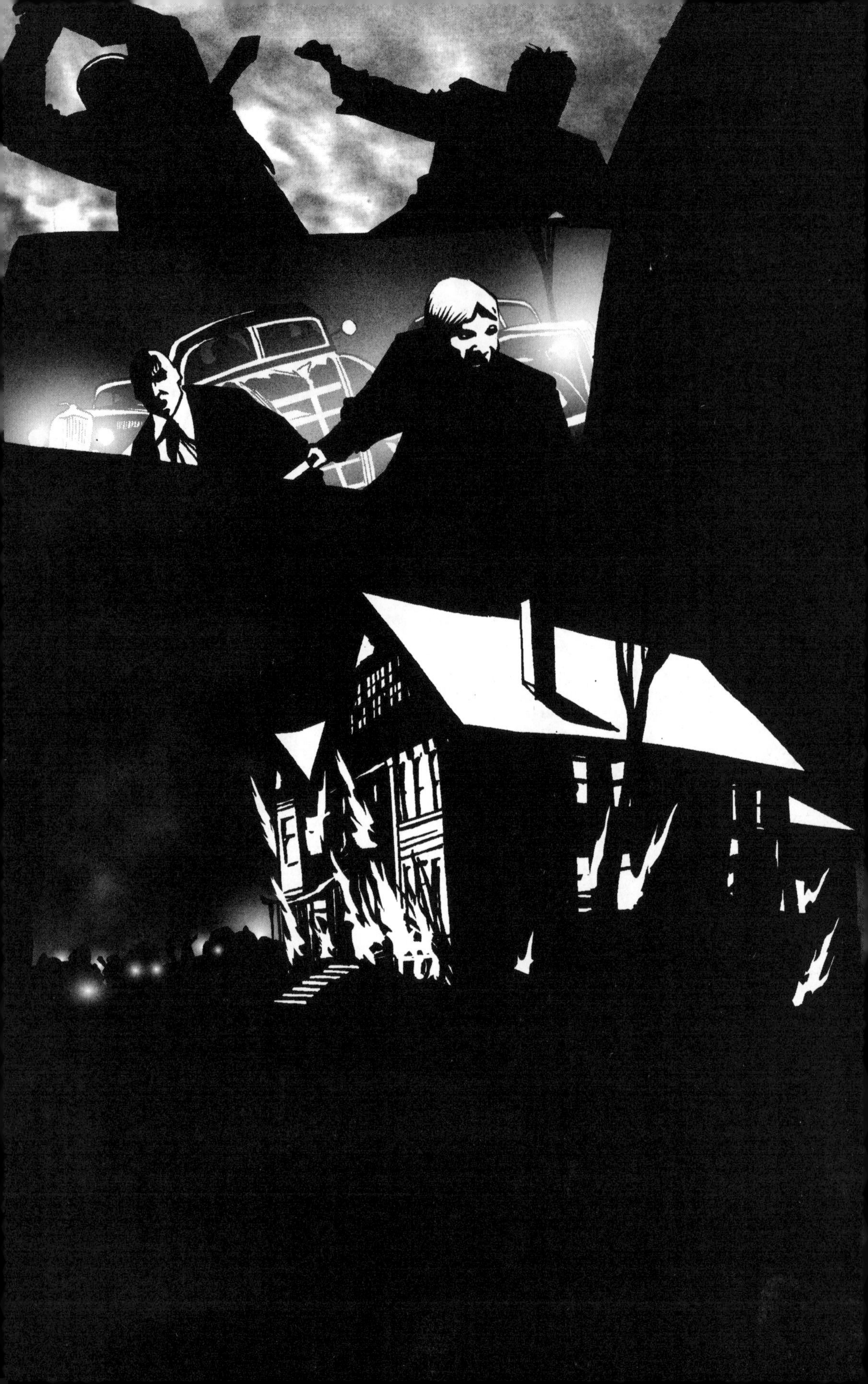

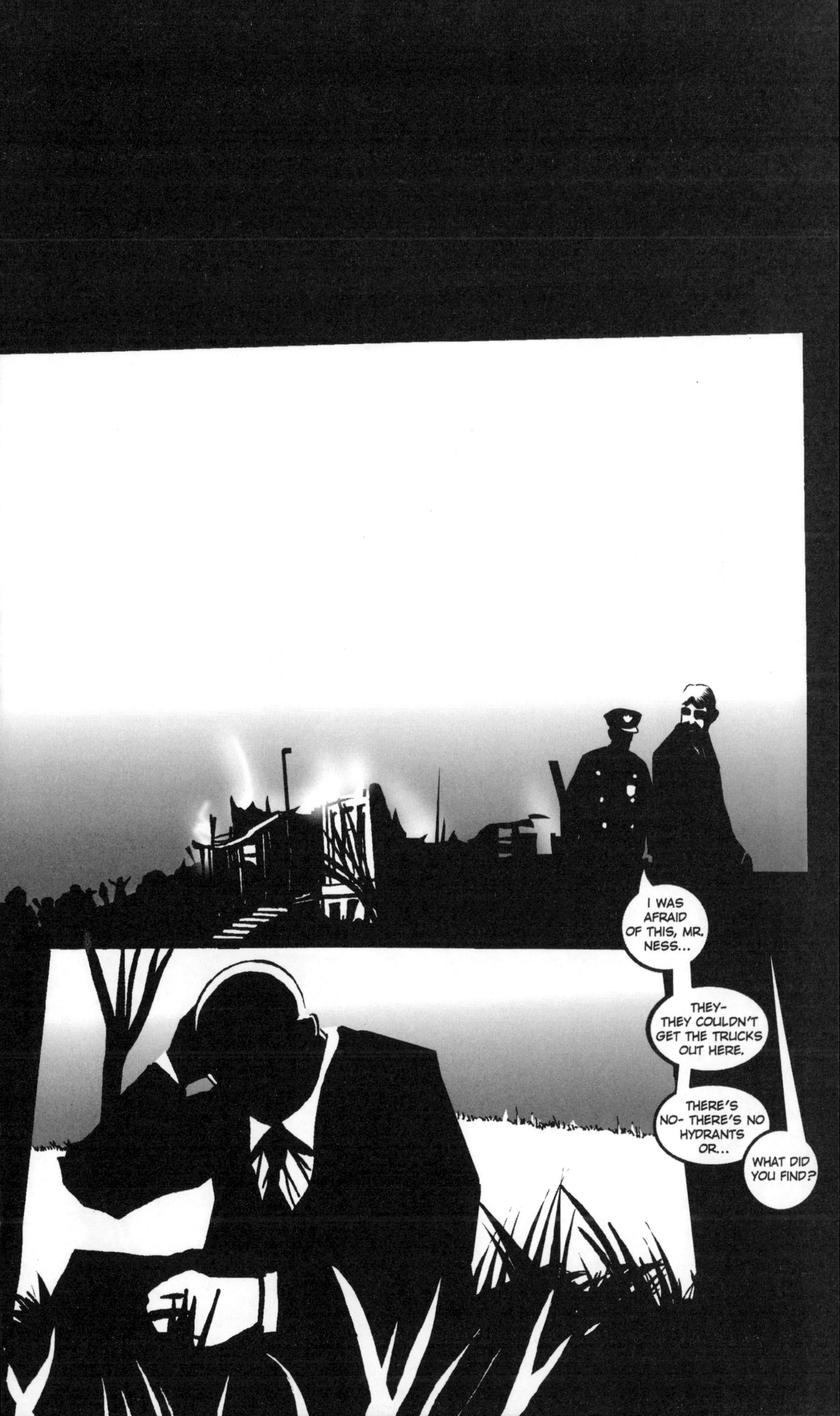
I WAS AFRAID OF THIS, MR. NESS...
THEY- THEY COULDN'T GET THE TRUCKS OUT HERE.
THERE'S NO- THERE'S NO HYDRANTS OR...
WHAT DID YOU FIND?

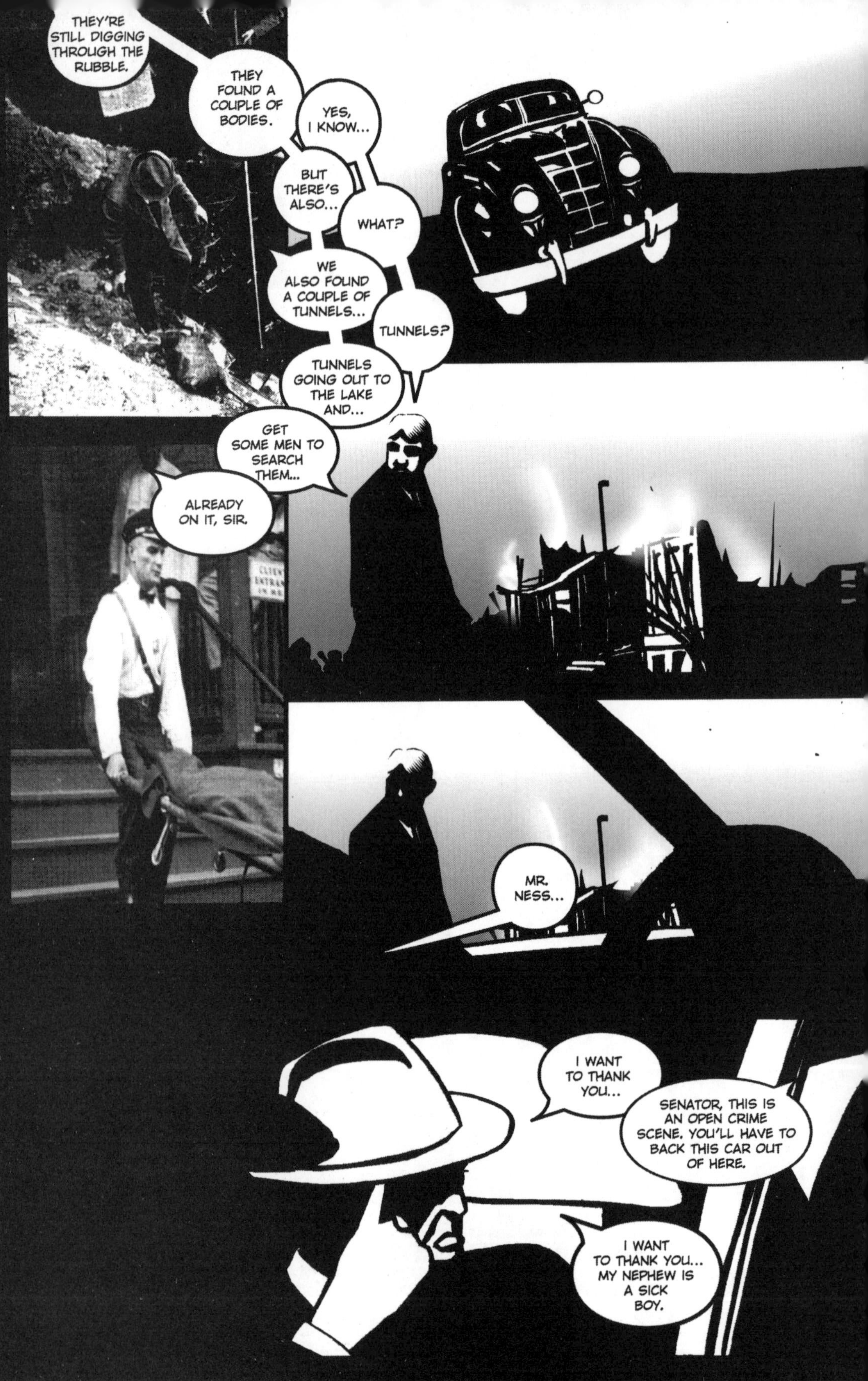
THEY'RE STILL DIGGING THROUGH THE RUBBLE.
THEY FOUND A COUPLE OF BODIES.
YES, I KNOW...
BUT THERE'S ALSO...
WHAT?
WE ALSO FOUND A COUPLE OF TUNNELS...
TUNNELS?
TUNNELS GOING OUT TO THE LAKE AND...
GET SOME MEN TO SEARCH THEM...
ALREADY ON IT, SIR.
MR. NESS...
I WANT TO THANK YOU...
SENATOR, THIS IS AN OPEN CRIME SCENE. YOU'LL HAVE TO BACK THIS CAR OUT OF HERE.
I WANT TO THANK YOU... MY NEPHEW IS A SICK BOY.

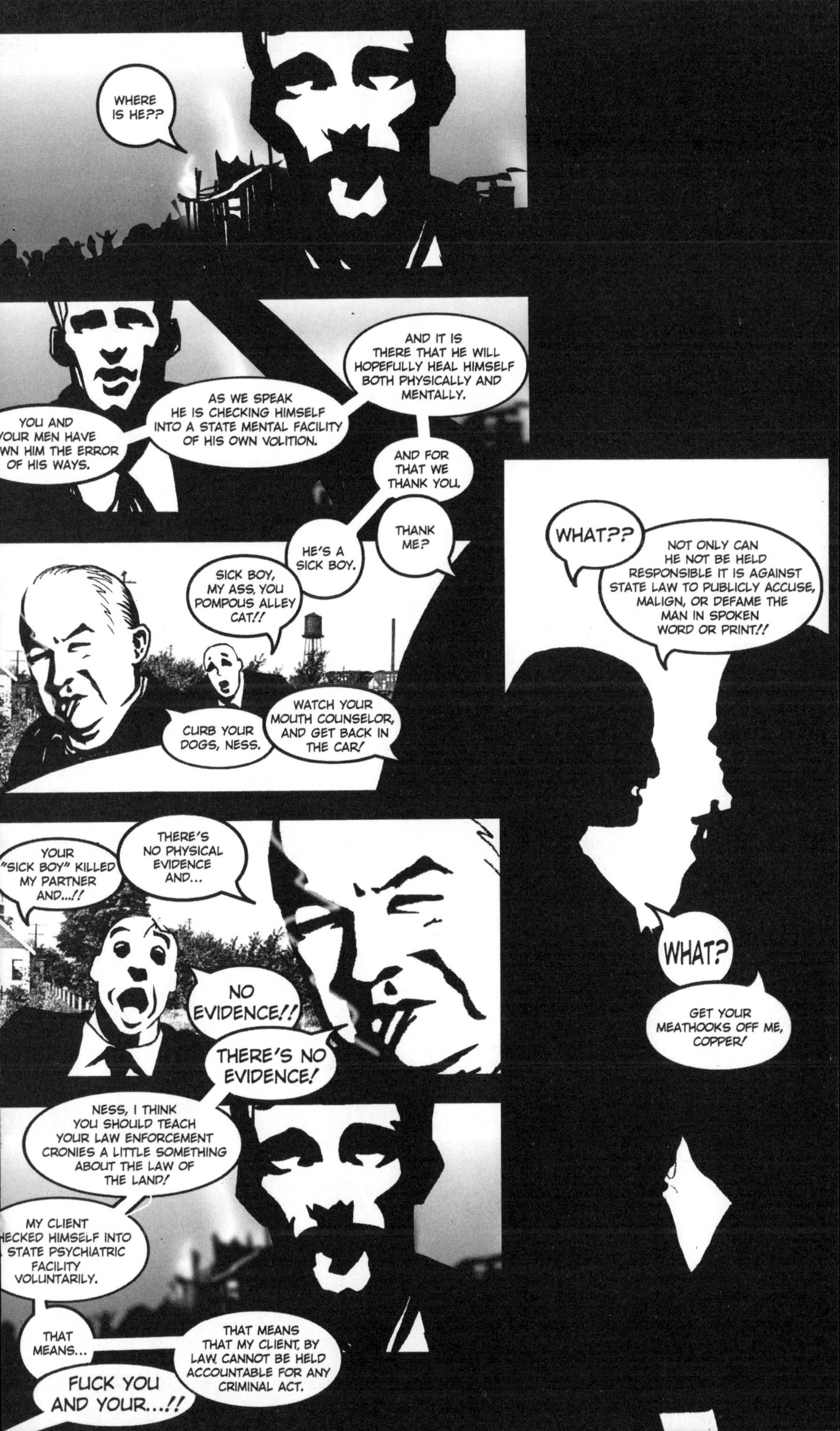
WHERE IS HE??
AS WE SPEAK HE IS CHECKING HIMSELF INTO A STATE MENTAL FACILITY OF HIS OWN VOLITION.
AND IT IS THERE THAT HE WILL HOPEFULLY HEAL HIMSELF BOTH PHYSICALLY AND MENTALLY.
AND FOR THAT WE THANK YOU.
THANK ME?
HE'S A SICK BOY.
SICK BOY, MY ASS, YOU POMPOUS ALLEY CAT!!
CURB YOUR DOGS, NESS.
WATCH YOUR MOUTH COUNSELOR, AND GET BACK IN THE CAR!
YOUR "SICK BOY" KILLED MY PARTNER AND...!!
THERE'S NO PHYSICAL EVIDENCE AND...
NO EVIDENCE!!
THERE'S NO EVIDENCE!
NESS, I THINK YOU SHOULD TEACH YOUR LAW ENFORCEMENT CRONIES A LITTLE SOMETHING ABOUT THE LAW OF THE LAND!
MY CLIENT
STATE PSYCHIATRIC FACILITY VOLUNTARILY.
THAT MEANS...
THAT MEANS THAT MY CLIENT, BY LAW, CANNOT BE HELD ACCOUNTABLE FOR ANY CRIMINAL ACT.
FUCK YOU AND YOUR...!!
WHAT??
NOT ONLY CAN HE NOT BE HELD RESPONSIBLE IT IS AGAINST STATE LAW TO PUBLICLY ACCUSE, MALIGN, OR DEFAME THE MAN IN SPOKEN WORD OR PRINT!!
WHAT?
GET YOUR MEATHOOKS OFF ME, COPPER!

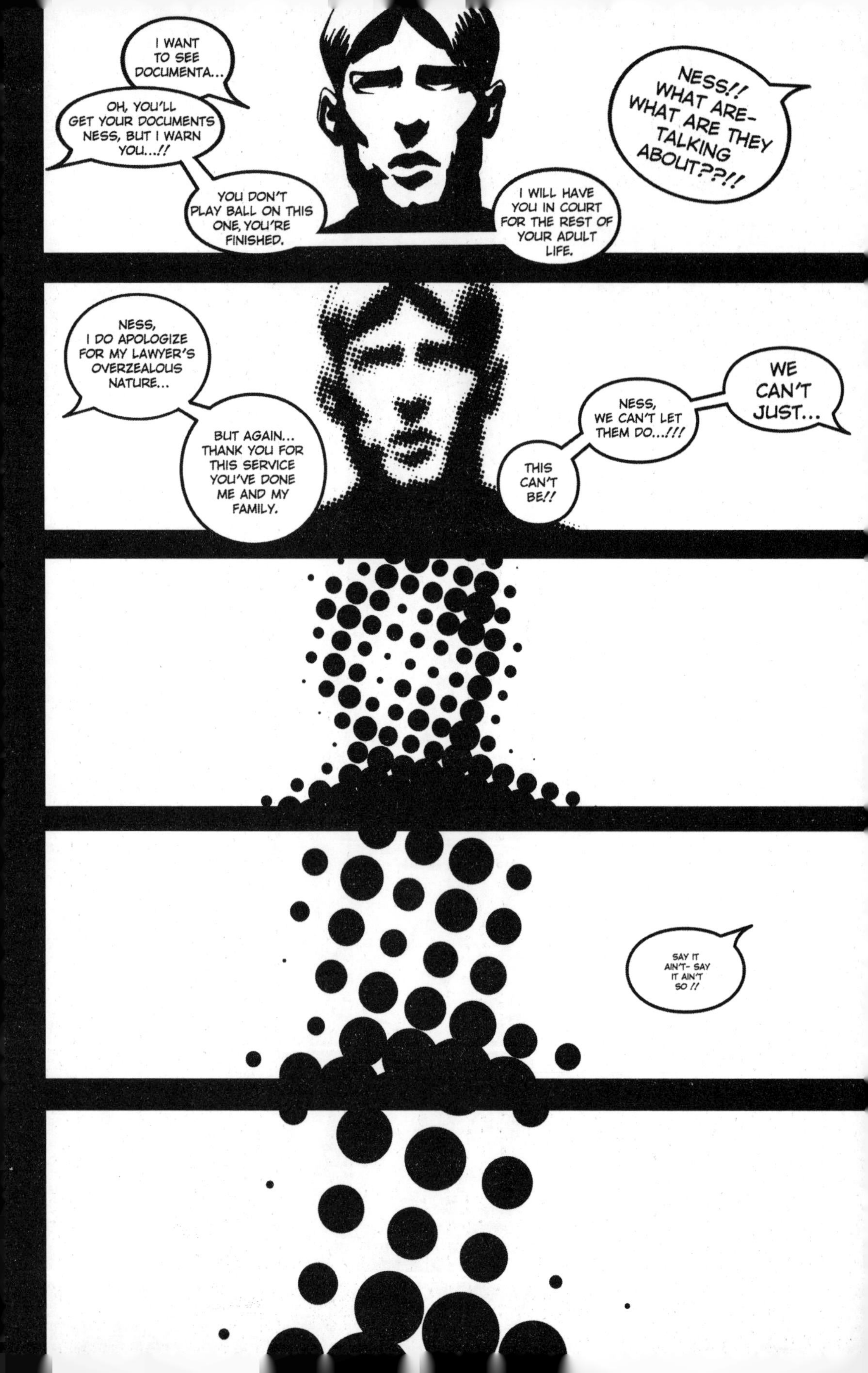
I WANT TO SEE DOCUMENTA...
OH, YOU'LL GET YOUR DOCUMENTS NESS, BUT I WARN YOU...!!
YOU DON'T PLAY BALL ON THIS ONE, YOU'RE FINISHED.
I WILL HAVE YOU IN COURT FOR THE REST OF YOUR ADULT LIFE.
NESS!! WHAT ARE- WHAT ARE THEY TALKING ABOUT??!!
NESS, I DO APOLOGIZE FOR MY LAWYER'S OVERZEALOUS NATURE...
BUT AGAIN... THANK YOU FOR THIS SERVICE YOU'VE DONE ME AND MY FAMILY.
THIS CAN'T BE!!
NESS, WE CAN'T LET THEM DO...!!!
WE CAN'T JUST...
SAY IT AIN'T- SAY IT AIN'T SO !!

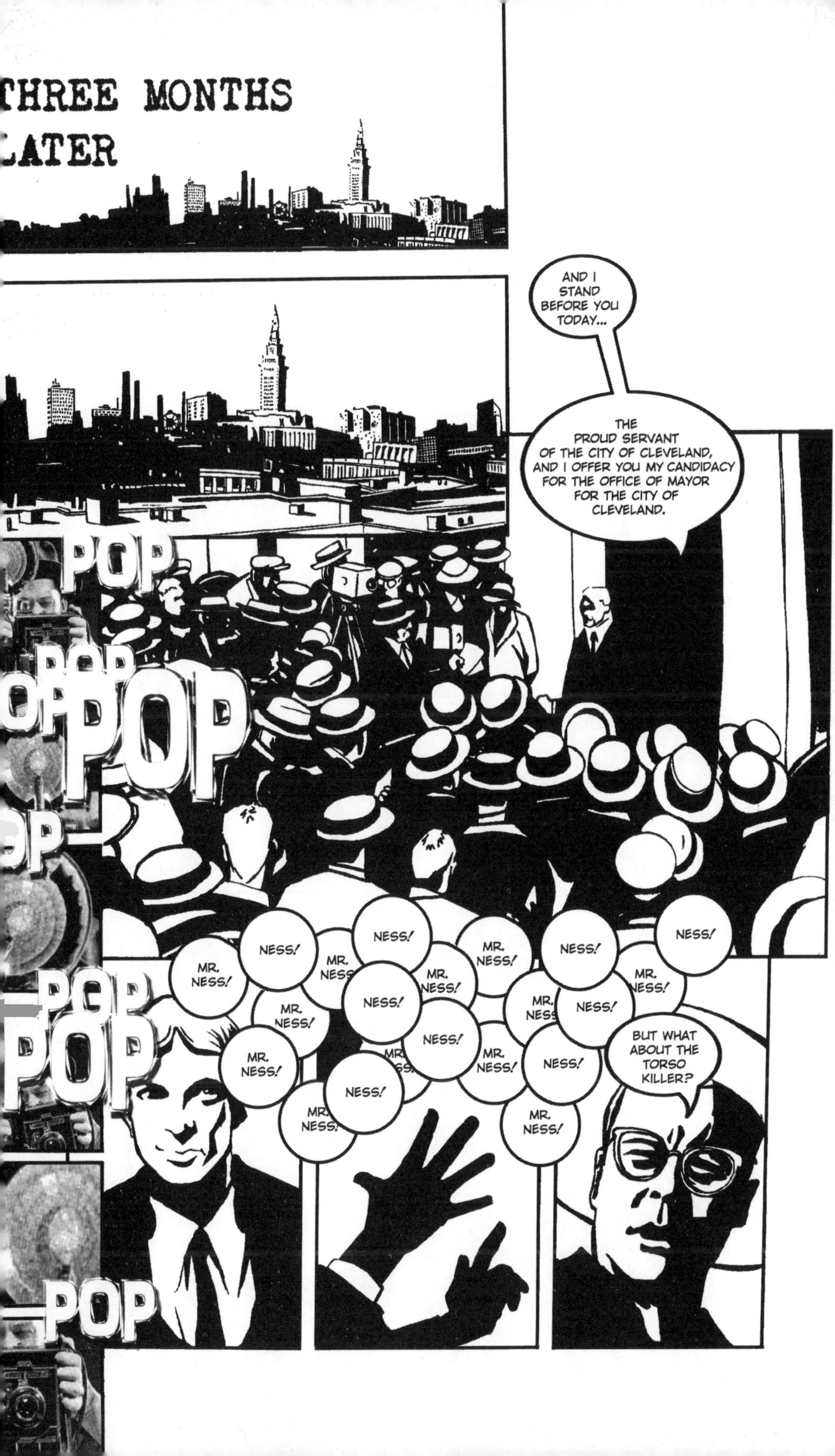
THREE MONTHS LATER
AND I STAND BEFORE YOU TODAY...
THE PROUD SERVANT OF THE CITY OF CLEVELAND, AND I OFFER YOU MY CANDIDACY FOR THE OFFICE OF MAYOR FOR THE CITY OF CLEVELAND.
POP
POP
POP
POP
MR. NESS!
NESS!
NESS!
MR. NESS!
NESS!
NESS!
MR. NESS!
MR. NESS!
NESS!
MR. NESS!
NESS!
MR. NESS!
NESS!
MR. NESS!
NESS!
MR. NESS!
BUT WHAT ABOUT THE TORSO KILLER?
POP
POP
POP

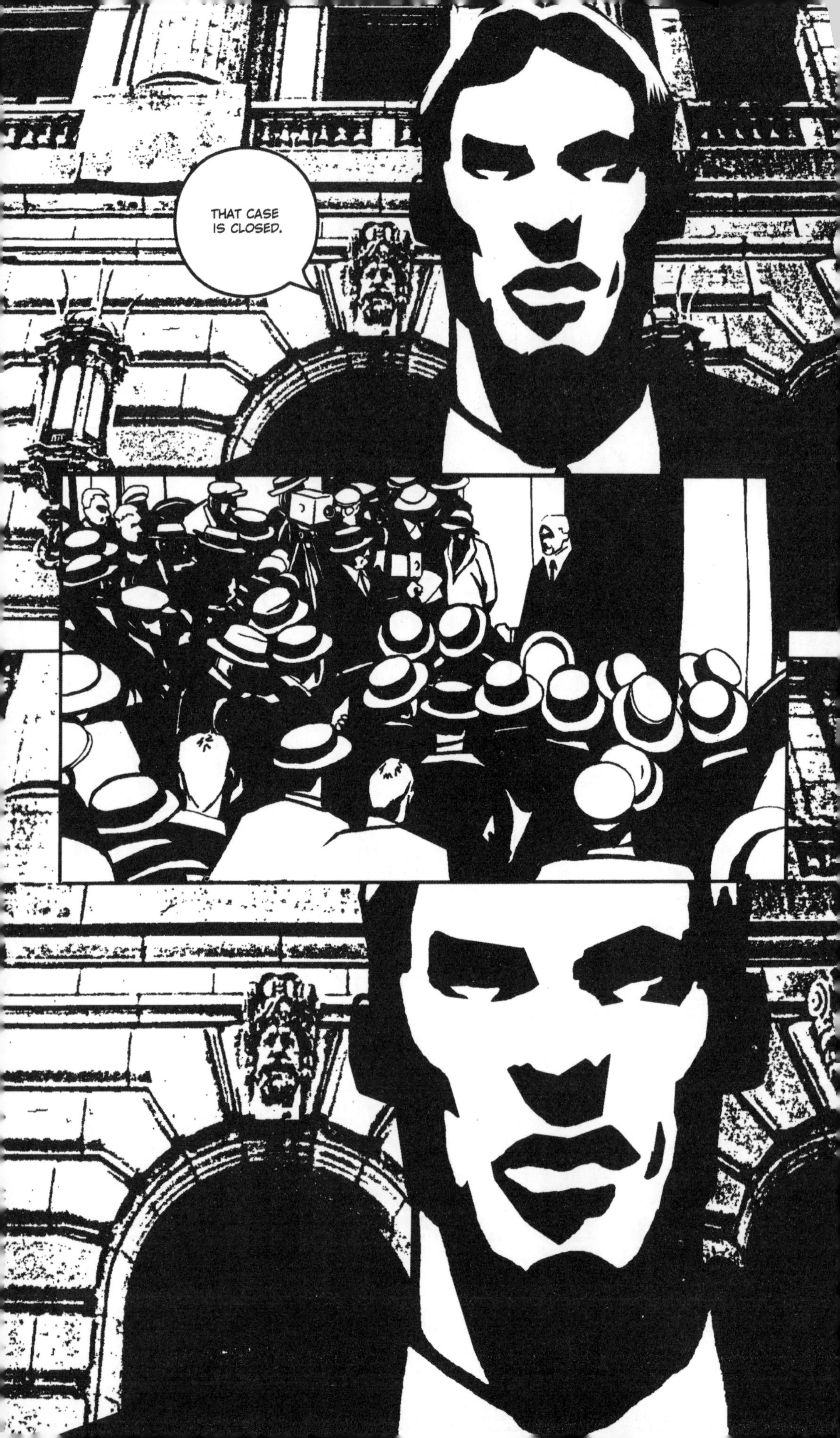
THAT CASE IS CLOSED.

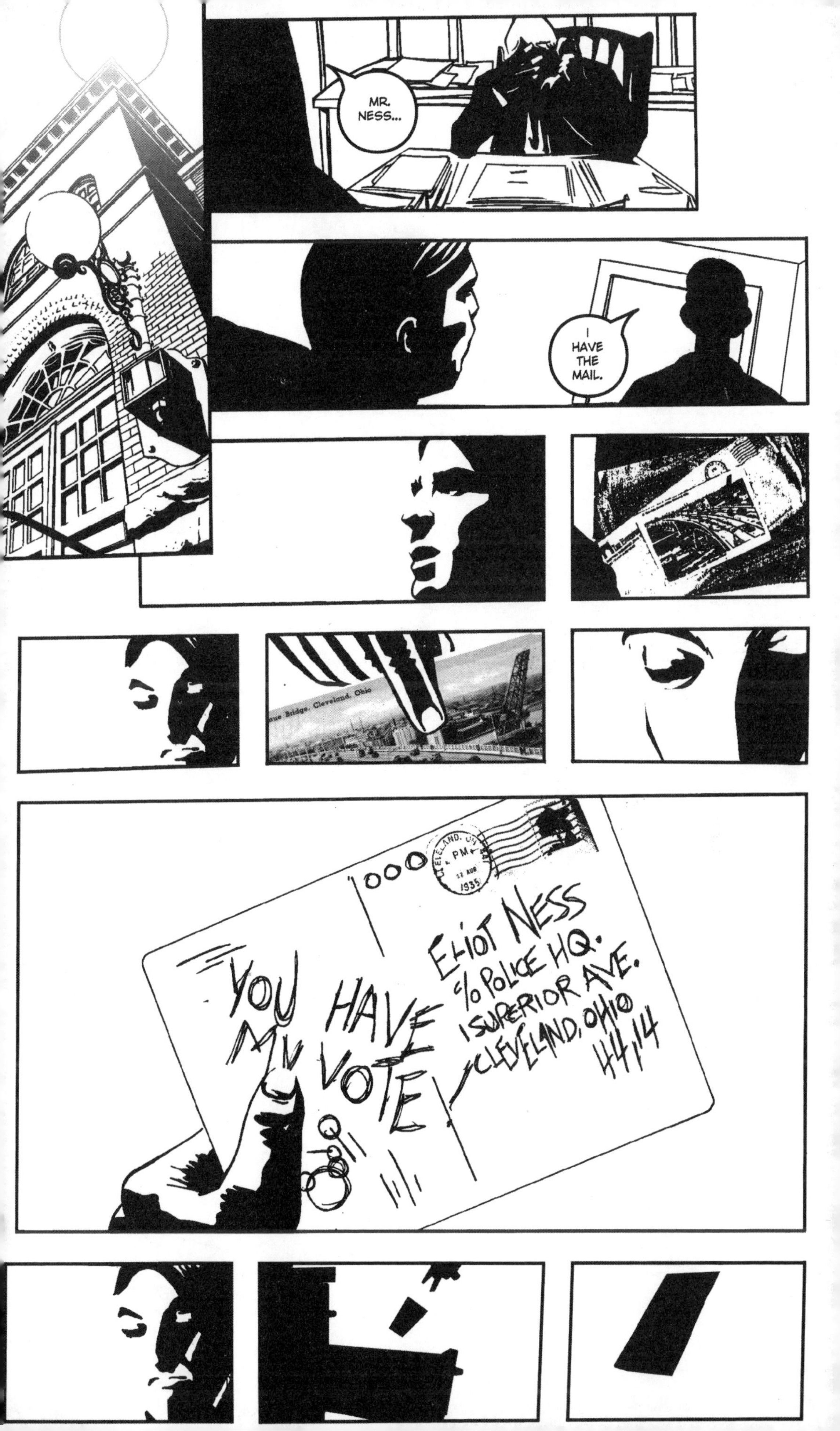
MR. NESS...
I HAVE THE MAIL.
Bridge, Cleveland, Ohio
PM
12 AUG
1935
YOU HAVE MY VOTE
ELIOT NESS
c/o POLICE HQ.
1 SUPERIOR AVE.
CLEVELAND, OHIO
44,14

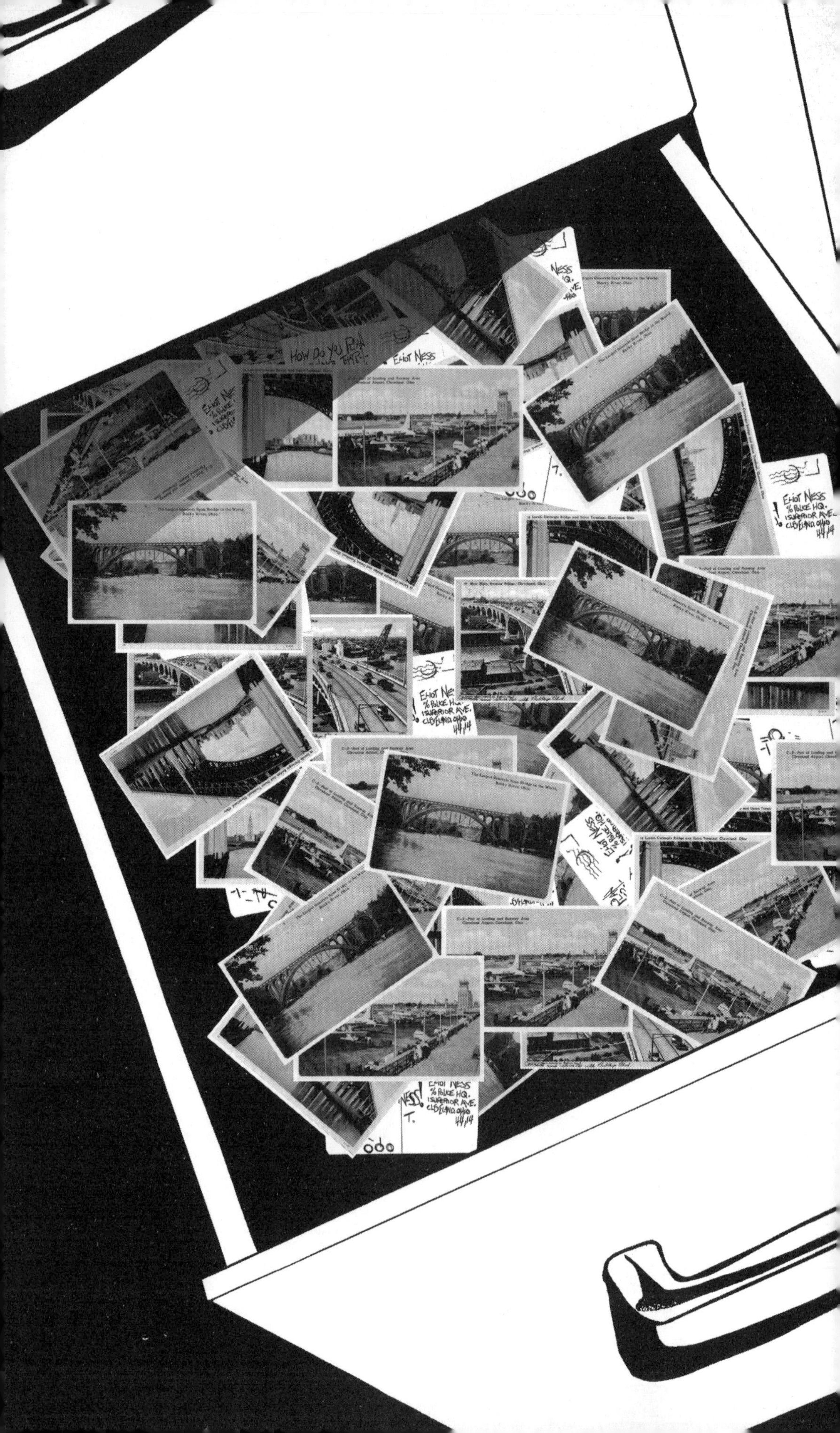

ELIOT NESS
% POLICE HQ.
1 SUPERIOR AVE.
CLEVELAND, OHIO
44114

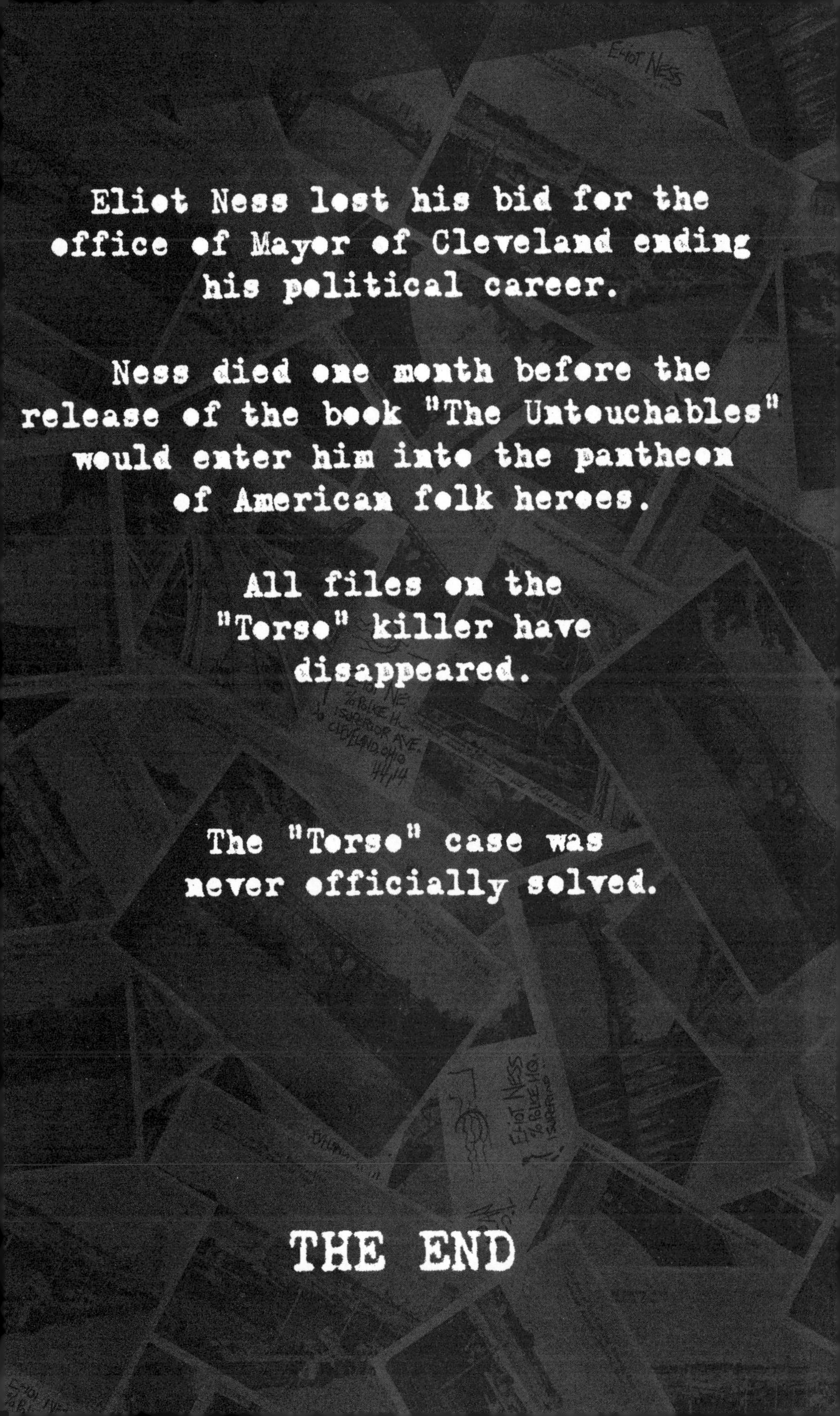
Eliot Ness lost his bid for the office of Mayor of Cleveland ending his political career.
Ness died one month before the release of the book "The Untouchables" would enter him into the pantheon of American folk heroes.
All files on the "Torso" killer have disappeared.
The "Torso" case was never officially solved.
THE END

the torso collection

The following images are courtesy of the Cleveland public library photography collection and The Cleveland Plain Dealer. The Press clippings are courtesy of the Cleveland State University Cleveland Press collection and newspaper archive.

We have literally hundreds of images and articles at our disposal. For this collection we have picked the items that stayed with us throughout the making of this book.

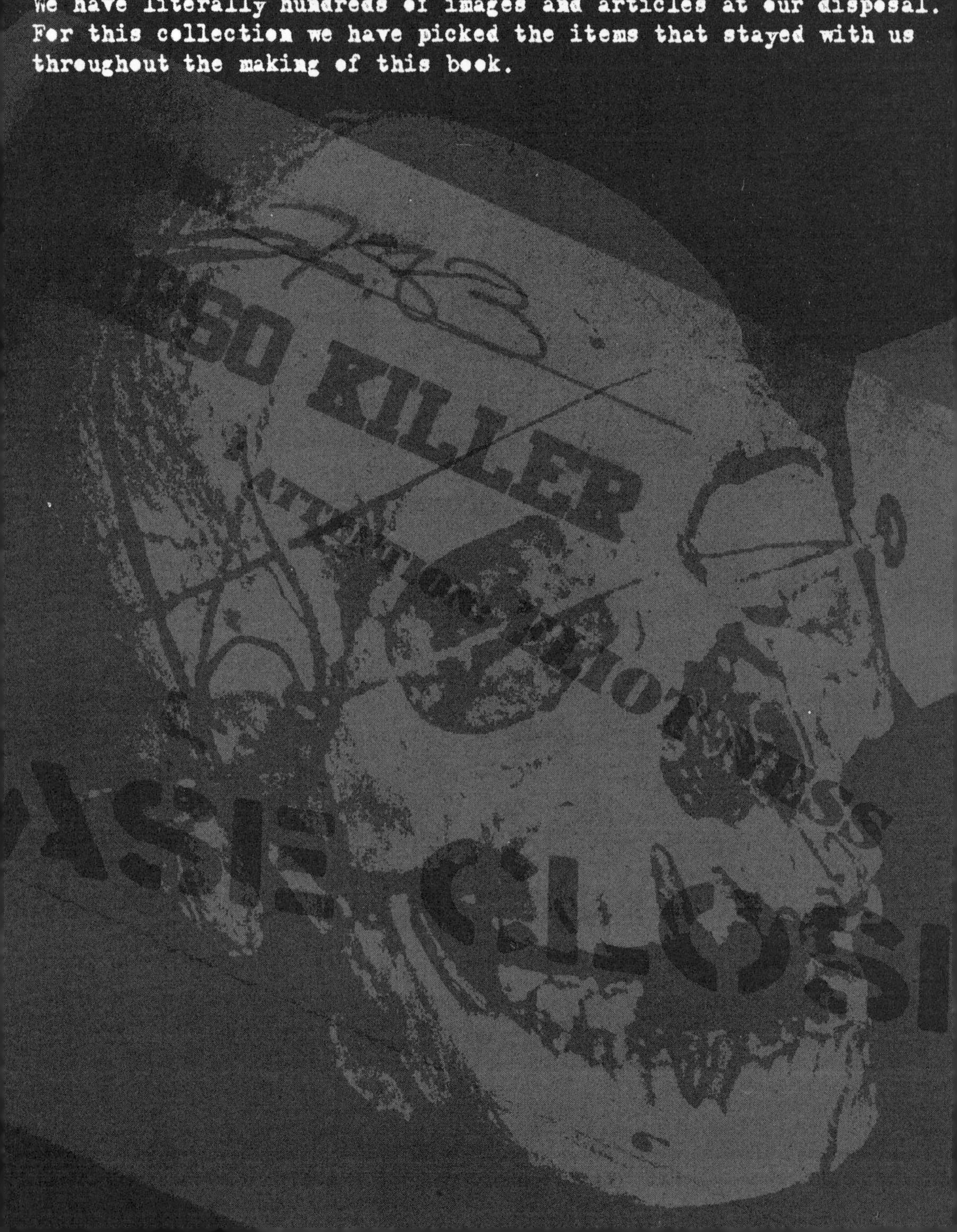
KILLER

the tattoo hustler and the torso death mask

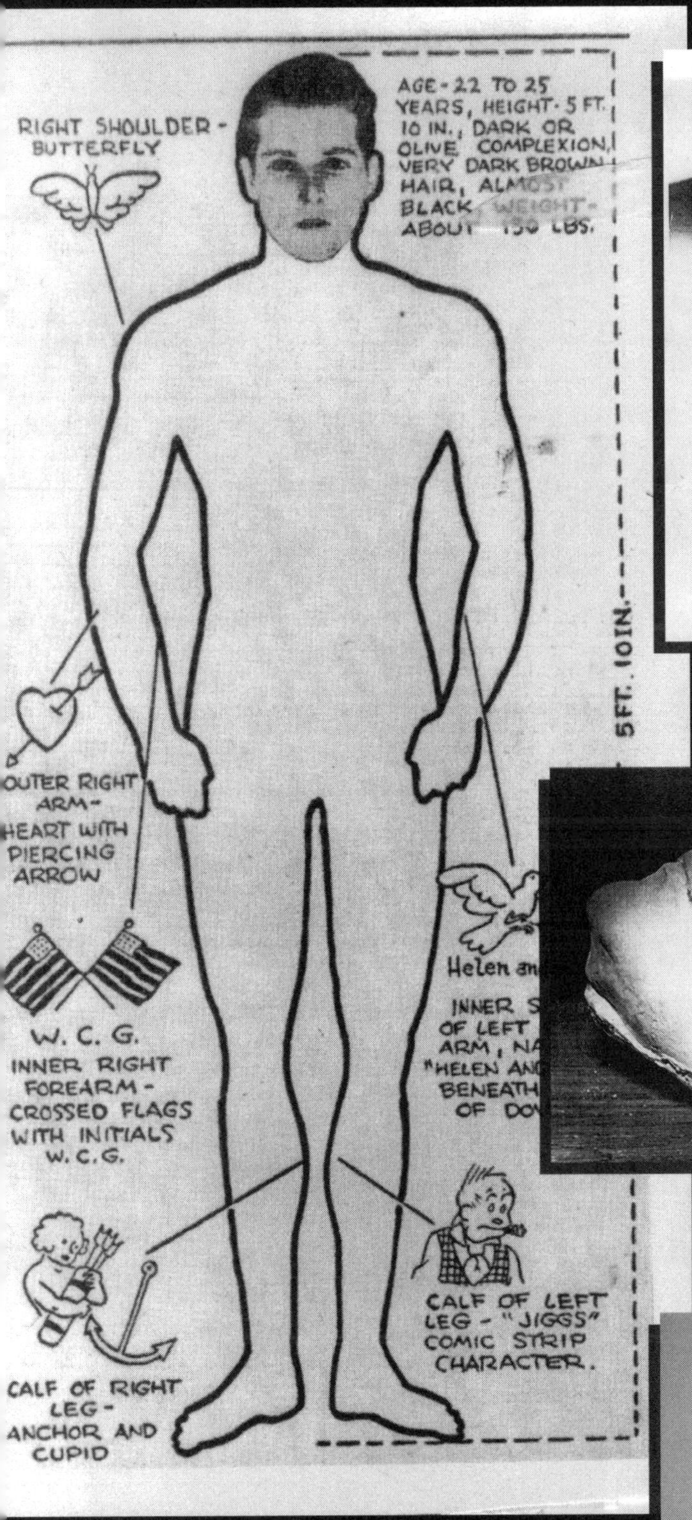

AGE - 22 TO 25 YEARS, HEIGHT - 5 FT. 10 IN., DARK OR OLIVE COMPLEXION, VERY DARK BROWN HAIR, ALMOST BLACK. WEIGHT - ABOUT 150 LBS.
RIGHT SHOULDER - BUTTERFLY
OUTER RIGHT ARM - HEART WITH PIERCING ARROW
W. C. G.
INNER RIGHT FOREARM - CROSSED FLAGS WITH INITIALS W. C. G.
Helen and
INNER S
OF LEFT
ARM, NA
"HELEN AND
BENEATH
OF DOV
5FT. 10IN.
CALF OF RIGHT LEG - ANCHOR AND CUPID
CALF OF LEFT LEG - "JIGGS" COMIC STRIP CHARACTER.

the hustler's head during autopsy

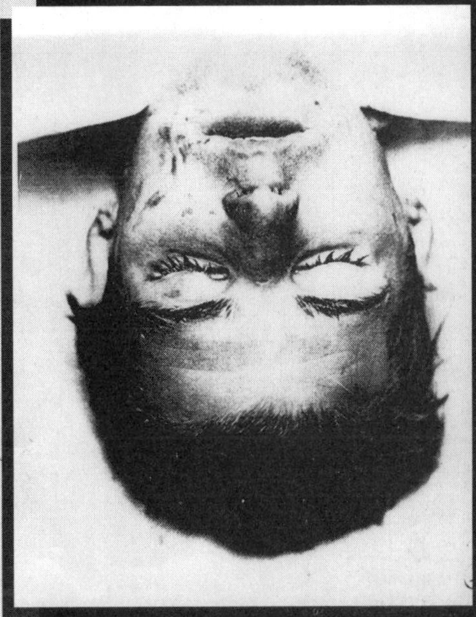

the death mask seen after creation

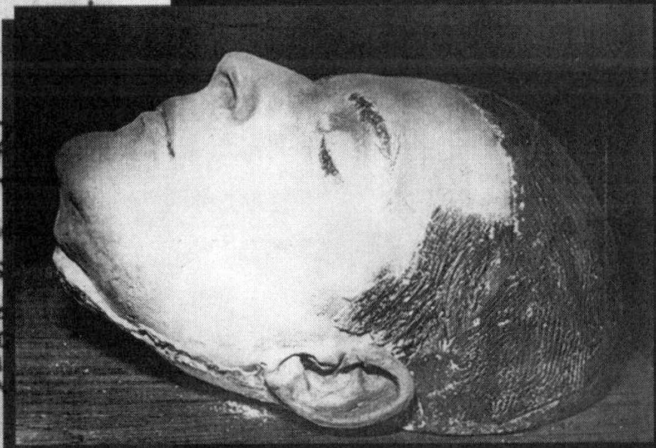

the death mask on display today

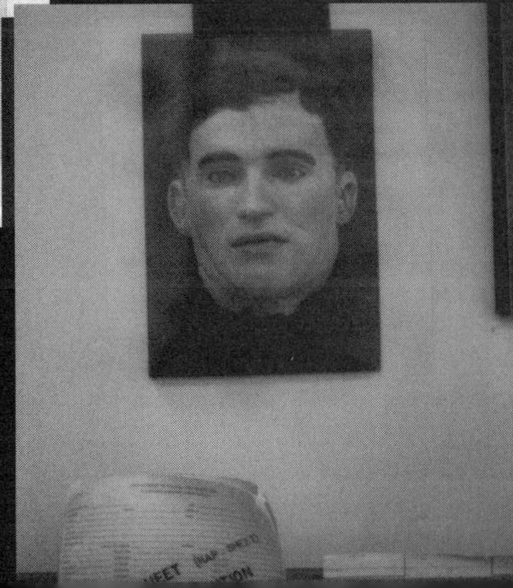

his diagram and a paper mache head were used to
y and gather information on the mysterious
attooed hustler. As described in this book,
he mask was hung in the downtown train station
r all to see. A handful of these "death masks"
e still on display in the Cleveland Justice
nter Police Historical Museum.

this is an actual police department graph documenting what information they did have on each of the murders.

Survey of "Torso Victims"

Case Number	#1	#2	#3	#4	#5	#6	#7
Name	?	Edward W. Andrassy	Florence Polillo alias Martin	?	?	?	?
Sex	Male	Male	Female	Male	Male	Male	Female
Color	White	White	White	White	White	White	White
Date Found	7/23/35	7/23/35	1/26/36 – 2/7/36	6/5/36 – 6/6/36	7/22/36	9/10/36	2/23/37
Duration of Death	7–8 Days	2–3 Days	2–3 Days	2–3 Days	1–2 Months	1–2 Days	3–6 Days
Approximate Date of Death	7/15/35	7/20/35	1/23/36	6/2/36	5/22/36	9/8/36	2/17/3[illegible]
Estimated Age	40–45 yrs.	28 yrs.	42 yrs.	25 yrs.	35–40 yrs.	25–30 yrs.	25–35 y[illegible]
Height	5 ft. 6 in.	5 ft. 11 in.	5 ft. 5 in.	5 ft. 11 in.	5 ft. 5 in.	5 ft. 10 in. (?)	?
Weight	160 lbs.	150 lbs.	160 lbs. (?)	150 lbs.	145 lbs. (?)	145 lbs. (?)	100–120 [illegible]
Location	Kingsbury Run at E. 49th St.	Kingsbury Run at E. 49th St.	2315–2325 E. 20th St.	Kingsbury Run E. 55th St.	Big Creek Clinton Road	Kingsbury Run at E. 37th St.	Lake Shore [illegible] at E 156th S[illegible]
Parts Recovered	Head Body	Head Body Genitalia	Upper Half Torso Lower Half Torso Four Extremities	Head Body	Head Body	Upper Half Torso Lower Half Torso Thighs + Legs	Upper Hal[illegible]
Parts Missing	Left Testicle (?)		Head			Head Both Upper Extr. Genitalia	Head Lower Hal[illegible] All 4 Extr[illegible]
Neck	Disarticulated Mid-Portion	Disarticulated Mid-Portion	Disarticulated C.4–5	Disarticulated C.[illegible]	Disarticulated C.3–4	Disarticulated C.3–4	Disarticu[illegible] C7–T1
Body			Disarticulated L2–3. Also Longitudinal Section			Disarticulated L.4.	Disarticu[illegible] L1. (Thru bo[illegible]
Extremities	Intact	Intact (Rope Burns on Wrists)	All Extremities Disarticulated also at Knee Joints	Intact	Intact	All Extremities Disarticulated also at Knee Joints	All Ext[illegible] Disartic[illegible]
Cut Surfaces Soft Tissues	Sharply Cut Muscles Retracted	Sharply Cut Muscles Retracted	All Surfaces sharply cut. No Retraction of Muscles. Few "Hesitation" Marks.	Sharply Cut. Few "Hesitation" Marks at Neck.	?	Sharply Cut. Few "Hesitation" Marks on Neck. No Retraction of Muscles.	Sharply [illegible] Numerou[illegible] Marks o[illegible]
Genitalia	Left Testicle Excised (?)	Scrotum and Penis Amputated	Mons veneris + symphysis [illegible]	Intact	?	Genitalia Amputated	
Blood in Body	?	Heart and Large Vessels Empty	Heart and Large Vessels Empty	Heart and Large Vessels Empty	!	Heart and Large Vessels Empty	Blood in Hea[illegible] Large [illegible]
Contents of Stomach		Recently Ingested Vegetable Meal.		Small Amount of Undigested Food (Baked Beans) in Stomach.		Kernels of Corn in Stomach	
Identifying Marks	Two Scars Middle Third Right Thigh 1" and 1½" diam.	Appendectomy Scar Small Scar Forehead Gold-Capped Left Upper Lateral Incisor Tooth.	Vaccination Mark Right Thigh. Mid-Line Lower Abdominal Laparotomy Wound.	Tattoo Marks. 1) Butterfly 2) Picture of "Jiggs" 3) Heart and Arrow 4) Flag with "W.C.M." 5) Cupid and Anchor 6) Dove with "Helen + Paul"	?	None	None (Exc[illegible] [illegible]
Cause of Death	Decapitation	Decapitation	? Decapitation	Decapitation	? Decapitation	?	

detective walter myrle holding possible murder weapons of one of the torso murder suspects.

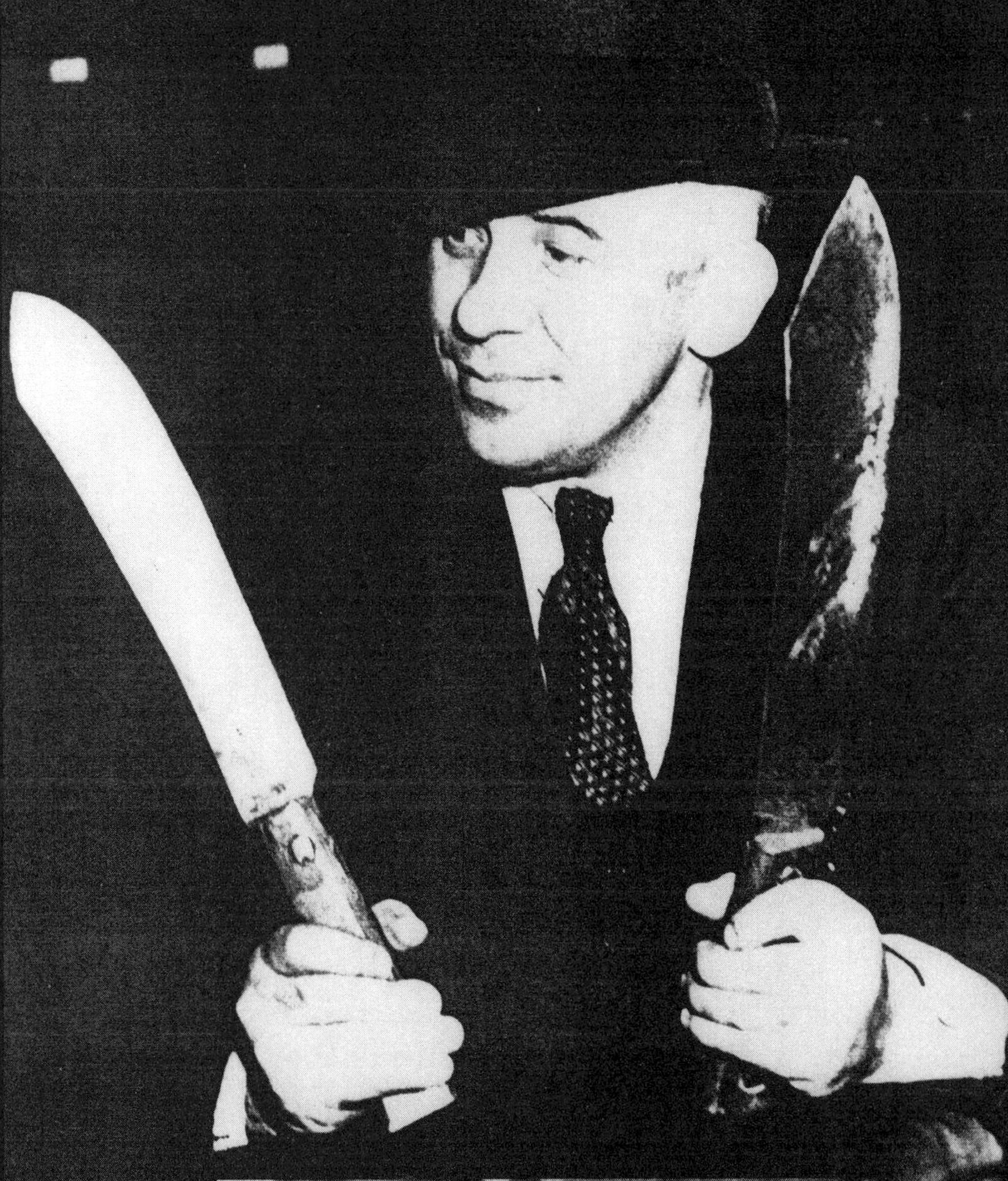

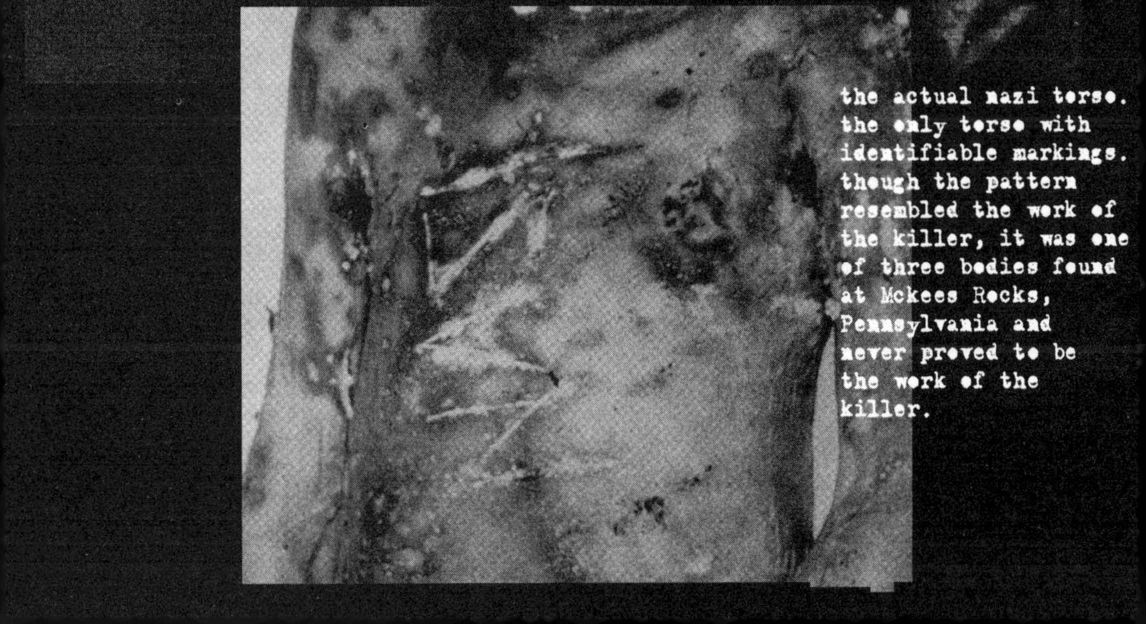

the actual nazi torso. the only torso with identifiable markings. though the pattern resembled the work of the killer, it was one of three bodies found at Mckees Rocks, Pennsylvania and never proved to be the work of the killer.

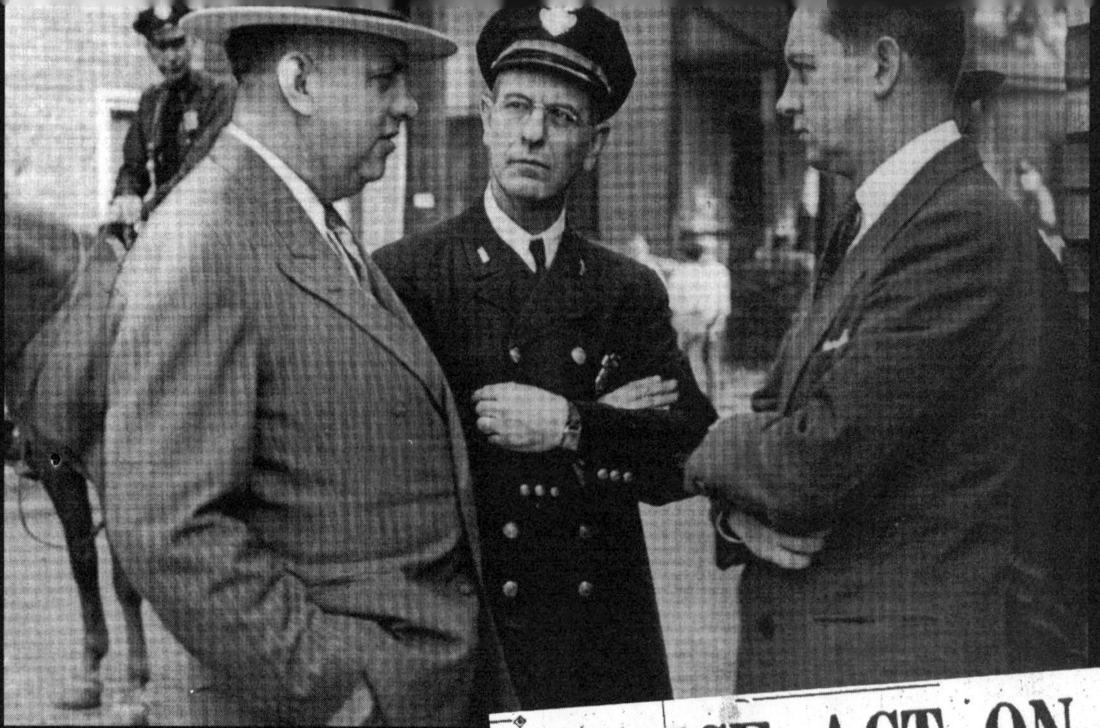

eliot ness

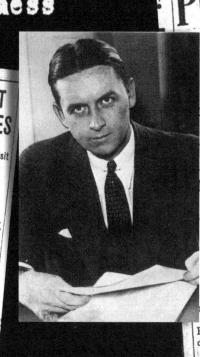

?POLICE ACT ON ORDER OF NES

ove Into Kingsbury Run, Laboratory Maniac Butcher, Bring in and Question All Residents in Valley

EARFUL HOBOES AVOID GUL

ool Dragged Again for Head and Hand Knife Fiend's Sixth Victim; Hat May Be Clew

Safety Director Eliot Ness today took personal cha investigation of the mystery of the headless dead.

As his first step he ordered a clean-out of the Kin Run area where four of the decapitation murders hav done.

A small army of police moved into the run area f 24th street eastward to bring in the score or more of nent residents" there—the men who manage somehow out working, to live in shacks and old piano box lean-to's.

Every transient in the ar be brought in. They we questioned on what they m heard along the hoboes' the wireless communicatio ready has warned tramp Cleveland and its mad bu

Director Ness went over ord gathered in the weir six killings, personally Detectives Peter Marylo Zalewski who for weeks assigned to the case.

The Murder The

Out of the conference theories of the killer:

HITLER SCORES SOVIET SETUP

Attacks Russia's Consideration of Workers; Lauds "German Peace"

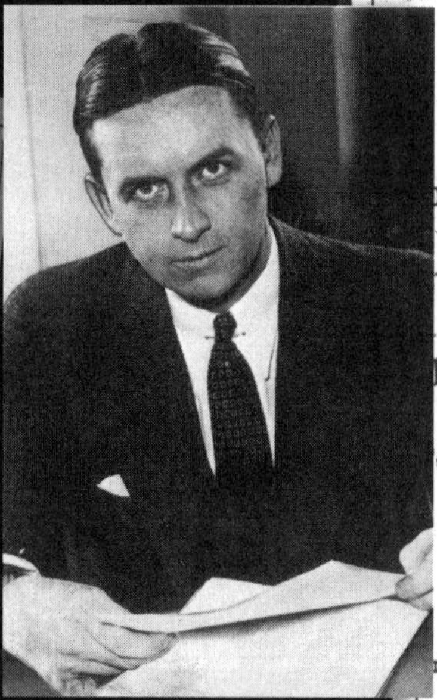

DEC. 13, 1935

IESS TO FIGHT IN FRONT LINES

v Safety Director to Visit lations, View Vice Dens In Crime War

ntinued From Page One)

ain permits from their cap- and then the chief himself they are granted a personal w with the safety director. nan can be refused an audi- h me by any superior offi- id Mr. Ness. "This, of pplies only to interviews at

orks both ways. If I wish iew any member of the vill notify the chief, and will notify the command- of the precinct."

said one of the purposes er is to curtail visits to favor-seekers, members wishing to be transfer- ne precinct to another, n quest of political fav- rpose, he said, is to im- e and discipline.

rking Director

to be a working safe- aid the former chief of x investigators for the of Ohio, "I- ...

erred today wi ... ue, traffic com ... and means of ... atalities in the ... suggestion to C ... nembers of the ... permits from the ... cers for intervie ... ss said he "wishe ... ned through th ...

He said "Nothing ... al to morale than ... of the department

Inside, the policemen who had

(Continued on Page 4, Column 1)

'Let's Go,' Ness Says, as He Shows His G-Man Training

Eliot Ness last night showed the county of Cuyahoga in general and Sheriff John M. Sulzmann in particular that his reputation as a zealous, courageous law enforcement officer is no publicity build-up.

Cleveland's 32-year-old safety director walked, unarmed, at the head of a column of 62 heavily-armed men to thrust open the doors of the Harvard Club into the faces of men who had threatened to "knock off the heads" and "mow down" anyone ... the place.

... know, evidently, that the slight figure in a camel's-hair topcoat, had led the federal government's "untouchables" in their desperate war that smashed Scarface Al Capone's beer racket in Chicago.

The plug-ugly didn't look down at the gold badge whose color blended with that of Ness' coat. The badge had inscribed on it: "City of Cleveland—Director of Public Safety."

Ness just smiled at the "hard guy" and walked away.

You might have thought he was a ... successful in an athletic ...

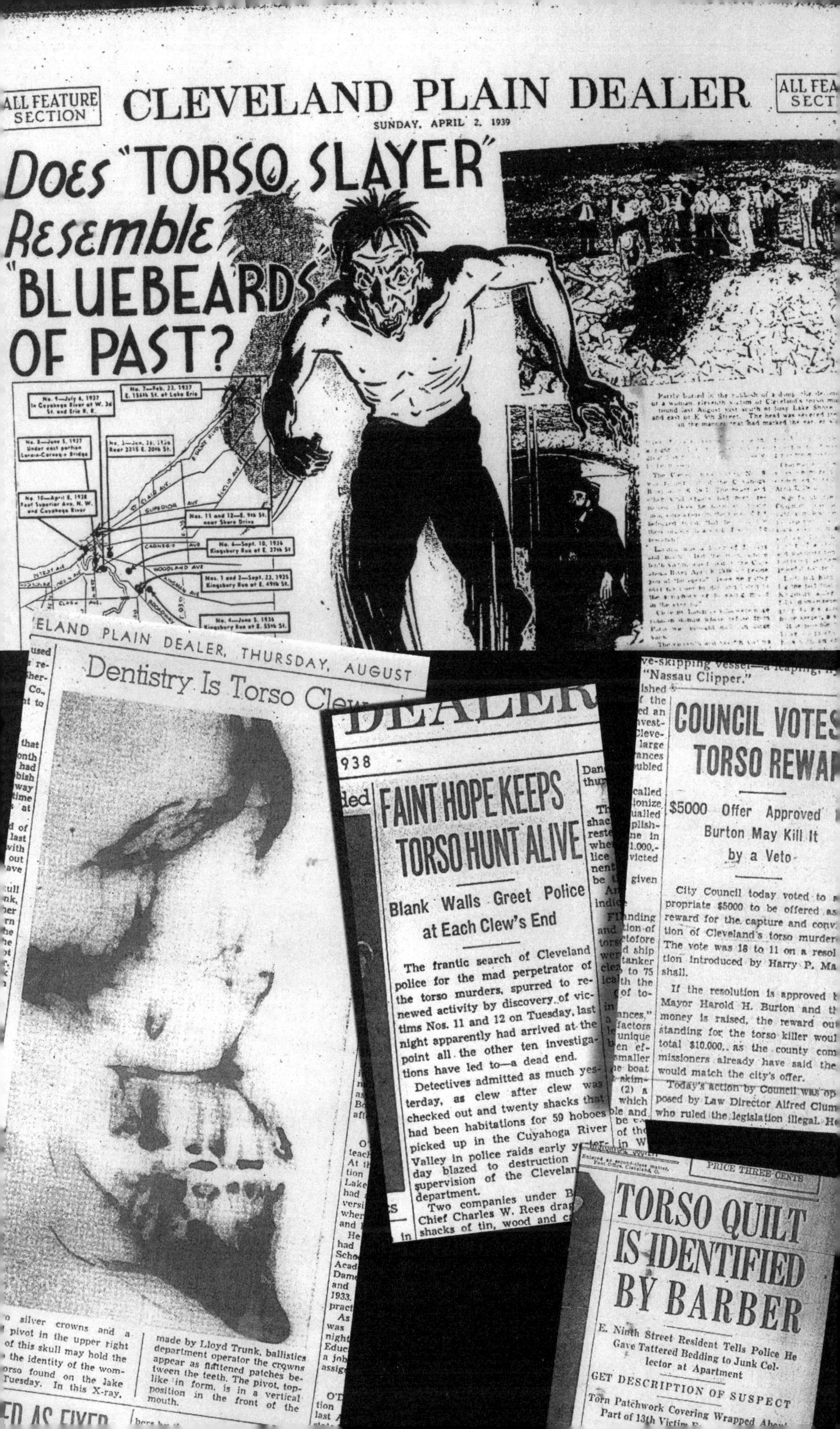

ALL FEATURE SECTION

CLEVELAND PLAIN DEALER

SUNDAY, APRIL 2, 1939

ALL FEATURE SECTION

Does "TORSO SLAYER" Resemble "BLUEBEARDS" OF PAST?

No. 9—July 6, 1937
In Cuyahoga River at W. 3d St. and Erie R. R.
No. 7—Feb. 23, 1937
E. 156th St. at Lake Erie
No. 8—June 5, 1937
Under east portion Lorain-Carnegie Bridge
No. 5—Jan. 26, 1936
Rear 2315 E. 20th St.
No. 10—April 8, 1938
Foot Superior Ave. N. W. and Cuyahoga River
Nos. 11 and 12—E. 9th St. near Shore Drive
No. 6—Sept. 10, 1936
Kingsbury Run at E. 37th St.
Nos. 1 and 2—Sept. 23, 1935
Kingsbury Run at E. 49th St.
No. 4—June 5, 1936
Kingsbury Run at E. 55th St.
ST. CLAIR AVE.
SUPERIOR AVE.
EUCLID AVE.
CARNEGIE AVE.
WOODLAND AVE.
KINSMAN AVE.
BROADWAY

Partly buried in the rubbish of a dump, the ... of a woman, eleventh victim of Cleveland's torso ... found last August just south of ... Lake Shore ... and east of E. 9th Street. The head was severed ...

ELAND PLAIN DEALER, THURSDAY, AUGUST

Dentistry Is Torso Clew

...o silver crowns and a ... pivot in the upper right ... of this skull may hold the ... the identity of the wom... torso found on the lake ... Tuesday. In this X-ray, made by Lloyd Trunk, ballistics department operator the crowns appear as flattened patches between the teeth. The pivot, top-like in form, is in a vertical position in the front of the mouth.

DEALER

...938

FAINT HOPE KEEPS TORSO HUNT ALIVE

Blank Walls Greet Police at Each Clew's End

The frantic search of Cleveland police for the mad perpetrator of the torso murders, spurred to renewed activity by discovery of victims Nos. 11 and 12 on Tuesday, last night apparently had arrived at the point all the other ten investigations have led to—a dead end.

Detectives admitted as much yesterday, as clew after clew was checked out and twenty shacks that had been habitations for 59 hoboes picked up in the Cuyahoga River Valley in police raids early yesterday blazed to destruction ... supervision of the Clevelan... department.

Two companies under B... Chief Charles W. Rees drag... shacks of tin, wood and c...

...ve-skipping vessel—a leaping, ... "Nassau Clipper."

COUNCIL VOTES TORSO REWA...

$5000 Offer Approved; Burton May Kill It by a Veto

City Council today voted to ... propriate $5000 to be offered as reward for the capture and conv... tion of Cleveland's torso murde... The vote was 18 to 11 on a resol... tion introduced by Harry P. Ma... shall.

If the resolution is approved b... Mayor Harold H. Burton and th... money is raised, the reward ou... standing for the torso killer woul... total $10,000, as the county com... missioners already have said the... would match the city's offer.

Today's action by Council was op... posed by Law Director Alfred Clum... who ruled the legislation illegal. H...

Entered as second-class matter, Post Office, Cleveland, O.

PRICE THREE CENTS

TORSO QUILT IS IDENTIFIED BY BARBER

E. Ninth Street Resident Tells Police He Gave Tattered Bedding to Junk Collector at Apartment

GET DESCRIPTION OF SUSPECT

Torn Patchwork Covering Wrapped Ab... Part of 13th Victim ...

...ED AS FIXER

Dec. 21,1938

Chief of Police Matowitz,

You can rest easy now as I have came out to sunny California for the winter. I felt bad operating on those people but science must advance. I shall soon astonde the medical profession-- a man with only a D.C.

What did their lives mean in comperasion to hundreds of sick x and disease twisted bodies. Just laboratory guinea pigs found on any public street. No one missed them when I failed. My last case was sucessful. I know now the feeling of PasteurThoreau and other pioneers.

Right now I have a volunteer who will absolutely prove my theory. They called me mad and a butcherer but the "truth will out".

I have failed but once here. The body has not been found and never will be but the head minus features is buried in a gully on Century Blvd. between Western and Century Crenshaw. I feel it is my duty to dispose of the bodies I do .It is God's will not to let them suffer.

X

Mad butcher's letter says he's in L. A.

Los Angeles police today prepared to search for the buried body of a possible local victim of Cleveland's "mad butcher of Kingsbury run."

Photostatic copy of a letter which was mailed from Los Angeles was bounced back to police here by Cleveland officers, who believed the writer of the boastful note might be the same man whose torso murders terrorized that city.

The letter claimed that the writer killed for the advancement of science, and "had failed but once here."

This "failure," minus features, is supposed to be buried in a gully near Century boulevard, between Western avenue and Crenshaw boulevard, apparently in the vicinity of the 77th street police pistol range.

Capt. H. J. Wallis of the homicide squad was inclined to believe the letter the work of a crank, who had read of the Cleveland murders. But he assigned Det. Lieuts. Lloyd Hurst and Frank Ryan to investigate, and they said trusties from the city jail would be taken to the spot described to dig as soon as the weather clears.

The letter was mailed from here December 22 at 11 p. m. from the Arcade annex post office.

The letter read:

"You can rest easy now as I have come out to sunny California for the winter. I felt bad operating on those people but science must advance. I shall soon astound the medical profession—a man with only a D. C. (doctor of chiropractic.)

"What are their lives in comparison to hundreds of sick and diseased, twisted bodies? Just laboratory guinea pigs found on any public street. No one missed them when I failed.

"My last case was successful. I know now the feeling of Pasteur, Thoreau and other pioneers.

"Right now I have a volunteer who will absolutely prove my theory. They called me mad and a butcher but the truth will out.

"I have failed but once here. The body has not been found and never will be but the head minus features is buried in a gully on Century boulevard between Western and Crenshaw.

"I feel it is my duty to dispose of the bodies. I do. It is God's will not to let them suffer."

The 13 victims of the Cleveland slayer have been both men and

(Continued on Page 8, Col. 5)

FEATURE INDEX

this is a copy of the actual letter.

this controversial letter has never been proven to be from the torso kil[ler] but it is chilling none the less. this letter is one of the reasons many casual observers connect the torso killer to the black dalia killer. but examination of the time lines and methods of thes[e] two killers prove otherwi[se]

they were different men.

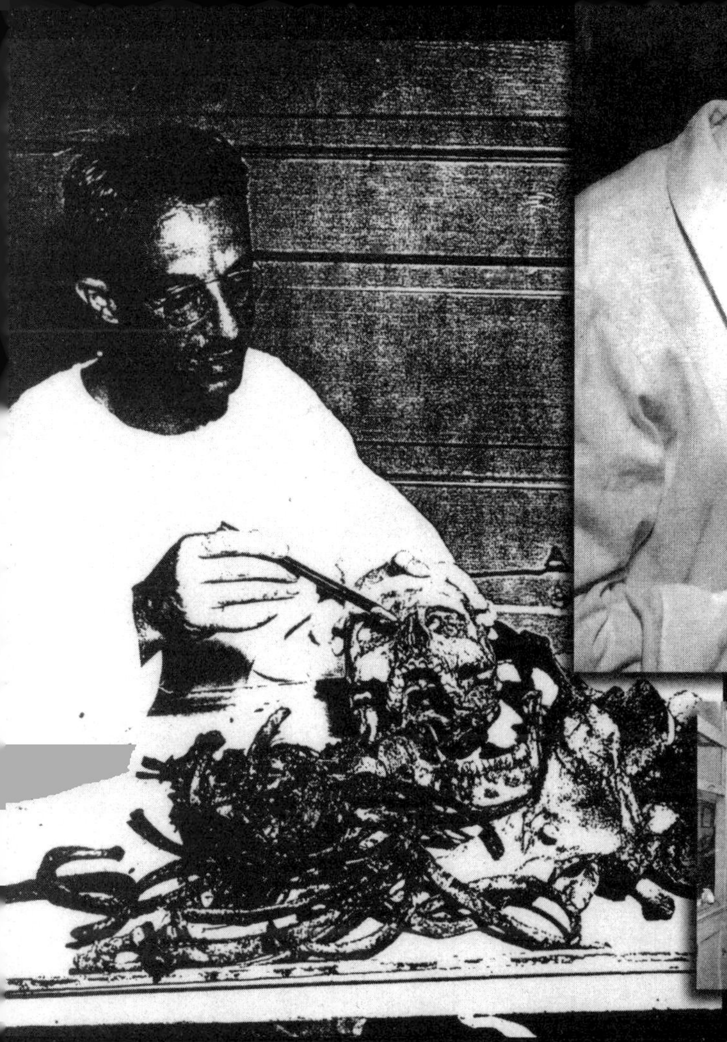

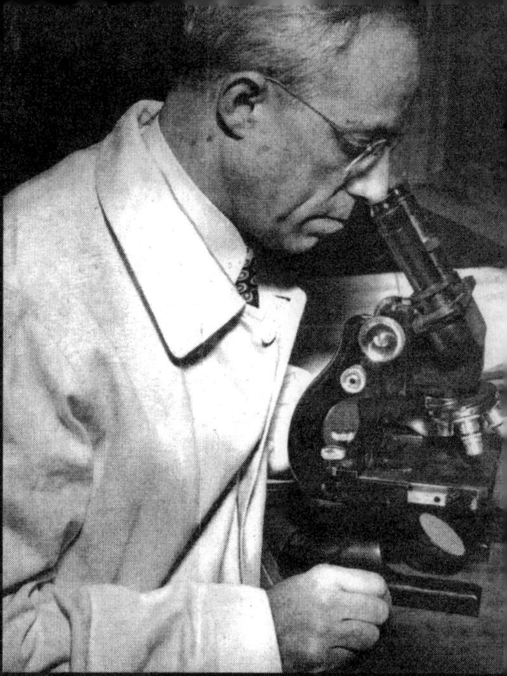

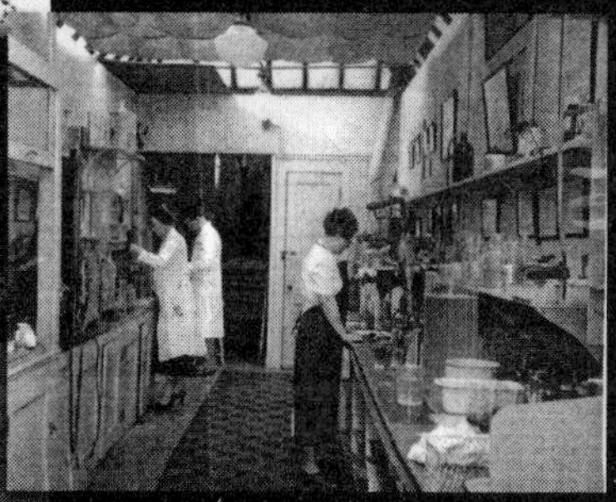

dr. gerber

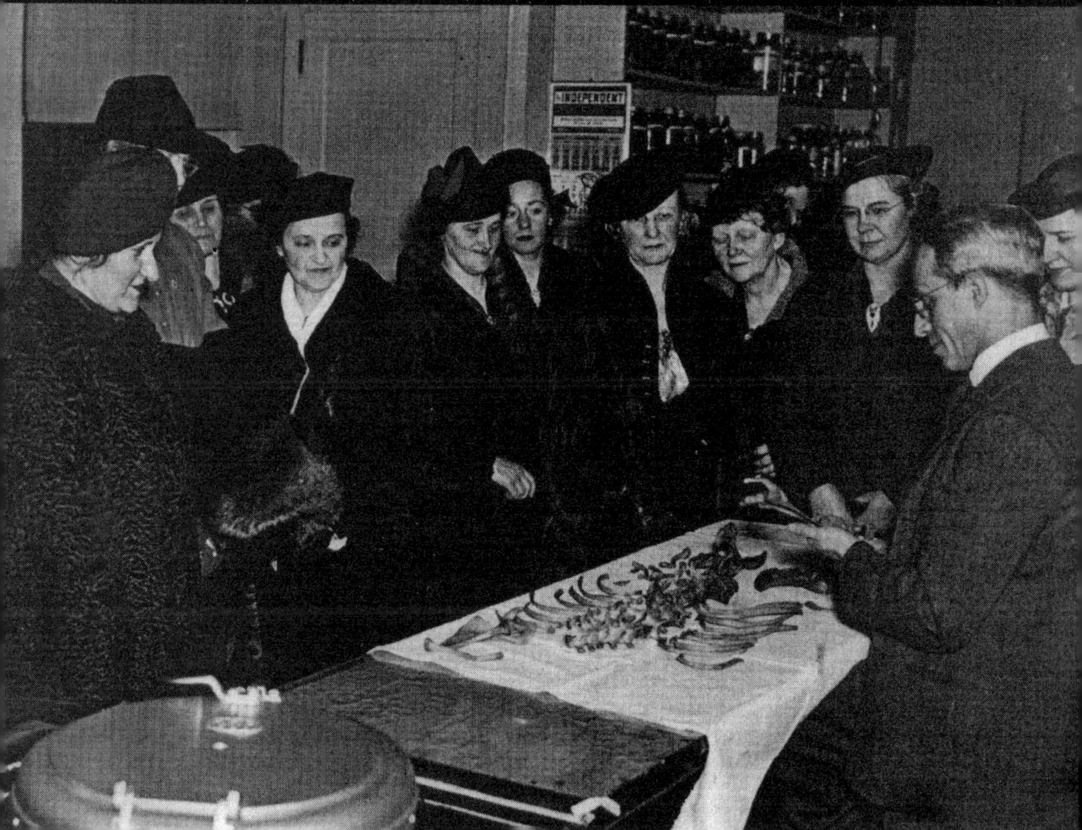
INDEPENDENT

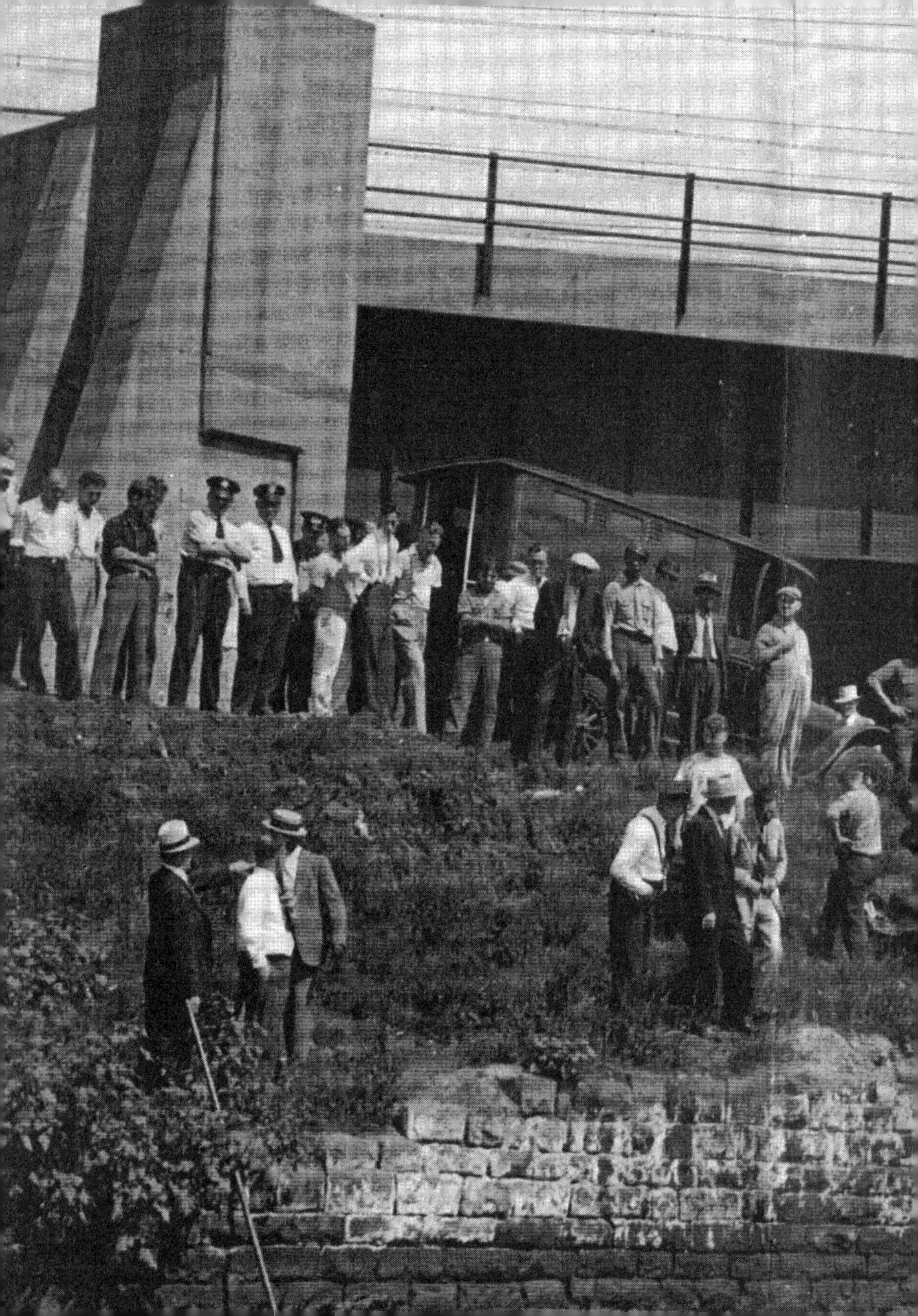

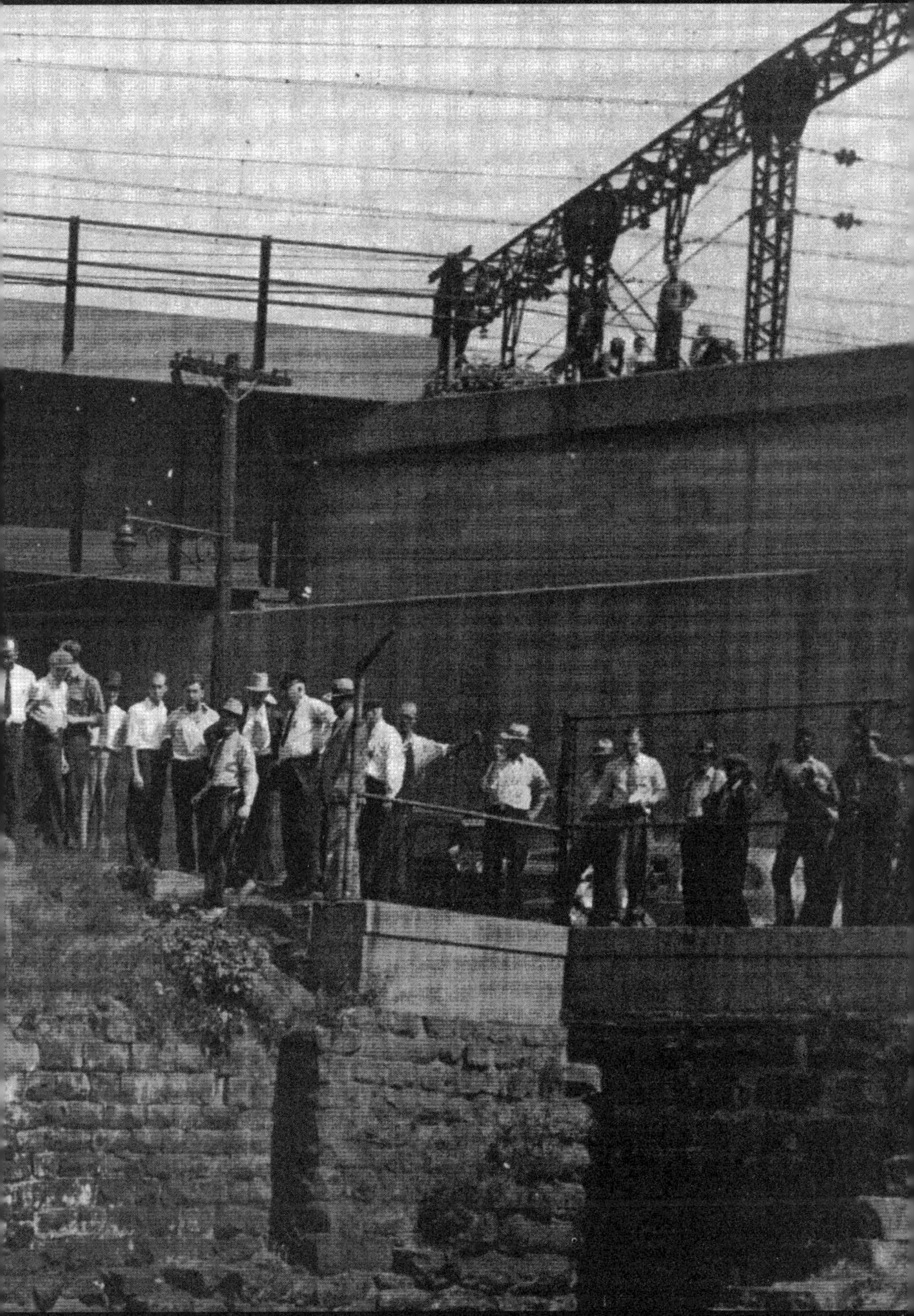

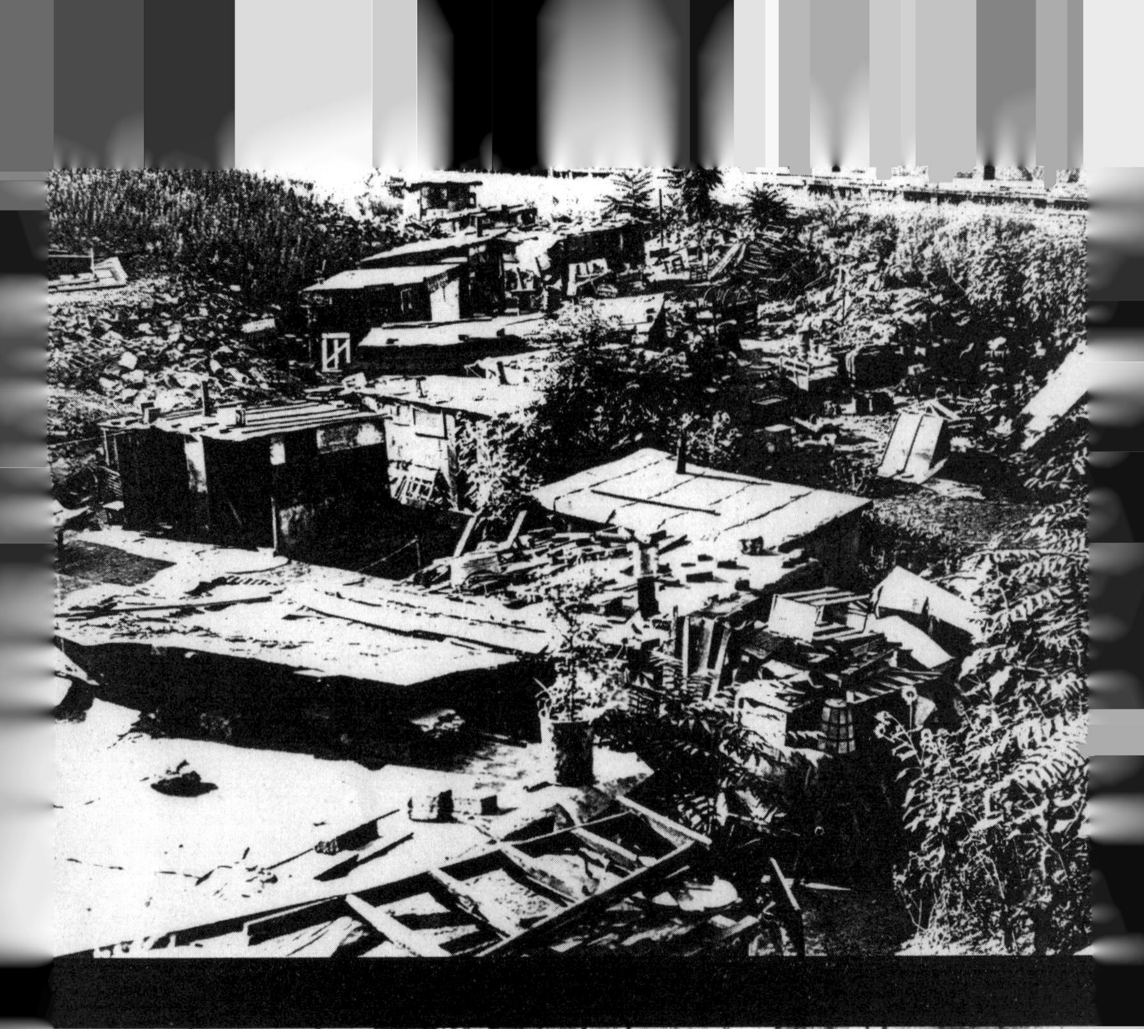

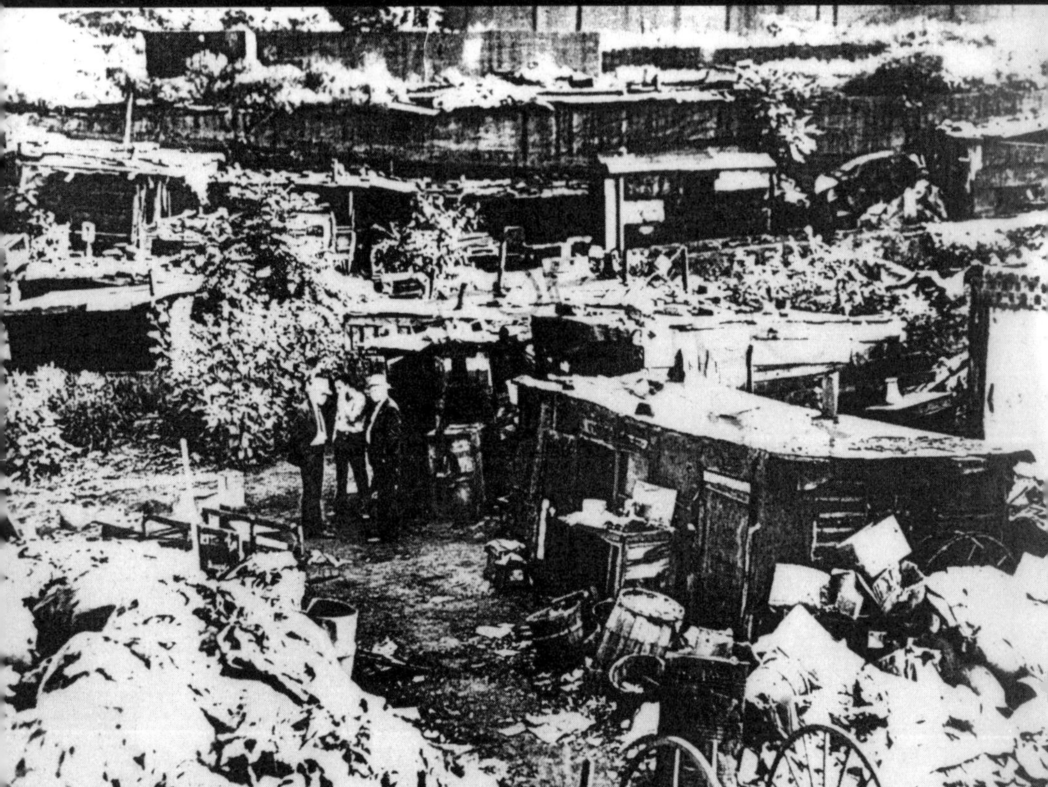

s is the section of the graphic
el that most people thought was
e up for dramatic purposes. but
was not. there was a shantytown
cleveland as described in the
el. and eliot ness in a fit of
stration over the murders had
burned to the ground and its
idents incarcerated.

s was crucified by the press
this for weeks and months to
e for this, and with the torso
ler's identity never made public,
entire city found ness' behavior
s night to be unforgivable.

POLICE, LED BY NESS, NAB 35 VAGRANTS

Squads Surround Cliff Shacks and Take in Dwellers for Fingerprints

Swooping down on a cluster of shanties, sprawled on the hillside of Commercial and Canal Roads S. W., 25 detectives and uniformed men led by Safety Director Eliot Ness shortly after 1 a. m. today corralled 35 vagrants and took them to Central Police Station for ques-

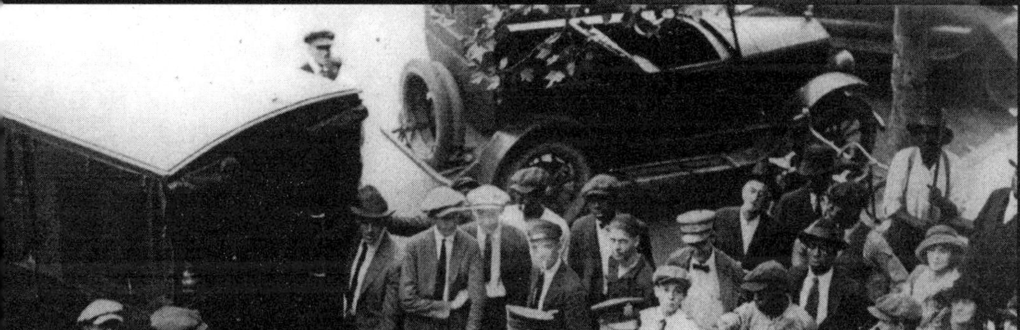

Kennedy and the university which offers the courses.

WRECKING SHANTYTOWNS

IT is a week now since Safety Director Eliot Ness, with considerable fanfare, made a personally supervised raid upon the packing box huts underneath the Eagle ramp in search of the torso killer.

Some promising clues have been uncovered in other parts of the city since then, but the torso killer is still at large. The net result of the director's raid seems to have been the wrecking of a few miserable huts and the confinement of their occupants

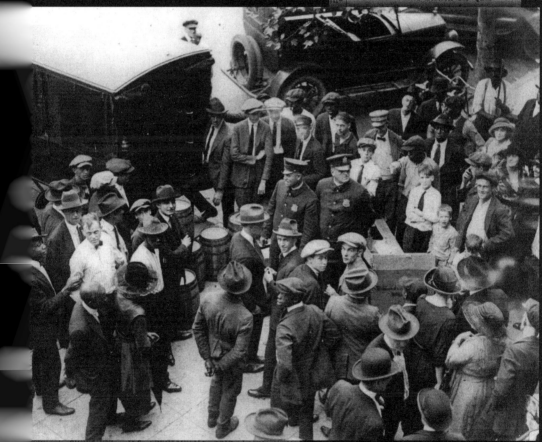

many believe that the
burning of the
shantytown destroyed the
previously golden boy
eliot ness' political
career forever.

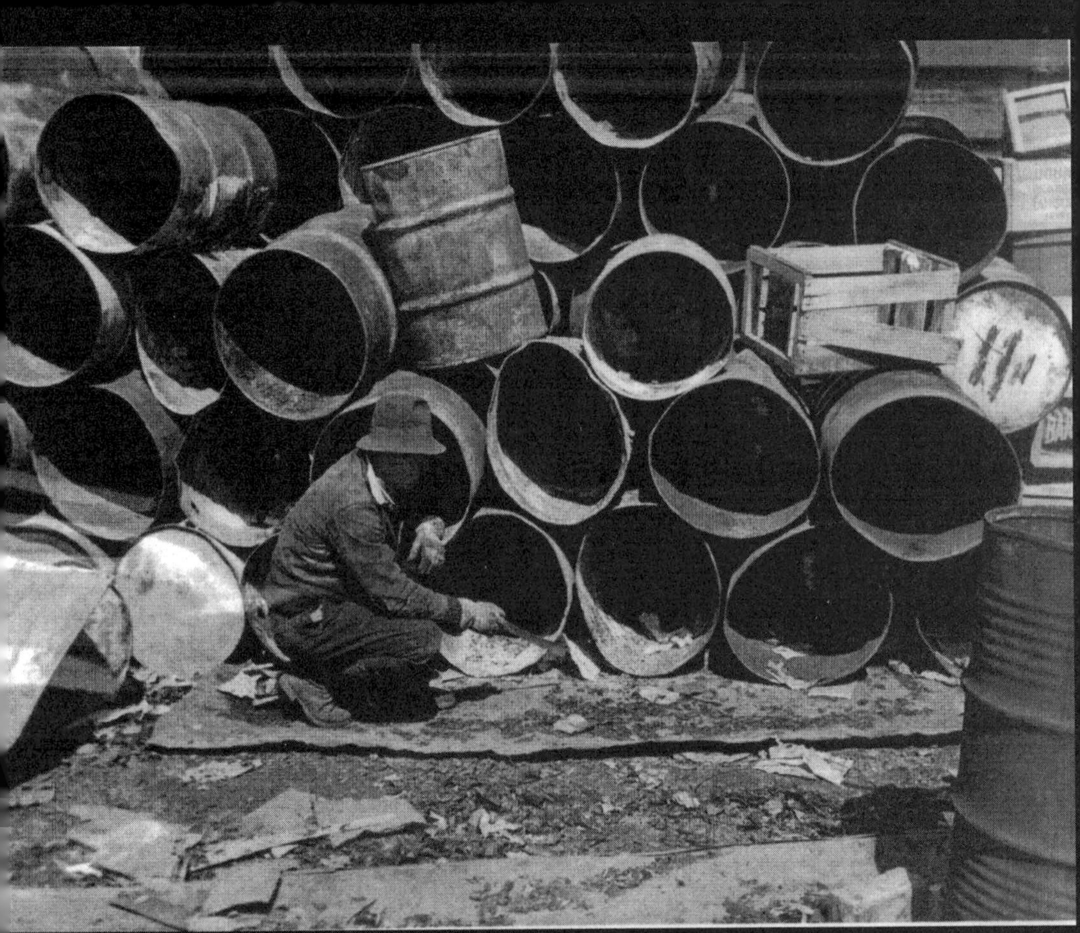

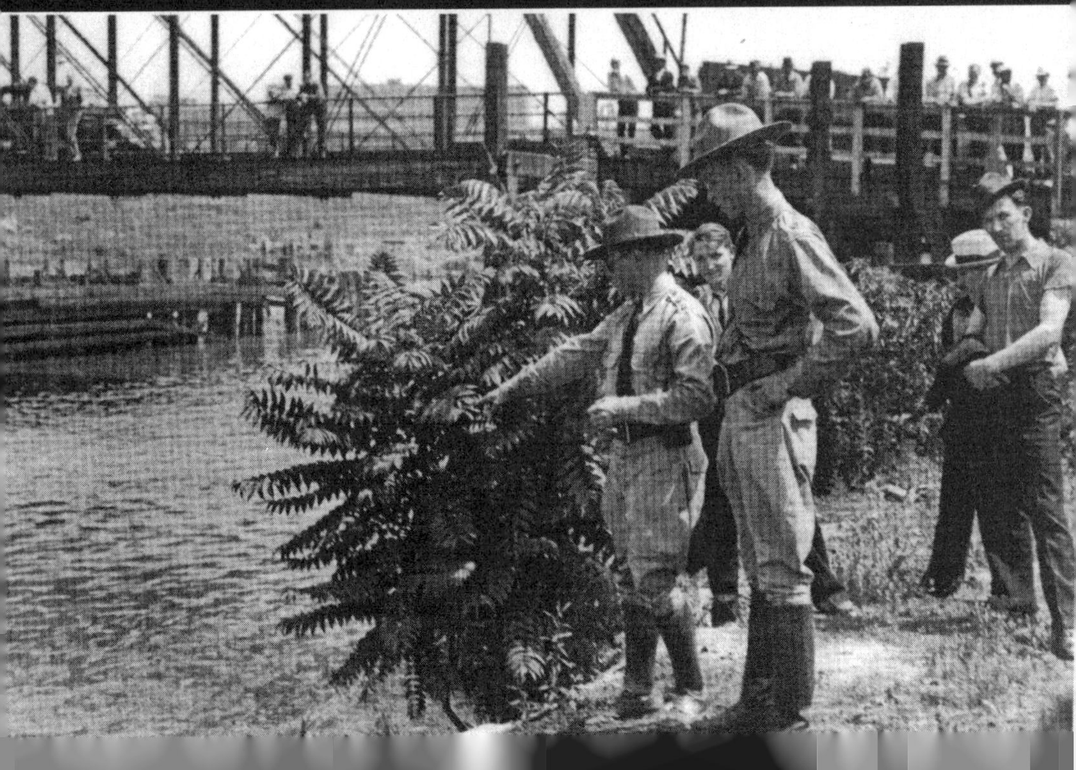

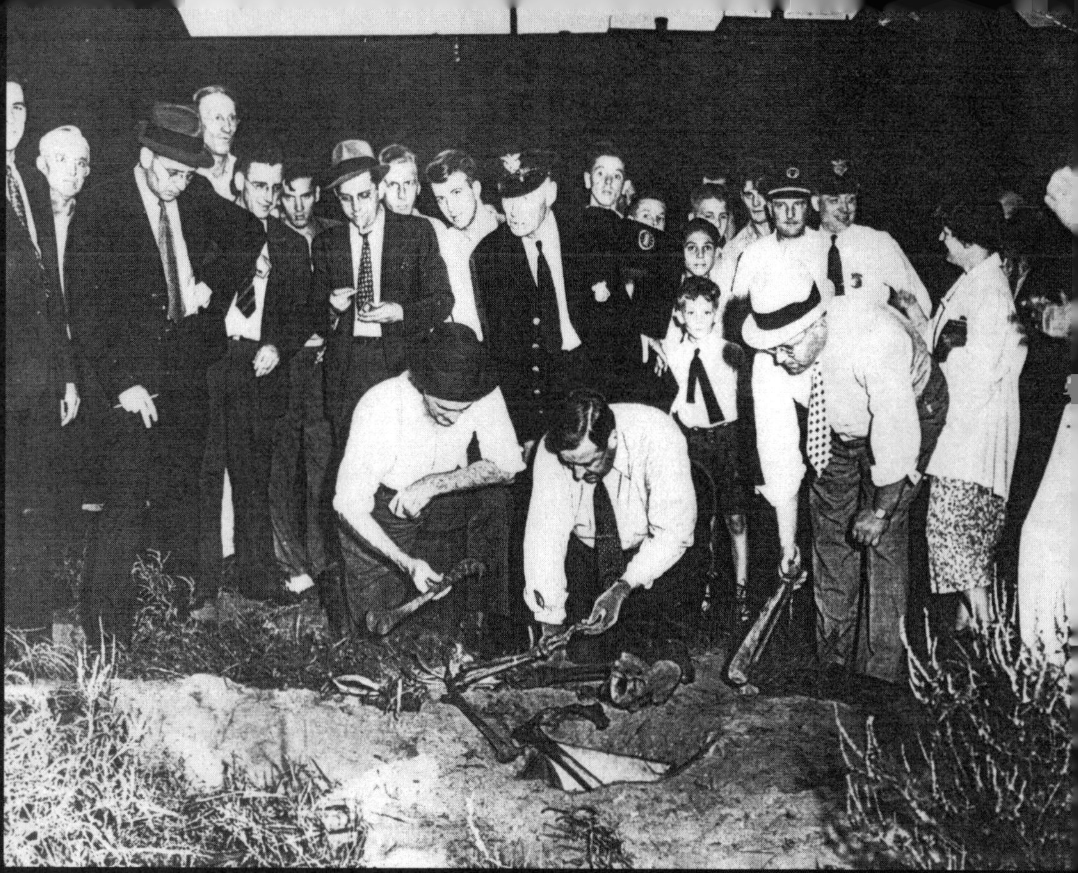

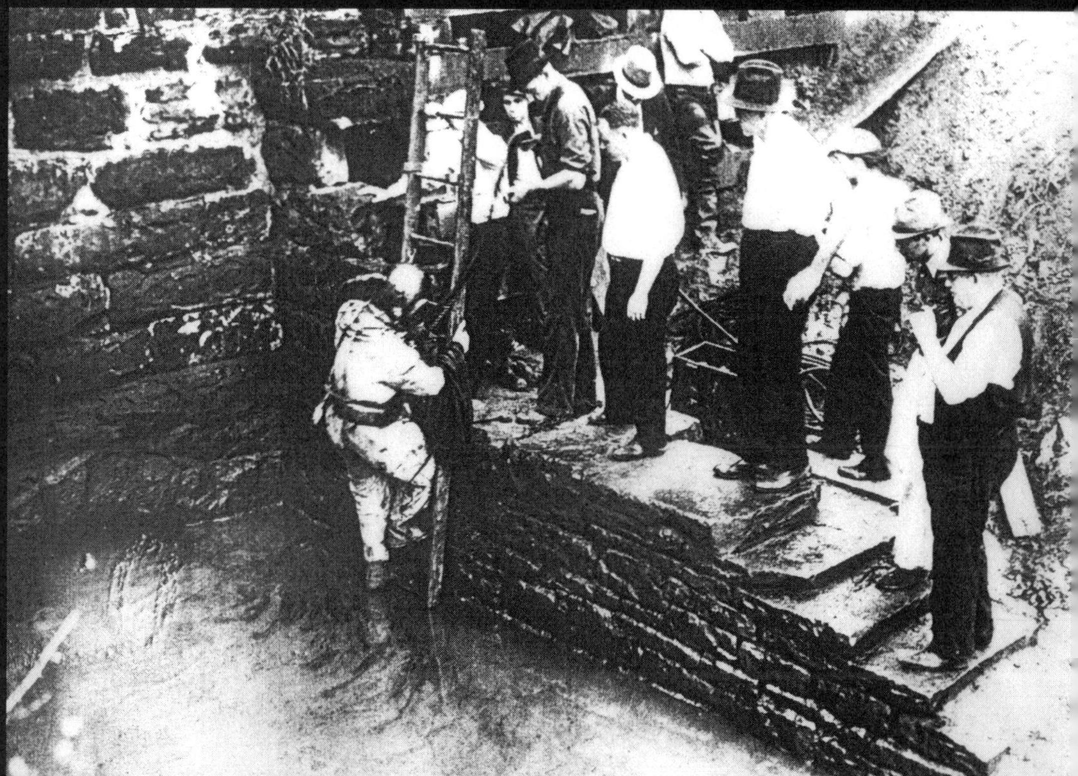

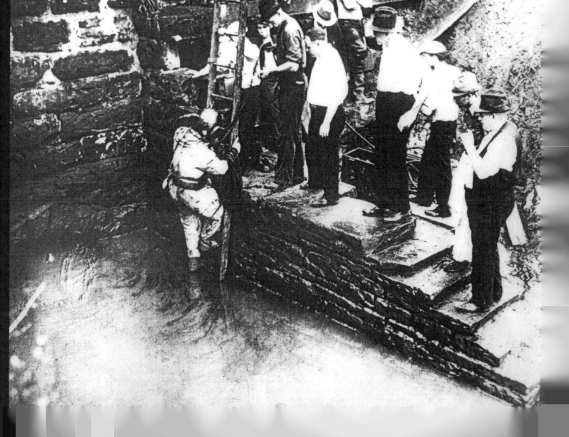

acknowledgements

brian

thanks to:
jim valentino, larry marder, anthony bozzi,
joe quesada, david mack, bill jemas,
anne gordon, mike sangiacomo, jared bendis,
mark ricketts, michael avon oeming,
chris silbermann, justin silvera, david engel,
marc andreyko and todd mcfarlane.

marc

thanks to:
todd mcfarlane, david engel, teddy tennenbaum,
craig titley, don murphy, rick benattar, jordan
fields, jim wedaa, nicole clemens, mike mendez,
brian swardstrom, shep rosenman, guy ferland,
david carson, steve kessler, scott putman and
shana landsburg, ben and tracy raab,
and lesa lakin richardson.

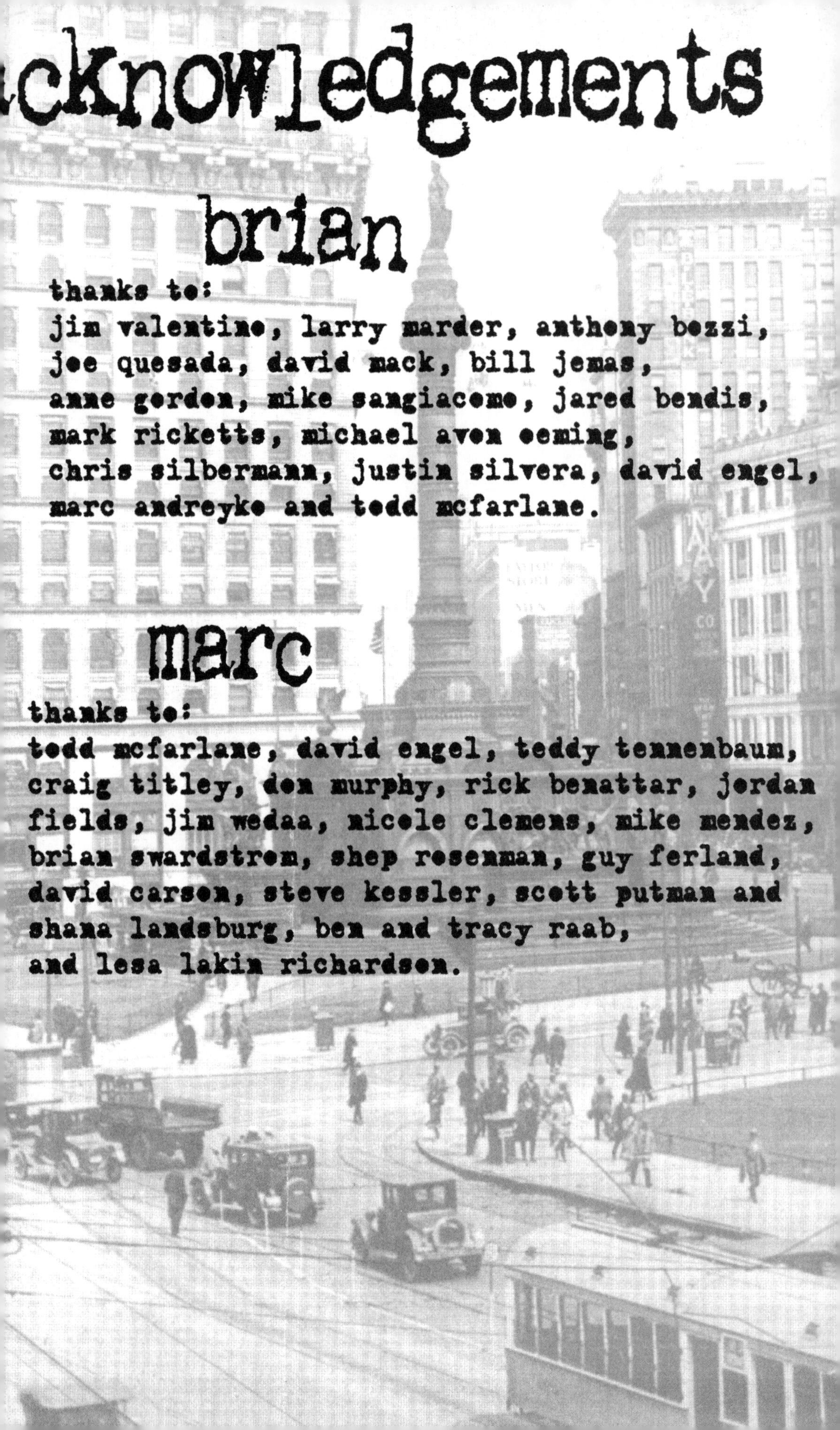